THE **GLOBAL** SOLUTION

Print + Online

GLOBAL⁴ delivers all the key terms and core concepts for the **Global Business** course.

GLOBAL Online provides the complete narrative from the printed text with additional interactive media and the unique functionality of **StudyBits**—all available on nearly any device!

What is a StudyBit™? Created through a deep investigation of students' challenges and workflows, the StudyBit™ functionality of **GLOBAL Online** enables students of different generations and learning styles to study more effectively by allowing them to learn their way. Here's how they work:

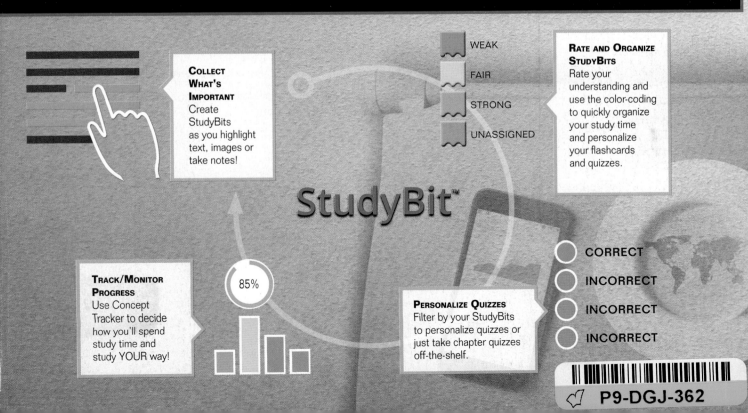

COLLECT WHAT'S IMPORTANT Create StudyBits as you highlight text, images or take notes!

WEAK

FAIR

STRONG

UNASSIGNED

RATE AND ORGANIZE STUDYBITS Rate your understanding and use the color-coding to quickly organize your study time and personalize your flashcards and quizzes.

StudyBit™

TRACK/MONITOR PROGRESS Use Concept Tracker to decide how you'll spend study time and study YOUR way!

85%

PERSONALIZE QUIZZES Filter by your StudyBits to personalize quizzes or just take chapter quizzes off-the-shelf.

CORRECT

INCORRECT

INCORRECT

INCORRECT

CENGAGE

GLOBAL4
Mike W. Peng

Senior Vice President, General Manager:
   Erin Joyner

Product Manager: Bryan Gambrel

Content/Media Developer: Colin Grover

Product Assistant: Rhett Ransom

Marketing Manager: Charisse Darin

Marketing Coordinator: Audrey Jacobs

Content Project Manager: D. Jean Buttrom

Sr. Art Director: Bethany Bourgeois

Cover Designer: Lisa Kuhn, Curio Press, LLC /
   Chris Miller, Cmiller Design

Internal Designer: Tippy McIntosh

Cover Images: Rawpixel.com/Shutterstock.com,
   KlingSup/Shutterstock.com, fleur_de_papier
   /Shutterstock.com, Sergey Peterman
   /Shutterstock.com

Internal Design Images: Compass icon for cases,
   jongcreative/Shutterstock.com; In Focus
   graphic, Mauro Fabbro/Shutterstock.com;
   PengAtlas Map, T. Lesia/Shutterstock.com;
   Debate graphic, kstudija/Shutterstock.com

Intellectual Property
   Analyst: Diane Garrity
   Project Manager: Sarah Shainwald

Production Service: MPS Limited

For product information and technology assistance, contact us at
Cengage Customer & Sales Support, 1-800-354-9706
For permission to use material from this text or product,
submit all requests online at **www.cengage.com/permissions**
Further permissions questions can be emailed to
permissionrequest@cengage.com

Library of Congress Control Number: 2017948122

Student Edition ISBN: 978-1-337-40683-3
Student Edition with Online ISBN: 978-1-337-40682-6

Cengage
20 Channel Center Street
Boston, MA 02210
USA

Cengage is a leading provider of customized learning solutions with employees residing in nearly 40 different countries and sales in more than 125 countries around the world. Find your local representative at **www.cengage.com.**

Cengage products are represented in Canada by Nelson Education, Ltd.

To learn more about Cengage Solutions, visit **www.cengage.com**

Purchase any of our products at your local college store or at our preferred online store **www.cengagebrain.com**

Printed in the United States of America
Print Number: 04   Print Year: 2018

COURTESY OF MIKE PENG

Mike W. Peng is the Jindal Chair of Global Business Strategy at the Jindal School of Management, University of Texas at Dallas. He is also a National Science Foundation (NSF) CAREER Award winner and a Fellow of the Academy of International Business (AIB). At UT Dallas, he has been the number-one contributor to the list of 50 top journals tracked by *Financial Times*, which has consistently ranked UT Dallas as a top 20 school in research worldwide.

Professor Peng holds a bachelor's degree from Winona State University, Minnesota, and a PhD from the University of Washington, Seattle. He had previously served on the faculty at the Ohio State University, University of Hawaii, and Chinese University of Hong Kong. He has taught in five states in the United States (Hawaii, Ohio, Tennessee, Texas, and Washington), as well as in China, Hong Kong, and Vietnam. He has also held visiting or courtesy appointments in Australia, Britain, China, Denmark, Hong Kong, and the United States, and lectured around the world.

Professor Peng is one of the most-prolific and most-influential scholars in international business (IB). Both the United Nations and the World Bank have cited his work. During the decade 1996–2006, he was the top seven contributor to IB's number-one premier outlet: *Journal of International Business Studies*. In 2015, he received the *Journal of International Business Studies* Decade Award. A *Journal of Management* article found him to be among the top 65 most widely cited management scholars, and an *Academy of Management Perspectives* study reported that he is the fourth-most-influential management scholar among professors who have obtained their PhD since 1991. Overall, Professor Peng has published more than 140 articles in leading journals and five books. Since the launch of *GLOBAL*, he has not only published in top IB journals, such as the *Academy of Management Journal, Journal of International Business Studies, Journal of World Business*, and *Strategic Management Journal*, but also in leading outlets in entrepreneurship (*Entrepreneurship Theory and Practice*), ethics (*Journal of Business Ethics*), human resources (*International Journal of Human Resource Management*), and engineering management (*IEEE Transactions on Engineering Management*).

Used in more than 30 countries, Professor Peng's best-selling textbooks, *Global Business, Global Strategy,* and *GLOBAL*, are global market leaders that have been translated into Chinese, Portuguese, and Spanish. A European adaptation (with Klaus Meyer) and an Indian adaptation (with Deepak Srivastava) have been successfully launched.

Truly global in scope, Professor Peng's research has investigated firm strategies in Africa, Asia Pacific, Europe, and North America. He is best known for his development of the institution-based view of strategy and his insights about the rise of emerging economies such as China in global business. With more than 29,000 Google citations and an H-index of 69, he is listed among *The World's Most Influential Scientific Minds* (compiled by Thomson Reuters based on citations covering 21 fields)—in the field of economics and business, he is one of the only 70 world-class scholars listed and the *only* IB textbook author listed.

Professor Peng is active in leadership positions. He has served on the editorial boards of the *AMJ, AMP, AMR, JIBS, JMS, JWB,* and *SMJ;* and guest-edited a special issue for the *JMS*. At AIB, he co-chaired the AIB/*JIBS* Frontiers Conference in San Diego (2006), guest-edited a *JIBS* special issue (2010), chaired the Emerging and Transition Economies track for the Nagoya conference (2011), and chaired the Richard Farmer Best Dissertation Award Committee for the Washington conference (2012). At the Strategic Management Society (SMS), he was elected to be the Global Strategy Interest Group Chair (2008). He also co-chaired the SMS Special Conferences in Shanghai (2007) and in Sydney (2014). He served one term as Editor-in-Chief of the *Asia Pacific Journal of Management*. He managed the successful bid to enter the Social Sciences Citation Index (SSCI), which reported *APJM*'s first citation impact to be 3.4 and rated it as the top 18 among 140 management journals (by citation impact factor) for 2010. In recognition of his significant contributions, *APJM* has named its best paper award the Mike Peng Best Paper Award. Currently, he is a Consulting Editor at *APJM*.

Professor Peng is also an active consultant, trainer, and keynote speaker. He has provided on-the-job training to more than 400 professors. He has consulted and been a keynote speaker for multinational enterprises (such as AstraZeneca, Berlitz, Mass Transit Railway Hong Kong, Nationwide, SAFRAN, and Texas Instruments), nonprofit organizations (such as World Affairs Council of Dallas-Fort Worth), educational and funding organizations (such as Canada Research Chair, Harvard Kennedy School of Government, US National Science Foundation, and Natural Science Foundation of China), and national and international organizations (such as the UK Government Office for Science, US-China Business Council, US Navy, and The World Bank).

Professor Peng has received numerous honors, including an NSF CAREER Grant ($423,000), a US Small Business Administration Best Paper Award, a (lifetime) Distinguished Scholar Award from the Southwestern Academy of Management, a (lifetime) Scholarly Contribution Award from the International Association for Chinese Management Research (IACMR), and a Best Paper Award named after him. He has been quoted by *The Economist, Newsweek, Dallas Morning News, Texas CEO Magazine, Smart Business Dallas, Atlanta Journal-Constitution, The Exporter Magazine, The World Journal, Business Times* (Singapore), *CEO-CIO* (Beijing), *Sing Tao Daily* (Vancouver), and *Brasil Econômico* (São Paulo), as well as on the Voice of America.

MIKE W. PENG

GLOBAL⁴

BRIEF CONTENTS

SERGEY PETERMAN/SHUTTERSTOCK.COM

CONTENTS

Part 1
Laying Foundations

MARCIO MACHADO/GETTY IMAGES

Part 2
Acquiring Tools

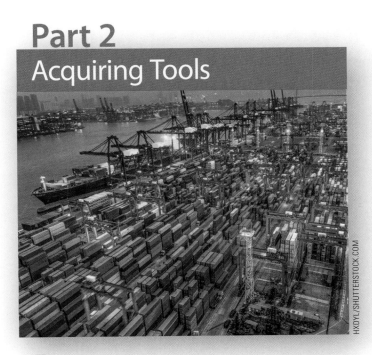

HXDYL/SHUTTERSTOCK.COM

8. Capitalizing on Global & Regional Integration 120

Part 3
Managing around the World

SUCCESSO IMAGES/SHUTTERSTOCK.COM

9. Growing & Internationalizing the Entrepreneurial Firm 138

10. Entering Foreign Markets 152

15. Managing Corporate Social Responsibility Globally 234

GLOBAL
ONLINE

ACCESS TEXTBOOK CONTENT ONLINE—
INCLUDING ON SMARTPHONES!

1 Globalizing Business

LEARNING OBJECTIVES

After studying this chapter, you will be able to . . .

1-1 Explain the concepts of international business and global business.

1-2 Give three reasons why it is important to study global business.

1-3 Articulate the fundamental question that the study of global business seeks to answer and the two perspectives from which to answer it.

1-4 Identify three ways of understanding what globalization is.

1-5 Appreciate the size of the global economy and the strengths of multinationals.

1-6 Understand the organization of this book.

After you finish this chapter, go to

PAGE 18 for

STUDY TOOLS

EMERGING MARKETS/ETHICAL DILEMMA
Opening Case: Shanghai Disneyland

On June 16, 2016, the world's biggest Disneyland opened in Shanghai with a great deal of fanfare. It features a supersize castle that is 200-feet tall. In comparison, the height for similar castles in Anaheim, California, and Orlando, Florida, is 77 feet and 180 feet, respectively. Approximately 80% of the Shanghai rides, such as the Tron Lightcycle Roller Coaster, are unique. Chinese elements are extensively found. The flagship restaurant, the Wandering Moon Teahouse, has sections representing different regions of China. Some old staples found in other Disney parks, such as Main Street USA, Jungle Cruise, and Space Mountain, have been banished—in fear of criticisms for cultural imperialism. "Authentically Disney and distinctly Chinese" is an interesting tagline coined by Robert Iger, chairman and CEO of The Walt Disney Company ("Disney" hereafter). More than 330 million people live within a three-hour drive or train ride. Disney is eager to turn them into lifelong customers not only for the $5.5 billion theme park, but also for movies, games, toys, clothes, books, TV programs, cruises, and resorts.

Mickey's journey to the Middle Kingdom has been a tortuous one. The two-decade courtship started in the late 1990s, when Jiang Zemin was president of China and Michael Eisner chairman and CEO of Disney. At that time, Disney was starting to have some success in China, with its cartoon series aired on Sunday evenings by major TV stations. Then Disney launched a movie about the exiled Tibetan spiritual leader the Dalai Lama, *Kundun*, which attracted the wrath of the Chinese government. "All of our business in China stopped overnight," Eisner recalled. Out of desperation, Disney hired as a consultant former Secretary of State Henry Kissinger, who spearheaded American efforts to establish diplomatic ties with China in the 1970s and was regarded as a trustworthy friend by the Chinese. The Chinese government only agreed to reopen China after intense lobbying by Kissinger and humiliating apologies by Eisner, who admitted *Kundun* was "a stupid mistake" in meetings with Chinese officials. Financially, *Kundun* was indeed a stupid mistake. It burned through a $30 million budget to reap only $5 million box office receipts.

Eisner then introduced Iger, Disney's international president at that time, to be in charge of negotiations for a theme park. The negotiations were slow and painful. Looking back, Iger, who succeeded Eisner as CEO in 2005 and as chairman in 2012, recalled in a *New York Times* interview that he had "engaged with three [Chinese] presidents, a few premiers, a number of vice premiers, a number of [Communist] Party secretaries, and five or six mayors of Shanghai."

By 2009, the Chinese government finally gave its blessing, but only after Disney agreed to be a *minority* partner. Disney took a 43% stake in the Shanghai Disney Resort. Shanghai Disney Resort would not only include the flagship Shanghai Disneyland, but also two additional theme parks, two themed hotels,

shopping malls, and entertainment facilities—when completed it would be three times the size of Hong Kong Disneyland. Disney's joint venture (JV) partner, the state-owned Shanghai Shendi Group controlled by the Shanghai government, owned a 57% stake. In the management company that actually ran the property, Disney gave up a 30% piece. In comparison, the Hong Kong government gave a 48% share to Disney for the JV that owned Hong Kong Disneyland, and the government itself took 52%. Disney gave up no management control in Hong Kong.

Why was Disney so eager to go to China? Although China's pull in terms of market size and potential is obvious, Disney is also pushed by its lackluster performance in other areas such as cable, movies, and some of its other theme parks. In April 2011, Shanghai Disneyland broke ground, with Iger and Chinese officials scooping up loose dirt, Mickey and Minnie Mouse frolicking in Chinese costumes, and a children's choir singing *When You Wish Upon a Star*—in Mandarin. Despite such hoopla, there was no guarantee that Disney's high-profile entry would be profitable. Exhibit A: Disneyland Paris, which opened in 1992, is still struggling to reach profitability.

For Shanghai Disneyland, the attention to detail was meticulous. In addition to the tremendous efforts to showcase local responsiveness, with 80% of the rides being uniquely tailored to local interests, Iger also pre-tasted the food (such as Donald Duck-shaped waffles) and decided which characters would appear in the parade. When first unveiled in March 2016, Shanghai Disneyland's website registered 5 million hits within 30 minutes. The first two weeks of tickets sold out in hours.

Yet as Shanghai Disneyland celebrated its first Chinese New Year in January 2017, disappointing news came. In its first six months ending on December 31, 2016, 5.6 million guests came. Although impressive, these numbers fell *far* short of rosy initial projections of an estimated 15 million visitors for the first year. If attendance continued at its current pace, then the first full-year result would barely reach over 10 million. In the Disney universe, 10 million visitors in the first year would not be too bad, as Hong Kong only attracted seven million in 2015—its 11th year. In comparison, in 2015, Tokyo reported 17 million; Anaheim 18 million; and Orlando 19 million. Although these sister parks are a lot more established, Shanghai Disneyland clearly has a long way to go. As the Magic Kingdom embarks on its residence in the Middle Kingdom, one thing is clear: this China business is not going to be Mickey Mousy.

Sources: "Disney gets a second chance in China," *Bloomberg Businessweek*, 18 April 2011: 21–22; "Middle Kingdom v Magic Kingdom," *Guardian*, 15 June 2016: www.theguardian.com; "How China won the keys to Disney's Magic Kingdom," *New York Times*, 14 June 2016: www.nytimes.com; M. W. Peng, "Mickey goes to Shanghai," in *Global Business*, 4th ed. (Boston: Cengage, 2017) 339–340; "Shanghai Disneyland welcomes 5.6 million visitors in first six months, is kind of a disappointment," *Shanghaiist*, 17 January 2017: www.shanghaiist.com.

How do firms such as Disney compete around the globe? How can competitors such as Europa Park, Happy Valley, Legoland, Lotte World, Sea World, Six Flags, Tivoli, and Universal Studios fight back? What determines the success and failure of these firms—and numerous others—around the world? This book will address these and other important questions on global business.

Ask yourself: Which country made the shirt you are wearing? Which country made the mobile device you have? Why are Airbus jets, Apple iPhones, Corona beer, Microsoft software, Starbucks coffee, and Toyota cars found in many places that you travel to? Can you join the men and women who are the real movers and shakers driving these successful firms? What are their secrets? Of course, there are numerous other firms around the world that are not so successful. How can you learn the lessons from these unsuccessful firms and avoid the mistakes made by their managers? Tackling these interesting questions, *GLOBAL 4* will be with you as you embark on your global business studies and launch your career. Enjoy the ride!

1-1 WHAT IS GLOBAL BUSINESS?

Traditionally, **international business (IB)** is defined as a business (firm) that engages in international (cross-border) economic activities. It can also refer to the action of doing business abroad. A previous generation of IB textbooks almost always takes the foreign entrant's perspective. Consequently, such books deal with issues such as how to enter foreign markets and how to select alliance partners. The most frequently discussed foreign entrant is the **multinational enterprise (MNE)**, defined as a firm that engages in **foreign direct investment (FDI)** by

directly investing in, controlling, and managing value-added activities in other countries.[1] Of course, MNEs and their cross-border activities are important. But they cover only one side of IB—the foreign side. Students educated by these books often come away with the impression that the other side of IB—namely, domestic firms—does not exist. But domestic firms obviously do not just sit around in the face of foreign entrants such as MNEs. They actively compete and/or collaborate with foreign entrants.[2] In other words, focusing on the foreign entrant side captures only one side of the coin at best.

There are *two* key words in IB: international (I) and business (B). However, previous textbooks all focus on the international aspect (the foreign entrant) to the extent that the business part (which also includes domestic business) almost disappears. This is unfortunate because IB is fundamentally about B in addition to being I. To put it differently, the IB course in the undergraduate and MBA curricula at numerous business schools is probably the *only* course with the word "business" in the course title. All other courses you take are labeled management, marketing, finance, and so on, representing one functional area but not the overall picture of business. Does it matter? Of course! It means that your IB course is an *integrative* course that has the potential to provide you with an overall business perspective grounded in a global environment (as opposed to a relatively narrow functional view). Consequently, it makes sense that your textbook should give you both the I and B parts, not just the I part.

To cover both the I and B parts, **global business** is defined in this book as business around the globe—thus the title of this book: *GLOBAL*. For the B part, the activities include *both* international (cross-border) activities covered by traditional IB books and domestic (non-IB) business activities. Such deliberate blurring of the traditional boundaries separating international and domestic business is increasingly important today, because many previously national (domestic) markets are now

international business (IB) (1) A business (firm) that engages in international (cross-border) economic activities or (2) the action of doing business abroad.

multinational enterprise (MNE) A firm that engages in foreign direct investment and operates in multiple countries.

foreign direct investment (FDI) Investment in, controlling, and managing value-added activities in other countries.

global business Business around the globe.

globalized. For example, not long ago, competition among college business textbook publishers was primarily on a nation-by-nation basis. The Big Three—Cengage Learning (our publisher), Prentice Hall, and McGraw-Hill—primarily competed in the United States. A different set of publishers competed in other countries. As a result, textbooks studied by British students would be authored by British professors and published by British publishers; textbooks studied by Brazilian students would be authored by Brazilian professors and published by Brazilian publishers; and so on. Now Cengage (under British and Canadian ownership), Pearson Prentice Hall (under British ownership), and McGraw-Hill (under US ownership) have significantly globalized their competition, thanks to rising demand for high-quality business textbooks in English. Around the globe, they compete against each other in many markets, publishing in multiple languages. For instance, *GLOBAL* and its sister books—*Global Business, Global Strategy,* and *International Business* (a European adaptation)—are published by different subsidiaries in Chinese, Spanish, and Portuguese in addition to English, reaching customers in over 30 countries. Despite such worldwide spread of competition, in each market—down to each school—textbook publishers have to compete locally. In other words, no professor teaches globally, and all students study locally. This means that *GLOBAL* has to win adoption for every class every semester. Overall, it becomes difficult to tell in this competition what is international and what is domestic. Thus, "global" is a better word to capture the essence of this competition.

GLOBAL also differs from other IB books because most focus on competition in developed economies. Here, by contrast, we devote extensive space to competitive battles waged throughout **emerging economies**, a term that has gradually replaced the term "developing countries" since the 1990s. Another commonly used term is **emerging markets** (see PengAtlas Map 1). How important are emerging economies? Collectively, they command 48% of world trade, attract 60% of FDI inflows, and generate 40% FDI outflows. Overall, emerging economies contribute approximately 50% of the global **gross domestic product (GDP)**.[3] In 1990, they accounted for less than a third of a much smaller world GDP.

NERTHUZ/SHUTTERSTOCK.COM

ISTOCK.COM/HENRIK5000

Note that this percentage is adjusted for **purchasing power parity (PPP)**, which is an adjustment to reflect the differences in cost of living.

Of many emerging economies, Brazil, Russia, India, and China—commonly referred to as **BRIC**—command more attention. With South Africa, BRIC becomes **BRICS**. As a group, BRICS countries have 40% of the world's population, cover a quarter of the world's land area, and contribute more than 25% of global GDP (on a PPP basis). In addition to BRICS, other interesting terms include BRICM (BRIC + Mexico), BRICET (BRIC + Eastern Europe and Turkey), and Next Eleven (N-11—consisting of Bangladesh, Egypt, Indonesia, Iran, Korea, Mexico, Nigeria, Pakistan, the Philippines, Turkey, and Vietnam).

Overall, the Great Transformation of the global economy is embodied by the tremendous shift in economic weight and engines of growth toward emerging economies in general and BRIC(S) in particular. Led by BRIC(S), emerging economies accomplished "the biggest economic transformation in modern economy," according to the *Economist*.[4] In China, per capita income doubled in about ten years, an achievement that took Britain 150 years and the United States 50 years as they industrialized. Throughout emerging economies, China is not alone. While groupings such as BRIC(S) and N-11 are always arbitrary, they serve a useful purpose—namely, highlighting their economic and demographic scale and trajectory that enable them to challenge developed economies in terms of weight and influence in the global economy.

Of course, the Great Transformation is not a linear story of endless and uniform high-speed growth. Most emerging economies have experienced some significant slow down recently.[5] It is possible that they may not be able to repeat their extraordinary growth sprint

emerging economy (emerging market) A developing country.

gross domestic product (GDP) The sum of value added by resident firms, households, and governments operating in an economy.

purchasing power parity (PPP) A conversion that determines the equivalent amount of goods and services different currencies can purchase. This conversion is usually used to capture the differences in cost of living in different countries.

BRIC An acronym for the emerging economies of Brazil, Russia, India, and China.

BRICS An acronym for the emerging economies of Brazil, Russia, India, China, and South Africa.

EXHIBIT 1.1 THE GLOBAL ECONOMIC PYRAMID

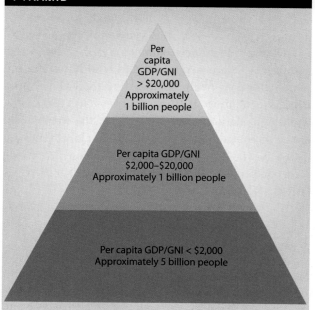

Per capita GDP/GNI > $20,000
Approximately 1 billion people

Per capita GDP/GNI $2,000–$20,000
Approximately 1 billion people

Per capita GDP/GNI < $2,000
Approximately 5 billion people

Sources: C. K. Prahalad and S. Hart, "The fortune at the bottom of the pyramid," *Strategy+Business* 26 (2002): 54–67; S. Hart, *Capitalism at the Crossroads* (Philadelphia: Wharton School Publishing, 2005) 111. GNI refers to gross national income.

during the decade between 1998 (the Asian economic crisis) and 2008 (the global financial crisis). For example, in 2007, Brazil accomplished an annual economic growth of 6%, Russia 8%, India 10%, and China 14%. In 2017, they would be very lucky if they could achieve half of these enviable growth rates. However, it seems that emerging economies *as a group* are destined to grow both their absolute GDP and their percentage of world GDP relative to developed economies. The debate centers on how much and how fast (or how slow) they will grow in the future (see Closing Case).

The global economy can be viewed as a pyramid shown in Exhibit 1.1. The top consists of about one billion people with per capita annual income of $20,000 or higher. These are mostly people who live in the developed economies of the **Triad**, which consists of North America, Western Europe, and Japan. Another billion people making $2,000 to $20,000 a year form the second tier. The vast majority of humanity—about five billion people—make less than $2,000 a year and comprise the **base of the pyramid (BoP)**. Most MNEs (and most traditional IB books) focus on the top and second tiers and end up ignoring the BoP. An increasing number of such low-income countries have shown increasingly more economic opportunities as income levels have risen.[6] Today's students—and tomorrow's business leaders—will ignore these opportunities in BoP markets at their own peril. This book will help ensure that you will not ignore these opportunities.

1-2 WHY STUDY GLOBAL BUSINESS?

Global business (or IB) is one of the most exciting, challenging, and relevant subjects offered by business schools. There are at least three compelling reasons why you should study it—and study hard (Exhibit 1.2). First, you don't want to be a loser. Mastering global business knowledge helps advance your employability and career in an increasingly competitive global economy. An ignorant individual is unlikely to emerge as a winner in global competition.

Second, expertise in global business is often a prerequisite to join the top ranks of large firms, something many ambitious students aspire to. It is now increasingly difficult, if not impossible, to find top managers at large firms who do not possess significant global competence. Eventually you will need hands-on global experience, not merely knowledge acquired from this course. However, in order to set yourself apart as an ideal candidate to be selected for an executive position, you will need to demonstrate that you are interested in global business and have mastered such knowledge during your education. This is especially true if you are interested in gaining experience as an **expatriate manager** (or "expat" for short)—a manager who works abroad (see Chapter 13 for details).

Triad Three regions of developed economies (North America, Western Europe, and Japan).

base of the pyramid (BoP) The vast majority of humanity, about five billion people, who make less than $2,000 a year.

expatriate manager (expat) A manager who works outside his or her native country.

EXHIBIT 1.2 WHY STUDY GLOBAL BUSINESS?

▶ To advance your employability and your career in the global economy

▶ To better prepare for possible expatriate assignments abroad

▶ To build stronger competence in interacting with foreign suppliers, partners, and competitors; and in working for foreign-owned employers in your own country

Thanks to globalization, low-level jobs not only command lower salaries, but are also more vulnerable. On the other hand, top-level jobs, especially those held by expats, are both financially rewarding and relatively secure. Expats often command a significant **international premium** in compensation—a significant pay raise when working overseas. In US firms, their total compensation package can be approximately $300,000 to $400,000 (including benefits; not all is take-home pay).

Even if you do not want to be a sought-after, globe-trotting expat, we assume that you do not want to join the ranks of the unemployed due to the impact of globalization and technology (see Exhibit 1.3).

Lastly, even if you do not aspire to compete for the top job at a large firm or work overseas, and even if you work at a small firm or are self-employed, you may find yourself dealing with foreign-owned suppliers and buyers, competing with foreign-invested firms in your home market, and perhaps even selling and investing overseas. Alternatively, you may find yourself working for a foreign-owned firm, your domestic employer may be acquired by a foreign player, or your unit may be ordered to shut down for global consolidation. Any of these is a very likely scenario, because approximately 80 million people worldwide, including 18 million Chinese, six million Americans, and one million British, are employed by foreign-owned firms. In the private sector, Taiwan-based Foxconn is the largest employer in China, India-based Tata Group is the

largest employer in the UK, IBM is the second largest employer in India, and Coca-Cola is the largest employer in Africa. Understanding how global business decisions are made may facilitate your own career in such firms. If there is a strategic rationale to downsize your unit, you would want to be prepared and start polishing your résumé right away. In other words, it is your career that is at stake. Don't be the last to know! To avoid the fate humorously portrayed in Exhibit 1.3, a good place to start is to study hard and do well in your IB course. Of course, don't forget to put *this* course on your résumé as a highlight of your education. (In Focus has additional advice on what language and what fields to study.)

1-3 A UNIFIED FRAMEWORK

Global business is a vast subject area. It is one of the few courses that will make you appreciate why your university requires you to take a number of diverse courses in general education. We draw on major social sciences such as economics, geography, history, psychology, political science, and sociology. We also draw on a number of business disciplines such as finance, marketing, and strategy. The study of global business is thus very interdisciplinary.[7] It is easy to lose sight of the forest while scrutinizing various trees or even branches. The subject is not difficult, and most students find it to be fun. The number-one student complaint is about the overwhelming amount of information. Truth be told, this is also *my* number-one complaint as your author. You may have to read and learn this material, but I have to bring it all together in a way that makes sense and in a compact book that does not go on and on and on for 900 pages. To make your learning more focused, more manageable, and hopefully more fun, in this book we develop a unified framework consisting of one fundamental question and two core perspectives (shown in Exhibit 1.4).

1-3a One Fundamental Question[8]

What is it that we do in global business? Why is it so important that practically all students in business schools around the world are either required or recommended to take this course? While there are certainly a lot of questions to raise, a relentless interest in what determines the

EXHIBIT 1.3 THE IMPACT OF GLOBALIZATION AND TECHNOLOGY

WWW.CARTOONSTOCK.COM

> **international premium** A significant pay raise commanded by expatriates when working overseas.

What Language and What Fields Should I Study?

On September 3, 2007, Markéta Straková of Tabor, the Czech Republic, wrote to *BusinessWeek* columnists Jack Welch and Suzy Welch:

> I am thinking of studying Portuguese, but in your opinion, what language should I learn to succeed in the world of business? And what fields of study hold the most potential?

Jack Welch was the former chairman and CEO of General Electric (GE), and Suzy Welch was the former editor of *Harvard Business Review*. They wrote back in the same issue of *BusinessWeek*:

> You're on to something with Portuguese, since it will give you a leg up in several markets with good potential, such as Brazil and some emerging African nations. Spanish is also a good choice, as it will allow you to operate with more ease throughout Latin America, and, increasingly, the United States. But for our money—and if you can manage the much higher order of commitment—Chinese is the language to learn. China is already an economic powerhouse. It will only gain strength. Anyone who can do business there with the speed and intimacy that fluency affords will earn a real competitive edge.
>
> As for what to study—and if you want to be where the action is now and for the next couple of decades—consider the industries focused

> on alternative sources of energy. Or learn everything you can about the confluence of three fields: biotechnology, information technology, and nanotechnology. For the foreseeable future, the therapies, machines, devices, and other products and services that these fields bring to market will revolutionize society—and business.
>
> That said, when it comes to picking an education field and ultimately a career, absolutely nothing beats pursuing the path that truly fascinates your brain, engages your energy, and touches your soul. Whatever you do, do what turns your crank. Otherwise your job will always be just work, and how dreary is that?

Source: J. Welch and S. Welch, "Ideas: The Welch way," *BusinessWeek*, 3 September 2007: 104.

EXHIBIT 1.4 **A UNIFIED FRAMEWORK FOR GLOBAL BUSINESS**

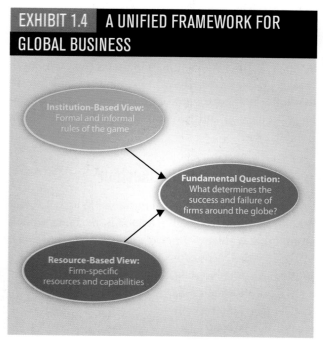

success and failure of firms around the globe serves to focus the energy of our field. Global business is fundamentally about not limiting yourself to your home country. It is about treating the global economy as your potential playground (or battlefield). Some firms may be successful domestically but fail miserably overseas. Other firms successfully translate their strengths from their home markets to other countries. If you were expected to lead your firm's efforts to enter a particular foreign market, wouldn't you want to find out what drives the success and failure of other firms in that market?

Overall, the focus on firm performance around the globe defines the field of global business (or IB) more than anything else. Numerous other questions all relate in one way or another to this most fundamental question. Therefore, all chapters in this book are centered on this fundamental question: What determines the success and failure of firms around the globe?

Given its equal treatment of companies no matter where they're from, it is not surprising that Hong Kong attracts businesses from all over the world.

1-3b First Core Perspective: An Institution-Based View[9]

An **institution-based view** suggests that the success and failure of firms are enabled and constrained by institutions. By **institutions**, we mean the rules of the game. Doing business around the globe requires intimate knowledge about both formal rules (such as laws) and informal rules (such as values) that govern competition in various countries as an **institutional framework**. Firms that do not do their homework and thus remain ignorant of the rules of the game in a certain country are not likely to emerge as winners.

Formal institutions include laws, regulations, and rules. For example, Hong Kong's laws are well known for treating all comers, whether from neighboring mainland China (whose firms are still technically regarded as "nondomestic") or far-away Chile, the same as they treat indigenous Hong Kong firms. Such equal treatment enhances the potential odds for foreign firms' success. It is thus not surprising that Hong Kong attracts a lot of outside firms. Other rules of the game discriminate against foreign firms and undermine their chances for success. India's recent attraction as a site for FDI was

only possible after its regulations changed from confrontational to accommodating. Prior to 1991, India's rules severely discriminated against foreign firms. For example, in the 1970s, the Indian government demanded that Coca-Cola either hand over the recipe for its secret syrup, which it does not even share with the US government, or get out of India. Painfully, Coca-Cola chose to leave India. Its return to India since the 1990s speaks volumes about how much the rules of the game have changed in India.

Informal institutions include cultures, ethics, and norms. They also play an important part in shaping the success and failure of firms around the globe (see Opening Case). For example, individualistic societies, particularly the English-speaking countries such as Australia, Britain, and the United States, tend to have a relatively higher level of entrepreneurship as reflected in the high number

institution-based view A leading perspective in global business that suggests that firm performance is, at least in part, determined by the institutional frameworks governing firm behavior around the world.

institution Formal and informal rules of the game.

institutional framework Formal and informal institutions that govern individual and firm behavior.

of business start-ups. Why? Because the act of founding a new firm is a widely accepted practice in individualistic societies. Conversely, collectivistic societies such as Japan often have a hard time fostering entrepreneurship. Most people there refuse to stick their neck out to found new businesses because it is contrary to the norm.

Overall, an institution-based view suggests that institutions shed a great deal of light on what drives firm performance around the globe. Next, we turn to our second core perspective.

1-3c Second Core Perspective: A Resource-Based View[10]

The institution-based view suggests that the success and failure of firms around the globe are largely determined by their environment. However, insightful as this perspective is, there is a major drawback. If we push this view to its logical extreme, then firm performance around the globe would be *entirely* determined by environments. The validity of this extreme version is certainly questionable.

The **resource-based view** helps overcome this drawback. While the institution-based view primarily deals with the *external* environment, the resource-based view focuses on a firm's *internal* resources and capabilities. It starts with a simple observation: In a harsh, unattractive environment, most firms either suffer or exit. However, against all odds, a few superstars thrive in such an environment. For instance, despite the former Soviet Union's obvious hostility toward the United States during the Cold War, PepsiCo began successfully operating in the former Soviet Union in the 1970s (!). In another example, airlines often lose money. But a small number of players, such as Southwest in the United States, Ryanair in Ireland, Hainan in China, and IndiGo in India, have been raking in profits year after year. In the fiercely competitive fashion industry, Zara has been defying gravity. How can these firms succeed in such a challenging environment? What is special about them? A short answer is that Hainan, IndiGo, PepsiCo, Ryanair, Southwest, and Zara must have certain valuable and unique *firm-specific* resources and capabilities that are not shared by competitors in the same environment.

Doing business outside one's home country is challenging. Foreign firms have to overcome a **liability of foreignness**, which is the *inherent* disadvantage that foreign firms experience in host countries because of their nonnative status.[11] Just think about all the differences in regulations, languages, cultures, and norms. Think about the odds against Toyota and Honda when they tried to eat some of General Motors' and Ford's lunch in the American heartland. Against such significant odds, the primary weapons that foreign firms such as Toyota and Honda employ are *overwhelming* resources and capabilities that can offset their liability of foreignness. Today, many of us take it for granted that the best-selling car in the United States rotates between the Toyota Camry and the Honda Civic, that Coca-Cola is the best-selling soft drink in Mexico, and that Disney is the world's number-one theme park operator (see Opening Case). We really shouldn't. Why? Because it is *not* natural for these foreign firms to dominate nonnative markets. These firms must possess some very rare and powerful firm-specific resources and capabilities that drive these remarkable success stories. This is a key theme of the resource-based view, which focuses on how winning firms develop unique and enviable resources and capabilities and how competitor firms imitate and then innovate in an effort to outcompete the winning firms.

1-3d A Consistent Theme

Given our focus on the fundamental question of what determines the success and failure of firms around the globe, we will develop a unified framework by organizing the material in *every* chapter according to the two core perspectives, namely, the institution-based and resource-based views.[12] For example, our Opening Case on Shanghai Disneyland illustrates both views at work. From an institution-based view, it is clear that Disney needs to thoroughly understand the rules of the game in China. Being insensitive about local politics and norms (such as the *Kundun* incident) can land the firm in big trouble. From a resource-based view, Disney needs to possess valuable and rare capabilities that the Chinese, who are craving for world-class entertainment, cannot get elsewhere. With our unified framework—an innovation in IB textbooks—we will not only explore the global business "trees," but also see the global business "forest."

1-4 WHAT IS GLOBALIZATION?

Globalization, generally speaking, is the close integration of countries and peoples of the world. This abstract five-syllable word is now frequently heard and debated. Those who approve of globalization count its contributions to include greater economic growth, higher standards of

---

resource-based view A leading perspective in global business that suggests that firm performance is, at least in part, determined by its internal resources and capabilities.

liability of foreignness The inherent disadvantage that foreign firms experience in host countries because of their nonnative status.

globalization The close integration of countries and peoples of the world.

ISTOCK.COM/MIPAN

living, increased technology sharing, and more exten-sive cultural integration. Critics argue that globalization undermines wages in rich countries, exploits workers in poor countries, gives MNEs too much power, destroys the environment, and undermines national sovereignty. So what exactly is globalization? This section outlines three views on globalization, recommends the pendulum view, and introduces the idea of semiglobalization.

1-4a Three Views on Globalization

Depending on what sources you read, globalization could be one of the following:

▶ A new force sweeping through the world in recent times

▶ A long-run historical evolution since the dawn of human history

▶ A pendulum that swings from one extreme to another from time to time

An understanding of these views helps put the debate about globalization in per-spective. First, opponents of glo-balization suggest that it is a new phenomenon beginning in the late 20th century, driven by recent technological inno-vations and a Western ideo-logy focused on exploiting and dominating the world

ISTOCK.COM/ROMAOSLO

through MNEs. The arguments against globalization fo-cus on an ideal world free of environmental stress, social injustice, and sweatshop labor, but present few clear alter-natives to the present economic order. Advocates and anti-globalization protesters often argue that globalization needs to be slowed down, if not stopped.

A second view contends that globalization has always been part and parcel of human history. Historians debate whether globalization started 2,000 or 8,000 years ago. MNEs existed for more than two millennia, with their earli-est traces discovered in Phoenician, Assyrian, and Roman times. International competition from low-cost countries is nothing new. In the first century A.D., the Roman emperor Tiberius was so concerned about the massive quantity of low-cost Chinese silk imports that he imposed the world's first known import quota of textiles. To-day's most successful MNEs do not come close to wielding the historical clout of some earlier MNEs, such as the East India Company during colonial times. In a nutshell, globalization is nothing new and will always exist.

A third view suggests that globalization is the "closer integration of the countries and peoples of the world which has been brought about by the enormous reduction of the costs of transportation and communication and the breaking down of artificial barriers to the flows of goods, services, capital, knowledge, and (to a lesser extent) people across borders."[13] Globalization is neither recent nor one-directional. It is, more accurately, a process similar to the swing of a pendulum.

1-4b The Pendulum View on Globalization

The third, pendulum view probably makes the most sense, because it can help us understand the ups and downs of globalization. The current era of globalization originated in the aftermath of World War II, when major Western nations committed to global trade and investment. However, between the 1950s and the 1970s, this view was not widely shared. Communist countries, such as the former Soviet Union and China, sought to develop self-sufficiency. Many noncommunist developing countries such as Argentina, Brazil, India, and Mexico focused on fostering and protecting domestic industries. But refusing to participate in global trade and investment ended up breeding uncompetitive industries. In contrast, four developing economies in Asia—namely, Hong Kong, Singapore, South Korea, and Taiwan—earned their stripes as the "Four Tigers" by participating in the global economy. They became the *only* economies once recognized as less developed (low-income) by the World Bank to have subsequently achieved developed (high-income) status.

Inspired by the Four Tigers, more countries and regions—such as China in the early 1980s, Latin America in the mid 1980s, Central and Eastern Europe in the late 1980s, and India in the 1990s—realized that joining the world economy was a must. As these countries started to emerge as new players in the world economy, they became collectively known as "emerging economies." As a result, globalization rapidly accelerated.

However, globalization, like a pendulum, is unable to keep going in one direction. Rapid globalization in the 1990s and the 2000s saw some significant backlash. First, the rapid growth of globalization led to the historically inaccurate view that globalization is new. Second, it created fear among many people in developed economies that they would lose jobs. Finally, some factions in emerging economies complained against the onslaught of MNEs, alleging that they destroy not only local companies, but also local cultures and values.

The December 1999 protests in Seattle and the September 2001 terrorist attacks in New York and Washington are undoubtedly some of the most visible and most extreme acts of anti-globalization forces at work. As a result, international travel was curtailed, and global trade and investment flows slowed in the early 2000s. Then in the mid 2000s, worldwide GDP, cross-border trade, and per capita GDP all soared to historically high levels. It was during that period that "BRIC" became a buzzword.

Unfortunately, the party suddenly ended in 2008. The 2008–2009 global economic crisis was unlike anything the world had seen since the Great Depression (1929–1933). The crisis showed, for better or worse, how interconnected the global economy has become. Deteriorating housing markets in the United States, fueled by unsustainable subprime lending practices, led to massive government bailouts of failed firms. The crisis quickly spread around the world, forcing numerous governments to bail out their own troubled banks. Global output, trade, and investment plummeted while unemployment skyrocketed. The 2008–2009 crisis became known as the Great Recession. Many people blamed globalization for the Great Recession.

After unprecedented government intervention in developed economies, confidence was growing that the global economy had turned the corner.[14] However, starting in 2010, the Greek debt crisis and then the broader PIGS debt crisis

("PIGS" refers to Portugal, Ireland or Italy, Greece, and Spain) erupted. The already slow recovery in Europe thus became slower, and unemployment hovered at very high levels. In 2016, a majority of citizens in Britain, frustrated by slow growth, high unemployment, endless needs to bail out troubled countries, and the influx of immigrants, voted to exit the European Union (EU)—resulting in Brexit (British exit of the EU) (see Chapter 8 for details).

Also in 2016, Americans voted Donald Trump into power. Departing from earlier American presidents' interest in globalization and free trade, Trump has openly called for protectionism, nationalism, and isolation. He withdrew US participation in the Trans-Pacific Partnership (TPP), demanded to renegotiate the North American Free Trade Agreement (NAFTA), threatened a trade war with China, and tightened immigration and border control.

In contrast, Chinese leaders became defenders of globalization. In January 2017, President Xi Jinping made his first appearance in Davos, Switzerland, an annual gathering of the world's pro-globalization political and business elite. His speech argued that "[n]o one will emerge as a winner in a trade war" and likened protectionism to "locking oneself in a dark room."[15] In the same month, Premier Li Keqiang, for the first time among all Chinese leaders, contributed an article to *Bloomberg Businessweek*, whose title summed it well: "Economic openness serves everyone better."[16] It is a great irony that at a time of global uncertainty and anxiety for capitalists, the world's most powerful communist leaders presented themselves as champions of open markets and globalization. In the 1980s, it was the (then) Chinese leaders who were lectured by American politicians about the merits of abandoning isolationism and joining the global economy. However, that is exactly why the *pendulum* view on globalization is so powerful (see Exhibit 1.5).

The Great Recession, Brexit, and Trump remind all firms and managers of the importance of **risk management**—the identification and assessment of risks and the preparation to minimize the impact of high-risk, unfortunate events. As a technique to prepare and plan for multiple scenarios (either high risk or low risk), **scenario planning** is now extensively used around the world. For

Under President Xi Jinping, China has emerged as a leading defender of globalization. In a recent speech, Xi argued that "No one will emerge as a winner in a trade war."

example, what if Britain did completely break ties with the EU? What if NAFTA was dismantled?

Like the proverbial elephant, globalization is seen by everyone yet rarely comprehended. Remember all of us felt sorry when we read the story of a bunch of blind men trying to figure out the shape and form of the elephant. We really shouldn't. Although we are not blind, our task is more challenging than the blind men who study a standing animal. Our beast—globalization—does not stand still and often rapidly moves, back and forth (!). Yet, we try to live with it, avoid being crushed by it, and even attempt to profit from it. Overall, relative to the other two views, the view of globalization as a pendulum is more balanced, more realistic, and thus more insightful. In other words, globalization has both rosy and dark sides, and it changes over time.

1-4c Semiglobalization

Despite the hype, globalization is not complete. Do we really live in a globalized world? Are selling and investing abroad just as easy as at home? Obviously not. Most measures of market integration, such as trade and FDI, have recently scaled new heights, but still fall far short of pointing to a single, globally integrated market. Given some countries' recent retreat from globalization, such measures are likely to be reduced. In other words, what we have may be labeled **semiglobalization**, which is more complex

	Leading countries in favor of *more* globalization	Leading countries in favor of *less* globalization
1980s	United States, Britain	China
2010s	China	United States, Britain

EXHIBIT 1.5 THE PENDULUM SWINGS ON GLOBALIZATION

risk management Identification and assessment of risks and preparation to minimize the impact of high-risk, unfortunate events.

scenario planning A technique to prepare and plan for multiple scenarios (either high or low risk).

semiglobalization A perspective that suggests that barriers to market integration at borders are high, but not high enough to completely insulate countries from each other.

Debate: Are US Multinationals Good for America?

Ethical Dilemma

Most debates on multinational enterprises (MNEs) around the world focus on their impact on host countries that receive foreign direct investment (FDI). Recent debates highlight the role of homegrown MNEs in the US economy itself. On the positive side, US MNEs are productive, innovative, employing more skilled workers, and paying higher wages—at least 6% more than non-MNEs in the United States. Shareholders pocket the fruits of these firms' global success, and executives—especially those from successful firms—enjoy increased power, more pay, and higher-profile global celebrity status.

However, on the non-positive side, in the past decade US MNEs have been decoupling from the US economy. They still have headquarters in the United States, are still listed on US stock exchanges, and most of their shareholders are still American (foreigners own approximately 15% of US equities). But their expansion has been mostly overseas. Between 2009 and 2013, only 400,000 (5%) of the net jobs created in America were created by US MNEs. In 2007, Delphi filed for Chapter 11 bankruptcy protection in order to slash its US headcount from 32,000 to 7,000. Its bankruptcy filing was careful to exclude its 115,000 foreign-based headcount, which was destined to grow. IBM reportedly endeavored to reduce the number of permanent employees located in the United States from 30% to 20% of its total global headcount by the end of 2017.

US MNEs are also increasingly shy about paying US taxes. One of their leading concerns is one of the world's highest corporate income tax rates imposed by Uncle Sam, and many other countries lure them away with lower taxes. Legally, Google Ireland is not a branch of the US-based Google Corporation. Although 100% owned by Google Corporation, Google Ireland is a separate, legally independent corporation registered in Ireland. Technically, Google Ireland is an *Irish* firm. Although Google Corporation intentionally lets Google Ireland earn a lot of profits, the US Internal Revenue Service (IRS) cannot tax a dime that Google Ireland makes unless Google Ireland sends back (repatriates) the profits to Google Corporation. Google Corporation does not have just one subsidiary. It has many around the world. Overall, 54% of Google's profits are parked overseas and are not taxable by the IRS. Google is not alone. The list of leading US firms that have left (or invested) a *majority* of their profits overseas includes Chevron, Cisco, Citigroup, Exxon Mobil, GE, HP, Johnson & Johnson, Microsoft, P&G, PepsiCo, and Pfizer.

Overall, in their eagerness to chase new markets, cheap labor, and lower taxes by "going global," many US MNEs, according to critics, have abandoned some of their most important corporate social

Apple (every day) keeps the taxman away

STOP tax dodging

LAURA HUTTON/SHUTTERSTOCK.COM

responsibility (CSR). They stand accused of unleashing "carnage" on ordinary Americans, in the words of President Trump during his inaugural speech in January 2017. The solution? "Domesticate" such globe-trotting multinationals, according to the *Economist*. Lower taxes would draw them back, and open threats with "a big border tax" (again, Trump's own words) would make them think twice before "doing business as usual." The list of US MNEs being publicly named and shamed by Trump includes Boeing, Carrier (part of United Technologies), General Motors, Northrop Grumman, and others. Getting the message, Apple, Ford Motor Company, IBM, and other US MNEs, including those named above, have pledged to grow thousands of jobs at home. Non-US firms such as Alibaba, Fiat Chrysler, and Toyota have also played along by pledging to invest in the United States and grow jobs there—at least to avoid being Trump's next Twitter victim.

Are these pledges "smoke screens," or are they the beginning of a new era? Are these moves good or bad for the US economy? Of course, given the complexity, "good" is simply a shorthand for benefits outweighing drawbacks, and "bad" is the other way around. Abandoning the benefits of low-cost labor and employing high-cost American labor would jack up the price of goods and services. Few would appreciate this outcome. An official Made-in-USA "Make America Great Again" hat costs $25, but a Made-in-China hat only costs $15 (or less). If US MNEs shifted a quarter of their foreign jobs back home at US wage levels, their profits would drop 12%, and dividends would plummet. Clearly, shareholders and executives are not going to be happy. Debates on how to strike the balance thus rage on.

Sources: "IBM's big jobs dodge," *Bloomberg Businessweek*, 30 January 2017: 30; "Trump's uncertainty principle," *Bloomberg Businessweek*, 30 January 2017: 6–7; "Go bankrupt, then go overseas," *Business Week*, 24 April 2006: 52–53; "In retreat," *Economist*, 28 January 2017: 11; "The retreat of the global company," *Economist*, 28 January 2017: 18–22; M. W. Peng, *Global Business*, 4th ed. (Boston: Cengage, 2017).

than extremes of total isolation and total globalization. Semiglobalization suggests that barriers to market integration at borders are high, but not high enough to insulate countries from each other completely.[17]

Semiglobalization calls for more than one way of strategizing around the globe. Total isolation on a nation-state basis would suggest localization—a strategy of treating each country as a unique market. An MNE marketing products to 100 countries will need to come up with 100 versions. This strategy is clearly too costly. Total globalization, on the other hand, would lead to standardization—a strategy of treating the entire world as one market. The MNE can just market one version of "world car" or "world drink." But the world obviously is not that simple. Between total isolation and total globalization, semiglobalization has no single right way of doing business around the globe, resulting in a wide variety of experimentations. Overall, (semi)globalization is neither to be opposed as a menace nor to be celebrated as a panacea; it is to be *engaged*.

1-5 A GLANCE AT THE GLOBAL ECONOMY

Twenty-first-century business leaders face enormous challenges (see Debate). This book helps overcome some of these challenges. As a backdrop for the remainder of this book, this section offers a basic understanding of the global economy. The global economy in 2015 was an approximately $75 trillion economy (total global GDP calculated at official, nominal exchange rates—alternatively, $110 trillion on a PPP basis).[18] Although there is no need to memorize a lot of statistics, it is useful to remember this $75 trillion (or $110 trillion) figure to put things in perspective.

One frequent observation in the globalization debate is the enormous size and power of multinationals (see Debate). Take a look at the largest MNE within one sizable country: Volkswagen's worldwide sales would represent 10% of German GDP, Samsung's sales 17% of South Korean GDP, and BP's sales 26% of British GDP.[19] Exhibit 1.6 shows the most recent top ten firms. If the

ISTOCK.COM/ZONECREATIVE

EXHIBIT 1.6 TOP TEN LARGEST FIRMS IN THE WORLD (MEASURED BY SALES)		
	Corporate name	Country
1	Walmart Stores	United States
2	State Grid	China
3	China National Petroleum Corporation	China
4	Sinopec Group	China
5	Royal Dutch Shell	Netherlands
6	Exxon Mobil	United States
7	Volkswagen	Germany
8	Toyota Motor	Japan
9	Apple	United States
10	BP	United Kingdom

Source: Adapted from *Fortune*, "Global 500," 1 August 2016: F-1. Data refer to 2015.

largest MNE, Walmart, were an independent country, it would be the 27th largest economy—its sales were smaller than Belgium's GDP but larger than Venezuela's. The sales of the largest EU-based MNE, Royal Dutch Shell, were larger than the GDP of each of the following EU member countries: Austria, Denmark, Finland, Ireland, and Portugal. The sales of the largest Asia-based MNE, State Grid, were larger than the GDP of each of the following Asian economies: Hong Kong, Malaysia, Phillipines, Singapore, and Thailand. Today, over 82,000 MNEs manage at least 810,000 subsidiaries overseas.[20] Total annual sales for the largest 500 MNEs reach $28 trillion (more than one third of global output).[21]

Exhibit 1.7 documents the change in the makeup of the 500 largest MNEs. Although MNEs from the Triad (North America, Europe, and Japan) dominate the list, their share has been shrinking—thanks to the Great Transformation (discussed earlier). Among MNEs from emerging economies, those from BRIC contribute 122 firms to the *Fortune* Global 500 list. In particular, MNEs from China have come on strong.[22] With 57 *Fortune* Global 500 company headquarters, Beijing now has the heaviest concentration of such headquarters. In comparison, Tokyo has 41 *Fortune* Global 500 headquarters (the world's second heaviest concentration). London, New York, and Paris each have 17 (third heaviest concentration). Clearly, global rivals cannot afford to ignore emerging multinationals such as those based in Beijing, and students studying this book need to pay attention to these emerging multinationals.

 1-6 ORGANIZATION OF THE BOOK

This book has three parts. Part 1 is *foundations*. Following this chapter, Chapters 2, 3, and 4 deal with the two leading perspectives: institution-based and resource-based views. Part 2 covers *tools*, focusing on trade (Chapter 5), foreign investment (Chapter 6), foreign exchange (Chapter 7), and global and regional integration (Chapter 8). Part 3 focuses on *managing* around the world. We start with the internationalization of small, entrepreneurial firms (Chapter 9), followed by ways to enter foreign markets (Chapter 10), to make alliances and acquisitions work (Chapter 11), to strategize, structure, and learn (Chapter 12), to manage human resources (Chapter 13), to deal with marketing and supply chain management (Chapter 14), and finally to manage corporate social responsibility (Chapter 15).

EXHIBIT 1.7   RECENT CHANGES IN THE *FORTUNE* GLOBAL 500

	2005	2010	2015
Developed economies			
United States	170	133	134
European Union	165	149	124
Japan	70	68	54
Switzerland	12	15	15
Canada	14	11	11
Australia	8	8	8
Emerging economies			
China	20	61	103
India	6	8	7
Brazil	4	7	7
Russia	5	7	5
BRIC	35	83	122

Sources: Compiled from various *Fortune* issues. The most recent *Fortune* Global 500 list (for 2015) was published in *Fortune*, 1 August 2016.

EMERGING MARKETS/ETHICAL DILEMMA
Closing Case: Two Scenarios of the Global Economy in 2050

Focusing on the future of the global economy, two scenarios have emerged with a view toward 2050. Known as "continued globalization," the first scenario is a rosy one. Spearheaded by Goldman Sachs, whose chairman of its Asset Management Division, Jim O'Neil, coined the term "BRIC" nearly two decades ago, this scenario suggests that—in descending order—China, the United States, India, Brazil, and Russia will become the largest economies by 2050 (Exhibit 1.8). BRIC countries together may overtake the US by 2015 and the Group of Seven (G-7) by 2032, and China may individually dethrone the US by 2026. In PPP terms, BRIC's share of global GDP, which rose from 18% in 2001 to 25% currently, may reach 40% by 2050. In addition, by 2050, the N-11 as a group may become significantly larger than the United States and almost twice the size of the Euro area.

Goldman Sachs' predictions have been largely supported by other influential forecasting studies. For example, the Organization for Economic Cooperation and Development (OECD) predicted

that by 2060, China, India, and the United States will become the top three economies. The combined GDP of China and India will be larger than that of the entire OECD area (Exhibit 1.9). In 2011, China and India accounted for less than one-half of GDP of the seven major (G-7) OECD economies. By 2060, the combined GDP of China and India may be 1.5 times larger than the G-7. India's GDP will be a bit larger than the United States', and China's a lot larger.

Despite such dramatic changes, one interesting constant is the relative rankings of income per capita. Goldman Sachs predicted that by 2050, the G-7 countries will still be the richest, led by the United States, Canada, and the United Kingdom (Exhibit 1.10). Ranked eighth globally ($63,486—all dollar figures in this paragraph refer to 2010 US dollars), Russia may top the BRIC group, with income per capita approaching that of Korea. By 2050, per capita income in China ($40,614) and India ($14,766) will continue to lag behind developed economies—at, respectively, 47% and 17% of the US level ($85,791). These predictions were supported by the OECD, which noted that by 2060, Chinese and Indian per capita

EXHIBIT 1.8   BRIC AND THE US WILL BECOME THE LARGEST ECONOMIES BY 2050

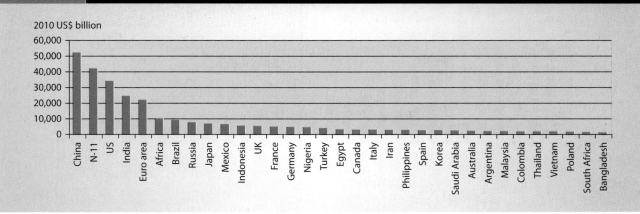

2010 US$ billion

Source: Goldman Sachs, "An update on the long-term outlook for the BRICs and beyond," *Monthly Insights from the Office of the Chairman, Goldman Sachs Asset Management* (January 2012): 3. "N-11" refers to the Next Eleven identified by Goldman Sachs: Bangladesh, Egypt, Indonesia, Iran, Korea, Mexico, Nigeria, Pakistan, Philippines, Turkey, and Vietnam.

EXHIBIT 1.9   CONTRIBUTIONS TO GLOBAL GDP, 2011 AND 2060

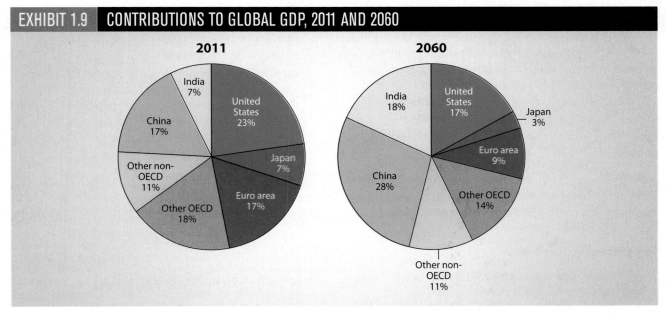

Source: OECD, "Looking to 2060: A global vision of long-term growth," *Economics Department Policy Note* 5, November 2012: 8. Note: The comparisons are based on 2005 purchasing power parity (PPP).

income would only reach 59% and 27% of the US level, respectively.

Underpinning this scenario of "continued globalization" are three assumptions: (1) Emerging economies as a group will maintain strong (albeit gradually reduced) growth; (2) geopolitical events and natural disasters (such as climate changes) will not create significant disruption; and (3) regional, international, and supranational institutions will continue to function reasonably. This scenario envisions a path of growth that is perhaps more volatile than that of the past 20 years, but ultimately leads to considerably higher levels of economic integration and much higher levels of incomes in countries nowadays known as emerging economies.

The second scenario can be labeled "de-globalization." It is characterized by (1) prolonged recession, high unemployment, droughts, climate shocks, disrupted food supply, and conflicts over energy (such as "water wars"), on the one hand; and (2) public unrest, protectionist policies, and the unraveling of

certain institutions that we take for granted (such as the EU and NAFTA), on the other hand. As protectionism rises, global economic integration suffers.

The upshot? Weak economic growth around the world. While global de-integration would harm economies worldwide, regional de-integration would harm countries of Europe, especially those outside a likely residual core of the EU. Brexit will make Britain a weaker economy. Unable to keep growing sustainably, BRIC may become "broken bricks" and may fail to reach their much-hyped potential. For example, in the 1950s and 1960s, Russian economic growth was also very impressive, fueling Soviet geopolitical ambitions that eventually turned out to be unsupportable. In the late 1960s, Burma (now Myanmar), the Philippines, and Sri Lanka were widely anticipated to become the next Asian Tigers, only to falter badly. Over the long course of history, it is rare to sustain strong growth in a large number of countries over more than a decade. It is true that the first decade of the 21st century—prior to the Great Depression—witnessed

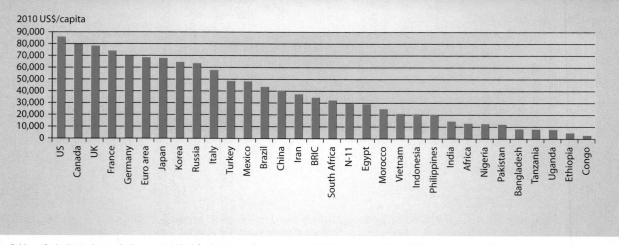

Source: Goldman Sachs, "An update on the long-term outlook for the BRICs and beyond," *Monthly Insights from the Office of the Chairman, Goldman Sachs Asset Management* (January 2012): 4. See footnote to Exhibit 1.8 for N-11.

some spectacular growth in BRIC and many other emerging economies. A key question concerns how unique the current times are. Historically, "failure to sustain growth has been the general rule," according to a pessimistic expert.

In both scenarios, one common prediction is that global competition will heat up. Competition under the "de-globalization" scenario would be especially intense since the total size of the "pie" will not be growing sufficiently (if not negatively). At the same time, firms would operate in partially protected markets, which result in additional costs for market penetration. Competition under the "continued globalization" scenario would also be intense, but in different ways. The hope is that a rising "tide" may be able to lift "all boats."

Case Discussion Questions

1. Which of the two scenarios is more plausible for the global economy in 2050? Why? How does that affect *you* as a consumer, as a professional, and as a citizen of your country?

2. From a resource-based view, what should firms do to better prepare for the two scenarios?

3. ***ON ETHICS:*** From an institution-based view, what should firms do to better prepare for the two scenarios? (*Hint:* For example, if they believe in "continued globalization," they may be more interested in lobbying for reduced trade barriers. But if they believe in "de-globalization," they may lobby for higher trade barriers.)

Source: "In retreat," *Economist*, January 28, 2017: 11; "The retreat of the global company," *Economist*, 28 January 2017: 18–22; Foresight Horizon Scanning Centre, *World Trade: Possible Futures* (London: UK Government Office for Science, 2009); Goldman Sachs, "An update on the long-term outlook for the BRICs and beyond," *Monthly Insights from the Office of the Chairman, Goldman Sachs Asset Management*, January 2012; A. Musacchio and E. Werker, "Mapping frontier economies," *Harvard Business Review*, December 2016: 41–48; OECD, "Looking to 2060: A global vision of long-term growth," *Economics Department Policy Note* 5, November 2012; M. W. Peng and K. Meyer, *Winning the Future Markets for UK Manufacturing Output* (London: UK Government Office for Science, 2013); R. Sharma, "Broken BRICS: Why the rest stopped growing," *Foreign Affairs*, November 2012: 2–7.

STUDY TOOLS 1

LOCATED AT THE BACK OF YOUR BOOK:

☐ Rip out and study the Chapter Review Card at the end of the book

LOG IN TO WWW.CENGAGEBRAIN.COM TO:

☐ Review key term flashcards

☐ Complete a practice quiz to test your knowledge of key concepts

☐ View animated PengAtlas Maps

☐ Complete interactive content, watch chapter videos, and take a graded quiz

☐ Track your knowledge of key concepts in Global Business

☐ Read and discuss additional case study content

2 Understanding Politics, Laws, & Economics

LEARNING OBJECTIVES

After studying this chapter, you will be able to . . .

2-1 Identify two types of institutions.

2-2 Explain how institutions reduce uncertainty.

2-3 Identify the two core propositions underpinning an institution-based view of global business.

2-4 List the differences between democracy and totalitarianism.

2-5 List the differences among civil law, common law, and theocratic law.

2-6 Articulate the importance of property rights and intellectual property rights.

2-7 List the differences among market economy, command economy, and mixed economy.

2-8 Explain why it is important to understand the different institutions when doing business abroad.

After you finish this chapter, go to

PAGE 34 for

STUDY TOOLS

ETHICAL DILEMMA
Opening Case: The Newest Transition Economy

The term "transition economy" was coined in the mid-1990s to refer to former Soviet Union and Central and Eastern European countries (such as Hungary, Poland, and Russia) as well as Asian countries (such as China and Vietnam), which were undergoing major transitions from state socialism toward market capitalism. Specifically, institutional transitions are defined as fundamental and comprehensive changes introduced to the formal and informal rules of the game that affect firms as players. How firms—both domestic and foreign, established and newly founded—navigate the uncertain waters of such transitions has been a major theme in the global business field since the 1990s.

Fast-forward to 2017. The United States has emerged to become the newest "transition economy," with numerous rules of the game being significantly changed by the Trump administration. Politically, the country has remained a functioning democracy. The peaceful transition of power in January 2017, despite a divisive campaign, continues the country's admirable tradition that started during President George Washington's time. Elsewhere, such a peaceful transition of power cannot be taken for granted. Speaking of coincidence, the tiny African nation of Gambia also elected a new president in late 2016, but the incumbent president who lost the election refused to leave. Political chaos and violence erupted. Thousands of people fled. On January 21, 2017, the incumbent president had to be militarily dislodged by foreign troops from the Economic Community of West African States (ECOWAS) so that the newly elected president could be sworn in—literally at the same time when Donald Trump was sworn in.

Economically, the changes unleashed by the Trump administration are numerous and wide-ranging. Turning inward, the United States would shy away from embracing the long-cherished principles of globalization and free trade. US participation in the Trans-Pacific Partnership (TPP), a free trade deal that negotiators from the United States and 11 other countries labored over for seven years and that had been signed (but not yet ratified by Congress) in 2016, was withdrawn by the stroke of a pen in an executive order during the first week of the new administration. Although well established since 1994, the North American Free Trade Agreement (NAFTA) would be renegotiated, if not dismantled. Firms such as Carrier, General Motors (GM), and Toyota that took advantage of NAFTA were publically named and shamed for "shipping US jobs" to Mexico. They were coerced to agree to invest in the US economy. Otherwise, these firms were threatened with—in Trump's own words—a "big border tax," which would be a violation of NAFTA. Getting the message, Fiat Chrysler and Ford Motor Company quickly announced expansion plans in the United States to avoid Trump's wrath. Looming on the horizon is a trade war with China, the world's largest trader and one of the United States' leading trading partners.

Politically, Trump's rapid-fire executive orders banning refugees from seven Muslim-majority countries, erecting a wall along the border with Mexico, and emphasizing "extreme vetting" touched off a storm of protests. Firms ranging from low-tech agribusinesses to high-tech Silicon Valley fast movers, which rely on immigrant labor and talents, had to brace themselves. Trump's actions also generated a series of lawsuits from various groups, alleging that the presidential actions were unconstitutional and disrespecting the rule of law. Although such allegations were not unusual for presidents in countries such as Gambia, it is rare for a US president to be so labeled. One thing "a president who prides himself on changing all the rules and throwing away the established norms," according to *Bloomberg Businessweek*, has accomplished is to introduce tremendous uncertainties amid all these transitions.

Affecting politics, laws, and economics, uncertainties are a hallmark of all transition economies, whose future direction, by definition, is unpredictable. Will the future of the United States as the newest transition economy be "great again" as promised by President Trump, or join the ranks of "failed states" as prophesized by a leading American political scientist, Francis Fukuyama (whose most famous earlier work is his 1992 book *The End of History and the Last Man*)?

Sources: "The arc of Trump," *Bloomberg Businessweek*, 28 November 2016: 6–7; "Silicon Valley's new reality show," *Bloomberg Businessweek*, 12 December 2016: 6–7; "Pharma's worst nightmare," *Bloomberg Businessweek*, 23 January 2017: 18–19; "The looming Trump trade disaster," *Bloomberg Businessweek*, 23 January 2017: 8; "The patriotic response to populism," *Bloomberg Businessweek*, 9 January 2017: 8; "Trump's uncertainty principle," *Bloomberg Businessweek*, 30 January 2017: 6–7; "Trump vs. the rule of law," *Bloomberg Businessweek*, 6 February 2017: 6–7; "Troops enter Gambia as new president is sworn in," *New York Times*, 19 January 2017: www.nytimes.com; F. Fukuyama, "America: The failed state," *Prospect Magazine*, January 2017: www.prospectmagazine.co.uk; M. W. Peng, *Business Strategies in Transition Economies* (Thousand Oaks, CA: Sage, 2000); "Auto industry's no. 1 preoccupation: Trump," *Wall Street Journal*, January 23, 2017: www.wsj.com.

What are the benefits and costs of institutional transitions? How do the rules of the game and their changes affect domestic and foreign firms as players? Why are the stakes so high? As the Opening Case illustrates, the answer boils down to institutions, popularly known as the "rules of the game" (first introduced in Chapter 1). As economic players, individuals and firms play by these rules. However, institutions are not static and they may change, as evidenced by the ongoing changes in the United States. Such

institutional transitions are "fundamental and comprehensive changes introduced to the formal and informal rules of the game that affect firms as players."[1]

Overall, the success and failure of firms around the globe are to a large extent determined by firms' ability to understand and take advantage of the different rules of the game. In other words, how firms play the game and win (or lose), at least in part, depends on how the rules are made, enforced, and changed. This calls for firms to constantly monitor, decode, and adapt to the changing rules of the game in order to survive and prosper. As a result, such an institution-based view has emerged as a leading perspective on global business.[2] This chapter first introduces the institution-based view. Then, we focus on *formal* institutions (such as political, legal, and economic systems). *Informal* institutions (such as cultures, ethics, and norms) will be discussed in Chapter 3.

2-1 UNDERSTANDING INSTITUTIONS

Building on the "rules of the game" metaphor, Douglass North, a Nobel laureate in economics, more formally defines institutions as "the humanly devised constraints that structure human interaction."[3] An institutional framework is made up of both the formal and informal institutions governing individual and firm behavior. Richard Scott, a leading sociologist, identifies three pillars that support these institutions: regulatory, normative, and cognitive.[4]

Shown in Exhibit 2.1, formal institutions include laws, regulations, and rules. Their primary supportive pillar, the **regulatory pillar**, is the coercive power of governments. For example, out of patriotic duty, many individuals may pay taxes. However, many other individuals pay taxes out of fear—if they did not pay and got caught, they would go to jail. In other words, it is the coercive power of governments' tax laws that forms the regulatory pillar to compel many individuals to pay taxes.

On the other hand, informal institutions include norms, cultures, and ethics. Informal institutions are supported by two pillars: normative and cognitive. The **normative pillar** refers to how the values, beliefs, and actions—collectively known as norms—of other relevant players influence the behavior of focal individuals and firms. For example, a recent norm among Western firms is the rush to invest in China and India. This norm has prompted many Western firms to imitate each other without a clear understanding of how to make such moves work. Cautious managers who resist such herding are often confronted by board members and investors with the question "Why are we not in China and India?" In other words, "Why don't we follow the norm?"

The **cognitive pillar** is the second support for informal institutions. It refers to the internalized (or taken-for-granted) values and beliefs that guide individual and firm behavior. For example, whistleblowers reported Enron's wrongdoing out of belief in what is right and wrong. While most employees may not feel comfortable with organizational wrongdoing, the social norm in any firm is to shut up and not to rock the boat. Essentially, whistleblowers choose to follow their internalized personal belief on what is right by overcoming the social norm that encourages silence. In Enron's case, the normative pillar suggests silence, whereas the whistleblowers' actions are supported by their strong cognitive pillar regarding what is right and wrong.

Formal and informal institutional forces stem primarily from home countries and host countries. In addition, international and regional organizations such as the World Trade Organization (WTO), the International Monetary Fund (IMF), and the European Union (EU) may also influence firm conduct in terms of do's and don'ts. See Chapters 7 and 8 for more details.

---

institutional transition Fundamental and comprehensive changes introduced to the formal and informal rules of the game that affect organizations as players.

regulatory pillar The coercive power of governments exercised through laws, regulations, and rules.

normative pillar The mechanisms through which norms influence individual and firm behavior.

cognitive pillar The internalized, taken-for-granted values and beliefs that guide individual and firm behavior.

EXHIBIT 2.1	DIMENSIONS OF INSTITUTIONS	
Degree of formality	**Examples**	**Supportive pillars**
Formal institutions	Laws Regulations Rules	Regulatory (coercive)
Informal institutions	Norms Cultures Ethics	Normative Cognitive

ISTOCK.COM/XYNO

2-2 WHAT DO INSTITUTIONS DO?

While institutions do many things, their key role is to *reduce uncertainty*. Specifically, institutions influence the decision-making process of both individuals and firms by signaling what conduct is legitimate and acceptable and what is not. Basically, institutions constrain the range of acceptable actions. Why is it so important to reduce uncertainty? Because uncertainty can be potentially devastating. Political uncertainty such as an uprising may render long-range planning obsolete. Political deadlocks in Washington have made the US government "less stable, less effective, and less predictable," which led Standard & Poor's—a private but influential rating agency—to downgrade its AAA credit rating to AA+.[5] Economic uncertainty such as failure to carry out transactions as spelled out in contracts may result in economic losses. See the Closing Case for the ongoing political and economic uncertainty in Russia.

Uncertainty surrounding economic transactions can lead to **transaction costs**, which are the costs associated with economic transactions or, more broadly, the costs of doing business. Nobel laureate Oliver Williamson makes the comparison to frictions in mechanical systems: "Do the gears mesh, are the parts lubricated, is there needless slippage or other loss of energy?" He goes on to suggest that transaction costs can be regarded as "the economic counterpart of frictions: Do the parties to exchange operate harmoniously, or are there frequent misunderstandings and conflicts?"[6]

An important source of transaction costs is **opportunism**, defined as the act of seeking self-interest with guile. Examples include misleading, cheating, and confusing other parties in transactions that will increase transaction costs. Attempting to reduce such transaction costs, institutional frameworks increase certainty by spelling out the rules of the game so that violations (such as failures to fulfill contracts) can be mitigated with relative ease (such as through formal courts and arbitration).

Without stable institutional frameworks, transaction costs may become prohibitively high, and certain transactions simply would not take place. For example, in the absence of credible institutional frameworks that

protect investors, domestic investors may choose to put their money abroad. Although Africa is starving for capital, rich people in Africa put a striking 39% of their assets outside of Africa.[7]

Institutions are not static. Institutional transitions in some emerging economies are so pervasive that these countries are simply called transition economies. Examples include those countries that are moving from central planning to market competition, such as China, Cuba, Poland, and Russia. Institutional transitions in these countries as well as other emerging economies such as Brazil, India, and South Africa create both huge challenges and tremendous opportunities for domestic and international firms. The Opening Case suggests that the United States has become a new transition economy.

Having outlined the definitions of various institutions and their supportive pillars as well as the key role of institutions in uncertainty reduction, next we will introduce the first core perspective on global business: an institution-based view.

2-3 AN INSTITUTION-BASED VIEW OF GLOBAL BUSINESS

Shown in Exhibit 2.2, an institution-based view of global business focuses on the dynamic interaction between institutions and firms, and considers firm behavior as the outcome of such an interaction. Specifically, firm behavior is often a reflection of the formal and informal constraints of a particular institutional framework. In short, institutions matter.

How do institutions matter? The institution-based view suggests two core propositions (see Exhibit 2.3). First, managers and firms *rationally* pursue their interests and make choices within institutional constraints. In Brazil, government tax revenues at all levels reach 35% of GDP, much higher than Mexico's 18% and China's 16%. Not surprisingly, the gray market in Brazil

transaction cost Cost associated with economic transactions or, more broadly, the cost of doing business.

opportunism The act of seeking self-interest with guile.

ISTOCK.COM/DEVONYU

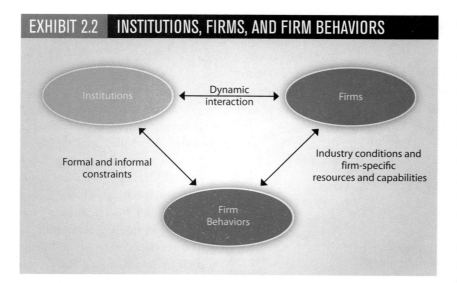

accounts for a much higher percentage of the economy than in Mexico and China.[8] Likewise, in the United States, firms such as Fiat Chrysler, Ford, GM, and Toyota were eager to take advantage of NAFTA's provisions to remove tariffs for cross-border movements of vehicles and parts. Under the threat of a "big border tax," their response to curtail expansion in Mexico and to beef up investments in the United States also made sense (see Opening Case). Both Brazilian firms' migration to the gray market and US and non-US automakers' interest in taking advantage of NAFTA are rational responses when they pursue their interests within formal institutional constraints in these countries.

Second, while formal and informal institutions combine to govern firm behavior, informal constraints play a *larger* role in reducing uncertainty and providing constancy for managers and firms in situations where formal constraints are unclear or fail. For example, when the former Soviet Union collapsed and with it the formal regime, the growth of many entrepreneurial firms was facilitated by informal constraints based on personal relationships and connections (called *blat* in Russian) among managers and officials.

Many observers have the impression that relying on informal connections is relevant only to firms in emerging economies and that firms in developed economies pursue only market-based strategies. This is far from the truth. Even in developed economies, formal rules make up only a small (though important) part of institutional constraints, and informal constraints are pervasive. Just as firms compete in product markets, firms also fiercely compete in the political marketplace characterized by informal

political system The rules of the game on how a country is governed politically.

relationships.[9] Basically, if a firm cannot be a market leader, it may still beat the competition on other grounds—namely, the nonmarket, political environment. In September 2008, a rapidly failing Merrill Lynch was able to sell itself to Bank of America for $50 billion. Supported by US government officials, this mega deal was arranged over 48 hours (shorter than the time most people take to buy a car) and the negotiations took place *inside* the Federal Reserve building in New York. In contrast, Lehman Brothers failed to secure government support and had to file for bankruptcy. In December 2016, Donald Trump's former campaign manager set up a lobbying firm, Avenue Strategies. It quickly landed 11 clients, including an Ohio payday lender, a Cleveland law firm, and an incoming governor of Puerto Rico.[10] Guess what Avenue Strategies will be selling? Overall, the skillful use of a country's institutional frameworks to acquire advantage is at the heart of the institution-based view.

While there are numerous formal and informal institutions, in this chapter we focus on *formal* institutions. (Informal institutions will be covered in Chapter 3.) Chief among formal institutions are political systems, legal systems, and economic systems. We introduce each in turn.

2-4 POLITICAL SYSTEMS

A **political system** refers to the rules of the game on how a country is governed politically. At the broadest level, there are two primary political systems: democracy and totalitarianism. This section first outlines these two systems and then discusses their ramifications for political risk.

2-4a Democracy

Democracy is a political system in which citizens elect representatives to govern the country on their behalf. Usually, the political party with the majority of votes wins and forms a government. Democracy was pioneered by the Athenians in ancient Greece. In today's world, Great Britain has the longest experience of running a democracy (by history), and India has the largest democracy (by population).

A fundamental aspect of democracy that is relevant to global business is an individual's right to freedom of expression and organization. For example, starting up a firm is an act of economic expression, essentially telling the rest of the world: "I want to be my own boss! And I want to make some money!" In most modern democracies, the right to organize economically has been extended not only to domestic individuals and firms, but also to *foreign* individuals and firms that come to do business. While those of us fortunate enough to have been brought up in a democracy take the right to establish a firm for granted, we should be reminded that this may not necessarily be the case under other political systems. Before the 1980s, if someone dared to formally establish a private firm in the former Soviet Union, he or she would have been arrested and *shot* by the authorities.

Marchers carry images of late Cuban President Fidel Castro at the 2016 International Workers' Day Parade in Havana, Cuba. Raúl Castro, who assumed control of Cuba from brother Fidel in 2008, continues to operate the country as a communist dictatorship.

2-4b Totalitarianism

On the opposite end of the political spectrum from democracy is **totalitarianism** (also known as **dictatorship**), which is defined as a political system in which one person or party exercises absolute political control over the population. There are four major types of totalitarianism:

- *Communist totalitarianism* centers on a communist party. This system was embraced throughout Central and Eastern Europe and the former Soviet Union until the late 1980s. It is still practiced in China, Cuba, Laos, North Korea, and Vietnam.

- *Right-wing totalitarianism* is characterized by its intense hatred of communism. One party, typically backed by the military, restricts political freedom because its members believe that such freedom would lead to communism. In the decades following World War II, Argentina, Brazil, Chile, South Africa, South Korea, and Taiwan practiced right-wing totalitarianism. Most of these countries have recently become democracies.

- *Theocratic totalitarianism* refers to the monopolization of political power in the hands of one religious party or group. Iran and Saudi Arabia are leading examples.

- *Tribal totalitarianism* refers to one tribe or ethnic group (which may or may not be the majority of the population) monopolizing political power and oppressing other tribes or ethnic groups. Rwanda's bloodbath in the 1990s was due to some of the most brutal practices of tribal totalitarianism.

2-4c Political Risk

While the degree of hostility toward business varies among different types of totalitarianism (some can be more pro-business than others), totalitarianism in general is not as good for business as democracy. Totalitarian countries often experience wars, riots, protests, chaos, and breakdowns. As a result, these countries often suffer from a high level

democracy A political system in which citizens elect representatives to govern the country on their behalf.

totalitarianism (dictatorship) A political system in which one person or party exercises absolute political control over the population.

Testing the Dell Theory of Peace in East Asia

Thomas Friedman, a *New York Times* columnist, suggested in his 2005 bestseller *The World Is Flat* a Dell theory of peace: No two countries that are both part of a major global supply chain, like Dell's, will ever fight a war against each other as long as they are both part of the same global supply chain. Countries involved in major global supply chains focus on just-in-time deliveries of goods and services, which raise standards of living for all involved. In the case of Dell, the following countries are involved: China, Costa Rica, Germany, Israel, Japan, Malaysia, the Philippines, South Korea, Taiwan, Thailand, and the United States.

East Asia is both a manufacturing hub for IT giants such as Dell and a hot neighborhood for territorial disputes. In 2012, the Japanese government ignored warnings from China and purchased from a right-wing politician five barren rocks in the East China Sea, which the Chinese call Diaoyu and the Japanese call Senkaku. (For compositional simplicity, we will call them the Diaoyu/Senkaku islands in the rest of In Focus.) Totaling less than three square miles, the uninhabited islands have long been disputed. In 1972, China and Japan agreed to shelve the issue indefinitely. Fast-forward to 2012: the Japanese government nationalized the islands, in fear of a right-wing politician whose plans for the islands would certainly have provoked China. But an assertive China argued that even the Japanese government's purchase was an unacceptable change in the status quo. Anti-Japanese riots and boycotts erupted in some Chinese cities in August and September 2012, vandalizing stores selling Japanese products, burning Japanese-branded cars, and setting a Panasonic factory on fire. Sales of Toyota, Honda, Nissan, and Mazda cars in China plummeted in the remainder of 2012. Chinese business and tourist visitors also canceled visits and vacations, and hotels, resorts, and restaurants in Japan were also hurt—All Nippon Airlines (ANA) alone suffered 46,000 seat cancellations. In all, between 0.5% and 1% of Japanese GDP was shaved off—all for a bunch of barren rocks.

Since then, Chinese and Japanese ships and aircraft routinely face off each other in the disputed waters and airspace surrounding the Diaoyu/Senkaku islands. Will such a new cold war turn hot? Most experts believe this to be unlikely, simply because China needs Japanese products as much as Japan needs to sell them. Japan provides some of the most critical components for made-in-China exports—think of the Sharp LCD screens and Toshiba flash memory drives that power the Apple iPhones assembled in China. Japan is also one of the largest foreign direct investors in China, employing approximately 1.5 million workers in 4,600 factories throughout the country. One-tenth of Japan's foreign direct investment (FDI) stock is in China. Because the two economies are complementary, there is a great deal of economic integration characterized by dense trade, investment, and personnel flows. Neither side risks disrupting these flows through conflicts without crippling its own economy—or both economies. Although there is no guarantee that cooler heads would always prevail in Beijing and Tokyo, Thomas Friedman and peace lovers of the world—a group that presumably includes *all* readers of this book—certainly hope that the Dell theory of peace will continue to be supported in East Asia and beyond.

Sources: "Japan, China, and a pile of rocks," *Bloomberg Businessweek*, 22 October 2012: 20–21; "Battered in China, Japan Inc. seeks refuge," *Bloomberg Businessweek*, 11 February 2013: 11–12; "Hot oil on troubled waters," *Economist*, 17 May 2014: 38; "Beijing's brand ambassador," *Foreign Affairs*, July 2013: 10–17; "Japan is back," *Foreign Affairs*, July 2013: 2–8; T. Friedman, *The World Is Flat* (New York: Farrar, Straus and Giroux, 2005); R. Katz, "Mutual assured production: Why trade will limit conflict between China and Japan," *Foreign Affairs*, July 2013: 18–24.

of **political risk**, which is a risk associated with political changes that may negatively impact domestic and foreign firms.[11] The most extreme political risk may lead to nationalization (expropriation) of foreign assets. This happened in many totalitarian countries from the 1950s through the 1970s. It has not become a thing of the past. Recently, Argentina expropriated the assets of YPF—the subsidiary of a major Spanish oil firm Repsol. Zimbabwe demanded that foreign mining companies cede 51% of their equity without compensation. It is hardly surprising that foreign firms are sick and tired and would rather go to "greener pastures" elsewhere.

Firms operating in democracies also confront political risk, but such risk is qualitatively different than that in totalitarian countries. Shown in the Opening Case, significant transitions have been introduced by the Trump

political risk Risk associated with political changes that may negatively impact domestic and foreign firms.

Debate: Is Democracy Good for Economic Development?

Emerging Markets/Ethical Dilemma

Democracy is good. Dictatorship is bad. Although crude, these two statements fairly accurately summarize the political sentiments in many parts of the world. It is not hard to understand why. Compared with dictatorships, on average, democracies are richer, less corrupt, and less likely to go to war. Beyond such nontrivial benefits, deep down, democracies allow people to make their own political choices. In the second half of the 20th century, the march of democracy was impressive. This powerful idea took root in some of the most difficult terrains. In Germany, Nazism had to be defeated militarily. In India, the world's largest population of poor people had to be taught how to vote. In Japan, emperor worship had to be curtailed and military adventurism destroyed. In South Africa, apartheid had to be dismantled. Throughout Asia and Africa, decolonization gave birth to a number of new democracies. A series of autocratic governments gave themselves up to democracy: Spain (1975), Argentina (1983), Brazil (1985), South Korea (1987), Taiwan (1988), and Chile (1989). The collapse of the Soviet Union (1991) resulted in the proliferation of young democracies throughout Central and Eastern Europe as well as Central Asia. Recently, the Arab Spring expanded democracy to North Africa: Algeria (2011), Egypt (2011), and Libya (2011). Overall, there is no doubt that democracy has spread around the world: from 69 countries in the 1980s to 120 in the 2000s.

CHRISDORNEY/SHUTTERSTOCK.COM

However, according to the *Economist*, democracy is "going through a difficult time." In new democracies such as Egypt, Iraq, Libya, Thailand, and Ukraine, an unenviable pattern emerges: it seems easier to get rid of the old regime than to establish a functioning democratic government. The new regime fumbles, the economy suffers, jobs disappear, and people find their conditions to be as bad as they were before. Civil disturbance broke out in Iraq and Libya, military coups smashed democracy in Egypt and Thailand, and foreign intervention (from Russia) pushed Ukraine's vulnerable democracy to its limits.

At the same time, established democracies have not been good role models. The United States has become a joke for dysfunctional politics—with partisan politicians shutting down the federal government once (2013) and threatening to default on its debt twice (2011 and 2013). The democratically elected President Donald Trump has attracted waves of protests (2016 and 2017). The European Union is hardly a paradise for democracy either. The fateful decision to introduce the euro in 1999 was largely dictated to the public. In the only two EU countries that held a democratic referendum on whether to adopt the euro—Denmark and Sweden—voters resoundingly said, "No." Not surprisingly, many ordinary people in Europe who had to cough up higher taxes to plug the hole of the recent euro mess were mad. When British voters were offered a chance to vote "Remain in" or "Leave" the EU, a majority of them (52%) voted in favor of Brexit. The economic impact was immediate and devastating. Within days of the referendum, the pound took a severe pounding, plummeting to its lowest level against the dollar in three decades. Overall, far from marching to dominate the world, democracy seems to have lost its forward momentum lately.

One of the litmus tests is: Is democracy good for economic development? Although champions of democracy shout, "Yes," the fastest-growing major economy in the last three decades, China, remains totalitarian. The growth rate of India, the world's largest democracy, in the same period is only about half of China's. With little democracy, Hong Kong has achieved enviably higher per capita income than its old colonial master, Britain, which enjoys the world's oldest democracy—US$52,000 versus US$37,000, according to the World Bank, based on purchasing power parity. In another example, Russia grew faster under Putin's more-authoritarian rule during the 2000s, compared with the 1990s when Russia was presumably more democratic under Yeltsin. In contrast, the economies of most established democracies have been stagnant or declining—the Great Recession of 2008–2009 can serve as Exhibit A here. Many Westerners have been tremendously disillusioned by their governments' actions to use taxpayer dollars, euros, and pounds to bail out banks—without much democratic consultation with the taxpayers.

Many Chinese willingly put up with the dictatorship that governs China if the regime delivers jobs, wealth, and economic growth. Of course, they do not have a choice anyway. But tellingly, the 2013 Pew Survey of Global Attitudes found that 85% of Chinese were "very satisfied" with their country's direction, compared with only 31% of Americans, 30% of British, and 20% of Japanese. Some Chinese elites argue that their model is more efficient than democracy in delivering growth. Just witness the new skyscrapers, highways, and airports that are thrown up in an amazingly short period of time. In two years, China implemented pension coverage to an additional 240 million rural residents—a process that would take decades in a democracy.

Despite the regime's heavy hand in control, paradoxically, obsession with control forces it to pay close attention to public opinion, which serves as meaningful constraints on the regime's behavior.

Despite democracies' unenviable scorecard on economic development lately, no one outside China has seriously argued for totalitarianism in order to facilitate economic development. In an influential paper concerned about the decline of US competitiveness and the rise of Chinese competitiveness, strategy guru Michael Porter nevertheless wrote, "We do not want to copy China, whose speed comes partly from a political system unacceptable to Americans." If democracy in the 21st century aspires to be as successful as it was in the 20th century, faith in democracy will need to be translated into strengths in economic development. So stay tuned.

Sources: "Welcome to Thailand, land of coups," *Bloomberg Businessweek*, 2 June 2014: 17; "The patriotic response to populism," *Bloomberg Businessweek*, 9 January 2017: 8; "Has the Arab Spring failed?" *Economist*, 13 July 2013: 11; "The battle for Egypt," *Economist*, 17 August 2013: 11; "What's wrong with democracy," *Economist*, 1 March 2014: 47–52; "When will the rainbow end?" *Economist*, 3 May 2014: 41–43; "Young people and democracy," *Economist*, 4 February 2017: 51–52; M. Porter and J. Rivkin, "Choosing the United States," *Harvard Business Review* (March 2012): 80–93.

administration. Although firms such as Boeing, Carrier, and GM highly exposed to Trump's wrath suffered some drop in their stock price, there was no general collapse of stock price in the United States or flight of capital out of the country. Instead, Wall Street enjoyed a rally, and the dollar became stronger. Overall, investors are confident that despite the disruption, the American democracy is mature enough to manage the transition process.

Obviously, when two countries are at each other's throats, we can forget about doing business between them (see In Focus). No two democracies have reportedly gone to war with each other. In this regard, the recent advance of democracy and retreat of totalitarianism is highly beneficial for global business. It is not a coincidence that globalization took off in the 1990s, a period during which both communist and right-wing totalitarianism significantly lost its power and democracy expanded around the world (see Chapter 1). The Debate features one of the most crucial questions regarding political systems: Is democracy conducive to economic development?

 ## 2-5 LEGAL SYSTEMS

A **legal system** refers to the rules of the game on how a country's laws are enacted and enforced. By specifying the do's and don'ts, a legal system reduces transaction costs by minimizing uncertainty and combating opportunism. This section first introduces three different legal traditions and then discusses crucial issues associated with property rights and intellectual property.

> **legal system** The rules of the game on how a country's laws are enacted and enforced.
>
> **civil law** A legal tradition that uses comprehensive statutes and codes as a primary means to form legal judgments.
>
> **common law** A legal tradition that is shaped by precedents from previous judicial decisions.

2-5a Civil Law, Common Law, and Theocratic Law

Laws in different countries typically are not enacted from scratch but are often transplanted—voluntarily or otherwise—from three legal traditions (or legal families): civil law, common law, and theocratic law. Each is introduced here.

Civil law was derived from Roman law and strengthened by Napoleon's France. It is "the oldest, the most influential, and the most widely distributed around the world."[12] It uses comprehensive statutes and codes as a primary means to form legal judgments. Over 80 countries practice civil law. **Common law**, which is English in origin, is shaped by precedents and traditions from previous judicial decisions. Common law has spread to all English-speaking countries, most of which were at one time British colonies.

Relative to civil law, common law has more flexibility because judges have to resolve specific disputes based on their *interpretation* of the law, and such interpretation may give new meaning to the law, which will in turn shape future cases. Civil law has less flexibility because judges have the power only to *apply* the law. Thus civil law is less confrontational because comprehensive statutes and codes serve to guide judges. Common law, on the other hand, is more confrontational because plaintiffs and defendants, through their lawyers, must argue and help judges to favorably interpret the law largely based on precedents. This confrontation is great material for movies. You may have seen common law in action in Hollywood movies such as *A Few Good Men*, *Devil's Advocate*, and *Legally Blond*. In contrast, you probably have rarely seen a civil law court in action in movies—you have not missed much because civil law lacks the drama and its proceedings tend to be boring.

The third legal family is **theocratic law**, a legal system based on religious teachings. Examples include Jewish and Islamic laws. Although Jewish law is followed by some elements of the Israeli population, it is *not* formally embraced by the Israeli government. Islamic law is the only surviving example of a theocratic legal system that is formally practiced by some governments, including those in Iran and Saudi Arabia. Despite the popular characterization of Islam as anti-business, it is important to note that Mohammed was a merchant trader and that the tenets of Islam are pro-business in general. However, the holy book of Islam, the Koran, does advise against *certain* business practices. In Saudi Arabia, McDonald's operates "ladies only" restaurants in order to comply with the Koran's ban on direct, face-to-face contact between unrelated men and women (who often wear a veil) in public. Moreover, banks in Saudi Arabia have to maintain two retail branches: one for male customers staffed by men and another for female customers staffed by women. This requirement obviously increases property, overhead, and personnel costs. To reduce costs, some foreign banks such as HSBC staff their back office operations with both male and female employees who work side by side.

Overall, legal systems form the first regulatory pillar that supports institutions. They directly impose do's and don'ts on businesses around the globe. Of a legal system's numerous components, two of these, property rights and intellectual property, are discussed next.

2-6 PROPERTY RIGHTS AND INTELLECTUAL PROPERTY RIGHTS

2-6a Property Rights

One fundamental economic function that a legal system serves is to protect **property rights**, which are the legal rights to use an economic property (resource) and to derive income and benefits from it. Examples of property include homes, offices, and factories.

What difference do property rights supported by a functioning legal system make? A lot. Why did developed economies become developed? (Remember, for example, the United States was a "developing" or "emerging" economy 100 years ago.) While there are many answers, a leading answer, most forcefully put forward by Hernando de Soto, a Peruvian economist, focuses on the protection of property rights.[13] In developed economies, every parcel of land, every building, and every trademark is represented in a property document that entitles the owner to derive income and benefits from it. That property document is also important when violators are prosecuted through legal means.

When a legal system is stable and predictable, tangible property also makes other, less tangible economic activities possible. For example, property can be used as collateral for credit. The single most important source of funds for new start-ups in the United States is the mortgage of entrepreneurs' houses. But this cannot be done without documented right to the property. If you live in a house but cannot produce a title document specifying that you are the legal owner of the house (which is a very common situation throughout the developing world, especially in shantytowns), no bank in the world will allow you to use your house as collateral for credit. To start up a new firm, you end up borrowing funds from family members, friends, and other acquaintances through *informal* means. But funds through informal means are almost certainly more limited than funds that could have been provided formally by banks. Insecure property rights are why, in general, the average firm size in the developing world is smaller than that in the developed world. Insecure property rights also result in using technologies that employ little fixed capital ("cash and carry" is the best) and do not entail long-term investment (such as research and development [R&D]). These characteristics of firms in developing economies do not bode well in global competition where leading firms reap benefits from economies of scale, capital-intensive technologies, and sustained investment in R&D. What the developing world lacks and desperately needs is formal protection of property rights in order to facilitate economic growth.

2-6b Intellectual Property Rights

While the term "property" traditionally refers to *tangible* pieces of property such as land, **intellectual property (IP)** specifically refers to *intangible*

theocratic law A legal system based on religious teachings.

property right Legal right to use an economic property (resource) and to derive income and benefits from it.

intellectual property (IP) Intangible property that results from intellectual activity (such as the content of books, videos, and websites).

property that is the result of intellectual activity (such as the content of books, videos, and websites). **Intellectual property rights (IPR)** are legal rights associated with the ownership of intellectual property. IPR primarily include rights associated with patents, copyrights, and trademarks.

▶ **Patents** are legal rights awarded by government authorities to inventors of new products or processes. The inventors are given exclusive (monopoly) rights for a period of time to derive income from such inventions through activities such as manufacturing, licensing, or selling.

▶ **Copyrights** are the exclusive legal rights of authors and publishers to publish and disseminate their work. For example, the book you are reading now is protected by copyright.

▶ **Trademarks** are the exclusive legal rights of firms to use specific names, brands, and designs to differentiate their products from others.

IPR need to be asserted and enforced through a *formal* system designed to provide an incentive for people and firms to innovate.[14] To be effective, the system must also punish violators. But the intangible nature of IPR makes enforcement difficult. **Piracy**, or unauthorized use of IPR, is widespread around the world. Acts of piracy range from unauthorized sharing of music files to deliberate counterfeiting of branded products.

Overall, an institution-based view suggests that the key to understanding IPR violation is realizing that violators are not amoral monsters but ordinary people and firms. When filling out a survey on "What is your dream career?" no high school graduate anywhere in the world will answer "Counterfeiting." Nevertheless, thousands of individuals and firms *voluntarily* choose to be involved in this business worldwide. Why? Because IPR protection is weak in many countries. In other words, given an institutional environment of weak IPR protection,

In June 2016, songwriters Martin Harrington and Thomas Leonard filed a $20 million copyright lawsuit against British pop star Ed Sheeran, claiming that the singer copied their song "Amazing" note-for-note in his 2014 hit song "Photograph."

JSTONE/SHUTTERSTOCK.COM

violators have made a rational decision by investing in the skills in and knowledge of counterfeiting (see Proposition 1 in Exhibit 2.3). For example, counterfeiters in China will be criminally prosecuted only if their profits exceed approximately $10,000. No counterfeiters are dumb enough to keep records to show that they make that much money. If caught, they can usually get away by paying a small fine. Stronger IPR protection may significantly reduce the incentive to be involved in piracy and counterfeiting. However, IP reforms to criminalize *all* counterfeiting activities regardless of the amount of profits, which have been discussed in China, may significantly reduce counterfeiters' incentive.

2-7 ECONOMIC SYSTEMS

2-7a Market, Command, and Mixed Economies

An **economic system** refers to the rules of the game on how a country is governed economically. A pure **market economy** is characterized by the "invisible hand" of market forces first noted in 1776 by Adam Smith in *The Wealth of Nations*. The government takes a *laissez faire* (hands-off) approach. Theoretically, all factors of production should thus be privately owned. The government performs only functions the private sector cannot perform, such as providing roads and defense.

intellectual property right (IPR) Legal right associated with the ownership of intellectual property.

patent Exclusive legal right of inventors to derive income from their inventions through activities such as manufacturing, licensing, or selling.

copyright Exclusive legal right of authors and publishers to publish and disseminate their work.

trademark Exclusive legal right of firms to use specific names, brands, and designs to differentiate their products from others.

piracy The unauthorized use of intellectual property rights.

economic system The rules of the game on how a country is governed economically.

market economy An economy that is characterized by the "invisible hand" of market forces.

A pure **command economy** is defined by a government taking, in the words of Vladimir Lenin, the "commanding heights" in the economy. Theoretically, all factors of production should be state owned and state controlled, and all supply, demand, and pricing are planned by the government. During the heydays of communism, the former Soviet Union and China approached such an ideal.

A **mixed economy**, by definition, has elements of both a market economy and a command economy. It boils down to the relative distribution of market forces versus command forces. In practice, no country has ever completely embraced Adam Smith's ideal *laissez faire* approach. Question: Which economy has the highest degree of economic freedom (the lowest degree of government intervention in the economy)? Hint: Given extensive government intervention (such as bailouts) since 2008, it is obviously *not* the United States. Answer: A series of surveys report that it is Hong Kong (the post-1997 handover to Chinese sovereignty does not make a difference). The crucial point here is that there is still some noticeable government intervention in the economy, even in Hong Kong. During the aftermath of the 1997 economic crisis when the share price of all Hong Kong firms took a nose dive, the Hong Kong government took a highly controversial course of action. It used government funds to purchase 10% of the shares of all the blue chip firms listed in the Hang Seng index. This action slowed down the sliding of share prices and stabilized the economy, but it turned all the blue chip firms into state-owned enterprises (SOEs)—at least 10% owned by the state. In 2008, US and European governments did something similar, nationalizing a large chunk of their failing banks and financial services firms via bailouts and turning them into SOEs.

Likewise, no country has ever had a complete command economy, not even in the Eastern Bloc during the Cold War. Poland never nationalized its agriculture. Hungarians were known to have second (and private!) jobs, while all of them theoretically worked only for the state. Black markets hawking agricultural produce and small merchandise existed in practically all former communist countries. While the former Soviet Union and Central and Eastern European countries have recently thrown away communism, ongoing practitioners

ISTOCK.COM/HENRIK5000

HEARTLAND ARTS/SHUTTERSTOCK.COM

of communism such as China and Vietnam have embraced market reforms. Cuba has a lot of foreign-invested hotels. Even North Korea is now interested in attracting foreign investment.

Overall, the economic system of most countries is a mixed economy. In practice, when we say a country has a market economy, it is really a shorthand version for a country that organizes its economy *mostly* (but not completely) by market forces and that still has certain elements of a command economy. China, France, Russia, Sweden, and the United States all claim to have a market economy now, but the meaning is different in each country. In other words, "free markets" are not totally free. It boils down to a matter of degree. It seems prudent to drop the "F" word ("free") from the term "free market economy." Instead, it makes sense to acknowledge the variety of capitalism, with each version of "market economy" differing in some ways.[15]

2-7b What Drives Economic Development?

Regardless of the economic system used, developing the economy is one of the aims for most governments. The differences in economic development around the globe are striking (see PengAtlas Map 4). The highest and lowest per capita income countries in the world are Norway ($76,450) and Burundi ($110). Why are some countries such as Norway so developed (rich) while others such as Burundi are so underdeveloped (poor)? More generally, what drives economic development in different countries? Scholars and policy makers have been debating this important question since Adam Smith. Various debate points boil down to three explanations: (1) culture, (2) geography, and (3) institutions.

The culture side argues that rich countries tend to have a smarter and harder working population driven by a stronger motivation for success,

> **command economy** An economy in which theoretically all factors of production are state owned and state controlled, and all supply, demand, and pricing are planned by the government.
>
> **mixed economy** An economy that has elements of both a market economy and a command economy.

such as the Protestant work ethic identified by Max Weber over a century ago. Still, it is difficult to imagine that Norwegians are, on average, over *700 times* smarter and harder working than Burundians. This line of thinking, bordering on racism, is no longer acceptable in the 21st century.

The geography school of thought suggests that rich countries tend to be well endowed with natural resources. But one can easily point out that some poor countries also possess rich natural resources while some rich countries are very poor in natural resources. The Democratic Republic of the Congo (formerly Zaire) is rich in diamonds, oil and natural gas, water, timber, and minerals, while Denmark and Japan lack significant natural resources. In addition, some countries are believed to be cursed by their poor geographic location, which may be landlocked (such as Malawi) and/or located near the hot equator zone and infested with tropical diseases (such as Burundi). This argument is not convincing either, because some landlocked countries (such as Switzerland) are phenomenally well developed and some countries near the equator (such as Singapore) have accomplished enviable growth. Clearly, geography is important, but it is not destiny.

A third side of the debate argues that institutions are "the basic determinants of the performance of an economy."[16] Because institutions provide the incentive structure of a society, formal political, legal, and economic systems have a significant impact on economic development by affecting the incentives and the costs of doing business.[17] In short, rich countries are rich because they have developed better market-supporting institutional frameworks. Consider these points:

▶ The presence of formal, market-supporting institutions encourages individuals to specialize and firms to grow in size. This is the "division of labor" thesis first advanced by Adam Smith (see Chapter 5). Specialization is economically advantageous because firms are able to grow to capture the gains from transactions with distant trading partners. For example, as China's market institutions progress, many Chinese firms have grown substantially. In 2016, 103 Chinese firms were among the *Fortune* Global 500 largest firms in the world (measured by sales). There were none in 1984.

▶ A lack of strong, formal, market-supporting institutions forces individuals to trade on an informal basis with a small neighboring group. The term "cash and carry" says it all (!). This forces firms to remain small and local in nature, as are most firms in Africa. Over 40% of Africa's economy is reportedly informal, the highest proportion in the world.[18]

▶ Formal, market-supporting institutions that protect property rights fuel more innovation, entrepreneurship, and thus economic growth. While spontaneous innovation has existed throughout history, why has its pace accelerated significantly since the Industrial Revolution starting in the 1700s? A big factor was the Statute of Monopolies enacted in Great Britain in 1624, which was the world's first patent law to formally protect the IPR of inventors and make innovation financially lucrative.[19] This law has been imitated around the world. Its impact is still felt today, as we now expect continuous innovation to be the norm—think of the doubling of computing power every couple of years. This would not have happened had there not been a system of IPR protection that protects and rewards innovation.

These arguments, of course, are the backbone of the institution-based view of global business, which has clearly won this debate.

 ## 2-8 MANAGEMENT SAVVY

Focusing on *formal* institutions, this chapter has sketched the contours of an institution-based view of global business. How does the institution-based view help us answer our fundamental question of utmost concern to managers worldwide: What determines the success and failure of firms around the globe? In a nutshell, this chapter suggests that firm performance is determined, at least in part, by the institutional frameworks governing firm behavior. It is the growth of the firm that, in the aggregate, leads to the growth of the economy. Not surprisingly, most developed economies are supported by strong, effective, and market-supporting formal institutions, and most underdeveloped economies are pulled back by weak, ineffective, and market-depressing formal institutions. In other words, when markets work smoothly in developed economies, formal market-supporting institutions are almost invisible and taken for granted. However, when markets work poorly, the absence of strong formal institutions may become conspicuous.

For managers doing business around the globe, this chapter suggests two broad implications for action (see Exhibit 2.4). First, managerial choices are made rationally within the constraints of a given institutional framework. Therefore, managers aiming to enter a new country need to do their homework by having a thorough understanding of the formal institutions affecting their business. The rules for doing business in a democratic market economy are certainly different from the rules in a totalitarian command economy. In short, "when in Rome, do as the Romans do." Although this is a good start, managers also need to understand *why* "Romans" do things in a certain way by studying the formal institutions governing "Roman" behavior.

Second, while this chapter has focused on the role of formal institutions, managers should follow the advice of the second proposition of the institution-based view: In situations where formal constraints are unclear or fail, informal constraints such as relationship norms will play a *larger* role in reducing uncertainty. If, for example, you are doing business in a country with a strong propensity for informal, relational exchanges, it may not be a good idea to insist on formalizing the contract right away. Such

a plan could backfire. Because such countries often have relatively weak legal systems, personal relationship building is often used to substitute for the lack of strong legal protection. Attitudes such as "business first, relationship afterwards" (have a drink *after* the negotiation) may clash with the norm that puts things the other way around (lavish entertainment first, talk about business later). We often hear that, because of their culture, the Chinese prefer to cultivate personal relationships (*guanxi*) first. This is *not* entirely true. Investing in personal relationships up front may simply be the initial cost one has to pay if interested in eventually doing business together, given the absence of a strong and credible legal and regulatory regime in China. In other words, the value on personal relationships has as much to do with the absence of institutional constraints as it does with cultural norms. In fact, personal relationships are key to business in a broad range of countries from Argentina to Zimbabwe, each with *different* cultural traditions. So the interest in cultivating what the Chinese call *guanxi*, the Russians call *blat* or *sistema*, or the Vietnamese call *guan he* is not likely to be driven by culture alone, but more likely by these countries' common lack of formal market-supporting institutions.

EXHIBIT 2.4	IMPLICATIONS FOR ACTION

▶ When entering a new country, do your homework and have a thorough understanding of the formal institutions governing firm behavior.

▶ When doing business in countries with a strong propensity for informal relational exchanges, insisting on formalizing the contract right away may backfire.

EMERGING MARKETS/ETHICAL DILEMMA
Closing Case: Carlsberg Confronts Political Risk in Russia

In the early 1900s, Danish firms rushed to invest in Czarist Russia, building engine factories, cement plants, and slaughterhouses. Their advanced technologies gave them competitive advantages in the vast Russian market that gradually opened to foreign direct investment (FDI). Then came the Russian Revolution of 1917, and all was lost as these businesses were expropriated. For the next seven decades, Russia had essentially zero FDI.

When Soviet rule came to an end in 1991, Danish firms rushed in again. After all, Russia was the crucial "R" in BRICS (Brazil, Russia, India, China, and South Africa). The world's fourth largest beer maker, Carlsberg was particularly successful, building a 38% market share and becoming the undisputed leader in Russia. As part of its commitment to Russia, Carlsberg sponsored the national hockey league and the Sochi Olympic Games. In 2013, Russia contributed 35% of Carlsberg's global revenues.

The success in Russia, however, exposed Carlsberg to the political and economic volatilities of Russia. In the 1990s,

when Russia was experimenting with democracy, the economy collapsed. By official estimates, GDP fell by approximately 40%. In the early 2000s, the economy was surging at 7% annually, but remained highly volatile. Russia was heavily dependent on exports of oil and gas, and thus on the world market prices of these commodities. Moreover, as Russia became richer and stronger (in part thanks to high oil prices), the government seemed to become more assertive vis-à-vis foreign firms. For example, the government put pressure on foreign oil companies such as BP to relinquish control over their operations to Russian partners.

Although brewing is not a politically sensitive industry, institutional transitions still had a profound impact on Carlsberg. Russian leaders from the czars to Vladmir Putin periodically attempted to convince their citizens to drink less alcohol. As Putin unleashed fresh efforts to reduce alcohol consumption by increasing alcohol tax, the beer market shrank. In addition, new laws banned TV, radio, and outdoor advertising of alcohol. Also banned was the selling of alcohol in street kiosks, which traditionally enjoyed 26% of off-trade sales (retail sales other than those in restaurants, bars, and hotels) of beer in Russia.

Such changes deeply impacted brewers such as Carlsberg. First, demand surged ahead of the first implementation date of the new tax as consumers stocked up their supplies, only to sharply drop in the next quarter as supplies purchased earlier were gradually consumed. Such ups and downs created enormous stress for logistics and supply chain management. Second, market resources had to be reallocated to, for example, in-store displays and online marketing. Third, constraints on sales channels and advertising shifted the pattern of consumption, leading to sales drops. Then the economic crisis—thanks to the collapsing oil price—further knocked off the demand for beer, especially in the premium segment. By 2014, capacity utilization in Carlsberg's Russian breweries did not exceed 60%, prompting speculation about possible brewery closures.

In 2014, Carlsberg was hit by the deteriorating Russian economy, worsening political relationships between Russia and the West, and the collapse of the ruble. The trade sanctions imposed by the European Union and the United States did not hit Carlsberg directly, because most of the beer it sold in Russia was made locally. Yet the economic crisis did: beer consumption dropped, and the value of its Russian investments depreciated when the ruble dropped in value. Therefore, every time there was bad news from Russia, Carlsberg's share price took a hit. In the second half of 2014, its shares lost 20% value.

Doing business in Russia was never easy. Foreign firms deployed different coping mechanisms. In fear of greater political risk such as the possible introduction of capital controls, some foreign investors such as Danish building materials giant Rockwool divested major assets in Russia. When the ruble

MONTICELLO/SHUTTERSTOCK.COM

collapsed, importers faced grave losses because their sales were invoiced in the ruble, but their costs in a foreign currency. As a coping mechanism, French-Japanese automaker Renault Nissan simply stopped taking orders as it could not appropriately price the cars, which had major imported components. In 2015, Carlsberg reduced overcapacity by closing two breweries. Despite the challenges, Carlsberg remained committed to Russia, hoping for an economic recovery and a warming up of the geopolitical relationship between its host country and the West.

Political risk aside, Russia's fundamental strengths remain. Although its GDP is smaller that of China and Brazil, it is larger than that of India. Russia's per capita GDP (approximately $16,000 at purchasing power parity) is one-third higher than that of Brazil, three times that of China, and five times that of India. In Europe, Russia not only has the second largest beer market, but also the second largest car market (both behind Germany). Worldwide, Russia has more college graduates (as a percentage of population) than any other country, offering a highly educated workforce. Simply put, Russia may be too big and too rich to ignore.

Case Discussion Questions

1. Why is investment in Russia considered politically risky?

2. Despite the risk, why do foreign multinationals such as Carlsberg eager to invest in Russia?

3. **ON ETHICS**: If you were a Carlsberg board member, would you vote "yes" or "no" for a new project to acquire a local brewery in Russia?

Sources: Adapted from M. W. Peng and K. E. Meyer, *International Business*, 2nd ed. (London: Cengage EMEA, 2016) 54–55. Underlying sources include "Manufacturers face 'bloodbath' in Russia, says Renault Nissan boss," *BBC News*, 19 December 2014; *Carlsberg Annual Report*, 2011–2016, various issues; *Carlsberg Shareholder News*, 2012–2014, various issues; "BP in Russia: Dancing with bears," *Economist*, 5 February 2011; M. W. Peng, "The peril and promise of Russia," in *Global Business*, 4th ed. (Boston: Cengage, 2017) 35–36.

STUDY TOOLS 2

LOCATED AT THE BACK OF YOUR BOOK:

☐ Rip out and study the Chapter Review Card at the end of the book

LOG IN TO WWW.CENGAGEBRAIN.COM TO:

☐ Review key term flashcards

☐ Complete a practice quiz to test your knowledge of key concepts

☐ View animated PengAtlas Maps

☐ Complete interactive content, watch chapter videos, and take a graded quiz

☐ Track your knowledge of key concepts in Global Business

☐ Read and discuss additional case study content

GLOBAL
ONLINE

PREPARE FOR TESTS ON
THE STUDYBOARD!

○ CORRECT

○ INCORRECT

○ INCORRECT

○ INCORRECT

**Personalize Quizzes
from Your StudyBits**

**Take Practice
Quizzes by Chapter**

CHAPTER QUIZZES

▶ Chapter 1

Chapter 2

Chapter 3

Chapter 4

3 Emphasizing Cultures, Ethics, & Norms

LEARNING OBJECTIVES

After studying this chapter, you will be able to . . .

3-1 Explain where informal institutions come from.

3-2 Define culture and articulate its two main manifestations.

3-3 Articulate three ways to understand cultural differences.

3-4 Explain why understanding cultural differences is crucial for global business.

3-5 Explain why ethics is important.

3-6 Identify ways to combat corruption.

3-7 Identify norms associated with strategic responses when firms deal with ethical challenges.

3-8 Explain how you can acquire cross-cultural literacy.

After you finish this chapter, go to

PAGE 51 for

STUDY TOOLS

Opening Case: Partying in Saudi Arabia and Xinjiang, China

Enjoying food together is part of the fun everywhere around the world. When venturing to locations far away from home, international businesspeople can often expect invitations to go to interesting parties. Two Swiss engineers, A and B, working for the French engineering giant Alstom at a location in Saudi Arabia, were told at midday that there would be a farewell dinner party after work. A tray the size of a wagon wheel, containing a bed of rice with a huge piece of grilled lamb on top, was set on the floor of the workshop. (Of course the floor had been cleaned earlier.) Since there were neither chairs nor utensils, colleagues just sat down on the floor around the tray and started eating—with their bare hands.

Swiss engineer A was a vegetarian. He nervously told his Swiss colleague B: "I won't squat on the floor like that, and I won't eat anything either." By then everybody else already had a piece of lamb in hand. One Saudi colleague held the lamb while another pulled out a chunk and passed it to B, who sat down and joined the festivities: "Here, that's a great piece, you must eat!" B encouraged A by saying: "Come on, let's just sit down. You don't have to eat lamb, but you can at least scoop up a handful of rice—it's so yummy!"

After A sat down and meat was passed around, the atmosphere became quite interesting and relaxing. Saudi colleagues respected A's vegetarian style and did not push him to eat lamb. A chatted with them about what kind of rice it was and what was in the rice. It was typical Saudi rice with raisins, and the taste was quite fantastic. B never knew lamb could be so delicious, and was having a good time. The Saudi colleagues gained immense joy from entertaining A and B—an experience that A later told B that he also enjoyed.

On a trip to Xinjiang University in Xinjiang Uyghur Autonomous Region in northwest China, my family and I were invited to a Kazakh dinner inside a Kazakh yurt (a traditional tent). On a huge tray, the main dish served was *beshbarmak*—meaning "five fingers" in Kazakh and a number of other Central Asian languages. Choice cuts of boiled lamb meat from the most tender and tasty parts of an unlucky sheep slaughtered just an hour ago were served on a huge tray, mixed with slices of purple onions. On top of the dish, the boiled head of the sheep stared at the oldest person at the table, who fortunately was not yours truly, but was a senior Chinese professor who accompanied us.

By tradition, the dish was to be enjoyed with "five fingers" only. The oldest and most senior person was supposed to use a knife to slice the meat off the face of the sheep to hand to everybody at the table—literally, to "give face." Receivers were to thank the most senior person profusely. Meat distribution was based on seniority, starting with the second oldest person. The ears were given to the youngest person at the table, my 11 year-old son, for him to "listen to his parents." (He gave thanks, but told me afterwards that he did not dare to eat the ears.) We enjoyed using our hands, but after we all had a bite and licked our fingers, the hosts graciously gave us utensils. We all had an amazing, unforgettable experience.

Sources: Author's interviews in Xinjiang, China; M. W. Peng, *Global 2* (Boston: Cengage, 2013); M. W. Peng and K. E. Meyer, *International Business* (London: Cengage EMEA, 2011).

Why do the Saudis and the Kazakhs prefer to pull meat from a common tray instead of being served on an individual plate? Why do the Kazakhs invite the most senior person to serve meat? Why is such meat distribution based on seniority? Why do local hosts have immense joy when visitors enjoy such festivities? More fundamentally, how do informal institutions govern individual behavior and firm behavior in different countries?

This chapter continues our coverage on the institution-based view, which began with formal institutions in Chapter 2. Here we focus on informal institutions represented by cultures, ethics, and norms. As informal institutions, cultures, ethics, and norms play an important part in shaping the success and failure of firms around the globe. Remember that the institution-based view suggests two propositions. First, managers and firms rationally pursue their interests within a given institutional framework. Second, in situations where formal institutions are unclear or fail, informal institutions play a larger role in reducing uncertainty. The first proposition deals with both formal and informal institutions. The second proposition hinges on the informal institutions we are about to discuss in this chapter.

3-1 WHERE DO INFORMAL INSTITUTIONS COME FROM?

Recall that any institutional framework consists of both formal and informal institutions. While formal institutions such as politics, laws, and economics (see Chapter 2) are crucial, they only make up a small (although important) part of the rules of the game that govern individual and firm behavior. As pervasive features of every economy, informal institutions can be found almost *everywhere*.

Where do informal institutions come from? They come from socially transmitted information and are a part of the heritage that we call cultures, ethics, and norms. Those within a society tend to perceive their own culture, ethics, and norms as "natural, rational, and morally right."[1] This self-centered mentality is known as **ethnocentrism**. For example, many Americans believe in "American exceptionalism," a view that holds the United States to be exceptionally well endowed to lead the world. The Chinese call China *zhong guo*, which literally means "the country in the middle" or "middle kingdom."

Recall from Chapter 2 that informal institutions are underpinned by the normative and cognitive pillars, while formal institutions are supported by the regulatory pillar. While the regulatory pillar clearly specifies the do's and don'ts, informal institutions, by definition, are more elusive. Yet, they are no less important. Thus it is imperative that we pay attention to three different informal institutions: culture, ethics, and norms.

3-2 CULTURE

Out of many informal institutions, culture is probably the most frequently discussed. Before we can discuss its two major components—language and religion—first we must define culture.

3-2a Definition of Culture

Although hundreds of definitions of culture have appeared, we will use the definition proposed by the world's foremost cross-cultural expert, Geert Hofstede, a Dutch professor. He defines **culture** as "the collective programming of the mind which distinguishes the members of one group or category of people from another."[2] Before proceeding, it is important to make two points to minimize confusion. First, although it is customary to talk about the American culture, no strict one-to-one correspondence between cultures and nation-states exists. Many subcultures exist within multiethnic countries such as Australia,

ethnocentrism A self-centered mentality held by a group of people who perceive their own culture, ethics, and norms as natural, rational, and morally right.

culture The collective programming of the mind that distinguishes the members of one group or category of people from another.

Belgium, Brazil, Britain, Canada, China, India, Indonesia, Russia, South Africa, Switzerland, and the United States (see In Focus). Second, culture has many layers, such as regional, ethnic, and religious. Even firms may have a specific organizational culture (such as the IKEA culture). Acknowledging the validity of these two points, we will, however, follow Hofstede by using the term "culture" to discuss *national* culture unless otherwise noted. While this is a matter of expediency, it is also a reflection of the institutional realities of the world with about 200 nation-states.[3]

Culture is made up of numerous elements. Although culture is too complex to dissect in the space we have here, we will highlight two major components of culture that impact global business: language and religion.

3-2b Language

Approximately 6,000 languages are spoken in the world. Chinese is the largest language in terms of the number of native speakers (20% of the world population). English is a distant second (8% of the world population), followed closely by Spanish (6%) and Hindi (5%). Yet,

Shakira attends the 2016 premiere of Disney's *Zootopia*. The Colombian-born pop star recorded the film's Grammy Award–nominated theme song, "Try Everything."

Marketing to Hispanics in the United States

According to the US Census Bureau definition, the term "Hispanics" refers to individuals of Latin American descent living in the United States who may be of any race or ethnic group (such as white or black). Now approximately 52 million people (15% of the US population), Hispanics represent the largest minority group in the United States. To put things in perspective, the US Hispanic population is larger than the population of Australia, Denmark, Finland, Norway, and Sweden combined. Their buying power jumped from $1 trillion in 2010 to $1.5 trillion by 2015. The print media advertising revenues for the US Hispanic market, $1.5 billion, have now surpassed the advertising revenues for the entire UK magazine market.

MONKEY BUSINESS IMAGES/SHUTTERSTOCK.COM

How to effectively market products and services to this sizable group of customers is a leading challenge among many marketers. Although most US Hispanics speak some English, Spanish is likely to remain their language of preference. Approximately 38% of Hispanics surveyed report English-language ads to be less effective than Spanish-language ads in terms of recall. Half of US Hispanics who watch TV during prime time watch Spanish language programming. Calling itself the "Hispanic heart of America," the Spanish-language TV network Univision is now the fifth largest TV network in the United States, behind ABC, CBS, Fox, and NBC.

The typical debate in international marketing, standardization versus localization, is relevant here within a country. Direct translation of English-language campaigns is often ineffective, because it tends to miss the emotional and cultural nuances. Savvy marketers thus call for "transcreation." For instance, Taco Bell's tagline "Think outside the bun" evolved into a Hispanic adaption: *"No solo de pan vive el hombre"* ("A man does not live by bread alone"). Volkswagen completely changed its "Drivers Wanted" English slogan and marketed to US Hispanics with a new slogan, *"Agarra Calle"* ("Hit the Road"), with a specific, Spanish-language website, agarracalle. com. When marketing its minivans on TV, Chrysler showed a grandfather figure engaged in a puppet show at a child's birthday party—a traditional way for Hispanics to entertain children.

Interestingly, although about 60% of the US Hispanic population can trace their roots to Mexican heritage, direct importation of ads used in Mexico may not necessarily be successful either. The reasons are twofold. First, the US Hispanic culture, with influences from numerous other Latin American countries, is much more diverse than the Mexican culture. Second, mainstream (Anglo) media in the United States has asserted substantial influence on US Hispanics. A case in point is that 40% of Spanish-dominant Hispanics regularly watch English-language TV. Univision has started English-language programming to capture its younger, US-born viewers.

Overall, US Hispanics possess a distinctive cultural identity that is neither mainstream (Anglo) American nor pure Mexican. One size does not fit all. Any firm interested in marketing products and services to the "US market" needs to use both caution and creativity when marketing to Hispanics.

Sources: "Where pizza gets some Latin spice," *Bloomberg Businessweek*, 8 October 2012: 26–27; "Won in translation," *Bloomberg Businessweek*, 5 September 2013: 53–57; N. Kumar and J. Steenkamp, "Diaspora marketing," *Harvard Business Review* (October 2013): 127–131; N. Singh and B. Bartikowski, "A cross-cultural analysis of print advertising targeted to Hispanic and non-Hispanic American consumers," *Thunderbird International Business Review* 51 (2009): 151–164; US Census Bureau, "Hispanics in the United States," December 2016: www.census.gov.

the dominance of English as a global business language, or **lingua franca**, is unmistakable.[4] This is driven by two factors. First, English-speaking countries contribute the largest share (approximately one-third) of global output. Such economic dominance not only drives trade and investment ties between English-speaking countries and the rest of the world, but also generates a constant stream of products and services marketed in English. Think about the ubiquitous Hollywood movies, *Economist*

magazine, and Google's search engine. In the online world, the dominance of English is more extraordinary: one in three log on in English.

Second, recent globalization has called for the use of one common language. For firms headquartered in English-speaking countries as well as Scandinavia and the Netherlands (where English is widely

lingua franca A global business language.

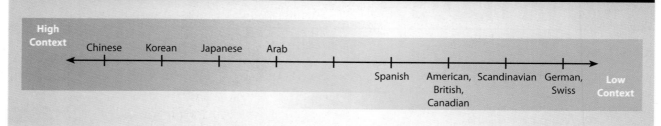

EXHIBIT 3.1   HIGH-CONTEXT VERSUS LOW-CONTEXT CULTURES

taught and spoken), using English to manage operations around the globe poses little difficulty. However, settling on a global language for the entire firm is problematic for firms headquartered in Latin countries (such as France) or Asian countries (such as South Korea), in which English is not widely spoken. Yet, even in these firms, it is still difficult to insist on a language other than English as the global corporate *lingua franca*. Around the world, nonnative speakers of English who can master English increasingly command a premium in jobs and compensation, and this fuels a rising interest in English. Think, for example, of the Taiwanese-born Hollywood director Ang Lee, Hong Kong-born kung-fu master Jackie Chan, Colombian-born pop star Shakira, and Austrian-born actor and politician Arnold Schwarzenegger.

On the other hand, the dominance of English may also lead to a disadvantage. Although native speakers of English have a great deal of advantage in global business, an expatriate manager who does not know the local language misses a lot of cultural subtleties and can only interact with locals fluent in English. Weak (or no) ability in foreign languages makes it difficult or even impossible to detect translation errors, which may result in embarrassments. For example, Rolls-Royce's Silver Mist was translated into German as "Silver Excrement." Coors Beer translated its slogan "Turn it loose!" into Spanish as "Drink Coors and get diarrhea!" Electrolux advertised its powerful vacuum machines in the United States with a slogan: "Nothing sucks like an Electrolux!" To avoid such embarrassments, you will be better off if you can pick up at least one foreign language during your university studies.

3-2c Religion

Religion is another major manifestation of culture. Approximately 85% of the world's population report having some religious belief. PengAtlas Map 5 shows the geographical distribution of different religious heritages. The four leading religions are Christianity

> **context** The background against which interaction takes place.

(approximately 1.7 billion adherents), Islam (1 billion), Hinduism (750 million), and Buddhism (350 million). Of course, not everybody claiming to be an adherent actively practices a religion. For instance, some Christians may go to church only *once* every year—at Christmas.

Because religious differences have led to numerous challenges, knowledge about religions is crucial even for *non*-religious managers. For example, in Christian-dominated countries, the Christmas season represents the peak in shopping and consumption. Half of toy sales for a given year in the United States occur during the month before Christmas. Since American kids consume half of the world's toys and virtually all toys are made outside the United States (mostly in Asia), this means 25% of the world's toy output is sold in one country in a month, thus creating enormous production, distribution, and coordination challenges. For toy makers and stores, missing the boat from Asia, whose transit time is at least two weeks, can literally devastate an entire holiday season and probably the entire year.

3-3 CLASSIFYING CULTURAL DIFFERENCES

Before reading this chapter, every reader already knows that cultures are different. There is no controversy in stating that the Indian culture is different from the Russian culture. But how are the Indian and Russian cultures *systematically* different? This section outlines three ways to understand cultural differences: (1) the context approach, (2) the cluster approach, and (3) the dimension approach.

3-3a The Context Approach

Of the three main approaches to cultural difference, the context approach is the most straightforward. It focuses on a single dimension: context.[5] **Context** is the background against which interaction takes place. Exhibit 3.1

ISTOCK.COM/HENRIK5000

EXHIBIT 3.2 CULTURAL CLUSTERS[1]

Ronen and Shenkar clusters	GLOBE clusters	Huntington civilizations
Anglo	Anglo	Western (1)[2]
Arab	Middle East	Islamic
Eastern Europe	Eastern Europe	Slavic-Orthodox
Far East	Confucian Asia	Confucian (Sinic)
Germanic	Germanic Europe	Western (2)
Latin America	Latin America	Latin American
Latin Europe	Latin Europe	Western (3)
Near East	Southern Asia	Hindu
Nordic	Nordic Europe	Western (4)
Sub-Saharan Africa	Sub-Saharan Africa	African
Independents: Brazil, India, Israel, Japan		Japanese

Notes:

1. This table is the *first* time these three major systems of cultural clusters have been compiled side by side. Viewing them together can allow us to see their similarities. However, there are also differences. Across the three systems (columns), even though clusters sometimes share the same labels, there are still differences. For example, Ronen and Shenkar's Latin America cluster does not include Brazil (which is regarded as an "independent"), whereas GLOBE and Huntington's Latin America includes Brazil.

2. For the Western civilization, Huntington does not use such labels as Western 1, 2, 3, and 4 as in the table. They are added by the present author to establish some rough correspondence with the respective Ronen and Shenkar and GLOBE clusters.

Sources: R. House, P. Hanges, M. Javidan, P. Dorfman, and V. Gupta (eds.), Culture, Leadership, and Organization: the GLOBE Study of 62 Societies (Thousand Oaks, Sage, 2004); S. Huntington, The Clash of Civilizations and the Remaking of World Order (New York: Simon & Schuster, 1996); S. Ronen and O. Shenkar, "Clustering countries on attitudinal dimension," *Academy of Management Review* 10 (1985): 435–454; S. Ronen and O. Shenkar, "Mapping world cultures," *Journal of International Business Studies*, 44 (2013): 867–897.

outlines a spectrum of countries along the dimension of low versus high context. In **low-context cultures** such as North American and Western European countries, communication is usually taken at face value without much reliance on unspoken conditions or assumptions, which are features of context. In other words, "no" means "no." In **high-context cultures** such as Arab and Asian countries, communication relies heavily on unspoken conditions or assumptions, which are as important as the words used. "No" does not necessarily mean "no," and you must rely much more on the context in order to understand just what "no" means.

Why is context important? Failure to understand the differences in interaction styles may lead to misunderstandings. For example, in Japan, a high-context culture, negotiators prefer not to flatly say "no" to a business request. They will say something like "We will study it" or "We will get back to you later." Their negotiation partners are supposed to understand the context of these unenthusiastic responses and interpret them as essentially "no," even though the word "no" is never explicitly said. By contrast, lawyers in the United States, a low-context culture, are included in negotiations to essentially help remove the context—a contract should be as straightforward as possible, and there should be no room for parties to read between the lines. But negotiators from high-context cultures such as China often prefer *not* to involve lawyers until the very last phase of contract drafting. In high-context cultures, initial rounds of negotiations are supposed to create the context for mutual trust and friendship. For individuals brought up in high-context cultures, decoding the context and acting accordingly becomes second nature. Straightforward communication and confrontation, typical in low-context cultures, often baffle them.

3-3b The Cluster Approach

The cluster approach groups countries that share similar cultures together as one **cluster**. Exhibit 3.2 shows three influential sets of clusters. This table is the first time these three major systems of cultural clusters are compiled side by side. Viewing them together

low-context culture A culture in which communication is usually taken at face value without much reliance on unspoken conditions or assumptions.

high-context culture A culture in which communication relies heavily on the underlying unspoken conditions or assumptions, which are as important as the words used.

cluster A group of countries that have similar cultures.

can allow us to see their similarities and differences. The first is the Ronen and Shenkar clusters, proposed by management professors Simcha Ronen and Oded Shenkar.[6] In alphabetical order, these clusters are (1) Anglo, (2) Arabic, (3) Eastern Europe, (4) Far East, (5) Germanic, (6) Latin America, (7) Latin Europe, (8) Near East, (9) Nordic, and (10) sub-Saharan Africa. Brazil, India, Israel, and Japan are classified as independents.

The second set of clusters is called the GLOBE clusters, named after the Global Leadership and Organizational Behavior Effectiveness project led by management professor Robert House.[7] The GLOBE project identifies ten clusters and covers 62 countries. Seven clusters use identical labels as the Ronen and Shenkar clusters: (1) Anglo, (2) Eastern Europe, (3) Germanic Europe, (4) Latin America, (5) Latin Europe, (6) Nordic Europe, and (7) sub-Saharan Africa. In addition, GLOBE has the clusters of (8) Confucian Asia, (9) Middle East, and (10) Southern Asia.

The third set of clusters is the Huntington civilizations, popularized by political scientist Samuel Huntington. A **civilization** is "the highest cultural grouping of people and the broadest level of cultural identity people have."[8] Huntington divides the world into eight civilizations: (1) African, (2) Confucian (Sinic), (3) Hindu, (4) Islamic, (5) Japanese, (6) Latin American, (7) Slavic-Orthodox, and (8) Western. While this classification shares a number of similarities with the Ronen and Shenkar and GLOBE clusters, Huntington's Western civilization is a very broad cluster that is subdivided into Anglo, Germanic, Latin Europe, and Nordic clusters by Ronen and Shenkar and by GLOBE.

An underlying idea of the cluster approach is that people and firms are more comfortable doing business with other countries within the same cluster/civilization. Having a common language, history, and religion reduces the liability of foreignness when operating in another country but within the same cluster/civilization (see Chapter 1). For example, Hollywood movies are more likely to succeed in English-speaking countries. Most foreign investors in China are from Hong Kong and Taiwan— they are not very "foreign." Brazilian firms enjoy doing business in Africa's Angola and Mozambique, which are also Portuguese-speaking countries.

civilization The highest cultural grouping of people and the broadest level of cultural identity people have.

power distance The extent to which less powerful members within a culture expect and accept that power is distributed unequally.

individualism The idea that the identity of an individual is fundamentally his or her own.

collectivism The idea that an individual's identity is fundamentally tied to the identity of his or her collective group.

3-3c The Dimension Approach

While both the context and cluster approaches are interesting, the dimension approach is more influential. The reasons for such influence are probably twofold. First, insightful as the context approach is, it represents only one dimension. What about other dimensions? Second, the cluster approach has relatively little to offer regarding differences of countries *within* one cluster. For example, what are the differences between Argentina and Chile, both of which belong to the same Latin America cluster according to Ronen and Shenkar and GLOBE? By focusing on multiple dimensions of cultural differences both within and across clusters, the dimension approach aims to overcome these limitations. While there are several competing frameworks, the work of Hofstede and his colleagues is by far the most influential and thus our focus here.

Shown in Exhibit 3.3, Hofstede and his colleagues have proposed five dimensions. **Power distance** is the extent to which less powerful members within a country expect and accept that power is distributed unequally. In high power distance Brazil, the richest 10% of the population pockets approximately 50% of the national income, and everybody accepts this as "the way it is." In low power distance Sweden, the richest 10% only obtains 22% of the national income. Major differences occur even within the same cluster. For example, in the United States, subordinates often address their bosses on a first name basis, a reflection of a relatively low power distance. While your boss, whom you call Mary or Joe, still has the power to fire you, the distance appears to be

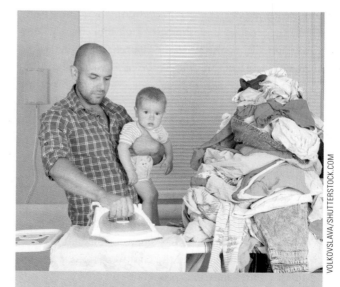

In low masculinity societies, men are increasingly likely to assume the roles of nurses, teachers, and househusbands.

VOLKOVSLAVA/SHUTTERSTOCK.COM

EXHIBIT 3.3 | HOFSTEDE DIMENSIONS OF CULTURE

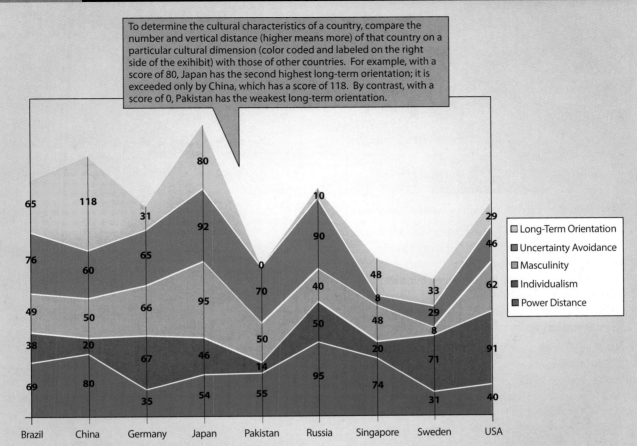

To determine the cultural characteristics of a country, compare the number and vertical distance (higher means more) of that country on a particular cultural dimension (color coded and labeled on the right side of the exihibit) with those of other countries. For example, with a score of 80, Japan has the second highest long-term orientation; it is exceeded only by China, which has a score of 118. By contrast, with a score of 0, Pakistan has the weakest long-term orientation.

Legend:
- Long-Term Orientation
- Uncertainty Avoidance
- Masculinity
- Individualism
- Power Distance

Countries (left to right): Brazil, China, Germany, Japan, Pakistan, Russia, Singapore, Sweden, USA

Sources: Adapted from G. Hofstede, "Cultural constraints in management theories," *Academy of Management Executive* 7, no. 1 (1993): 81–94; G. Hosftede, *Cultures and Organizations: Software of the Mind* (New York: McGraw-Hill, 1997) 25, 26, 53, 84, 113, 166. For updates, see www.geerthofstede.com.

shorter than if you have to address this person as Mrs. Y or Dr. Z. In low power distance American universities, all faculty members, including the lowest-ranked assistant professors, are commonly addressed as "Professor A." In high power distance British universities, only full professors are allowed to be called "Professor B" (everybody else is called "Dr. C" or "Ms. D" if D does not have a PhD). German universities are perhaps most extreme: Full professors with PhDs need to be honored as "Prof. Dr. X." Your author would be "Prof. Dr. Peng" if I were to teach at a German university.

Individualism refers to the idea that an individual's identity is fundamentally his or her own, whereas **collectivism** refers to the idea that an individual's identity is fundamentally tied to the identity of his or her collective group, be it a family, village, or company. In individualistic societies, led by the United States, ties between individuals are relatively loose and individual achievement and freedom are highly valued. In collectivist societies such as many countries in Africa, Asia, and Latin America, ties between individuals are relatively close

and collective accomplishments are often sought after. In Chinese restaurants, most dishes are served "family style" to be shared by all the people around the table. In American restaurants, most dishes are served "individual style" to be only enjoyed by particular persons who order them. Shown in our Opening Case, sharing food and passing meat by hand is frequently done among people in collectivistic cultures such as the Saudis and the Kazakhs.

The **masculinity** versus **femininity** dimension refers to sex role differentiation. In every traditional society, men tend to have occupations that reward assertiveness, such as politics, military, and management. Women, on the other hand, usually work in caring professions such as teaching and nursing in addition to being

masculinity A relatively strong form of societal-level sex-role differentiation whereby men tend to have occupations that reward assertiveness and women tend to work in caring professions.

femininity A relatively weak form of societal-level sex-role differentiation whereby more women occupy positions that reward assertiveness and more men work in caring professions.

Debate: Criticizing Hofstede's Framework

Despite the influence of Hofstede's framework, debate continues to rage. Criticisms include:

▶ Cultural boundaries are not the same as national boundaries.

▶ Although Hofstede was careful to remove some of his own cultural biases, "the Dutch software" of his mind, as he acknowledged, "will remain evident to the careful reader." Being more familiar with Western cultures, Hofstede might inevitably be more familiar with dimensions relevant to Westerners. Thus, crucial dimensions relevant to Easterners (Asians) could be missed.

▶ Hofstede's research was based on surveys of more than 116,000 IBM employees working at 72 national subsidiaries from 1967 to 1973. This had both pros and cons. On the positive side, it took place not only in the same industry, but also in the same company. Otherwise, it would have been difficult to determine whether findings were due to differences in national cultures or industry or organizational cultures. However, because of such a single firm/single industry design, it was possible that Hofstede's findings captured what was unique to that industry or to IBM. Given anti-American sentiments in some countries, some individuals might refuse to work for an American employer. Thus, it was difficult to ascertain whether employees working for IBM were true representatives of their respective national cultures.

▶ Because the original data are now over 40 years old, critics contend that Hofstede's framework would simply fail to capture aspects of recent cultural change.

Hofstede responded to all four criticisms. First, he acknowledged that his focus on national culture was a matter of expediency with all its trappings. Second, since the 1980s, Hofstede

COURTESY OF GEERT HOFSTEDE

and colleagues relied on a questionnaire derived from cultural dimensions most relevant to the Chinese, and then translated it from Chinese to multiple languages. That was how he uncovered the fifth dimension, long-term orientation (originally labeled "Confucian dynamism"). In response to the third and fourth criticisms, Hofstede pointed out a large number of more recent studies conducted by other scholars, using a variety of countries, industries, and firms. Most results were supportive of his findings. Overall, while Hofstede's work is not perfect, on balance, its values seem to outweigh its drawbacks.

Sources: T. Fang, "Asian management research needs more self-confidence," *Asia Pacific Journal of Management* 27 (2010): 155–170; G. Hofstede, "What did GLOBE really measure?" *Journal of International Business Studies* 37 (2006): 882–896; G. Hofstede, "Asian management in the 21st century," *Asia Pacific Journal of Management* 24 (2007): 411–420; M. Javidan, R. House, P. Dorfman, P. Hanges, and M. Luque, "Conceptualizing and measuring cultures and their consequences," *Journal of International Business Studies* 37 (2006): 897–914; B. Kirkman, K. Lowe, and C. Gibson, "A quarter century of *Culture's Consequences*," *Journal of International Business Studies* 37 (2006): 285–320; R. Maseland and A. van Hoorn, "Explaining the negative correlation between values and practices," *Journal of International Business Studies* 40 (2009): 527–532; B. McSweeney, "Hofstede's model of national cultural differences and their consequences," *Human Relations* 55 (2002): 89–118; L. Tang and P. Keveos, "A framework to update Hofstede's cultural value indices," *Journal of International Business Studies* 39 (2008): 1045–1063; R. Tung and A. Verbeke, "Beyond Hofstede and GLOBE," *Journal of International Business Studies* 41 (2010): 1259–1274.

---

uncertainty avoidance The extent to which members of a culture accept or avoid ambiguous situations and uncertainty.

homemakers. High masculinity societies (led by Japan) continue to maintain a sharp role differentiation along gender lines. In low masculinity societies (led by Sweden), women are increasingly likely to become politicians, scientists, and executives, and men frequently assume the role of nurses, teachers, and *househusbands*.

Uncertainty avoidance refers to the extent to which members in a culture accept or avoid ambiguous situations and uncertainty. Members of high uncertainty avoidance cultures (led by Greece) place a premium on job security and retirement benefits. They also tend to resist change, which often creates uncertainty. Low uncertainty avoidance cultures (led by Singapore) are characterized by a greater willingness to take risks and less resistance to change.

Long-term orientation emphasizes perseverance and savings for future betterment. China, which has the world's longest continuous written history of approximately 4,000 years and the highest contemporary savings rate, leads the pack. On the other hand, members of short-term orientation societies (led by Pakistan) prefer quick results and instant gratification.

Overall, Hofstede's dimensions are interesting and informative. It is also important to note that Hofstede's dimensions are not perfect and have attracted some criticisms (see Debate). However, it is fair to suggest that these dimensions represent a *starting point* for us as we try to figure out the role of culture in global business.

3-4 CULTURE AND GLOBAL BUSINESS

A great deal of global business activity is consistent with the context, cluster, and dimension approaches to cultural differences. For instance, the average length of contracts is longer in low-context countries (such as Germany) than in high-context countries (such as Vietnam), where a lot of agreements are unspoken and not necessarily put in a legal contract.

Also, as pointed out by the cluster approach, firms are a lot more serious in preparation when doing business with countries in other clusters compared to how they deal with fellow countries within the same cluster. Countless new books in English have recently been published on "how to do business in China." Two decades ago, gurus wrote about "how to do business in Japan." However, has anyone ever seen a book in English on "how to do business in Canada?"

Hofstede's dimension approach can be illustrated by numerous real-world examples. For instance, managers in high power distance countries such as France and Italy have a greater tendency for centralized authority. Although widely practiced in low power distance Western countries, asking for feedback and participation from subordinates—known as empowerment—is often regarded as a sign of weak leadership and low integrity in high power distance countries such as Egypt, Russia, and Turkey.

Individualism and collectivism also affect business activities. Individualist US firms may often try to differentiate themselves, whereas collectivist Japanese firms tend to follow each other. Because entrepreneurs stick their necks out by founding new firms, individualistic societies tend to foster a relatively higher level of entrepreneurship.

Likewise, masculinity and femininity affect managerial behavior. The stereotypical manager in high masculinity societies is "assertive, decisive, and aggressive," and the word "aggressive" carries positive connotations. In contrast, high femininity societies generally consider "aggressive" a negative term, and managers are "less visible, intuitive rather than decisive, and accustomed to seeking consensus."[9]

Managers in low uncertainty avoidance countries such as Britain rely more on experience and training, whereas managers in high uncertainty avoidance countries such as China rely more on rules. In addition, cultures with a long-term orientation are likely to nurture firms with long horizons. In comparison, Western firms often focus on relatively short-term profits (often on a *quarterly* basis).

Overall, there is strong evidence for the importance of culture. Sensitivity to cultural differences does not guarantee success but can at least avoid blunders. For instance, a Chinese manufacturer exported to the West a premium brand of battery called White Elephant without knowing the meaning of this phrase in Western culture. In another example, when a French manager (a man) was transferred to a US subsidiary and met his American secretary (a woman) for the first time, he greeted her with an effusive cheek-to-cheek kiss, a harmless "Hello" in France. However, the secretary later filed a complaint for sexual harassment. More seriously, Mitsubishi Motors encountered major problems when operating in the United States. While Japan leads the world in masculinity, the company's US facilities had more female participation in the labor force, typical of a country with a relatively higher level of femininity. Yet, its US division reportedly tolerated sexual discrimination and sexual harassment behaviors. Mitsubishi ended up paying $34 million to settle these charges.

CREATISTA/SHUTTERSTOCK.COM

long-term orientation A perspective that emphasizes perseverance and savings for future betterment.

Cross-cultural differences can be interesting (see Opening Case). But they can also be unethical, all depending on the institutional frameworks in which firms are embedded (see Closing Case). This is discussed next.

3-5a Definition and Impact of Ethics

Ethics refers to the principles, standards, and norms of conduct that govern individual and firm behavior. Ethics is not only an important part of informal institutions, but is also deeply reflected in formal laws and regulations. To the extent that laws reflect a society's minimum standards of conduct, there is a substantial overlap between what is ethical and legal as well as between what is unethical and illegal. However, in some cases, what is legal may be unethical. For example, mass layoffs are legal, but are widely viewed as unethical in many countries.

Recent scandals have pushed ethics to the forefront of global business discussions. Numerous firms have introduced a **code of conduct**—a set of guidelines for making ethical decisions. But firms' ethical motivations are still subject to debate. Three views have emerged:

▶ A *negative view* suggests that firms may simply jump onto the ethics bandwagon under social pressure to *appear* more legitimate without necessarily becoming better.

▶ A *positive view* maintains that some (although not all) firms may be self-motivated to do it right regardless of social pressure.

▶ An *instrumental view* believes that good ethics may simply be a useful instrument to help make money.

Perhaps the best way to appreciate the value of ethics is to examine what happens after some crisis. As a reservoir of goodwill, the value of an ethical reputation is *magnified* during a time of crisis. After the 2008 terrorist attacks on the Taj Mahal Palace Hotel in Mumbai, India, that killed 31 people (including 20 guests), the hotel received only praise. Why? The surviving guests were overwhelmed by employees' dedication to duty and their desire to protect guests in the face of terrorist attacks. Eleven employees laid down their

ethics The principles, standards, and norms of conduct that govern individual and firm behavior.

code of conduct A set of guidelines for making ethical decisions.

ethical relativism A perspective that suggests that all ethical standards are relative.

ethical imperialism The absolute belief that "there is only one set of Ethics (with a capital E), and we have it."

A 2008 terrorist attack on the Taj Mahal Palace Hotel in Mumbai, India, killed 31 people, yet the hotel received an outpouring of praise in the wake of the attack. Why do you think that is?

lives while helping between 1,200 and 1,500 guests safely escape. Paradoxically, catastrophes may allow more ethical firms such as the Taj, which is renowned for its integrity and customer service, to shine.[10] The upshot seems to be that ethics pays.

3-5b Managing Ethics Overseas

Managing ethics overseas is challenging because what is ethical in one country may be unethical elsewhere. There are two schools of thought.[11] First, **ethical relativism** follows the cliché, "When in Rome, do as the Romans do." If Muslim countries discriminate against women, so what? Likewise, if industry rivals in Mexico can fix prices, who cares? Isn't that what "Romans" do in "Rome"? Second, **ethical imperialism** refers to the absolute belief that "There is only one set of Ethics (with a capital E), and we have it." Americans are especially renowned for believing that their ethical values should be applied universally. For example, since sexual discrimination and price fixing are wrong in the United States, they must be wrong everywhere. In practice, however, neither of these schools of thought is realistic. At the extreme, ethical relativism would have to accept any local practice, whereas ethical imperialism may cause resentment and backlash among locals.

Three middle-of-the-road guiding principles have been proposed by Thomas Donaldson, a business ethicist. These are shown in Exhibit 3.4. First, respect for human dignity and basic rights—such as concern for health, safety, and the need for education rather than working at a young age—should determine the absolute, minimal ethical thresholds for *all* operations around the world.

Second, firms should respect local traditions. If a firm bans giving gifts, it can forget about doing business in China and Japan. While hiring employees' children and relatives instead of more qualified applicants is illegal in the United States under equal opportunity laws, it is routine practice for Indian companies and is expected to strengthen employee loyalty. What should US companies setting up subsidiaries in India do? Donaldson advises that such nepotism is not necessarily wrong, at least not in India.

Finally, respect for institutional context calls for a careful understanding of local institutions. Codes of conduct banning bribery are not very useful unless accompanied by guidelines for the scale and scope of *appropriate* gift giving/receiving (see Exhibit 3.5). Citigroup allows employees to accept noncash gifts whose nominal value is less than $100. The *Economist* allows its journalists to accept any gift that can be consumed in a single day; a bottle of wine is acceptable, but a case of wine is not.[12] Overall, these three principles, although far from perfect, can help managers make decisions about which they may feel relatively comfortable.

 ## 3-6 ETHICS AND CORRUPTION

Ethics helps to combat **corruption**, often defined as the abuse of public power for private benefits usually in the form of bribery, in cash or in kind.[13] Competition should be based on products and services, but corruption distorts that basis, causing misallocation of resources and slowing economic development. Corruption discourages foreign direct investment (FDI). If the level of corruption in Singapore (very low) were to increase to the level in Mexico (in the middle range), it reportedly would have the same negative impact on FDI inflows as raising the tax rate by 50%.[14]

> **corruption** The abuse of public power for private benefits, usually in the form of bribery.

EXHIBIT 3.4 MANAGING ETHICS OVERSEAS: THREE APPROACHES

▶ Respect for human dignity and basic rights

▶ Respect for local traditions

▶ Respect for institutional context

Sources: T. Donaldson, "Values in tension: Ethics away from home," *Harvard Business Review* (September-October 1996): 4–11; J. Weiss, *Business Ethics*, 4th ed. (Cincinnati: South-Western Thomson, 2006).

EXHIBIT 3.5 TEXAS INSTRUMENTS (TI) GUIDELINES ON GIFTS IN CHINA

▶ These China-Specific Guidelines are based on TI's Global Standard Guidelines, taking into consideration China's local business climates, legal requirements, customs, and cultures as appropriate. Employees of TI entities in China ("TIers") should comply with both these China-Specific Guidelines and Global Standard Guidelines. In any event of conflict, the stricter standard will apply.

▶ Acceptable gifts include calendars, coffee cups, appointment books, notepads, small pocket calculators, and ball point pens.

▶ Gifts with excessive value refer to those that are worth more than RMB 200 yuan (approximately $32), and need approval from Asia Finance Director.

▶ If you are not sure when you can accept or offer any gift, the following two Quick Tests are recommended:

  a. "Reciprocity" Test. Ask this question: Based on your knowledge of TI's policy and culture, would TI under similar circumstances allow you to provide a TI business partner a gift of an equivalent nature? If the answer is no, then politely refuse the offer.

  b. "Raise Eyebrow" or "Embarrassments" Test. Ask these questions: Would you "raise eyebrows" or feel uncomfortable in giving or receiving the gift in the presence of others in a work area? Would you feel comfortable in openly displaying the gift you are offering or receiving? Would you feel embarrassed if it were seen by other TI business partners or by your colleagues/supervisor?

▶ No cash or cash equivalent gift cards may be given. Gift cards that are redeemable only for a specific item (and not cash) with a fixed RMB value, such as a Moon Cake card,* are permitted as long as the gift is otherwise consistent with these Guidelines.

* Moon Cake is a special dessert for the Mid-Autumn Festival, which is a major holiday for family reunion in September.

Source: Adapted from Texas Instruments, *Comprehensive Guidelines on Gifts, Entertainment, and Travel in China* (2014).

In the global fight against corruption, the Foreign Corrupt Practices Act (FCPA) was enacted by the US Congress in 1977. It bans bribery of foreign officials. Many US firms complain that the act has unfairly restricted them. They also point out that overseas bribery expenses were often tax deductible (!) in many EU countries such as Austria, France, and Germany until the late 1990s. Even with the FCPA, however, there is no evidence that US firms are inherently more ethical than others. The FCPA itself was triggered in the 1970s by investigations of many corrupt US firms. Even the FCPA makes exceptions for small grease payments to get through customs abroad. Overall, the FCPA can be regarded as an institutional weapon in the global fight against corruption. Recall that every institution has three supportive pillars: regulatory, normative, and cognitive (Exhibit 2.1). Despite the FCPA's formal *regulatory* teeth, for a long time it had neither a *normative* pillar nor a *cognitive* pillar. Until recently, the norm among other OECD firms was to pay bribes first and get tax deductions later, a clear sign of ethical relativism. Only in 1997 did the OECD Convention on Combating Bribery of Foreign Public Officials commit all 30 member countries (essentially all developed economies) to criminalize bribery. The regulation went into force in 1999. A more ambitious campaign is the UN Convention against Corruption, which was signed by 106 countries in 2003 and came into force in 2005. If every country criminalizes bribery and every firm resists corruption, their combined power will eradicate it.[15] But this will not happen unless FCPA-type legislation is institutionalized and *enforced* in every country.

3-7 NORMS AND ETHICAL CHALLENGES

As an important informal institution, **norms** are the prevailing practices of relevant players—the proverbial "everybody else"—that affect the focal individuals and firms. How firms strategically respond to ethical challenges is often driven, at least in part, by norms. Shown in Exhibit 3.6, four broad strategic responses are (1) reactive strategy, (2) defensive strategy, (3) accommodative strategy, and (4) proactive strategy.

A **reactive strategy** is passive. Firms do not

norm The prevailing practices of relevant players that affect the focal individuals and firms.

reactive strategy A response to an ethical challenge that often involves denial and belated action to correct problems.

defensive strategy A response to an ethical challenge that focuses on regulatory compliance.

accommodative strategy A response to an ethical challenge that involves accepting responsibility.

EXHIBIT 3.6	STRATEGIC RESPONSES TO ETHICAL CHALLENGES	
Strategic responses	**Strategic behaviors**	**Examples in the text**
Reactive	Deny responsibility; do less than required	GM (the 2000s)
Defensive	Admit responsibility but fight it; do the least that is required	Nike (the 1990s)
Accommodative	Accept responsibility; do all that is required	Toyota (the 2010s), Ford (the 2000s)
Proactive	Anticipate responsibility; do more than is required	BMW (the 1990s)

feel compelled to act when problems arise, and denial is usually the first line of defense. In the absence of formal regulation, the need to take action is neither internalized through cognitive beliefs, nor embodied in any practicable norm. For example, as early as in 2005, General Motors (GM) had been aware that the ignition switch of some of its cars could accidentally shut off the engine. Yet, it refused to take any actions and proceeded to produce and sell the cars for a decade. Sure enough, accidents happened and people were killed and injured due to the faulty switches. Only when victims' families sued and Congressional pressures increased did GM belatedly recall millions of cars in 2014.

A **defensive strategy** focuses on regulatory compliance. In the 1990s, media and activist groups charged Nike with running sweatshops, although there was no existing regulation prohibiting sweatshops. Nike's initial response was "We don't make shoes," because Nike did not directly own and manage the factories. Its contractors in Indonesia and Vietnam were in charge. This response, however, failed to convey any ethical responsibility. Only when several senators began to suggest legislative solutions—regulations with which Nike would need to comply—did Nike become more serious.

An **accommodative strategy** features emerging organizational norms to accept responsibility and a set of increasingly internalized cognitive beliefs and values toward making certain changes. In other words, higher levels of ethical and moral responsibility, beyond simply the minimum of what is legally required, are accepted. During 2009 and 2010, Toyota initially was reluctant to recall 12 million vehicles, some of which had a tendency to suffer from unintended acceleration. In 2011, Toyota again recalled 1.7 million vehicles for fuel leaks. This time,

Toyota became more accommodative, aggressively carrying out recalls before they turned into a bigger mess.

Companies can change their strategic response. In 2000, when Ford Explorer vehicles equipped with Firestone tires had a large number of fatal rollover accidents, Ford evidently took the painful lesson from its Pinto fire fiasco in the 1970s. In the 1970s Ford marketed the Pinto car, being aware of a design flaw that could make the car susceptible to exploding in rear-end collisions. Similar to GM's recent scandal, Ford had not recalled the Pinto until Congressional, consumer, and media pressures heated up. In 2000, Ford aggressively initiated a speedy recall, launched a media campaign featuring its CEO, and discontinued the 100-year-old relationship with Firestone. While critics argued that Ford's accommodative strategy simply attempted to place the blame squarely on Firestone, the institution-based view (especially Proposition 1 in Chapter 2) suggests that such highly rational actions are to be expected. Even if Ford's public relations campaign was only window dressing designed to make the company look good to the public, it publicized a set of ethical criteria against which Ford could be judged and opened doors for more scrutiny by concerned stakeholders. It is probably fair to say that Ford was a better corporate citizen in 2000 than it was in 1975.

Finally, firms that take a **proactive strategy** anticipate institutional changes and do more than is required. In 1990, the German government proposed a "take-back" policy, requiring automakers to design cars whose components can be taken back by the same manufacturers for recycling. With this policy in mind, BMW anticipated its emerging responsibility. It not only designed easier-to-disassemble cars, but also enlisted the few high-quality dismantler firms as part of an exclusive recycling infrastructure. Further, BMW actively participated in public discussions and succeeded in establishing its approach as the German national standard for automobile disassembly. Other automakers were thus required to follow BMW's lead. However, other automakers had to fight over smaller, lower-quality dismantlers or develop in-house dismantling infrastructures from scratch. Through such a proactive strategy, BMW set a new industry standard for environmentally friendly norms.

3-8 MANAGEMENT SAVVY

The institution-based view emphasizes the importance of informal institutions—cultures, ethics, and norms—as the soil in which business around the globe either thrives or stagnates. How does this perspective answer our fundamental question: What determines the success and

---

failure of firms around the globe? The institution-based view argues that firm performance is determined, at least in part, by the informal cultures, ethics, and norms governing firm behavior.

This emphasis on informal institutions suggests two broad implications for savvy managers around the globe. First, managers should enhance their **cultural intelligence**, defined as an individual's ability to understand and adjust to new cultures. Acquisition of cultural intelligence passes through three phases: (1) awareness, (2) knowledge, and (3) skills. *Awareness* refers to the recognition of both the pros and cons of your own cultural mental software and the appreciation of people from other cultures. *Knowledge* refers to the ability to identify the symbols, rituals, and taboos in other cultures. Knowledge is also known as cross-cultural literacy. While you may not share (or may disagree) with their values, you will at least have a road map of the informal institutions governing their behavior. Finally, *skills* are good practices based on awareness and knowledge of other cultures (see Exhibit 3.7).

While skills can be taught in a classroom, the most effective way to learn them is total immersion in a foreign culture. Even for gifted individuals, learning a new language and culture well enough to function at a managerial level will take at least several months of full-time studies. Most employers do not give their expatriates that much time to learn before sending them abroad. Most expatriates are thus inadequately prepared, and the costs for firms, individuals, and families are tremendous (see Chapter 13). This means that you, a student studying this book, are advised to invest in your own career by picking up at least one foreign language, spending one semester (or year) abroad, and reaching out to make

proactive strategy A strategy that anticipates ethical challenges and addresses them before they happen.

cultural intelligence An individual's ability to understand and adjust to new cultures.

some international friends who are taking classes with you (and perhaps even sitting next to you). Such an investment will make you stand out among the crowd and propel your future career to new heights.

Savvy managers should also be aware of the prevailing norms and their transitions globally. The norms around the globe in the 21st century are more culturally sensitive and more ethically demanding than, say, in the 1970s (see Closing Case). This is not to suggest that every local norm needs to be followed. Failing to understand the changing norms or adapting to them in an insensitive and unethical way may lead to unsatisfactory or disastrous results. The best managers expect norms to shift over time and constantly decipher changes in the informal rules of the game in order to take advantage of new opportunities. How BMW managers proactively shape the automobile recycling norms in Germany serves as a case in point. Firms that fail to realize the passing of old norms and adapt accordingly are likely to fall behind or even go out of business.

EMERGING MARKETS/ETHICAL DILEMMA
Closing Case: Monetizing the Maasai Tribal Name

Living in Kenya and Tanzania, the Maasai, with their recognizable red attire, represent one of the most iconic tribes in Africa. As seminomadic pastoralists, the Maasai have for ages raised cattle and hunted with some small-scale agriculture near Africa's finest game parks such as Serengeti. Known as fierce warriors, the Maasai have won the respect of rival tribes, colonial authorities, and modern governments of Kenya and Tanzania. Together with lions, giraffes, and zebras, a Maasai village is among the "must-see" places for a typical African safari trip.

Those of you who cannot travel so far as to visit Africa can still get a taste of the colorful Maasai culture. Jaguar Land Rover marketed a limited-edition version of its Freelander 4×4 named Maasai. Louis Vuitton developed a line of menswear and womenswear fashion inspired by the Maasai dress. Diane von Furstenberg produced a red pillow and cushion line simply called Maasai. Switzerland-based Maasai Barefoot Technology (MBT) developed a line of round-bottom shoes to simulate the challenge of Maasai walking barefoot on soft earth. Italian pen maker Delta named its high-end, red-capped fountain pen Maasai. A single pen retails at $600, "which is like three or four good cows," according to a Maasai tribesman. These are just high-profile examples. Experts estimate that perhaps 10,000 firms around the world use the Maasai name, selling everything from hats to legal services.

All this sounds fascinating, except for one catch. While these firms made millions, neither a single Maasai individual nor the tribe ever received a penny from the companies using their name. This has caused a huge ethical and legal debate. Legally, the Maasai case is weak. The tribe has never made any formal effort to enforce intellectual property rights (IPR) of its culture and identity. With approximately 2 million tribal members spread between Kenya and Tanzania, just who can officially represent the Maasai is up in the air. An expert laughed at this idea, saying, "Look, if it could work, the French budget deficit would be gone by demanding royalties on French fries."

However, from an ethical standpoint, all the firms named above claim to be interested in corporate social responsibility (CSR). If they indeed are interested in the high road to business ethics, expropriating—or, if you may, "ripping off" or "stealing"—the Maasai name without compensation is a huge embarrassment.

Although steeped in tradition, the Maasai are also constantly in touch with the modern world. Their frequent interactions with tourists have made them aware of how much value there is in the Maasai name. But they are frustrated by their lack of knowledge about the rules of the game concerning IPR. Fortunately, they have the help of Ron Layton, a New Zealander and former diplomat who now runs nonprofit Light Years IP, which advises groups in the developing world such as the Maasai. Layton previously helped the Ethiopian government wage a legal battle with Starbucks, which marketed Harrar, Sidamo, and Yirgacheffe coffee lines from different regions of Ethiopia without compensation. Although Starbucks projects an image of being very serious about CSR, it initially fought these efforts before eventually agreeing to recognize Ethiopia's claims.

Emboldened by the success in fighting Starbucks, Layton worked with Maasai elders such as Issac ole Tialolo to establish a nonprofit registered in Tanzania called Maasai Intellectual Property Initiative (MIPI). Together, they crafted MIPI bylaws that reflected traditional Maasai cultural values while satisfying the requirements of Western courts—in preparation for an eventual legal showdown. Layton himself made no money from MIPI—his only income was the salary from his own nonprofit Light Years IP. A $1.25 million grant from the US Patent and Trademark Office (USPTO) helped to defray some of

Left: A Massai man poses for a portrait in Amboseli, Kenya. Right: A model walks the runway in a Maasai-inspired outfit at a Louis Vuitton fashion show.

the expenses. The challenge now is to have more tribal leaders and elders sign up with MIPI so that it comes to be viewed both externally and internally as the legitimate representative of the Maasai tribe. How the tribe can monetize its name remains to be seen.

Case Discussion Questions

1. **ON ETHICS**: Assuming you can afford (and are interested in) some of the "Maasai" products, would you like to pay *more* for these products if royalties are paid to the Maasai? If so, how much more?

2. **ON ETHICS**: As CEO of one of the firms mentioned, how are you going to respond to the criticism that your firm is "ripping off," or "stealing," from the Maasai?

3. **ON ETHICS**: If you were a judge in the home country of any of these firms named, how would you proceed with the legal dispute (assuming MIPI can eventually represent the tribe and press legal charges)?

Sources: "Maasai™," *Bloomberg Businessweek*, 24 October 2013: 84–88; ca.mbt.com; V. Kaster, "Maasai tribe wants control over commercial uses of its name," 6 March 2014; "Mailing yourself a copy of your creative work DOES NOT protect your copyright," IP Legal Freebies blog, 30 January 2013: www.iplegalfreebies.wordpress.com; www.dvf.com; www.jaguarlandrover.com.

STUDY TOOLS 3

LOCATED AT THE BACK OF YOUR BOOK:

☐ Rip out and study the Chapter Review Card at the end of the book

LOG IN TO WWW.CENGAGEBRAIN.COM TO:

☐ Review key term flashcards

☐ Complete a practice quiz to test your knowledge of key concepts

☐ View animated PengAtlas Maps

☐ Complete interactive content, watch chapter videos, and take a graded quiz

☐ Track your knowledge of key concepts in Global Business

☐ Read and discuss additional case study content

4 Leveraging Resources & Capabilities

LEARNING OBJECTIVES

After studying this chapter, you will be able to . . .

4-1 Define resources and capabilities.

4-2 Explain how value is created from a firm's resources and capabilities.

4-3 Articulate the difference between keeping an activity in-house and outsourcing it.

4-4 Explain how to use a VRIO framework to understand a firm's resources and capabilities.

4-5 Identify four things you need to do as part of a successful career and business strategy.

After you finish this chapter, go to

PAGE 64 for

STUDY TOOLS

Opening Case: LEGO's Secrets

LEGO is everywhere—toys, games, books, magazines, competitions, retail stores, theme parks, and now movies. If all of the approximately 400 billion colorful interlocking bricks ever produced by LEGO were to be divided equally among the world's population, each person would have 86 bricks (!). *Fortune* magazine half-joked that "at least ten billion are under sofa cushions and three billion are inside vacuum cleaners." By itself, a single LEGO brick is lifeless. But snap two of these plastic blocks together, and suddenly they take on a life of their own. A world of nearly infinite possibilities opens up. Igniting the imaginations of millions of children and adults around the world, the little LEGO brick has become a universal building block for fostering creativity. Accolades such as "the toy of the (20th) century" and "the most popular toy of all time" are routine for LEGO. Around the world, LEGO fan clubs abound, often with their own conferences and competitions. "With the possible exception of Apple, arguably no brand sparks as much cult-like devotion as LEGO," noted one expert. What are LEGO's secrets?

Relentless innovation and experimentation are one of the foremost characteristics of LEGO. Derived from the Danish phase *leg godt* ("play well"), LEGO was founded in 1932 by Ole Kirk Christiansen, a carpenter from Billund, Denmark—a rural town three hours away from Copenhagen. (LEGO Group is still headquartered in Billund today.) As a firm self-styled "to stimulate children's imagination and creativity" and "to nurture the child in each of us," LEGO is known for its willingness to entertain numerous experiments in order to capture the hearts and minds of its fickle primary customers—boys age 7 to 16—as well as the wallets of their parents. You may not know that LEGO started out making wooden toys. In 1947, it became the first Danish toymaker to experiment with plastics, even though trade magazines predicted at the time that plastics would never replace wooden toys. The now-ubiquitous LEGO brick was not the company's original invention. Actually, it was based on "self-locking bricks," which were patented in the UK in 1939 and released to the public domain in 1947. LEGO tinkered with the brick, and initial efforts were not successful. The bricks snapped together, but could not be separated easily. LEGO continued to experiment, eventually hitting a stud-and-tube coupling design that the company patented in Denmark in 1958. When a child snapped two bricks together, they would click into place and stick together. The two bricks would stay together until separated with an easy tug. Because such bricks would not come apart, kids could build from the ground up, leveraging what LEGO continues to call "clutch power." While the brick proved to be one of the toy industry's greatest innovations, LEGO's experiments marched on, with numerous hits and also numerous misses in the six decades since the finalization of the basic brick design.

Another LEGO hallmark is insisting on excellence. Coming from the founder, "Only the best is good enough" is a company motto engraved on a plaque that graces the entrance to LEGO Group headquarters' cafeteria even today. The seemingly simple tight fit of two bricks—and their easy separation—calls for extremely precise manufacturing. Because the size of each brick is so tiny, misalignment in the range of a few millimeters can easily create misfit when bricks are stacked together. Competitors can produce LEGO look-alikes that tolerate higher levels of variations, but kids often quickly figure out that LEGO is the best after playing with competing products for a short while. This is not to say LEGO's quality is perfect. On average, 18 out of 1 million bricks produced fail to meet LEGO's quality standards and have to be tossed. In addition to tight fit and easy separation, LEGO bricks are also known for being virtually indestructible. More than half a million people (mostly parents) have liked the Facebook page "For those who have experienced the pain caused by stepping on LEGO."

LEGO is famous in the business world for generating a *system*, not merely a product. Long before the days when computer programs were supposed to be backward compatible (a new version of Windows must allow users to open old files), LEGO made its bricks backward compatible—new bricks would click with old bricks of the 1950s vintage. As a result, kids (and adults) can mix and match old and new sets, and the LEGO universe can grow exponentially. Likewise, the bewildering array of new LEGO gadgets and experiences—such as board games, online games, competitions, books, magazines, theme parks, retail stores, and movies—unleash a powerful and mutually reinforcing ecosystem (or product family) centered on the brick.

Of course, numerous other secrets reside within LEGO, each contributing to its success. Dozens of books and hundreds of articles have been written, slicing and dicing LEGO in a variety of ways in order to probe its secrets. In the end, what exactly these secrets are remains elusive.

Sources: Author's interviews of LEGO customers and LEGO store personnel in Copenhagen and Dallas; "Lego in Asia," *Economist*, 16 November 2013: 72; "Unpacking Lego," *Economist*, 8 March 2014: 71; D. C. Robertson, *Brick by Brick: How LEGO Rewrote the Rules of Innovation and Conquered the Global Toy Industry* (New York: Crown Business, 2013).

Why is LEGO so popular and successful? Why do competitors have a hard time chipping away its market share? The answer is that there must be certain resources and capabilities specific to LEGO that are not shared by competitors. This insight has been developed into a resource-based view, which has emerged as one of the two core perspectives on global business.[1]

One leading tool in global business is **SWOT analysis**. A SWOT analysis identifies a firm's strengths (S), weaknesses (W), opportunities (O), and threats (T). The institution-based view of global business we discussed in Chapters 2 and 3 deals with the *external* opportunities and threats, enabled and constrained by formal and informal rules of the game. The resource-based view, on the other hand, concentrates on a firm's *internal* strengths and weaknesses. In this chapter, we first define resources and capabilities. Then we discuss the value chain analysis concentrating on the decision to keep an activity in-house or outsource it. We then focus on a VRIO framework centered on value (V), rarity (R), imitability (I), and organization (O).

4-1 UNDERSTANDING RESOURCES AND CAPABILITIES

A basic proposition of the resource-based view is that a firm consists of a bundle of productive resources and capabilities. **Resources** are defined as "the tangible and intangible assets a firm uses to choose and implement its strategies."[2] There is some debate regarding the definition of capabilities. Some scholars define them as a firm's capacity to dynamically deploy resources, suggesting a potentially crucial distinction between resources and capabilities and resulting in a "dynamic capabilities" view.[3]

While scholars may debate the fine distinctions between resources and capabilities, these distinctions are likely to "become badly blurred" in practice.[4] For example, is LEGO's R&D prowess a resource or capability? How about its abilities in precision manufacturing? For current and would-be managers, the key is to understand how these attributes help improve firm performance, not to figure out whether they should be labeled as resources or capabilities. Therefore, in this book, we will use the terms "resources" and "capabilities" *interchangeably* and often in *parallel*. In other words, **capabilities** are defined here the same as resources.

All firms, even the smallest ones, possess a variety of resources and capabilities. How do we meaningfully classify such diversity? One useful way is to separate the resources and capabilities into two categories: tangible and intangible (Exhibit 4.1). **Tangible resources and capabilities** are assets that are observable and quantifiable. They can be broadly organized in categories such as financial, physical, technological, and organizational resources and capabilities.

By definition, **intangible resources and capabilities** are harder to observe and more difficult (or even impossible) to quantify (see Exhibit 4.1). Yet, it is widely acknowledged that they must be there, because no firm is likely to generate competitive advantage by relying on tangible resources and capabilities alone. Examples of intangible assets include human, innovation, and reputational resources and capabilities. Note that all resources and capabilities discussed here are merely *examples* (see In Focus). They do not represent an exhaustive list. Firms will forge ahead to discover and leverage new resources and capabilities.

SWOT analysis An analytical tool for determining a firm's strengths (S), weaknesses (W), opportunities (O), and threats (T).

resource (capability) The tangible and intangible assets a firm uses to choose and implement its strategies.

tangible resource and capability Assets that are observable and easily quantified.

intangible resource and capability Assets that are hard to observe and difficult to quantify.

EXHIBIT 4.1 EXAMPLES OF RESOURCES AND CAPABILITIES	
Intangible	Tangible
Human	Financial
Innovation	Physical
Reputational	Technological

PETR VACLAVEK/SHUTTERSTOCK.COM

ISTOCK.COM/CLAUDIO BALDINI

Natura Makes Brazil Look Beautiful

Many people agree that Brazil is beautiful. Likewise, Brazilians are widely considered to be among the world's most beautiful people. However, beauty has to be maintained. Brazilian women's spending on beauty products is legendary. Although Brazil has the fifth largest population (with 200 million people) and the seventh largest economy in the world, it is one of the top markets for beauty products—second only to the United States. Beauty products spending per woman in Brazil matches that in Britain, which has a much higher income. While Brazil is obviously the attractive "B" in BRIC, beauty products are among Brazil's most attractive consumer markets, with multinationals such as Avon, Estée Lauder, L'Oreal, Mary Kay, P&G, Shiseido, and Unilever salivating over a share of the growing spoils. Emerging as the leading foreign player, Avon now sells more cosmetics in Brazil than in the United States. Yet, the queen of Brazil's highly attractive and competitive market is the homegrown Natura. Natura is everywhere in Brazil—its cosmetics, perfume, and hygiene products are in 60% of all households, and it leads the market with a 14% share in terms of sales (a total of $3 billion). Founded in 1969 and listed on the São Paulo Stock Exchange since 2004, Natura is already the world's 20th most valuable cosmetics brand. But because 90% of its sales are in Brazil and almost 100% of its sales are in Latin America, few people outside the region have heard about it.

How has Natura been able to dominate such a large and diverse market? Its recipe has at least two ingredients. First, by definition, Natura is green. About 70% of its products are plant based, and approximately 10% come from the Amazon region, where it purchases from village cooperatives and indigenous tribes. In addition to soccer and beaches, many people associate Brazil with the rainforest and biodiversity, which seems to be an obvious advantage for a firm that calls itself Natura and uses a heavy dose of ingredients from the Amazon. Natura is also among the first cosmetics firms in the world to pay attention to the specific hair-care

ROMARIOIEN/SHUTTERSTOCK.COM

needs of black women, which are often ignored by more mainstream firms.

Second, Natura relies on a small army of 1.2 million direct sales agents, who work like the legendary Avon Ladies. Since 2006, Natura's agents have actually been beating the Avon Ladies—Natura's number-one foreign rival in the country. With $3 billion in sales, Natura's total number of employees is only 6,200. By comparison, Avon worldwide has $10 billion sales but has 37,000 employees (and 6.4 million Avon Ladies). Thanks to Brazil's sky-high labor costs and tax rates, Natura has deliberately kept its employee base small in order to save costs. Since 1974, its marketing has relied on direct sales, leveraging hard-working women who go the extra mile to deliver products (sometimes literally penetrating into the jungles of the Amazon). Direct sales thus give Natura a cost advantage relative to its number-one domestic rival, O Boticário, which relies on a traditional retail format. An additional beauty of direct sales is that Natura's sales force is directly in touch with end users, whose needs, wants, and aspirations can be conveyed back to corporate headquarters for new product development.

Facing the onslaught of multinational cosmetics giants, Natura has realized that its best defense is offense. In 2005, Natura opened its first boutique in Paris, announcing its arrival in the cosmetics capital of the world. Although progress has been slow overseas (in part thanks to the hot growth back home, which dominates executive attention and capital allocation), Natura is indeed committed to making a big push globally. While Brazil is famous for commodity exports such as coffee and soybeans and one high-tech firm (Embraer, which is renowned for its regional jets), no Brazilian consumer products have made a big splash overseas. Can Natura leverage Brazil's positive country-of-origin effect of being beautiful? Stay tuned.

Sources: J. Chelekis and S. Mudambi, "MNCs and micro-entrepreneurship in emerging economies: The case of Avon in the Amazon," *Journal of International Management* 16 (2010): 412–424; J. Chelekis and S. Mudambi, "Direct selling at the base of the pyramid," in M. W. Peng, *Global Business*, 3rd ed. (Boston: Cengage, 2014) 28–30; "Consumer goods: Looks good," *Economist*, 28 September 2013 (special report): 14–15.

4-2 RESOURCES, CAPABILITIES, AND THE VALUE CHAIN

If a firm is a bundle of resources and capabilities, how do they come together to add value? A value chain analysis allows us to answer this question. Shown in Panel A of Exhibit 4.2, most goods and services are produced through a chain of vertical activities (from upstream to downstream) that add value—in short, a **value chain**. The value chain typically consists of two areas: primary activities and support activities.

Each activity requires a number of resources and capabilities. Value

value chain A series of activities used in the production of goods and services that make a product or service more valuable.

chain analysis forces managers to think about firm resources and capabilities at a very micro, activity-based level. Given that no firm is likely to be good at all primary and support activities, the key is to examine whether the firm has resources and capabilities to perform a *particular* activity in a manner superior to competitors—a process known as **benchmarking** in SWOT analysis. If managers find that their firm's particular activity is unsatisfactory, a decision model (shown in Exhibit 4.3) can remedy the situation.

4-3 WHEN AND WHEN NOT TO OUTSOURCE

In the first stage of the decision model, managers ask, "Do we really need to perform this activity in-house?" Exhibit 4.4 introduces a framework to take a hard look at this question, the answer to which boils down to (1) whether an activity is industry-specific or common across industries, and (2) whether this activity is proprietary (firm-specific) or not. The answer is "No," when the activity is found in Cell 2 in Exhibit 4.4 with a great deal of commonality across industries and little need for keeping it proprietary—known in the recent jargon as a high degree of **commoditization**. The answer may also be "No" if the activity is in Cell 1 in Exhibit 4.4, which is industry-specific but also has a high level of commoditization. Then, the firm may want to outsource this activity, sell the unit involved, or lease the unit's services to other firms (see Exhibit 4.3). This is because operating multiple stages of uncompetitive activities in the value chain may be prohibitively costly.

Think about steel, definitely a crucial component for automobiles. But the question for automakers is: "Do we need to make steel by ourselves?" The requirements for steel are common across end-user industries—that is, the

steel for automakers is essentially the same for construction, defense, and other steel-consuming end users (ignoring minor technical differences for the sake of our discussion). For automakers, while it is imperative to keep the auto-making activity (especially engine and final assembly) proprietary (Cell 3 in Exhibit 4.4), there is no need to keep

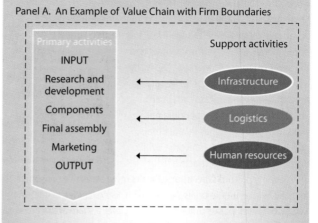

EXHIBIT 4.2 THE VALUE CHAIN

Panel A. An Example of Value Chain with Firm Boundaries

Panel B. An Example of Value Chain with Some Outsourcing

Note: Dashed lines represent firm boundaries.

benchmarking Examining whether a firm has the resources and capabilities to perform a particular activity in a manner superior to competitors.

commoditization A process of market competition through which unique products that command high prices and high margins gradually lose their ability to do so, thus becoming commodities.

EXHIBIT 4.3 A TWO-STAGE DECISION MODEL IN VALUE CHAIN ANALYSIS

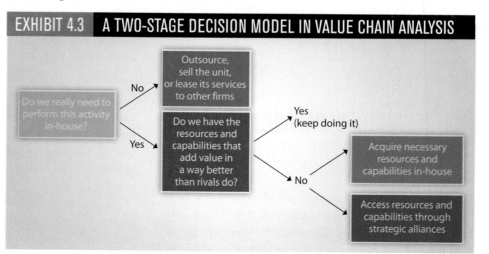

EXHIBIT 4.4   IN-HOUSE VERSUS OUTSOURCE

Note: At present, there are no clear guidelines for Cell 4, where firms either choose to perform activities in-house or outsource.

EXHIBIT 4.5   LOCATION, LOCATION, LOCATION

Note: "Captive sourcing" is a new term that is conceptually identical to "foreign direct investment (FDI)," a term widely used in global business. See Chapter 6 for details.

steelmaking in-house. Therefore, although many automakers, such as Ford and GM, historically were involved in steelmaking, none of them does it now. In other words, steelmaking is outsourced and steel is commoditized.

Outsourcing is defined as turning over an activity to an outside supplier that will perform it on behalf of the focal firm. For example, many consumer products companies (such as Nike and Apple), which possess strong capabilities in upstream activities (such as design) and downstream activities (such as marketing), have outsourced manufacturing to suppliers in low-cost countries. A total of 70% of the value of Boeing's new 787 Dreamliner is provided by outside suppliers. This compares with 51% for existing Boeing aircraft.[5] Recently, not only is manufacturing often outsourced but a number of service activities, such as IT, HR, and logistics, are also outsourced. The driving force is that many firms, which used to view certain activities as a very special part of their industries (such as airline reservations and bank call centers), now believe that these activities have relatively generic attributes that can be shared across industries. Of course, this changing mentality is fueled by the rise of service providers, such as IBM and Infosys in IT, Manpower in HR, Foxconn in contract manufacturing, and DHL in logistics. These specialist firms argue that such activities can be broken off from the various client firms (just as steelmaking was broken off from automakers decades ago) and leveraged to serve multiple clients with greater economies of scale. Such outsourcing enables client firms to become "leaner and meaner" organizations, which can better focus on their core activities (see Exhibit 4.2, Panel B).

If the answer to the question "Do we really need to perform this activity in-house?" is "Yes" (Cell 3 in Exhibit 4.4), but the firm's current resources and capabilities are not up to the task, then there are two choices

(see Exhibit 4.3). First, the firm may want to acquire and develop capabilities in-house so that it can perform this particular activity better. Second, if a firm does not have enough skills to develop these capabilities in-house, it may want to access them through alliances.

Conspicuously lacking in both Exhibits 4.3 and 4.4 is the *geographic* dimension—domestic versus foreign locations. Because the two terms "outsourcing" and "offshoring" have emerged rather recently, there is a great deal of confusion, especially among some journalists, who often casually equate them. So, to minimize confusion, we go from two terms to four terms in Exhibit 4.5, based on locations and modes (in-house versus outsource):

▶ **Offshoring**—international/foreign outsourcing.

▶ **Onshoring**—domestic outsourcing.

▶ **Captive sourcing**—setting up subsidiaries to perform in-house work in foreign locations.

▶ Domestic in-house activity.

Outsourcing—especially offshoring—has no shortage of controversies (see Debate). Despite this set of new labels, we need to be aware that "captive sourcing" is conceptually identical to foreign direct investment (FDI), which is nothing new in the world of global business (see Chapters 1 and 6). We also need to be aware that "offshoring" and "onshoring" are simply international and domestic variants of outsourcing, respectively. Offshoring low-cost IT

outsourcing Turning over an activity to an outside supplier that will perform it on behalf of the focal firm.

offshoring Outsourcing to an international or foreign firm.

onshoring Outsourcing to a domestic firm.

captive sourcing Setting up subsidiaries abroad so that the work done is in-house but the location is foreign. Also known as foreign direct investment (FDI).

Debate: For and Against Offshoring

Emerging Markets/Ethical Dilemma

Offshoring—or, more specifically, international outsourcing—has emerged as a leading corporate movement in the 21st century. However, it is debatable whether such offshoring proves to be a long-term benefit or hindrance to Western firms and economies.

Proponents argue that offshoring creates enormous value for firms and economies. Western firms are able to tap into low-cost yet high-quality labor, translating into significant cost savings. Firms can also focus on their core capabilities, which may add more value than dealing with non-core (and often uncompetitive) activities. In turn, offshoring service providers, such as Infosys, TCS, and Wipro, develop their core competencies in information technology (IT), especially **business process outsourcing (BPO)**. A McKinsey study that focused on offshoring between the United States and India reported that for every dollar spent by US firms in India, US firms save 58 cents (see Exhibit 4.6). Overall, $1.46 of new wealth is created, of which the US economy captures $1.13 through cost savings and increased exports to India. India captures the other 33 cents through profits, wages, and additional taxes. While acknowledging that some US employees may lose their jobs, proponents suggest that on balance, offshoring is a win-win solution for both US and Indian firms and economies.

Critics make three points on strategic, economic, and political grounds. Strategically, if "even core functions like engineering, R&D, manufacturing, and marketing can be moved outside," what is left of the firm? US firms have gone down this path before—in manufacturing—with disastrous results. In the 1960s, Radio Corporation of America (RCA) invented the color TV and then outsourced its production to Japan, a low-cost country at that time. Fast forward to the 2000s and the United States no longer has any US-owned color TV producers. Critics argue that offshoring nurtures rivals. Why are Indian IT/BPO firms now emerging as strong rivals? It is in part because they built up their capabilities doing work for EDS and IBM in the 1990s, particularly by working to help the IT industry prevent the "millennium bug" (or Y2K) problem.

Economically, critics question whether developed economies, on the whole, actually gain more. While shareholders and corporate highflyers embrace offshoring, it increasingly results in job losses in high-end areas such as design, R&D, and IT/BPO. While white-collar individuals who lose jobs will naturally hate it, the net impact on developed economies may still be negative.

Finally, critics make the political argument that many large firms in developed economies are unethical and are interested only in the cheapest and most exploitable labor. Not only is work commoditized, but people are also degraded as tradable commodities that can be jettisoned. As a result, large firms that outsource work to emerging economies are often accused of destroying jobs at home, ignoring corporate social responsibility, violating customer privacy (for example, by sending medical records, tax returns, and credit card numbers to be processed overseas), and in some cases undermining national security. Not surprisingly, the debate often becomes emotional and explosive when such accusations are made.

For firms in developed economies where this debate primarily takes place, the choice is not really offshoring versus nonoffshoring, but where to draw the line on offshoring. There is relatively little debate in emerging economies because they clearly stand to gain from offshoring. Taking a page from the Indian playbook, the

business process outsourcing (BPO) The outsourcing of business processes such as loan origination, credit card processing, and call center operations.

EXHIBIT 4.6	BENEFIT OF $1 US SPENDING ON OFFSHORING TO INDIA				
Benefit to the United States		**$**	**Benefit to India**		**$**
Savings accruing to US investors/customers		0.58	Labor		0.10
Exports of US goods/services to providers in India		0.05	Profits retained in India		0.10
Profit transfer by US-owned operations in India back to the United States		0.04	Suppliers		0.09
Net direct benefit retained in the United States		0.67	Central government taxes		0.03
Value from US labor re-employed		0.46	State government taxes		0.01
Net benefit to the United States		1.13	*Net benefit to India*		0.33

Source: D. Farrell, "Offshoring: Value creation through economic change," *Journal of Management Studies* (2005) 42: 675–683.

C SQUARED STUDIOS/PHOTODISC/GETTY IMAGES

Philippines, with numerous English-speaking professionals, is trying to eat some of India's lunch. Northeast China, where Japanese is widely taught, is positioning itself as an ideal location for call centers for Japan. Central and Eastern Europe gravitates toward serving Western Europe. Central and South American countries want to grab call center contracts for the large Hispanic market in the United States (see Chapter 3 In Focus).

Sources: D. Farrell, "Offshoring," *Journal of Management Studies* 42 (2005): 675–683; M. Gottfredson, R. Puryear, and S. Phillips, "Strategic sourcing," *Harvard Business Review* (February 2005): 132; P. Jensen, M. Larsen, and T. Pedersen, "The organizational design of offshoring," *Journal of International Management* 19 (2013): 315-323; S. Mudambi and S. Tallman, "Make, buy, or ally?" *Journal of Management Studies* 47 (2010): 1434–1456; D. Mukherjee, A. Gaur, and A. Dutta, "Creating value through offshore outsourcing," *Journal of International Management* 19 (2013): 377-389; C. Weigelt and M. Sarkar, "Performance implications of outsourcing for technological innovations," *Strategic Management Journal* 33 (2012): 189–216.

EXHIBIT 4.7 THE VRIO FRAMEWORK AND FIRM PERFORMANCE

Is a resource or capability . . .

Valuable?	Rare?	Costly to imitate?	Exploited by organization?		Competitive implications	Firm performance
No	—	—	No	→	Competitive disadvantage	Below average
Yes	No	—	Yes	→	Competitive parity	Average
Yes	Yes	No	Yes	→	Temporary competitive advantage	Above average
Yes	Yes	Yes	Yes	→	Sustained competitive advantage	Persistently above average

Sources: J. Barney, *Gaining and Sustaining Competitive Advantage*, 2nd ed. (Upper Saddle River, NJ: Prentice Hall, 2002) 173; R. Hoskisson, M. Hitt, and R. D. Ireland, *Competing for Advantage* (Cincinnati: Cengage, 2004) 118.

work to India, the Philippines, and other emerging economies has been widely practiced. Interestingly, eastern Germany; northern France; and the Appalachian, Great Plains, and southern regions of the United States have emerged as new hotbeds for onshoring. In job-starved regions such as Michigan, high-quality IT workers may accept wages 35% lower than at headquarters in Silicon Valley.

One interesting lesson we can take away from Exhibit 4.5 is that even for a single firm, value-adding activities may be geographically dispersed around the world, taking advantage of the best locations and modes to perform certain activities. For instance, a Dell laptop may be designed in the United States (domestic in-house activity), its components may be produced in Taiwan (offshoring) as well as the United States (onshoring), and its final assembly may be done in China (captive sourcing/FDI). When customers call for help, the call center may be in India, Ireland, Jamaica, or the Philippines, manned by an outside service provider—Dell may have outsourced the service activities through offshoring.

Of course, decisions on offshoring are not one-off. More recently as the cost of manufacturing in China rises because of rising labor cost and unreliable quality, some Western firms have brought some of the work back to their home countries—a process known as **reshoring**.

Overall, a value chain analysis engages managers to ascertain a firm's strengths and weaknesses on an activity-by-activity basis, *relative to rivals*, in a SWOT analysis. The recent proliferation of new labels is intimidating, causing some gurus to claim that "21st century offshoring really is different."[6] In reality, it is not. Under the skin of the new vocabulary, we still see the time-honored SWOT analysis at work. The next section introduces a VRIO framework on how to do this.

4-4 FROM SWOT TO VRIO

Recent progress in the resource-based view has gone beyond the traditional SWOT analysis. The new work focuses on the value (V), rarity (R), imitability (I), and organizational (O) aspects of resources and capabilities, leading to a **VRIO framework**. Summarized in Exhibit 4.7, addressing these four important questions has a number of ramifications for competitive advantage.

4-4a The Question of Value

Do firm resources and capabilities add value? The preceding value chain analysis suggests that this is the most fundamental question to

reshoring Moving formerly offshored activities back to the home country of the focal firm.

VRIO framework The resource-based framework that focuses on the value (V), rarity (R), imitability (I), and organizational (O) aspects of resources and capabilities.

start with. Only value-adding resources can lead to competitive advantage, whereas non-value-adding capabilities may lead to competitive *disadvantage*. With changes in the competitive landscape, previous value-adding resources and capabilities may become obsolete. The evolution of IBM is a case in point. IBM historically excelled in making hardware, including tabulating machines in the 1930s, mainframes in the 1960s, and PCs in the 1980s. However, as competition for hardware heated up, IBM's capabilities in hardware not only added little value, but also increasingly stood in the way for it to move into new areas. Since the 1990s, IBM has been focused more on lucrative software and services, where it has developed new value-adding capabilities, aiming to become an on-demand computing *service* provider for corporations. As part of this new strategy, IBM purchased PricewaterhouseCoopers, a leading technology consulting firm, and sold its PC division to Lenovo.

The relationship between valuable resources and capabilities and firm performance is straightforward. Instead of becoming strengths, non-value-adding resources and capabilities, such as IBM's historical expertise in hardware, may become weaknesses. If firms are unable to get rid of non-value-adding assets, they are likely to suffer from below-average performance.[7] In the worst case, they may become extinct, a fate IBM narrowly skirted during the early 1990s. According to IBM's CEO Ginni Rometty, "Whatever business you're in, it's going to commoditize over time, so you have to keep moving it to a higher value and change."[8]

4-4b The Question of Rarity

Simply possessing valuable resources and capabilities may not be enough. The next question asks: How rare are valuable resources and capabilities? At best, valuable but common resources and capabilities will lead to competitive parity, but not an advantage. Consider the identical aircraft made by Boeing and Airbus used by numerous airlines. They are certainly valuable, yet it is difficult to derive competitive advantage from these aircraft alone. Airlines have

> "Whatever business you're in, it's going to commoditize over time, so you have to keep moving it to a higher value and change."

LOPOLO/SHUTTERSTOCK.COM

causal ambiguity The difficulty of identifying the actual cause of a firm's successful performance.

to work hard on how to use these same aircraft *differently*.

Only valuable and rare resources and capabilities have the potential to provide some temporary competitive advantage. Overall, the question of rarity is a reminder of the cliché: If everyone has it, you can't make money from it. For example, the quality of the American Big Three automakers is now comparable with that of the best Asian and European rivals. However, even in their home country, the Big Three's quality improvements have not translated into stronger sales. Embarrassingly, in 2009 both GM and Chrysler, despite the decent quality of their cars, had to declare bankruptcy and be bailed out by the US government (and also by the Canadian government). The point is simple: Flawless high quality is now expected among car buyers, is no longer rare, and thus provides little advantage.

4-4c The Question of Imitability

Valuable and rare resources and capabilities can be a source of competitive advantage only if competitors have a difficult time imitating them. While it is relatively easy to imitate a firm's *tangible* resources (such as plants), it is a lot more challenging and often impossible to imitate *intangible* capabilities (such as tacit knowledge, superior motivation, and managerial talents).

Imitation is difficult. Why? In two words: **causal ambiguity**, which refers to the difficulty of identifying the causal determinants of successful firm performance. What exactly has caused LEGO to be such an enduring and continuously relevant toy company (see Opening Case)? LEGO has no shortage of competitors and imitators. Its performance has not always been enviable. Yet, in the past eight decades LEGO has always been able to turn around by finding new paths to growth (sometimes by returning to roots, as evidenced by its most recent turnaround).

A natural question is: How does LEGO do it? Usually a number of resources and capabilities will be nominated, such as a commitment to customer relationships, a willingness to change, a strong leadership team, and a multinational presence. While all of these are plausible, what *exactly* is it? This truly is a million dollar question, because knowing the answer to this question is not only intriguing to scholars and students, it can also be hugely profitable for LEGO's rivals. Unfortunately, outsiders usually have a hard time understanding what a firm does inside its boundaries. We can try, as many rivals have, to identify LEGO's recipe for success by drawing up a long list of possible reasons, labeled as "resources and capabilities" in our classroom discussion. But in the end, as outsiders we are not sure.

What is even more fascinating for scholars and students and more frustrating for rivals is that often managers of a focal firm such as Apple do not know exactly what contributes to its success. When interviewed, they can usually generate a long list of what they do well, such as a strong organizational culture, a relentless drive, and many other attributes. To make matters worse, different managers of the same firm may have a different list. When probed as to which resource or capability is "it," they usually suggest that it is all of the above in *combination*. After Apple made a record-breaking $18 billion profit in the fourth quarter of 2014 (never before had so much money been made by a single firm in three months), its CEO Tim Cook told the media that it was "hard to comprehend."[9] This is probably one of the most interesting and paradoxical aspects of the resource-based view: If insiders have a hard time figuring out what unambiguously contributes to their firm's performance, it is not surprising that outsiders' efforts in understanding and imitating these capabilities are usually flawed and often fail.

Overall, valuable and rare but imitable resources and capabilities may give firms some temporary competitive advantage, leading to above-average performance for some period of time. However, such advantage is not likely to be sustainable. Shown by the examples of Apple, LEGO (Opening Case), Natura (In Focus), and Alibaba (Closing Case), only valuable, rare, and *hard-to-imitate* resources and capabilities may potentially lead to sustained competitive advantage.

4-4d The Question of Organization

Even valuable, rare, and hard-to-imitate resources and capabilities may not give a firm a sustained competitive advantage if it is not properly organized.[10] Although movie stars represent some of the most valuable, rare, and hard-to-imitate (as well as highest paid) resources, *most* movies flop. More generally, the question of organization asks: How can a firm (such as a movie studio) be organized to develop and leverage the full potential of its resources and capabilities?

Numerous components within a firm are relevant to the question of organization. In a movie studio, these components include talents in "smelling" good ideas, photography crews, musicians, singers, makeup artists, animation specialists, and managers on the business side. These components are often called **complementary assets**,[11] because by themselves they are difficult to generate box office hits. For the favorite movie you saw most recently, do you still remember the names of its photographers and makeup artists? Of course not—you probably only remember the names of the stars. However, stars alone cannot generate hit movies. It is the *combination* of star resources and complementary assets that create hit movies. "It may be that not just a few resources and capabilities enable a firm to gain a competitive advantage but that literally thousands of these organizational attributes, bundled together, generate such advantage."[12]

Known as the ability to use one's two hands equally well, **ambidexterity** in the management literature describes capabilities to simultaneously deal with paradoxes. For example, in emerging economies, ambidexterity to manage both market forces and government forces simultaneously—as a bundle of complementary resources—is key to navigate the competitive waters.[13] In other words, to attain competitive advantage, market-based and nonmarket-based (political) capabilities need to complement each other. This is not only important for foreign firms, but also crucial for domestic firms. Case in point: The Tata Nano, the much-hyped, cheapest car that presumably would allow many Indians to become first-time car owners and create thousands of jobs, could not be made in its originally planned factory in the Indian state of West Bengal. Thousands of farmers who lost their land used to build the Nano factory protested. Political pressures forced Tata to abandon the plan and start another factory in another state, Gujarat, at a great cost. The fact that such an influential and otherwise respected firm can mess up its political relations *domestically* underscores the importance of ambidexterity as capabilities to manage

complementary asset The combination of numerous resources and assets that enable a firm to gain a competitive advantage.

ambidexterity Ability to use one's both hands equally well. In management jargon, this term has been used to describe capabilities to simultaneously deal with paradoxes (such as exploration versus exploitation).

both market-based and nonmarket-based relationships. Otherwise, strong market performers, such as Tata in India, may nevertheless hit a wall when messing up government relations.

Another idea is **social complexity**, which refers to the socially complex ways of organizing typical of many firms. Many multinationals consist of thousands of people scattered in many different countries. How they overcome cultural differences and are organized as one corporate entity and achieve corporate goals is profoundly complex. Oftentimes, it is their invisible relationships that add value.[14] Such organizationally embedded capabilities are thus very difficult for rivals to imitate. This emphasis on social complexity refutes what is half-jokingly called the "LEGO" view of the firm, in which a firm can be assembled (and dissembled) from modules of technology and people (a la LEGO toy blocks). By treating employees as identical and replaceable blocks, the "LEGO" view fails to realize that social capital associated with complex relationships and knowledge permeating many firms can be a source of competitive advantage.

Overall, only valuable, rare, and hard-to-imitate capabilities that are organizationally embedded and exploited can lead to sustained competitive advantage and persistently above-average performance. Because capabilities cannot be evaluated in isolation, the VRIO framework presents four interconnected and increasingly difficult hurdles (Exhibit 4.7). In other words, these four V, R, I, and O aspects come together as one *package*.

 ## 4-5 MANAGEMENT SAVVY

How does the resource-based view answer the big question in global business: What determines the success and failure of firms around the globe? The answer is straightforward. Fundamentally, some firms outperform others because winners possess some valuable, rare, hard-to-imitate, and organizationally embedded resources and capabilities that competitors do not have. This view is especially insightful when we see firms such as LEGO (Opening Case), Natura (In Focus), and Alibaba (Closing Case) persistently succeed, while numerous others struggle.

Shown in Exhibit 4.8, the resource-based view suggests four implications for action. First, the proposition that firms "compete on resources and capabilities" is not novel. The subtlety comes when managers attempt, via the VRIO framework, to distinguish resources and capabilities that are valuable,

social complexity The socially intricate and interdependent ways that firms are typically organized.

rare, hard-to-imitate, and organizationally embedded from those that do not share these attributes. In other words, the VRIO framework can greatly aid the time-honored SWOT analysis, especially the S (strengths) and W (weaknesses) parts. Managers, who cannot pay attention to everything, must have some sense of what *really* matters. Managers commonly fail to assess how their resources and capabilities compare with those of their rivals. As a result, most firms end up having a mixed bag of both good and mediocre capabilities. Using the VRIO framework, a value chain analysis helps managers make decisions on what capabilities to focus on in-house and what to outsource. Increasingly, what really matters is not tangible resources that are relatively easy to imitate, but intangible capabilities that are harder for rivals to wrap their arms around. Therefore, managers need to identify, develop, and leverage valuable, rare, hard-to-imitate, and organizationally embedded resources and capabilities, which are often intangible. It is thus not surprising that capabilities not meeting these criteria are increasingly outsourced.

Second, relentless imitation or benchmarking, while important, is not likely to be successful in the long run. By the time Elvis Presley died in 1977, there were a little over 100 Elvis impersonators. After his death, the number skyrocketed.[15] But obviously none of these imitators achieved any fame remotely close to the star status attained by the King of Rock 'n' Roll. Imitators have a tendency to mimic the most visible, the most obvious, and, consequently, the *least* important practices of winning firms. At best, follower firms that meticulously replicate every resource possessed by winning firms at best can hope to attain competitive parity. Firms endowed with sufficient resources to imitate others may be better off developing their own unique capabilities. The best-performing firms such as LEGO (Opening Case) often create new ways of adding value.

Third, even a sustainable competitive advantage will not last forever, particularly in today's global competition. All a firm can hope for is a competitive advantage that can be sustained for as long as possible.

Over time, all advantages may erode. As noted earlier, each of IBM's product-related advantages associated with tabulating machines, mainframes, and PCs was sustained for a period of time. But, eventually, these advantages disappeared. Even IBM's newer focus on software and servers is challenged by cloud computing heavyweights such as Amazon.[16] Therefore, the lesson for all firms, including current market leaders, is to develop strategic *foresight*—over-the-horizon radar is a good metaphor. Such strategic foresight enables firms to anticipate future needs and move early to identify, develop, and leverage resources and capabilities for future competition.

Finally, here is a very personal and relevant implication for action. As a student who is probably studying this book in a developed (read: high-wage and thus high-cost!) country such as the United States, you may be wondering: What do I get out of this? How do I cope with the frightening future of global competition? There are two lessons you can draw. First, the whole debate on offshoring, a part of the larger debate on globalization, is very relevant and directly affects your future as a manager, a consumer, and a citizen (see Chapter 1). So don't be a couch potato. Be active, get involved, and be prepared because it is not only their debate, it is *yours* as well. Second, be very serious about the VRIO framework of the resource-based view. While the resource-based view has been developed to advise firms, there is no reason you cannot develop that into a resource-based view of the *individual*. In other words, you can use the VRIO framework to develop yourself into an "untouchable"—a person whose job cannot be outsourced, as defined by Thomas Friedman in *The World Is Flat* (2005). An untouchable individual's job cannot be outsourced because he or she possesses valuable, rare, and hard-to-imitate capabilities that are indispensable to an employer. This won't be easy. But you really don't want to be mediocre. A generation ago, American parents told their kids: Eat your food—kids in China and India are starving. Now, Friedman would advise you: Study this book and leverage your education—students in China and India are starving for your job.[17]

EMERGING MARKETS
Closing Case: The Rise of Alibaba

Founded in 1999 by former English teacher Jack Ma, Alibaba has risen to become the largest e-commerce firm not only in China, but also in the world. The value of goods sold on Alibaba platforms eclipses that of Amazon and eBay *combined*. Alibaba started as a business-to-business (B2B) portal connecting overseas buyers and small Chinese manufacturers. Inspired by eBay, Alibaba next launched Taobao, a consumer-to-consumer (C2C) portal that today features nearly a billion products and is the one of the 20 most-visited websites worldwide. Finally, with Tmall, Alibaba offers an Amazon-like business-to-consumer (B2C) portal that helps global brands such as Levi's and Disney reach the middle class in China.

The rise of Alibaba has been breathtaking. China is the world's largest e-commerce market (bigger even than the United States'), and Alibaba controls four-fifths of all e-commerce in China. On Single's Day 2013 (November 11—an annual marketing invention created to encourage singles to "be nice" to themselves), Alibaba sold more than $5.7 billion worth of products. While preparing to initiate an initial public offering (IPO) in New York, Alibaba was predicted by the *Economist* to "be among the world's most valuable companies."

DREW ANGERER/GETTY IMAGES

On September 19, 2014, Alibaba's initial public offering (IPO) on the New York Stock Exchange was indeed the world's largest, raising $25 billion. On Single's Day 2016, the company's one-day sales reached $18 billion.

From a resource-based perspective, the rise of Alibaba is a story of focus and innovation. "eBay may be a shark in the ocean," Ma once said, "but I am a crocodile in the Yangtze River. If we fight in the ocean, I lose. But if we fight in the river, I win."

The Crocodile of Yangtze, as Ma became known, has largely focused on China to avoid head-on competition with the eBays of the world elsewhere. In China, eBay has been forced to retreat. In a low-trust society such as China, where people generally shy away from buying from strangers online and hesitate to use credit cards in general, Alibaba has pioneered the Alipay system. This novel online payment system relies on escrow (releasing money to a seller only once the buyer is happy with the goods received). This not only facilitates transactions for Alibaba as well as its buyers and sellers, but also helps build trust at the societal level. Alifinance, Alibaba's financing arm, has become a notable microlender to small firms, which are typically underserved by China's state-owned banks. Alifinance now plans to lend to individuals as well. Perhaps Alibaba's greatest treasure lies in its vast amount of data regarding the creditworthiness of the millions of China's middle class and thousands of firms that do business via Alibaba—clearly a Big Data gold mine.

Led by Jack Ma, Alibaba has emerged as a high-profile global leader in e-commerce. In 2016, the Group of 20 (G-20) leaders met in Hangzhou, where Alibaba is headquartered. During the conference, Ma proposed a globally connected e-commerce plan. He was soon after appointed special adviser on youth entrepreneurship and small business to the United Nations Conference on Trade and Development (UNCTAD).

Formidable as Alibaba is, it is not without its challenges. Its business model grows on PC-based e-commerce. As China moves toward becoming the world's largest market for smartphones, it is fast moving to mobile commerce—at a speed faster than any other major economy. According to Alibaba's own prospectus, "We face a number of challenges to successfully monetizing our mobile user traffic." In other words, Alibaba is but one of several contenders. Until fairly recently, Alibaba and two other Chinese Internet giants largely minded their own business as the "three kingdoms," referring to a historical era during which China was divided three ways. While Alibaba dominated e-commerce, Baidu was king of search engines, and Tencent made a killing on online games. The truce among the three kingdoms seems to have ended with the arrival of mobile commerce, as all three rush to establish dominance in this new market frontier. Famous for elbowing out Google in China, Baidu is listed on NASDAQ and is Microsoft's partner in China. In addition to online games, Tencent is known for its WeChat social messaging app, which is widely popular. There is no guarantee Alibaba will win in this contest.

While he is eager to fight it out for China's mobile commerce traffic, the Crocodile of the Yangtze has also been eyeing the wider global ocean. Some 12% of Alibaba's sales are already overseas. Its most attractive overseas markets are likely to be low-trust, underbanked emerging economies in Asia, Africa, and Latin America. But sharks such as eBay and Amazon will not go down without a fight. In 2016, Alibaba spent $1 billion to acquire Singapore-based Lazada Group, the "Amazon of Southeast Asia." This represents a major step forward in Alibaba's internationalization. Looking to the future, whether Alibaba deserves to be one of the world's most valuable companies will depend on how it can defend its e-commerce dominance at home in the mobile era and how it can grow its business abroad.

Case Discussion Questions

1. What are the characteristics of Alibaba's resources and capabilities that are valuable, unique, hard-to-imitate, and organizationally embedded?

2. Why has Alibaba become globally famous by focusing on its domestic market?

3. Sometimes the IPO of widely successful firms flops—Facebook's disappointing IPO comes to mind. Does Alibaba deserve to be one of the world's most valuable companies?

Sources: "Alibaba plays defense against Tencent," *Bloomberg Businessweek*, 26 August 2013: 38–40; 2013; "Tencent's worth," *Economist*, 21 September 2013: 66–68; "The Alibaba phenomenon," *Economist*, 23 March 2013: 15; "The world's greatest bazaar," *Economist*, 23 March 2013: 27–30; "From bazaar to bonanza," *Economist*, 10 May 2014: 63–65; "After the float," *Economist*, 6 September 2014: 66–67; "Just spend," *Economist*, 19 November 2016: 65; "Jack Ma," *Fortune*, 1 December 2016: 85; "Alibaba expected to be approved for IPO," *South China Morning Post*, 12 July 2014: B4; "Jack Ma named special advisor on youth entrepreneurship at United Nations trade body," *South China Morning Post*, 21 September 2016: www.scmp.com.

STUDY TOOLS 4

LOCATED AT THE BACK OF YOUR BOOK:

☐ Rip out and study the Chapter Review Card at the end of the book

LOG IN TO WWW.CENGAGEBRAIN.COM TO:

☐ Review key term flashcards

☐ Complete a practice quiz to test your knowledge of key concepts

☐ View animated PengAtlas Maps

☐ Complete interactive content, watch chapter videos, and take a graded quiz

☐ Track your knowledge of key concepts in Global Business

☐ Read and discuss additional case study content

5 Trading Internationally

LEARNING OBJECTIVES

After studying this chapter, you will be able to . . .

5-1 Use the resource-based and institution-based views to explain why nations trade.

5-2 Understand the classical and modern theories of international trade.

5-3 Explain the importance of political realities governing international trade.

5-4 Identify factors that should be considered when your firm participates in international trade.

After you finish this chapter, go to

PAGE 85 for

STUDY TOOLS

ETHICAL DILEMMA
Opening Case: Why Are US Exports So Competitive?

The rise of China as the leading exporter has been widely reported (see Closing Case). Yet, what has been little reported by the media is that the United States has also rocketed ahead of Germany and become the world's second largest merchandise (goods) exporter.* Never mind all that talk about the "decline" of US competitiveness (!). An important part of your university education is to foster a critical thinking mindset by relying on data and forming evidence-based judgments, as opposed to being excessively influenced by media fads, fake news, and alternative facts. Shown in Exhibit 5.1, the data suggest a story that is different from that typically portrayed by certain media and politicians.

In 2015, the United States exported $1.51 trillion in goods. Of China's $2.28 trillion exports in goods, only about two-thirds of the value added was contributed by China (the rest were imported components assembled in China). The United States contributed approximately 90% of the value added of its exports. Do your math: the value added of US exports ($1.36 trillion) was very close to the value added of Chinese exports ($1.52 trillion). In addition, the United States again outsold the long-time export champion Germany (which exported $1.33 trillion) and the formidable export powerhouse Japan (which exported $625 billion). Don't forget: the United States accomplished such enviable export success during the very difficult aftermath of the Great Recession, in which every nation was eager to export its way out of recession. What were the top US export categories? Refined petroleum products, civilian aircraft, semiconductors, passenger cars, and telecom equipment. The top five export states were Texas (which exported one-sixth of the nation's total exports), California, Washington, New York, and Illinois. The US Department of Commerce proudly noted that "fueling our economic recovery, exports are a bright spot in the US economy."

Why are US exports so competitive? What is unique about US exports? What has been driving their recent rise in a bleak global economic environment? On top of the Great Recession, one can add more recent troubles such as the Japanese earthquake, the euro zone crisis, the Middle East turmoil, the Russian sanctions, the Ebola crisis, the Chinese slow down, and Brexit. To make a long story short, first, US exports have to deliver *value*. Consider civilian aircraft. One crucial reason that the new Boeing 787 Dreamliner became the hottest-selling airliner prior to its launch is its ability to reduce fuel consumption by 15%—music to the ears of airline executives. Second, US exports

also have to be *rare* and *hard to imitate*. There is no shortage of global rivals tearing apart US products and trying to reverse engineer them. European, Russian, and Chinese aerospace firms are doing this at this moment by trying to "out-Boeing" Boeing. Although Airbus has been quite successful, neither Russian nor Chinese civilian aircraft makers have much presence in export markets. Finally, US exporters have to *organize* themselves in a more productive and efficient manner relative to their global rivals. It is hard enough to design and manufacture world-class aircraft, but it is no less challenging to operate service, training, and maintenance networks for airlines that cannot afford any equipment breakdown for a long period—on a worldwide basis and for 20 to 30 years after the initial sale.

While the products themselves have to be competitive, Uncle Sam also helps. At least ten federal agencies offer export assistance: the Departments of Commerce, State, Treasury, Energy, and Agriculture as well as the Office of US Trade Representative (USTR), Export-Import Bank (Ex-Im Bank), US Agency for International Development (USAID), Overseas Private Investment Corporation (OPIC), and Small Business Administration (SBA). Only approximately 1% of all US firms export, and 58% of them export to just one country. Clearly, more assistance will be helpful to facilitate more firms to join the export game.

Going beyond routine export assistance, new initiatives focus on negotiating free trade agreements (FTAs). As of this writing, the United States has 12 FTAs in force with 18 countries: Australia, Bahrain, Chile, DR–CAFTA (Dominican Republic–Central America FTA, which covers Costa Rica, Dominican Republic, El Salvador, Guatemala, Honduras, and Nicaragua), Israel, Jordan, Morocco, NAFTA (which covers Canada and Mexico), Oman, Peru, Singapore, and South Korea. In addition, two FTAs with Panama and Colombia were negotiated, but they are still pending congressional approval. FTAs typically reduce trade barriers to US exports and create a more stable and transparent trading environment. In this regard, the Trump

EXHIBIT 5.1	TOP FIVE MERCHANDISE (GOODS) EXPORTING NATIONS			
Rank based on value	2008	2011	2013	2015
1	Germany	China	China	China
2	China	United States	United States	United States
3	United States	Germany	Germany	Germany
4	Japan	Japan	Japan	Japan
5	Netherlands	Netherlands	Netherlands	Netherlands

Sources: The first three columns are adapted from M. W. Peng, *Global Business*, 1st, 2nd, and 3rd eds. (Cincinnati: Cengage, 2009, 2011, 2014); and M. W. Peng, *Global*, 3rd ed. (Cincinnati: Cengage, 2016). 2015 data are from the World Trade Organization, *World Trade Statistical Review 2016* (Geneva: WTO, 2016).

* This case only deals with *merchandise (goods)* exports. In service exports, the United States is even more competitive—it is the world champion.

administration's actions to withdraw from the Trans-Pacific Partnership (TPP), a massive FTA negotiated among 12 member countries over seven years, and to threaten to dismantle NAFTA are likely to be counterproductive.

In addition to formal institutions, informal norms and values also play a role behind US exports. Although some gurus write about the decline of US influence, the informal norms of consuming and appreciating US products seem to proliferate overseas. Around the world, it is *cool* to consume made-in-USA products. In Paris metro (underground) stations, almost every other poster seems to be about a Hollywood blockbuster. In Accra, the middle class flock into Ghana's first KFC and lick their fingers greased by grown-in-USA chicken. In Beijing, the Chinese president takes off and lands in a "Chinese Air Force One," which is a Boeing 747. If you are studying *this* book outside the United States, then you are a US export customer too. Enjoy!

Sources: This case draws on a long line of my own research on US export strategy, starting with my PhD dissertation and more recently with contributions to *Dallas Morning News* and *Texas CEO Magazine*—cited below. "Yum's big game of chicken," *Bloomberg Businessweek*, 29 March 2012: 64–69; "The real way a trade deal gets done," *Bloomberg Businessweek*, 24 October 2011: 30–32; "Texas exports spike higher on energy goods," *Dallas Morning News*, 23 February 2012; "Picking the world champion of trade," *Economist*, 18 January 2014: 72–73; M. W. Peng, *Behind the Success and Failure of US Export Intermediaries* (Westport, CT: Quorum, 1998); M. W. Peng, "What happens if NAFTA goes away," *Texas CEO Magazine*, January 2017: 26–27; US Commercial Service, 2015, export.gov.

Why are American merchandise exports so competitive in the world? Why are American service exports—ranging from movies to university degrees—even more competitive? More generally, how does international trade contribute to a nation's economic growth and prosperity? International trade is the oldest and still the most important building block of international business. It has never failed to generate debates. Debates on international trade tend to be very ferocious, because so much is at stake. We begin by addressing a crucial question: Why do nations trade? Then we outline how the two core perspectives introduced in earlier chapters—namely, resource-based and institution-based views—can help answer this question. The remainder of the chapter deals with the theories and realities of international trade. As before, implications for action follow.

3DMI/SHUTTERSTOCK.COM

trouble of trading internationally? Without getting into details, we can safely say that there must be economic gains from trade. More importantly, such gains must be shared by *both* sides. Otherwise, there would be no willing exporters and importers. In other words, international trade is a win–win deal. Exhibit 5.2 shows that world trade growth generally outpaces GDP growth. Historically, the growth of world merchandise trade has grown approximately 1.5 times faster than world GDP growth, although in the 1990s it grew more than twice as fast. However, since the 2008 Global Financial Crisis, the ratio of trade growth to GDP growth has fallen to about 1:1. The year 2016 marked the first time since 2001 that this ratio has dropped below 1, to a ratio of 0.6:1.

Why are there gains from trade?[1] How do nations benefit from such gains? The remainder of this chapter will answer these questions. Before proceeding, it is important to realize that it is misleading to say that *nations* trade.[2] A more accurate expression would be *firms* from different nations trade.[3] Unless different governments directly buy and sell from each other (such as arms sales), the majority of trade is conducted by firms that pay little attention to country-level ramifications. For example, Walmart imports large quantities of goods into the United States and does not export much. Walmart thus directly contributes to the US trade deficit. **Trade deficit** occurs when a nation imports more than it exports. When we discuss US–China trade, we are really referring to thousands

5-1 WHY DO NATIONS TRADE?

Internationally, trade means **export** (sell abroad) and **import** (buy from abroad). International trade consists of both merchandise (goods) trade and service trade. **Merchandise (goods) trade** is the buying and selling of tangible products, while **service trade** is the buying and selling of intangible services.

International trade is far more complex than domestic trade. So why do nations go through the

ISTOCK.COM/HENRIK5000

export To sell abroad.

import To buy from abroad.

merchandise (goods) trade Tangible products being bought and sold.

service trade Intangible services being bought and sold.

trade deficit An economic condition in which a nation imports more than it exports.

EXHIBIT 5.2   WORLD TRADE GROWTH AND GDP GROWTH (ANNUAL % CHANGE AND RATIO)

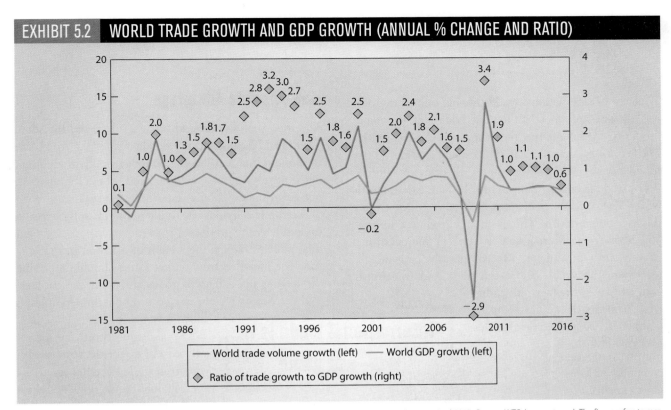

Source: World Trade Organization, "Trade recovery expected in 2017 and 2018, amid policy uncertainty," press release, 12 April 2017, Geneva: WTO (www.wto.org). The figure refers to merchandise (goods) trade.

of US firms buying from and selling to China, which also has thousands of firms buying from and selling to the United States. Unlike the United States, China has a **trade surplus**, which occurs when a nation exports more than it imports. The aggregation of such importing and exporting by firms on both sides leads to the country-level **balance of trade**—namely, whether a country has a trade surplus or deficit. Overall, we need to be aware that when we ask, "Why do nations trade?" we are really asking, "Why do *firms* from different nations trade?"

Having acknowledged the limitations of the expression "nations trade," we will still use it. Why? Because it is commonly used and serves as a shorthand version of the more accurate but more cumbersome expression "firms from different nations trade." This clarification does enable us to use the two *firm-level* perspectives introduced earlier—resource-based and institution-based views—to shed light on why nations trade.

Recall from Chapter 4 that valuable, rare, inimitable, and organizationally derived (VRIO) products determine a firm's competitive advantage. Applying this insight, we can suggest that valuable, rare, and inimitable products generated by organizationally strong firms in one nation such as China and the United States can lead to the competitive advantage of their exports

(see Opening Case and Closing Case).[4] Further, recall from Chapters 2 and 3 that numerous politically and culturally derived rules of the game, known as institutions, constrain individual and firm behavior. Institutions can either limit or facilitate trade. For example, although American movies dominate the world market, Canada, France, and South Korea use regulations to limit the market share of American movies in order to protect their domestic movie industries. On the other hand, we also see the rise of rules that facilitate trade, such as those promoted by the World Trade Organization (WTO) (see Chapter 8).

Overall, why are there economic gains from international trade? According to the resource-based view, it is because some firms in one nation generate exports that are valuable, unique, and hard to imitate that firms and consumers from other nations find it beneficial to import.[5] How do nations benefit from such gains? According to the institution-based view, different rules governing trade are designed to determine how such gains are shared (or not shared). The remainder of this chapter expands on these two perspectives.

trade surplus An economic condition in which a nation exports more than it imports.

balance of trade The country-level trade surplus or deficit.

5-2 THEORIES OF INTERNATIONAL TRADE

Theories of international trade provide one of the oldest, richest, and most influential bodies of economic literature. Although the publication of Adam Smith's *The Wealth of Nations* in 1776 is usually considered the foundation of modern economics, theories of international trade predate Adam Smith. In fact, Adam Smith wrote *The Wealth of Nations* to challenge an earlier theory: mercantilism. This section introduces six major theories of international trade: (1) mercantilism, (2) absolute advantage, (3) comparative advantage, (4) product life cycle, (5) strategic trade, and (6) national competitive advantage of industries. The first three are often regarded as classical trade theories, and the last three are viewed as modern trade theories.

> **international trade is a win–win game**

5-2a Mercantilism

Widely practiced during the 17th and 18th centuries, the theory of **mercantilism** viewed international trade as a zero-sum game. It suggested that the wealth of the world (measured in gold and silver at that time) was fixed, so a nation that exported more than it imported would enjoy the net inflows of gold and silver and become richer. On the other hand, a nation experiencing a trade deficit would see its gold and silver flowing out and, consequently, would become poorer. The upshot? Self-sufficiency would be best.

Although mercantilism is the oldest theory in international trade, it is not an extinct dinosaur. Very much alive, mercantilism is the direct intellectual ancestor of modern-day **protectionism**, which is the idea that governments should actively protect domestic industries from imports and vigorously promote exports. Even today, many modern governments may still be mercantilist at heart.

mercantilism A theory that holds that the wealth of the world (measured in gold and silver) is fixed and that a nation that exports more than it imports will enjoy the net inflows of gold and silver and become richer.

protectionism The idea that governments should actively protect domestic industries from imports and vigorously promote exports.

free trade The idea that free market forces should determine the buying and selling of goods and services with little or no government intervention.

theory of absolute advantage A theory that suggests that under free trade, each nation gains by specializing in economic activities in which it is the most efficient producer.

absolute advantage The economic advantage one nation enjoys because it can produce a good or service more efficiently than anyone else.

5-2b Absolute Advantage

The theory of absolute advantage, advocated by Adam Smith in 1776, opened the floodgates for the free trade movement that is still going on today. Smith argued that in the aggregate, the "invisible hand" of the free market, not government, should determine the scale and scope of economic activities. By trying to be self-sufficient and to (inefficiently) produce a wide range of goods, mercantilist policies *reduce* the wealth of a nation in the long run. The idea that free market forces should determine the buying and selling of goods and services with little or no government intervention is called **free trade**.

Specifically, Smith proposed a **theory of absolute advantage**: with free trade, a nation gains by specializing in economic activities in which it has an absolute advantage. What is absolute advantage? A nation that is more efficient than anyone else in the production of any good or service is said to have an **absolute advantage** in the production of that good or service. For instance, Smith argued that Portugal enjoyed an absolute advantage over England in producing grapes and wines because Portugal had better soil, water, and weather. Likewise, England had an absolute advantage over Portugal in raising sheep and producing wool. It cost England more to grow grapes: an acre of land that could raise high-quality sheep and produce fine wool would only produce an inferior grape and a lower quality wine.

Everyone has heard of port wine, one of Portugal's most famous exports, but who has heard of any world-famous English wine? Smith recommended that England specialize in sheep and wool, that Portugal specialize in grapes and wines, and that they trade with each other. Here are two of Smith's greatest insights. First, by specializing in the production of goods for which each has an absolute advantage, both can produce more. Second, both can benefit more by trading. By specializing, England produces more wool than it can use, and Portugal produces more wine than it can drink. When both countries trade, England gets more (and better) wine and Portugal gets more (and better) wool than either country could produce on its own. In other words, international trade is not a zero-sum game as mercantilism suggests. Instead, international trade is a *win–win* game.

How can this be? Smith's England–Portugal example offers a general sense, but let us use a specific example with hypothetical numbers (see Exhibits 5.3 and 5.4). For the sake of simplicity, assume that there are only two nations in the world: China and the United States. They perform only two economic activities: growing wheat and making aircraft. Production of wheat or aircraft, naturally, requires resources such as labor, land, and technology. Assume that both countries are equally endowed with 800 units of resources. Between the two activities, the United States has an absolute advantage in the production of aircraft: it takes 20 resources to produce an aircraft (for which China needs 40 resources), and the total US capacity is 40 aircraft if it does not produce wheat (point D in Exhibit 5.3). China has an absolute advantage in the production of wheat: it takes 20 resources to produce 1,000 tons of wheat (for which the United States needs 80 resources), and the total Chinese capacity is 40,000 tons of wheat if it does not make aircraft (point A). It is important to note that the United States can grow wheat and China can make aircraft, albeit inefficiently. Both nations need wheat and aircraft. Without trade, each nation would have to produce *both* by spending half of their resources on each—China at point B (20,000 tons of wheat and 10 aircraft) and the United States at point C (5,000 tons of wheat and 20 aircraft). Interestingly, if they stay at points A and D, respectively, and trade one-quarter of their output with each other (that is, 10,000 tons of Chinese wheat with 10 American aircraft), these two countries, and by implication the global economy, both produce more and consume more (see Exhibit 5.4). In other words, the numbers show that there are *net* gains from trade based on absolute advantage.

5-2c Comparative Advantage

According to Adam Smith, each nation should look for absolute advantage. However, what can nations do when they do *not* possess absolute advantage? Continuing our two-country example of China and the United States, what if China is absolutely more inefficient than the United States in the production of *both* wheat and aircraft (which is the real case today)? What should they do? Obviously, the theory of absolute advantage runs into a dead end.

EXHIBIT 5.3   ABSOLUTE ADVANTAGE

EXHIBIT 5.4	ABSOLUTE ADVANTAGE			
Total units of resources = 800 for each country			**Wheat**	**Aircraft**
1. Resources required to produce 1,000 tons of wheat and one aircraft		China	20 resources	40 resources
		US	80 resources	20 resources
2. Production and consumption with no specialization and without trade (each country devotes *half* of its resources to each activity)		China (point B)	20,000 tons	10 aircraft
		US (point C)	5,000 tons	20 aircraft
		Total production	*25,000 tons*	*30 aircraft*
3. Production with specialization (China specializes in wheat and produces no aircraft, and the United States specializes in aircraft and produces no wheat)		China (point A)	40,000 tons	0
		US (point D)	0	40 aircraft
		Total production	*40,000 tons*	*40 aircraft*
4. Consumption after each country trades one-fourth of its output while producing at points A and D, respectively (scenario 3 above)		China	30,000 tons	10 aircraft
		US	10,000 tons	30 aircraft
		Total consumption	*40,000 tons*	*40 aircraft*
5. *Gains* from trade: Increase in consumption as a result of specialization and trade (scenario 4 versus scenario 2 above)		China	+10,000 tons	0
		US	+5,000 tons	+10 aircraft

EXHIBIT 5.5 COMPARATIVE ADVANTAGE

British economist David Ricardo responded to Smith in 1817 by developing a **theory of comparative advantage**. This theory suggests that even though the United States has an absolute advantage in both wheat and aircraft over China, as long as China is not equally less efficient in the production of both goods, China can still choose to specialize in the production of one good (such as wheat) in which it has comparative advantage. **Comparative advantage** is defined as the relative (not absolute) advantage in one economic activity that one nation enjoys in comparison with other nations. Exhibits 5.5 and 5.6 show that China's comparative advantage lies in its *relatively less inefficient* production of wheat. If China devotes all resources to wheat, it can produce 10,000 tons, which is four-fifths of the 12,500 tons that the United States can produce. However, at a maximum, China can produce only 20 aircraft, which is merely half of the 40 aircraft that the United States can make. By letting China specialize in the production of wheat and importing some wheat from China, the United States is able to leverage its strengths by devoting

theory of comparative advantage A theory that suggests that a nation gains by specializing in production of one good in which it has comparative advantage.

comparative advantage The relative (not absolute) advantage in one economic activity that one nation enjoys in comparison with other nations.

opportunity cost The cost of pursuing one activity at the expense of another activity.

factor endowment The extent to which different countries possess various factors of production such as labor, land, and technology.

factor endowment theory (Heckscher–Ohlin theory) A theory that suggests that nations will develop comparative advantages based on their locally abundant factors.

its resources to aircraft. For example, if the United States devotes four-fifths of its resources to aircraft and one-fifth to wheat (point C in Exhibit 5.5), and if China concentrates 100% of its resources on wheat (point E), and if the two trade with each other, then both countries produce and consume more than what they would produce and consume if they inefficiently devoted half of their resources to each activity (see Exhibit 5.6).

Again, the numbers show that there are *net* gains from trade—this time from comparative advantage. One crucial concept here is **opportunity cost**, which refers to the cost of pursuing one activity at the expense of another activity, given the alternatives. For the United States, the opportunity cost of concentrating on wheat at point A in Exhibit 5.5 is tremendous relative to producing aircraft at point D, because it is only 25% more productive in wheat than China but is 100% more productive in aircraft.

Relative to absolute advantage, the theory of comparative advantage seems counterintuitive. But comparative advantage is actually far more realistic and useful when applied in the real world than is absolute advantage. Why? While it is easy to identify an absolute advantage in a highly simplified, two-country world (like the one in Exhibit 5.3), how can each nation decide what to specialize in when there are over 200 nations in the world? It is simply too challenging to ascertain that one nation is absolutely better than all others in one activity. Is the United States *absolutely* better than not only China but also all other 200 nations in aircraft production? European nations that produce Airbus planes obviously beg to differ. The theory of comparative advantage suggests that even without an absolute advantage, the United States can still specialize profitably in aircraft as long as it is relatively more efficient than others. This insight has greatly lowered the threshold for specialization because absolute advantage is no longer required.

Where do absolute and comparative advantages come from? In a word: productivity. Smith looked at *absolute* productivity differences, and Ricardo emphasized *relative* productivity differences. In this sense, absolute advantage is really a special case of comparative advantage. But what leads to such productivity differences? In the early 20th century, Swedish economists Eli Heckscher and Bertil Ohlin argued that absolute and comparative advantages stem from different **factor endowments**—namely, the extent to which different countries possess various factors of production such as labor, land, and technology. This **factor endowment theory** (or **Heckscher–Ohlin theory**) proposed that nations will develop comparative advantages based on their *locally abundant* factors, such as plentiful labor supply in China and innovative commercialization of basic research in the United States.

EXHIBIT 5.6 | COMPARATIVE ADVANTAGE

Total units of resources = 800 for each country		Wheat	Aircraft
1. Resources required to produce 1,000 tons of wheat and one aircraft	China US	80 resources 64 resources	40 resources 20 resources
2. Production and consumption with no specialization and without trade (each country devotes *half* of its resources to each activity)	China (point F) US (point B) *Total production*	5,000 tons 6,250 tons *11,250 tons*	10 aircraft 20 aircraft *30 aircraft*
3. Production with specialization (China devotes all resources to wheat, and the United States devotes one-fifth of its resources to wheat and four-fifths of its resources to aircraft)	China (point E) US (point C) *Total production*	10,000 tons 2,500 tons *12,500 tons*	0 32 aircraft *32 aircraft*
4. Consumption after China trades 4,000 tons of wheat for 11 US aircraft while producing at points E and C, respectively (scenario 3 above)	China US *Total consumption*	6,000 tons 6,500 tons *12,500 tons*	11 aircraft 21 aircraft *32 aircraft*
5. *Gains* from trade: Increase in consumption as a result of specialization and trade (scenario 4 versus scenario 2 above)	China US	+1,000 tons +250 tons	+1 aircraft +1 aircraft

Mi MIX
Innovation on full display

CENGAGE

Contrary to the product life cycle theory, many of today's cutting-edge mobile phones are being pioneered in Asia. The Xiaomi Mi Mix, for example, features a ceramic body and a nearly bezel-less display.

5-2d Product Life Cycle

The three classical theories—mercantilism, absolute advantage, and comparative advantage—all paint a *static* picture: if England has an absolute or comparative advantage in textiles, which it does mostly because of its factor endowments such as favorable weather and soil, it should keep making textiles. But factor endowments and trade patterns change over time, so the assumption that trade is static does not always hold in the real world. Adam Smith's England, over 200 years ago, was a major exporter of textiles, but today England's textile industry is rather insignificant. So what happened?

While one may argue that the weather in England has changed and the soil has become less fertile for sheep (and wool), it is difficult to believe that weather and soil have changed so much in 200 years, which is a relatively short period for long-run climatic changes. Now consider another example that has nothing to do with weather or soil change. Since the 1980s, the United States has changed from being a net exporter to a net importer of personal computers (PCs), while Malaysia has gone from being a net importer to a net exporter. Why have patterns of trade in PCs changed over time? Classical theories would have a hard time answering this intriguing question.

In 1966, American economist Raymond Vernon developed the **product life cycle theory**, which is the first *dynamic* theory to account for changes in the patterns of trade over time. Vernon divided the world into three categories: lead innovation nation (which, according to him, is typically the United States), other developed nations, and developing nations. Further, every product has three life cycle stages: new, maturing, and standardized. Shown in Exhibit 5.7, the first stage involves production of a new product (such as TV) that commands a price premium. Such production will concentrate in the United States, which exports to other developed nations. In the second, maturing stage, demand and ability to produce grow in other developed nations such as Australia and Italy, so it becomes worthwhile to produce there. In the third stage, the previously new product is standardized (or commoditized).

> **product life cycle theory** A theory that suggests that patterns of trade change over time as production shifts and as the product moves from new to maturing to standardized stages.

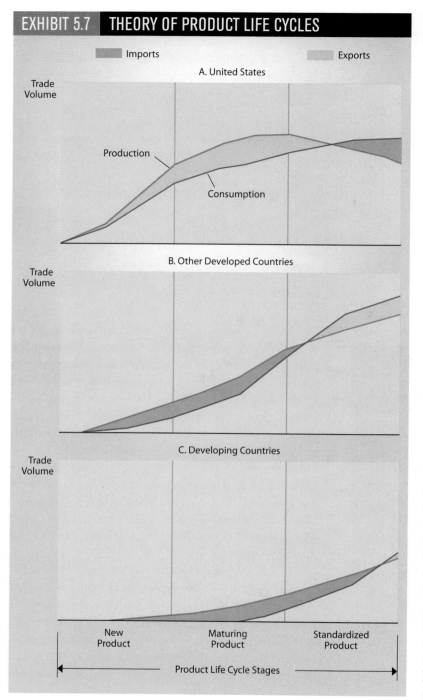

EXHIBIT 5.7 THEORY OF PRODUCT LIFE CYCLES

Imports   Exports

A. United States

Trade Volume

Production
Consumption

B. Other Developed Countries

Trade Volume

C. Developing Countries

Trade Volume

New Product   Maturing Product   Standardized Product

Product Life Cycle Stages

---

theory has been criticized on two accounts. First, it assumes that the United States will always be the lead innovation nation for new products. This may be increasingly invalid. For example, the fanciest mobile (cell) phones are now routinely pioneered in Asia and Europe. Second, this theory assumes a stage-by-stage migration of production, taking at least several years, if not decades. In reality, however, an increasing number of firms now launch new products such as iPhones *simultaneously* around the globe.

5-2e Strategic Trade

Except for mercantilism, none of the theories discussed above say anything about the role of governments. Since the days of Adam Smith, government intervention is usually regarded by economists as destroying value because, they contend, it distorts free trade. But government intervention is extensive and is not going away. Can government intervention actually add value? Since the 1970s, a new theory, strategic trade theory, has been developed to address this question.

Strategic trade theory suggests that strategic intervention by governments in certain industries can enhance their odds for international success. What are these industries? They tend to be highly capital-intensive industries with high barriers to entry, where domestic firms may have little chance of entering and competing without government assistance. These industries also feature substantial **first-mover advantages**—namely, advantages that first entrants enjoy and do not share with late entrants. A leading example is the commercial aircraft industry. Founded in 1915 and strengthened by large military orders during World War II, Boeing has long dominated this industry. In the jumbo jet segment, Boeing's first-mover advantages associated with its 400-seat 747, first launched in the late 1960s, are still significant today. Alarmed by such US dominance, British, French, German, and Spanish governments realized in the late 1960s that if they did not intervene, individual European aerospace firms might be driven out of business by US rivals. So these European governments agreed to launch and subsidize Airbus. In five decades, Airbus has risen from scratch to splitting the global market 50–50 with Boeing.

Thus, much production will now move to low-cost developing nations that export to developed nations. In other words, comparative advantage may change over time.

While this theory was first proposed in the 1960s, some later events such as the migration of PC production have supported its prediction. However, this

strategic trade theory A theory that suggests that strategic intervention by governments in certain industries can enhance their odds for international success.

first-mover advantage Advantage that first entrants enjoy and do not share with late entrants.

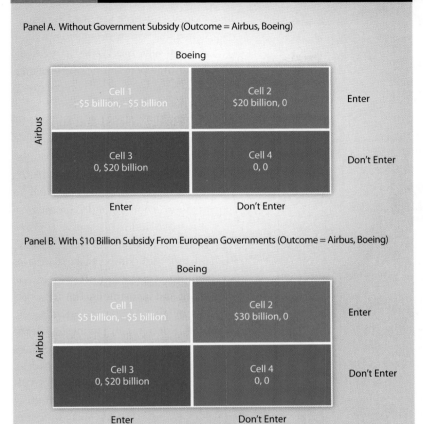

EXHIBIT 5.8 ENTERING THE VERY LARGE, SUPER-JUMBO MARKET?

Panel A. Without Government Subsidy (Outcome = Airbus, Boeing)

Boeing

Airbus	Cell 1 −$5 billion, −$5 billion	Cell 2 $20 billion, 0	Enter
	Cell 3 0, $20 billion	Cell 4 0, 0	Don't Enter
	Enter	Don't Enter	

Panel B. With $10 Billion Subsidy From European Governments (Outcome = Airbus, Boeing)

Boeing

Airbus	Cell 1 $5 billion, −$5 billion	Cell 2 $30 billion, 0	Enter
	Cell 3 0, $20 billion	Cell 4 0, 0	Don't Enter
	Enter	Don't Enter	

DEGTYARYOV ANDREY LEONIDOVICH/SHUTTERSTOCK.COM

How do European governments help Airbus? Let us use the super-jumbo aircraft, which is larger than the Boeing 747, as an example. Both Airbus and Boeing are interested in entering this market. However, the demand in the next 20 years is only about 400 to 500 aircraft, and a firm needs to sell at least 300 just to break even, which means that only one firm can be supported profitably. Shown in Exhibit 5.8 (Panel A), the outcome will be disastrous if both enter because each will lose $5 billion (Cell 1). If one enters and the other does not, the entrant will make $20 billion (Cells 2 and 3). It is also possible that both will choose not to enter (Cell 4). If a number of European governments promise Airbus a subsidiary of, say, $10 billion if it enters, then the picture changes to Panel B. Regardless of what Boeing does, Airbus finds it lucrative to enter. In Cell 1, if Boeing enters, it will lose $5 billion as before, whereas Airbus will make $5 billion

($10 billion subsidy minus $5 billion loss). So Boeing has no incentive to enter. Therefore, the more likely outcome is Cell 2, where Airbus enters and enjoys a profit of $30 billion. Therefore, the subsidy has given Airbus a *strategic* advantage, and the policy to assist Airbus is known as a **strategic trade policy**. This has indeed been the case, as the 550-seat A380 entered service in 2007 and became a formidable competitor for the Boeing 747.

Strategic trade theorists do not advocate a mercantilist policy to promote all industries. They propose to help only a few strategically important industries, such as those centered on clean energy like electric cars and batteries.[6] Still, this theory has been criticized on two accounts. First, many scholars and policy makers are uncomfortable with government intervention. What if governments are not sophisticated and objective enough to do this job? Second, many industries claim that they are strategically important. For example, after 9/11, American farmers successfully argued that agriculture is a strategic industry because the food supply needs to be guarded against terrorists, and extracted more subsidies. Overall, where to draw the line between strategic and non-strategic industries is tricky.

5-2f National Competitive Advantage of Industries

The most recent theory is known as the **theory of national competitive advantage of industries**. This is popularly known as the **diamond theory** because its principal architect, Harvard strategy professor Michael Porter, presents it in a diamond-shaped diagram, as shown in Exhibit 5.9.[7] This theory focuses on why certain *industries* (but not others) within a nation are competitive internationally. For example, while Japanese electronics and automobile industries are global winners, Japanese service industries are notoriously inefficient. Porter is interested in finding out why.

> **strategic trade policy** Economic policy that provides companies a strategic advantage through government subsidies.
>
> **theory of national competitive advantage of industries (or diamond theory)** A theory that suggests that the competitive advantage of certain industries in different nations depends on four aspects that form a "diamond" shape when diagrammed.

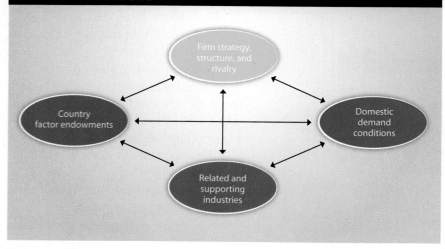

Source: M. Porter, "The competitive advantage of nations," *Harvard Business Review* (March-April 1990): 77.

Porter argues that the competitive advantage of certain industries in different nations depends on four aspects, which form a diamond. First, he starts with factor endowments, which refer to the natural and human resources noted by the Heckscher–Ohlin theory. Some countries (such as Saudi Arabia) are rich in natural resources but short on population, while others (such as Singapore) have a well-educated population but few natural resources. Not surprisingly, Saudi Arabia exports oil, and Singapore exports semiconductors (which need abundant skilled labor). While building on these insights from previous theories, Porter argues that factor endowments are not enough.

Second, tough domestic demand propels firms to scale new heights. Why are American movies so competitive worldwide? One reason may be the level of extraordinary demand in the US market for exciting movies. Endeavoring to satisfy domestic demand, US movie studios unleash *High School Musical 3* after *High School Musical* and *High School Musical 2,* and *The Hunger Games: Mockingjay* after *The Hunger Games* and *The Hunger Games: Catching Fire*, each time packing in more excitement. Most movies—in fact, most products—are created to satisfy domestic demand first. Thus, the ability to satisfy a tough domestic crowd may make it possible to successfully deal with less demanding overseas customers.

Third, domestic firm strategy, structure, and rivalry in one industry play a huge role in its international success or failure. One reason the Chinese toy, shoes, and light manufacturing industries are so competitive globally is because their *domestic* rivalry is probably the most intense in the world. Most makers of toys, shoes, socks, clothes, lamps,

candles, coffee makers, and DVD players in China do not make much money. However, the few top firms in China that win the tough competition domestically may have a relatively easier time penetrating overseas markets, because overseas competition is less demanding (see In Focus).

Finally, related and supporting industries provide the foundation upon which key industries can excel. In the absence of strong related and supporting industries such as engines, avionics, and materials, an aerospace industry cannot become globally competitive. Each of these related and supporting industries requires years (and often decades) of hard work and investment. For instance, inspired by the Airbus experience, the Chinese, Korean, and Japanese governments poured money into their own aerospace industries. Eventually, they all realized that Europe's long history and excellence in a series of critically related and supporting industries made it possible for Airbus to succeed. A lack of such industries made it unrealistic for the Chinese, Korean, and Japanese aerospace industries to succeed in making commercial aircraft.

Overall, Porter argues that the dynamic interaction of these four aspects explains what is behind the competitive advantage of leading industries in different nations. This theory is the first *multilevel* theory to realistically connect firms, industries, and nations, whereas previous theories work on only one or two levels. However, it has not been comprehensively tested. Some critics argue that the diamond places too much emphasis on domestic conditions. The recent rise of India's IT industry suggests that its international success is not entirely driven by domestic demand, which is relatively tiny compared with overseas demand—it is overseas demand that matters a lot more in this case.

5-2g Evaluating Theories of International Trade

In case you are tired after studying the six theories, you have to appreciate that we have just gone through over 300 years of research, debates, and policy changes around the world in about eight pages (!). As a student, that is not a small accomplishment. Exhibit 5.10 enables you to see the "forest." Keep the following four points in mind as you look at the forest.

EXHIBIT 5.10 THEORIES OF INTERNATIONAL TRADE: A SUMMARY

Classical theories	Main points	Strengths and influences	Weaknesses and debates
Mercantilism	▸ International trade is a zero-sum game; trade deficits are dangerous ▸ Governments should protect domestic industries and promote exports	▸ Forerunner of modern-day protectionism	▸ Inefficient allocation of resources ▸ Reduces the wealth of the nation in the long run
Absolute advantage	▸ Nations should specialize in economic activities in which they have an absolute advantage and trade with others ▸ By specializing and trading, each nation produces more and consumes more ▸ The wealth of all trading nations and the world increases	▸ Birth of modern economics ▸ Forerunner of the free trade movement ▸ Defeats mercantilism, at least intellectually	▸ When one nation is absolutely inferior to another, the theory is unable to provide any advice ▸ When there are many nations, it may be difficult to find an absolute advantage
Comparative advantage	▸ Nations should specialize in economic activities in which they have a comparative advantage and trade with others ▸ Even if one nation is absolutely inferior to another, the two nations can still gainfully trade ▸ Factor endowments underpin comparative advantage	▸ More realistic guidance to nations (and their firms) interested in trade but having no absolute advantage ▸ Explains patterns of trade based on factor endowments	▸ Relatively static, assuming that comparative advantage and factor endowments do not change over time

Modern theories			
Product life cycle	▸ Comparative advantage first resides in the lead innovation nation, which exports to other nations ▸ Production migrates to other advanced nations and then developing nations in different product life cycle stages	▸ First theory to incorporate dynamic changes in patterns of trade ▸ More realistic with trade in industrial products in the 20th century	▸ The United States may not always be the lead innovation nation ▸ Many new products are now launched simultaneously around the world
Strategic trade	▸ Strategic intervention by governments may help domestic firms reap first-mover advantages in certain industries ▸ First-mover firms, aided by governments, may have better odds at winning internationally	▸ More realistic and positively incorporates the role of governments in trade ▸ Provides direct policy advice	▸ Ideological resistance from many free trade scholars and policy makers ▸ Invites all kinds of industries to claim they are strategic
National competitive advantage of industries	▸ Competitive advantage of different industries in a nation depends on the four interacting aspects of a diamond ▸ The four aspects are (1) factor endowments; (2) domestic demand; (3) firm strategy, structure, and rivalry; and (4) related and supporting industries	▸ Most recent, most complex, and most realistic among various theories ▸ As a multilevel theory, it directly connects firms, industries, and nations	▸ Has not been comprehensively tested ▸ Overseas (not only domestic) demand may stimulate the competitiveness of certain industries

▸ The classical pro-free trade theories seem like common sense today, but they were *revolutionary* in the late 1700s and the early 1800s when the world was dominated by mercantilistic thinking.

▸ All theories simplify to make their point. Classical theories rely on highly simplistic assumptions of a model consisting of only two nations and two goods.

▸ The theories also assume perfect **resource mobility**—the assumption that a resource used in producing for one industry can be shifted and put to use in another industry (for example, one resource removed from wheat production can be moved to make aircraft). In reality, not all resources can be moved. Farm hands, for example, will have a hard time assembling modern aircraft.

▸ Classical theories assume no foreign exchange issues and zero transportation costs.

resource mobility The assumption that a resource used in producing a product in one industry can be shifted and put to use in another industry.

Debate: Should Canada Diversify Its Trade?

Ethical Dilemma

Canada has the 11th largest economy (measured by nominal GDP) or the 14th largest (measured by PPP) in the world.

The bilateral trading relationship between Canada and the United States is the world's largest, with approximately $600 billion in volume. The two-way traffic that crosses the Ambassador Bridge between Windsor, Ontario, and Detroit, Michigan, alone equals all US trade with Japan. Approximately three-fourths of Canadian exports go to the United States, which also provides half of Canadian imports. While enjoying a $32 billion surplus in trading with the United States, Canadians have been frustrated by the occasional disputes, such as salmon runs, magazine content, softwood lumber, and food labeling. Recently, Canadians are alarmed that the Trump administration has sought to renegotiate NAFTA, with a threat to ultimately dismantle it.

Thanks to geography, Canada and the United States will always trade a lot. But Canadians have also sought to diversify their trading relationship away from too much reliance on the United States. They have focused on two areas. The first is to cultivate trade ties with major Asian economies, such as China and Japan. As Canada's second largest trading partner, China now absorbs 5% of Canadian exports and contributes 10% of Canadian imports. The second area is to negotiate more free trade agreements (FTAs) beyond NAFTA. Canada has FTAs with Chile,

GERALD MCDONALD PHOTOGRAPHY/SHUTTERSTOCK.COM

Colombia, Costa Rica, Israel, Jordan, and Panama. While Canada is negotiating with a number of other countries, one of the major breakthroughs is the Comprehensive Economic and Trade Agreement (CETA) with the EU announced in 2013. As a bloc, the EU is the largest economy in the world. CETA would not only eliminate 99% of tariffs on both sides, but would also open competition for large government contracts in Canada to European firms and contracts in the EU to Canadian firms. CETA is likely to boost the Canada–EU bilateral trade by 23%, thus reducing Canada's reliance on the United States, whose share has decreased but still remains dominant.

Sources: "Canada and the United States," *Economist*, 19 December 2011: 41; "Canada doesn't get any sexier than this," *Economist*, 26 October 2013: 18; "The Canada-EU trade deal," *Economist*, 26 October 2013: 44; "Canada turns to WTO over US label law," *Globe and Mail*, 8 October 2009: B7; M. W. Peng, "What happens if NAFTA goes away?" *Texas CEO Magazine*, January 2017: 26–27.

So is free trade still as beneficial as Smith and Ricardo suggested in the real world of many countries, numerous goods, imperfect resource mobility, fluctuating exchange rates, high transportation costs, and product life cycle changes? The answer is still *Yes!* In Focus shows how difficult life can be when an American family tries to spend a year without buying imports "Made in China." Worldwide data support the *basic* arguments for free trade.[8] (See Closing Case for disagreements.)

Instead of relying on simple factor analysis, modern theories rely on more realistic product life cycles, first-mover advantages, and the diamond to explain and predict patterns of trade. Overall, classical and modern theories have significantly contributed to today's ever deepening trade links around the world. Yet, the victory of pro-free trade theories is not complete. The political realities, outlined next, indicate that mercantilism is still alive and well (see Closing Case).

5-3 REALITIES OF INTERNATIONAL TRADE

Although most theories support free trade, plenty of trade barriers exist. While some trade barriers are being dismantled, many will remain (see Debate). Let us examine why this is the case. To do so, we will first discuss the two broad types of trade barriers: tariff barriers and nontariff barriers.

EXHIBIT 5.11   TARIFF ON RICE IMPORTS IN JAPAN

Panel A. No International Trade

Panel B. Imports with No Tariff

Panel C. Imports with Tariff

P_1: Japanese domestic price without imports. P_2: World price (and Japanese domestic price with no tariff). P_3: Japanese domestic price with import tariff.

5-3a Tariff Barriers

A **tariff barrier** is a means of discouraging imports by placing a tariff (tax) on imported goods. As a major tariff barrier, an **import tariff** is a tax imposed on a good brought in from another country. Exhibit 5.11 uses rice tariffs in Japan to show *unambiguously* that net losses, known as **deadweight costs**, occur when import tariffs are imposed.

ISTOCK.COM/ELENATHEWISE

▸ Panel A: In the absence of international trade, the domestic price is P_1 and domestic rice farmers produce Q_1, determined by the intersection of domestic supply and demand curves.

▸ Panel B: Because Japanese rice price P_1 is higher than world price P_2, foreign farmers export to Japan. Japanese farmers reduce output to Q_2. Japanese consumers enjoy more rice at Q_3 at a much lower price P_2.

▸ Panel C: The government imposes an import tariff, effectively raising the price from P_2 to P_3. Japanese farmers increase production from Q_2 to Q_4, and consumers pay more at P_3 and consume less by reducing consumption from Q_3 to Q_5. Imports fall from Q_2Q_3 in Panel B to Q_4Q_5 in Panel C.

Classical theorists such as Smith and Ricardo would have advised Japan to enjoy the gains from trade in Panel B. But political realities land Japan in Panel C, which, by limiting trade, introduces total inefficiency represented by the area consisting of A, B, C, and D. However, Japanese rice farmers gain the area of A, and the government pockets tariff revenues in the area of C. Therefore:

$$\text{Net losses} = \text{Total inefficiency} - \text{Net gain}$$
$$\text{(deadweight)} = \text{Area } (A + B + C + D)$$
$$- \text{Area } (A + C)$$
$$= \text{Area } (B + D)$$

The net losses (areas B and D) represent unambiguous economic inefficiency to the nation as a whole. Japan is not alone in this regard. In 2010, an Apple iPad that retailed for $600 in the United States cost $1,000 in Brazil, after adding a 60% import tariff.[9] In 2009, the United States slapped a 35% import tariff on tires made in China. Brazilian iPad lovers and American tire buyers have to pay more, and some may be unable to afford the products. While not being able to put your arms around an iPad will have no tangible damage, some economically struggling US drivers who should have replaced their worn-out tires may be forced to delay replacing their tires—and some may be *killed* should they be involved in accidents before they are able to afford the now more expensive tires.[10] The Trump administration's threat to impose a 45% tariff on Chinese imports, if implemented, will severely reduce the standard of living for a lot of Americans (see In Focus).

tariff barrier A means of discouraging imports by placing a tariff (tax) on imported goods.

import tariff A tax imposed on imports.

deadweight cost Net losses that occur in an economy as the result of tariffs.

Can an American Family Spend a Year without "Made in China" Goods?

Once upon a time, an average American family—a middle-aged couple Sara and Kevin, a four-year-old son, and a one-year-old daughter living in Louisiana—decided to do an experiment: Could the family last for a year without buying "Made in China" goods? One day after Christmas, Sara, a business reporter, faced in her living room a small mountain of "Made in China" presents such as toys, gadgets, and shoes. Realizing that Christmas had become "a Chinese holiday," she suddenly "wanted China out" as her New Year's resolution.

"No, it's not for Chinese workers," Sara explained to her mother. "Is it for American workers, then? For the ones who have lost jobs to China?" her mother asked. "No, it's not for them either." "Then what is it?" "It's an experiment," Sara explained calmly, "to see if it can be done." With one Chinese ancestor whom Sara could trace 300 years back, she had no political agenda against China. "Do we not like China?" Sara's son asked. "We like China," she answered, "but we want to give other countries a chance to sell us things."

After 12 long months, Sara's experiment proved: (1) An American family could spend a year without buying anything "Made in China." (2) Such a life would be extraordinarily challenging. Sara and Kevin coughed up huge additional costs not only in paying more for goods, but also in spending countless hours on the phone asking customer service representatives where the goods were made. The inconveniences were endless. These parents could no longer buy new toys for their kids—except LEGO toys made in Denmark, Switzerland, and the United States. For Halloween, Sara sewed two costumes for her children instead of buying any. She found out that, just like Christmas, Halloween was a "Chinese" holiday too. So was the Fourth of July. When her son's feet outgrew his $9 "Made in China" shoes, Sara shelled out $68 for shoes made in Italy. Sara and Kevin could not buy a new coffeemaker to replace the "Made in China" one that broke—all coffeemakers were made in you know where. They ended up boiling water for their coffee. Sara's home office printer ran out of ink, and she could not find any cartridge that was not made in China. She knowingly—and semi-unethically—asked Kevin to print her papers from his printer at work.

Despite Sara's strong will and her generally cooperative family, exceptions in two areas had to be made. First, not buying stuff "Made in China" did not mean not accepting *gifts* made there. To avoid too much hassle, Sara let her family accept gifts made in China. Otherwise, Sara's kids would have become the most unpopular ones at birthday parties, because other kids' parents who would buy toys as gifts to bring over would view her as too "difficult." For his own birthday gift, Kevin expressed an interest in an inflatable backyard swimming pool. But as a loving father, he was really requesting this for the kids—summer in Louisiana is long and hot.

AQUIR/SHUTTERSTOCK.COM

Because all such pools were made in China, Sara was frustrated. Then she creatively decided to beg her sister-in-law to buy a pool for Kevin as a birthday gift, invoking her policy that gifts "Made in China" were okay. Sara's mother, never a fan of this new experiment, was critical of Sara's practice of "depriving" her grandchildren of their childhood joy—Sara essentially had to say "no" on all items on their Christmas wish lists. Upon hearing Sara's flexibility about gifts, grandma immediately shipped over a huge box of Christmas toys.

Second, not buying stuff "Made in China" only meant not buying anything with that label. To Sara's horror, she discovered some parts of her hard-to-find "Made in USA" lamp were made in China. Intending to return the lamp, she called the owner of the lamp maker. The owner informed her that only four companies still made lamps in the United States, and all used some parts from China. The 100% "Made in USA" lamp simply did not exist. Then Sara felt good about keeping the lamp. Also, some parts of the LEGO toys Sara bought for her kids were made in China. For the same reason, she let her kids play with them.

On Christmas day, Sara counted the gifts: the rest of the world contributed 42 items, and China still managed to show up via 11 items—all courtesy of her mother and siblings. Looking back, on the one hand, Sara and Kevin became more thoughtful shoppers. The house was cleaner, because it was no longer filled with little things they didn't really need but could not resist until the boycott. Her kids developed a habit of resisting instant gratification and reading (product labels). On the other hand, Sara was thankful that her ancient TV had not died during the boycott year. Life without a coffeemaker was hard, but life without a TV would probably be unbearable. In addition, lots of little things in life, such as birthday candles, video games, holiday decorations, and mousetraps, came from China. Sara and her family were not sure they would want to go on without them. Upon reflection on whether the family would go on with (mostly) China-free living, Sara reasoned that "the idea of swearing off Chinese products forever feels like holding a perpetual grudge against 1.3 billion people. I'm not sure I have the energy for that."

On January 1 of the new year, Sara and Kevin delivered what they had promised: kids could pick *any* three toys of their own choosing from a store. Guess what? Both kids chose "Made in China" toys. The family then lived happily ever after.

Sara wrote a book and became a minor celebrity interviewed by American and Chinese media. When answering the question as to whether life without China was possible, she answered: "Not a chance!"

Source: Extracted from S. Bongiorni, *A Year Without "Made in China." One Family's True Life Adventure in the Global Economy* (New York: Wiley, 2007).

Given the well-known net losses, why are tariffs imposed? The answer boils down to the political realities. Although everybody in a country suffers because of higher prices, it is very costly to politically organize individuals and firms that are geographically scattered to advance the case for free trade. On the other hand, certain special interest groups tend to be geographically concentrated and skillfully organized to advance their interest. Although farmers represent less than 5% of the Japanese population, they represent disproportionate votes in the Diet (Japanese parliament). Why? Diet districts were drawn up in the aftermath of World War II when most Japanese lived in rural areas. Although the majority of the population now lives in urban areas, such districts were never re-zoned. Thus when the powerful farm lobby speaks, the Japanese government listens. The upshot? A whopping 777% tariff on imported rice.[11]

5-3b Nontariff Barriers

Today, tariff barriers are often criticized around the world, and nontariff barriers are now increasingly the weapon of choice in trade wars. A **nontariff barrier (NTB)** discourages imports using means other than tariffs on imported goods. NTBs include subsidies, import quotas, export restraints, local content requirements, administrative policies, and antidumping duties.

Subsidies are government payments to domestic firms. Much like their Japanese counterparts, European farmers are masters of extracting subsidies even though they constitute only 2% of the EU population. The Common Agricultural Policy (CAP) costs European taxpayers $47 billion a year, eating up 40% of the EU budget.

Import quotas are restrictions on the quantity of goods that can be brought into a country. Import quotas are worse than tariffs because foreign goods can still be imported if tariffs are paid. Quotas are thus the most straightforward denial of absolute or comparative advantage. For example, between 2003 and 2009, Australia annually exported 770,000 head of live cattle to Indonesia, to the delight of Indonesian beef lovers. However, since 2009, import permits suddenly became harder to obtain. A quota of only 500,000 head of imported cattle was set for 2011.[12]

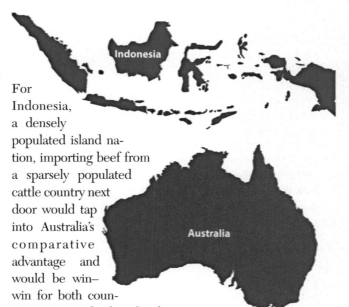

For Indonesia, a densely populated island nation, importing beef from a sparsely populated cattle country next door would tap into Australia's comparative advantage and would be win–win for both countries. But with the shrinking quota, Aussie cattle exporters are devastated, and Indonesian beef lovers have to put up with skyrocketing prices—and some of them may have to quit eating beef at all.

Because import quotas are protectionist pure and simple, they force countries to shoulder certain political costs in today's largely pro-free trade environment. In response, **voluntary export restraints (VERs)** have been developed to show that, on the surface, exporting countries *voluntarily* agree to restrict their exports. In essence, though, VERs are export quotas. One of the most (in)famous examples is the set of VERs that the Japanese government agreed to in the 1980s to restrict US-bound automobile exports. The VERs, of course, were a euphemism because the Japanese did not really volunteer to restrict their exports. Only when faced with concrete protectionist threats did the Japanese reluctantly agree.

nontariff barrier (NTB) A means of discouraging imports using means other than taxes on imported goods.

subsidy A government payment to domestic firms.

import quota A restriction on the quantity of goods brought into a country.

voluntary export restraint (VER) An international agreement that shows that an exporting country voluntarily agrees to restrict its exports.

Another NTB is **local content requirements**, which are rules stipulating that a certain proportion of the value of the goods made in one country must originate from that country. The Japanese automobile VERs are again a case in point. Starting in the 1980s, because of VERs, Japanese automakers switched to producing cars in the United States through foreign direct investment (FDI). Initially, such factories were "screwdriver plants," because a majority of components were imported from Japan and only local screwdrivers were needed to tighten the bolts. To deal with this issue, many countries impose local content requirements, mandating that a domestically produced product will still be treated as an "import" subject to tariffs and NTBs unless a certain fraction of its value (such as the 51% specified by the Buy America Act) is produced locally.

Administrative policies are bureaucratic rules that make it harder to import foreign goods. India recently banned Chinese toys, citing safety concerns. Argentina has recently ordered importers of foreign cars to find export buyers of Argentine wines; otherwise, port authorities would not release imported cars. Foreign print publications, including time-sensitive newspapers and magazines, are held at the Buenos Aires airport unless subscribers go there to pay an additional fee.

Finally, the arsenal of trade weapons also includes **antidumping duties** levied on imports that have been "dumped," or sold below cost in order to unfairly drive domestic firms out of business.

> **local content requirement** A rule that stipulates that a certain proportion of the value of a good must originate from the domestic market.
>
> **administrative policy** A bureaucratic rule that makes it harder to import foreign goods.
>
> **antidumping duty** A cost levied on imports that have been "dumped," or sold below cost, to unfairly drive domestic firms out of business.

5-3c Economic Arguments against Free Trade

Overall, trade barriers reduce or eliminate international trade. While certain domestic industries and firms benefit, the entire country—or at least a majority of its consumers—tends to suffer. Given these well-known negative aspects, why do people make arguments against free trade? This section outlines economic arguments against free trade, and the next section deals with political arguments. Two prominent economic arguments against free trade are (1) the need to protect domestic industries and (2) the need to shield infant industries.

The oldest and most frequently used economic argument against free trade is the urge to protect domestic industries, firms, and jobs from allegedly "unfair" foreign competition—in short, protectionism. Calls for protection are not limited to commodity producers. Highly talented individuals, such as American mathematicians and Japanese sumo wrestlers, have also called for protection. Foreign math PhDs grab 40% of US math jobs, and recent US math PhDs face a jobless rate of 12%. Many American math PhDs have thus called for protection of their jobs. Similarly, Japanese sumo wrestlers insist that foreign sumo wrestlers should not be allowed to throw their weight around in Japan.

The second argument is the infant industry argument. Young domestic firms need government protection. Otherwise, they stand no chance of surviving and will be crushed by mature foreign rivals. It is thus imperative that governments level the playing field by assisting infant industries. While this argument is sometimes legitimate, governments and firms have a tendency to abuse it. Some protected infant industries may never grow up—why bother? When Airbus was a true infant in the 1960s, it undoubtedly deserved some subsidies. By the 2000s, Airbus had become a giant that could take on Boeing. (In some years, Airbus has outsold Boeing.) However, Airbus continues to ask for subsidies, which European governments continue to provide.

France

5-3d Political Arguments against Free Trade

Political arguments against free trade are based on advancing a nation's political, social, and environmental agenda regardless of possible economic gains from trade.

These arguments include national security, consumer protection, foreign policy, and environmental and social responsibility.

First, national security concerns are often invoked to protect defense-related industries. France has always insisted on maintaining an independent defense industry to produce nuclear weapons, aircraft carriers, and combat jets. While the French can purchase such weapons at much lower costs from the United States, which is eager to sell them, the French answer has usually been "No, thanks!"

Second, consumer protection has frequently been used as an argument for nations to erect trade barriers. For example, American hormone-treated beef was banned by the EU in the 1990s because of the alleged health risks. Even though the United States won a WTO battle on this, the EU still has refused to remove the ban.

Third, trade intervention is often used to meet foreign policy objectives. **Trade embargoes** are politically motivated trade sanctions against foreign countries to signal displeasure. For example, the United States recently enforced embargoes against Iran, Russia, Sudan, and Syria. In 2009, DHL paid a record fine of $9.4 million for sending illegal shipments to these countries. According to a US Treasury Department statement, DHL "may have conferred a significant economic advantage to these sanctioned countries that potentially created extraordinarily adverse harm." What are such dangerous shipments? Condoms, Tiffany jewelry, and radar detectors for cars, according to the same Treasury Department statement.[13]

Finally, environmental and social responsibility can be used as political arguments to initiate trade intervention against certain countries. In a "shrimp-turtle" case, the United States banned shrimp imports from India, Malaysia, Pakistan, and Thailand. Although the shrimp were not harvested from US waters, they were caught using a technique that also accidentally trapped and killed sea turtles, an endangered species protected by the United States. India, Malaysia, Pakistan, and Thailand were upset and brought the case to the WTO, alleging that the United States invoked an environmental law as a trade barrier.

5-4 MANAGEMENT SAVVY

How does this chapter answer the big question in global business, adapted for the context of international trade: What determines the success and failure of firms' exports around the globe? The two core perspectives lead to two answers. Fundamentally, the various economic theories underpin the resource-based view, suggesting that successful exports are valuable, unique, and hard-to-imitate products generated by certain firms from a nation.

EXHIBIT 5.12 IMPLICATIONS FOR ACTION

▶ Discover and leverage comparative advantage of world-class locations.

▶ Monitor and nurture the current comparative advantage of certain locations, and take advantage of new locations.

▶ Be politically active to demonstrate, safeguard, and advance the gains from international trade.

However, the political realities stress the explanatory and predictive power of the institution-based view: as rules of the game, laws and regulations promoted by various special interest groups can protect certain domestic industries, firms, and individuals; erect trade barriers; and make the nation as a whole worse off (see Closing Case).

Listed in Exhibit 5.12, three implications for action emerge. First, location, location, location! In international trade, a savvy manager's first job is to leverage the comparative advantage of world-class locations. Shown in In Focus and Closing Case, one crucial reason behind China's rise as the world's top merchandise exporting nation is that many non-Chinese managers at non-Chinese firms have discovered China's comparative advantage as a low-cost production location. As a result, they set up factories and export from China—*two-thirds* of the value added of Chinese exports is generated by such foreign-invested firms.

Second, comparative advantage is not fixed. Managers need to constantly monitor and nurture the current comparative advantage of a location and take advantage of new promising locations. Managers who fail to realize when a location no longer has a comparative advantage are likely to fall behind. For example, numerous German managers have moved production out of Germany, citing the country's reduced comparative advantage in basic manufacturing. However, they still concentrate top-notch, high-end manufacturing in Germany, leveraging its excellence in engineering.

Third, managers need to be politically savvy if they appreciate the gains from trade. While managers at many uncompetitive firms have long mastered the game of using politicians to gain protection, managers at competitive firms tend to shy away from politics. But they often fail to realize that free trade is *not* free—it requires constant efforts to demonstrate and advance the gains from such trade. For example, the US-China Business Council, a pro-free trade (in particular, pro-China trade) group consisting of 250 large US corporations, has frequently spoken out in defense of trade with China.[14]

trade embargo Politically motivated trade sanctions against foreign countries to signal displeasure.

Closing Case: The China Trade Debate

Since 2011, China has dethroned Germany to become the world's champion merchandise (goods) exporter. Why does the rest of the world buy so many "Made in China" products? From a resource-based view, Chinese exports win markets because they deliver value, are rare, and possess hard-to-imitate attributes (see In Focus). From an institution-based view, China's accession to the World Trade Organization (WTO) in 2001 has certainly provided a booster to its rise as a trading nation.

Substantiating free trade theories' claim that international trade is a *win–win* game, active trading has not only made China richer, but also made its trading partners richer. Since China's accession to the WTO in 2001, neighboring economies that actively trade with China (such as Hong Kong, Singapore, South Korea, and Taiwan) and distant economies that export to China large quantities of minerals and agricultural commodities (such as Australia, Canada, and New Zealand) have benefitted more. So has the United States. During the period of 2000–2015, among developed economies, only Australia, New Zealand, and Singapore enjoyed higher GDP per capita gains than the United States. Since 2001, US exports to China soared by 500%, doubling the growth of US exports to the rest of the world. Cheaper Chinese imports shave off US consumer prices by 1–1.5%. In other words, every American family enjoys an extra $850 every year. Overall, US-China trade supports approximately 2.6 million US jobs and adds 1.2% to US GDP (Exhibit 5.13).

However, not all is rosy. The US trade deficit with China has provoked an enormous debate (Exhibit 5.14). Despite enviable export success (see Opening Case), the United States, due to its extraordinary appetite for imports, runs the world's largest merchandise trade deficit. In 2015, it reached $760 billion (5% of GDP). The lion's share, $334 billion (1.9% of GDP), was contributed by merchandise trade deficit with China. Should this level of trade deficit be of concern?

Armed with classical theories, free traders argue that this is not a grave concern. They argue that the United States and China mutually benefit by developing a deeper division of labor based on comparative advantage. They point out that in addition to China, the United States runs trade deficits with all of its major trading partners—Canada, the EU, Japan, and Mexico. The real US trade deficit with China is often overstated, because substantial value of Chinese exports is imported. If the value of such imported components is subtracted from China's exports, then the US trade deficit with China would be reduced in half, to less than 1% of US GDP—about the same as the US trade deficit with the EU. Quantitatively, such a level is manageable. Conceptually, former Treasury Secretary Paul O'Neill went so far as

EXHIBIT 5.13	POSITIVE IMPACT OF US-CHINA ECONOMIC RELATIONSHIP	
	Gains to US employment	**Boost to US GDP**
Direct exports to China	1,467,000	0.7%
Indirect exports to China*	296,000	0.1%
Income from US foreign direct investment (FDI) in China	688,000	0.3%
Inward FDI from China	104,000	0.1%
TOTAL	**2,555,000**	**1.2%**

* Indirect exports are US exports to other Asian countries that are re-exported to China

Source: Adapted from US-China Business Council, *Understanding the US-China Trade Relationship* (Washington: USCBC, January 2017) 12.

to say that trade deficit was "an antiquated theoretical construct." Paul Krugman, the 2008 Nobel laureate in economics, argued:

International trade is not about competition, it is about mutually beneficial exchange.... Imports, not exports, are the purpose of trade. That is, what a country gains from trade is the ability to import things it wants. Exports are not an objective in and of themselves: the need to export is a burden that a country must bear because its import suppliers are crass enough to demand payment.

Critics strongly disagree. They argue that international trade is about competition—about markets, jobs, and incomes. Fingering China as the primary contributor to the reduction of US manufacturing jobs from 17 million in 2000 to 12 million in 2016, Donald Trump as a candidate frequently threatened China with a trade war. A serious academic study published in the *American Economic Review* attributed one quarter of such decline to the "China syndrome." Economic Armageddon between the top two economies in the world with a 45% tariff on all Chinese imports could shave off 13% from China's exports and 1.4% of its GDP growth. But the United States could hardly hope to do better, and the poorest Americans would be the hardest hit. The *Economist* opined:

Were Americans unable to buy cheap imports, they would be poorer, with less to spend on other things. They would also be less specialized, and hence less productive at work ... If China exploits its workers and pollutes its rivers so that poor Americans can enjoy cheap goods, it is not obvious that America is getting a raw deal.

Case Discussion Questions

1. How do the US economy, US firms, and US consumers like you benefit from trade with China?

2. How are the US economy, US firms, and US consumers like you hurt by trade with China?

EXHIBIT 5.14 DEBATE ON THE US TRADE DEFICIT WITH CHINA

US trade deficit with China is a huge problem	US trade deficit with China is not a huge problem
Greedy exporters	*Eager foreign investors*
▶ Unscrupulous Chinese exporters are eager to gut US manufacturing jobs and drive US rivals out of business, resulting in massive unemployment.	▶ Two-thirds of Chinese exports are generated by foreign-invested firms in China, and numerous US firms have invested in and benefited from such operations in China.
The demon who has caused deflation	*Thank China (and Walmart) for low prices*
▶ Cheap imports sold at "the China price" push down prices and cause deflation.	▶ Consumers benefit from cheap prices brought from China by US firms such as Walmart. Trade with China pushes consumer prices down by 1–1.5%, and gives every American family $850 every year.
Intellectual property (IP) violator	*Inevitable step in development*
▶ China is a major violator of IP rights, and US firms lose billions of dollars every year.	▶ True, but the US did that in the 19th century (to Britain). IP protection has been improving in China—US films' box office revenues there grew from $2.1 billion in 2011 to $6.8 billion in 2015.
Currency manipulator	*Currency issue is not relevant*
▶ The yuan is severely undervalued, giving Chinese exports an "unfair" advantage in being priced at an artificially low level.	▶ The yuan is somewhat undervalued, but (1) US and other foreign firms producing in China benefit, and (2) the US also manipulates its own currency via quantitative easing.
Trade deficit will make the United States poorer	*Trade deficit does not cause a fall in the standard of living*
▶ Since imports have to be paid, the United States borrows against its future with disastrous outcomes.	▶ As long as the Chinese are willing to invest in the US economy (such as Treasury bills and foreign direct investment [FDI]), what's the worry?
Something has to be done	*Remember the gains from trade argued by classic theories?*
▶ If the Chinese don't do it "our way," the United States should introduce drastic measures (such as slapping a 45% tariff on all Chinese imports).	▶ Tariffs will not necessarily bring back US jobs, and will lead to retaliation from China, the third largest *importer* of US goods (behind Canada and Mexico). China will sue the US at the WTO, which the US will lose. Trade wars are lose-lose.

3. **ON ETHICS**: Prior to studying this case, how often have you heard about the benefits outlined in Question 1? How often have you heard about how Chinese imports "destroy" US jobs? What are the implications of such excessive (one-sided) negative reporting?

4. **ON ETHICS**: If you were appointed to be head of the new National Trade Council, how would you advise the president regarding the China trade policy?

Sources: D. Autor, D. Dorn, and G. Hanson, "The China syndrome," *American Economic Review* 103 (2013): 2121–2168; "America's trade deficit," *BusinessWeek*, 3 October 2005: 31; "Picking the world champion of trade," *Economist*, 18 January 2014: 72–73; "Trading places," *Economist*, 5 April 2014: 49; "America's trade with China," *Economist*, 28 January 2017: 12–13; "Rules of engagement," *Economist*, 28 January 2017: 59 -60; "Why free trade matters to companies like Caterpillar," *Fortune*, 26 July 2010: 40; P. Krugman, "What do undergrads need to know about trade?" *American Economic Review* 83 (1993): 23–26; G. Locke, "A message from the US Ambassador to China," *China Business Review*, October 2011: 16; M. W. Peng, D. Ahlstrom, S. Carraher, and W. Shi, "An institution-based view of global IPR history," *Journal of International Business Studies* (2017, in press); US-China Business Council, *Understanding the US-China Trade Relationship* (Washington: USCBC, January 2017); US Trade Representative, *2016 Report to Congress on China's WTO Compliance* (Washington: USTR, January 2017); World Trade Organization, *World Trade Statistical Review 2016* (Geneva: WTO, 2016).

STUDY TOOLS 5

LOCATED AT THE BACK OF YOUR BOOK:

☐ Rip out and study the Chapter Review Card at the end of the book

LOG IN TO WWW.CENGAGEBRAIN.COM TO:

☐ Review key term flashcards

☐ Complete a practice quiz to test your knowledge of key concepts

☐ View animated PengAtlas Maps

☐ Complete interactive content, watch chapter videos, and take a graded quiz

☐ Track your knowledge of key concepts in Global Business

☐ Read and discuss additional case study content

6 Investing Abroad Directly

KRIANGKRAI THITIMAKORN/SHUTTERSTOCK.COM

LEARNING OBJECTIVES

After studying this chapter, you will be able to . . .

6-1 Identify and define the key terms associated with foreign direct investment (FDI).

6-2 Use the resource-based and institution-based views to answer why FDI takes place.

6-3 Explain how FDI results in ownership advantages.

6-4 Identify the ways your firm can acquire and neutralize location advantages.

6-5 List the benefits of internalization.

6-6 Identify different political views on FDI and understand its benefits and costs to host and home countries.

6-7 List three things you need to do as your firm considers FDI.

After you finish this chapter, go to

PAGE 101 for

STUDY TOOLS

Opening Case: Nordic Multinationals

Nordic countries have small populations (6 million in Denmark, 9 million in Sweden, 5 million in Finland, and 5 million in Norway). But they are big in breeding multinational enterprises (MNEs) that actively invest abroad and compete globally. Denmark boasts world leaders in beer (Carlsberg), fur (Kopenhagen Fur), medical insulin (Novo Nordisk), shipping (Maersk), toys (LEGO), and wind turbines (Vestas). Tiny Denmark, an agricultural superpower, is home to 30 million pigs—five pigs for every Dane. Leading global players include Arla, Danish Crown, Rose Poultry, and DuPont Danisco (a household name with over 100 years of history, Danisco was acquired by DuPont in 2011). Sweden is a world leader in fighter jets (SAAB), mining equipment and machine tools (Sandvik and Atlas Copco), retail (IKEA and H&M), telecom equipment (Ericsson), and trucks (Scania). Finland leads the world in elevators and escalators (Kone), games (Ravio, the creator of *Angry Birds*), and telecom (Nokia, whose mobile phones were a global sensation until pushed aside by smartphones like Apple's iPhone). Norway has world-class competitors in oil services (Statoil) and fishing (Aker BioMarine and Havfisk—formerly Aker Seafoods). Although technically not an MNE, Norway's Government Pension Fund Global (GPFG) is the largest sovereign wealth fund (SWF) in the world, owning 1% of all listed shares globally (see Debate).

Nordic multinationals often collaborate and sometimes merge with each other. TeliaSonera is the result of a merger between Telia of Sweden and Sonera of Finland in 2002. TeliaSonera is the fifth largest telecom operator in Europe and the world's first operator of 4G networks. If you climb on top of Mount Everest and want to call down to brag about your views, it will be TeliaSonera that connects you from such a remote corner to the rest of civilization.

Small domestic markets have propelled many Nordic firms to go international at a relatively young age. Although most of them export aggressively, they often find that merely exporting is not enough to help penetrate new markets and facilitate growth. Therefore, it is not unusual to see Nordic firms directly invest abroad and manage operations in areas ranging from neighboring Western European countries to distant shores such as Australia, Brazil, India, China, and South Africa.

Three common characteristics make Nordic multinationals stand out among global peers. First, they are committed to relentless innovation. Second, they foster a consensus-based approach to management, which promotes trust and cooperation. Finally, they share a passion for replacing labor with machines. In some advanced Nordic farms, robots milk cows automatically with no human intervention. At one Swedish farm your author visited, two owners—with the aid of milking robots—managed 70 productive milk cows.

Sources: Author's interviews in Copenhagen, Denmark; Helsinki, Finland; Stockholm and Mora, Sweden; "Global niche players," *Economist*, 2 February 2013 (special report: The Nordic countries): 8–10; "Adventures in the skin trade," *Economist*, 3 May 2014: 62; "Bringing home the bacon," *Economist*, 4 January 2014: 52; "Norway's global fund: How to not spend it," *Economist*, 24 September 2016: 67–68; C. Mutlu, "TeliaSonera: A Nordic investor in Eurasia," in M. W. Peng, *Global Strategy*, 3rd ed. (Boston: Cengage, 2014) 404–408.

Why are Nordic firms interested in undertaking foreign direct investment (FDI)? What are the benefits to these firms and to the host economies in which they invest? What are the drawbacks? Recall from Chapter 1 that FDI is defined as putting money into activities that control and manage value-added activities in other countries. Also recall from Chapter 1 that firms that engage in FDI are known as multinational enterprises (MNEs). In 2015, global FDI flows rose by 40%, to $1.8 trillion, the highest level since the global economic and financial crisis of 2008–2009. Firms from developed economies such as those from Nordic countries (see Opening Case) contributed two-thirds of FDI outflows, and those from emerging economies generated the other one-third. Overall, developed and emerging economies had a 55–45 split in FDI inflows.[1]

This chapter starts by first defining key terms related to FDI. Then we address a crucial question: Why do firms engage in FDI? We outline how the core perspectives introduced earlier—namely, resource-based and institution-based views—can help answer this question.[2] We then look at a debate over whether countries should welcome certain foreign investment. Finally, we outline factors a firm should address as it considers engaging in FDI.

6-1 UNDERSTANDING THE FDI VOCABULARY

Part of FDI's complexity is associated with its vocabulary. This section will try to reduce the complexity by setting the terms straight.

6-1a The Key Word Is *Direct*

International investment happens primarily in two ways: FDI and **foreign portfolio investment (FPI)**. FPI refers to holding securities, such as stocks and bonds, of companies in countries outside one's own but does not entail the active management of foreign assets. Essentially, FPI is foreign *indirect* investment. In contrast, the key word in FDI is *direct*—namely, the direct, hands-on management of foreign assets. Some of you reading this book may have some FPI—that is, you own some foreign stocks and bonds. However, as a student taking this course, it is by definition impossible that you are also engaging in FDI at the same time, because that requires you to be a manager who is getting your feet wet by actively managing foreign operations rather than just learning about them.

For statistical purposes, the United Nations defines FDI as an equity stake of 10% or more in a foreign-based enterprise. A lower percentage invested in a foreign firm is considered FPI. Without a sufficiently large equity, it is difficult to exercise **management control rights**—namely, the rights to appoint key managers and establish control mechanisms. Many firms invest abroad for the explicit purpose of managing foreign operations, and they need a large equity (sometimes up to 100%) to be able to do that.

6-1b Horizontal and Vertical FDI

FDI can be horizontal or vertical. Recall the value chain from Chapter 4, whereby firms perform value-adding activities stage by stage in a vertical fashion, from upstream to downstream. When a firm takes the same activity at the same value-chain stage from its home country and *duplicates* it in a host country through FDI, we call this horizontal FDI (see Exhibit 6.1). For example, BMW assembles cars in Germany. Through horizontal FDI, it does the same thing in host countries such as Britain. Overall, **horizontal FDI** refers to producing the same products or offering the same services in a host country as firms do at home.

If a firm moves upstream or downstream in different value chain stages in a host country through FDI, we label this **vertical FDI** (see Exhibit 6.2). For example, if BMW (hypothetically) only assembled cars and did not manufacture components in Germany but entered into components manufacturing through FDI in Russia (an earlier activity in the value chain), this would be **upstream vertical FDI**. Likewise, if BMW did not engage in car distribution in Germany but invested in car dealerships in Egypt (a later activity in the value chain), it would be **downstream vertical FDI**.

6-1c FDI Flow and Stock

Other words often associated with FDI are "flow" and "stock." **FDI flow** is the amount of FDI moving in a given period (usually a year) in a certain direction. **FDI inflow** usually refers to FDI moving into a country in a year, and **FDI outflow** typically refers to FDI moving out of a country in a year. PengAtlas Map 8 illustrates the top ten economies for FDI inflows and outflows. **FDI stock** is the total accumulation of inward FDI in a country or outward FDI from a country. Hypothetically, between two countries A and B, if firms from A undertake $10 billion of FDI in B in Year 1 and another $10 billion in Year 2, then we can say that in each of these two years, B receives annual FDI *inflows* of $10 billion and, correspondingly, A generates annual FDI *outflows* of $10 billion. If we assume that firms from no other countries undertake FDI in country B and prior to Year 1 no FDI was possible, then the

foreign portfolio investment (FPI) Holding securities, such as stocks and bonds, of firms in other countries but without a controlling interest.

management control right The right to appoint key managers and establish control mechanisms.

horizontal FDI A type of FDI in which a firm produces the same products or offers the same services in a host country as at home.

vertical FDI A type of FDI in which a firm moves upstream or downstream in different value chain stages in a host country.

upstream vertical FDI A type of vertical FDI in which a firm engages in an upstream stage of the value chain.

downstream vertical FDI A type of vertical FDI in which a firm engages in a downstream stage of the value chain.

FDI flow The amount of FDI moving in a given period (usually a year) in a certain direction.

FDI inflow FDI moving into a country in a year.

FDI outflow FDI moving out of a country in a year.

FDI stock The total accumulation of inbound FDI in a country or outbound FDI from a country across a given period of time (usually several years).

total *stock* of FDI in B by the end of Year 2 is $20 billion. Essentially, flow is a snapshot of a given point in time, and stock represents the cumulative volume.

6-1d MNE versus Non-MNE

An MNE, by definition, is a firm that engages in FDI when doing business abroad.[3] An MNE is sometimes called a multinational corporation (MNC) or a transnational corporation (TNC). To avoid confusion, we will stick with the term "MNE" throughout the book. Note that non-MNE firms can also do business abroad by exporting and importing, licensing and franchising, outsourcing, or engaging in FPI. What sets MNEs apart from non-MNEs is FDI. An exporter has to undertake FDI in order to become an MNE. In other words, BMW would not be an MNE if it manufactured all of its cars in Germany and exported them around the world. BMW became an MNE only when it started to directly invest abroad.

Although some people argue that MNEs are a new organizational form that emerged after World War II, it is simply not the case. MNEs have existed for at least 2,000 years, with some of the earliest examples found in the Phoenician, Assyrian, and Roman times. In 1903, when Ford Motor Company was founded, it exported its sixth car. Ford almost immediately engaged in FDI by having a factory in Canada that produced its first output in 1904. It is true that MNEs have experienced significant growth since World War II. In 1970, there were approximately 7,000 MNEs worldwide. By 2010, over 82,000 MNEs managed approximately 810,000 foreign affiliates.[4] Clearly, there is a proliferation of MNEs lately.

Germany

| EXHIBIT 6.1 | HORIZONTAL FDI |

Operations in home country — Operations in host country

| EXHIBIT 6.2 | VERTICAL FDI |

Operations in home country — Operations in host country

6-2 WHY DO FIRMS BECOME MNEs BY ENGAGING IN FDI?

Having set the terms straight, we need to address a fundamental question: Why do so many firms—ranging from those in the ancient world to today's BMW, Samsung, and Walmart—become MNEs by engaging in

FDI? Without getting into details, we can safely say that there must be economic gains from FDI. More importantly, given the tremendous complexities associated with FDI, such gains must significantly outweigh the costs. What are the sources of such gains? The answer, as suggested by British scholar John Dunning and illustrated in Exhibit 6.3, boils down to firms' quest for ownership (O) advantages, location (L) advantages, and internalization (I) advantages—collectively known as **OLI advantages**.[5] The two core perspectives introduced earlier—resource-based and institution-based views—enable us to probe into the heart of this question.

In the context of FDI, **ownership** refers to possession and leveraging by an MNE of certain valuable, rare, hard-to-imitate, and organizationally embedded (VRIO) assets overseas. Owning the proprietary technology and the management know-how that goes into making a BMW helps ensure that the MNE can beat rivals abroad.

Location advantages are those enjoyed by firms because they do business in a certain place. Features unique to a place, such as its natural or labor resources or its location near particular markets, provide certain advantages to firms doing business there. For example, Vietnam has emerged as a convenient location for MNEs that want to diversify away from coastal

In 2015, the top ten regions with the highest FDI outflows were the United States ($300 billion), Japan ($129 billion), China ($128 billion), the Netherlands ($113 billion), Ireland ($102 billion), Germany ($94 billion), Switzerland ($70 billion), Canada ($67 billion), Hong Kong ($55 billion), and Luxembourg ($39 billion).

China with rising labor costs. From a resource-based view, an MNE's pursuit of ownership and location advantages can be regarded as flexing its muscles—its resources and capabilities—in global competition.

Internalization refers to the replacement of cross-border markets (such as exporting and importing) with one firm (the MNE) locating and operating in two or more countries. For example, BMW could sell its technology to an Indonesian firm for a fee. This would be a non-FDI-based market entry mode technically called **licensing** and can be done with intellectual property as well as technology. Instead, BMW chooses to assemble cars in Indonesia via FDI. In other words, external market transactions (in this case, buying and selling of technology through licensing) are replaced by internalization. From an institution-based view, internalization is a response to the imperfect rules governing international transactions, known as **market imperfections** (or **market failure**). Evidently, Indonesian regulations governing the protection of intellectual property such as BMW's proprietary technology do not give BMW sufficient confidence that those rights will be protected. Therefore, internalization is a must.

Overall, firms become MNEs because FDI provides OLI advantages that they otherwise would not obtain. The next three sections explain why this is the case.

OLI advantages The advantages of ownership (O), location (L), and internalization (I) that come from engaging in FDI.

ownership Possessing and leveraging of certain valuable, rare, hard-to-imitate, and organizationally embedded (VRIO) assets overseas in the context of FDI.

location Advantages enjoyed by a firm that derive from the places in which it operates.

internalization The replacement of cross-border markets (such as exporting and importing) with one firm (the MNE) located in two or more countries.

licensing Buying and selling technology and intellectual property rights.

market imperfection (market failure) The imperfect rules governing international market transactions.

EXHIBIT 6.3   AN OLI FRAMEWORK FOR WHY FIRMS ENGAGE IN FDI

6-3 OWNERSHIP ADVANTAGES

All investments, including both FDI and FPI, entail ownership of assets. So what is unique about FDI? This section highlights the benefits of direct ownership and compares FDI to licensing when considering market entries abroad.

6-3a The Benefits of Direct Ownership

Remember that *direct* is the key word in foreign direct investment. FDI requires a significant equity ownership position. The benefits of direct ownership lie in the *combination* of equity ownership rights and management control rights. Specifically, the ownership rights provide the much-needed management control rights. In contrast, FPI represents essentially insignificant ownership rights and no management control rights. To compete successfully, firms need to deploy overwhelming resources and capabilities to overcome their liabilities of foreignness (see Chapters 1 and 4). FDI provides one of the best ways to facilitate such extension of firm-specific resources and capabilities abroad.

6-3b FDI versus Licensing

Basic choices when entering foreign markets include exporting, licensing, and FDI. Successful exporting may provoke protectionist responses from host countries, thus forcing firms to choose between licensing and FDI. Between licensing and FDI, which is better? Exhibit 6.4 shows three reasons that may compel firms to prefer FDI to licensing.

First, FDI affords a high degree of direct management control that reduces the risk of firm-specific resources and capabilities being appropriated. One of the leading risks abroad is **dissemination risk**, defined as the possibility of unauthorized diffusion of firm-specific know-how. If a foreign company grants a license to a local firm to manufacture or market a product, the licensee (or an employee of the licensee) may disseminate the know-how by using it against the wishes of the foreign company. For example, Pizza Hut found out that its long-time licensee in Thailand disseminated its know-how and established a direct competitor, simply called The Pizza Company, which controlled 70% of the market in Thailand.[6] While owning and managing proprietary assets through FDI does not completely shield firms from dissemination risks (after all, their employees can quit and join competitors), FDI

EXHIBIT 6.4 WHY FIRMS PREFER FDI TO LICENSING

▸ FDI reduces dissemination risks.

▸ FDI provides tight control over foreign operations.

▸ FDI facilitates the transfer of tacit knowledge through "learning by doing."

---

is better because licensing does not provide management control at all. Understandably, FDI is extensively used in knowledge-intensive, high-tech industries such as automobiles, electronics, chemicals, and IT.

Second, FDI provides more direct and tighter control over foreign operations. Even when licensees (and their employees) harbor no opportunistic intention to steal secrets, they may not always follow the wishes of the foreign firm that provides the know-how. Without FDI, the foreign firm cannot control its licensee. For example, Starbucks entered South Korea by licensing its format to ESCO. Although ESCO soon opened ten stores, Starbucks felt that ESCO was not aggressive enough in growing the chain. But without FDI, there was little Starbucks could do. Eventually, Starbucks switched from licensing to FDI, which allowed it to directly promote the more aggressive growth of the chain in South Korea.

Finally, certain knowledge (or know-how) calls for FDI as opposed to licensing. Even if there is no opportunism on the part of licensees and if they follow the wishes of the foreign firm, certain know-how may simply be too difficult to transfer to licensees without FDI. There are two basic categories of knowledge: explicit and tacit. Explicit knowledge is codifiable—specifically, it can be written down and transferred without losing much of its richness. Tacit knowledge, on the other hand, is noncodifiable, and its acquisition and transfer require hands-on practice. For example, a driving manual represents a body of explicit knowledge. However, mastering the manual without any road practice does not make you a good driver. Tacit knowledge is more important and harder to transfer and learn—it can only be

> **dissemination risk** The possibility of unauthorized diffusion of firm-specific know-how.

acquired by doing (in this case, practice driving under the supervision of an experienced driver). Likewise, operating a Walmart store involves a great deal of knowledge, some explicit (often captured in an operational manual) and some tacit. As such, simply giving foreign licensees—via a licensing agreement—a copy of the Walmart operational manual will not be enough. Foreign employees will need to learn directly from experienced Walmart personnel by actually doing the job.

From a resource-based standpoint, it is Walmart's tacit knowledge that gives it competitive advantage (see Chapter 4). Walmart owns such crucial tacit knowledge and has no incentive to give that knowledge away to licensees without having some management control over how that knowledge is used. Therefore, properly transferring and controlling tacit knowledge calls for FDI. Overall, ownership advantages enable the firm, now becoming an MNE, to more effectively extend, transfer, and leverage firm-specific capabilities abroad.

6-4 LOCATION ADVANTAGES

Given the well-known liability of foreignness, foreign locations must offer compelling advantages to make it worthwhile to undertake FDI. We may regard the continuous expansion of international business (IB), such as FDI, as an unending saga in search of location advantages.[7] This section highlights the sources of location advantages and outlines ways to acquire and neutralize those advantages.

6-4a Location, Location, Location

Certain locations possess geographical features that are difficult to match by others. For example, although Austria politically and culturally belongs to the West, the country is geographically located in the heart of Central and Eastern Europe (CEE). In fact, Austria's capital Vienna is actually *east* of Prague, the Czech Republic, and Ljubljana, Slovenia. Therefore, Vienna attracts significant FDI from MNEs to set up regional headquarters for CEE. Due to its proximity to the United States, Mexico attracts numerous automakers to set up production there. Thanks to such FDI, 82% of Mexico's vehicle production is exported (see In Focus).

Beyond natural geographical advantages, location advantages also arise from the clustering of economic activities in certain locations, referred to as **agglomeration** (see In Focus). For instance, the Netherlands grows and

agglomeration Clustering of economic activities in certain locations.

exports two-thirds of the worldwide exports of cut flowers. Slovakia produces more cars per capita than any other country in the world, thanks to the quest for agglomeration benefits by global automakers. Dallas attracts all of the world's major telecom equipment makers and many telecom service providers, making it the Telecom Corridor. Overall, agglomeration advantages stem from:

▸ Knowledge spillover, or the diffusion of knowledge from one firm to others among closely located firms that attempt to hire individuals from competitors.

▸ Industry demand that creates a skilled labor force whose members may work for different firms without moving out of the region.

▸ Industry demand that facilitates a pool of specialized suppliers and buyers also located in the region.

6-4b Acquiring and Neutralizing Location Advantages

Note that from a resource-based view, location advantages do *not* entirely overlap with country-level advantages such as the factor endowments discussed in Chapter 5. Location advantages refer to the advantages that one firm obtains when operating in a location due to its *firm-specific* capabilities. In 1982, General Motors (GM) ran its Fremont, California, plant into the ground and had to close it. Reopening the same plant in 1984, Toyota initiated its first FDI project in the United States in a joint venture (JV) with GM. Since then, Toyota (together with GM) has leveraged this plant's location advantages by producing award-winning cars that American customers particularly like—the Toyota Corolla and Tacoma. The point is this: it is Toyota's unique capabilities, applied to the California location, that literally have saved the plant from its demise. The California location in itself does not provide location advantages per se, as shown by GM's inability to make it work prior to 1982.

Automobile FDI in Brazil and Mexico

Brazil and Mexico are, respectively, the top one and two largest economies in Latin America in terms of GDP. Globally, Brazil and Mexico are, respectively, the seventh- and eighth-largest car producers and the fourth- and 16th-largest automobile markets. Almost all of their production is undertaken by global automakers via foreign direct investment (FDI). Audi, Fiat, Ford, General Motors (GM), Honda, Nissan, Renault, Toyota, and Volkswagen (VW) have assembly factories in both countries. In addition, Hyundai, MAN, and Mercedes-Benz produce in Brazil. BMW, Chrysler, Isuzu, Kia, and Mitsubishi operate assembly plants in Mexico. Clearly, there is significant agglomeration in the automobile industry in both countries. For multinationals striving for ownership, location, and internalization (OLI) advantages, their efforts in leveraging O and I advantages are similar in both countries. However, they have pursued location (L) advantages in these two countries in different ways.

Brazil attracts FDI primarily due to its huge domestic market, while Mexico pulls in FDI due to its proximity to the United States. As a result, only 13% of Brazil's vehicle production is exported (67% of such exports go to its neighbors in Mercusor—a customs union with Argentina, Paraguay, Uruguay, and Venezuela). In contrast, 64% of Mexico's vehicle production is exported to the United States, and all together 82% of its output is exported. Brazil maintains high import tariffs on cars and components (except when 65% of the value is imported from one of the Mercosur partners or from Mexico—with which Brazil had a bilateral free trade deal in cars and components). As a result, only 21% of the content of Brazil's exports is imported. This ratio of imported content among exports is 47% for Mexico, indicating a much more open and less protectionist environment in which automakers can import a great deal more components tariff-free.

ANDREI KOBYLKO/SHUTTERSTOCK.COM

The differences in the production, export, and import patterns, of course, are not only shaped by the resources and capabilities of multinationals, but also by government policies in both host countries of FDI. Whether Brazil or Mexico gains more is subject to intense debate in these two countries and beyond. One side of the argument posits that Mexico is only leveraging its low-cost labor and has not fostered a lot of domestic suppliers. Indeed, most first-tier suppliers in Mexico are foreign owned and they import a great deal of components to be assembled into final products. As a result, most final assembly plants are *maquiladora* type, otherwise known as "screw driver plants." With little technology spillovers to local suppliers, the innovation ability of the Mexican automobile industry is thus limited.

Brazil, on the other hand, has pushed automakers to work closely with domestically-owned suppliers or with foreign-owned suppliers that have to source locally. Brazilian subsidiaries of multinational automakers, aided by suppliers, have endeavored to search for solutions to meet unique local demands, such as ethanol fuel. Brazil is a world leader in ethanol—a sustainable biofuel based on sugarcane. By law, no light vehicles in Brazil are allowed to run on pure gasoline. Led by Volkswagen's Gol 1.6 Total Flex in 2003, the Brazilian automobile industry has introduced flexible-fuel vehicles that can run on any combination of ethanol and gasoline. All multinational automakers producing in Brazil have eagerly participated in the flex movement. Starting with 22% of car sales in 2004, flex cars reached a record 94% by 2010. By 2012, the cumulative production of flex cars and light vehicles reached 15 million units. Advocates of Brazil's FDI policy argue that such successes have generated new opportunities for locally-owned component producers and local research institutions.

The other side of the debate points out Mexico's shining accomplishments as an export hub with more open trade and investment-friendly policies. Mexico has successfully leveraged its NAFTA membership and free trade agreements with more than 40 countries. Such institutional support is helpful, but at the end of the day, "Made in Mexico" vehicles have to be hard to beat in performance and price in export markets. Mexico largely succeeds in this because of its persistent efforts to keep its wage levels low, its labor skills high, and its infrastructure modernized.

Brazil, on the other hand, suffers from the notorious *custo Brasil* (Brazil cost)—the exorbitant cost of living and doing business in Brazil. In office between 2011 and 2016, President Dilma Rousseff created new tariffs, subsidies, and protectionist policies for several Brazilian industries, including automobiles. According to some critics, the Brazilian automobile industry simply could not stand on its own in the absence of such protectionism. Brazil even threatened to tear up the agreement with Mexico that allowed free trade in cars and components, because—thanks to its uncompetitive automobile industry—it suffered from an embarrassing trade deficit. In 2012, Brazil renegotiated the deal with Mexico, imposing import quotas on "Made in Mexico" cars and components. More recently, the Brazilian government introduced Inovar Autos, an automotive plan intended to encourage firms to hit specific targets in localization of production and R&D by 2017 through additional tax benefits. Critics argue that this is just one more round of protectionism and government meddling that is ultimately counterproductive.

Sources: "Two ways to make a car," *Economist*, 10 March 2012: 48–49; "The price is wrong," *Economist*, 28 September 2013 (special report): 5; P. Figueiredo, "The role of dual embeddedness in the innovative performance of MNE subsidiaries: Evidence from Brazil," *Journal of Management Studies* 48 (2011): 417–440; M. Kotabe, R. Parente, and J. Murray, "Antecedents and outcomes of modular production in the Brazilian automobile industry," *Journal of International Business Studies* 38 (2007): 84–106; United Nations, *World Investment Report 2014* (New York and Geneva: UN, 2014) 65–69.

Firms do not operate in a vacuum. When one firm enters a foreign country through FDI, its rivals are likely to increase FDI in that host country either to acquire location advantages themselves or to at least neutralize the first mover's location advantages. These actions to imitate and follow competitors are especially likely in oligopolies—industries (such as aerospace and semiconductors) populated by a small number of players. The automobile industry is a typical oligopolistic industry (see In Focus). Volkswagen was the first foreign entrant in China, starting production in 1985 and enjoying a market share of 60% in the 1990s. Now, every self-respecting global automaker has entered China trying to eat some of Volkswagen's lunch. Overall, competitive rivalry and imitation, especially in oligopolistic industries, underscores the importance of acquiring and neutralizing location advantages around the world.

6-5 INTERNALIZATION ADVANTAGES

Known as internalization, another set of great advantages associated with FDI is the ability to replace the external market relationship with one firm (the MNE) owning, controlling, and managing activities in two or more countries. Internalization is important because of significant imperfections in international market transactions. The institution-based view suggests that markets are governed by rules, regulations, and norms that are designed to reduce uncertainties. Uncertainties introduce transaction costs—costs associated with doing business (see Chapter 2). This section outlines the necessity of combating market failure and describes the benefits brought by internalization.

6-5a Market Failure

International transaction costs tend to be higher than domestic transaction costs. Because laws and regulations are typically enforced on a nation-state basis, enforcement can be an issue on the international level.[8] Suppose two parties from different countries are doing business. If the party from country A behaves opportunistically, the other party from country B will have a hard time enforcing the contract. Suing the other party in a foreign country is not only costly, but also uncertain. In the worst case, such imperfections are so grave that markets fail to function, and many firms simply choose not to do business abroad to avoid being burned. High transaction costs can therefore result in market failure in cases where the market imperfections actually prohibit transactions altogether. However, recall from Chapter 5 that there are gains from trade. Not doing business together prevents firms from reaping such gains. In response, MNEs emerge to overcome and combat such market failure through FDI.

6-5b Overcoming Market Failure Through FDI

How do MNEs combat market failure through internalization? Let us use an example involving an oil importer, BP in Britain, and an oil exporter, Nigerian National Petroleum Corporation (NNPC) in Nigeria. For the sake of our discussion, assume that BP does all of its business in Britain and NNPC does all of its business in Nigeria—in other words, neither of them is an MNE. BP and NNPC negotiate a contract specifying that NNPC will export a certain amount of crude oil from Nigeria to BP's oil refinery facilities in Britain for a certain amount of money. Shown in Exhibit 6.5, this is both an export contract (from NNPC's perspective) and an import contract (from BP's standpoint) between two firms. In other words, it is an international market transaction.

An international market transaction between an importer and an exporter like BP and NNPC may suffer from high transaction costs. What is especially costly is

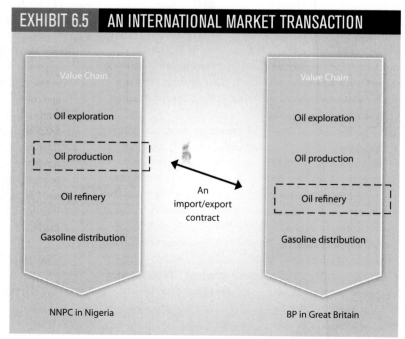

EXHIBIT 6.5 AN INTERNATIONAL MARKET TRANSACTION

Value Chain

Oil exploration
Oil production
Oil refinery
Gasoline distribution

NNPC in Nigeria

An import/export contract

Value Chain

Oil exploration
Oil production
Oil refinery
Gasoline distribution

BP in Great Britain

the potential opportunism on both sides. For example, NNPC may demand a higher than agreed upon price, citing a variety of reasons such as inflation, natural disasters, or simply rising oil prices after the deal is signed. BP then has to either pay more than the agreed-upon price or refuse to pay more and suffer from the huge costs of keeping expensive refinery facilities idle. In other words, NNPC's opportunistic behavior can cause a lot of losses for BP.

Opportunistic behavior can go both ways in a market transaction. In this particular example, BP can also be opportunistic. It may refuse to accept a shipment after its arrival from Nigeria citing unsatisfactory quality, but the real reason may be BP's inability to sell refined oil downstream because gasoline demand is going down. People in Britain are driving less due to the recession—the jobless do not need to commute to work that much. NNPC is thus forced to find a new buyer for a huge tanker load of crude oil on a last-minute, "fire sale" basis with a deep discount, losing a lot of money.

Overall, once one side in a market (export/import) transaction behaves opportunistically, the other side will not be happy and will threaten or initiate law suits. Because the legal and regulatory frameworks governing such international transactions are generally not as effective as those governing domestic transactions, the injured party will generally be frustrated while the opportunistic party can often get away with it. All of these are examples of transaction costs that increase international market inefficiencies and imperfections, ultimately resulting in market failure.

In response, FDI combats such market failure through internalization, which involves replacing the external market with in-house links. The MNE reduces cross-border transaction costs and increases efficiencies by replacing an external market relationship with a single organization spanning both countries.[9] In our example, there are two possibilities for internalization: BP could undertake *upstream* vertical FDI by owning oil production assets in Nigeria, or NNPC could undertake *downstream* vertical FDI by owning oil refinery assets in Britain (see Exhibit 6.6). FDI essentially transforms the international trade between two independent firms in two countries to **intrafirm trade** between two subsidiaries in two countries controlled by the same MNE. By coordinating cross-border activities better, the MNE can thus achieve internalization advantages relative to non-MNEs.

Overall, the motivations for FDI are complex. Based on resource-based and institution-based views,

EXHIBIT 6.6   COMBATING MARKET FAILURE THROUGH FDI: ONE COMPANY (MNE) IN TWO COUNTRIES

Value Chain

Oil exploration
Oil production
Oil refinery
Gasoline distribution

Nigeria

Value Chain

Oil exploration
Oil production
Oil refinery
Gasoline distribution

Great Britain

we can see FDI as a reflection of both a firm's motivation to extend its firm-specific capabilities abroad and its responses to overcome market imperfections and failures.

6-6   REALITIES OF FDI

The realities of FDI are intertwined with politics. This section starts with three political views on FDI and follows with a discussion of pros and cons of FDI for home and host countries.

6-6a   Political Views on FDI

There are three primary political views on FDI. First, the **radical view on FDI** is hostile to FDI. Tracing its roots to Marxism, the radical view treats FDI as an instrument of imperialism and a vehicle for exploiting domestic resources, industries, and people by foreign capitalists and firms. Governments embracing the radical view often nationalize MNE assets or simply ban (or discourage) inbound MNEs. Between the 1950s and the early 1980s, the radical view was influential throughout Africa, Asia, Eastern Europe, and Latin America.

intrafirm trade International trade between two subsidiaries in two countries controlled by the same MNE.

radical view on FDI A political view that sees FDI as an instrument of imperialism and a vehicle for foreign exploitation.

On the other hand, the **free market view on FDI** suggests that FDI, unrestricted by government intervention, will enable countries to tap into their absolute or comparative advantages by specializing in the production of certain goods and services. Similar to the win–win logic for international trade as articulated by Adam Smith and David Ricardo (see Chapter 5), free market–based FDI should lead to a win–win situation for both home and host countries. Since the 1980s, a series of countries such as Brazil, China, Hungary, India, Ireland, and Russia have adopted more FDI-friendly policies.

However, a totally free market view does not really exist in practice. Most countries embrace the **pragmatic nationalism view on FDI**, considering both the pros and cons of FDI and approving FDI only when its benefits outweigh its costs. The French government, invoking "economic patriotism," has torpedoed several foreign takeover attempts of French companies. The Chinese government insists that automobile FDI has to take the form of JVs with MNEs so that Chinese automakers can learn from their foreign counterparts. The US government has expressed alleged "national security concerns" over the FDI made by Chinese telecom equipment makers Huawei and ZTE.

Overall, more countries in recent years have changed their policies to be more favorable to FDI. Restrictive policies toward FDI succeed only in driving out foreign investors to countries with more favorable policies (see Closing Case). Even hard-core countries such as Cuba and North Korea that had a radical view on FDI are now experimenting with some FDI. However, there is some creeping increase of restrictions in the form of policies discouraging inbound FDI in some countries. For example, France and Russia have recently issued decrees reinforcing control for FDI in the interest of public security or national defense.

EXHIBIT 6.7   EFFECTS OF FDI ON HOME AND HOST COUNTRIES

Effects of FDI

Recipients versus sources

	Benefits	Costs
Host (recipient) countries	Cell 1 Capital inflow, technology, management, job creation	Cell 2 Loss of sovereignty, competition, capital outflow
Home (source) countries	Cell 3 Earnings, exports, learning from abroad	Cell 4 Capital outflow, job loss

6-6b Benefits and Costs of FDI to Host Countries

Underpinning pragmatic nationalism is the need to assess the various benefits and costs of FDI to host (recipient) countries and home (source) countries (see Closing Case). In a nutshell, Exhibit 6.7 outlines these considerations. This section focuses on *host* countries, and the next section deals with *home* countries.

Cell 1 in Exhibit 6.7 shows four primary benefits to host countries. First, *capital inflow* can help improve a host country's balance of payments. The balance of payments measures a country's payments to and receipts from other countries. Chinese firms undertake FDI by acquiring US-based assets. By bringing more capital into the United States, such FDI helps improve the US balance of payments. (See Chapter 7 for more details.)

Second, *technology*, especially more advanced technology from abroad, can create **technology spillovers** that benefit domestic firms and industries. Technology spillover is the domestic diffusion of foreign technical knowledge and processes.[10] After observing such technology, local rivals may recognize its feasibility and strive to imitate it. This is known as the **demonstration effect**, sometimes also called the **contagion** (or **imitation**) **effect**. It underscores the important role that MNEs play in stimulating competition in host countries.

Third, *advanced management know-how* may be highly valued. In many developing countries, it is often difficult for the development of management know-how to reach a world-class level in the absence of FDI.

Finally, FDI creates a total of 80 million jobs, which represent approximately 4% of the global workforce.[11] FDI creates jobs both directly and indirectly. Direct benefits arise when MNEs employ individuals locally.

free market view on FDI A political view that holds that FDI, unrestricted by government intervention, will enable countries to tap into their absolute or comparative advantages by specializing in the production of certain goods and services.

pragmatic nationalism view on FDI A political view that approves FDI only when its benefits outweigh its costs.

technology spillover The domestic diffusion of foreign technical knowledge and processes.

demonstration effect (contagion or imitation effect) The effect that occurs when local rivals recognize the feasibility of foreign technology and imitate it.

In Ireland, more than 50% of manufacturing employees work for MNEs.[12] In the UK, the largest private sector employer is an MNE: India's Tata has over 50,000 employees in the UK working for a variety of businesses such as Jaguar, Land Rover, Tata Steel (formerly Corus), Tata Tea (formerly Tetley), and Tata Consultancy Services. Indirect benefits include jobs created when local suppliers increase hiring and when MNE employees spend money locally, which also results in more jobs.

Cell 2 in Exhibit 6.7 outlines three primary costs of FDI to host countries: loss of sovereignty, adverse effects on competition, and capital outflow. The first concern is the loss of some (but not all) economic sovereignty associated with FDI. Because of FDI, decisions to produce and market products and services in a host country are being made by foreigners. Even if locals serve as heads of MNE subsidiaries, they represent the interest of foreign firms. Will foreigners and foreign firms make decisions that are in the best interest of host countries (see Debate)? This is truly a million-dollar question. According to the radical view, the answer is "No!" because foreigners and foreign firms are likely to maximize their own profits by exploiting people and resources in host countries. Such deep suspicion of MNEs leads to policies that discourage or even ban FDI. On the other hand, countries embracing free market and pragmatic nationalism views agree that despite some acknowledged differences between foreign and host country interests, the interests of MNEs and host countries overlap sufficiently. Host countries are thus willing to live with some loss of sovereignty.

A second concern is associated with the negative effects on local competition. While we have just discussed the positive effects of MNEs on local competition, it is possible that MNEs may drive some domestic firms out of business. Having driven domestic firms out of business, in theory, MNEs may be able to monopolize local markets. While this is a relatively minor concern in developed economies, it is a legitimate concern for less developed economies where MNEs are generally so much larger and financially stronger when compared with local firms (see In Focus and Closing Case). For example, as Coca-Cola and PepsiCo extended their "cola wars" from the United States to countries around the world, they have almost "accidentally" wiped out much of the world's indigenous beverages companies, which are—or were—much smaller.

A third concern is associated with capital outflow. When MNEs make profits in host countries and repatriate (send back) such earnings to headquarters in home countries, host countries experience a net outflow in the capital account in their balance of payments.

Bolivia

As a result, some countries have restricted the ability of MNEs to repatriate funds. In some parts of the developing world, tension over foreign ownership can turn into political action. Given the recent worldwide trend toward more FDI-friendly policies, many people thought optimistically that nationalization and expropriation against MNE assets were a thing of the past. However, the optimists had a rude awakening recently. In 2006, Venezuelan president Hugo Chavez ordered Chevron, ENI, Royal Dutch Shell, Total, and other oil and gas MNEs to convert their operations in the country into forced JVs with the state-owned Venezuelan firm PDVSA, and PDVSA would hold at least 60% of the equity. When France's Total and Italy's ENI rejected the terms, the Venezuelan government promptly seized their fields. Also in 2006, Bolivia seized control of the MNEs' oil fields. Soon after, Ecuador expropriated the oil fields run by America's Occidental Petroleum. More recently, in 2012, Argentina nationalized YPF, which was owned by Spain's Repsol. It is important to note that the anti-MNE actions in Latin America were not sudden impulsive policy changes. The politicians leading these actions were all democratically elected. These actions were the result of lengthy political debates concerning FDI in the region, and such takeovers were mostly popular among the public. Until the 1970s, the treatment and dealings with MNEs among Latin American governments was largely harsh and confrontational. Only in the 1990s, when these countries became democratic, did they open their oil industry to inbound FDI. So the 180-degree policy reversal is both surprising (considering how recently these governments welcomed MNEs) and not surprising (considering historical dealings with MNEs in the region). Some argue that the recent actions represent the swing of a pendulum (see Chapter 1 on the pendulum of globalization).

TOMMASO79/SHUTTERSTOCK.COM

Debate: Welcoming versus Restricting Sovereign Wealth Fund Investments

Emerging Markets/Ethical Dilemma

A **sovereign wealth fund (SWF)** is a state-owned investment fund composed of financial assets such as stocks, bonds, real estate, or other financial instruments funded by foreign exchange assets. Although the term "SWF" was only coined in 2005 by Andrew Rozanov, a senior manager at State Street Global Advisors, outside the United States investment funds that we now call SWFs were first created in 1953 by Kuwait. Both the United States and Canada have had their own SWFs—at least at the state and provincial level, such as the Alaska Permanent Fund and Alberta Heritage Fund. In the United States, the Texas Permanent School Fund was established in 1854.

In the recent global financial crisis, SWFs came to the rescue. For example, in 2007, the Abu Dhabi Investment Authority injected $7.5 billion (4.9% of equity) into Citigroup. In 2008, China Investment Corporation (CIC) invested $5 billion for a 10% equity stake in Morgan Stanley.

Such large-scale investments have ignited the debate on SWFs. On the one hand, SWFs have brought much-needed cash to rescue desperate Western firms. On the other hand, concerns are raised by host countries, which are typically developed economies. One primary concern is national security in that SWFs may be politically (as opposed to commercially) motivated. Another concern is SWFs' inadequate transparency. Governments in several developed economies, in fear of the "threats" from SWFs, have been erecting anti-SWF measures to defend their companies.

Foreign investment certainly has both benefits and costs to host countries. However, in the absence of any evidence that the costs outweigh benefits, the rush to erect anti-SWF barriers is indicative of protectionist (or, some may argue, even racist) sentiments. For executives at hard-pressed Western firms, it would not seem sensible to ask for government bailouts on the one hand, and to reject cash from SWFs on the other hand. Most SWF investment is essentially free cash with few strings attached. For example, CIC, which now holds 10% of Morgan Stanley equity, did not demand a board seat or a management role. For Western policy makers, it makes little sense to spend taxpayers' dollars to bail out failed firms, run huge budget deficits, and then turn away SWFs. Commenting on inbound Chinese investment

AFRICA STUDIO/SHUTTERSTOCK.COM

in the United States (including SWF investment), then Secretary of the Treasury Henry Paulson argued in *Foreign Affairs*:

> *These concerns [on Chinese investment] are misplaced . . . the United States would do well to encourage such investment from anywhere in the world— including China—because it represents a vote of confidence in the US economy and it promotes growth, jobs, and productivity in the United States.*

Lastly, thanks to the financial crisis in 2008–2009, recent SWF investment in developed economies suffered major losses. Such a "double whammy"—both the political backlash and the economic losses—has severely discouraged SWFs. Some SWFs, especially those from the Gulf, are increasingly investing in their domestic public services (health care, education, and infrastructure). As a result, the competition for funds puts a premium on maintaining a welcoming climate. As part of the efforts to foster such a welcoming climate in times of great political and economic anxiety, the US–China Strategic and Economic Dialogue (S&ED) in July 2009 confirmed:

> *The United States confirms that the Committee on Foreign Investment in the United States (CFIUS) process ensures the consistent and fair treatment of all foreign investment without prejudice to the place of origin. The United States welcomes sovereign wealth fund investment, including that from China.*

In September 2008, major SWFs of the world at a summit in Santiago, Chile, agreed to a voluntary code of conduct known as the Santiago Principles. These principles are designed to alleviate some of the concerns for host countries of SWF investment and to enhance the transparency of such investment. These principles represent an important milestone of SWFs' evolution. Since then, SWF assets have grown faster than the assets of any other institutional investor group, including private equity and hedge funds. Today more than 70 major SWFs manage approximately $6.4 trillion in assets. In the EU, between 15% and 25% of listed firms have

sovereign wealth fund (SWF) A state-owned investment fund composed of financial assets such as stocks, bonds, real estate, or other financial instruments funded by foreign exchange assets.

SWF shareholders. Norway's Government Pension Fund Global, the world's largest SWF, owns an average of 2.5% of every European listed firm and 1% of all the listed equities in the world.

Sources: R. Agulera, J. Capape, and J. Santiso, "Sovereign wealth funds," *Academy of Management Perspectives* 30 (2016): 5–23; D. Drezner, "Sovereign wealth funds and the (in)security of global finance," *Journal of International Affairs* 62 (2008): 115–130; "More money than Thor," *Economist*, 14 September 2013: 73; "Norway's global fund: How to not spend it," *Economist*, 24 September 2016: 67–68; V. Fotak and W. Megginson, "Are SWFs welcome now?" *Columbia FDI Perspectives*, No. 9, 21 July 2009: www.vcc.columbia.edu; H. Paulson, "The right way to engage China," *Foreign Affairs*, September/October 2008: www.foreignaffairs.org; A. Rozanov, "Who holds the wealth of nations?" *Central Banking Journal*, May 2005; Sovereign Wealth Fund Institute, "About sovereign wealth fund," 2014: www.swfinstitute.org; United Nations, *World Investment Report 2014* (New York and Geneva: UN) 19–20; US Department of the Treasury, *The First US-China Strategic and Economic Dialogue Economic Track Joint Fact Sheet*, 28 July 2009, Washington.

6-6c Benefits and Costs of FDI to Home Countries

As exporters of capital, technology, management, and, in some cases, jobs, home (source) countries often reap benefits and endure costs associated with FDI that are *opposite* to those experienced by host countries. Cell 3 of Exhibit 6.7 shows three benefits to home countries:

▶ Repatriated earnings from profits from FDI.

▶ Increased exports of components and services to host countries.

▶ Learning via FDI from operations abroad.

Cell 4 in Exhibit 6.7 shows that the costs of FDI to home countries primarily center on capital outflow and job loss. First, since host countries enjoy capital inflow because of FDI, home countries naturally suffer from some capital outflow. Less confident home country governments often impose capital controls to prevent or reduce FDI from flowing abroad.

The second concern is now more prominent: job loss. Many MNEs simultaneously invest abroad by adding employment overseas and curtail domestic production by laying off employees. It is not surprising that restrictions on FDI outflows have been increasingly vocal, called for by politicians, union members, journalists, and activists in many developed economies. For example, President Donald Trump called Carrier Corporation to discourage it from investing in Mexico and hiring workers there at the expense of US jobs.

valuable, unique, and hard to imitate by rival firms. Second, from an institution-based view, the political realities either enable or constrain FDI from reaching its full economic potential. Therefore, the success and failure of FDI also significantly depend on institutions governing FDI as "rules of the game."

Shown in Exhibit 6.8, three implications for action emerge. First, you should carefully assess whether FDI is justified in light of other possibilities such as outsourcing and licensing. This exercise needs to be conducted on an activity-by-activity basis as part of the value chain analysis (see Chapter 4). If ownership and internalization advantages are not deemed critical, then FDI is not recommended.

Second, once a decision to undertake FDI is made, you should pay attention to the old adage, "location, location, location!" The quest for location advantages has to fit with the firm's strategic goals. For example, if a firm is searching for innovation hot spots, then low-cost locations that do not generate sufficient innovations will not be attractive (see Chapters 10 and 12). High-cost locations such as Denmark would be ideal for wind turbine makers in search of cutting-edge innovations (see Opening Case).

Finally, given the political realities around the world, be aware of the institutional constraints. Savvy MNE managers should not take FDI-friendly policies for granted. Setbacks are likely. The global economic slowdown has made many developed economies less attractive to invest, and the credit crunch means that firms are less able to invest abroad. Attitudes toward

6-7 MANAGEMENT SAVVY

The big question in global business, adapted to the context of FDI, is: What determines the success and failure of FDI around the globe? The answer boils down to two components. First, from a resource-based view, some firms are good at FDI because they leverage ownership, location, and internalization advantages in a way that is

EXHIBIT 6.8 IMPLICATIONS FOR ACTION

▶ Carefully assess whether FDI is justified in light of other foreign entry modes such as outsourcing and licensing.

▶ Pay careful attention to the location advantages in combination with the firm's strategic goals.

▶ Be aware of the institutional constraints and enablers governing FDI, and enhance legitimacy in host countries.

certain forms of foreign investment (such as sovereign wealth funds discussed in the Debate feature) are changing, which may lead FDI policies to become more protectionist. In the long run, the interests of MNEs in host countries can be best safeguarded if MNEs accommodate, rather than neglect or dominate, the interests of host countries (see Closing Case). In practical terms, contributions to local employment, job training, education, and pollution control will tangibly demonstrate MNEs' commitment to host countries.[13]

Closing Case: FDI in the Indian Retail Industry

India's retail industry is the country's largest provider of jobs, accounting for 40 million jobs and 10% of GDP. India has the world's highest density of retail outlets. There are more than 15 million retail outlets in India, compared to 900,000 in the United States, whose market is 13 times bigger by revenue. At present, 92% of retail sales in India are made in tiny mom-and-pop shops (*kirana*). In Indian jargon, this is known as the "unorganized sector." By contrast, the "organized sector," made up of modern supermarkets, commanded only 8% of the country's $600 billion retail sales in 2015. This is low by international standards. In China, Thailand, and the United States, the organized sector accounts respectively for 25%, 40%, and 85% of all retail sales. But the growth in India is likely to be phenomenal, with total retail sales estimated to reach $1.3 trillion by 2020.

CORNFIELD/SHUTTERSTOCK.COM

With a booming economy, a fast-growing middle class, and fragmented local competitors, the Indian retail industry is the world's biggest untapped retail market. Not surprisingly, foreign giants such as Carrefour, IKEA, Metro, Tesco, and Walmart are all interested. However, there is a catch: FDI in Indian retail comes alongside a hugely controversial and emotionally charged debate. Although India has been welcoming FDI in general since 1991, the retail industry is conspicuous in being one of the last four industries with FDI restrictions—the other three are the more sensitive atomic energy, gambling, and agriculture.

India's retail industry, according to the *Economist*, is now "the most glaring example of the need for foreign investment." One of the leading arguments is that super-efficient retail operations will enhance productivity and efficiency throughout the entire supply chain. Retail labor productivity in India—one of the lowest in the world—is only about 6% of that in the United States. At present, about a third of groceries spoil while in transit or in *kirana* shops—a catastrophe in a country where so many go hungry.

For years, a side door has been open to FDI. Until 2011, foreign firms could take up to 51% equity in single-brand shops that sell their own products, such as Nike, Nokia, and Starbucks. Foreign firms could also set up wholesale and sourcing subsidiaries that supply local mass retail partners. In 2010, Walmart set up a joint venture (JV) with Bharti to operate nine Best Price wholesale stores. But the JV dissolved in 2013, and Walmart is now the solo operator of Best Price wholesale stores.

Until November 2011, FDI in multi-brand stores—an Indian term for supermarkets—had been banned altogether. To attract more FDI, the government announced that foreign firms could now own 51% of multi-brand retailers (up from zero) and 100% of single-brand retailers (up from 51%). But multi-brand retail investors were required to invest a minimum of $100 million, with at least half of that in back-end infrastructure such as refrigeration and transportation—sectors that were particularly underdeveloped in India. The reforms were only to be implemented in 53 cities with populations of more than one million. Consumers would benefit from increased competition. The shares of listed local retailers soared on speculation that they might be bought out by foreign firms. Farmers would gain from greater investment in the supply chain. Currently farmers have little bargaining power, fetching only one-third of the final price paid by consumers. In comparison, farmers in countries with a higher percentage of organized retail can grab two-thirds. In India, it is the middlemen—wholesalers and distributors—who grab the lion's share of the fruits of farmers' labor, pocketing two-thirds of the final price paid by consumers. Easy profits provide little incentive for middlemen to enhance efficiency and invest in modern supply chain (such as cold storage), and food spoils along the way. Going directly to farmers, foreign retailers would then pay farmers higher prices and invest in a modern supply chain to minimize food spoilage. Some middlemen's jobs and livelihood would indeed be threatened.

A huge political brawl erupted after the announcement. Thousands of shopkeepers, supported by middlemen, protested against the alleged onslaught of multinationals and cited the controversial "Walmart Effect" in the United States and elsewhere. While members of parliament debated the merits and the drawbacks of retail FDI, protesters sought to physically disrupt the work of parliament. Some activists even argued that giant foreign retailers such as Walmart might represent "dark" foreign interests intending to "recolonize" India—after all, the East Indian Company had first come as a trader several hundred years ago. Interested in shopkeepers' votes, a humiliated government announced in December 2011 that it would suspend FDI reforms on *multi-brand* retail.

In January 2012, the Indian government confirmed that single-brand retailers could be 100% foreign owned—with a condition that 30% of the value be sourced from Indian small and medium-sized enterprises (SMEs). The single-brand retailer IKEA, which had been eager to enter India, announced that it had to postpone its plan because it could not meet the sourcing requirement. Instead, IKEA would focus on expanding in China and Russia, where no such restrictions existed.

Even in the case of FDI in single-brand retailers, the process was not smooth. The federal policy was an enabling legal framework, which would need to be approved by each of the 36 states. Some states gave support and allowed FDI in single-brand retail in their territories, and some states declined. In 2012, the state government of Delhi, National Capital Territory (NCT), gave its support. Then in 2014, a new state government from a different party was elected and sought to reverse the support for such FDI. However, the (federal) Ministry of Commerce and Industry rejected such policy reversal within a state (NCT), in fear that foreign investors would think of India as an "unpredictable banana republic." Once a state gave its consent to support FDI, asserted the Ministry, the state could not withdraw its support merely because of a change of the party in power.

In 2016, the federal government made another push: 100% foreign ownership would be allowed in multi-brand food retailing—with a catch that such food products would be sourced and processed in India. As in 2011, debates erupted again. Supporters hailed this move as a concrete step to implement the new "Make in India" initiative. Opposition forced the government to agree with a major concession: "nothing personal"—no personal care and household products would be permitted. But retailers complained that selling low-margin food products alone would not make business sense and that they needed to be given the freedom to experiment with nonfood products. To overcome such hesitation, the government no longer imposed a minimal investment amount. Further, a nontrivial incentive was offered: 100% income tax exemption for the first five years and 25% for the next five. Given FDI's tumultuous history in this industry and India's diverse politics and stakeholders, how many foreign investors will show up remains to be seen.

Case Discussion Questions

1. What are the possible benefits of FDI in the Indian retail industry?

2. What are the possible drawbacks of FDI in this industry?

3. India is a tantalizing market with huge potential and with onerous restrictions. As an executive at Walmart, Tesco, or IKEA whose domestic growth at home is sluggish, how would you approach this market?

Sources: "Retailers like Walmart, Tesco to gain as govt allows 100% FDI in multi-brand processed food retailing," *Economic Times*, 1 March 2016: economictimes.indiatimes.com; "Government won't include personal care products under FDI in food retail," *Economic Times*, 27 August 2016: economictimes.indiatimes.com; "FDI in retailing of food products is the most significant," *Economic Times*, 21 June 2016: economictimes.indiatimes.com; "Send for the supermarketers," *Economist*, 16 April 2011: 67–68; "The supermarket's last frontier," *Economist*, 3 December 2011: 75–76; "Delhi government can't de-notify FDI in retail, says Centre," *Hindu*, 21 January 2014: www.thehindu.com; India Brand Equity Foundation, *Retail*, 2016: www.ibef.org; "Wal-Mart, thwarted by India's retail restrictions, goes big: wholesale," *Los Angeles Times*, 23 July 2015: www.latimes.com; Ministry of Commerce and Industry, "Press note no. 1 (2012 series)," 10 January 2012.

STUDY TOOLS 6

LOCATED AT THE BACK OF YOUR BOOK:

☐ Rip out and study the Chapter Review Card at the end of the book

LOG IN TO WWW.CENGAGEBRAIN.COM TO:

☐ Review key term flashcards

☐ Complete a practice quiz to test your knowledge of key concepts

☐ View animated PengAtlas Maps

☐ Complete interactive content, watch chapter videos, and take a graded quiz

☐ Track your knowledge of key concepts in Global Business

☐ Read and discuss additional case study content

7 Dealing with Foreign Exchange

LEARNING OBJECTIVES

After studying this chapter, you will be able to . . .

7-1 List the factors that determine foreign exchange rates.

7-2 Articulate and explain the steps in the evolution of the international monetary system.

7-3 Identify strategic responses firms can take to deal with foreign exchange movements.

7-4 Identify three things you need to know about currency when doing business internationally.

After you finish this chapter, go to

PAGE 119 for

STUDY TOOLS

ETHICAL DILEMMA
Opening Case: The All-Mighty Dollar

For seven decades, the dollar has reigned supreme in the global economy. Although the US share of the global economy has fallen—relative to its rivals—and its politics have turned inward, the dollar remains indispensable. While the United States contributes 23% of global GDP (measured at official exchange rates), 12% of merchandise trade, and 35% of market capitalization, 60% of the world's foreign exchange holdings are in dollars—followed by 26% in euros, 4% in pounds, 3% in yen, and 1% in yuan. Measured at purchasing power parity (PPP), China (including Hong Kong and Macau) has caught up, running neck and neck with the United States, each with approximately 16% of global GDP (China's contribution using official exchange rates is 14%). The United States is the biggest export market for 32 countries, down from 44 in 1994. The comparative numbers for China grow from 2 to 43. Yet, no American firm bothers to list in Shanghai, while a small number of elite Chinese firms such as Alibaba enjoy a badge of honor for their ability to successfully chase the dollar by listing in New York. Widely viewed as a major source of soft power, the dollar helps American firms trade or invest abroad with less currency risk. Whenever an economic crisis erupts, the dollar is typically the safe haven to which investors rush. Swiss bankers, Mexican drug lords, and corrupt Chinese officials all prefer to hold and transact using the all-mighty dollar.

What is the proper role of the dollar? This is a trillion-dollar question. The recent economic turmoil has intensified the global debate. In terms of international trade competitiveness, a strong dollar makes it harder for US firms to export and to compete on price when combating imports at home (see Exhibit 7.1). Conversely, a weak dollar may facilitate more US exports and stem import growth. Since the Plaza Accord of 1985, after which the dollar declined sharply against the Japanese yen, the United States has been pursuing a "cheap (weak) dollar" policy.

While critics in an influential *Economist* (2015) report argue that the dominance of the dollar in the face of fading US economic supremacy is "unsustainable," its would-be contenders are in a worse shape. The euro, the same *Economist* report opined, "is a currency whose very existence cannot be taken for granted." Thanks to Brexit, the pound has taken a severe pounding. The yen is a forgotten currency to which nobody outside Japan has paid much attention for two decades. The newest darling, the yuan, is on the lips of many bankers from Hong Kong to London. But it is an underachiever. Despite progress, the yuan is not fully internationalized. Only less than 10% of China's trade with the world uses the yuan. The presence of yuan payments over the SWIFT system used by global banks is only 1%—as opposed to the dollar's 50%. The freely traded part

EXHIBIT 7.1	A STRONG DOLLAR VERSUS A WEAK DOLLAR

A Strong (Appreciating) Dollar

Advantages	Disadvantages
▸ US consumers benefit from low prices on imports	▸ US exporters have a hard time competing on price abroad
▸ Lower prices on foreign goods help keep US price level and inflation level low	▸ US firms in import-competing industries have a hard time competing with low-cost imports
▸ US tourists enjoy lower prices abroad	▸ Foreign tourists find it more expensive when visiting the US
▸ US firms find it easier to acquire foreign targets	

A Weak (Depreciating) Dollar

Advantages	Disadvantages
▸ US exporters find it easier to compete on price abroad	▸ US consumers face higher prices on imports
▸ US firms face less competitive pressure to keep prices low	▸ Higher prices on imports contribute to higher price level and inflation level in the US
▸ Foreign tourists enjoy lower prices in the US	▸ US tourists find it more expensive when traveling abroad
▸ Foreign firms find it easier to acquire US targets	▸ Governments, firms, and individuals outside the US holding dollar-denominated assets suffer from value loss of their assets
▸ The US can print more dollars (quantitative easing) to export its problems to the rest of the world	

of China's stock markets is only the size of Switzerland's. In other words, although China is a giant in trade and FDI, it is "a mid-sized power in finance, currencies, and financial markets," according to the same *Economist* report.

Overall, the rise of the yuan will be slower than commonly predicted. At best, according to experts in *Foreign Affairs*, the yuan will assume a place among secondary reserve currencies, such as the euro, the pound, the yen, and the Swiss franc. But it is "a far cry from displacing the dollar." There are generally long lags between a country's emergence as a leading economic power and the widespread use of its currency by foreigners. As early as in 1872, the US economy became larger than Britain's. But it took 70 years (including two World Wars) for the dollar to displace the pound as the reigning international currency. So, what are the two lessons from history? First, a country that does not grow its economy cannot continue to provide adequate liquidity to the global economy indefinitely. At some point, the tension between the real economic clout and the financial muscle will cause the fault line to collapse. Second, the process will take a very long time. At present, thanks to the economic weaknesses in the rest of the world and the strengths of the US economy (January 2017 unemployment rate was only at 4.7%, less than 1% away from full employment), the dollar recently enjoyed the rise to a 14-year high against a basket of six major currencies. Boeing, 3M, and United Technologies issued warnings about the damage in export markets done by the strong dollar. In summary, a strong dollar was bad for US growth, potentially threatening 400,000 jobs. The all-*naughty* dollar might wash away a lot of President Donald Trump's job-creation efforts.

Sources: "Whose money will the world follow?" *Bloomberg Businessweek*, 18 May 2015: 10–11; "A serious pounding," *Bloomberg Businessweek*, 12 December 2016: 17–18; "Donald and the dollar," *Bloomberg Businessweek*, 12 December 2016: 15; "Dollar so ripped, it might actually rip," *Bloomberg Businessweek*, 9 January 2017: 12–13; "A longer march," *Economist*, 3 October 2015: 12–14; "Dominant and dangerous," *Economist*, 3 October 2015: 8; "The sticky superpower," *Economist*, 3 October 2015: 3–6; B. Eichengreen, "When currencies collapse," *Foreign Affairs*, January 2012: 117–134; S. Mallaby and O. Wethington, "The future of the yuan," *Foreign Affairs*, January 2012: 135–146.

Why is the value of currencies so important in the global economy? What determines foreign exchange rates? How do foreign exchange rates affect trade and investment undertaken by firms such as Alibaba, Boeing, 3M, and United Technologies? Finally, how can firms respond strategically? This chapter addresses these crucial questions. At the heart of our discussion lie the two core perspectives introduced earlier: the institution-based and resource-based views. Essentially, the institution-based view suggests that domestic and international institutions (such as the International Monetary Fund [IMF]) influence foreign exchange rates and affect capital movements. In turn, the resource-based view sheds light on how firms can profit from favorable foreign exchange movements by developing their own firm-specific resources and capabilities.

We start with a basic question: What determines foreign exchange rates? Then, we track the evolution of the international monetary system culminating in the IMF, and continue with firms' strategic responses.

South America

7-1 WHAT DETERMINES FOREIGN EXCHANGE RATES?

foreign exchange rate The price of one currency in terms of another.

appreciation An increase in the value of the currency.

depreciation A loss in the value of the currency.

A **foreign exchange rate** is the price of one currency, such as the dollar ($), in terms of another, such as the euro (€). Exhibit 7.2 provides some examples. An **appreciation** is an increase in the value of the currency, and a **depreciation** is a loss in the value of the currency. This section addresses a key question: What determines foreign exchange rates?

7-1a Basic Supply and Demand

The concept of an exchange rate as the price of a commodity—in this case, a country's currency—helps us understand its determinants. Basic economic theory suggests that a commodity's price is fundamentally determined by its supply and demand. Strong demand will lead to price hikes, and oversupply will result in price drops. Of course, here we are dealing with a most unusual commodity—money—but the basic principles still apply. When the United States sells products to China, US exporters often demand that they be paid in US dollars because the Chinese yuan is useless (or, using the technical term, nonconvertible) in the United States. Chinese importers of US products must somehow generate US dollars in order to pay for US imports. The easiest way to generate US dollars is to *export* to the United States, whose buyers pay in US dollars. In this example, the dollar is the common transaction currency involving both US imports and US exports. As a result, the demand for dollars is much stronger than the demand for yuan (while holding the supply constant). A wide variety of users, such as Chinese exporters, Colombian drug dealers, and Russian bankers, prefer to hold and transact in US dollars, thus fueling the demand for dollars. Such a strong demand explains why the US dollar is the most sought after currency in the postwar decades (see Opening Case). At present, about 60% of the world's foreign exchange holdings are in US dollars, followed by 26% in euros, 4% in pounds, 3% in yen, and 1% in yuan.

EXHIBIT 7.2 EXAMPLES OF KEY CURRENCY EXCHANGE RATES

	US dollar (US$)	Euro (€)	UK pound (£)	Swiss franc (CHF)	Mexican peso (Mex$)	Japanese yen (¥)	Canadian dollar (C$)
Canadian dollar (C$)	1.32	1.41	1.65	1.31	0.06	0.012	—
Japanese yen (¥)	114	122	142	114	5.29	—	86.48
Mexican peso (Mex$)	21.53	23.10	26.95	21.51	—	0.189	16.36
Switzerland franc (CHF)	1.00	1.07	1.25	—	0.05	0.009	0.76
UK pound (£)	0.80	0.86	—	0.80	0.04	0.007	0.61
Euro (€)	0.93	—	1.17	0.93	0.04	0.008	0.71
US dollar (US$)	—	1.07	1.25	1.00	0.05	0.009	0.76

Source: Adapted from "Key currency cross rates," *Wall Street Journal*, 24 January 2017: www.wsj.com. Reading vertically, the first column means US$1 = C$1.32 = ¥114 = Mex$21.53 = 1 CHF = £0.80 = €0.93. Reading horizontally, the last row means €1 = US$1.07; £1 = US$1.25; 1 CHF = US$1; Mex$1 = US$0.05; ¥1 = US$0.009; C$1 = US$0.76.

EXHIBIT 7.3 WHAT DETERMINES FOREIGN EXCHANGE RATES?

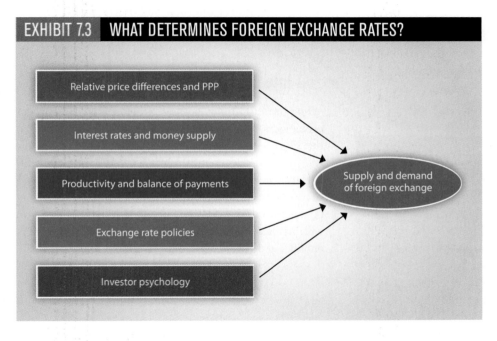

The next question is: What determines the supply and demand of foreign exchange? Because foreign exchange involves such a unique commodity, its markets are influenced by not only economic but also political and psychological factors. Exhibit 7.3 sketches the five underlying building blocks, which are discussed next.

7-1b Relative Price Differences and Purchasing Power Parity

Some countries (such as Switzerland) have famously expensive prices, and others (such as the Philippines) are known to have cheap prices. How do these price differences affect exchange rates? An answer is provided by the theory of purchasing power parity (PPP). Recall from Chapter 1 that PPP is a conversion that determines the equivalent amount of goods and services different currencies can purchase. This conversion is usually used to capture the differences in cost of living between countries. PPP is essentially the "law of one price." The theory suggests that in the absence of trade barriers (such as tariffs), the price for identical products sold in different countries must be the same. Otherwise, traders may buy low and sell high, eventually driving different prices for identical products to the same level around the world. The PPP theory argues that in the long run, exchange rates should move toward levels that would equalize the prices of an identical basket of goods in any two countries.

Exhibit 7.4 shows that in 2017, a Big Mac cost $5.06 in the United States, but just $2.83 in China. We can determine the local price in yuan by using the local price in dollars reported ($2.83) and the official exchange rate of 6.88 yuan to the dollar. The local price was 19.47 yuan (which is 6.88 yuan × $2.83). If the Big Mac indeed cost the same, the de facto exchange rate based on the Big Mac index became 3.85 yuan to the dollar (which is 19.47 yuan/$5.06). According to this calculation, the yuan was 44% "undervalued" against the dollar ([6.88 − 3.85] Y 6.88). But the yuan, which several years ago used to be the most undervalued currency, was only the 12th most undervalued currency in the Big Mac universe (not every one of the undervalued currencies is shown in Exhibit 7.4). The Russian ruble, the Mexican peso, and the Indian rupee were the most undervalued currencies (in that order). In other words, the Big Mac in Russia and Mexico and the chicken-based Maharaja Mac in India (where the beef-based Big Mac is not available) had the best "value" in the world, based on official exchange rates. They only cost $2.15, $2.23, and $2.49, respectively.[1] Overall, four observations emerge:

▶ The Big Mac index confirms that prices in some European countries are very expensive. A Big Mac in Switzerland was the most expensive in the world, costing $6.35.

▶ Big Macs in emerging economies are cheap in dollar terms. This makes sense because a Big Mac is a product with both traded and non-traded inputs. To simplify our discussion, let us assume that the costs for traded inputs (such as flour for the bun) are the same, it is obvious that non-traded inputs (such as labor and real estate) are cheaper in emerging economies.

▶ The Big Mac is not a traded product. No large number of American hamburger lovers would travel to Russia simply to get the best deal on the Big Mac, and then somehow take with them large quantities of the made-in-Russia Big Mac (perhaps in portable freezers). If they did that, the Big Mac price in Russia would be driven up and the price in the United States pushed down—remember supply and demand?

▶ After having a laugh, we shouldn't read too much into this index. PPP signals where exchange rates may move in the *long run*. But it does not suggest that the yuan should appreciate by 44% or the Swiss franc should depreciate by 25% next year. According to the *Economist*, anyone interested in the PPP theory "would be unwise to exclude the Big Mac index from their diet, but Super Size servings (of this index) would equally be a mistake."[2]

7-1c Interest Rates and Money Supply

While the PPP theory suggests the long-run direction of exchange rate movement, what about the short run? In the short run, variations in interest rates have a powerful effect. If one country's interest rates are high relative to other countries, that country will attract foreign funds. Because inflows of foreign funds usually need to be converted to the home currency, a high interest rate will increase the demand for the home currency, thus enhancing its exchange value.

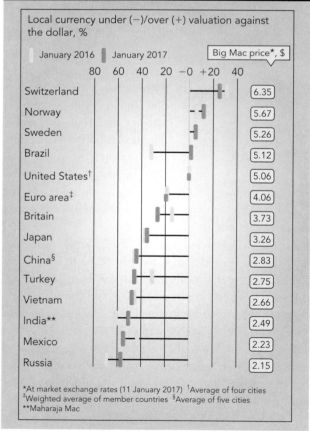

EXHIBIT 7.4 THE BIG MAC INDEX

Local currency under (−)/over (+) valuation against the dollar, %

	January 2016	January 2017	Big Mac price*, $
Switzerland			6.35
Norway			5.67
Sweden			5.26
Brazil			5.12
United States[†]			5.06
Euro area[‡]			4.06
Britain			3.73
Japan			3.26
China[§]			2.83
Turkey			2.75
Vietnam			2.66
India**			2.49
Mexico			2.23
Russia			2.15

Scale: 80 60 40 20 −0 +20 40

*At market exchange rates (11 January 2017) [†]Average of four cities
[‡]Weighted average of member countries [§]Average of five cities
**Maharaja Mac

Sources: "The all-meaty dollar," *Economist*, 14 January 2017: 66. © The Economist Newspaper Limited.

NAPOCSKA/SHUTTERSTOCK.COM

A young woman eats a Big Mac in Budapest, Hungary, where the hamburger costs $3.05—an undervaluation of 39.6%.

EXHIBIT 7.5 THE SIMPLIFIED US BALANCE OF PAYMENTS (BILLION DOLLARS)

I. Current Account

1. Exports of goods (merchandise)	1,460	
2. Imports of goods (merchandise)	−2,210	
3. Balance on goods (merchandise trade—lines 1 + 2)		**−750**
4. Exports of services	752	
5. Imports of services	−503	
6. Balance on services (service trade—lines 4 + 5)		**249**
7. Balance on goods and services (trade deficit/surplus—lines 3 + 6)		**−501**
8. Primary income receipts on US-owned assets abroad	802	
9. Secondary income receipts (mostly government grants and private remittances)	128	
10. Primary income payments on foreign-owned assets in the US	−621	
11. Secondary income payments (mostly government grants and private remittances)	−289	
12. Balance on current account (deficit/surplus—lines 7 + 8 + 9 + 10 + 11)		**−481**

II. Financial Account

13. US-owned private assets abroad (increase/financial outflow = −)	−331	
14. Foreign-owned private assets in the US	759	
15. Financial derivatives, net transaction (net US cash payments = −)	−22	
16. Balance on financial account (lines 13 + 14 + 15)		**406**
17. Overall balance of payments (Official reserve transactions balance—lines 12 + 16)		**−75**

Source: This is a simplified table adapted from US Department of Commerce, Bureau of Economic Analysis, *US International Transactions: Fourth Quarter and Year 2016*, Table 1, 21 March 2017, Washington: BEA (www.bea.gov [accessed 28 April 2017]). This table refers to 2016. The official table has 109 lines. Numbers may not add due to rounding.

7-1d Productivity and Balance of Payments

A rise in a country's productivity relative to other countries will improve its competitive position in international trade. This is the basic proposition of the theories of absolute and comparative advantage discussed in Chapter 5. In turn, more FDI will be attracted to the country, fueling demand for its home currency. One recent example is China. Most of the China-bound FDI inflows in dollars, euros, and pounds have to be converted to the local currency, boosting the demand for the yuan and hence its value.

Recall from Chapter 5 that changes in productivity will change a country's balance of trade. A country highly productive in manufacturing may generate a merchandise trade surplus, whereas a country less productive in manufacturing may end up with a merchandise trade deficit. These have ramifications for the **balance of payments (BOP)**, which is officially known as a country's international transaction statement and includes merchandise trade, service trade, and capital movement. Exhibit 7.5 shows that the United States had a merchandise trade deficit of $750 billion and a service trade surplus of $249 billion in 2016. In addition to merchandise and service trade, we add receipts on US assets abroad (such as repatriated earning from US multinational enterprises [MNEs] in Ireland and dividends paid by Japanese firms to American shareholders), subtract payments on US-based foreign assets (such as repatriated earnings from Canadian MNEs in the United States to Canada and dividends paid by US firms to Dutch shareholders), and government grants and private remittances (such as US foreign aid

In addition, a country's rate of inflation relative to that prevailing abroad affects its ability to attract foreign funds and hence its exchange rate. A high level of inflation is essentially too much money chasing too few goods in an economy. Technically, it is an expansion of a country's money supply. When a government faces budgetary shortfalls, it may choose to print more currency—known as "quantitative easing" as a recent euphemism. More currency tends to stimulate inflation. Inflation, in turn, would cause the currency to depreciate. Why does this chain of events happen? As the supply of a given currency (such as the Mexican peso) increases while the demand stays the same, the per unit value of that currency (such as one peso) goes down. Therefore, the exchange rate is highly sensitive to changes in monetary policy. It responds swiftly to changes in money supply. To avoid losses from holding assets in a depreciated currency, investors sell them for assets denominated in other currencies. Such massive sell-offs may worsen the depreciation. This happened in Britain during the aftermath of its 2016 Brexit referendum. Expressing a lack of confidence, numerous investors sold off assets held in pound sterling, forcing it to depreciate 18% against the dollar.[3]

balance of payments (BOP) A country's international transaction statement, which includes merchandise trade, service trade, and capital movement.

thrown at Iraq and the money that Mexican farm hands in America sent home). After doing all of the math, we can see that the United States ran a $481 billion current account deficit. Technically, the current account balance consists of exports minus imports of merchandise and services, plus primary income receipts on a country's assets abroad minus payments on foreign assets in the focal country, plus secondary income receipts minus payments (mostly government transfers and private remittances).

A current account deficit has to be financed by financial account—consisting of purchases and sales of assets. This is because a country needs to balance its accounts in much the same way as a family deals with its finances. Any deficit in a family budget has to be financed by drawing from savings or by borrowing. In a similar fashion, the overall US deficit of $75 billion was financed by drawing from savings and borrowing (for example, selling US government securities such as Treasury bonds to foreign central banks such as the People's Bank of China).

To make a long story short, a country experiencing a current account surplus will see its currency appreciate. Conversely, a country experiencing a current account deficit will see its currency depreciate. This will not happen overnight, but will take place over a span of years and decades. The current movement between the yuan (appreciating) and the dollar (depreciating) is but one example. In the 1950s and 1960s, the rise of the dollar was accompanied by a sizable US surplus on merchandise trade. By the 1970s and 1980s, the surplus gradually turned into a deficit. By the 1990s and 2000s, the US current account deficit increased, forcing the dollar to depreciate relative to other currencies such as the yuan, the euro, and the Canadian dollar. Broadly speaking, the value of a country's currency is an embodiment of its economic strengths as reflected in its productivity and BOP positions.

Some foreign exchange investors use sophisticated software to buy and sell automatically. This software uses historical trends, market condition analysis, and real-time data to make hundreds of trades per day.

allow it to determine exchange rates, usually on a daily basis via the foreign exchange market. However, few countries adopt a **clean** (or **free**) **float**, which would be a pure market solution. Most countries practice a **dirty** (or **managed**) **float**, with selective government interventions. Of the major currencies, the US, Canadian, and Australian dollars, the yen, and the pound have been under managed float since the 1970s (after the collapse of the Bretton Woods system, which we will discuss in the next section). Since the late 1990s, Brazil, China, Hungary, Mexico, Poland, South Korea, and numerous other countries have also joined the managed float regime. Despite complaints from the US government, China currently does *not* fix its currency. Since 2005, China has been allowing the yuan to float—from 8.3 yuan to the dollar in 2005 to 6.88 yuan to the dollar in 2017 (a 17% appreciation).

The severity of intervention is a matter of degree. Heavier intervention moves the country closer to a fixed exchange rate policy, and less intervention enables a country to approach the free float ideal. A main objective for intervention is to prevent erratic fluctuations that may trigger macroeconomic turbulence. Some countries do not adhere to any particular rates. Others choose **target exchange rates**, which are specified upper and lower bounds within which the exchange rate is allowed to fluctuate. These are also known as **crawling bands**. A country that uses target exchange rates—an approach called "snake in a tube"—will intervene only when the snake (the exchange rate) crawls out of the tube (the upper or lower bounds). Technically, the

7-1e Exchange Rate Policies

There are two major exchange rate policies: floating rate and fixed rate. The **floating** (or **flexible**) **exchange rate policy** is the willingness of a government to let demand and supply conditions determine exchange rates. Governments adopting this policy tend to believe in the free market and yuan is now allowed to float, but only within a limited tube (up to 0.5% fluctuation per day).

The second major exchange rate policy is the **fixed exchange rate policy**. A country adopting a fixed rate policy fixes the exchange rate of its domestic currency relative to other currencies. A specific version of fixed rate policy involves pegging the domestic currency, which means to set the exchange rate of the domestic currency in terms of another currency (the peg). Many developing countries, for example, peg their currencies to the US dollar. There are two benefits to a peg policy. First, a peg stabilizes the import and export prices. Second, many countries with high inflation have pegged their currencies to the dollar in order to restrain domestic inflation because the United States has relatively low inflation.

ISTOCK.COM/DIMOS

7-1f Investor Psychology

While theories on price differences (PPP), interest rates and money supply, balance of payments, and exchange rate policies predict long-run movements of exchange rates, they often fall short of predicting short-run movements. What then determines short-run movements? They are largely driven by investor psychology, some of which is fickle and thus very hard to predict. Professor Richard Lyons at the University of California, Berkeley, is an expert on exchange rate theories. He was baffled when he observed currency trading firsthand:

> *As I sat there, my friend traded furiously all day long, racking up over $1 billion in trades each day. This was a world where the standard trade was $10 million, and a $1 million trade was a "skinny one." Despite my belief that exchange rates depend on macroeconomics, only rarely was news of this type his primary concern. Most of the time he was reading tea leaves that were, at least to me, not so clear. . . . It was clear my understanding was incomplete when he looked over, in the midst of his fury, and asked me: "What should I do?" I laughed. Nervously.*[4]

Investors—currency traders (such as the one Lyons observed), foreign portfolio investors, and average citizens—may move in the same direction at the same time, like a herd, resulting in a **bandwagon effect**. The bandwagon effect seemed to be at play in August 2014, when the Argentinean peso plunged against key currencies such as the US dollar, the euro, and the pound sterling. Essentially, a large number of individuals and firms exchanged the peso for the key foreign currencies in order to minimize their exposure to Argentina's sovereign default (its second since 2001)—a phenomenon known as **capital flight**. This would push down the demand for, and thus the value of, the domestic currency. Then, more individuals and companies joined the "herd," further depressing the exchange rate and worsening an economic crisis.

Overall, economics, politics, and psychology are all at play. The stakes are high, yet consensus is rare regarding the determinants of foreign exchange rates. As a result, predicting the direction of currency movements remains an art or, at best, a highly imprecise science.

7-2 EVOLUTION OF THE INTERNATIONAL MONETARY SYSTEM

Having outlined the basic determinants of exchange rates, let us examine the history of the international monetary system, divided into three eras: the gold standard, the Bretton Woods system, and the post–Bretton Woods system.

7-2a The Gold Standard (1870–1914)

The **gold standard** was in place from 1870 to

fixed exchange rate policy A government policy to set the exchange rate of a currency relative to other currencies.

bandwagon effect The effect of investors moving in the same direction at the same time, like a herd.

capital flight A phenomenon in which a large number of individuals and companies exchange domestic currencies for a foreign currency.

gold standard A system in which the value of most major currencies was maintained by fixing their prices in terms of gold.

1914 and fixed the value of most major currencies in terms of gold. Gold was used as the **common denominator** for all currencies, which means that all currencies were pegged at a fixed rate to gold. The gold standard was essentially a global peg system with little volatility and a great deal of predictability and stability. To be able to redeem its currency in gold at a fixed price, every central bank needed to maintain gold reserves. The system provided powerful incentives for countries to run current account surpluses, resulting in net inflows of gold.

TONCHIK1981/GETTY IMAGES

7-2b The Bretton Woods System (1944–1973)

The gold standard was abandoned in 1914 when several World War I (WWI) combatant countries printed excessive amounts of currency to finance their war efforts. After WWI, especially during the Great Depression (1929–1933), countries engaged in competitive devaluations in an effort to boost exports at the expense of trading partners. But no country could win such a race to the bottom, and the gold standard had to be jettisoned.

Toward the end of World War II (WWII), at an allied conference in Bretton Woods, New Hampshire, a new system, known simply as the **Bretton Woods system**, was agreed upon by 44 countries. The system was centered on the US dollar as the new common denominator. All currencies were pegged at a fixed rate to the dollar. Only the dollar was convertible to gold at $35 per ounce. Other currencies were not required to be gold convertible.

The Bretton Woods system propelled the dollar to the commanding heights of the global economy. This system reflected the higher US productivity level and the large trade surplus the United States had with the rest of the world in the first two postwar decades. At the end of WWII, the US economy contributed approximately 70% of the global GDP and was the export engine and growth engine of the world.

common denominator A currency or commodity to which the value of all currencies are pegged.

Bretton Woods system A system in which all currencies were pegged at a fixed rate to the US dollar.

post–Bretton Woods system A system of flexible exchange rate regimes with no official common denominator.

7-2c The Post–Bretton Woods System (1973–Present)

By the late 1960s and early 1970s, a combination of rising productivity elsewhere and US inflationary policies led to the demise of Bretton Woods. First, in the 1960s, President Lyndon Johnson increased government spending in order to finance both the Vietnam War and Great Society welfare programs. He did this not by additional taxation but by increasing money supply. These actions led to rising inflation levels and strong pressures for the dollar to depreciate. Second, the United States ran its first post-1945 trade deficit in 1971 as (West) Germany and other countries caught up to the United States in productivity and increased their exports. This pushed the (West) German mark to appreciate and the dollar to depreciate, a situation very similar to the yen–dollar relationship in the 1980s and the yuan–dollar relationship in the 2000s.

As currency traders bought more German marks, Germany's central bank, the Bundesbank, had to buy billions of dollars to maintain the dollar/mark exchange rate fixed by Bretton Woods. Being stuck with massive amounts of the dollar that were worth less now, Germany unilaterally allowed its currency to float in 1971.

The Bretton Woods system also became a pain in the neck for the United States because the exchange rate of the dollar was not allowed to unilaterally change. Per Bretton Woods agreements, the US Treasury was obligated to dispense one ounce of gold for every $35 brought to it by a foreign central bank such as the Bundesbank. Consequently, the United States was hemorrhaging gold into the coffers of foreign central banks. In order to stop the flow of gold out of the Treasury, President Richard Nixon unilaterally announced in 1971 that the dollar was no longer convertible into gold. After tense negotiations, the major countries collectively agreed in 1973 to allow their currencies to float, thus ending the Bretton Woods system. In retrospect, the Bretton Woods system had been built on two conditions. First, the US inflation rate had to be low. Second, the United States could not run a trade deficit. When both of these conditions were violated, the system's demise was inevitable.

As a result, today we live with a **post–Bretton Woods system**, which has no official common denominator and is characterized by the diversity of exchange rate systems discussed earlier (various floating systems and fixed rates). Diversity and flexibility are its strengths. Its drawbacks are turbulence and uncertainty. Although the US dollar has not been the official common denominator since the early

Ukrainian President Petro Poroshenko (left) speaks with IMF director Christine Lagarde during a 2017 summit in Davos, Switzerland.

1970s, the dollar has retained a significant amount of soft power as a key currency (see Opening Case). In November 2008 and then in April 2009, in the midst of the worst financial crisis in recent times, leaders of the Group of 20 (G-20) held two summits: first in Washington, DC, and then in London. Both summits called for an overhaul of the world's financial structure. These summits were labeled by the media as an effort to construct "Bretton Woods II."[5] The dust has yet to settle on the outcome of these efforts.

7-2d The International Monetary Fund

While the Bretton Woods system is no longer with us, one of its most enduring legacies is the **International Monetary Fund (IMF)**, founded in 1944 as a Bretton Woods institution. (The World Bank is the other Bretton Woods institution.) The IMF's mandate is to promote international monetary cooperation, exchange stability, and orderly exchange arrangements.

Lending is a core responsibility of the IMF, which provides loans to countries experiencing balance of payments problems. The IMF can be viewed as a lender of last resort to help member countries out of financial difficulty. Where does the IMF get its funds? The answer boils down to the same principle as how insurance companies obtain their funds to pay out insurance claims. Similar to insurance companies collecting premiums from subscribers to accumulate the funds necessary to cover claims, the IMF collects funds from member countries. Each member country is assigned a **quota** that determines its financial contribution to the IMF (technically known as its "subscription"), its capacity to borrow from the IMF, and its voting power. The quota is broadly based on a country's relative size in the global economy.

By definition, the IMF makes loans, not grants. IMF loans usually have to be repaid in one to five years. Although payments have been extended in some cases, no member country has defaulted. An ideal IMF loan scenario would be a balance of payments crisis that threatens to severely disrupt a country's financial stability, such as when it imports more than it exports and cannot pay for imports. The IMF could step in and inject funds in the short term to help stabilize the financial system.

While an IMF loan provides short-term financial resources, it also comes with strings attached. Those strings are long-term policy reforms that recipient countries must undertake as conditions of receiving the loan. These conditions usually entail belt tightening and push governments to undertake painful reforms that they otherwise probably would not have undertaken. For example, when the IMF (together with the EU) provided a loan to Greece in 2010, the Greek government agreed to cut pensions and wages for public sector employees by 15% to 20% in order to pay for government debt.[6] Since the 1990s, the IMF has helped Mexico (1994), Russia (1996 and 1998), Asia (Indonesia, South Korea, and Thailand, 1997), Turkey (2001), Brazil (2002), Iceland (2008), Ukraine (2008), Hungary (2008), Greece (2010), and several others.

While the IMF has noble goals, its actions are not without criticisms that call for reforms. A new alternative international organization, which is simply called the New Development Bank (NDB), has recently been set up by the BRICS countries (see Debate).

7-3 STRATEGIC RESPONSES

From an institution-based view, knowledge about foreign exchange rates and the international monetary system (including the role of the IMF) helps paint a broad picture of the rules of the game that govern financial transactions around the world. Armed with this knowledge, savvy managers need to develop firm-specific resources and capabilities so they can rise to the challenge, or at least avoid having their firms crushed by unfavorable currency movements (see Opening and Closing Cases). This section outlines the strategic responses of two types of firms: financial and nonfinancial companies.

International Monetary Fund (IMF) An international organization that was established to promote international monetary cooperation, exchange stability, and orderly exchange arrangements.

quota The weight a member country carries within the IMF, which determines the amount of its financial contribution (technically known as its "subscription"), its capacity to borrow from the IMF, and its voting power.

Debate: International Monetary Fund versus New Development Bank and Asian Infrastructure Investment Bank

Emerging Markets/Ethical Dilemma

The complexity of the IMF's actions means that it cannot please everyone. Debates about the IMF rage throughout the world. First, critics argue that the IMF's lending may *facilitate* moral hazard, which means recklessness when people and organizations (including governments) do not have to face the full consequences of their actions. Moral hazard is inherent in all insurance arrangements, including the IMF. Basically, knowing that the IMF would come to the rescue, certain governments may behave more recklessly. For example, between 1958 and 2001, Turkey was rescued by 18 IMF loans.

A second criticism centers on the IMF's lack of accountability. Although the IMF can dictate terms over a host country that is being rescued and receiving loans, none of the IMF officials is democratically elected and most of them do not have deep knowledge of the host country. Consequently, they sometimes make disastrous decisions. For example, in 1997–1998, the IMF forced the Indonesian government to drastically cut back on food subsidies for the poor. Riots exploded the next day. Hundreds of people were killed and numerous properties damaged. Then, the IMF reversed its position by restoring food subsidies. However, in some quarters, the bitterness was all the greater. A lot of protesters argued: If food subsidies could have been continued, why were they taken away in the first place?

A third and perhaps most challenging criticism is that the IMF's "one-size-fits-all" strategy—otherwise known as the "bitter medicine"—may be inappropriate. Since the 1930s, in order to maintain more employment, most Western governments have abandoned the idea of balancing their budgets. Deficit spending has been used as a major policy weapon to pull a country out of an economic crisis. Yet, the IMF often demands governments in more vulnerable developing countries, in the midst of a major crisis, to balance their budgets by slashing spending (such as cutting food subsidies). These actions often make the crisis far worse than it needs to be. After the IMF came to "rescue" countries affected by the

1997 Asian financial crisis, the unemployment rate was up threefold in Thailand, fourfold in South Korea, and tenfold in Indonesia.

However, the momentum of the criticisms, the severity of the global crisis, and the desire to better serve the international community have facilitated a series of IMF reforms since 2009. Some of these reforms represent a total (180-degree) change from its previous directions, resulting in an "IMF 2.0" dubbed by *Time*. For example, the IMF now starts to promote more fiscal spending in order to stimulate the economy and to ease money supply and reduce interest rates, given the primary concern for the global economy now is deflation and recession, but not inflation. Obviously, the IMF's change of heart is affected by the tremendous stimulus packages unleashed by developed economies since 2008, which result in skyrocketing budget deficits. If the developed economies can (hopefully) use greater fiscal spending and budget deficits to pull themselves out of a crisis, the IMF simply cannot lecture developing economies that receive its loans to balance their budgets in the middle of a crisis. Further, given the stigma of receiving IMF loans and listening to and then implementing IMF lectures, many countries avoid the IMF until they run out of options. In response, in April 2009, the IMF unleashed a new Flexible Credit Line (FCL), which would be particularly useful for crisis *prevention* by providing the flexibility to draw on it at any time, with no strings attached—a radical contrast to its earlier requirement. Mexico, Colombia, and Poland have used the FCL so far.

Further, the IMF 2.0 has become three times bigger—leaders in the G20 Summit in London in 2009 agreed to enhance the IMF's funding from $250 billion to $750 billion. Of the $500 billion new funding (technically Special Drawing Rights [SDRs]), the United States, the EU, and Japan each was expected to contribute $100 billion. China signed up for $40 billion. Request for injection of substantial funding from emerging economies resulted in the calls for better representation of these countries. However, enhancing voting rights for emerging economies would lead to reduced shares for developed economies. As a result, progress is slow. Even with the new changes, Brazil, with 1.72% of the votes (up from the previous 1.38%), still carries less weight than Belgium (1.86%, down from the previous 2.09%). Despite having the world's second largest economy, China has failed to be admitted as one of the top five IMF shareholders—with 3.81% of the votes, it has become the sixth largest, behind the United States (16.75%), Japan (6.23%), Germany (5.81%), France (4.29%), and the UK (4.29%). Overall, Western countries, which have been overrepresented at the IMF, have refused to make room at the table for emerging economies.

In July 2014 at the sixth BRICS summit in Fortaleza, Brazil, BRICS countries—consisting of Brazil, Russia, India, China, and South Africa—agreed to launch a New Development Bank (NDB) as an alternative to the IMF. Launched in 2015 and headquartered in Shanghai, the NDB, previously known as the BRICS Development Bank, represents a significant block of countries that have 2.8 billion people (40% of the world's population), cover a quarter of the world's land area, and account for more than 25% of global GDP. Unlike the IMF, which assigns votes to member countries differently, the NDB assigns each of the five participating countries one vote (each country contributing $10 billion initial paid-in capital for a total of $50 billion). While the NDB will focus on infrastructure and sustainable development projects, BRICS have also set up a $100 billion Contingent Reserve Arrangement (CRA), with China contributing $41 billion, Brazil, Russia, and India each $18 billion, and South Africa $5 billion. Designed to provide protection against global liquidity pressures, the CRA is a precautionary instrument in response to actual or potential short-term balance of payments problems.

The NDB and the CRA were set up due to BRICS' frustration with the IMF. This is because in the IMF, BRICS only wield a combined total of 11% of the votes (after recent IMF reforms). Further, the NDB and the CRA were set up in response to the IMF's enforcement of conditions on countries seeking emergency loans. The founding statement signed by BRICS leaders has stated: "International governance structures designed within a different power configuration show increasingly evident signs of losing legitimacy and effectiveness." In a couple of decades and with expanding membership, the NDB may indeed become a rival of the IMF.

In addition, in 2015, China took the lead to launch a new Asian Infrastructure Investment Bank (AIIB) with 50 founding member countries. Not only did all other BRICS countries sign up, but most Asian developing countries also joined. Mostly interesting is that 13 members of NATO (such as Britain, France, and Germany) and US allies in Asia (such as Australia, New Zealand, and South Korea) also signed up, despite intense US lobbying for them not to join the China-led bank. At AIIB, China is supplying 30% of the capital and is imitating the US's veto rights at the IMF. How the NDB and the AIIB can coordinate the internal interests among diverse members and manage tricky external relationships with the IMF, the World Bank, and the United States remains to be seen.

Sources: R. Desai and J. Vreeland, "What the new bank of BRICS is all about," *Washington Post*, 17 July 2014: www.washingtonpost.com; "New fund, old fundamentals," *Economist*, 2 May 2009: 78; "Beyond Bretton Woods 2," *Economist*, 6 November 2010: 85–87; "The 70-year itch," *Economist*, 5 July 2014: 12; "A longer march," *Economist*, 3 October 2015: 12–14; R. Fuller, 2014, "Refusing to share: How the West created BRICS New Development Bank," www.rt.com; A. Ghosh, M. Chamon, C. Crowe, J. Kim, and J. Ostry, "Coping with the crisis: Policy options for emerging market countries," IMF staff position paper (Washington: IMF, 2009); C. Lagarde, "I try to spark new ideas," *Harvard Business Review* (November 2013): 111–114; New Development Bank, "About us," 2016: www.ndb.int; R. Rajan, "The future of the IMF and the World Bank," *American Economic Review* 98 (2008): 110–115; J. Stiglitz, *Globalization and Its Discontents* (New York: Norton, 2002); "International Monetary Fund 2.0," *Time*, 20 April 2009.

7-3a Strategies for Financial Companies

One of the leading strategic goals for financial companies is to profit from the foreign exchange market. The **foreign exchange market** is where individuals, firms, governments, and banks buy and sell currencies of other countries. Unlike a stock exchange, the foreign exchange market has no central, physical location. This market is truly global and transparent. Buyers and sellers are geographically dispersed but constantly linked, and quoted prices change as often as 20 times a *minute*.[7] Each week, the market opens first in Sydney, then Tokyo, Hong Kong, and Singapore. Gradually, Frankfurt, Zurich, Paris, London, New York, Chicago, and San Francisco wake up and come online.

Operating on a 24/7 basis, the foreign exchange market is the largest and most active market in the world. On average, the worldwide volume is approximately $5.3 trillion per *day*.[8] To put this mind-boggling number in perspective, the amount of one single *day* of foreign exchange transactions is more than three times the amount of entire worldwide FDI inflows in one *year* and more than one-third of worldwide merchandise exports in one *year*. Specifically, the foreign exchange market has two functions: (1) to service the needs of trade and investment and (2) to trade in its own commodity—namely, foreign exchange.

There are three primary types of foreign exchange transactions: spot transactions, forward transactions, and swaps. **Spot transactions** are the classic single-shot exchange of one currency for another. For example, Australian tourists visiting Italy go to a bank to exchange their Australian dollars for euros, essentially buying euros with Australian dollars.

Forward transactions allow participants to buy and sell currencies now for future delivery, typically in 30, 90, or 180 days after the date of the transaction. The primary benefit of forward transactions

foreign exchange market The market where individuals, firms, governments, and banks buy and sell currencies of other countries.

spot transaction The classic single-shot exchange of one currency for another.

forward transaction A foreign exchange transaction in which participants buy and sell currencies now for future delivery.

is to protect traders and investors from being exposed to the unfavorable fluctuations of the spot rate, an act known as **currency hedging**. Currency hedging is essentially a way to minimize the foreign exchange risk inherent in all non-spot transactions, which include most trade and FDI deals.[9] Traders and investors expecting to make or receive payments in a foreign currency in the future are concerned that they may be forced to make either a greater payment or receive less in terms of the domestic currency should the spot rate change. For example, if the forward rate of the euro (€/US$) is exactly the same as the spot rate, the euro is flat. If the forward rate of the euro per dollar is *higher* than the spot rate, the euro has a **forward discount**. If the forward rate of the euro per dollar is *lower* than the spot rate, the euro then has a **forward premium**.

Let's apply this to a hypothetical example. Assume that today's exchange rate of €/US$ is 1, that a US firm expects to be paid €1 million six months later, and that the euro is at a 180-day forward discount of 1.1 (or €1/US$1.1). The US firm could take out a forward contract now, and at the end of six months the euro earnings would be converted into $909,091 (€1 million/1.1). Does such a currency hedging move make sense? Maybe. The move makes sense if the firm knows in advance that the future spot rate will be higher. So in six months if the spot rate is 1.25, then the forward contract provides the US firm with $909,091 instead of $800,000 (€1 million/1.25). The difference is $109,091 (or 14% of $800,000). However, the move would backfire if after six months the spot rate were actually below 1.1. If the spot rate remained at 1, the firm could have earned $1 million *without* the forward contract, instead of only $909,091 with the contract. This simple example suggests a powerful observation: Currency hedging *requires* firms to have expectations or forecasts of future spot rates relative to forward rates.

Another major type of foreign exchange transactions is a swap. A **currency swap** is the conversion of one currency into another at Time 1, with an

agreement to revert it back to the original currency at a specified Time 2 in the future. Deutsche Bank may have an excess balance of pounds but needs dollars now. At the same time, Union Bank of Switzerland (UBS) may have more dollars than it needs at the moment and is looking for more pounds. The two banks can negotiate a swap agreement in which Deutsche Bank agrees to exchange pounds for dollars with UBS today and dollars for pounds at a specific point in the future.

The primary participants of the foreign exchange market are large international banks such as Deutsche Bank, UBS, and Citigroup, which trade among themselves. How do these banks make money by trading money? They make money by capturing the difference between their **offer rate** (the price to sell) and **bid rate** (the price to buy)—the bid rate is *always* lower than the offer rate. In other words, banks buy low and sell high. The difference between the offer rate and the bid rate is technically called the **spread**. For example, Citigroup may quote offer and bid rates for the Swiss franc at $1.0877 and $1.0874, respectively, and the spread is $0.0003. That is, Citigroup is willing to sell 1 million francs for $1,087,700 and buy 1 million francs for $1,087,400. If Citigroup can simultaneously buy and sell 1 million francs, it can make $300 (the spread of $0.0003 × 1 million francs). Given the instantaneous and transparent nature of the electronically linked foreign exchange market around the globe (one new quote in London can reach New York before you finish reading this *sentence*), the opportunities can come and go very quickly. The globally integrated nature of this market leads to three outcomes:

▸ A razor-thin spread.

▸ Quick (often literally split-second) decisions on buying and selling.

▸ Ever-increasing volume in order to make more profits.

To envision the quick decisions, remember the observation by Lyons mentioned earlier. To get a sense of the ever-increasing volume, recall the daily volume of over $5 trillion. In the example above, $300 is obviously "small peanuts" for Citigroup. Do a little math: How much trading in Swiss francs does Citigroup have to do in order to make $1 million in profits for itself?

---

currency hedging A transaction that protects traders and investors from exposure to the fluctuations of the spot rate.

forward discount A condition under which the forward rate of one currency relative to another currency is higher than the spot rate.

forward premium A condition under which the forward rate of one currency relative to another currency is lower than the spot rate.

currency swap A foreign exchange transaction between two firms in which one currency is converted into another at Time 1, with an agreement to revert it back to the original currency at a specified Time 2 in the future.

offer rate The price at which a bank is willing to sell a currency.

bid rate The price at which a bank is willing to buy a currency.

spread The difference between the offer price and the bid price.

Chinese Exporters Cope with Currency Fluctuation in Africa

In 2000, trade between China and Africa was only $10 billion. In 2010, the volume rocketed ahead to reach $127 billion. While China has become Africa's number-one trading partner, the downside of such intense trading is the complications of having to deal with currency fluctuation. The vast majority of the trade deals between China and Africa are conducted in US dollars, which have fluctuated substantially. Since the dollar is likely to depreciate and the yuan is likely to correspondingly appreciate further, Chinese exporters with costs in yuan and payments in dollars stand to lose. While currency hedging using forward contracts is an obvious coping strategy, many small exporters cannot afford the expenses. In addition, currency hedging is not risk-free. Wrong bets may end up burning firms big time.

To better cope with currency fluctuation, one straightforward mechanism for Chinese exporters is to insist on payment in yuan. The question is: Why would African importers agree to pay in yuan? Two compelling reasons emerge. First, Chinese exporters can save approximately 7% to 10% of their costs if they are paid in yuan. If they can share some of these gains with their African trading partners with lower prices, the new deal to use yuan as the common transaction currency becomes a win–win solution for both sides. Second, an increasing number of Chinese firms have engaged in foreign direct investment (FDI) in Africa. Their subsidiaries in Africa would be comfortable to use yuan to buy supplies, components, and manufactured products from home.

Getting paid in yuan would significantly eliminate the headache of currency fluctuation for Chinese exporters. By 2014, approximately 10% of China's foreign trade was already being settled in yuan. Little by little, China's currency is gaining ground in Africa and elsewhere. However, adding all international payments together, the yuan in 2014 only ranked 14th in the world, behind Russia's ruble and Thailand's baht, according to SWIFT, a company that specializes in transfer of funds between banks. Therefore, the rise of the "redback" as a major currency for international trade in Africa and beyond still has a long way to go.

Sources: G. Allard, "Chinese OFDI in Africa," in I. Alon, M. Fetscherin, and P. Gugler (eds.), *Chinese International Investments* (New York: Palgrave, 2012) 279–299; "Renminbi is popular in Africa," *21st Century Business Insights*, 16 September 2011: 26; "Yuan for the money," *Economist*, 9 February 2013: 14–15; "The red and the green," *Economist*, 26 April 2014: 44; "A longer march," *Economist*, 3 October 2015: 12–14.

7-3b Strategies for Nonfinancial Companies

How do nonfinancial companies cope with the potential losses they may incur due to fluctuations in the foreign exchange market, broadly known as **currency risks**? There are three primary strategies: (1) invoicing in their own currencies, (2) currency hedging (as discussed above), and (3) strategic hedging. The most basic way is to invoice customers in your own currency. By invoicing in dollars, many US firms have enjoyed such protection from unfavorable foreign exchange movements. As the euro becomes a more powerful currency, firms based in countries that use the euro now increasingly demand that they be paid in euros. In Focus illustrates how some Chinese exporters insist on getting paid in yuan from African importers.

Currency hedging is risky because, as discussed in the previous section, in trying to predict currency movements your bets could be all wrong.

Strategic hedging means spreading out activities in a number of countries in different currency zones in order to offset any currency losses in one region through gains in other regions. Therefore, strategic hedging can be considered as currency diversification. It reduces exposure to unfavorable foreign exchange movements. Strategic hedging is conceptually different from currency hedging. Currency hedging focuses on using forward contracts and swaps to contain currency risks, a financial management activity that can be performed by in-house financial specialists or outside experts (such as currency traders). Strategic hedging refers to

> **currency risk** The potential for loss associated with fluctuations in the foreign exchange market.
>
> **strategic hedging** Spreading out activities in a number of countries in different currency zones to offset any currency losses in one region through gains in other regions.

dispersing operations geographically—through sourcing or FDI—in multiple currency zones. By definition, this is more strategic because it involves managers from many functional areas such as production, marketing, and sourcing in addition to those from finance.

Overall, the importance of foreign exchange management for firms of all stripes interested in doing business abroad cannot be over-stressed. Firms whose performance is otherwise stellar can be devastated by unfavorable currency movements (see Closing Case). For example, the Swiss franc appreciated 25% against the euro between 2010 and 2012. Swiss manufacturers thus had a hard time competing with relatively cheap imports. On the other hand, thanks to crises in countries such as Greece, Ireland, and Portugal, the euro depreciated sharply against the dollar during the same period. Euro-zone exporters such as Daimler-Benz (maker of Mercedes cars) and EADS (manufacturer of Airbus jets) could not be happier.

From a resource-based view, it seems imperative that firms develop resources and capabilities that can combat currency risks in addition to striving for excellence in areas such as operations and marketing.[10] Developing such expertise is no small accomplishment, because, as noted earlier, predicting currency movements remains an art or at least a highly imprecise science. These challenges mean that firms able to profit from (or at least avoid being crushed by) unfavorable currency movements will possess valuable, rare, and hard-to-imitate capabilities that are the envy of rivals.

7-4 MANAGEMENT SAVVY

The big question in global business, adapted to the context of foreign exchange movements, is: What determines the success and failure of currency management around the globe? The answer boils down to two components. First, from an institution-based standpoint, the changing rules of the game—economic, political, and psychological—enable or constrain firms. For example, Swiss exporters' frustration with the appreciation of the Swiss franc relative to the euro stems from the centuries-old policy of Switzerland to maintain its political and economic independence. While all of Switzerland's neighbors have joined the EU and adopted the euro, Switzerland will not. Second, from a resource-based perspective, how firms develop valuable, unique, and hard-to-imitate capabilities in currency management may make or break them.

EXHIBIT 7.6 **IMPLICATIONS FOR ACTION**

- ▶ Fostering foreign exchange literacy is a must.
- ▶ Risk analysis of any country must include an analysis of its currency risks.
- ▶ A currency risk management strategy is necessary—via invoicing in one's own currency, currency hedging, or strategic hedging.

Shown in Exhibit 7.6, three implications for action emerge. First, foreign exchange literacy must be fostered. Savvy managers need to pay attention not only to the broad, long-run movements informed by PPP, productivity changes, and BOP, but also to the fickle short-run fluctuations triggered by interest rate changes and investor mood swings.

Second, risk analysis of any country must include its currency risks. Previous chapters have advised managers to pay attention to political, regulatory, and cultural risks of various countries. Here, a crucial currency risk dimension is added. An otherwise attractive country may suffer from devaluation of its currency. For example, prior to 2008, foreign and domestic banks in emerging European countries such as Hungary, Latvia, and Poland let numerous home buyers take out mortgage loans denominated in the euro, while a majority of these customers' assets and incomes were in local currencies. Unfortunately, local currencies in these countries were severely devaluated in the 2008–2009 crisis, making many home buyers unable to come up with the higher mortgage payments. Domestic and foreign banks in the region suffered from severe losses.

Finally, a country's high currency risks do not necessarily suggest that the country needs to be avoided totally. Instead, it calls for a prudent currency risk management strategy via invoicing in one's own currency, currency hedging, or strategic hedging. Not every firm has the power to invoice in its own currency. Smaller, internationally inexperienced firms may outsource currency hedging to specialists such as currency traders. Strategic hedging may be unrealistic for smaller, inexperienced firms. On the other hand, many larger, internationally experienced firms (such as 3M) choose not to touch currency hedging, citing its unpredictability. Instead, they focus on strategic hedging. Although no one has found a fixed formula, firms without a well thought-out currency management strategy will be caught off guard when currency movements take a nasty turn.

LEUNGCHOPAN/SHUTTERSTOCK.COM

Closing Case: Bellini Do Brasil's Foreign Exchange Challenges

Danilo Bellini, owner and CEO of Bellini do Brasil, a sophisticated furniture manufacturer based in the South Brazilian provincial town of Bento Gonçalves in the state of Rio Grande do Sul, was drinking coffee with his export manager, Carlo di Toni. Both set on complaining about the political and economic situation. The former president, Dilma Rousseff, was impeached in August 2016, and the new president, Michel Temer, also came under pressure since the electoral tribunal initiated an investigation into allegedly illegal campaign financing. At the same time, the largest corruption scandal the country had ever seen brought dozens of politicians and business people behind bars. In chorus, the exchange rate bounced like a yo-yo, much to the disappointment of hard-working businessmen such as Danilo and Carlo. If all of that was not enough, the election of Donald Trump caused further disarray and sent currencies plummeting from Mexico to Brazil.

Brazil's Foreign Exchange Policy

After more than a decade of high inflation, low growth, and debt default, the Brazilian government introduced a new currency, the real (R$), in 1994. The new currency was initially pegged to the US dollar at parity (R$1 = US$1) and could oscillate within an adjustable band until 1999. At that time, the effects of the Asian and the Russian crises also increased pressure on Brazil, which still suffered from repetitive trade deficits. Then, the real depreciated rapidly and reached R$2.25 to the dollar in January 2002. When it became increasingly likely that José Ignácio Lula da Silva would be elected Brazil's new president, hot money quickly left Brazil, and the real dropped to R$3.83 to the dollar in October 2002. Contrary to initial expectations, Lula's government gained the confidence of the international financial markets. Brazil's monetary policy aimed to quickly crush inflationary pressures by raising interest rates. During the 2003 crisis, the Central Bank's reference nominal interest rates topped 26%. Even at the beginning of 2017, nominal interest rates were around 13% and real interest rates close to 8%, one of the highest worldwide. Brazil's conservative fiscal and monetary policy quickly showed positive results. After paying back its last IMF loan in 2005, the country obtained the investment grade rating in 2008. Billions of US dollars have poured into the country since then. In addition, higher export sales, partly triggered by record commodity prices, led to solid foreign exchange reserves of US$365 billion by December 2016. However, such stabilization came at a cost: the real was appreciating between 2004 and 2012, undercutting Brazil's export competitiveness. Therefore, about 2,700 exporters (approximately 12% of all exporters as of 2004) quit international markets between 2004 and 2011.

Things have markedly changed since 2013, when the commodity price boom came to an end. Brazil, being the third largest iron ore producer worldwide after China and Australia, seriously suffered from the collapse of the iron ore price—thanks to the Chinese slowdown. The Brazilian currency nosedived in parallel from R$1.55 to the dollar in July 2011 to R$4.15 in January 2016 (Exhibit 7.7).

The economic and political crisis only exacerbated the extreme volatility of the Brazilian currency. After Rousseff was reelected in October 2014 by a narrow margin, she quickly fell into disgrace, with approval ratings falling to as low as 13% in 2016. Her alleged manipulation of the federal budget and economic mismanagement eventually led to her impeachment process between December 2015 and August 2016. In parallel, Brazilian prosecutors and judges uncovered a hitherto unseen corruption scheme, which dragged the national oil company Petrobras and major construction companies, such as Odebrecht, Camargo Correa, and Andrade Gutierrez, into the abyss. Almost the entire economy followed suit with a GDP decline of 3.8% in 2015 and 3.5% in 2016.

"Custo Brasil:" Cost of Doing Business in Brazil

As if the economic and political crisis and the ensuing foreign exchange pressures were not enough, other problems, colloquially summarized as *"Custo Brasil"* ("Brazil cost"), gave Danilo and Carlo headaches. While port and road infrastructure, critical to the export industry, lagged behind, hourly compensation costs in manufacturing were several times higher than those in China. The government increased minimum wages from R$ 200 in 2002 to R$ 880 in 2016. According to World Bank data, in Brazil businesses took 2,038 hours to prepare and pay taxes in 2015, which compares unfavorably against China (259 hours) and the United States (175 hours). Worse, taxes levied on interstate business transactions within Brazil make it often cheaper to import than to buy from suppliers located in another state. In 2016, Global Manufacturing Competitiveness Index ranked Brazil only 29th (a score of 46), while China was ranked first (a score of 100).

Strategically Balancing Exporting and Importing

Bellini do Brasil was founded by descendants of Italian immigrants who populated the Gaucho Highlands region in South Brazil in the second half of the 19th century. Bellini recognized that the more lucrative export markets would only be reachable by focusing on upscale furniture. Cognizant of its Italian roots, Bellini hired Natale, an Italian design company that designed sophisticated kitchens and high-end leather sofas for the world market. The terms of their deal looked very promising as Natale offered Bellini to honor its services through a modest upfront fee plus yearly royalty payments.

EXHIBIT 7.7   BRAZILIAN REAL (R$) TO US DOLLAR (US$) EXCHANGE RATE

Sources: Adapted from www.tradingeconomics.com/brazil/currency; www.xe.com/currency/brl-brazilian-real; various newspaper articles.

For the products it designed, Natale recommended using high-quality components and special chemicals, which Bellini started importing initially from Italy and Switzerland. Bellini also upgraded its plant near Bento Gonçalves and placed new orders for Italian and German machinery equipment in 2012, taking advantage of a favorable exchange rate of R$1.8 to the dollar. The European machinery exporters facilitated a low-interest loan from their European house banks, which helped Bellini avoid the exorbitant interest rates common in Brazil.

Importing an increasing share of furniture components and manufacturing equipment was also a wise strategic move in times of an appreciating real, making Bellini's products more competitive at home and abroad. Danilo explained:

We have a well-developed regional supply chain with really good products in South Brazil. However, after 2005 and until around 2012, importing was way cheaper than buying from our local suppliers. . . .

By purchasing from foreign suppliers, we ended up learning a lot about international trade. . . . Increasingly we figured out how seemingly tiny differences in imported components and materials could result in tremendous efficiency gains in manufacturing and quality improvements in our final products. On top of this, importing components helped us expand our product range. . . .

However, things changed unexpectedly. Not only did the commodity price boom come to an end, but Brazil also suffered from a deep domestic political and economic crisis, which led to one of the worst economic performances among emerging economies. The real followed suit and has plummeted since 2013 (Exhibit 7.7). Although exports would generally benefit from currency devaluations, noted Carlo, recent data from the Brazilian furniture industry showed rather a mixed picture (Exhibit 7.8). Danilo interrupted Carlo's thoughts, pondering . . .

EXHIBIT 7.8   DOMESTIC AND EXPORT SALES BY BRAZILIAN FURNITURE FIRMS

Year	Exchange Rate (US$1)	Sales in RS	Sales in Brazil	Exports from RS	Exports from Brazil
2015	R$3.32	US$2.0 billion	US$10.8 billion	US$183.5 million	US$601.6 million
2014	R$2.35	US$3.5 billion	US$19.0 billion	US$216.8 million	US$689.5 million
2013	R$2.16	US$3.6 billion	US$19.8 billion	US$210.9 million	US$702.9 million
2012	R$1.95	US$3.6 billion	US$19.7 billion	US$205.7 million	US$723.4 million
2011	R$1.67	US$3.8 billion	US$20.9 billion	US$203.5 million	US$763.3 million

Sources: Sales include furniture and mattresses. RS = state of Rio Grande do Sul, where Bellini do Brasil is located. Adapted from MOVERGS, Sindimóveis-BG / SEFAZ / RS / CGI / MDIC / SECEX; World Bank Indicators for average exchange rates.

Look, Carlo, don't forget we have to pay royalties and interest payments. Remember we have to import components for our products and spare parts for machinery—and all this is invoiced in dollars or euros. Since 2015, our payments for these things virtually went through the roof. When we signed contracts in 2011, we committed to monthly payments of R$ 5 million to our international partners. But now we pay close to R$ 8 million. Last year, sometimes we had to pay more than R$ 10 million. This eats up all our combined export profits and on the domestic market we also lose money, month after month. . . .

Firmly believing that there must be a way to save their company, Danilo and Carlo discussed possible coping strategies to get out of this trap. Yet, this was easier said than done, as royalty, interest, and down payments on loans constituted long-term commitments. Expensive imports of components and specialized chemicals had become an integral part of Bellini's differentiation strategy that allowed it to be so successful in the past. Using cheaper, domestically sourced materials to substitute for imports now might delay already scheduled deliveries and jeopardize its competitive edge.

Sipping bitter coffee, both Danilo and Carlo scratched their heads as they endeavored to overcome Bellini do Brasil's foreign exchange challenges.

Case Discussion Questions

1. How do you evaluate Bellini do Brasil's situation from the resource-based and institution-based views? How may resources and institutions enable or hinder Danilo and Carlo to turn around the company?

2. Which strategic response alternatives to its foreign exchange challenges should Bellini consider?

3. What would you do if you were Danilo? What would you propose if you were Carlo?

Sources: This case was written by Dr. **Dirk Boehe** (University of Adelaide, Australia). All corporate and individual names are fictitious. Brazilian Central Bank, www.bacen .gov.br; Brazilian Ministry of Economic Development, www.mdic.gov.br; Deloitte Global Manufacturing Competitiveness Index, www2.deloitte.com/content/dam /Deloitte/us/Documents/manufacturing/us-gmci.pdf; Exchange rate and commodity price data: www.tradingeconomics.com; "What is the Petrobras scandal that is engulfing Brazil?" *Financial Times*, 1 April 2016; Furniture Industry Association of the State of Rio Grande do Sul, www.movergs.com.br; World Bank, www.doingbusiness.org.

STUDY TOOLS 7

LOCATED AT THE BACK OF YOUR BOOK:

☐ Rip out and study the Chapter Review Card at the end of the book

LOG IN TO WWW.CENGAGEBRAIN.COM TO:

☐ Review key term flashcards

☐ Complete a practice quiz to test your knowledge of key concepts

☐ View animated PengAtlas Maps

☐ Complete interactive content, watch chapter videos, and take a graded quiz

☐ Track your knowledge of key concepts in Global Business

☐ Read and discuss additional case study content

8 Capitalizing on Global & Regional Integration

LEARNING OBJECTIVES

After studying this chapter, you will be able to . . .

8-1 Make the case for global economic integration.

8-2 Explain the evolution of the GATT and the WTO, including current challenges.

8-3 Make the case for regional economic integration.

8-4 List the accomplishments, benefits, and costs of the European Union.

8-5 Identify the five organizations that promote regional trade in the Americas and describe their benefits and costs.

8-6 Identify the four organizations that promote regional trade in the Asia Pacific and describe their benefits and costs.

8-7 Articulate how regional trade should influence your thinking about global business.

After you finish this chapter, go to

PAGE 137 for

STUDY TOOLS

ETHICAL DILEMMA
Opening Case: Brexit

On June 23, 2016, in a referendum Britain voted by 52% to 48% to leave the European Union (EU), sending shock waves throughout the world. Although no country had exited from the EU before, it turns out that the intense debate on whether Britain should stay in or leave the EU has been going on for *decades*. Britain's relationship with the EU has always been rocky. In both 1963 and 1967, Britain applied to join the European Economic Community (EEC), the EU's predecessor. But French President Charles de Gaulle vetoed both applications in an effort to preserve the French–German dominance. In 1969, after de Gaulle relinquished French presidency, Britain applied for the third time. In 1973, it successfully joined the EEC. However, within Britain, Euroscepticism quickly rose and forced the government to run a referendum on whether Britain should leave or remain in the EEC in 1975. With 67% supportive votes, Britain's membership was confirmed in that referendum. In other words, although the term "Brexit"—British exit from the EU—was recently coined in 2012, the 2016 referendum was in fact a *second* referendum on "Leave or Remain."

Given substantial Eurosceptic sentiments, Britain has always been less enthusiastic than many other EU members in pushing for deeper integration. In 1979, Britain opted out of the mechanism that ultimately led to the creation of the euro. In 1999, when the Schengen passport free travel zone abolishing border control was implemented for a majority of the EU members, Britain (together with Ireland) opted out, insisting on maintaining passport control at the border. Despite Britain's nonparticipation of Schengen, a significant number of migrants, most from new EU members in Eastern Europe, such as Poland and Romania, have moved to the country. In 2011, Britain vetoed a new treaty supported by 26 EU members to enhance the "economic governance" for the EU. All EU treaties had to be signed off by all members. Thus, Britain's veto torpedoed the whole treaty, causing an uproar throughout the EU. In 2013, Prime Minister David Cameron announced that he would put the UK membership in the EU for a referendum. Although his "bulldog spirit" won praise from Britain's Eurosceptics crowd, he was—according to a *Foreign Affairs* article in 2013—"gambling with his country's future."

The 2016 Leave campaign was led by the UK Independence Party (UKIP), which was founded in 1991. From a fringe movement in early years, UKIP has become an influential force in British politics. By definition, UKIP is nationalist at its core. Opposition to Britain's continued EU membership is central to the party's identity. UKIP criticizes the EU as a fundamentally undemocratic institution, and stresses the need to regain what it describes as the UK's lost national sovereignty from the EU. It views the EU as being responsible for "flooding" Britain with 3.2 million EU migrants, in particular those from Eastern Europe.

The Remain campaign was supported by Cameron's Conservative government. In a departure from the usual collective voice of the cabinet, Cameron allowed Conservative cabinet ministers and members of Parliament to freely campaign for Leave, if they so chose. This was probably due to Cameron's confidence that the Leave campaign would not succeed.

Succeed the Leave campaign did. Within hours, Cameron resigned. After three weeks, Theresa May became the new prime minister, with a mandate to lead the country out of the EU. Within a few days after the referendum, the economic impact was immediate and devastating. The pound took a severe pounding, plummeting to its lowest level against the dollar in three decades. FTSE 250 fell by 14%. Trading of Barclays and Royal Bank of Scotland stocks was suspended. Worldwide, $3 trillion of global share-price value dissipated.

While markets gradually recovered, realities set in. The EU absorbs 54% of all UK exports, and three million UK jobs depend on exports to the EU. Although growing fast, exports to leading emerging economies known as BRICS (Brazil, Russia, India, China, and South Africa) only command 8% of UK exports, of which 3% goes to China. With or without EU membership, the EU will be Britain's largest trading partner—the question is, *on what terms*. Likewise, in foreign direct investment (FDI) Britain has been successful in attracting multinationals undertaking an "EU platform" strategy to invest in one location to serve the entire EU. For example, in 2015 Nissan made 450,000 cars in Britain, 80% of which were exported to the rest of the EU. As a nonmember, Britain is likely to lose a significant chunk of such FDI. After the Brexit result, Nissan seriously reconsidered whether to establish a new plant in continental Europe or to continue investing in the current Sunderland plant, which employed 6,700 people. In financial services, London's fabled banks may lose their "passporting rights," which allow these firms in one EU member country to serve customers in the other 27 members without setting up local offices. The upshot? London may lose 70,000 financial services jobs, and its rivals in Dublin, Frankfurt, and Paris may benefit as banks such as Barclays, Citigroup, Deutsche Bank, HSBC, and JPMorgan Chase create more jobs there.

Exactly on what terms will Britain leave the EU? Nobody seemed to know, and the new prime minister received a well-earned nickname, "Theresa Maybe," from the *Economist*. In January 2017, May finally gave a speech to outline a clean (or "hard") break with the EU by leaving the single market and customs union—otherwise Britain would continue to have little control over migration and to pay into the EU budget. At the same time, she promised a "truly global Britain," essentially embracing a "World Trade Organization (WTO) option" that would enable Britain as a WTO member to seek the best possible trade deals outside the EU.

Long fed up with British fickleness, EU leaders are frustrated with seemingly endless concessions Britain demanded. "What else do you need to make you happy?" they often asked UK negotiators. More seriously, EU leaders such as German Prime Minister Angela Merkel warned that Britain could not "cherry-pick" and could not expect "to leave this family . . . to get rid of all obligations while holding on to privileges." As Britain embarks upon the uncertain road to Brexit, the *Economist* opined that "it will survive. But the chances are that it will be a poorer, more inward-looking place—its drawbridge up, its influence diminished."

Sources: "After Brexit, here's what's next for Europe," *Bloomberg Businessweek*, 4 July 2016: 8–9; "May spells out her ambitious wish list," *Bloomberg Businessweek*, 23 January 2017: 14; D. Champion, "Is Project Europe doomed?" *Harvard Business Review*, September 2016: 114–115; "An aggravating absence," *Economist*, 2 July 2016: 17–20; "Business," *Economist*, 2 July 2016: 8; "The politics of anger," *Economist*, 2 July 2016: 9; "The road to Brexit," *Economist*, 8 October 2016: 13; "The fallacy of the fallback," *Economist*, 7 January 2017: 58; "Theresa Maybe," *Economist*, 7 January 2017: 12; "A hard road," *Economist*, 21 January 2017: 9–10; "Lost passports," *Economist*, 21 January 2017: 63; M. Matthijs, "David Cameron's dangerous game," *Foreign Affairs*, September 2013: 10–16; M. W. Peng and K. E. Meyer, *Winning the Future Markets for UK Manufacturing Output* (London: UK Government Office for Science, 2013); "Nissan to review UK investment decision based on Brexit deal," *Politico*, 20 January 2017: www.politico.eu.

Why did Britain join the **European Union (EU)** in the first place? How did British firms (such as HSBC), EU firms (such as Deutsche Bank), and non-EU firms (such as Nissan) benefit from Britain's EU membership? In Brexit negotiations, what is the "**World Trade Organization (WTO) option**" often discussed? More broadly, what are the advantages and disadvantages of WTO membership? In two words, the answer is: economic integration—both regionally and globally. **Regional economic integration** refers to efforts to reduce trade and investment barriers within one region, such as the EU. **Global economic integration**, in turn, refers to efforts to reduce trade and investment barriers around the globe, such as the WTO.

This chapter is fundamentally about how the two core perspectives in global business interact. Specifically, how do changes in the rules of the game for global and regional economic integration, as emphasized by the institution-based view, lead firms to better develop and leverage their capabilities, as highlighted by the resource-based view? In other words, how do firms around the world such as HSBC and Nissan capitalize on global and regional economic integration? We start with a description of global economic integration. Then, we introduce regional economic integration around the world. Finally, we offer some practical tips for managers.

European Union (EU) The official title of European economic integration since 1993.

World Trade Organization (WTO) The official title of the multilateral trading system and the organization underpinning this system since 1995.

regional economic integration Efforts to reduce trade and investment barriers within one region.

global economic integration Efforts to reduce trade and investment barriers around the globe.

General Agreement on Tariffs and Trade (GATT) A multilateral agreement governing the international trade of goods (merchandise).

8-1 INTEGRATING THE GLOBAL ECONOMY

Current frameworks of regional and global economic integration date back to the end of World War II (WWII). The world community was mindful of the mercantilist trade policies in the 1930s, which worsened the Great Depression and eventually led to WWII. Two new developments after the war were initiated to prevent a repeat of these circumstances. Globally, the **General Agreement on Tariffs and Trade (GATT)** was created in 1948 as a multilateral agreement governing the international trade of goods (merchandise). In Europe, regional integration started in 1951. The agreement and ensuing integration proved so successful that they are now considerably expanded. GATT became the WTO, which was established in 1995 as the global multilateral trading system and the organization that supports it. Economic integration in Europe led to the EU.

8-1a Political Benefits for Global Economic Integration

Recall from Chapters 5 and 6 that, theoretically, economic gains occur when firms from different countries can freely trade and invest. But these insights were not accepted by most governments until the end of WWII. In the late 1920s and the early 1930s, virtually all governments tried to protect domestic industries by imposing protectionist policies through tariffs and quotas. Collectively, these beggar-thy-neighbor policies triggered retaliation that further restricted trade. Trade wars eventually turned into WWII.

The postwar urge for global economic integration grew out of the painful lessons of the 1920s and the 1930s. While emphasizing economic benefits, global economic integration is *political* in nature. Its fundamental goal is to promote peace (see Exhibit 8.1). Simply put, people who buy and sell from each other are usually reluctant to fight or kill each other. For example, Japan decided to attack Pearl Harbor in 1941 only *after* the United States cut off oil sales to Japan in protest of Japanese aggression in China. Global economic integration also seeks to build confidence. The mercantilist trade policies in the 1930s were triggered by a lack of confidence. So confidence building is key to avoiding the tragedies of the 1930s. Governments, if they are confident that other countries will not raise trade barriers, will not be tempted to do the same.

ISTOCK.COM/R.R

Recently, as the global economy endeavors to recover from the worst economic crisis (now called the Great Recession) since the Great Depression, there is a grave danger of rising protectionism around the globe. Hopefully, leaders of the 21st century will be smarter and wiser than leaders of the 1920s and the 1930s. While protectionism may lead to short-term gains at the expense of trading partners, the world as a whole "has been there, done that"—with disastrous outcomes and tremendous wartime losses. This is a lesson that protectionist leaders such as Donald Trump need to be aware of.

8-1b Economic Benefits for Global Economic Integration

There are at least three compelling economic reasons for global economic integration. The first is to handle disputes constructively. The WTO's dispute resolution mechanisms (discussed later in this chapter) are designed to help countries do just that. Although there is an escalation in the number of disputes brought to the WTO, such an increase, according to the WTO, "does not reflect increasing tension in the world. Rather, it reflects the closer economic ties throughout the world, the WTO's expanding membership, and the fact that countries have faith in the system to solve their differences."[1] In other words, it is much better to bring disputes to the WTO than to declare war on each other.

A second benefit is that global economic integration makes life easier for all participants. Officially, the GATT/WTO system is called a **multilateral trading system** because it involves all participating countries (the key word being *multilateral*) and not just two countries (*bilateral*). A crucial principle in the multilateral trading system is **nondiscrimination**. Specifically, a country cannot make distinctions in trade among its trading partners. Every time a country lowers a trade barrier, it has to do the same for *all* WTO member countries, except when giving preference to regional partners (an exception we discuss later). Such nondiscrimination makes things easier for all members.

Finally, global economic integration raises incomes, generates jobs, and stimulates economic growth. The WTO estimates that cutting global trade barriers by a third may raise worldwide income by approximately $600 billion. That is equivalent to adding an economy the size of Canada to the world. Benefits are not limited to countries as a whole. Individuals also benefit because more and better jobs are created. In the United States, 12 million people owe their jobs to exports. In China, 18 million people work for foreign-invested firms, which have the highest level of profits and pay among all China-based firms.

multilateral trading system The global system that governs international trade among countries—otherwise known as the GATT/WTO system.

nondiscrimination A principle that a country cannot discriminate among its trading partners.

EXHIBIT 8.1	BENEFITS OF GLOBAL ECONOMIC INTEGRATION

Political benefits

▶ Promotes peace by promoting trade and investment

▶ Builds confidence in a multilateral trading system

Economic benefits

▶ Disputes are handled constructively

▶ Rules make life easier and discrimination impossible for all participating countries

▶ Free trade and investment raise incomes and stimulate economic growth

World Trade Organization Director-General Roberto Azevedo (left) poses with Jordanian Ambassador Saja Majali following Jordan's acceptance of the WTO's Trade Facilitation Agreement on February 22, 2017.

FABRICE COFFRINI/GETTY IMAGES

Of course, global economic integration has its problems. Critics may not be happy with the environmental impact and with the distribution of the benefits from more trade and investment among the haves and have-nots in the world. However, when weighing all of the pros and cons, most governments and people agree that global economic integration generates enormous benefits, ranging from preserving peace to generating jobs.

8-2 ORGANIZING WORLD TRADE

8-2a General Agreement on Tariffs and Trade: 1948–1994

Created in 1948, the GATT (unlike the WTO) was technically an agreement, but *not* an organization. Its major contribution was to reduce the level of tariffs by sponsoring rounds of multilateral negotiations. As a result, the average tariff in developed economies dropped from 40% in 1948 to 3% in 2005. Between 1950 and 1995, when the GATT was phased out to become the WTO, world GDP grew about fivefold, but world merchandise exports grew about 100 times (!). During the GATT era, trade growth consistently outpaced GDP growth.

Despite the GATT's phenomenal success in bringing down tariff barriers, by the 1980s three concerns had surfaced that made it clear that reforms would be necessary. First, because of the GATT's declared focus on merchandise trade, neither trade in services nor intellectual property (IP) protection was covered. Both of these areas were becoming more important. Second, the many loopholes in merchandise trade needed reforming. The most (in)famous loophole was the Multi-fiber Arrangement (MFA) designed to *limit* free trade in textiles, a direct violation of the letter and spirit of the GATT. Finally, although the GATT had been successful in reducing tariffs, the global recessions in the 1970s and the 1980s led many governments to invoke nontariff barriers (NTBs) such as subsidies and local content requirements (see Chapter 5). Unlike tariff barriers, which were relatively easy to verify and challenge, NTBs were more subtle but pervasive, thus triggering a growing number of trade disputes. The GATT, however, lacked effective dispute resolution mechanisms. Therefore, at the end of the Uruguay Round in 1994, participating countries agreed to upgrade the GATT and launch the WTO.

8-2b World Trade Organization: 1995–Present

Established on January 1, 1995, the WTO is the GATT's successor. This transformation turned the GATT from a provisional treaty serviced by an ad hoc secretariat to a full-fledged international organization headquartered in Geneva, Switzerland. Significantly broader in scope than the GATT, the WTO has several new features:

▸ An agreement governing the international trade of services, the **General Agreement on Trade in Services (GATS)**.

▸ An agreement governing IP rights, the **Trade-Related Aspects of Intellectual Property Rights (TRIPS)**.

▸ Trade dispute settlement mechanisms, which allow for the WTO to adjudicate trade disputes among countries in a more effective and less time-consuming way.

▸ Trade policy reviews, which enable the WTO and other member countries to peer review a country's trade policy.

General Agreement on Trade in Services (GATS) A WTO agreement governing the international trade of services.

Trade-Related Aspects of Intellectual Property Rights (TRIPS) A WTO agreement governing intellectual property rights.

ISTOCK.COM/CARMEN MARTINEZ BANUS

8-2c Trade Dispute Settlement

One of the main objectives for establishing the WTO was to strengthen trade dispute settlement mechanisms. The old GATT mechanisms experienced long delays, blocking by accused countries, and inadequate enforcement. The WTO addresses all three of these problems. First, it sets time limits for a panel, consisting of three neutral countries as peers, to reach a judgment. Second, it removes the power of the accused countries to block any unfavorable decision. WTO decisions will be final. Third, in terms of enforcement, although the WTO has earned the nickname of "the world's supreme court in trade," it does *not* have real enforcement capability. The WTO simply recommends that the losing country change its laws or practices and authorizes the winning country to use tariff retaliation to compel the offending country to comply with the WTO rulings.

Understandably, enforcement by the WTO is controversial because the losing country experiences some loss of sovereignty. Fundamentally, a WTO ruling is a *recommendation,* but not an order. No higher-level entity can order a sovereign government to do something against its wishes. In other words, the offending country retains full sovereignty in its decision whether or not to implement a WTO recommendation. Because the WTO has no real power to enforce its rulings, a country that has lost a dispute case can choose from one of two options: change its laws or practices to be in compliance, or defy the ruling by doing nothing and suffer trade retaliation by the winning country known as "punitive duties." Most of the WTO's trade dispute rulings, however, are resolved without resorting to trade retaliation. This suggests that—per Proposition 1 in the institution-based view (see Chapter 2)—most member countries have reached a *rational* decision that after losing a case, being in (often painful) compliance with a WTO decision has more benefits than "rocking the boat."

8-2d The Doha Round: "The Doha Development Agenda"

The **Doha Round** was the only round of trade negotiations sponsored by the WTO. In 1999, a WTO meeting in Seattle intended to start a new round of trade talks was not only devastated by 30,000 protesters, but was also derailed by significant differences between developed and developing countries. Undeterred by the backlash, member countries went ahead to launch a new round in Doha, Qatar, in November 2001.

The Doha Round was significant for two reasons. First, it was launched in the aftermath of the 9/11 attacks.

Members had a strong resolve to make free trade work around the globe in order to defeat the terrorist agenda to divide and terrorize the world. Second, this was the first round in the history of GATT/WTO to specifically aim at promoting economic development in developing countries. Consequently, the official title of the Doha Round was the "Doha Development Agenda." Doha was ambitious: it would (1) reduce agricultural subsidies in developed countries to facilitate exports from developing countries; (2) slash tariffs, especially in industries that developing countries might benefit from (such as textiles); (3) free up trade in services; and (4) strengthen IP protection. In the Doha Round, *not* all meetings were held in Doha. Subsequent meetings took place in locations such as Bali, Indonesia; Cancun, Mexico; Geneva, Switzerland; and Hong Kong, China.

Unfortunately, numerous countries failed to deliver on promises made in Doha. The "hot potato" turned out to be agriculture. Australia, Argentina, and most developing countries demanded that Japan, the EU, and the United States reduce farm subsidies. Japan rejected any proposal to cut rice tariffs. The EU refused to significantly reduce farm subsidies. The United States actually *increased* farm subsidies. On the other hand, many developing countries, led by India, refused to tighten IP protection, citing their needs for cheap generic drugs to combat deceases such as HIV/AIDS. Overall, developing countries refused to offer concessions in IP and service trade in part because of the failure of Japan, the EU, and the United States to reduce farm subsidies.

Eventually, at the Geneva meeting in 2006, the Doha Round was thus officially suspended. Hopes of lifting millions out of poverty through free trade were derailed. Labeled "the biggest threat to the postwar (multilateral) trading system" by the *Economist,*[2] the fiasco disappointed almost every country involved. Naturally, finger pointing started immediately. To be fair, no country was totally responsible for the collapse of the Doha Round, and all members collectively were culpable. The sheer complexity of reaching an agreement on "everything" among 153 member countries (in 2006) was simply mind boggling.

What happens next? Officially, Doha was "suspended" but not

> **Doha Round** A round of WTO negotiations to reduce agricultural subsidies, slash tariffs, and strengthen intellectual property protection that started in Doha, Qatar, in 2001. Officially known as the "Doha Development Agenda," it was suspended in 2006 due to disagreements.

Debate: Food versus Trade

Emerging Markets/Ethical Dilemma

In December 2013 in Bali, Indonesia, 159 members of the WTO struck a trade facilitation agreement (TFA)—a pledge to cut red tape at customs posts around the world. This would be the only tangible achievement of the Doha Round, which was launched in 2001. Limited in scope, the deal would simplify customs red tape rather than tackling the far thornier problem of agricultural subsidies and intellectual property. Still, it would add up to $400 billion a year to a struggling global economy.

Unfortunately, in July 2014, the TFA collapsed. This was because India withdrew its support. The "hot potato" again turned out to be food subsidies. India, like many developing countries, strengthened "food security" policies (a euphemism for agricultural subsidies) in response to recent swings in food prices. Such subsidies would soon grow large enough to violate WTO rules, which dictate that

TIMOLINA/SHUTTERSTOCK.COM

no developing country could subsidize more than 10% of the total value of harvests to farmers. Already spending $19 billion (1% of GDP) on such subsidiaries, India is likely to exceed the 10% limit in the near future. When that happens, India could be subject to a WTO challenge. While the Bali deal was signed by a previous government, the new Narendra Modi administration, elected into power in early 2014, insisted that it would not sacrifice food security on the altar of global trade. Even the WTO's efforts to let India have four extra years (until 2017) of immunity from challenge were not viewed to be good enough. In other words, India would not trade food for trade.

India is hardly the only protectionist country when it comes to agricultural subsidies. According to the *Economist*, "the rich countries are the worst culprits." Japanese rice and sugar tariffs are, respectively, 778% and 328%. The EU dishes out 40% of its budget to farmers. But by giving up the gains from more smooth trade, India is also hurting itself. Its massive food subsidies lead to huge stockpiles of unwanted, rotting produce and fan corruption. In the end, with Doha dead (technically "suspended") and Bali (a subset of Doha) scuttled, the WTO had no concrete deal to show when it celebrated its 20th anniversary in 2015.

Sources: "The Indian problem," *Economist*, 23 November 2013: 17; "Unaccustomed victory," *Economist*, 14 December 2013: 78; "Bailing out from Bali," *Economist*, 9 August 2014: 58–59; "No more grand bargains," *Economist*, 9 August 2014: 10.

"terminated" or "dead." Members repeatedly tried again but failed again. Most recently in 2013 in Bali, Indonesia, 159 members finally struck a trade facilitation agreement (TFA)—a pledge to cut red tape at customs posts in all countries. Although the TFA was far narrower and less ambitious than the sweeping deal envisioned when Doha was first launched, it was viewed as Doha's first big win. Unfortunately, in 2014, the TFA collapsed. This was because India withdrew its support. The "hot potato" again turned out to be food subsidies (see Debate).

Multilateral trade negotiations are notoriously challenging.[3] In 1990, the Uruguay Round of the GATT was similarly suspended, only to rise again in 1994 with a far-reaching agreement that launched the WTO. Whether history will repeat itself remains to be seen. On the other hand, although global deals may be hard to do, regional deals are moving "at twice the speed and with half the

fuss."[4] The upshot is stagnation of multilateralism and acceleration of regionalism—a topic to which we turn next.

8-3 INTEGRATING REGIONAL ECONOMIES

There is now a proliferation of regional trade deals. This section first introduces the benefits for regional economic integration and discusses its major types.

8-3a The Pros and Cons of Regional Economic Integration

Similar to global economic integration, the benefits of regional economic integration center on both political and economic dimensions (see Exhibit 8.1). Politically, regional economic integration promotes peace by fostering closer economic ties and building confidence. Only in the last seven decades did the Europeans break away from their centuries-old habit of war and violence among themselves. A leading cause of this dramatic behavioral change is economic integration. In addition, regional integration enhances the collective political weight of a region, which has also helped fuel postwar European integration, particularly when dealing with superpowers such as the United States.

EXHIBIT 8.2   TYPES OF REGIONAL ECONOMIC INTEGRATION

Political Union — Integration of political and economic affairs

Economic Union — Common economic policies

Common Market — Free movement of goods, people, and capital

Customs Union — Common external tariffs

Free Trade Area — Removal of intragroup tariffs

Economically, the three benefits associated with regional economic integration are similar to those associated with global economic integration (see Exhibit 8.1). First, disputes are handled constructively. Second, consistent rules make life easier and discrimination impossible for participating countries within one region. Third, free trade and investment raise incomes and stimulate economic growth.[5]

However, not everything is rosy in regional integration. A case can be made *against* it. Politically, regional integration is centered on preferential treatments for firms within a region, leading to discrimination against firms outside a region and thus undermining global integration. Of course, in practice, global deals such as Doha are so challenging to accomplish that regional deals emerge as realistic alternatives. Economically, regional integration may result in some loss of sovereignty. This is one of the leading causes of Brexit (see Opening Case).

The simultaneous existence of both pros and cons means that some countries are cautious about joining regional economic integration. Norway and Switzerland chose not to join the EU. Even when countries are part of a regional deal, they sometimes choose not to participate in some areas. For example, three EU members—Britain, Denmark, and Sweden—refused to adopt the euro. Overall, different levels of enthusiasm call for different types of regional economic integration, which are outlined next.

8-3b Types of Regional Economic Integration

Exhibit 8.2 shows five main types of regional economic integration. A **free trade area (FTA)** is a group of countries that remove trade barriers among themselves. One of the newest examples is the Eurasian Union consisting of Belarus, Kazakhstan, and Russia, which was created in 2014. In an FTA, each member still maintains different external policies regarding nonmembers. For example, three NAFTA members have each pursued *different* FTA agreements with the EU.

A **customs union** is one step beyond an FTA. In addition to all the arrangements of an FTA, a customs union imposes common external policies on nonparticipants. Two examples are Andean Community and Mercosur in South America.

A **common market** has everything a customs union has, but also permits the free movement of goods and people. Today's EU used to be a common market. An **economic union** has all the features of a common market, but members

free trade area (FTA) A group of countries that remove trade barriers among themselves.

customs union One step beyond a free trade area, a customs union imposes common external policies on nonparticipating countries.

common market Combining everything a customs union has, a common market additionally permits the free movement of goods and people.

economic union Having all the features of a common market, members also coordinate and harmonize economic policies (in areas such as monetary, fiscal, and taxation) to blend their economies into a single economic entity.

also coordinate and harmonize economic policies (monetary, fiscal, and taxation) in order to blend their economies into a single economic entity. Today's EU is an economic union. One possible dimension of an economic union is to establish a **monetary union**, which has been accomplished by 19 EU members through the adoption of the euro (see the next section).

A **political union** is the integration of political and economic affairs of a region. The United States and the former Soviet Union are two examples. The EU at present is not a political union. Overall, each of these five major types is an intensification of the level of regional economic integration from the one before. Next, we look at concrete examples of these arrangements.

8-4 REGIONAL ECONOMIC INTEGRATION IN EUROPE

At present, the most ambitious economic integration takes place in Europe. This section (1) outlines its origin and evolution, (2) introduces its current structure, and (3) discusses its challenges.

8-4a Origin and Evolution

Although European economic integration is often noted for its economic benefits, its origin was political in nature. In an effort to stop the vicious cycle of hatred and violence, Belgium, France, (West) Germany, Italy, Luxembourg, and the Netherlands in 1951 signed the European Coal and Steel Community (ECSC) Treaty, which was the first step toward what is now the EU. There was a good reason for the six founding members and the two industries to be involved. France and Germany were the main combatants in both WWI and WWII (and major previous European wars), each having lost millions of soldiers and civilians. Reflecting the public mood, statesmen in both countries realized that such killing needed to stop. One of the best ways to prevent hostilities is to let France and Germany economically embrace each other so tightly that neither could get an arm free to punch the other. Italy always had the misfortune of being dragged along and devastated whenever France and Germany went to war. The three small countries known as Benelux (Belgium, the Netherlands, and Luxembourg) had the unfortunate geographic location of being sandwiched between France and Germany, and were usually wiped out when France and Germany slugged it out. Naturally, Italy and Benelux would be happy to do anything to stop France and Germany from fighting again. Also, the industry focus on coal and steel was not an accident. These industries traditionally supplied the raw materials for war. Integrating them might help prevent future hostilities from breaking out.

In 1957, six member countries of ECSC signed the Treaty of Rome, which launched the European Economic Community (EEC)—later known as the European Community (EC). Starting as an FTA, the EEC/EC progressed to become a customs union and eventually a common market. In 1991, 12 member countries signed the Treaty on European Union in Maastricht, the Netherlands (in short, the "Maastricht Treaty") to complete the single market and establish an economic union. The title the "European Union" (EU) was officially adopted in 1993 when the Maastricht Treaty went into effect. Recently, the Lisbon Treaty, signed in 2007 and enacted in 2009, amended the Maastricht Treaty that served as a constitutional basis for the EU.

8-4b The EU Today

Headquartered in Brussels, Belgium, today's EU (see PengAtlas Map 9) has 28 member countries, 500 million citizens, and $18 trillion GDP. Contributing about 26% of the world's GDP, the EU is the world's largest economy, the largest exporter and importer of goods and services, and the largest trading partner with major economies such as the United States, China, and India. Here is how the EU describes itself in an official publication:

> The European Union is not a federation like the United States. Nor is it simply an organization for cooperation between governments, like the United Nations. Neither is it a state intended to replace existing states, but it is much more than any other organization. The EU is, in fact, unique. Never before have countries voluntarily agreed to set up common institutions to which they delegate some of their sovereignty so that decisions on specific matters of joint interest can be made democratically at a higher, in this case European, level. This pooling of sovereignty is called "European integration."[6]

The EU today is an economic union. Internal trade barriers have been mostly removed. In aviation, the EU now has a single market, which means all European carriers compete on equal terms across the EU (including domestic routes in a foreign country). US airlines are not allowed to fly between pairs of cities within Germany. However,

monetary union A group of countries that use a common currency.

political union The integration of political and economic affairs of a region.

non-German, EU airlines (such as Ireland's Ryanair) can fly between any pair of cities within Germany. On the ground, it used to take Spanish truck drivers 24 hours to cross the border into France due to paperwork and checks. Since 1992, passport and customs control within most (but not all) member countries of the EU has been disbanded, and checkpoints at border crossings are no longer manned. The area covered by EU countries became known as the **Schengen** passport-free travel zone, named after Schengen, Luxembourg, where the agreement was signed in 1985. Now, Spanish trucks can move from Spain to France nonstop, similar to how American trucks go from Texas to Oklahoma. At present, 22 of the 28 EU member countries are in the Schengen zone. Six other members are not yet in: Britain and Ireland chose to opt out, and four new members—Bulgaria, Cyprus, Romania, and Slovenia—have yet to meet requirements. (Interestingly, three non-EU member countries—Iceland, Norway, and Switzerland—are also in the Schengen area.)

As an economic union, one of the EU's proudest accomplishments—but also one of its most significant headaches—is the introduction of a common currency, the **euro**, initially in 12 of the EU 15 countries. Since then, seven more countries have joined the **euro zone**. Today, the 19-member euro zone accounts for 330 million people and 21% of world GDP (relative to 24% for the United States). The euro was introduced in two phases. First, it became available in 1999 as "virtual money" only used for financial transactions, but not in circulation. Second, in 2002, the euro was introduced as banknotes and coins.

Adopting the euro has three great benefits (Exhibit 8.3). First, it reduces currency conversion costs. Travelers and businesses no longer need to pay processing fees to convert currencies for tourist activities or hedging purposes (see Chapter 7). Second, direct and transparent price comparison is now possible, thus channeling more resources toward more competitive firms. Third, adopting the euro imposes strong macroeconomic discipline. Prior to adopting the euro, different governments independently determined exchange rates. Italy, for example, sharply devalued its lira in the 1990s. While Italian exports became cheaper and more competitive, other EU members (especially France) were furious. But Italy can no longer devalue its currency, although it has been engulfed in an economic crisis. Also, when confronting recessions, governments often printed more currency and increased spending. Such actions cause inflation,

PengAtlas Map

ISTOCK.COM/HENRIK5000

AARON AMAT/SHUTTERSTOCK.COM

which may spill over to neighboring countries. By adopting the euro, euro zone countries agreed to abolish monetary policy (such as manipulating exchange rates and printing more currency) as a tool to solve macroeconomic problems. These efforts in theory would provide macroeconomic stability. Overall, the euro has boosted intra-EU trade by about 10%. Commanding a quarter of global foreign currency reserves, the euro has quickly established itself as the only credible rival to the dollar.

However, there are also significant costs involved. The first, noted above, is the loss of ability to implement independent monetary policy. Since 2008, economic life in many EU countries without the option of devaluation is tough. The possibility of leaving the euro zone has surfaced in public discussion in some countries. The second cost is the lack of flexibility in implementing fiscal policy in areas such as deficit spending. When a country runs into fiscal difficulties, it may be faced with inflation, high interest rates, and a run on its currency. When a number of countries share a common currency, the risks are spread. But some countries can become "free riders," because they may not need to fix their own fiscal problems—other, more responsible members will have to shoulder the burden.

8-4c The EU's Challenges

Politically, the EU and its predecessors—the ECSC, the EEC, and the EC—have delivered more than 60 years of peace and prosperity and have turned some Cold War enemies into members. Although some people complain about the EU's huge expenses and bureaucratic meetings, they need to be reminded that one day spent on meetings is one day member countries are not shooting at one another. Given that most European countries, until WWII, had been involved in wars as their primary conflict resolution mechanism, negotiating to resolve differences via EU platforms is not only cheaper but also far more peaceful. For this extraordinary accomplishment, the EU—in the middle of a major economic crisis—received the Nobel *Peace* Prize in 2012.

Schengen A passport-free travel zone within the EU.

euro The currency currently used in 19 EU countries.

euro zone The 19 EU countries that currently use the euro as the official currency.

EXHIBIT 8.3 BENEFITS AND COSTS OF ADOPTING THE EURO

Benefits	Costs
▶ Reduces currency conversion costs	▶ Unable to implement independent monetary policy
▶ Facilitates direct price comparison	▶ Limits the flexibility in fiscal policy (in areas such as deficit spending)
▶ Imposes monetary disciplines on governments	

Economically, the EU has launched a single currency and has built a single market in which people, goods, services, and capital can move freely—known as the "four freedoms of movement"—within the core Schengen area (although not throughout the entire EU). Although the accomplishments are enviable in the eyes of other regional organizations, the EU has been engulfed in a midlife crisis.[7] Significant challenges lie ahead, especially in terms of (1) enlargement concerns, (2) internal divisions, and (3) existential crisis.

The EU enlargement has caused significant concerns. The EU's largest expansion took place in 2004, with ten new members. Eight of them—the Czech Republic, Estonia, Hungary, Latvia, Lithuania, Poland, Slovakia, and Slovenia—were former eastern bloc Central and Eastern Europe (CEE) countries. Three of these—Estonia, Latvia, and Lithuania—had previously been part of the Soviet Union. Such expansion was a political triumph, but it was also an economic burden. The ten new members constituted 20% of the overall population but contributed only 9% to GDP and had an

Germany

average GDP per capita that was 46% of the average for the (pre-2004) EU 15. In 2007, Bulgaria and Romania joined and brought the average down further. In 2013, Croatia joined. With low growth and high unemployment throughout the EU and severe economic crisis in the so-called PIGS (Portugal, Ireland/Italy, Greece, and Spain) countries, many EU citizens are tired of taking on additional burdens to absorb new members. Many EU 15 countries have restricted immigration from new members.

Another major debate regarding enlargement is Turkey, whose average income is even lower. In addition, its large Muslim population is also a concern for a predominantly Christian EU. If Turkey were to join, its population of 73 million would make it the second most populous EU country behind only Germany, whose population is 83 million now (but is declining). The weight of EU countries in voting is based (mostly) on population. Given the high birth rates in Turkey and low birth rates in Germany and other EU countries, if Turkey were to join the EU, by 2020 it would become the most populous and thus the most powerful member by commanding most significant voting power. Turkey's combination of low incomes, high birth rates, and Muslim majority visibly concern current member countries, especially given the history of Christian–Muslim tensions in Europe. Turkey's military coup in 2016 and the government's crackdown in its aftermath have made Turkey's prospects to join the EU even dimmer.

Internally, there is a significant debate on whether the EU should be an economic and political union, or just an economic union. One school of thought, led by France, argues that an economic union should inevitably evolve toward a political union, through which Europe speaks as "one voice." Its proponents frequently invoke the famous term enshrined in the 1957 Treaty of Rome, "ever closer union."[8] Another school of thought,

VCHAL/SHUTTERSTOCK.COM

Turkey has long sought membership in the European Union, but unfavorable demographics, Christian–Muslim tensions, and a 2016 coup attempt have dimmed its prospects substantially.

led by Britain, views the EU as primarily an economic union that should focus on free trade, pure and simple. The profound frustration associated with the fear of losing national sovereignty in the march toward an "ever closer union" has directly contributed to Brexit (see Opening Case).

The 2010–2012 bailouts to rescue Greece have intensified this debate. Although Germany reluctantly agreed to lead bailout efforts, it demanded that the EU-wide "economic governance" be strengthened and that insolvent countries lose some of their economic sovereignty by having their budgets approved (or vetoed) by the EU. While this is viewed as a step toward closer political union, Germany does not share France's political motivation for an "ever closer union." In fact, the German media has called for Germany to withdraw from the euro zone in order to avoid the burden of paying for other countries' problems. However, abandoning the euro is not realistic for Germany. This is because a revived Deutsche Mark would certainly appreciate and severely undermine Germany's export competitiveness. Germany ends up being a "reluctant hegemon."[9]

Finally, since 2008, the EU's challenges have been magnified. Externally, in 2014, with Russia's intervention in Ukraine, the EU felt compelled to join the US-led sanctions on Russia, inflicting economic wounds on itself by abandoning hard-won markets in Russia. Internally, a total of eight members were engulfed in embarrassing financial crises that had to be bailed out by other members (and the IMF): Hungary (2008), Latvia (2008), Romania (2009), Greece (2010, 2011, 2012), Ireland (2010), Portugal (2011), Cyprus (2011), and Spain (2012). Not surprisingly, Germany and other relatively well-off EU countries, in the middle of their own Great Recession, were reluctant to foot the bill to bail out other countries. Each crisis was painful in its own ways, but the Greek crisis was particularly gut-wrenching, resulting in calls for Greece to exit or to be expelled—a "Grexit" scenario.

Although Grexit has not materialized, Brexit—a newer word directly inspired by Grexit—has been taking place (see Opening Case). Now that one country sets a precedent that it is possible to leave the EU, certain politicians and groups frustrated with the EU's problems are now openly advocating Frexit (for France), Gexit (for Germany), and Nexit (for the Netherlands) in addition to Grexit.

On top of all these political moves advocating exit, the migrant crisis, which began in 2015, has severely undermined EU solidarity. Basically, millions of refugees from Muslim-majority countries such as Syria, Iraq, Afghanistan, and Libya have illegally but desperately crossed the Mediterranean or traveled overland through Southeast Europe to reach EU countries. Although such refugees typically arrive in a Southern European country such as Greece and Italy first, their preferred destinations are often wealthy Northern European countries, especially Germany. In response to the migrant crisis with endless unauthorized crossings, border controls were *reintroduced* in seven Schengen countries (Austria, Denmark, France, Germany, Norway, Poland, and Sweden). This has directly caused the collapse of Schengen—free movement of people, one of the core "four freedoms of movement." Overall, with the second largest economy (Britain) leaving, with other countries threatening to leave, and with endless internal crises and external threats, the EU is facing an existential crisis. This severe setback is part of the recent backlash against globalization—and in the EU, against regional integration.

8-5 REGIONAL ECONOMIC INTEGRATION IN THE AMERICAS

8-5a North America: North American Free Trade Agreement (NAFTA)

NAFTA is an FTA among Canada, Mexico, and the United States. Launched in 1994, NAFTA has no shortage of hyperbole and controversy. Because of the very different levels of economic development, NAFTA was labeled "one of the most radical free trade experiments in history."[10] Politically, the Mexican government was interested in cementing market liberalization reforms by demonstrating its commitment to free trade. Economically, Mexico was interested in securing preferential treatment for 80% of its exports. Consequently, by the stroke of a pen, Mexico declared itself a *North* American country. Many Americans, on the other hand, thought it was not the best time to open the borders, as the US unemployment rate was 7% at that time. Texas billionaire H. Ross Perot, a presidential candidate in 1992, described NAFTA's potential destruction of thousands of US jobs as a "giant sucking sound."

As NAFTA celebrated its 20th anniversary, NAFTA's supporters largely won the argument. In two decades, trilateral merchandise trade grew from $290 billion in 1993 to $1.1 trillion in 2016—a nearly fourfold increase. Approximately $3 billion goods and services cross the border every day now. That is an astonishing $2 million every *minute*. US trade with Canada tripled and US trade with Mexico increased by five times—while US trade with the rest of the world grew 280%. In two decades, Mexico's GDP per capita almost tripled to $10,650 (ranked 64th in the world, based on nominal GDP)—over 40% higher than China's $7,000. While many Americans and Canadians think of Mexicans as "poor" and "infested with crimes"—thanks to the negative (and typically one-sided) media—Mexico is the second largest importer of US goods (next only to Canada), imports more US goods than China, and absorbs more US exports than Britain, France, and Germany combined.[11] Running the 14th largest economy in the world with a number of advanced manufacturing industries such as automobile, pharmaceuticals, and aerospace, Mexico, according to the *Economist*, has been "NAFTA's biggest beneficiary."[12]

What about jobs? In brief, job destruction on a large scale never materialized. *Maquiladora* (export assembly) factories blossomed under NAFTA, with jobs peaking at 1.3 million in 2000. Yet, no "giant sucking sound" was heard. Approximately 300,000 US jobs were lost due to NAFTA, but about 100,000 jobs were added. The net loss was small, since the US economy generated 20 million new jobs during the first decade of NAFTA. A hard count on jobs misses another subtle, but important, benefit.

NAFTA has allowed US firms to *preserve* more US jobs, because 40% of the value of US imports from Mexico and 25% from Canada is actually made in USA—in comparison, only 10% of the value of US imports from China is made in USA. Without NAFTA, entire industries might be lost rather than just the labor-intensive portions.

However, not all is rosy. First, thanks to Chinese competition, many US, Canadian, European, and Japanese multinationals have shifted some

ISTOCK.COM/HENRIK5000

ISTOCK.COM/NIKADA

of their factory work to China, which has now replaced Mexico as the second largest exporter to the United States (after Canada). Second, President Donald Trump, when he was a candidate, attacked NAFTA as a "disaster" and "the worst trade deal." Unhappy about work done in Mexico, he threatened US firms such as Carrier and GM with "a big border tax," which would be a violation of NAFTA (see Closing Case).

8-5b South America: Andean Community, Mercosur, USAN/UNASUR, and CAFTA

Despite NAFTA's imperfections, it is much more effective than the two customs unions in South America: **Andean Community** and **Mercosur**. Members of Andean Community (launched in 1969) and Mercusor (launched in 1991) are mostly countries on the *western* (Pacific-facing) and *eastern* (Atlantic-facing) sides of the Andean mountains, respectively (see PengAtlas Map 10). There is much mutual suspicion and rivalry between both organizations as well as within each of them. Mercosur is relatively more protectionist and suspicious of the United States, whereas Andean Community is more pro–free trade.

Neither regional initiative has been effective, in part because only about 5% and 20% of members' trade is within the Andean Community and Mercosur, respectively. Their largest trading partner, the United States, lies outside the region. An FTA with the United States, not among themselves, would generate the most significant benefits. For this reason, Chile, Colombia, Panama, and Peru signed bilateral FTAs with the United States and reaped the benefits of higher economic growth than other countries.[13]

In 2008, Andean Community and Mercusur countries agreed to form the **Union of South American Nations** (**USAN**, more commonly known by its Spanish acronym, **UNASUR**, which refers to *Unión de Naciones Suramericanas*). Inspired by the EU, USAN/UNASUR announced its intention to eventually adopt a common currency, parliament, and passport. However, progress has been slow.

One regional accomplishment is the **United States–Dominican Republic–Central America Free Trade Agreement (CAFTA)**, which took effect in 2005. Modeled after NAFTA, CAFTA is between "a whale and six minnows" (five Central American countries—Costa Rica, El Salvador, Guatemala, Honduras, and Nicaragua—

plus the Dominican Republic). Although small, the six CAFTA countries collectively represent the second largest US export market in Latin America (behind only Mexico). Globally, CAFTA is the tenth largest US export market, importing more US goods than Russia, India, and Indonesia *combined*.[14]

8-6 REGIONAL ECONOMIC INTEGRATION IN THE ASIA PACIFIC

This section introduces regional integration efforts between Australia and New Zealand, in Southeast Asia, and throughout Asia and the Pacific. Their scale and scope differ from one another tremendously.

8-6a Australia–New Zealand Closer Economic Relations Trade Agreement (ANZCERTA or CER)

The **Australia–New Zealand Closer Economic Relations Trade Agreement (ANZCERTA or CER)**, launched in 1983, turned the historic rivalry between Australia and New Zealand into a partnership. As an FTA, the CER removed tariffs and NTBs. For example, both countries agreed not to charge exporters from the other country for dumping. Citizens from both countries also could freely work and reside in the other country. Thanks to the relatively high level of geographic proximity and cultural homogeneity, CER has been very successful.

8-6b Association of Southeast Asian Nations (ASEAN)

Founded in 1967, the **Association of Southeast Asian Nations (ASEAN)** was inspired by the EU's success. In 1992, the ASEAN Free Trade Area (AFTA) was set up. ASEAN suffers from a problem similar to the one that Latin American countries face: ASEAN's main trading partners—the United States, the EU, Japan, and China—are outside the region. Intra-ASEAN trade usually accounts for less than a quarter of total trade. The benefits of AFTA, thus, may be limited.

In response, ASEAN in 2002 signed an ASEAN–China Free Trade Agreement (ACFTA), which was launched in 2010. Given the increasingly strong competition in terms of Chinese exports and China-bound FDI that could have come to ASEAN, ACFTA hopes to turn such rivalry into a partnership. ACFTA is estimated to boost ASEAN's exports to China by 48% and China's exports to ASEAN by 55%, thus raising ASEAN's GDP by 0.9% and China's by 0.3%. Similar FTAs are being negotiated with Japan and South Korea.

8-6c Asia–Pacific Economic Cooperation (APEC) and Trans-Pacific Partnership (TPP)

While ASEAN was deepening its integration, Australia was afraid that it might be left out and suggested in 1989 that ASEAN and CER countries form the **Asia–Pacific Economic Cooperation (APEC)**. Given the lack of a global heavyweight in both ASEAN and CER, Japan was invited. While the Japanese happily agreed to join, ASEAN and CER countries also feared that Japan might dominate the group and create a de facto "yen bloc." During WWII, Japan invaded most countries in the region, bombed Darwin and attacked Sydney harbor in Australia (see the movie *Australia*). Bitter memories of Japanese wartime atrocities seemed to die hard. At that time, China was far less significant economically than it is now, and thus could hardly counterbalance Japan.

Then the United States requested to join APEC, citing its long West Coast that would qualify it as a Pacific country. Economically, the United States did not want to be left out of the most dynamically growing region in the world. Politically, the United States was interested in containing Japanese influence in any Asian regional deals. While the United States could certainly serve as a counterweight for Japan, the US membership would also change the character of APEC, which had been centered on ASEAN and CER. To make its APEC membership less odd, the United States brought on board two of its NAFTA partners, Canada and Mexico. Canada and Mexico were equally interested in the economic benefits, but probably cared less about the US political motives. Once the floodgates for membership were open, Chile, Peru, and Russia all eventually got in, emphasizing their long Pacific coastlines.

ISTOCK.COM/HENRIK5000

Australia–New Zealand Closer Economic Relations Trade Agreement (ANZCERTA or CER) A free trade agreement between Australia and New Zealand.

Association of Southeast Asian Nations (ASEAN) The organization underpinning regional economic integration in Southeast Asia.

Asia-Pacific Economic Cooperation (APEC) The official title for regional economic integration involving 21 member economies around the Pacific.

IN FOCUS: *Emerging Markets/Ethical Dilemma*

Does the TPP Have a Future?

Launched in 2005 by four small member countries of APEC (Brunei, Chile, New Zealand, and Singapore), the Trans-Pacific Partnership (TPP) is a multilateral free trade agreement (FTA). A number of additional countries (all APEC members)—Australia, Canada, Malaysia, Mexico, Peru, Japan, the United States, and Vietnam—negotiated to join the TPP. Although smaller and less complex than APEC (and certainly simpler than the WTO), the TPP talks ran into a similar bunch of problems: (1) agriculture, (2) intellectual property (IP), (3) investor-state dispute settlement (ISDS), and (4) domestic politics.

As ever, the United States and Japan fought over agricultural subsidies, especially in beef and pork—a small problem in the larger scheme of things. In the United States, less than 1% of GDP comes from beef and pork production. In Japan, a country with 46 million households, only 100,000 households are involved in the beef and pork sectors. Eventually, Japan agreed to drop its beef tariffs from 39% to 9%, but over 15 years—to the frustration of US and Australian cattle ranchers.

In IP, the United States sought the TPP to agree with tighter IP protection that would go beyond TRIPS. This made sense from a US standpoint. In 2010, 40% of worldwide payments made to IP rights holders—nearly $100 billion—went to Americans and American firms. These sums matched the profits from the export of aircraft, grain, and business services, the three leading US export sectors. Unfortunately, other countries were not so interested. Weaker IP protection enables faster diffusion of innovation (such as generic drugs) to less developed countries—a US practice for about 100 years in the nineteenth century when the United States was a developing country itself.

Designed to deter governments from expropriating foreign assets, ISDS allows foreign firms to launch arbitration to sue governments that allegedly deny their rights under an FTA. For example, Lone Pine, a US firm, sued the Canadian province of Quebec for its ban on fracking. Philip Morris sued the Australian government for its requirements for nasty pictures of lung cancer victims on cigarette packages. Taking the painful lesson, Australia opposed having ISDS in the TPP. In comparison, the WTO only allows national governments, not private firms, to launch such cases. In the end, TPP's dispute-settlement mechanisms specifically bar tobacco firms from claiming compensation from public-health policies that limit their business.

After seven years of arduous negotiations, the final agreement was signed by all 12 countries in Auckland, New Zealand, on February 4, 2016. It would have to be ratified by every TPP member within two years of signing. However, as of this writing (February 2017), only Japan ratified it. Although advocated by the Obama administration, chances of the TPP

POOL/GETTY IMAGES

passing the US Congress are zero. The reason is that during the bitter 2015–2016 presidential campaign, all three major candidates opposed it. Democratic candidate Bernie Sanders, after seeing the text, rendered his judgment: "It's even worse than I thought." Another Democratic candidate, Hillary Clinton, who had supported the TPP as Secretary of State, in an effort to grab Sanders' votes changed her course and was no longer supportive of it. Republican candidate Donald Trump, who did not like any trade deal (including NAFTA), called the TPP "insanity." On January 23, 2017, the first full working day as president, Trump formally withdrew the US signature from the TPP. Japanese Prime Minister Shinzo Abe flatly admitted, "TPP is meaningless without the United States."

Even if the TPP did enter into force, because all members are APEC members, what the relationship is between APEC and TPP remains to be seen. By pointedly excluding China (the second largest economy in APEC and in the world), how meaningful the TPP can be is also a huge question mark. Making an institution-based argument focusing on the "rules of the game," President Obama warned that "if we don't pass this agreement—if America doesn't write those rules—then countries like China will."

Exhibit A: In October 2014, at the APEC summit meeting in Beijing, with Obama in attendance, Chinese President Xi Jingping openly called for the establishment of a Free Trade Area of the Asia-Pacific (FTAAP) consisting of all 21 members of APEC. Exhibit B: In November 2016, within days after Trump's election (but before his inauguration), Australia, Malaysia, and other TPP members changed the course and embraced a rival China-led agreement—the Regional Comprehensive Economic Partnership (RCEP), which Beijing had been advocating for years with few followers. The RCEP, which deliberately excludes the United States, would enable China to assert significant influence on trade rules and norms. Exhibit C: In January 2017, a few days after Trump's inauguration, a senior Chinese diplomat noted at a press conference, "If anyone were to say China is playing a leadership role in the world, I would say it's not China rushing to the front, but rather the front runners have stepped back leaving the place to China." So stay tuned.

Sources: "A mega trade deal," *Bloomberg Businessweek*, 12 October 2015: 12–13; "Trade's coming rough turn," *Bloomberg Businessweek*, 16 January 2017: 8–9; "Bridge over troubled water," *Economist*, 15 November 2014: 15; "The Pacific age," *Economist*, 15 November 2014: special report; "A serviceable deal," *Economist*, 4 November 2015: 76; "Weighing anchor," *Economist*, 10 October 2015: 71–72; B. Gordon, "Trading up in Asia," *Foreign Affairs*, July 2012: 17–22; R. Katz, "The Trans-Pacific Partnership: Lessons from negotiations," NBR Analysis Brief, September 2014, Seattle: National Bureau of Asian Research; "Trans-Pacific Partnership text released, waving green flag for debate," *New York Times*, 5 November 2015; M. W. Peng, D. Ahlstrom, S. Carraher, and W. Shi, "An institution-based view of global IPR history," *Journal of International Business Studies* (2017, in press); "Diplomat says China would assume world leadership if needed," Reuters, 23 January 2017.

Today, APEC's 21 member economies (shown in PengAtlas Map 11) span four continents, are home to 2.6 billion people, contribute 46% of world trade, and command 54% of world GDP, making it the largest regional integration grouping by geographic area and by GDP. While it is nice to include "everyone," APEC may be too big. Essentially as a talking shop, APEC (nicknamed "a perfect excuse to chat") provides a forum for members to make commitments that are largely rhetorical. In part because APEC is too big and too difficult to get anything meaningful done, a new and smaller **Trans-Pacific Partnership (TPP)** has been developing (see In Focus).

 8-7 MANAGEMENT SAVVY

Of the two major perspectives on global business (institution-based and resource-based views), this chapter has focused on the institution-based view. In order to address the question "What determines success and failure around the globe?" the entire chapter has been devoted to an introduction of the rules of the game as institutions governing global and regional economic integration. How does this knowledge help managers? Managers need to combine the insights from the institution-based view with those from the resource-based view to come up with strategies and solutions on how their firms can capitalize on the opportunities presented by global and regional economic integration. Listed in Exhibit 8.4, two broad implications for action emerge.

First, given the slowdown of multilateralism and the acceleration of regionalism, managers are advised to focus their attention more at regional than global levels.[15] To a large extent, they are already doing that. The largest multinational enterprises may have a presence all over the world, but their center of gravity (measured by revenues) is often still their home region (such as within the EU or NAFTA). Thus, they are not really

---

EXHIBIT 8.4 IMPLICATIONS FOR ACTION

▶ Think regional, downplay global.

▶ Understand the rules of the game and their transitions at both global and regional levels.

---

global. Regional strategies make sense because most countries within a region share some cultural, economic, and geographic similarities that can lower the liability of foreignness when moving within the region, as opposed to moving from one region to another. From a resource-based standpoint, most firms are better prepared to compete at a regional rather than a global level.[16] Despite the hoopla associated with global strategies, managers, in short, need to think local and downplay—while not necessarily abandon—global.

Second, managers also need to understand the rules of the game and their transitions at both global and regional levels. While trade negotiations involve a lot of politics that many managers could hardly care less about, managers who ignore these rules and their transitions do so at their own peril. When the MFA was phased out in 2005, numerous managers at textile firms, who had become comfortable under the MFA's protection, decried the new level of competition and complained about their lack of preparation. In fact, they had 30 *years* to prepare for such an eventuality. When the MFA was signed in 1974, it was agreed that it would be phased out by 2005. The typical attitude that "we don't care about (trade) politics" can lead to a failure in due diligence. The best managers expect their firm strategies to shift over time, constantly work to decipher the changes in the big picture, and are willing to take advantage of the new opportunities brought by global and regional trade deals.

> **Trans-Pacific Partnership (TPP)**
> A multilateral free trade agreement being negotiated by 12 Asia Pacific countries.

Closing Case: What If NAFTA Goes Away?

In effect since 1994, the North American Free Trade Agreement (NAFTA) has no shortage of controversies. As Trump has assumed power, the criticisms against NAFTA, potentially culminating in its repeal, force us to entertain a previously unthinkable scenario: What happens if NAFTA goes away? The answer to this question obviously boils down to what NAFTA has brought to the United States.

In two decades, trilateral merchandise trade among three member countries grew from $290 billion in 1993 to $1.1 trillion in 2016—a nearly fourfold increase. Approximately $3 billion goods and services cross the border every *day*—an astonishing $2 million every *minute*. US trade with Canada tripled and US trade with Mexico increased by five times—while US trade with the rest of the world grew 280%. Canada and Mexico are, respectively, the second and third largest exporters to the United States (China is the first). Canada and Mexico are, respectively, the first and second largest importers of US goods. Mexico alone imports more US goods than China, and absorbs more US imports than Britain, France, and Germany *combined*. Canada imports even more "Made in USA" goods.

What about jobs? In brief, no "giant sucking sound" has been heard. Approximately 300,000 US jobs—an average of 15,000 per year—were lost due to NAFTA in its first two decades, but about 100,000 jobs were added. The net loss was small, as the US economy generated at least 25 million new jobs during the same period. In 2015, the Congressional Research Service acknowledged some worker and firm adjustment costs brought by NAFTA. But overall, it reported conclusively that "NAFTA did not cause the huge job losses feared by the critics." At present some eight million US jobs depend on trade with Canada and another six million on trade with Mexico. Even for every job lost, the economy gains $450,000 in the form of higher productivity and lower consumer prices, which benefit all.

But a hard count on jobs misses another subtle but important benefit. NAFTA has allowed US firms to *preserve* more US jobs, because 40% of the value of US imports from Mexico and 25% from Canada is actually made in USA—in comparison, only 10% of the value of US imports from China is made in USA. In 1994, US imports from Mexico only contained 5% of the value made in USA. Clearly NAFTA has facilitated seamless supply chain integration, with goods, components, and parts crossing the border multiple times to be eventually assembled in one member country. Without NAFTA, entire industries may be lost rather than just the labor-intensive portions.

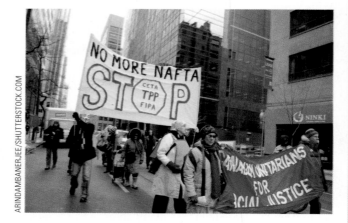

ARINDAMBANERJEE/SHUTTERSTOCK.COM

So what if NAFTA goes away? First, relax: not all the benefits discussed above will be lost. As an institutional framework, NAFTA merely represents some relatively new rules of the game that are man-made and artificial. Given their natural geographic proximity and historical links, the three North American neighbors had been trading for ages before 1994. Their tightly knit economies cannot and will not immediately stop trading. In a hypothetical post-NAFTA era, these three economies will still gain by trading, but the gains will be smaller. Americans and Canadians can still enjoy plenty of yummy avocadoes from Mexico (the world's top avocado producer), but they will have to cough up more money for their beloved guacamole.

Second, if the Trump administration unilaterally imposes high import tariffs, Canada and Mexico will certainly respond in kind. Given the reality of NAFTA supply chain, a tariff is like erecting a wall in the middle of a *factory*. Hard-fought export market share in Canada and Mexico will shrink. Thousands of jobs in manufacturing, logistics, and other services will disappear. For example, the Center for Automotive Research estimated that a 35% tariff on vehicles imported from Mexico, which would contain 40% "Made in USA" parts, would result in the loss of 31,000 US jobs.

Third, because both Canada and Mexico have free trade agreements (FTAs) with the EU, the US withdrawal from NAFTA will significantly help increase EU firms' market share there. In other words, EU firms, propelled by their own FTAs with Canada and Mexico, will be delighted to take over the market share vacated by US firms. Beyond those from the EU, strong competitors from China, Japan, and Korea, despite having no help from FTAs, will be elbowing their way into Canada and Mexico. In other words, reducing the preferential treatments (especially low or zero tariffs) enjoyed by US firms under NAFTA will clip their wings in the competition for export markets in Canada and Mexico. Ironically, gutting NAFTA will help enhance the competitiveness of America's global rivals.

Finally, shutting down NAFTA does not bring back a large number of manufacturing jobs to the United States. The recent crises facing US manufacturing jobs, falling from 17 million to 11 million between 2000 and 2010, have little to do with NAFTA. Instead, competition with China and technological changes have largely contributed to such a decline. Therefore, blaming Mexico and dismantling a beneficial FTA do not solve the problems associated with manufacturing job losses.

There is widespread belief that Trump's nasty rhetoric on NAFTA is just "talk." Procedurally, Trump is required to seek congressional approval if he merely wants to renegotiate NAFTA. Congress is unlikely to support a policy to throw away so many benefits and to spark retaliatory trade sanctions in America's top two export markets—with so little gains. While NAFTA is not a panacea and has its problems, dismantling it would be "lunacy," according to *Texas Monthly*. In summary, NAFTA is unlikely to be gone completely. But renegotiation is certainly possible.

Case Discussion Questions

1. Because the three NAFTA member countries had been trading for ages before NAFTA, what are the benefits of an FTA such as NAFTA?

2. ***ON ETHICS:*** Pick your role as (1) a consumer, (2) a manufacturing worker, or (3) a banker in one member country. What has NAFTA done to *help* or *hurt* you and your community?

3. Pick a firm from your state or country that is active in at least two (preferably three) member countries via trade and investment. How does it prepare for the scenario that NAFTA benefits are curtailed?

Sources: Center for Automotive Research, *NAFTA Briefing: Trade Benefits to the Automotive Industry and Potential Consequences of Withdrawal from the Agreement* (Ann Arbor, MI, 2017); "Better than a wall," *Economist*, 4 February 2017: 66; E. Grieder, "Trumpeting trade," *Texas Monthly*, October 2016: www.texasmonthly.com; J. Ku and J. Yoo, "Don't sweat it Texas, NAFTA isn't going anywhere," *Houston Chronicle*, 30 November 2016: www.houstonchronicle.com; A. Kumar, "Did NAFTA spur Texas exports?" *Southwest Economy* (March 2006): 3–7; J. McBride, *NAFTA's Economic Impact* (New York: Council on Foreign Relations, 2016); M. W. Peng, "What happens if NAFTA goes away?" *Texas CEO Magazine*, January 2017: 26–27; M. W. Peng, "What happens to Texas if the US withdraws from NAFTA?" *Dallas Morning News*, 9 May 2017: 13A; "Border leaders think Trump's tough talk on NAFTA will die down," *Texas Tribune*, 11 November 2016: www.texastribune.org; "Trump calls NAFTA a 'disaster,' Texas Republicans beg to differ," *Texas Tribune*, 9 August 2016: www.texastribune.org; M. A. Villarreal and I. Fergusson, *The North American Free Trade Agreement (NAFTA)* (Washington: Congressional Research Service, 2015).

STUDY TOOLS 8

LOCATED AT THE BACK OF YOUR BOOK:

☐ Rip out and study the Chapter Review Card at the end of the book

LOG IN TO WWW.CENGAGEBRAIN.COM TO:

☐ Review key term flashcards

☐ Complete a practice quiz to test your knowledge of key concepts

☐ View animated PengAtlas Maps

☐ Complete interactive content, watch chapter videos, and take a graded quiz

☐ Track your knowledge of key concepts in Global Business

☐ Read and discuss additional case study content

9 Growing & Internationalizing the Entrepreneurial Firm

SUCCESSO IMAGES/SHUTTERSTOCK.COM

LEARNING OBJECTIVES

After studying this chapter, you will be able to . . .

 9-1 Define entrepreneurship, entrepreneurs, and entrepreneurial firms.

 9-2 Identify the institutions and resources that affect entrepreneurship.

 9-3 Highlight three characteristics of a growing entrepreneurial firm.

9-4 Describe how international strategies for entering foreign markets are different from those for staying in domestic markets.

9-5 Articulate what you should do to strengthen your entrepreneurial ability.

After you finish this chapter, go to

PAGE 151 for

STUDY TOOLS

Opening Case: Sriracha Spices Up American Food

Named after a seaside city in eastern Thailand, Sriracha is a generic name for a hot sauce made from a paste of chili peppers (jalapeños), garlic, vinegar, sugar, and salt. As a dipping sauce, Sriracha has been used in Thai and Vietnamese cuisine for ages. However, in the United States, most people would associate Sriracha with the specific brand produced by Huy Fong Foods, based in Irwindale (a suburb of Los Angeles), California. It is indeed Huy Fong's Sriracha Hot Chili Sauce—often affectionately called the "rooster sauce" due to the prominent logo of the rooster on its squeeze bottle—that has popularized this once niche food and spiced up mainstream American taste buds. So what exactly is Sriracha? What does it do? Huy Fong's website has provided an official answer:

Sriracha is made from sun ripen chilies which are ground into a smooth paste along with garlic and packaged in a convenient squeeze bottle. It is excellent in soups, sauces, pastas, pizzas, hot dogs, hamburgers, chow mein, or anything else to give it a delicious, spicy taste.

Founded in 1980 by a Vietnamese-Chinese immigrant David Tran, the firm was named after the freighter, *Huy Fong*, that carried him to the land of opportunity. Tran was born and raised in Vietnam. Already an entrepreneur back in Vietnam, he had a small business making a similar hot sauce there in the 1970s. But the Vietnam War made growth impossible. After the war, the Vietnamese government gave ethnic Chinese businessmen like Tran a hard time. In 1979, he left Vietnam. As a serial entrepreneur, Tran looked for opportunities in his new country. He quickly discovered that (in his view) there was no decent spicy food in the United States. Having identified this gap, he endeavored to fill it by making hot sauce again. By 1983, he came up with the winning recipe that has not changed much since.

Distinguished by a green cap and a clear plastic squeeze bottle, Huy Fong's Sriracha was first sold to Asian supermarkets and restaurants. While popular in the Asian community, Sriracha remained a niche product hardly noticed by mainstream America. Over time, the burgeoning Asian population in the United States made crossover into the mainstream possible. Sriracha created quite a sensation. In 2003, Walmart started selling it in its stores in Los Angeles and Houston. Eventually, Walmart would carry it in its more than 3,000 stores across the nation. Various restaurants, such as Applebee's, P. F. Chang's, Subway, and White Castle, introduced Sriracha-flavored dishes and dipping sauces. Potato chip king Lay's unleashed a sriracha-flavored potato chip. In 2010, *Bon Appétit*—an influential foodie magazine—named it Ingredient of the Year. In 2011, its first mainstream kitchen bible, *The Sriracha Cookbook*, was published by Randy Clemens. In 2012, *Cook's Illustrated* claimed Sriracha to be the best-tasting hot sauce, ahead of rivals such as Tobasco, Colula Hot Sauce, and Frank's Red Hot. While focusing on the United States, Sriracha has been exported to many countries around the world.

Sriracha's success has not only inspired a number of imitators and counterfeiters (!), but has also caught the attention of McIlhenny Co., the maker of the standard-bearer of American hot sauce, Tobasco, for the past 160 years. McIlhenny Co. used to dismiss Sriracha as "a West Coast thing." But now Paul McIlhenny, its sixth-generation CEO, can pick up a bottle of rooster sauce at his local Walmart in rural Louisiana. In response, a Tobasco-version of Sriracha is now available. Given such strong incumbents and a crowded field, what is Sriracha's secret? Again, Huy Fong's website has provided an official answer: "The secret? Continued high quality ingredients at low prices and great taste makes it a success in today's trend toward spicy foods."

Sources: "Burning sensation: How Sriracha hot sauce won the American kitchen," *Bloomberg Businessweek*, 21 February 2013: 67–69; www.huyfong.com; www.tobasco.com.

How do entrepreneurial firms such as Huy Fong grow? How do they enter international markets? What are the challenges and constraints they face? This chapter deals with these important questions. This is different from many international business (IB) textbooks that typically only cover large firms. To the extent that *every* large firm today started small and that some (although not all) of today's **small and medium-sized enterprises (SMEs)** may become tomorrow's multinational enterprises (MNEs), current and would-be managers will not gain a complete picture of the global business landscape if they only focus on large firms. SMEs are firms with fewer than 500 employees in the United States and with fewer than 250 employees in the European Union (other countries may have different definitions). Most students will join SMEs for employment. Some will also start up SMEs,

> **small and medium-sized enterprise (SME)** A firm with fewer than 500 employees in the United States or with fewer than 250 employees in the European Union.

thus further necessitating our attention on these numerous "Davids" (such as Huy Fong) instead of on the smaller number of "Goliaths."

This chapter will first define entrepreneurship. Next, we will outline how our two leading perspectives—institution-based and resource-based views—shed light on entrepreneurship. Then, we will introduce the characteristics of a growing entrepreneurial firm and multiple ways to internationalize. In addition, you will encounter a debate about a growing entrepreneurial phenomenon: bankruptcy. Do's and don'ts follow.

French in origin, the word "entrepreneurs" traditionally means intermediaries connecting others.

Although SMEs are not the exclusive domain of entrepreneurship, many people often associate entrepreneurship with SMEs because, on average, SMEs tend to be more entrepreneurial than large firms. To minimize confusion, the remainder of this chapter will follow that convention, although it is not totally accurate. That is, while we acknowledge that managers at large firms can be entrepreneurial, we will limit the use of the term "entrepreneurs" to owners, founders, and managers of SMEs. Further, we will use the term "entrepreneurial firms" when referring to SMEs. We will refer to non-SMEs (which are firms with more than 500 employees in the United States or firms with more than 250 employees in the European Union) as "large firms."

SMEs are important. Worldwide, they account for over 95% of the number of firms, create approximately 50% of total value added, and generate 60% to 90% of employment, depending on the country. Many entrepreneurs will try, and many SMEs will fail. Only a small number of entrepreneurs and SMEs will succeed.

9-1 ENTREPRENEURSHIP AND ENTREPRENEURIAL FIRMS

Although entrepreneurship is often associated with smaller and younger firms, no rule bans larger and older firms from being entrepreneurial. So what exactly is entrepreneurship? Recent research suggests that firm size and age are *not* defining characteristics of entrepreneurship. Instead, **entrepreneurship** is defined as "the identification and exploitation of previously unexplored opportunities."[1] Specifically, it is concerned with "the sources of opportunities; the processes of discovery, evaluation, and exploitation of opportunities; and the set of individuals who discover, evaluate, and exploit them."[2] French in origin, the word "entrepreneurs" traditionally means intermediaries connecting others.[3] Today, **entrepreneurs** are founders and owners of new businesses or managers of existing firms. **International entrepreneurship** is defined as "a combination of innovative, proactive, and risk-seeking behavior that crosses national borders and is intended to create wealth in organizations."[4]

9-2 INSTITUTIONS, RESOURCES, AND ENTREPRENEURSHIP

Shown in Exhibit 9.1, both the institution-based view and the resource-based view shed light on entrepreneurship. In this section, we will look at how institutions constrain or facilitate entrepreneurs and how firm-specific (and in many cases entrepreneur-specific) resources and capabilities determine their success and failure.

9-2a Institutions and Entrepreneurship

First introduced in Chapters 2 and 3, both formal and informal institutional constraints, as rules of the game, affect entrepreneurship.[5] The Opening Case illustrates how Vietnam's entrepreneur-hostile institutional framework drove away David Tran, and how the United States' entrepreneur-friendly institutional framework has offered rich soil on which his entrepreneurial firm Huy Fong Foods blossoms.

entrepreneurship The identification and exploitation of previously unexplored opportunities.

entrepreneur Founders and owners of new businesses or managers of existing firms who identify and exploit new opportunities.

international entrepreneurship A combination of innovative, proactive, and risk-seeking behavior that crosses national borders and is intended to create wealth in organizations.

Although entrepreneurship is thriving around the globe in general, its development is unequal.[6] Whether entrepreneurship is facilitated or retarded significantly depends on formal institutions governing how entrepreneurs start up new firms (see In Focus).[7] A World Bank survey, *Doing Business*, reports some striking differences in government regulations concerning how easy it is to start up new entrepreneurial firms in terms of registration, licensing, and incorporation (Exhibit 9.2). Using the relatively straightforward (or even "mundane") task of connecting electricity to a newly built commercial building, the World Bank finds that in general, governments in developed economies impose fewer procedures (an average of 4.6 procedures for OECD high-income countries) and a lower total cost (free in Japan and 5.1% of per capita GDP in Germany). On the other hand, entrepreneurs have to put up with harsher hurdles in poor countries. As a class of its own, Burundi imposes a total cost of 430 times of its per capita GDP for entrepreneurs to obtain electricity. Sierra Leone leads the world in requiring entrepreneurs to spend 441 days to obtain electricity.

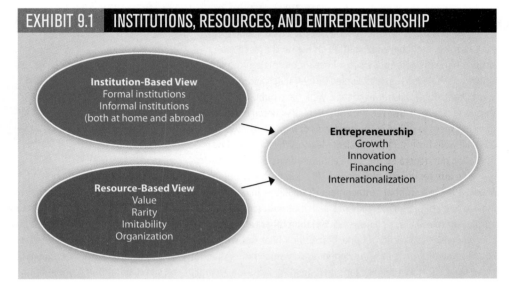

EXHIBIT 9.1 INSTITUTIONS, RESOURCES, AND ENTREPRENEURSHIP

Institution-Based View
Formal institutions
Informal institutions
(both at home and abroad)

Resource-Based View
Value
Rarity
Imitability
Organization

Entrepreneurship
Growth
Innovation
Financing
Internationalization

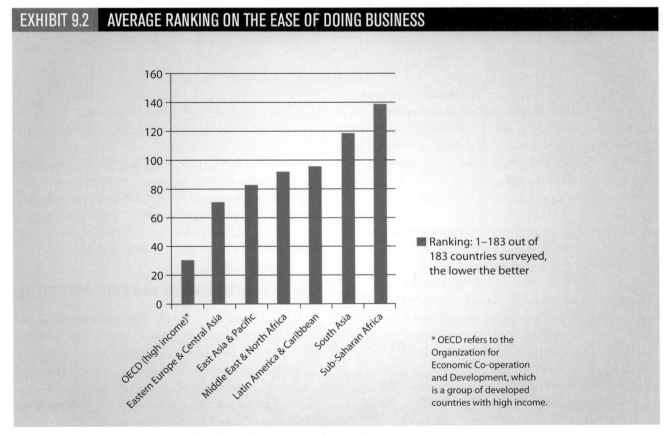

EXHIBIT 9.2 AVERAGE RANKING ON THE EASE OF DOING BUSINESS

■ Ranking: 1–183 out of 183 countries surveyed, the lower the better

* OECD refers to the Organization for Economic Co-operation and Development, which is a group of developed countries with high income.

Source: Data extracted from the World Bank, *Doing Business 2010* (database at www.doingbusiness.org).

IN FOCUS: *Emerging Markets*

One Rock Formation, Two Countries

North Mexico shares a great deal of similarities with South Texas, including landscape, weather, people, food, culture . . . and rock formation beneath the land. South Texas has hit the jackpot of sitting on top of Eagle Ford shale, whose rock formation contains significant shale gas deposits. Fueled by hydraulic fracturing—in short, "fracking"—thousands of shale wells have bubbled up throughout Texas. However, the entrepreneurial boom of fracking does not seem to spill over the border. As of May 2014, fewer than 25 shale wells have stood up in all of Mexico. Why has the same rock formation not generated the same entrepreneurial boom in Mexico?

The answer is institution-based. Oil is big business. But Mexicans have a stubborn attachment to smallness in business. Mexico has a higher percentage of small firms with ten or fewer employees as a share of all firms (95.5%) than other Latin American countries (80%–90% in Argentina, Brazil, and Chile). Known as the Peter Pan syndrome, many firms prefer to stay small rather than to grow, in an effort to minimize tax and regulatory intrusion. Overall, only 8% of bank loans in Mexico go to small and medium-sized enterprises (SMEs). Of about five million SMEs, only 900,000 are sufficiently formal to be creditworthy. Bank loans they obtain carry much higher interest rates than the interest rates for large firms.

JENS LAMBERT/SHUTTERSTOCK.COM

Another reason behind the conspicuous silence of fracking in Mexico is a lack of incentives. In Texas—as well as the rest of the United States—rights to what is discovered under one's farm or ranch belong to the private owner, whereas in Mexico the government owns what is under *your* farm or ranch. In other words, private land ownership in Mexico literally only covers the land, but nothing underneath it. As a result, there is hardly any incentive for any Mexican farmer or rancher to be curious about what lies beneath his or her land.

Sources: "Electronic arm-twisting," *Economist*, 17 May 2014: 68; "On shaky ground," *Economist*, 3 May 2014: 32; "The Peter Pan syndrome," *Economist*, 17 May 2014: 63–64.

Overall, it is not surprising that the more entrepreneur-friendly these formal institutional requirements are, the more flourishing entrepreneurship is, and the more developed the economies become—and vice versa (see PengAtlas Map 12). As a result, many developing economies are now reforming their formal institutions in order to become more entrepreneur-friendly (see PengAtlas Map 13).

In addition to formal institutions, informal institutions such as cultural values and norms also affect entrepreneurship. For example, because entrepreneurs necessarily take more risk, individualistic and low uncertainty-avoidance societies tend to foster relatively more entrepreneurs, whereas collectivistic and high uncertainty-avoidance societies may result in relatively fewer entrepreneurs. For example, among developed economies, Japan has the lowest rate of start-ups, one-third of America's rate and half of Europe's.[8] In another example, Russians make heavy use of social networks online, averaging 9.8 hours

per month—more than double the world average. While spending that much time online makes sense during the long and cold Russian winter, another important reason is the long-held Russian tradition of relying more on informal information networks for daily life. These informal norms help nurture social network entrepreneurs such as Russia's Vkontakte and attract foreign entrants such as Facebook.[9] Overall, the institution-based view suggests that both formal and informal institutions matter.[10] Later sections in this chapter will discuss how they matter.

9-2b Resources and Entrepreneurship

In addition to being subject to institutional constraints, entrepreneurial firms have a unique set of resources and capabilities.[11] A start-up primarily has entrepreneurial vision, drive, and leadership, which compensate for its shortage of tangible resources such as financial capital and formal organizational structure. The resource-based view, discussed in Chapter 4,

PengAtlas Map

ISTOCK.COM/HENRIK5000

sheds considerable light on entrepreneurship with a focus on its value (V), rarity (R), imitability (I), and organizational (O) aspects (see Exhibit 9.1). Like any other firm, an entrepreneurial firm must take the VRIO framework into account as it considers how to leverage its resources.

First, entrepreneurial resources must create *value*. For example, by offering cheap fares, convenient schedules, and Wi-Fi and power port on every seat, Megabus offers superb value to travelers for medium-haul trips that are too far for a leisurely drive but too close to justify the expenses and the increasing hassle to fly. On routes between New York and Boston and between Dallas and Austin, Megabus is rapidly changing the way Americans—especially the young—travel, so much so that it may help kill plans for the new high-speed rail that after all may not offer that much value.[12]

Second, resources must be *rare*. As the cliché goes, "If everybody has it, you can't make money from it." The best-performing entrepreneurs tend to have the rarest knowledge and insights about business opportunities. There is no shortage of hot sauce producers. But the ability to identify such a winning recipe as Huy Fong's David Tran did is rare (see Opening Case).

Third, resources must be *inimitable*. For example, in the ocean of e-commerce firms, the ability to do the "dirtiest job on the Internet" as an online moderator is very hard to imitate. After being exposed to, and then cleaning up, the most nasty and most undesirable racism and bigotry on a daily basis, sometimes online moderators "feel you need to spend two hours in the shower just because it is so disgusting."[13] But then that is why firms such as eModeration and ICUC Moderation can charge a lot of money to clean up comments and tweets for established organizations.

Fourth, entrepreneurial resources must be *organizationally* embedded.[14] For example, as long as there have been wars, there have been mercenaries ready to fight on behalf of the highest bidder. But only in modern times have private military companies (PMCs) become a global industry. Entrepreneurial PMCs thrive on their organizational capabilities to provide military and security services in dangerous environments, particularly in places like Iraq and Afghanistan where individuals shy away and even national militaries withdraw.

9-3 GROWING THE ENTREPRENEURIAL FIRM

This section discusses three major characteristics associated with a growing entrepreneurial firm: (1) growth, (2) innovation, and (3) financing. A fourth characteristic, internationalization, will be highlighted in the next section.

9-3a Growth

For many entrepreneurs such as David Tran in the Opening Case, the excitement associated with growing new firms such as Huy Fong is the very thing that attracts them in the first place. Recall from the resource-based view that a firm can be conceptualized as a bundle of resources and capabilities. The growth of an entrepreneurial firm can thus be viewed as an attempt to more fully use currently underutilized resources and capabilities. An entrepreneurial firm can leverage its (intangible) vision and drive in order to grow, even though it may be short on (tangible) resources such as financial capital.

9-3b Innovation

Innovation is at the heart of entrepreneurship. Evidence shows a positive relationship between a high degree of innovation and superior profitability. Innovation allows for a more sustainable basis for competitive advantage. Innovation can range from low-tech ones such as Huy Fong's humble Sriracha hot sauce (see Opening Case) to high-tech ones such as Aliababa's Taobao that can handle millions of online transactions daily.

Entrepreneurial firms are uniquely ready for innovation. Owners, managers, and employees at entrepreneurial firms tend to be more innovative and risk taking than those at large firms. In fact, many SMEs are founded by former employees of large firms who were frustrated by their inability to translate innovative ideas into realities at the large firms. Intel, for example, was founded by

The ABC television show Shark Tank features entrepreneurs and small-business owners pitching their innovative new products to the "Sharks"—successful and well-known businesspeople from a variety of industries.

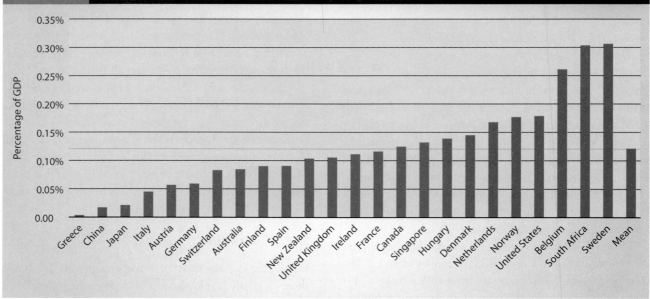

EXHIBIT 9.3 VENTURE CAPITAL INVESTMENT AS A PERCENTAGE OF GDP

Percentage of GDP

Greece, China, Japan, Italy, Austria, Germany, Switzerland, Australia, Finland, Spain, New Zealand, United Kingdom, Ireland, France, Canada, Singapore, Hungary, Denmark, Netherlands, Norway, United States, Belgium, South Africa, Sweden, Mean

Source: Adapted from M. Minniti, W. Bygrave, and E. Autio, *Global Entrepreneurship Monitor 2006 Executive Report* (Wellesley, MA: Babson College/GEM, 2006) 49.

three former employees of Fairchild Semiconductor. Innovators at large firms also have limited ability to personally profit from their innovations because property rights usually belong to their employers. In contrast, innovators at entrepreneurial firms are better able to reap the financial gains associated with innovation, thus fueling their motivation to charge ahead.

9-3c Financing

All start-ups need capital. What are the sources of capital? Three of the "4F" sources of entrepreneurial financing are founders, family, and friends. What is the other "F" source? The answer is . . . *fools* (!). While this is a joke, it strikes a chord in the entrepreneurial world. Given the well-known failure risks of start-ups (a *majority* of them will fail—see Closing Case), why would anybody other than a fool be willing to invest in a start-up? In reality, most outside strategic investors, who can be wealthy individual investors (often called angels), venture capitalists, banks, foreign entrants, or government agencies, are not fools. They often demand some assurance (such as collateral), examine business plans, and require a strong management team.

Muhammad Yunus

LEV RADIN/SHUTTERSTOCK.COM

Around the world, the extent to which entrepreneurs draw on resources from outside investors (such as venture capitalists) rather than family and friends varies. Exhibit 9.3 shows that Sweden, South Africa, Belgium, and the United States lead the world in venture capital (VC) investment as a percentage of GDP. In contrast, Greece and China have the lowest level of VC investment. Exhibit 9.4 illustrates a different picture: informal investment (mostly by family and friends) as a percentage of GDP. In this case, China leads the world with the highest level of informal investment as a percentage of GDP. In comparison, Brazil and Hungary, on the other hand, have the lowest level of informal investment. While there is a lot of noise in such worldwide data, the case of China (second lowest in VC investment and highest in informal investment) is easy to explain: China's lack of formal market-supporting institutions, such as venture capitalists and credit-reporting agencies, requires a high level of informal investment for Chinese entrepreneurs and new ventures, particularly during a time of entrepreneurial boom.[15]

A highly innovative solution, called microfinance, has emerged in response to the lack of financing for entrepreneurial opportunities in many developing countries.

EXHIBIT 9.4   INFORMAL INVESTMENT AS A PERCENTAGE OF GDP

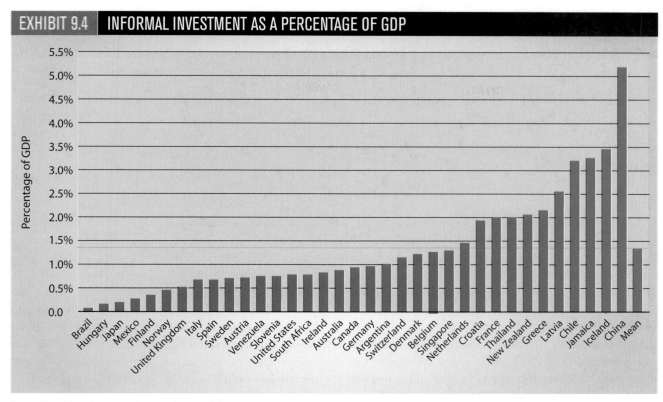

Source: Adapted from M. Minniti, W. Bygrave, and E. Autio, *Global Entrepreneurship Monitor 2006 Executive Report* (Wellesley, MA: Babson College/GEM, 2006) 53.

Microfinance involves lending small sums ($50–$300) used to start small businesses with the intention of ultimately lifting the entrepreneurs out of poverty. Starting in Bangladesh in the 1970s by Muhammad Yunus, microfinance has now become a global movement. Yunus himself won a Nobel Peace Prize in 2006.

9-4 INTERNATIONALIZING THE ENTREPRENEURIAL FIRM

There is a myth that only large MNEs do business abroad and that SMEs mostly operate domestically. This myth, based on historical stereotypes, is being increasingly challenged as more SMEs go international.[16] Further, some start-ups attempt to do business abroad from inception. These are often called **born global firms** (or **international new ventures**). This section examines how entrepreneurial firms internationalize.

9-4a Transaction Costs and Entrepreneurial Opportunities

Compared with domestic transaction costs (the costs of doing business), international transaction costs are qualitatively higher. Some costs are high due to numerous innocent differences in formal institutions and informal norms (see Chapters 2 and 3). Other costs, however, may be due to a high level of potential opportunism that is hard to detect and remedy. For example, when a small business in Texas with $5 million annual revenues receives an unsolicited order of $1 million from an unknown buyer in Alaska, most likely the Texas firm will fill the order and allow the Alaska buyer to pay within 30 or 60 days after receiving the goods—a typical practice among domestic transactions in the United States. But what if this order comes from an unknown buyer (importer in this case) in Azerbaijan? If the Texas firm ships the goods but foreign payment does not arrive on time (after 30, 60, or even more days), it is difficult to assess whether firms in Azerbaijan simply do not have the norm of punctual payment or that particular importer is being deliberately opportunistic. If the latter is indeed the case, suing the importer in a court in Azerbaijan where Azeri is the official language may be so costly that it is not an option for a small US exporter.

Maybe the Azerbaijani importer is an honest and capable firm with every intention and ability to pay. But because the Texas

microfinance Lending small sums ($50–$300) used to start small businesses with the intention of ultimately lifting the entrepreneurs out of poverty.

born global firm (International new venture) A start-up company that attempts to do business abroad from inception.

EXHIBIT 9.5 INTERNATIONALIZATION STRATEGIES FOR ENTREPRENEURIAL FIRMS

Entering foreign markets	Staying in domestic markets
▶ Direct exports	▶ Indirect exports (through export intermediaries)
▶ Franchising/licensing	▶ Supplier of foreign firms
▶ Foreign direct investment (strategic alliances, greenfield wholly owned subsidiaries, and/or foreign acquisitions)	▶ Franchisee or licensee of foreign brands
	▶ Alliance partner of foreign direct investors
	▶ Harvest and exit (through sell-off to and acquisition by foreign entrants)

firm may not be able to ascertain, prior to the transaction, that the Azerbaijani side will pay upon receiving the goods, the Texas firm may simply say "No, thanks!" Conceptually, this is an example of transaction costs being too high that many firms may choose not to pursue international opportunities. Therefore, entrepreneurial opportunities exist to lower transaction costs and bring distant groups of people, firms, and countries together. Exhibit 9.5 shows that while entrepreneurial firms can internationalize by entering foreign markets, they can also add an international dimension without actually going abroad. Next, we discuss how an SME can undertake some of these strategies.

9-4b International Strategies for Entering Foreign Markets

SMEs have three broad modes for entering foreign markets: (1) direct exports, (2) licensing/franchising, and (3) foreign direct investment (FDI) (see Chapters 6 and 10 for more details). First, **direct exports** involve the sale of products made by entrepreneurial firms in their home country to customers in other countries. This strategy is attractive because entrepreneurial firms are able to reach foreign customers directly. However, a major drawback is that SMEs may not have enough resources to turn overseas opportunities into profits. Many SMEs reach foreign customers through **sporadic (passive) exporting**, meaning sales prompted by unsolicited inquiries. To actively and systematically pursue export customers would be a different ball game.

direct export The sale of products made by firms in their home country to customers in other countries.

sporadic (passive) exporting The sale of products prompted by unsolicited inquiries from abroad.

letter of credit (L/C) A financial contract that states that the importer's bank will pay a specific sum of money to the exporter upon delivery of the merchandise.

licensing Firm A's agreement to give Firm B the rights to use A's proprietary technology (such as a patent) or trademark (such as a corporate logo) for a royalty fee paid to A by B. This is typically done in manufacturing industries.

Export transactions are complicated. One particular concern is how to overcome the lack of trust between exporters and importers when receiving an order from unknown importers abroad. For example, while the US exporter in Exhibit 9.6 does not trust the Chinese importer, banks on both sides can facilitate this transaction by a **letter of credit (L/C)**, which is a financial contract stating that the importer's bank (Bank of China in this case) will pay a specific sum of money to the exporter upon delivery of the merchandise. It has several steps.

▶ The US exporter may question the unknown Chinese importer's assurance that it will promptly pay for the merchandise. An L/C from the highly reputable Bank of China will assure the US exporter that the importer has good creditworthiness and sufficient funds for the transaction. If the US exporter is not sure whether Bank of China is a credible bank, it can consult its own bank, Bank of America, which will confirm that an L/C from Bank of China is as good as gold.

▶ With the assurance through an L/C, the US exporter can release the merchandise, which goes through a US freight forwarder, then a shipping company, and then a Chinese customs broker. Finally, the goods will reach the Chinese importer.

▶ Once the US exporter has shipped the goods, it will present to Bank of America the L/C from Bank of China and shipping documents. On behalf of the US exporter, Bank of America will then collect payment from Bank of China, which, in turn, will collect payment from the Chinese importer.

In short, instead of having unknown exporters and importers deal with each other, transactions are facilitated by banks on both sides that have known each other quite well because of numerous such dealings. In other words, the L/C reduces transaction costs by lowering the transaction risks.

A second way to enter international markets is licensing and/or franchising. Usually used in *manufacturing* industries, **licensing** refers to Firm A's agreement to give Firm B the rights to use A's proprietary technology

EXHIBIT 9.6 AN EXPORT/IMPORT TRANSACTION

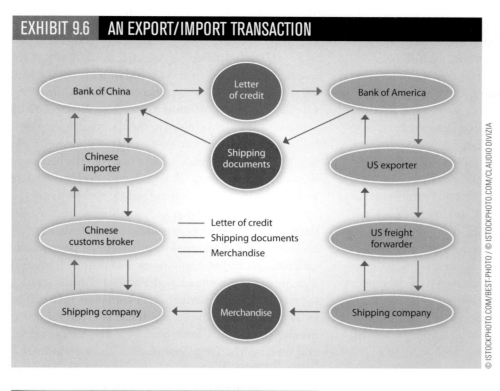

Letter of credit
Shipping documents
Merchandise

For example, a McDonald's franchise now costs the franchisee approximately one million dollars. But licensors and franchisors also take a risk because they may suffer a loss of control over how their technology and brand names are used. If McDonald's (hypothetical) franchisee in Finland produces sub-standard products that damage the brand and refuses to improve quality, McDonald's has two difficult choices: (1) sue its licensee in an unfamiliar Finnish court or (2) discontinue the relationship. Either choice is complicated and costly.

A third entry mode is FDI. FDI may involve strategic alliances with foreign partners (such as joint ventures), foreign acquisitions, and/or greenfield wholly owned subsidiaries. FDI has several distinct advantages. By planting some roots abroad, a firm becomes more committed to serving foreign markets. It is physically and psychologically closer to foreign customers. Relative to licensing and franchising, a firm is better able to control how its proprietary technology and brand name are used. However, FDI has a major drawback: its cost and complexity. It requires both a nontrivial sum of capital and a significant managerial commitment. Many SMEs are unable to engage in FDI.

In general, the level of complexity and resources required increases as a firm moves from direct exports to licensing/franchising and finally to FDI. Traditionally, it is thought that most firms will have to go through these different stages and that SMEs (perhaps with few exceptions) are unable to undertake FDI. Known as the **stage model**, this idea posits that SMEs that do eventually internationalize will do so through a slow, stage-by-stage process.

However, enough counterexamples of *rapidly* internationalizing entrepreneurial firms, known as born globals, exist to challenge stage models. Consider Logitech, now

With 15,000 restaurants in more than 30 countries—such as this Bangkok, Thailand, location—Dunkin' Donuts is among the United States' fastest growing franchises.

(such as a patent) or trademark (such as a corporate logo) for a royalty fee paid to A by B. Assume (hypothetically) that a US exporter cannot keep up with demand in Turkey. It may consider granting a Turkish firm the license to use its technology and trademark for a fee.

Franchising is essentially the same, except it is typically used in *service* industries such as fast food. A great advantage is that SME licensors and franchisors can expand abroad while risking relatively little of their own capital. Foreign firms interested in becoming licensees or franchisees have to put their own capital up front.

> **franchising** Firm A's agreement to give Firm B the rights to use A's proprietary assets for a royalty fee paid to A by B. This is typically done in service industries.
>
> **stage model** Model of internationalization that involves a slow step-by-step (stage-by-stage) process a firm must go through to internationalize its business.

a global leader in computer peripherals. It was established by entrepreneurs from Switzerland and the United States, where the firm set up dual headquarters. Research and development (R&D) and manufacturing were initially split between these two countries and then quickly spread to Ireland and Taiwan through FDI. Its first commercial contract was with a Japanese company.

Given that most SMEs still fit the stereotype of slow (or no) internationalization but some entrepreneurial SMEs seem to be born global, a key question is: What leads to rapid internationalization? The key differentiator between rapidly and slowly (or no) internationalizing SMEs seems to be the international experience of the entrepreneurs. If entrepreneurs have solid previous experience abroad (such as David Tran's earlier experience in Vietnam as portrayed in the Opening Case), then doing business in a different country is not so intimidating. Otherwise, the apprehension associated with the unfamiliar foreign business world may take over, and entrepreneurs may simply want to avoid trouble overseas.

While many entrepreneurial firms have aggressively gone abroad, it is probably true that a majority of SMEs will be unable to do so. They already have enough headaches struggling with the domestic market. However, as discussed next, some SMEs can still internationalize by staying at home.

9-4c International Strategies for Staying in Domestic Markets

Exhibit 9.5 also shows a number of strategies for entrepreneurial SMEs to internationalize without leaving their home country. The five main strategies are (1) export indirectly, (2) become suppliers for foreign firms, (3) become licensees or franchisees of foreign brands, (4) become alliance partners of foreign direct investors, and (5) harvest and exit through sell-offs.

First, whereas direct exports may be lucrative, many SMEs simply do not have the resources to handle such work. But they can still reach overseas customers through **indirect exports**, which involve exporting through domestically based export intermediaries. **Export intermediaries** perform an important middleman function by linking domestic sellers and overseas buyers who otherwise would not have been connected. Being entrepreneurs themselves, export intermediaries facilitate the internationalization of many SMEs.[17]

indirect export A way for SMEs to reach overseas customers by exporting through domestically based export intermediaries.

export intermediary A firm that acts as a middleman by linking domestic sellers and foreign buyers that otherwise would not have been connected.

A second strategy is to become a supplier for a foreign firm that enters a domestic market. For example, when Subway came to Northern Ireland, it secured a contract for chilled part-bake bread with a domestic bakery. This relationship was so successful that the firm now supplies Subway franchisees throughout Europe. SME suppliers thus may be able to internationalize by piggybacking on the larger foreign entrants.

Third, an entrepreneurial firm may consider becoming licensee or franchisee of a foreign brand. Foreign licensors and franchisors provide training and technology transfer—for a fee of course. Consequently, an SME can learn a great deal about how to operate at world-class standards. Further, licensees and franchisees do not have to be permanently under the control of licensors and franchisors. If enough learning has been accomplished, it is possible to discontinue the relationship and to reap greater entrepreneurial profits. In Thailand, Minor Group, which had held the Pizza Hut franchise for 20 years, broke away from the relationship. Its new venture, The Pizza Company, has become the market leader in Thailand.

A fourth strategy is to become an alliance partner of a foreign direct investor. Facing an onslaught of aggressive MNEs, many entrepreneurial firms may not be able to successfully defend their market positions. Then it makes great sense to follow the old adage, "If you can't beat them, join them!" While dancing with the giants is tricky, it is better than being crushed by them. (See Chapter 11 for examples of how smaller, domestic firms become alliance partners with MNEs.)

Finally, as a harvest and exit strategy, entrepreneurs may sell an equity stake or the entire firm to foreign entrants. An American couple, originally from Seattle, built a Starbucks-like coffee chain in Britain called Seattle Coffee. When Starbucks entered Britain, the couple sold the chain of 60 stores to Starbucks for a hefty $84 million. In light of the high failure rates of start-ups (see Closing Case), being acquired by foreign entrants may help preserve the business in the long run.

9-5 MANAGEMENT SAVVY

What determines the success and failure of entrepreneurial firms around the globe? The answer boils down to two components. First, the institution-based view argues that institutional frameworks explain a great deal about what is behind the differences in entrepreneurial and economic development around the world (see Debate). Second, the resource-based view posits that it is largely intangible resources such as vision, drive, and willingness to take risk that fuels entrepreneurship around the globe. Overall, the performance of

Debate: Europe's Entrepreneurship Deficit: Traits versus Institutions

Ethical Dilemma

"Traits versus institutions" is probably the oldest debate on entrepreneurship. It focuses on the question "What motivates entrepreneurs to establish new firms, while most others are simply content to work for bosses?" The "traits" school of thought argues that it is personal traits that matter. Compared with nonentrepreneurs, entrepreneurs seem more likely to possess a stronger desire for achievement and to be more willing to take risks and tolerate ambiguities. Overall, entrepreneurship inevitably deviates from the norm to work for others, and this deviation may be in the "blood" of entrepreneurs. One example is David Tran, who has founded businesses in both Vietnam and the United States (see Opening Case).

Critics, however, argue that some of these traits, such as a strong achievement orientation, are not necessarily limited to entrepreneurs, but instead are characteristic of many successful individuals. The diversity among entrepreneurs makes any attempt to develop a standard psychological or personality profile futile. Critics suggest what matters is institutions—namely, the environments of formal and informal rules of the game that enable or constrain entrepreneurship.

Historically Europe had neither a shortage of entrepreneurial talents nor market-friendly institutions. A leading debate in Europe now focuses on why so few Europeans are interested in entrepreneurship. *Global Entrepreneur Monitor* has reported that in Europe, an alarmingly small percentage of individuals are involved in "early stage entrepreneurship," representing only 2% of Italy's adult population, 4% of Germany's, and 6% of France's. These numbers compare very unfavorably with 8% in the United States, 14% in China, and 17% in Brazil. The lack of a risk-taking entrepreneurial culture is one reason. But another reason is a series of formal, institution-based barriers that scare away a lot of would-be entrepreneurs.

Europe has many successful large firms and many entrepreneurial SMEs. But the vast majority of Europe's large firms were born around the turn of the last century. What Europe lacks is successful SMEs that grow quickly and join the ranks of large firms. Of the world's 500 largest publicly listed firms, Europe gave birth to only 12 of them between 1950 and 2007, whereas the United States produced 52 during the same period. One reason that the United States has rocketed ahead of Europe in economic growth and job creation is the ability to produce new, fast-growing SMEs that quickly become giants, such as Amazon, Facebook, Google, and eBay. Although one of Google's founders,

BENNY MARTY/SHUTTERSTOCK.COM

Sergey Brin, was born in Europe, why was Google not made in Europe?

A known fact in entrepreneurship is that risks are high and bankruptcy is likely. However, Europe's personal bankruptcy laws are notoriously unfriendly to bankrupt entrepreneurs. In France, they are responsible for their debts for nine years after the bankruptcy. In Germany, six years. In the United States, failed entrepreneurs can walk away from their debts in less than a year (see Closing Case).

Another hurdle is labor laws. To remain viable, failed SMEs need to reduce staff quickly and cheaply. But in Europe even very recent hires expect to receive at least six months of severance pay. "In San Francisco and in China, a communist country, I pay one to two months," a frustrated French executive shared with a journalist. Anil de Mello is a Spanish entrepreneur. After the Great Recession of 2008–2009 during which his firm went bankrupt, Spanish social security pursued him for five *years* to capture funds it had paid to his employees as severance on his behalf. Although eager to start up another firm again, de Mello reasoned that he could not afford another bankruptcy in Spain. Instead, he founded his next new venture in Switzerland, whose labor laws are more entrepreneur friendly.

De Mello at least stays in Europe, but a large army of European entrepreneurs simply leave the continent. There are about 50,000 Germans in Silicon Valley, and approximately 500 start-ups in the San Francisco Bay area are founded by French entrepreneurs. Although some will strike it rich and most will fail, one conclusion seems foregone: the next Google will still not be made in Europe.

Sources: G. Cassar, "Are individuals entering self-employment overly optimistic?" *Strategic Management Journal* 31 (2010): 822–840. "A slow climb," *Economist*, 5 October 2013: 65 -66; "Les misérable," *Economist*, 28 July 2013: 19–22; "Start me up," *Economist*, 5 October 2013: 60–61; M. W. Peng, Y. Yamakawa, and S. Lee, "Bankruptcy laws and entrepreneur-friendliness," *Entrepreneurship Theory and Practice* 34 (2010): 517–530.

entrepreneurial firms depends on how they take advantage of formal and informal institutional resources and leverage their capabilities at home, abroad, or both.

Two clear implications for action emerge (Exhibit 9.7). First, institutions that help entrepreneurship development—both formal and informal—are important. As a result, savvy entrepreneurs have a vested interest in pushing for more entrepreneur-friendly formal institutions in various countries, such as rules governing how to set up new firms and how to reduce the pain for failed entrepreneurs and their firms (see Closing Case). Entrepreneurs also need to cultivate strong informal norms granting legitimacy to entrepreneurs. Talking to high school and college students, taking on internships, and providing seed money as angels for new ventures are some of the actions that entrepreneurs can undertake.

EXHIBIT 9.7	IMPLICATIONS FOR ACTION

▶ Push for institutions that facilitate entrepreneurship development, both formal and informal.

▶ When internationalizing, be bold but not *too* bold.

Second, when internationalizing, entrepreneurs are advised to be bold. Thanks to globalization, the costs of doing business abroad have fallen recently. But being bold does not mean being reckless. One specific managerial insight from this chapter is that it is possible to internationalize without actually venturing abroad. When the entrepreneurial firm is not ready to take on higher risk abroad, the more limited international involvement at home may be appropriate. In other words, be bold but not too bold.

EMERGING MARKETS/ETHICAL DILEMMA
Closing Case: Boom in Busts: Good or Bad?

Corporate bankruptcies* have climbed to new heights since the Great Recession of 2008–2009. Firms ranging from mighty ones such as Lehman Brothers and General Motors to tiny entrepreneurial outfits have dropped out left and right around the world. Because bankruptcies do not sound too good or inspiring, is there anything that we—the government, financial institutions, consumers, taxpayers, or the society at large—can do to prevent widespread bankruptcies?

Efforts trying to rescue failing firms from bankruptcies stem from an "anti-failure" bias widely shared among entrepreneurs, scholars, journalists, and government officials. Although a majority of entrepreneurial firms fail, this "anti-failure" bias leads to a strong interest in entrepreneurial success (remember how many times Google, Facebook, and Alibaba were written up by the press or your textbook author?). Yet scant attention has been devoted to the vast majority of entrepreneurial firms that end up in failure and bankruptcy. However, one perspective suggests that bankruptcies, which are undoubtedly painful to individual entrepreneurs and employees, may be *good* for the society. Consequently, bankruptcy laws need to be reformed to become more entrepreneur friendly by making it easier for entrepreneurs to declare bankruptcy and to move on. Consequently, financial, human, and physical resources stuck with failed firms can be redeployed in a socially optimal way.

CAROLYN FRANKS/SHUTTERSTOCK.COM

A leading debate is how to treat failed entrepreneurs who file for bankruptcy. Do we let them walk away from debt or punish them? Historically, entrepreneur friendliness and bankruptcy laws are like an "oxymoron," because bankruptcy laws are usually harsh and even cruel. The very term "bankruptcy" is derived from a harsh practice: in medieval Italy, if bankrupt entrepreneurs did not pay their debt, debtors would destroy the trading bench (booth) of the bankrupt—the Italian word for broken bench, *banca rotta*, has evolved into the English word "bankruptcy." The pound of flesh demanded by the creditor in Shakespeare's *The Merchant of Venice* is only a slight exaggeration. The world's first bankruptcy law, passed in England in 1542, considered a bankrupt individual a criminal and penalties ranged from incarceration to death sentence.

---

* The term "bankruptcies" in this case refers to corporate bankruptcies and does not deal with personal bankruptcies.

However, recently, many governments have realized that entrepreneur-friendly bankruptcy laws can not only lower exit barriers, but also lower entry barriers for entrepreneurs. Although we are confident that many start-ups will end up in bankruptcy, up front it is impossible to predict which ones will go under. Therefore, from an institution-based standpoint, if entrepreneurship is to be encouraged, there is a need to ease the pain associated with bankruptcy by means such as allowing entrepreneurs to walk away from debt, a legal right that bankrupt US entrepreneurs appreciate. In contrast, until the recent bankruptcy law reforms, bankrupt German entrepreneurs might remain liable for unpaid debt for up to 30 years. Further, German and Japanese managers of bankrupt firms can also be liable for criminal penalties, and numerous bankrupt Japanese entrepreneurs have committed suicide. Not surprisingly, many failed entrepreneurs in Germany and Japan try to avoid business exit despite escalating losses, and societal and individual resources cannot be channeled to more productive uses. Therefore, as rules of the "end game," harsh bankruptcy laws become grave exit barriers. They can also create significant entry barriers, as fewer would-be entrepreneurs may decide to launch their ventures.

At a societal level, if many would-be entrepreneurs, in fear of failure, abandon their ideas, there will not be a thriving entrepreneurial sector. Given the risks and uncertainties, it is not surprising that many entrepreneurs do not make it the first time. However, if they are given more chances, some of them will succeed. For example, approximately 50% of US entrepreneurs who filed bankruptcy resumed a new venture in four years. This high level of entrepreneurialism is, in part, driven by the relatively entrepreneur-friendly bankruptcy laws (such as the provision of Chapter 11 bankruptcy reorganization instead of straight liquidation). On the other hand, a society that severely punishes failed entrepreneurs (such as forcing financially insolvent firms to liquidate instead of offering a US Chapter 11–style reorganization option) is not likely to foster widespread entrepreneurship. Failed entrepreneurs have nevertheless accumulated a great deal of experience and lessons on how to avoid their mistakes. If they drop out of the entrepreneurial

game (or, in the worst case, kill themselves), their wisdom will be permanently lost. Overall, worldwide evidence from 29 countries—involving both developed and emerging economies from five continents—has identified a strong linkage between entrepreneur-friendly bankruptcy laws and new firm entries.

In summary, one side of the debate asserts that at a societal level, entrepreneurial failures may be beneficial. This is because only through a large number of entrepreneurial experimentations—although many will fail—can winning solutions emerge and economies develop. Thus, the boom in busts is not necessarily bad. On the other hand, President Donald Trump's history of walking away from six corporate bankruptcies (although never personal bankruptcy) recently energized the other side of the debate. Trump praised himself during the 2016 presidential campaign for playing the bankruptcy laws. Critics argue that people with lots of money such as Trump can easily avoid the consequences of big losses by cashing out at the first sign of trouble, because bankruptcy laws protect them. But workers, who have no such protection, are stuck with the mess or are simply out of work. Is that fair?

Case Discussion Questions

1. What are the pros and cons for entrepreneur-friendly bankruptcy laws?

2. Why can bankruptcy laws become exit barriers for an entrepreneurial firm? Entry barriers?

3. Having studied this case, how would you respond to a friend's comment: "Recent news about the boom in bankruptcies is so depressing"?

Sources: S. Lee, M. W. Peng, and J. Barney, "Bankruptcy law and entrepreneurship development," *Academy of Management Review* 32 (2007): 257–272; S. Lee, Y. Yamakawa, and M. W. Peng, "How does bankruptcy law affect entrepreneurship development?" SBA Best Research Papers Collection (Washington, DC: US Small Business Administration, 2007), www.sba.gov/advo/research/rs326tot.pdf; S. Lee, Y. Yamakawa, M. W. Peng, and J. Barney, "How do bankruptcy laws affect entrepreneurship development around the world?" *Journal of Business Venturing* 26 (2011): 505–520; R. Reich, "Donald Trump proves what's wrong with bankruptcy laws in America," *Politico*, 28 September 2015: www.politico.com; Y. Yamakawa, M. W. Peng, and D. Deeds, "Rising from the ashes: Cognitive determinants of venture growth after entrepreneurial failure," *Entrepreneurship Theory and Practice* 39 (2015): 209–236.

STUDY TOOLS 9

LOCATED AT THE BACK OF YOUR BOOK:

☐ Rip out and study the Chapter Review Card at the end of the book

LOG IN TO WWW.CENGAGEBRAIN.COM TO:

☐ Review key term flashcards

☐ Complete a practice quiz to test your knowledge of key concepts

☐ View animated PengAtlas Maps

☐ Complete interactive content, watch chapter videos, and take a graded quiz

☐ Track your knowledge of key concepts in Global Business

☐ Read and discuss additional case study content

10 Entering Foreign Markets

PE3K/SHUTTERSTOCK.COM

LEARNING OBJECTIVES

After studying this chapter, you will be able to . . .

 10-1 Identify ways in which institutions and resources affect the liability of foreignness.

 10-2 Match the quest for location-specific advantages with strategic goals.

 10-3 Compare and contrast first-mover and late-mover advantages.

 10-4 List the steps in the comprehensive model of foreign market entries.

10-5 Explain what you should do to make your firm's entry into a foreign market successful.

After you finish this chapter, go to

PAGE 166 for

STUDY TOOLS

Opening Case: Coca-Cola Pours into Africa

Founded in 1892, Coca-Cola first entered Africa in 1929. While Africa had always been viewed as "backwater," it has recently emerged as a major growth market commanding strategic attention. Of the $27 billion that Coca-Cola planned to invest in emerging economies between 2015 and 2025, $12 billion would be used to beef up plants and distribution facilities in Africa. Why does Coca-Cola show such strong commitments to Africa? Both the push and pull effects are at work.

The push comes from the necessity to find new sources of growth for this mature firm, which has promised investors 7%–9% earnings growth. In 1998, its stock reached a high-water mark at $88. But it dropped to $37 in 2003. Since 2004, the share price rallied again, rising from $43 to a new peak of $90 in November 2014 (adjusted for a 2:1 share split in 2012). Can Coca-Cola's stock reach higher?

Its home markets are unlikely to help. Between 2006 and 2011, US sales declined for five consecutive years. Further, health advocates accused Coca-Cola of contributing to an epidemic of obesity in the United States, and proposed to tax soft drinks to pay for health care. Although Coca-Cola defeated the tax initiative, it is fair to say the room for growth at home is limited. In Europe and Japan, sales are similarly flat. Elsewhere, in China, strong local rivals have made it tough for Coca-Cola to break out. Its acquisition of a leading local fruit juice firm was blocked by the government, which did not seem to bless Coca-Cola's further growth. In India, Pepsi is so popular that "Pepsi" has become the Hindi shorthand for all bottled soft drinks (including Coke!). In Latin America, sales are encouraging, but growth is limited. Mexicans on average are already guzzling 665 servings of Coca-Cola products every year, the highest in the world. There is only so much sugary water one can drink every day.

In contrast, Coca-Cola is pulled by Africa, where it has a commanding 29% market share versus Pepsi's 15%. With 65,000 employees and 160 plants, Coca-Cola is Africa's largest private-sector employer. Yet, annual per capita consumption of Coca-Cola products is only 39 servings in Kenya. For the continent as a whole, disposable income is growing. In 2014, 100 million Africans earned at least $5,000 per person. While Africa indeed has some of the poorest countries in the world, 12 African countries (with a combined population of 100 million) have a GDP per capita that is greater than China's. Coca-Cola is hoping to capitalize on Africa's improved political stability and physical infrastructure. Countries not fighting civil wars make Coke's operations less disruptive, and new roads penetrating the jungle can obviously elevate sales.

Coca-Cola is already in all African countries. The challenge now, according to chairman and CEO Muhtar Kent, will be to deep dive into "every town, every village, every township." This will not be easy. War, poverty, and poor infrastructure make it extremely difficult to distribute and market products in hard-to-access regions. Undaunted, Coca-Cola is in a street-by-street campaign to increase awareness and consumption of its products. The crowds and the poor roads dictate that some of the deliveries have to be done manually on pushcarts, trolleys, or horsebacks. Throughout the continent, Coca-Cola has set up 3,000 manual distribution centers. Taking a page from its playbook in Latin America, especially Mexico, Coca-Cola has aggressively courted small corner stores. Coca-Cola and its bottlers offer small corner store owners delivery, credit, and direct coaching—ranging from the tip not to ice down the Cokes until the midday rush in order to save electricity to helping on how to buy a house after vendors make enough money.

In Africa, US-style accusations of Coca-Cola's alleged contribution to the obesity problem are unlikely. After all, the primary concern in many communities is too few available calories of any kind. However, this does not mean that Coca-Cola faces no criticisms in Africa. It has to defend itself from critics who accuse it of depleting fresh water, encouraging expensive and environmentally harmful refrigeration, and hurting local competitors who hawk beverages. In response, Coca-Cola often points out the benefits it has brought. In addition to the 65,000 jobs created directly, one million local jobs are indirectly created by its vast system of distribution, which moves beverages deep into the slums and the bush a few crates at a time.

Sources: M. Blanding, *The Coke Machine* (New York: Avery, 2010); "Coke's last round," *Bloomberg Businessweek*, 1 November 2010: 54–61; "For India's consumers, Pepsi is the real thing," *Bloomberg Businessweek*, 20 September 2010: 26–27; "Can Coke surpass its record high of $88 a share?" *Bloomberg Businessweek*, 6 June 2011: 49–50; "Business in Africa," *Economist*, 9 September 2006: 60–62; "Index of happiness," *Economist*, 5 July 2008: 58; "A continent goes shopping," *Economist*, 18 August 2012: 57–58; D. Zoogah, M. W. Peng, and H. Woldu, "Institutions, resources, and organizational effectiveness in Africa," *Academy of Management Perspectives* 29 (2015): 7–31.

Why is Coca-Cola interested in Africa? In the face of its competitors such as PepsiCo, can Coca-Cola maintain its market leadership and even grow its market share? These are some of the key questions driving this chapter. Entering foreign markets is one of the most important topics in international business (IB). This chapter first draws on the institution-based and resource-based views to discuss ways to overcome the liability of foreignness.[1] Then we focus on three crucial dimensions: *where*, *when*, and *how*—known as the 2W1H dimensions. Our discussion culminates in a comprehensive model, followed by management savvy.

10-1 OVERCOMING THE LIABILITY OF FOREIGNNESS

PHOTOSTOCKIMAGE/SHUTTERSTOCK.COM

It is not easy to succeed in an unfamiliar environment. Recall from Chapter 1 that foreign firms have to overcome a liability of foreignness, which is the inherent disadvantage that foreign firms experience in host countries because of their nonnative status. Such a liability is manifested in at least two ways. First, numerous differences in formal and informal institutions govern the rules of the game in different countries. While local firms are already well versed in these rules, foreign firms have to invest significant resources to learn such rules. Some of the rules are in favor of local firms. For example, after working for years to familiarize itself with US defense procurement rules, European Aeronautic Defence and Space (EADS), the maker of Airbus, in 2008 won a major $35 billion contract to supply the US Air Force with next-generation refueling tankers. Then EADS (along with its US partner, Northrop Grumman) was disappointed to find out that Boeing was able to twist the arms of politicians and change the rules. In 2010, Boeing emerged as the winner of this rich prize and EADS (which more recently changed its name to the Airbus Group) had to drop out.

Second, although customers in this age of globalization supposedly no longer discriminate against foreign firms, the reality is that foreign firms are often still discriminated against, sometimes formally and other times informally. For example, activists in India accused both Coca-Cola and PepsiCo that their products contained higher-than-permitted levels of pesticides but did not test any Indian-branded soft drinks, even though pesticide residues are present in virtually all groundwater in India. Although both Coca-Cola and PepsiCo denied these charges, their sales suffered.

Against such significant odds, how do foreign firms crack new markets? The answer boils down to our two core perspectives introduced earlier (see Exhibit 10.1). The institution-based view suggests that firms need to undertake actions deemed legitimate and appropriate by the various formal and informal institutions governing market entries. Differences in formal institutions may lead to regulatory risks due to differences in political, economic, and legal systems (see Chapter 2). There may be numerous trade and investment barriers on a national or regional basis (see Chapters 5, 6, and 8). In addition, the existence of multiple currencies—and currency risks as a result—may be another formal barrier (see Chapter 7). Informally, numerous differences in cultures, norms, and values create another major source of liability of foreignness (see Chapter 3).

The resource-based view argues that foreign firms need to deploy *overwhelming* resources and capabilities that after offsetting the liability of foreignness, there is still significant competitive advantage left.[2] Applying the VRIO framework introduced in Chapter 4 to our Opening Case, we can suggest that Coca-Cola possesses some overwhelmingly valuable and rare capabilities in successfully penetrating African markets. It is very difficult to imitate Coca-Cola's commanding market presence and increasing commitment. Finally, deep diving into African markets and coaching small corner store owners represent a tremendous organizational asset in its African forays.

Overall, our two core perspectives shed a lot of light on firms' internationalization. Sometimes, instead of having to overcome the liability of foreignness, some firms may leverage their asset of foreignness (see Debate). Nevertheless, how to enter foreign markets remains an art rather than a science. Next, we investigate the 2W1H dimensions associated with foreign market entries.

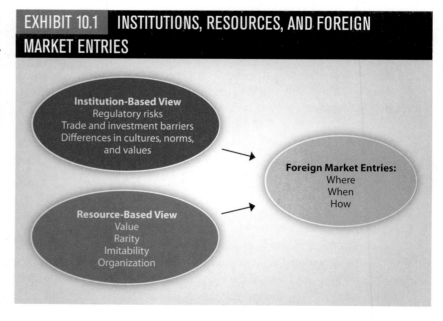

EXHIBIT 10.1 INSTITUTIONS, RESOURCES, AND FOREIGN MARKET ENTRIES

Institution-Based View
Regulatory risks
Trade and investment barriers
Differences in cultures, norms, and values

Resource-Based View
Value
Rarity
Imitability
Organization

Foreign Market Entries:
Where
When
How

Debate: Foreignness: Liability versus Asset

Emerging Markets/Ethical Dilemma

While we do not need to spill more ink on the term "liability of foreignness," one contrasting view argues that under certain circumstances, being foreign can be an *asset* (that is, a competitive advantage). German cars are viewed as of higher quality than locally made cars in the United States and Japan. In China, consumers discriminate against made-in-China luxury goods. Although these made-in-China luxury goods sport Western brands, they are viewed inferior to made-in-France handbags and made-in-Switzerland watches. American cigarettes are "cool" among smokers in Central and Eastern Europe. Anything Korean—ranging from handsets and TV shows to *kimchi* (pickled cabbage)-flavored instant noodles—are considered hip in Southeast Asia.

Conceptually, this is known as the **country-of-origin effect**, which refers to the positive or negative perception of firms and products from a certain country. Although IKEA is now registered and headquartered in Leiden, the Netherlands (and thus technically a *Dutch* company), it relentlessly displays Swedish flags in front of its stores in an effort to leverage the positive country-of-origin effect of Sweden. Pearl River's promotion of the Ritmüller brand, which highlights its German origin, suggests that the negative country-of-origin effect can be (at least partially) overcome. Pearl River is not alone in this regard. Here is a quiz: What is the country of origin of Häagen-Dazs ice cream? My students typically answer: Belgium, Denmark, Germany, the Netherlands, Switzerland, Sweden, or some other European countries. Sorry, all wrong. Häagen-Dazs is *American* since its founding. But many customers have been happily paying a premium price for such a "European" ice cream.

KAMUI29/SHUTTERSTOCK.COM

Whether foreignness is indeed an asset or a liability remains tricky. Tokyo Disneyland became wildly popular in Japan, because it played up its American image. But Paris Disneyland received relentless negative press coverage in France, because it insisted on its wholesome American look. To play it safe, Hong Kong Disneyland endeavored to strike the elusive balance between American image and Chinese flavor. All eyes are now on the newest Shanghai Disneyland in terms of such balance. Approximately 80% of the rides in Shanghai Disneyland are unique, and Main Street USA has been replaced by a new feature, Mickey Avenue.

country-of-origin effect The positive or negative perception of firms and products from a certain country.

Sources: Author's interviews; "How China won the keys to Disney's Magic Kingdom," *New York Times*, 14 June 2016: www.nytimes.com; S. Kabadayi and D. Lerman, "Made in China but sold at FAO Schwarz," *International Marketing Review* 28 (2011): 102–126; P. Magnusson, S. Westjohn, and S. Zdravkovic, "What? I thought Samsung was Japanese," *International Marketing Review* 28 (2011): 454–472; S. Samiee, "Resolving the impasse regarding research on the origins of products and brands," *International Marketing Review* 28 (2011): 473–485.

10-2 WHERE TO ENTER?

PengAtlas Map

ISTOCK.COM/HENRIK5000

Similar to real estate, the motto for IB is "location, location, location." In fact, such a *spatial* perspective (that is, doing business outside of one's home country) is one of the defining features of IB.[3] Two sets of considerations drive the location of foreign entries: (1) strategic goals and (2) cultural and institutional distances.

10-2a Location-Specific Advantages and Strategic Goals

Favorable locations in certain countries may give firms operating there what are called location-specific advantages.

EXHIBIT 10.2 MATCHING STRATEGIC GOALS WITH LOCATIONS

Strategic goals	Location-specific advantages	Examples in the text
Natural resource seeking	Possession of natural resources and related transport and communication infrastructure	Oil in the Middle East, Russia, and Venezuela
Market seeking	Abundance of strong market demand and customers willing to pay	Automakers and business jet makers in China
Efficiency seeking	Economies of scale and abundance of low-cost factors	Manufacturing in China
Innovation seeking	Abundance of innovative individuals, firms, and universities	IT in Silicon Valley and Bangalore; telecom in Dallas; perfumes in Paris

Location-specific advantages are the benefits a firm reaps from features specific to a particular place. Certain locations simply possess geographical features that are difficult for others to match. Leading seaports and airports (see PengAtlas Map 14) naturally attract a lot of foreign entrants. For example, Miami, the self-styled "Gateway of the Americas," is an ideal location both for North American firms looking south and Latin American firms coming north. Vienna is an attractive site as multinational regional headquarters for Central and Eastern Europe. Dubai is an ideal stopping point for air traffic between Europe and Asia and between Africa and Asia. Two billion people live within four hours of flying time from Dubai, and four billion can be reached within seven hours. Dubai's airport is already the third busiest international airport in terms of passengers behind only London Heathrow and Hong Kong airports.[4] Similarly, Rotterdam, the Netherlands, is the main hub for sea-bound transportation into and out of Europe. More than 500 liner services connect Rotterdam with over 1,000 ports worldwide. Overall, we may regard the continuous expansion of global business as an unending saga in search of location-specific advantages.

location-specific advantage
The benefit a firm reaps from the features specific to a place.

We learned in Chapter 6 about agglomeration—location-specific advantages that arise from the clustering of economic activities in certain locations (see In Focus). The basic idea dates back at least to Alfred Marshall, a British economist who first published it in 1890. Recall that location-specific advantages stem from (1) knowledge spillovers among closely located firms that attempt to hire individuals from competitors, (2) industry demand that creates a skilled labor force whose members may work for different firms without having to move out of the region, and (3) industry demand that facilitates a pool of specialized suppliers and buyers to also locate in the region. For example, due to agglomeration, Dallas has the world's heaviest concentration of telecom companies. US firms such as AT&T, HP, Raytheon, Texas Instruments (TI), and Verizon cluster there. Moreover, numerous leading foreign telecom firms such as Alcatel-Lucent, Ericsson, Fujitsu, Huawei, Siemens, STMicroelectronics, and ZTE have also converged in this region.

Given that different locations offer different benefits, it is imperative that a firm match its strategic goals with potential locations. The four strategic goals are shown in Exhibit 10.2.

▶ Firms seeking *natural resources* have to go to particular foreign locations where those resources are found. For example, the Middle East, Russia, and Venezuela are all rich in oil. Even when the Venezuelan government became more hostile, Western oil firms had to put up with it.

▶ *Market-seeking* firms go to countries that have a strong demand for their products and services. As China becomes the largest car market in the

Dallas skyline

Agglomeration of Wind Turbine Producers in Denmark

On a clear day, passengers with window seats on planes taking off and landing at Copenhagen International Airport can clearly see dozens of huge wind turbines offshore in Oresund (the strait that separates Denmark and Sweden). Chances are that these wind turbines are also developed and made in Denmark. Thanks to visionary government policies that offer generous subsidies, Denmark is a first mover and now a world leader in the wind turbine industry. At present, *one-third* of Danish energy consumption comes from wind. No other country comes close. Denmark's goal is to become the first country in the world to meet 50% of energy needs with wind power by 2020 and 100% by 2050. Underpinning these achievements and ambitions is a cluster of wind turbine manufacturers and suppliers in one part of Denmark—Jutland, the peninsula in western Denmark that is attached to the European mainland. (Copenhagen is located in the easternmost part of the country on the island of Zealand.)

Based in Aarhus (Denmark's second largest city), Vestas is the world leader in terms of installed turbines (60 GW), accounting for nearly one-fifth of the total capacity of all the installed turbines in the world. Founded in 1979, Vestas employs 15,000 people, including 4,000 in Denmark. About 80 kilometers west of Aarhus, in the small town of Brande, Siemens Wind Power is headquartered. Founded in 2004 following the acquisition of Bonus Energy, which was established in 1979, Siemens Wind Power (a division of Siemens) is another giant in this industry. It has 23 GW-installed turbines and 11,000 employees worldwide (of which 5,500 are in Denmark). In addition, major Danish-owned suppliers LM Wind Power and AH Industries are also nearby.

Attracted by the greatest agglomeration of know-how in this specialized but rapidly expanding industry, a number of international wind turbine manufacturers, such as India's Suzlon

SILKEBORG
Envision Energy

BRANDE
Siemens Wind Power

KOLDING
LM Wind Power

AARHUS
Vestas, Suzlon, Mitsubishi

COPENHAGEN

BJERT
AH Industries

and China's Envision Energy, have also undertaken foreign direct investment (FDI) in this region of Denmark. With an investment of $400 million, Japan's Mitsubishi Heavy Industries (MHI) has recently established a 50–50 joint venture with Vestas, named MHI Vestas Offshore Wind, which focuses on the huge 8.0 MW turbines. Anders Rebsdorf, director of Envision Energy (Denmark) located in Silkeborg, a town almost equidistant between the global headquarters of the two giants Vestas and Siemens Wind Power, articulated the firm's location choice:

> Our choice of Denmark is directly related to the country's strong cluster of know-how in the area of turbine design. It is also important that there are manufacturers of turbine components and experts in turbine service. The entire value chain is represented to a degree that is not found anywhere else. . . . If we are to earn the right to join the battle for international orders, then we must be visible where the competition is fierce.

Sources: "A wind energy hub," *Focus Denmark*, summer–autumn 2014: 24; "Titans of wind energy arm for battle," *Focus Denmark*, summer–autumn 2014: 18–23; MHI Vestas, "Our story," 1 November 2016: www.mhivestosoffshore.com; Vestas, "MHI Vestas Offshore Wind now operational," 1 April 2014: www.vestas.com; "Vestas, Mitsubishi form offshore joint venture," *Wall Street Journal*, 27 September 2013: www.wsj.com.

---

world, practically all the automakers in the world are now elbowing into it. General Motors (GM) has emerged as the leader. In 2010, GM for the first time sold more cars in China than in the United States.[5] As demand for business aviation takes off in China, business jet makers are now intensely eyeing the new market.

▶ *Efficiency-seeking* firms often single out the most efficient locations featuring a combination of scale economies and low-cost factors. It is the search for efficiency that induced numerous multinational

enterprises (MNEs) to enter China. China now manufactures two-thirds of the world's photocopiers, shoes, toys, and microwave ovens; and one-third of the desktop computers, mobile phones, television sets, and steel. Shanghai alone reportedly has a cluster of over 400 of the *Fortune* Global 500 firms. It is important to note that China does not present the absolutely lowest labor costs in the world, and Shanghai is the *highest* cost city in China. However, its attractiveness lies in its ability to enhance efficiency for foreign entrants by lowering *total* costs.

▶ *Innovation-seeking* firms target countries and regions renowned for generating world-class innovations, such as Silicon Valley and Bangalore (in IT), Dallas (in telecom), and Paris (in perfumes). Such entries can be viewed as "an option to maintain access to innovations resident in the host country, thus generating information spillovers that may lead to opportunities for future organizational learning and growth."[6] (See Chapter 12 for details.)

It is important to note that location-specific advantages may grow, change, and/or decline, prompting a firm to relocate. If policy makers fail to maintain the institutional attractiveness (for example, by raising taxes) and if companies overcrowd and bid up factor costs such as land and talents, some firms may move out of certain locations previously considered advantageous. For example, the Chinese government has raised minimum wages and tightened environmental regulations. Also, thanks to the "one child" policy that was first implemented in the 1980s, the number of low-skill youth entering the labor market has declined. These changes have eroded the location-specific advantages of coastal China centered on low cost. As a result, many labor-intensive, cost-conscious firms have either moved to inland China (where labor cost has remained relatively low) or Southeast Asian countries such as Indonesia, Malaysia, Thailand, and Vietnam (where labor cost is now lower than that of coastal China).

10-2b Cultural/Institutional Distances and Foreign Entry Locations

In addition to strategic goals, another set of considerations centers on cultural/institutional distances (see also Chapters 2 and 3). **Cultural distance** is the difference between two cultures along identifiable dimensions such as individualism. Considering culture as an informal part of institutional frameworks governing a particular country, **institutional distance** is "the extent of similarity or dissimilarity between the regulatory, normative, and cognitive institutions of two countries."[7] Broadly speaking, cultural distance is a *subset* of institutional distance. For example, many Western cosmetics products firms, such as L'Oréal and Victoria's Secret, have shied away from Saudi Arabia, citing its stricter rules of personal behavior. In essence, Saudi Arabia's cultural and institutional distance from Western cultures is too large.

Two schools of thought have emerged in overcoming these distances. The first is associated with the stage model. According to the stage model first introduced in Chapter 9, firms will enter culturally similar countries during their first stage of internationalization and will then gain more confidence to enter culturally distant countries in later stages. This idea is intuitively appealing: It makes sense for Belgian firms to enter France first and for Mexican firms to enter Texas first to take advantage of common cultural and language traditions. On average, business between countries that share a language is three times greater than between countries without a common language. Firms from common-law countries (English-speaking countries and Britain's former colonies) are more likely to be interested in other common-law countries. Colony–colonizer links (such as Britain's ties with the Commonwealth and Spain's with Latin America) boost trade significantly. Overall, certain performance benefits seem to exist when competing in culturally and institutionally adjacent countries.

Citing numerous counterexamples, a second school of thought argues that it is more important to consider strategic goals such as market and efficiency rather than culture and institutions. For example, despite the often hostile Congress and the typically unfriendly US media, many Chinese firms are eager to do business in the United States.[8] Because the United States is the largest market, cultural and institutional distances between China and the United States do not seem to matter. Overall, in the complex calculus underpinning entry decisions, location represents only one of several important considerations. As shown next, entry timing and modes are also crucial.

cultural distance The difference between two cultures along identifiable dimensions such as individualism.

institutional distance The extent of similarity or dissimilarity between the regulatory, normative, and cognitive institutions of two countries.

10-3 WHEN TO ENTER?

Entry timing refers to whether there are compelling reasons to be an early or late entrant in a particular country. Some firms look for **first-mover advantages**, defined as the benefits that accrue to firms that enter the market first and that later entrants do not enjoy.[9] Speaking of the power of first-mover advantages, "Xerox," "FedEx," and "Google" have now become *verbs*, such as "Google it." In many African countries, "Colgate" is the generic term for toothpaste. Unilever, a late mover, is disappointed to find out that some of its African customers call its own toothpaste "the red Colgate." However, first movers may also encounter significant disadvantages which, in turn, become **late-mover advantages**. Exhibit 10.3 shows a number of first-mover advantages:

PAULO M. F. PIRES/SHUTTERSTOCK.COM

▸ First movers may gain advantage through proprietary technology. Think about Apple's iPod, iPad, and iPhone.

▸ First movers may also make preemptive investments. A number of Japanese MNEs have cherry-picked leading local suppliers and distributors in Southeast Asia as new members of the expanded *keiretsu* networks (alliances of Japanese businesses with interlocking business relationships and shareholdings) and have blocked access to the suppliers and distributors by late entrants from the West.[10]

▸ First movers may erect significant entry barriers for late entrants, such as high switching costs due to brand loyalty. Buyers of expensive equipment are likely to stick with the same producers for components, training, and other services for a long time. That is why American, British, French, German, and Russian aerospace firms competed intensely for Poland's first post–Cold War order of fighters—America's F-16 eventually won.

▸ Intense domestic competition may drive some nondominant firms abroad to avoid clashing with dominant firms head-on in their home market. Matsushita, Toyota, and NEC were the market leaders in Japan, but Sony, Honda, and Epson all entered the United States in their respective industries ahead of the leading firms.

▸ First movers may build precious relationships with key stakeholders such as customers and governments. For example, Citigroup, JP Morgan Chase, and Metallurgical Corporation of China have entered Afghanistan, earning a good deal of goodwill from the Afghan government that is interested in wooing more foreign direct investment (FDI).[11]

EXHIBIT 10.3	FIRST-MOVER ADVANTAGES AND LATE-MOVER ADVANTAGES
First-mover advantages	**Examples in the text**
Proprietary, technological leadership	Apple's iPod, iPad, and iPhone
Preemption of scarce resources	Japanese MNEs in Southeast Asia
Establishment of entry barriers for late entrants	Poland's F-16 fighter jet contract
Avoidance of clash with dominant firms at home	Sony, Honda, and Epson went to the US market ahead of their Japanese rivals
Relationships with key stakeholders such as governments	Citigroup, JP Morgan Chase, and Metallurgical Corporation of China entered Afghanistan
Late-mover advantages	**Examples in the text**
Opportunity to free ride on first mover investments	Ericsson won big contracts in Saudi Arabia, free riding on Cisco's efforts
Resolution of technological and market uncertainties	BMW, GM, and Toyota had patience to wait until the Nissan Leaf resolved uncertainties about the electric car
First mover's difficulty to adapt to market changes	Greyhound is stuck with the bus depots, whereas Megabus simply uses curbside stops

first-mover advantage Benefit that accrues to firms that enter the market first and that later entrants do not enjoy.

late-mover advantage Benefit that accrues to firms that enter the market later and that early entrants do not enjoy.

The potential advantages of first movers may be counterbalanced by various disadvantages, which are also listed in Exhibit 10.3. Numerous first-mover firms—such as EMI in CT scanners and Netscape in Internet browsers—have lost market dominance in the long run. It is such late-mover firms as General Electric and Microsoft (Explorer), respectively, that win. Specifically, late-mover advantages are manifested in three ways:

▶ Late movers may be able to free ride on the huge pioneering investments of first movers. In Saudi Arabia, Cisco invested millions of dollars to rub shoulders of dignitaries, including the king, in order to help officials grasp the promise of the Internet in fueling economic development. But it lost out to late movers such as Ericsson that offered lower cost solutions. For instance, the brand new King Abdullah Economic City awarded an $84 million citywide telecom project to Ericsson whose bid was more than 20% lower than Cisco's—in part because Ericsson did not have to offer a lot of basic education and did not have to entertain that much. "We're very proud to have won against a company that did as much advance work as Cisco did," an elated Ericsson executive noted.[12]

▶ First movers face greater technological and market uncertainties. Nissan, for example, has launched the world's first all-electric car, the Leaf, which can run without a single drop of gasoline. However, there are tremendous uncertainties. After some of these uncertainties are removed, late movers such as BMW, GM, and Toyota have joined the game with their own electric cars.

▶ As incumbents, first movers may be locked into a given set of fixed assets or are reluctant to cannibalize existing product lines in favor of new ones. Late movers may be able to take advantage of the inflexibility of first movers by leapfrogging them. Although Greyhound, the incumbent in intercity bus service in the United States, is financially struggling, it cannot get rid of the expensive bus depots in inner cities that are often ill-maintained and dreadful. Megabus, the new entrant from Britain, simply has not bothered to build and maintain a single bus depot. Instead, Megabus uses curbside stops (like regular city bus stops), which have made travel by bus more appealing to a large number of passengers.

Overall, evidence points out both first-mover advantages and late-mover advantages. Unfortunately, a mountain of research is still unable to conclusively recommend a particular entry timing strategy. Although first movers may have an *opportunity* to win, their pioneering status is not a guarantee of success. For example, among the three first movers into the Chinese automobile industry in the 1980s, Volkswagen captured significant advantages, Chrysler had very moderate success, and Peugeot failed and had to exit. Although many of the late movers that entered in the 1990s struggled, GM, Honda, and Hyundai gained significant market shares. It is obvious that entry timing cannot be viewed in isolation, and entry timing per se is not the sole determinant of success and failure of foreign entries. It is through *interaction* with other strategic variables that entry timing has an impact on performance.

10-4 HOW TO ENTER?

In this section, we first consider on what scale—large or small—a firm may enter foreign markets. Then we look at a comprehensive model for entering foreign markets. The first step is to determine whether to pursue an equity or nonequity mode of entry. As we will see, this crucial decision differentiates MNEs (involving equity modes) from non-MNEs (relying on nonequity modes). Finally, we outline the pros and cons of various equity and nonequity modes.

10-4a Scale of Entry: Commitment and Experience

One key dimension in foreign entry decisions is the **scale of entry**, which refers to the amount of resources committed to entering a foreign market. Large-scale entries demonstrate a strategic commitment to certain markets. This helps assure local customers and suppliers ("We are here for the long haul!") while deterring potential entrants. The drawbacks of such a hard-to-reverse strategic commitment are (1) limited strategic flexibility elsewhere and (2) huge losses if these large-scale bets turn out to be wrong.

scale of entry The amount of resources committed to entering a foreign market.

EXHIBIT 10.4   THE CHOICE OF ENTRY MODES: A COMPREHENSIVE MODEL

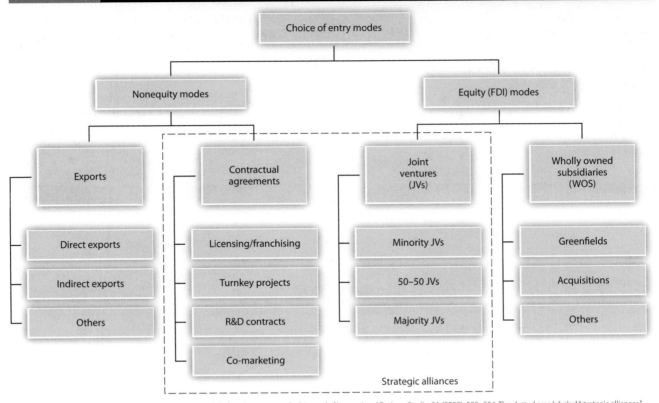

Source: Adapted from Y. Pan and D. Tse, "The hierarchical model of market entry modes," *Journal of International Business Studies* 31 (2000): 535–554. The dotted area labeled "strategic alliances," including both nonequity modes (contractual agreements) and equity modes (JVs), was added by the present author. See Chapter 11 for more details on strategic alliances.

Small-scale entries are less costly. They focus on organizational learning by getting a firm's feet wet—learning by doing—while limiting the downside risk.[13] For example, to enter the market of Islamic finance whereby no interest can be charged (according to the Koran), Citibank set up a subsidiary Citibank Islamic Bank. On a small scale, it was designed to experiment with different interpretations of the Koran on how to make money while not committing religious sins. Overall, the longer foreign firms stay in host countries, the less liability of foreignness they experience. The drawback of small-scale entries is a lack of strong commitment, which may lead to difficulties in building market share and capturing first-mover advantages.

10-4b Modes of Entry: The First Step on Equity versus Nonequity Modes

Managers are unlikely to consider the numerous **modes of entry**—methods used to enter a foreign market—at the same time. Given the complexity of entry decisions, it is imperative that managers *prioritize* and consider only a few key variables first and then consider other variables later. The comprehensive model shown in Exhibits 10.4 and 10.5 is helpful.

In the first step, considerations for small-scale versus large-scale entries usually boil down to the equity (ownership) issue. **Nonequity modes** include exports and contractual agreements, and tend to reflect relatively smaller commitments to overseas markets. **Equity modes**, on the other hand, are indicative of relatively larger, harder-to-reverse commitments. Equity modes call for the establishment of independent organizations overseas (partially or wholly controlled). Nonequity modes do not require such independent establishments. Overall, these modes differ significantly in terms of cost, commitment, risk, return, and control.

mode of entry Method used to enter a foreign market.

nonequity mode A mode of entering foreign markets through exports and/or contractual agreements that tends to reflect relatively smaller commitments to overseas markets.

equity mode A mode of entering foreign markets through joint ventures and/or wholly owned subsidiaries that indicates a relatively larger, harder-to-reverse commitment.

EXHIBIT 10.5 MODES OF ENTRY: ADVANTAGES AND DISADVANTAGES

Entry modes (examples in the text)	Advantages	Disadvantages
1. Nonequity modes: Exports		
Direct exports (*Pearl River exports pianos to over 80 countries*)	▶ Economies of scale in production concentrated in home country ▶ Better control over distribution	▶ High transportation costs for bulky products ▶ Marketing distance from customers ▶ Trade barriers and protectionism
Indirect exports (*Commodities trade in textiles and meats*)	▶ Concentration of resources on production ▶ No need to directly handle export processes	▶ Less control over distribution (relative to direct exports) ▶ Inability to learn how to compete overseas
2. Nonequity modes: Contractual agreements		
Licensing/franchising (*Coca-Cola in Brazil and Pizza Hut in Thailand*)	▶ Low development costs ▶ Low risk in overseas expansion	▶ Little control over technology and marketing ▶ May create competitors ▶ Inability to engage in global coordination
Turnkey projects (*Safi Energy in Morocco*)	▶ Ability to earn returns from process technology in countries where FDI is restricted	▶ May create efficient competitors ▶ Lack of long-term presence
Research and development (R&D) contracts (*IT work in India*)	▶ Ability to tap into the best locations for certain innovations at low costs	▶ Difficult to negotiate and enforce contracts ▶ May nurture innovative competitors ▶ May lose core innovation capabilities
Co-marketing (*McDonald's campaigns with movie studios and toy makers; airline alliances*)	▶ Ability to reach more customers	▶ Limited coordination
3. Equity modes: Partially owned subsidiaries		
Joint ventures (*Shanghai Volkswagen*)	▶ Sharing costs, risks, and profits ▶ Access to partners' knowledge and assets ▶ Politically acceptable	▶ Divergent goals and interests of partners ▶ Limited equity and operational control ▶ Difficult to coordinate globally
4. Equity modes: Wholly owned subsidiaries		
Greenfield projects (*Microsoft's R&D center in China; TI in Japan; Japanese auto transplants in the United States*)	▶ Complete equity and operational control ▶ Protection of know-how ▶ Ability to coordinate globally	▶ Potential political problems and risks ▶ High development costs ▶ Add new capacity to industry ▶ Slow entry speed (relative to acquisitions)
Acquisitions (*Fiat Chrysler*)	▶ Same as greenfield (above) ▶ Do not add new capacity ▶ Fast entry speed	▶ Same as greenfield (above), except adding new capacity and slow speed ▶ Post-acquisition integration problems

The distinction between equity and nonequity modes is not trivial. In fact, it is what defines an MNE: An MNE enters foreign markets via equity modes through FDI. A firm that merely exports/imports with no FDI is usually not regarded as an MNE. As discussed at length in Chapter 6, an MNE, relative to a non-MNE, enjoys the three-pronged advantages of ownership, location, and internalization—collectively known as the OLI advantages. Overall, the first step in entry mode considerations is crucial. A strategic decision has to be made in terms of whether or not to undertake FDI and to become an MNE.

10-4c Modes of Entry: The Second Step on Making Actual Selections

During the second step, managers consider variables within *each* group of nonequity and equity modes. If the decision is to export, then the next consideration is direct exports or indirect exports (see Chapter 9). Direct exports are the most basic mode of entry, capitalizing on economies of scale in production concentrated in the home country and providing better control over distribution. The world's largest piano maker, Pearl River, exports its pianos from China to over 80 countries. This strategy essentially treats foreign demand as an extension of domestic demand, and the firm is geared toward designing and producing first and foremost for the domestic market. While direct exports may work if the export volume is small, it is not optimal when the firm has many foreign buyers. Marketing 101 suggests that the firm needs to be closer, both physically and psychologically, to its customers, prompting the firm to consider more intimate overseas involvement such as FDI. Direct exports may also be accused of **dumping**, triggering antidumping actions.

As you will recall from Chapter 9, another export strategy is indirect exports—namely, exporting through domestically based export intermediaries. This strategy not only enjoys the economies of scale in domestic production (similar to direct exports), but is also relatively worry free. A significant amount of export trade in commodities such as textiles, woods, and meats, which compete primarily on price, is indirect through intermediaries.[14] Indirect exports have some drawbacks. For example, third parties such as export trading companies may not share the same agendas and objectives as exporters. Exporters choose intermediaries primarily because of information asymmetries concerning risks and uncertainties associated with foreign markets.[15] Intermediaries with international contacts and knowledge essentially make a living by taking advantage of such information asymmetries. They may have a vested interest in making sure that such asymmetries are not reduced. Intermediaries, for example, may repackage the products under their own brand and insist on monopolizing the communication with overseas customers. If the exporter is interested in knowing more about how its products perform overseas, indirect exports would not provide such knowledge.

The next group of nonequity entry modes involves the following types of contractual agreement: (1) licensing or franchising, (2) turnkey projects, (3) research and development contracts, and (4) co-marketing. Recall from Chapter 9 that in licensing/franchising agreements, the licensor/franchisor sells the rights to intellectual property such as patents and know-how to the licensee/franchisee for a royalty fee. The licensor/franchisor thus does not have to bear the full costs and risks associated with foreign expansion. Coca-Cola, for example, has licensed its trademark to clothing manufacturers in Brazil. On the other hand, the licensor/franchisor does not have tight control over production and marketing. Pizza Hut, for example, was disappointed when its franchise in Thailand discontinued the relationship and launched a competing pizza restaurant to eat Pizza Hut's lunch.

In **turnkey projects**, clients pay contractors to design and construct new facilities and train personnel. At project completion, contractors hand clients the proverbial key to facilities ready for operations—hence the term "turnkey." This mode allows firms to earn returns from process technology (such as power generation) in countries where FDI is restricted. The drawbacks, however, are twofold. First, if foreign clients are competitors, selling them state-of-the-art technology through turnkey projects may boost their competitiveness. Second, turnkey projects do not allow for a long-term presence after the key is handed to clients. To obtain a longer-term presence, build-operate-transfer agreements are now often used instead of the traditional build-transfer type of turnkey projects. A **build-operate-transfer (BOT) agreement** is a nonequity mode of entry used to build a longer-term presence by building and then operating a facility for a period of time before transferring operations to a domestic agency or firm. For example, Safi Energy, a consortium among GDF Suez (France), Mitsui (Japan), and Nareva Holdings (Morocco), has been awarded a BOT power-generation project in Morocco.[16]

> **dumping** Exporting products at prices that are below what it costs to manufacture them, with the intent to raise prices after eliminating local rivals.

> **turnkey project** A project in which clients pay contractors to design and construct new facilities and train personnel.

> **build-operate-transfer (BOT) agreement** A nonequity mode of entry used to build a longer-term presence by building and then operating a facility for a period of time before transferring operations to a domestic agency or firm.

PHOTO MELON/SHUTTERSTOCK.COM

Research and development (R&D) contracts refer to outsourcing agreements in R&D between firms. Firm A agrees to perform certain R&D work for Firm B. Firms thereby tap into the best locations for certain innovations at relatively low costs. However, three drawbacks may emerge. First, given the uncertain and multidimensional nature of R&D, these contracts are often difficult to negotiate and enforce. While delivery time and costs are relatively easy to negotiate, quality is often difficult to assess. Second, such contracts may cultivate competitors. A number of Indian IT firms, nurtured by such work, are now on a global offensive to take on their Western rivals. Finally, firms that rely on outsiders to perform a lot of R&D may lose some of their core R&D capabilities in the long run.

Co-marketing refers to efforts among a number of firms to jointly market their products and services. Toy makers and movie studios often collaborate in co-marketing campaigns with fast-food chains such as McDonald's to package toys based on movie characters in kids' meals. Airline alliances such as One World, Sky Team, and Star Alliance engage in extensive co-marketing through code sharing. The advantages are the ability to reach more customers. The drawbacks center on limited control and coordination.

Next are equity modes, all of which entail some FDI and transform the firm to become an MNE. A **joint venture (JV)** is a corporate child, a new entity jointly created and owned by two or more parent companies. It has three principal forms: Minority JV (less than 50% equity), 50–50 JV (equal equity), and majority JV (more than 50% equity). JVs, such as Shanghai Volkswagen, have three advantages. First, an MNE shares costs, risks, and profits with a local partner, so the MNE possesses a certain degree of control but limits risk exposure. Second, the MNE gains access to knowledge about the host country; the local firm, in turn, benefits from the MNE's technology, capital, and management. Third, JVs may be politically more acceptable in host countries.

In terms of disadvantages, JVs often involve

US shoe manufacturer Skechers had a record revenue year in 2016 thanks to 27.1% growth in international sales. Driving this growth was Sketchers' 212 joint venture stores across China (96 stores), Hong Kong (40 stores), India (35), Israel (6), South Korea (14), and Southeast Asia (21)—up from just 74 such stores in 2013.

partners from different backgrounds and with different goals, so conflicts are natural. Furthermore, effective equity and operational control may be difficult to achieve since everything has to be negotiated—in some cases, fought over. Finally, the nature of the JV does not give an MNE the tight control over a foreign subsidiary that it may need for global coordination. Overall, all sorts of nonequity-based contractual agreements and equity-based JVs can be broadly considered as strategic alliances (within the *dotted area* in Exhibit 10.4). Chapter 11 will discuss them in detail.

The last entry mode is to establish a **wholly owned subsidiary (WOS)**, defined as a subsidiary located in a foreign country that is entirely owned by the parent multinational. There are two primary means to set up a WOS. One is to establish **greenfield operations**, building new factories and offices from scratch (on a proverbial piece of "green field" formerly used for agricultural purposes). For example, Microsoft established a wholly owned greenfield R&D center in Beijing. There are three advantages. First, a greenfield WOS gives an MNE complete equity and management control, thus eliminating the headaches associated with JVs. Second, this undivided control leads to better protection of proprietary technology. Third, a WOS allows for centrally coordinated global actions. Sometimes, a subsidiary will be ordered to launch actions that by design will *lose* money. In the semiconductor market, TI faced competition from Japanese rivals

research and development (R&D) contract Outsourcing agreement in R&D between firms.

Co-marketing Efforts among a number of firms to jointly market their products and services.

joint venture (JV) A new corporate entity jointly created and owned by two or more parent companies.

wholly owned subsidiary (WOS) A subsidiary located in a foreign country that is entirely owned by the parent multinational.

greenfield operation Building factories and offices from scratch (on a proverbial piece of "green field" formerly used for agricultural purposes).

such as NEC and Toshiba that maintained low prices outside of Japan by charging high prices in Japan and using domestic profits to cross-subsidize overseas expansion. By entering Japan via a WOS and slashing prices there, TI incurred a loss but forced the Japanese firms to defend their home market. This was because Japanese rivals had a much larger market share in Japan. When the price level in Japan collapsed thanks to the aggressive price cutting unleashed by TI's WOS in the country, NEC and Toshiba would suffer much more significant losses. Consequently, Japanese rivals had to reduce the ferocity of their price wars outside of Japan. Local licensees/franchisees or JV partners are unlikely to accept such a subservient role as being ordered to *lose* money (!).

In terms of drawbacks, a greenfield WOS tends to be expensive and risky, not only financially but also politically. Its conspicuous foreignness may become a target for nationalistic sentiments. Another drawback is that greenfield operations add new capacity to an industry, which will make a competitive industry more crowded. For example, think of all the Japanese automobile plants built in the United States, which have severely squeezed the market share of US automakers and forced Chrysler and GM into bankruptcy. Finally, greenfield operations suffer from a slow entry speed of at least one to several years (relative to acquisitions).

The other way to establish a WOS is through an acquisition. Fiat's acquisition of Chrysler is a case in point. Although this is the last mode we discuss here, it represents approximately 70% of worldwide FDI. Acquisition shares all the benefits of greenfield WOS but enjoys two additional advantages: (1) adding no new capacity and (2) faster entry speed. In terms of drawbacks, acquisition shares all of the disadvantages of greenfield WOS except adding new capacity and slow entry speed. But acquisition has a unique and potentially devastating disadvantage: post-acquisition integration problems. (See Chapter 11.)

Overall, while we have focused on one entry mode at a time, firms in practice are not limited by any single entry mode (see Closing Case). For example, IKEA stores in China are JVs, and its stores in Hong Kong and Taiwan are separate franchises. In addition, entry modes may change over time. Starbucks, for instance, first used franchising. It then switched to JVs and, more recently, to acquisitions.

10-5 MANAGEMENT SAVVY

Foreign market entries represent a *foundation* for overseas actions. Without these crucial first steps, firms will remain domestic players. The challenges

associated with internationalization are daunting, the complexities enormous, and the stakes high. Returning to our fundamental question, we ask: What determines the success and failure in foreign market entries? The answer boils down to the two core perspectives: institution-based and resource-based views. Shown in Exhibit 10.6, three implications for action emerge from these perspectives. First, from an institution-based view, managers need to understand the rules of the game, both formal and informal, governing competition in foreign markets. Failure to understand these rules can be costly. Why do Chinese MNEs' high-profile acquisition attempts in the United States (such as CNOOC's bid for Unocal) and Australia (such as Chinalco's bid for Rio Tinto) often fail? Why do Arabic MNEs' similar attempts (such as DP World's bid for US ports) often fail too? While there are many reasons, one key reason is these foreign entrants' failure in understanding the informal, unwritten rules of the game that often have protectionist (or even racist) undertones in developed economies. Knowing these rules of the game does not mean these emerging multinationals need to be discouraged. They just need to do better homework, keep their heads low, and work on *low*-profile acquisitions, which are routinely approved in developed economies.

Second, from a resource-based view, managers need to develop *overwhelming* capabilities to offset the liability of foreignness. The key word is *overwhelming*. Merely outstanding, but not overwhelming, capabilities cannot ensure success in the face of strong incumbents—a painful lesson that DHL learned when it withdrew from the United States. In short, being good enough is not good enough.

Finally, managers need to match entries with strategic goals. If the goal is to deter rivals in their home markets through price slashing as TI did in Japan, then be prepared to fight a nasty price war and lose money. If the goal is to generate decent returns, then withdrawing from some tough nuts to crack may be necessary—as evidenced by Walmart's withdrawal from Germany and South Korea.

Closing Case: Thai Union's Foreign Market Entries

A family business founded in Thailand in 1977 by a Chinese immigrant, Thai Union Frozen Products Plc has become one of the world's largest seafood processors, with subsidiaries in France, India, Indonesia, Japan, Norway, the United States, and Vietnam. Thai Union's international growth started with exports to Japan and the United States in 1988. In Japan, a joint venture (JV) with a local trading partner soon followed. In the United States, Thai Union went step-by-step to build up its market presence.

BLOOMBERG/GETTY IMAGES

Exports were followed by sales offices. Acquisitions of Chicken of the Sea and Empress International then followed in the 2000s. In Europe, Thai Union made a big splash in 2010 by acquiring MW Brands, a French manufacturer and distributor of canned seafood. At €670 million, this acquisition was the second largest outward foreign direct investment (FDI) deal in the history of Thailand. In 2014, Thai Union added further European brands to its portfolio by acquiring King Oscar in Norway and MerAlliance in France.

Thai Union's strategy focuses on exploiting its lower cost base arising from (1) low-cost skilled labor in Thailand and seafood caught off the Thai coast, and (2) product diversification that enables full exploitation of the raw seafood. The best parts of fish and shrimp become high-end food products, and the residual is used, for example, for pet food.

The purchase of European firms is primarily motivated by market-seeking motives, but it also adds fishing and processing capacity. With the acquisition of MW Brands, the share of Europe in Thai Union's total sales jumped from 11% to over one-third, thus reducing its dependence on the US market. MW Brands became the market leader in Britain, France, Ireland, Italy, and the Netherlands, with brands such as Conserverie Parmentier, John West, Mareblu, and Petite Navire. These brands represent a strategic asset that could be further exploited in other European markets. In addition, the European acquisitions also supported efficiency-seeking motives by adding four processing plants in France, Ghana, Portugal, and Seychelles to its existing facilities in Indonesia, Thailand, the United States, and Vietnam. These acquisitions also increased the fishing fleet from four to nine vessels.

The ambitions of CEO Thiraphong Chansiri (son of the founder) do not end with such acquisitions in Europe. In 2015, Thai Union pursued a $1 billion bid for Bumble Bee Foods in the United States in an effort to move into higher margin, premium products. In short, if you are a seafood lover, Thai Union has probably come to a plate near you—or in front of you.

Case Discussion Questions

1. Other than Thai Union, have you heard any firm based in Thailand that has become one of the world's largest (in any industry)?

2. What are some of the unique resources and capabilities that Thai Union has?

3. How many foreign market entry modes does Thai Union use? What are their advantages and disadvantages?

4. Why does Thai Union use more acquisitions lately?

Sources: "Thai Union plans to real in more Western catches," *Financial Times*, 2 February 2015: www.ft.com; K. E. Meyer and O. Thaijongarak, "The dynamics of emerging economy MNEs: How the internationalization process model can guide future research," *Asia Pacific Journal of Management* 30 (2013); 1125–1153; M. W. Peng and K. E. Meyer, "Thai Union acquires market access," in *International Business*, 2nd ed. (London: Cengage EMEA, 2016) 349; www.mwbrands.com.

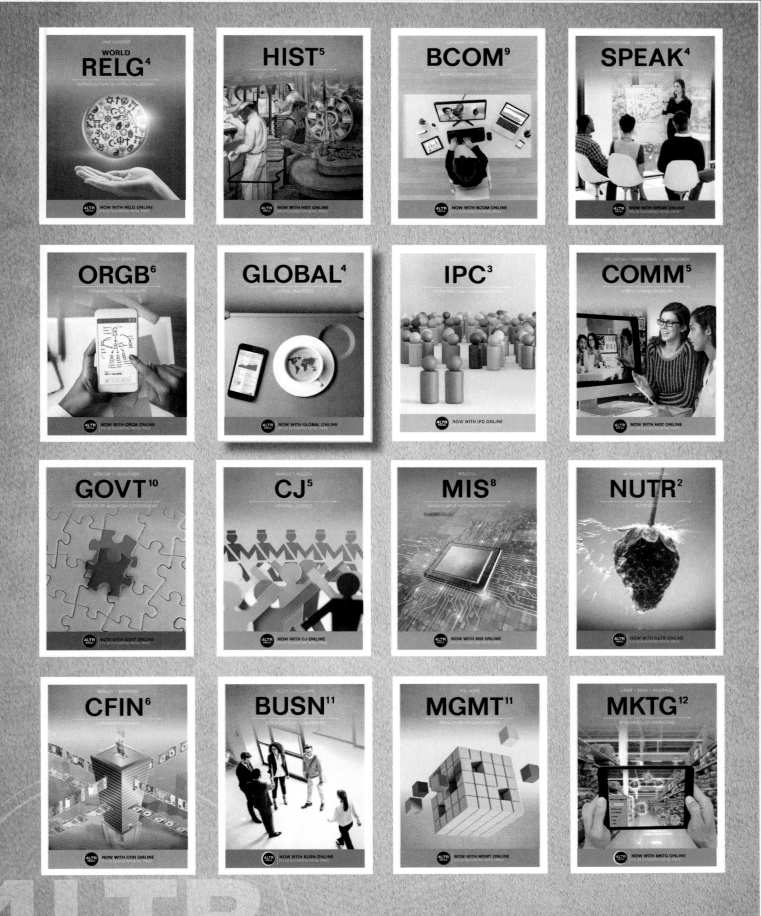

11 Making Alliances & Acquisitions Work

LEARNING OBJECTIVES

After studying this chapter, you will be able to . . .

11-1 Define alliances and acquisitions.

11-2 Articulate how institutions and resources influence alliances and acquisitions.

11-3 Describe how alliances are formed.

11-4 Outline how alliances are dissolved.

11-5 Discuss how alliances perform.

11-6 Explain why firms make acquisitions.

11-7 Describe what performance problems firms tend to encounter with acquisitions.

11-8 Articulate what you can do to make global alliances and acquisitions successful.

After you finish this chapter, go to

PAGE 183 for

STUDY TOOLS

Opening Case: Etihad Airways' Alliance Network

Founded in 2003 and based in Abu Dhabi, Etihad Airways is both inspired by Emirates Airlines and a direct competitor of Emirates, which is based in Dubai, a fellow emirate in the United Arab Emirates (UAE). Etihad, which means "union" in Arabic, quickly became the fastest growing airline in the history of commercial aviation. Currently, with over 120 aircraft, Etihad serves over 15 million passengers to nearly 120 destinations around the world. Now the world's fourth largest airline in terms of international passengers (and second largest in terms of freight tonnage), Emirates is a mammoth that has 246 aircraft and carries 52 million passengers to over 150 cities.

Etihad imitates the highly successful Emirates by (1) equipping itself with modern long-haul jets (such as Airbus A380 and Boeing 777 Extended Range [ER]) and (2) leveraging the enviable location of the Abu Dhabi International Airport, which is only an hour away by car from Dubai's storied airport. Given the small local population (three million in Abu Dhabi versus four million in Dubai), Etihad—like Emirates—can only grow by being a "super-connector" airline. In other words, most of the passengers neither travel from nor to Abu Dhabi. Blessed by its Middle East location, Abu Dhabi, just like Dubai, is an ideal stopping point for air traffic between Europe and Australasia and between Asia and Africa.

One area that Etihad has decisively deviated from its role model, Emirates, is an interest in weaving an alliance network. Other than a single alliance with Qantas, Emirates either has been very shy or does not care about collaboration. In an industry with three major multipartner networks—One World, Sky Team, and Star Alliance—airlines are no strangers to alliances. But Etihad's alliances are not what you think. Its talks to join these three mega networks did not go anywhere, because none of them were interested in

admitting an ambitious new member determined to eat their lunch. Instead, Etihad has built its own alliance network consisting of eight smaller airlines. In 2011, Etihad took a 29% equity share in Air Berlin, Europe's sixth largest airline. Since then, through a series of equity-based strategic investments, Etihad acquired stakes in Dublin, Ireland–based Aer Lingus (4% equity); Rome, Italy–based Alitalia (49%)—the largest airline in Italy; Belgrade, Serbia–based Air Serbia (49%)—the largest airline in Serbia, formerly known as Jat Airways; Mahe, Seychelles–based Air Seychelles (40%); Lugano, Switzerland–based Darwin Airline (34%)—recently rebranded as Etihad Regional; Mumbai, India–based Jet Airways (24%); and Brisbane, Australia–based Virgin Australia (20%).

Etihad CEO James Hogan, who is an Australian, is viewed as a "white knight" who bailed out a bunch of money-losing or cash-poor airlines, including the struggling flag carriers of Ireland, Italy, Serbia, and Seychelles. Hogan has argued that his multibillion-dollar investments in airlines that serve smaller markets made economic sense by increasing Etihad's passenger tally and securing economies of scale when competing with Emirates. But can Etihad turn such an alliance network profitable? The most challenging member is Alitalia, which lost €1.1 billion ($1.5 billion) in five years, and Etihad has spent €560 million to breathe some new life into it.

Always known for using nasty language, Michael O'Leary, CEO of Ireland's and Europe's largest airline, Ryanair, bluntly told journalists that Etihad "bought a lot of rubbish, and increasing their stake in Aer Lingus is consistent with that." Indeed, no other airline in the world is doing what Etihad is doing at this scale. Does Etihad, despite its deep pockets, have what it takes to turn around a whole bunch of also-rans? Stay tuned.

Sources: "Will Etihad's flock of also-rans fly?" *Bloomberg Businessweek*, 24 April 2014: 22–24; "Airline alliances: New world order," *CEO Middle East*, June 2013: 36–42; "Emirates—our destinations," 2016, emirates.com; "Etihad Airways route map," 2016, flights.etihad.com.

In its competition with Emirates and other airlines, why is Etihad Airways interested in weaving an alliance network? Is Etihad likely to acquire some of these alliance partners? These are some of the key questions driving this chapter. Alliances and acquisitions are two major strategies for growth used by firms around the world, thus necessitating our attention.[1] This chapter first defines alliances and acquisitions, followed by a discussion of how institution-based and resource-based views shed light on these topics. We then discuss the formation, evolution, and performance of alliances and acquisitions.

11-1 DEFINING ALLIANCES AND ACQUISITIONS

Strategic alliances are voluntary agreements of cooperation between firms. Remember that the dotted area in Exhibit 10.4 in Chapter 10 consists of nonequity-based contractual agreements and equity-based joint ventures (JVs). These

> **strategic alliance** Voluntary agreement of cooperation between firms.

EXHIBIT 11.1 THE VARIETY OF STRATEGIC ALLIANCES

can all be broadly considered as strategic alliances. Exhibit 11.1 illustrates this further, depicting alliances as degrees of *compromise* between pure market transactions and acquisitions. **Contractual (nonequity-based) alliances** are associations between firms that are based on contracts and do not involve the sharing of ownership. They include co-marketing, research and development (R&D) contracts, turnkey projects, strategic suppliers, strategic distributors, and licensing/franchising. **Equity-based alliances**, on the other hand, are based on ownership or financial interest between the firms. They include **strategic investment** (one partner invests in another—see Opening Case) and **cross-shareholding** (each partner invests in the other). Equity-based alliances also include JVs, which involve the establishment of a new legally independent entity (in other words, a new firm) whose equity is provided by two or more partners.

Although JVs are often used as examples of alliances, *not* all alliances are JVs. A JV is a corporate child produced by two or more parent firms, as is the case with Sony Ericsson. A non-JV, equity-based alliance can be regarded as two firms getting married but not having children. For example, Renault is a strategic investor in Nissan, but both automakers still operate independently. They have *not* given birth to a new car company.

An **acquisition** is a transfer of the control of operations and management from one firm (target) to another (acquirer), the former becoming a unit of the latter. For example, Volvo is now a unit of Geely. A **merger** is the combination of operations and management of two firms to establish a new legal entity. For instance, the merger between Fiat and Chrysler resulted in Fiat Chrysler Automobiles (see Closing Case).

Although the phrase "mergers and acquisitions" (M&As) is often used, in reality acquisitions dominate the scene. Only 3% of M&As are mergers. For practical purposes, "M&As" basically mean "acquisitions." Consequently, we use the two terms "M&As" and "acquisitions" interchangeably. Specifically, we focus on cross-border (international) M&As (Exhibit 11.2). This is not only because of our global interest, but also because of (1) the high percentage (about 30%) of international deals among all M&As and (2) the high percentage (about 70%) of M&As among foreign direct investment (FDI) flows.

11-2 HOW INSTITUTIONS AND RESOURCES AFFECT ALLIANCES AND ACQUISITIONS

What drives alliances? What drives acquisitions? The institution-based and resource-based views can shed considerable light on these important questions. The institution-based view suggests that as rules of the game, institutions influence how a firm chooses between

contractual (nonequity-based) alliance An association between firms that is based on a contract and does not involve the sharing of ownership.

equity-based alliance An association between firms that is based on shared ownership or financial interest.

strategic investment A business strategy in which one firm invests in another.

cross-shareholding A business strategy in which each partner in an alliance holds stock in the other firm.

acquisition The transfer of the control of operations and management from one firm (target) to another (acquirer), the former becoming a unit of the latter.

merger The combination of operations and management of two firms to establish a new legal entity.

EXHIBIT 11.2　THE VARIETY OF CROSS-BORDER MERGERS AND ACQUISITIONS

Source: United Nations, *World Investment Report 2000* (New York: UN, 2000) 100.

EXHIBIT 11.3　INSTITUTIONS, RESOURCES, ALLIANCES, AND ACQUISITIONS

suspect at least some tacit collusion when competitors cooperate. However, because integration within alliances is usually not as tight as acquisitions (which would eliminate one competitor), antitrust authorities are more likely to approve alliances as opposed to acquisitions. A proposed merger of American Airlines and British Airways was blocked by both US and UK antitrust authorities. But the two airlines were allowed to form an alliance that has eventually grown to become the multipartner One World. In another example, the proposed merger between AT&T and T-Mobile (a wholly owned subsidiary [WOS] of Deutsche Telekom in the United States) was torpedoed by US antitrust authorities. But the US government *blessed* AT&T and T-Mobile's collaboration in roaming and mobile payments.

Another way formal institutions affect alliances and acquisitions is through formal requirements on market entry modes. In many countries, governments discourage or simply ban acquisitions to establish WOSs, thereby leaving alliances with local firms as the only choice for FDI. For example, before NAFTA went into effect in 1994, the Mexican government not only limited multinationals' entries to JVs, but also dictated a maximum equity position of 49%.

Recently, two trends have emerged in the entry mode requirements dictated by formal government

alliances and acquisitions in terms of its strategy.[2] However, rules are not made just for one firm. The resource-based view argues that although a number of firms may be governed by the same set of rules, some excel more than others because of the differences in firm-specific capabilities that make alliances and acquisitions work (see Exhibit 11.3).

11-2a Institutions, Alliances, and Acquisitions

Alliances and acquisitions function within a set of formal legal and regulatory frameworks.[3] The impact of these formal institutions on alliances and acquisitions can be found along two dimensions: (1) antitrust concerns and (2) entry mode requirements. First, many firms establish alliances with competitors. For example, Siemens and Bosch compete in automotive components and collaborate in household appliances. Antitrust authorities

In 2016, Walmart formed a strategic alliance with JD.com, China's largest e-commerce company by revenue. The alliance spurred a wide range of cooperative ventures, including both online and offline retail initiatives.

SORBIS/SHUTTERSTOCK.COM

policies. The first is a general trend toward more liberal policies. Many governments that historically approved only JVs as an entry mode (such as those in Mexico and South Korea) now allow WOSs. As a result, JVs have declined and acquisitions have increased in emerging economies.[4]

Despite the general movement toward more liberal policies, a second noticeable trend is that many governments still impose considerable requirements, especially when foreign firms acquire domestic assets. The strategically important Chinese automobile assembly industry and the Russian oil industry permit only JVs, thus eliminating acquisitions as a choice. US regulations limit foreign carriers to a maximum 25% of the equity in any US airline, and EU regulations limit non-EU ownership of EU-based airlines to 49%.

Informal institutions also influence alliances and acquisitions. The first set of informal institutions centers on collective norms, supported by a normative pillar. A core idea of the institution-based view is that because firms want to enhance or protect their legitimacy, copying what other reputable organizations are doing—even without knowing the direct performance benefits of doing so—may be a low-cost way to gain legitimacy. Thus, when a firm sees competitors entering alliances, that firm may jump on the alliance bandwagon just to be safe rather than risk ignoring industry trends. When M&As appear to be the trend, even managers with doubts about the wisdom of M&As may nevertheless be tempted to hunt

for acquisition targets. Although not every alliance or acquisition decision is driven by imitation, this motivation seems to explain a lot of these activities. The flip side is that many firms rush into alliances and acquisitions without due diligence and then get burned big time.

A second set of informal institutions emphasizes the cognitive pillar, which is centered on internalized, taken-for-granted values and beliefs that guide alliances and acquisitions. For example, BAE Systems (formerly British Aerospace) has announced that *all* of its future aircraft development programs would involve alliances. Likewise, in the area of acquisitions, Span's Santander is a firm believer. It has undertaken a total of $70 billion of acquisitions throughout Europe, Latin America, and now North America.[5] Clearly, managers at BAE Systems and Santander believe that such alliances and acquisitions, respectively, are the right (and sometimes the only) thing to do, which have become part of their informal norms and beliefs.

11-2b Resources and Alliances

How does the VRIO framework that characterizes the resource-based view influence alliances?

VALUE Alliances must create value. The three global airline alliance networks—One World, Sky Team, and Star Alliance—create value by reducing ticket costs by 18% to 28% on two-stage flights compared with separate flights on the same route if the airlines were not allied.[6] Exhibit 11.4 identifies three broad categories of value creation in terms of how advantages outweigh disadvantages. First, alliances may reduce costs, risks, and uncertainties. As Emirates Airlines from Dubai rises to preeminence, Etihad Airways from Abu Dhabi,

EXHIBIT 11.4	STRATEGIC ALLIANCES: ADVANTAGES AND DISADVANTAGES
Advantages	**Disadvantages**
Reduce costs, risks, and uncertainties	Choosing wrong partners
Access complementary assets and learning opportunities	Potential partner opportunism
Possibility to use alliances as real options	Risk of helping nurture competitors (learning race)

a fellow emirate in the United Arab Emirates, has set up a number of alliances with smaller airlines around the world in an effort to eat some of Emirates' lunch (see Opening Case). Second, alliances allow firms such as Fiat and Chrysler to tap into complementary assets of partners and facilitate learning (see Closing Case).

Finally, an important advantage of alliances lies in their value as real options. Conceptually, an option is the right (but not obligation) to take some action in the future. Technically, a financial option is an investment instrument permitting its holder, having paid for a small fraction of an asset, the right to increase investment by eventually acquiring the asset if necessary. A **real option** is an investment in real operations as opposed to financial capital.[7] A real options view suggests two propositions:

▶ In the first phase, an investor makes a small, initial investment to buy an option, which leads to the right to future investment but is not an obligation to do so.

▶ The investor then holds the option until a decision point arrives in the second phase and then decides between exercising the option or abandoning it.

OLEKSANDR KOVAL/SHUTTERSTOCK.COM

For firms interested in eventually acquiring other companies but uncertain about such moves, working together in alliances affords an insider view to the capabilities of these partners. This is similar to trying on new shoes to see if they fit before buying them. Since acquisitions are not only costly but also very likely to fail, alliances permit firms to *sequentially* increase their investment should they decide to pursue acquisitions (see Closing Case). If after working together as partners a firm finds that an acquisition is not a good idea, there is no obligation to pursue it. Overall, alliances have emerged as great instruments of real options because of their flexibility to sequentially scale *up* or scale *down* the investment.

On the other hand, alliances have a number of non-trivial drawbacks. First, there is always a possibility of being stuck with the wrong partner. Firms are advised to choose a prospective partner with caution, preferably a known entity. Yet, the partner should also be sufficiently differentiated to provide some complementary (non-overlapping) capabilities. Many firms find it difficult to evaluate the true intentions and capabilities of their prospective partners until it is too late.

A second disadvantage is potential partner opportunism. While opportunism is likely in any kind of

economic relationship, the alliance setting may provide especially strong incentives for some (but not necessarily all) partners to be opportunistic. A cooperative relationship always entails some elements of trust that may be easily abused.

RARITY The ability to successfully manage interfirm relationships—often called **relational (or collaborative) capabilities**—tends to be rare. Managers involved in alliances require relationship skills rarely covered in the traditional business school curriculum, which typically emphasizes competition rather than collaboration. To truly derive benefits from alliances, managers need to foster trust with partners yet be on guard against opportunism.[8]

As much as alliances represent a strategic and economic arrangement, they also constitute a social, psychological, and emotional phenomenon. Words such as "courtship," "marriage," and "divorce" are often used when discussing alliances. Given that the interests of partner firms do not fully overlap and are often in conflict, managers involved in alliances live a precarious existence, trying to represent the interests of their respective firms while attempting to make the complex relationship work. Not surprisingly, sound relational capabilities necessary to successfully manage alliances are in short supply.[9]

IMITABILITY Imitability occurs at two levels in alliances: (1) firm level and (2) alliance level. First, as noted earlier, one firm's resources and capabilities may be imitated by partners. Another imitability issue refers to the trust and understanding among partners in successful alliances. Firms without such "chemistry" may have a hard time imitating such activities. CFM International, a JV set up by GE and Snecma to produce jet engines in France, has successfully operated for over 40 years. Rivals stuck in a bad relationship would have a hard time imitating such a successful relationship.

ORGANIZATION Some successful alliance relationships are organized in a way that is difficult to replicate. Tolstoy makes the observation in the opening sentence of *Anna Karenina*: "All happy families are alike; each

> **real option** An investment in real operations as opposed to financial capital.
>
> **relational (collaborative) capability** The ability to successfully manage interfirm relationships.

Emerging Acquirers from China and India

Multinational enterprises (MNEs) from emerging economies, especially China and India, have emerged as a new breed of acquirers around the world. Causing "oohs" and "ahhs," they have grabbed media headlines and caused controversies. Anecdotes aside, are the patterns of these new global acquirers similar? How do they differ? Only recently has rigorous academic research been conducted to allow for systematic comparison (Exhibit 11.5).

Overall, China's stock of outward foreign direct investment (OFDI) (1.7% of the worldwide total) is about three times India's (0.5%). One visible similarity is that both Chinese and Indian MNEs seem to use M&As as their primary mode of OFDI. Throughout the 2000s, Chinese firms spent $130 billion to engage in M&As overseas, whereas Indian firms made M&A deals worth $60 billion.

MNEs from China and India target different industries to support and strengthen their own most competitive industries at home. Given China's prowess in manufacturing, Chinese firms' overseas M&As primarily target energy, minerals, and mining—crucial supply industries that feed their manufacturing operations at home. Indian MNEs' world-class position in high-tech and software services is reflected in their interest in acquiring firms in these industries.

The geographic spread of these MNEs is indicative of the level of their capabilities. Chinese firms have undertaken most of their deals in Asia, with Hong Kong being their most favorable location. In other words, the geographic distribution of Chinese M&As is not global; rather, it is quite regional. This reflects a relative lack of capabilities to engage in managerial challenges in regions distant from China, especially in more developed economies. More recently, Chinese acquirers have become more active in developed economies, such as Haier's acquisition of GE Appliances and Wanda's acquisition of AMC Theaters in the United States, Midea's acquisition of Kuka in Germany, ChemChina's purchase of Pirelli in Italy, and COSCO's takeover of Piraeus Port in Greece. Indian MNEs have primarily made deals in Europe, with the UK as their leading target country. For example, acquisitions made by Tata Motors (Jaguar Land Rover) and Tata Steel (Corus Group) propelled Tata Group to become the number-one private-sector employer in the

EXHIBIT 11.5	COMPARING CROSS-BORDER M&AS UNDERTAKEN BY CHINESE AND INDIAN MNES	
	Chinese MNEs	**Indian MNEs**
Top target industries	Energy, minerals, and mining	High-tech and software services
Top target economies	Hong Kong	United Kingdom
Top target regions	Asia	Europe
Top acquiring companies involved	State-owned enterprises	Private business groups
Percent of successfully closed deals	47%	67%

Source: Extracted from S. Sun, M. W. Peng, B. Ren, and D. Yan, "A comparative ownership advantage framework for cross-border M&As," *Journal of World Business* 47 (2012): 4–16.

unhappy family is unhappy in its own way." Much the same can be said for business alliances. Each failed alliance has its own mistakes and problems, and firms in unsuccessful alliances (for whatever reason) often find it exceedingly challenging, if not impossible, to organize and manage their interfirm relationships better.

11-2c Resources and Acquisitions

VALUE Do acquisitions create *value*?[10] Overall, their performance record is sobering. As many as 70% of acquisitions reportedly fail. On average, the performance of acquiring firms does not improve after acquisitions.

Target firms, after being acquired and becoming internal units, often perform worse than when they were independent, stand-alone firms. The only identifiable group of winners is the shareholders of target firms, who may experience on average a 25% increase in their stock value.[11] This is due to **acquisition premium**, which is the difference between the acquisition price and the market value of target firms.

Acquirers of US firms pay, on average, a 20% to 30% premium, and acquirers of EU firms pay a slightly lower premium (about 18%).[12] Shareholders of acquiring firms experience a 4% loss in their stock value during the same

UK. Overall, Indian firms display a more global spread in their M&As and demonstrate a higher level of confidence and sophistication in making deals in developed economies.

From an institution-based view, the contrasts between Chinese and Indian acquirers are significant. The primary M&A players from China are state-owned enterprises (SOEs), which have their own advantages (such as strong support from the Chinese government) and trappings (such as resentment and suspicion from host-country governments). The movers and shakers of cross-border M&As from India are private business groups, which generally are not viewed with strong suspicion. The limited evidence suggests that M&As by Indian firms tend to create value for their shareholders. On the other hand, M&As by Chinese firms tend to destroy shareholder value—indicative of potential hubristic and managerial motives evidenced by empire building and agency problems.

Announcing high-profile deals is one thing, but completing them is another matter. Chinese MNEs have a particularly poor record in completing the overseas acquisition deals they announce. Fewer than half (47%) of their announced acquisitions were completed, which compares unfavorably to Indian MNEs' 67% completion rate and to a global average of 80%–90% completion rate. Chinese MNEs' lack of ability and experience in due diligence and financing is one reason, but another reason is the political backlash and resistance they encounter, especially in developed economies. The 2005 failure of CNOOC's bid for Unocal in the United States and the 2009 failure of Chinalco's bid for Rio Tinto's assets in Australia are but two high-profile examples.

Even assuming successful completion, integration is a leading challenge during the post-acquisition phase. Acquirers from China and India have often taken the "high road" to acquisitions, in which acquirers deliberately allow acquired target companies to retain autonomy, keep the top management intact, and then gradually encourage interaction between the two sides. In contrast, the "low road" to acquisitions would be for acquirers to act quickly to impose their systems and rules on acquired target companies. Although the "high road" sounds noble, this is a reflection of these acquirers' lack of international management experience and

capabilities. However, this "high road" or "light touch" approach has helped some of these acquirers to overcome initial reservations and resistance in developed economies. In 2016, when facing concerns from the German government in Midea's attempt to take over Kuka, a leading industrial robot maker, Midea promised to maintain existing plants and jobs until 2023—far longer than what other acquirers could promise—and to keep sensitive customer data walled off from the Chinese parent company. The deal eventually sailed through.

From a resource-based view, examples of emerging acquirers that can do a good job in integration and deliver value are rare. According to the *Economist*, Tata "worked wonders" at JLR by increasing 30% sales and keeping the factory at full capacity. This took place during a recession when European automakers were suffering. Fiat, for example, could only utilize 40% of its factory capacity in Italy (see Closing Case). According to *Bloomberg Businessweek*, Lenovo was able to "find treasure in the PC industry's trash" by turning around the former IBM PC division and using it to propel itself to become the biggest PC maker in the world. In ten years, it grew from a $3 billion company to a $40 billion one. However, Lenovo knew that worldwide PC sales were going down, thanks to the rise of mobile devices. In response, Lenovo recently bought "the mobile phone industry's trash"—Motorola Mobility division—from Google and endeavored to leverage the Motorola brand to become a top player in the smartphone world. This deal quickly made Lenovo the world's third best-selling smartphone maker after Samsung and Apple.

Sources: "Lenovo completes Motorola takeover after Google sale," BBC News, 30 October 2014: www.bbc.co.uk; "Jackpot! How Lenovo found treasure in the PC industry's trash," *Bloomberg Businessweek*, 12 May 2014: 46–51; "The new barbarians at the gate," *Bloomberg Businessweek*, 31 November 2016: 39–41; Y. Chen and M. Young, "Cross-border M&As by Chinese listed companies," *Asia Pacific Journal of Management* 27 (2010): 523–539; "The cat returns," *Economist*, 29 September 2012: 63; O. Hope, W. Thomas, and D. Vyas, "The cost of pride," *Journal of International Business Studies* 42 (2011): 128–151; J. Knoerich, "Why some advanced economy firms prefer to be taken over by Chinese acquirers," *Columbia FDI Perspectives* 187 (2016); S. Lebedev, M. W. Peng, E. Xie, and C. Stevens, "Mergers and acquisitions in and out of emerging economies," *Journal of World Business* 50 (2015): 651–662 ; Y. Yang, "I came back because the company needed me," *Harvard Business Review* (July 2014): 104–108; United Nations; *World Investment Report 2016* (Geneva: United Nations UN, 2016) 49.

period. The combined wealth of shareholders of both acquiring and target firms is only marginally positive, less than 2%.[13] Unfortunately, many M&As destroy value.

RARITY For acquisitions to add value, one or all of the firms involved must have rare and unique skills that enhance the overall strategy. Although acquirers from emerging economies generally have a hard time delivering value from their acquisitions, Lenovo, according to *Bloomberg Businessweek*, was able to "find treasure in the PC industry's trash" by turning around the former IBM PC division and using it to propel itself to become the biggest PC maker in the world (see In Focus).[14] Such skills

are not only rare among emerging acquirers, but also rare among established acquirers—think of DaimlerChrysler.

IMITABILITY While many firms undertake acquisitions, a much smaller number of them have mastered the art of post-acquisition integration. Consequently, firms that excel in integration possess *hard-to-imitate* capabilities that are advantages in acquisitions. For example, each of Northrop Grumman's acquisitions must conform to a carefully orchestrated plan of

> **acquisition premium** The difference between the acquisition price and the market value of target firms.

Nomura Securities, Japan's largest securities company, acquired Lehman Brothers' Asian and European assets in the wake of the Great Recession.

nearly 400 items, from how to issue press releases to which accounting software to use. Unlike its bigger defense rivals such as Boeing and Raytheon, Northrop Grumman thus far has not stumbled with any of its acquisitions.

ORGANIZATION Fundamentally, whether acquisitions add value boils down to how merged firms are organized to take advantage of the benefits while minimizing the costs. Pre-acquisition analysis often focuses on **strategic fit**, which is the effective matching of complementary strategic capabilities. Yet, many firms do not pay adequate attention to **organizational fit**, which is the similarity in cultures, systems, and structures. On paper, Nomura and Lehman Brothers' Asia and Europe operations seemed to have a great

strategic fit The effective matching of complementary strategic capabilities.

organizational fit The similarity in cultures, systems, and structures between two or more firms.

deal of strategic fit: Nomura was strong in Asia and weak in Europe. Lehman was strong in Europe and weak in Asia. (Lehman was also strong in its home region, North America, but its North American assets were sold to another firm and thus were not relevant to Nomura.) Why was the integration between the two such a mess? Mostly because of the almost total lack of organizational fit.

11-3 FORMATION OF ALLIANCES

The next few sections discuss in some detail the formation, evolution, and performance of alliances and acquisitions. First: How are alliances formed? A three-stage model in Exhibit 11.6 addresses this process.

In Stage One, a firm must decide if growth can be achieved through market transactions, acquisitions, or alliances. To grow by pure market transactions, the firm has to confront competitive challenges independently. This is highly demanding, even for resource-rich multinationals. As noted earlier in the chapter, acquisitions have some unique drawbacks, leading many managers to conclude that alliances are the way to go. For example, Dallas-based Sabre Travel Network have used alliances to enter Australia, Bahrain, India, Israel, Japan, and Singapore.

In Stage Two, a firm must decide whether to take a contractual or an equity approach. As noted in Chapters 6 and 10, the choice between contract and equity is crucial. The first driving force is shared capabilities. The more tacit (that is, hard to describe and codify) the capabilities, the greater the preference for equity involvement. The most effective way to learn *complex* processes is through learning by doing. A good example of this is learning to cook by actually cooking and not by simply reading cookbooks. Many business processes are the same way. A firm that wants to produce cars will find that the codified knowledge found in books, reports, and operating manuals is not enough. Much tacit knowledge can only be acquired via learning by doing, preferably with experts as alliance partners (see Opening Case and Closing Case).

A second driving force is the importance of direct monitoring and control. Equity relationships allow firms to have some direct control over joint activities on a continuing basis, whereas contractual relationships usually do not. In general, firms that fear their intellectual property may be expropriated prefer equity alliances (and a higher level of equity).

Eventually, firms need to specify a specific format that is either equity based or contractual (nonequity based), depending on the choice made in Stage Two. Exhibit 11.6 lists the different format options. Since

EXHIBIT 11.6   ALLIANCE FORMATION

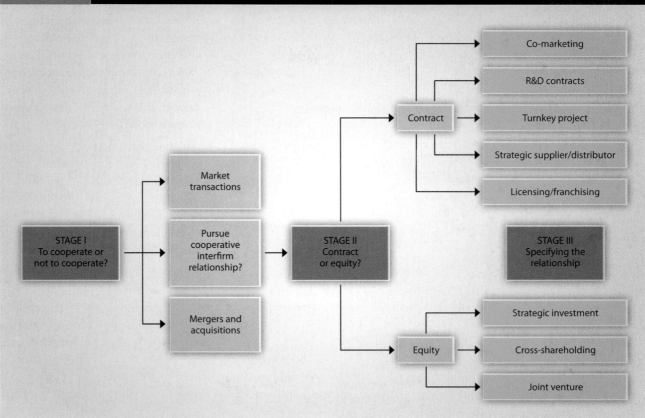

Source: S. Tallman and O. Shenkar, "A managerial decision model of international cooperative venture formation," *Journal of International Business Studies* 25 (1994): 101.

Chapter 10 has already covered this topic as part of the discussion on entry modes, we will not repeat it here.

 11-4   DISSOLUTION OF ALLIANCES

Alliances are often described as corporate marriages and, when terminated, as corporate divorces.[15] Exhibit 11.7 portrays an alliance dissolution model. To apply the metaphor of divorce, we focus on the two-partner alliance such as the Danone-Wahaha case (and ignore multipartner alliances such as One World). Following the convention in research on human divorce, the party who begins the process of ending the alliance is labeled the "initiator," while the other party is termed the "partner"—for lack of a better word.

The first phase is initiation. The process begins when the initiator starts feeling uncomfortable with the alliance (for whatever reason). Wavering begins as a quiet, unilateral process by the initiator, which was Danone in this case. After repeated demands to modify Wahaha's behavior failed, Danone began to sense that the alliance was probably unsalvageable. At this point, the display of discontent became bolder. Initially, Wahaha, the partner,

may simply not "get it." The initiator's "sudden" dissatisfaction may confuse the partner. As a result, initiation tends to escalate.

The second phase is going public. The party that breaks the news first has a first-mover advantage. By presenting a socially acceptable reason in favor of its cause, this party is able to win sympathy from key stakeholders, such as parent company executives, investors, and journalists. Not surprisingly, the initiator is likely to go public first. Alternatively, the partner may preempt by blaming the initiator and establishing the righteousness of its position—this was exactly what Wahaha did. Eventually, both Danone and Wahaha were eager to publicly air their grievances.

The third phase is uncoupling. Like human divorce, alliance dissolution can be friendly or hostile. In uncontested divorces, both sides attribute the separation more on, say, a change in circumstances. For example, Eli Lilly and Ranbaxy phased out their JV in India and remained friendly with each other. In contrast, contested divorces involve a party that accuses another. The worst scenario is "death by a thousand cuts" inflicted by one party at every turn. A case in point is the numerous lawsuits and arbitrations filed in many countries by Danone and Wahaha accusing each other of wrongdoing.

EXHIBIT 11.7 ALLIANCE DISSOLUTION

Source: M. W. Peng and O. Shenkar, "Joint venture dissolution as corporate divorce," *Academy of Management Executive* 16, no. 2 (2002): 95.

The last phase is aftermath. Like most divorced individuals, most (but not all) "divorced" firms are likely to search for new partners. Understandably, the new alliance is often negotiated more extensively. However, excessive formalization may signal a lack of trust—in the same way that pre-nuptials may scare away some prospective human marriage partners.

11-5 PERFORMANCE OF ALLIANCES

Although managers naturally focus on alliance performance, opinions vary on how to measure it. A combination of objective measures (such as profit and market share) and subjective measures (such as managerial satisfaction) can be used. Four factors may influence alliance performance: (1) equity, (2) learning and experience, (3) nationality, and (4) relational capabilities.

▶ The level of equity may be crucial in how an alliance performs. A greater equity stake may mean that a firm is more committed, which is likely to result in higher performance.

▶ Whether firms have successfully learned from partners is important when assessing alliance performance. Since learning is abstract, experience is often used as a proxy because it is relatively easy to measure. While experience certainly helps, its impact on performance is not linear. There is a limit beyond which further increase in experience may not enhance performance.

▶ Nationality may affect performance. For the same reason that marriages where both parties have similar backgrounds are more stable, dissimilarities in national culture may create strains in alliances. Not surprisingly, international alliances tend to have more problems than domestic ones.

▶ Alliance performance may fundamentally boil down to soft, hard-to-measure relational capabilities. The art of relational capabilities, which are firm specific and difficult to codify and transfer, may make or break alliances.

Overall, none of these four factors has an unambiguous, direct impact on performance. What has been found is that they may have some *correlations* with performance. It would be naïve to think that any of these four single factors would guarantee success. It is their *combination* that jointly increases the odds for the success of strategic alliances.

11-6 MOTIVES FOR ACQUISITIONS

What drives acquisitions? Exhibit 11.8 shows three potential motives for acquisition: (1) synergistic, (2) hubristic, and (3) managerial. All three can be explained by the institution-based and resource-based views. From an institution-based view, synergistic motives for acquisitions are often a response to formal institutional constraints and transitions that affect a company's search for synergy. It is not a coincidence that the number of cross-border acquisitions has skyrocketed in the last three decades. This is the same period during which trade and investment barriers have gone down and FDI has risen.

From a resource-based standpoint, the most important synergistic rationale is to leverage superior resources. Indian firms' cross-border acquisitions have primarily targeted high-tech and computer services in order to leverage their superior resources in these industries (see In Focus). Another motive is to access complementary resources, as evidenced by Fiat's interest in Chrysler's Jeep brand (see Closing Case).

While all the synergistic motives, in theory, add value, hubristic and managerial motives reduce value.

EXHIBIT 11.8 | MOTIVES FOR ACQUISITIONS

	Institution-Based Issues	Resource-Based Issues
Synergistic motives	▶ Respond to formal institutional constraints and transitions	▶ Leverage superior managerial capabilities ▶ Enhance market power and scale economies ▶ Access to complementary resources
Hubristic motives	▶ Herd behavior—following norms and chasing fads of M&As	▶ Managers' overconfidence in their capabilities
Managerial motives	▶ Self-interested actions such as empire building guided by informal norms and cognitions	

Hubris refers to overconfidence in one's capabilities. Managers of acquiring firms make two strong statements. The first is: "We can manage *your* assets better than you [target firm managers] can!" The second statement is even bolder. Given that purchasing a publicly listed firm requires paying an acquisition premium, managers of an acquiring firm essentially say, "We are smarter than the market!" Acquiring firm managers can quantitatively state exactly how much smarter they are relative to the market—as evidenced by the specific acquisition premium they are willing to pay. In other words, a 20% acquisition premium, by definition, is the acquiring firm's announcement: "We are 20% smarter than the market!"

To the extent that the capital market is efficient and that the market price of target firms reflects their intrinsic value, there is simply no hope to profit from such acquisitions. Even when we assume the capital market to be inefficient, it is still apparent that when the premium is too high, acquiring firms must have overpaid. This attitude is especially dangerous when multiple firms are bidding for the same target. The winning acquirer may suffer from what is called the "winner's curse" in auctions—the winner has overpaid. From an institution-based view, hubristic motives are at play when managers join the acquisition bandwagon. The fact that M&As come in waves speaks volumes about such herd behavior. After a few first-mover firms start making some deals in the industry, waves of late movers, eager to catch up, may rush in, prompted by a "Wow! Get it!" mentality. Not surprisingly, many of those deals turn out to be busts.

While the hubristic motives suggest that some managers may *unknowingly* overpay for targets, some managers may *knowingly* overpay for targets. Such self-interested actions are fueled by **managerial motives**, defined as managers' desire for power, prestige, and money, which may lead to decisions that do not benefit the firm overall in the long run. As a result, some managers may deliberately grow their firms through M&As for such personal gains. These are known as agency problems.

Overall, synergistic motives add value, and hubristic and managerial motives destroy value. They may *simultaneously* coexist. In Focus uses emerging multinationals as a new breed of cross-border acquirers to illustrate these dynamics. Next, we discuss the performance of M&As.

11-7 PERFORMANCE OF ACQUISITIONS

Why do as many as 70% of acquisitions reportedly fail?[16] Problems can be identified in both pre-acquisition and post-acquisition phases (Exhibit 11.9). During the pre-acquisition phase, because of executive hubris and/or managerial motives, acquiring firms may overpay targets—in other words, they fall into a "synergy trap." For example, in 1998, when Chrysler was profitable, Daimler-Benz paid $40 billion, a 40% premium over its market value, to acquire it. Given that Chrysler's expected performance was already built into its existing share price, at a *zero* premium, Daimler-Benz's willingness to pay for such a high premium was indicative of (1) strong managerial capabilities to derive synergy, (2) high levels of hubris, (3) significant managerial self-interests, or (4) *all of the above*. As it turned out, by the time Chrysler was sold in 2007, it only fetched $7.4 billion, destroying four-fifths of the value. In another case, in 2010, Microsoft paid $8.5 billion to buy Skype, which was 400 times greater than Skype's income. Although many readers of this book use Skype, Skype has remained an underachieving Internet icon—how many people have paid money to Skype each other? Not surprisingly, this acquisition, Microsoft's biggest, raised a lot of eyebrows.

Another primary pre-acquisition problem is inadequate screening and

hubris Exaggerated pride or overconfidence.

managerial motive Managers' desire for power, prestige, and money, which may lead to decisions that do not benefit the firm overall in the long run.

EXHIBIT 11.9　SYMPTOMS OF ACQUISITION FAILURES

	Problems for all M&As	Particular problems for cross-border M&As
Pre-acquisition: Overpayment for targets	▶ Managers over-estimate their ability to create value ▶ Inadequate pre-acquisition screening ▶ Poor strategic fit	▶ Lack of familiarity with foreign cultures, institutions, and business systems ▶ Nationalistic concerns against foreign takeovers (political and media levels)
Post-acquisition: Failure in integration	▶ Poor organizational fit ▶ Failure to address multiple stakeholder groups' concerns	▶ Clashes of organizational cultures compounded by clashes of national cultures ▶ Nationalistic concerns against foreign takeovers (firm and employee levels)

failure to achieve strategic fit. In September 2008, Bank of America, in a hurry to make a deal, spent only 48 hours before agreeing to acquire Merrill Lynch for $50 billion. Not surprisingly, failure to do adequate homework (technically, due diligence) led to numerous problems centered on the lack of strategic fit. Consequently, this acquisition was labeled by the *Wall Street Journal* as "a deal from hell."[17]

Acquiring international assets can be even more problematic, because institutional and cultural distances can be large and nationalistic concerns over foreign acquisitions may erupt (see In Focus). When Japanese firms acquired Rockefeller Center and movie studios in the 1980s and the 1990s, the US media reacted with indignation. In the 2000s, when DP World of the United Arab Emirates and CNOOC of China attempted to acquire US assets, they had to back off due to political backlash.

Numerous integration problems may surface during the post-acquisition phase (see Exhibit 11.10). Although "mergers of equals" sound nice, their integration tends to be awful (see Debate). Organizational fit is just as important as strategic fit. Many acquiring firms (such as Nomura) do *not* analyze organizational fit with targets (such as Lehman Brothers' assets in Asia and Europe). The result is a mess. Firms often fail to address the concerns of multiple stakeholders, including job losses and diminished power. Most firms focus on task issues such as standardizing reporting, and pay inadequate attention to people issues, which typically results in low morale and high turnover.

In cross-border M&As, integration difficulties may be much worse because clashes of organizational cultures are compounded by clashes of national cultures. Due to cultural differences, Chinese acquirers such as Geely often have a hard time integrating Western firms such as Volvo (see In Focus). But even when both sides are from the West, cultural conflicts may still erupt. When Four Seasons acquired a hotel in Paris, the simple American request that employees *smile* at customers was resisted by French employees and laughed at by the local media as "*la culture Mickey Mouse.*" After Alcatel acquired Lucent, the situation became "almost comically dysfunctional."[18] At an all-hands gathering at

EXHIBIT 11.10　A CHALLENGE IN POST-ACQUISITION INTEGRATION

"*As you know, some details of the new merger have yet to be resolved.*"

ROY DELAGADO/ARTIZANS.COM. REPRINTED BY PERMISSION.

Debate: Can Mergers of Equals Work?

Ethical Dilemma

Romanticized by the ideal of human marriages, mergers of equals between firms sound nice. But can they work? The answer is hardly. In 1998, Daimler and Chrysler announced their "merger of equals" (their own words). Very soon, it was clear who called the shots at DaimlerChrsyler AG. After two years, Chrysler's former boss Robert Eaton left. Jürgen Schrempp, Daimler's boss, shared with the media that the term "merger of equals" had been used only for "psychological reasons"—in other words, it was a lie. Not surprisingly, the two sides divorced each other later (in 2007).

In case you think the DaimlerChrysler tragedy was caused in part by the cross-cultural difficulties (which undoubtedly added to the challenges), mergers of equals between two firms from the same country may still be unworkable. In 1998, two US firms, Citibank and Travelers, merged with great fanfare to become Citigroup. Within two years, only one boss survived. Within five years, Citigroup had a divorce by spinning off Travelers, suggesting that the celebrated merger should not have taken place in the first place. In 2000, AOL Time Warner was born of a merger between "old economy" media firm Time Warner and "new economy" Internet firm American Online. The burst of the dot-com bubble in 2001 quickly revealed the shaky economics and the shaky power-sharing arrangements. In late 2001, Time Warner's former boss announced retirement. In 2009, AOL was spun off. The new boss of Time Warner called the merger "the biggest mistake in corporate history."

Why are mergers of equals so hard? Because both firms are not willing to let the other have an upper hand, and both bosses, whose egos are typically huge, are not willing to let the other be in charge. It is possible at least one of the two bosses is opportunistic in the beginning and determined to drive away another—as evidenced in the case of Schrempp at Daimler. But even in the absence of opportunism, when both bosses believe they can share power, a merger of equals can "effectively translate into rudderless behemoth," according to one expert. *Economist* put it more bluntly: "Forget the romance of power sharing. When it comes to the tricky business of making a merger work, someone must be in charge."

Sources: A. Cowen, "An expanded model of status dynamics," *Academy of Management Journal* 55 (2012): 1169–1186; "Riding the wave," *Economist*, 5 November 2013: 71; "Shall we?" *Economist*, 9 February 2013: 65; "Love on the rocks," *Economist*, 17 May 2014: 65; "Return of the big deal," *Economist*, 3 May 2014: 55–57; "The new rules of attraction," *Economist*, 15 November 2014: 66–67; J. Krug, P. Wright, and M. Kroll, "Top management turnover following mergers and acquisitions," *Academy of Management Perspectives* 28 (2014): 147–163.

---

an Alcatel-Lucent European facility, employees threw fruits and vegetables at executives announcing another round of restructuring.

Although acquisitions are often the largest capital expenditures most firms ever make, they frequently are the worst planned and executed activities of all. Unfortunately, while merging firms are sorting out the mess, rivals are likely to launch aggressive attacks. When Daimler-Benz struggled first with the chaos associated with its marriage with Chrysler and then was engulfed in its divorce with Chrsyler, BMW rocketed ahead of Mercedes-Benz to become the world's number-one luxury carmaker. Adding all of the above together, it is hardly surprising that most M&As fail.

 MANAGEMENT SAVVY

What determines the success and failure in alliances and acquisitions? Our two core perspectives shed light on this big question. The institution-based view argues that alliances and acquisitions depend on a thorough understanding and skillful manipulation of the rules of the game. The resource-based view calls for the development of firm-specific capabilities to make a difference in enhancing alliance and acquisition performance. As two alternatives, neither alliances nor acquisitions should be preordained, and careful analysis of the pros and cons of each should be undertaken before going forward with either one.

Consequently, three clear implications for action emerge (see Exhibit 11.11). First, managers need to understand and master the rules of the game—both formal and informal—governing alliances and acquisitions around the world. When negotiating its acquisition of IBM's PC assets, Lenovo clearly understood and tapped into the Chinese government's support for home-grown multinationals. IBM likewise understood the necessity for the new Lenovo to maintain an American image when it persuaded Lenovo to set up a second headquarters in the United States. This highly symbolic action made it easier to win approval from the US government. In contrast, GE and Honeywell proposed to merge and cleared US antitrust scrutiny, but failed to anticipate the EU antitrust authorities' incentive to kill the deal. In the end, the EU torpedoed the deal. The upshot is that, in addition to the economics of alliances and acquisitions, managers need to pay attention to the politics behind such high-stakes strategic moves.

Second, when managing alliances, managers need to pay attention to the soft relational capabilities that often make or break relationships. To the extent that business schools usually provide a good training on hard number-crunching skills, it is time for all of us to beef up on soft but equally important (perhaps even more important) relational capabilities.

Finally, when managing acquisitions, managers are advised not to overpay for targets and to focus on both strategic and organizational fit. Refusing to let the bidding war go out of hand and admitting failure in proposed deals by walking away are painful but courageous. Around the world between 10% and 20% of the proposed deals collapse.[19] Despite the media hoopla about the "power" of emerging multinationals from China, in reality more than half of their announced deals end in tears. Indian multinationals do better, but still one-third of their deals cannot close (see In Focus). This is not a problem that only affects emerging acquirers. Experienced acquirers such as AT&T, News Corporation, and Pfizer recently withdrew from their multibillion dollar deals to acquire, respectively, T-Mobile, Time Warner, and AstraZeneca. Given that 70% of acquisitions fail and that integration challenges loom large down the road even if deals close, acquisitions that fail to close may sometimes be a blessing in disguise.

EXHIBIT 11.11	IMPLICATIONS FOR ACTION

▶ Understand and master the rules of the game governing alliances and acquisitions around the world.

▶ When managing alliances, pay attention to the soft relationship aspects.

▶ When managing acquisitions, do not overpay, focus on both strategic and organizational fit, and thoroughly address integration concerns.

EMERGING MARKETS/ETHICAL DILEMMA

Closing Case: Fiat Chrysler: From Alliance to Acquisition

The year 2009 was one of the most tragic and unforgettable years in the history of the US automobile industry: two of the Big Three automakers, GM and Chrysler, went bankrupt in April. However, there was one glimmer of hope: Fiat was the "white knight" who came to Chrysler's rescue. Chrysler had recently gone through a traumatic divorce with Daimler in 2007. By 2009, nobody wanted Chrysler, which was pulled down by deteriorating products, hopeless finances, and the Great Recession. Its desperate call asking GM, Honda, Nissan-Renault, Toyota, and Volkswagen to help went nowhere. Only Fiat answered the call with $5 billion. As the "new Chrysler"—Chrysler Group LLC, which is different from the pre-bankrutpcy "old Chrysler," formerly called Chrysler LLC—emerged out of bankruptcy in June 2009, the US government (which spent $8 billion to bail out Chrysler) had 10% of equity. The Canadian government had 2%. The United Auto Workers (union) had 68%. Although Fiat only had 20%, clearly, as the senior partner in this new alliance, it was calling all the shots.

While Chrysler got itself another European partner, Fiat itself was a weak automaker. Would the relationship work? The DaimlerChrysler marriage consisted of a luxury automaker and a working-class truck and SUV maker, which had a hard time working together. The Fiat-Chrysler alliance at least consisted of two similar mass-market operations. Both offered each other a set of complementary skills and capabilities. In addition to cash, Chrysler needed attractive small cars. Fiat supplied Chrysler with its award-winning Alfa Romeo Giulietta small car and its excellent small-engine technology that would comply with the increasingly strict fuel-economy standards in the United States. In 2013, while

Chrysler's US factories were running at nearly full capacity, only 40% of the capacity of Fiat's Italian factories was being utilized. Thanks to Italian politics, Fiat could not close any major factories. Therefore, Fiat needed novel models from Chrysler to make them in Italy. Fiat recently assigned Chrysler's brand-new Jeep Renegade SUV to be built in Italy. In third-country markets, although each of these relatively smaller players was weak, their odds would be better by working together. In Brazil, which is Fiat's number-one market (where Fiat sold more cars than in Italy), Fiat faced major challenges from GM and Renault. Assistance from Chrysler in the form of newer models and technologies would certainly be valuable. In Asia (especially China), neither of them was very strong, although Chrysler's Jeep models did better. Combining forces allowed them to scale new heights in the tough but important Asian markets.

After several years of experimentation, both sides seemed satisfied with the alliance. Sergio Marchionne, who served as chairman and CEO for both Fiat and Chrysler, was instrumental in making sure both sides worked together. Many American managers at Chrysler used to resent European dominance, thanks to their bad experience with Daimler. This time, as Chrysler owed its existence to Marchionne, its managers tended to give him the benefit of the doubt as he turned Chrysler around. Instead of the more centralized German style, Marchionne practiced a more decentralized management style. He also hired third-country (non-US and non-Italian) executives to help reduce the binational cultural barriers. By 2011, Chrysler repaid $7.6 billion loans to the US and Canadian governments and bought out the shares both governments held. Overall, Fiat gradually increased its Chrysler shares, reaching 59% by 2013. In 2014, Fiat acquired the remaining shares and owned 100% of Chrysler.

Set up in 2014, the combined entity is called Fiat Chrysler Automobiles (FCA), which interestingly is headquartered neither in Turin, Italy (Fiat's home), nor Auburn Hills, Michigan

ERMESS/SHUTTERSTOCK.COM

(a Detroit suburb—Chrysler's base). Instead, it is registered in the Netherlands, which has emerged as "Europe's Delaware." (Many famous firms that you normally would not think of as "Dutch," such as Airbus Group and IKEA, are in fact registered there.) But FCA's CEO and the top management team are based in London—its operational headquarters. Cross-listed in both Borasa Italiana (BIT: FCA) and New York Stock Exchange (NYSE: FCAU), FCA is the world's seventh largest automaker. With combined annual output of 4.6 million cars, FCA is behind Toyota, GM, Volkswagen, Hyundai, Ford, and Nissan-Renault, but ahead of Honda and Peugeot. This is not bad for the 11th-ranked Chrysler (2.4 million vehicles per year prior to the full merger) and the 13th-ranked Fiat (2.1 million vehicles). FCA has a broad portfolio of brands, such as Alfa Romeo, Chrysler, Dodge, Ferrari, Fiat, Jeep, Maserati, and Ram Trucks. Whether tighter integration would enable FCA to challenge the global heavyweights remains to be seen.

Case Discussion Questions

1. From a resource-based view, what does Fiat have in turning around a struggling Chrysler that Daimler did not seem to have?

2. Prior to their merger in 1998, Daimler and Chrysler had not collaborated in any alliance relationship. This probably contributed to the eventual failure of DaimlerChrsyler. After Fiat made a strategic investment in Chrysler in 2009, both of them collaborated in an alliance, which eventually resulted in a merger. Does Fiat Chrysler have better odds for success than DaimlerChrysler?

3. What are some of the do's and don'ts that can be learned from this case?

Sources: "This 'baby Jeep' has an Italian accent," *Bloomberg Businessweek*, 7 March 2014: 23–24; "Hoping it will hold together," *Economist*, 24 August 2013: 57; "Here, there, and everywhere," *Economist*, 22 February 2014: 56–57; "Fiat Chrysler teams up with Amazon to sell cars online," Reuters, 18 November 2016: www.reuters.com; www.fcagroup.com.

12 Strategizing, Structuring, & Learning around the World

LEARNING OBJECTIVES

After studying this chapter, you will be able to . . .

12-1 Describe the relationship between multinational strategy and structure.

12-2 Explain how institutions and resources affect multinational strategy, structure, and learning.

12-3 Outline the challenges associated with learning, innovation, and knowledge management.

12-4 List three things you can do to make a multinational firm successful.

After you finish this chapter, go to

PAGE 200 for

STUDY TOOLS

EMERGING MARKETS
Opening Case: Launching the McWrap

It is hard to believe, but McDonald's is no longer the world's largest fast food chain—at least measured by the number of restaurants. Subway has rocketed ahead, with close to 44,000 restaurants worldwide versus McDonald's 36,000. Although McDonald's still sells more than Subway ($25 billion versus $18 billion in 2015), McDonald's seems to have lost momentum, with US sales slowing down noticeably. McDonald's, of course, not only competes with Subway, but also with the likes of Five Guys and Chipotle. In all three competitors, customers can see their food being prepared and feel that it is fresher and seemingly healthier. In the Fresh Wars, Subway has elevated its food preparers to become "sandwich artists." Chipotle has bragged about its "food with integrity," and released a short film critical of industrial farming—with a finger pointing at you know what.

In response, McDonald's has unleashed the McWrap, a high-profile salvo in the Fresh Wars in an effort to grab customer attention. At $3.99 in the United States, the McWrap is a ten-inch, white-flour tortilla wrapped around three ounces of chicken (grilled or crispy), lettuce, spring greens, sliced cucumbers, tomatoes, and cheddar jack cheese. Customers can choose their preferred dressing: ranch, sweet chili, or creamy garlic. Only made to order (not pre-made), the McWrap can be prepared under 60 seconds. When served, it comes with a cool cardboard wrapper whose top can be zipped open. The whole thing can fit vertically in a cup holder in a car. The two-year, nine-ingredient, focus-grouped efforts to fix McDonald's freshness problem are an amazing case study of how a multinational changes its strategy, taps into its global organization, and leverages its knowledge—all under the pressures of cost reduction and local responsiveness. Dissecting what is behind the launch of McWrap, we can see at least three things.

First, the idea did not come from the United States. It came from three operations in Europe. In 2004, McDonald's in the Czech Republic started selling the Chicken Roll Up. In 2005, McDonald's in Poland introduced a tortilla sandwich, inspired by the kebab, a popular street food. In 2009, Austria pioneered the nifty cardboard container that can be unzipped. Thanks to a European food studio (which would be called an R&D lab in many other firms), these local innovations were noticed and diffused to the rest of the McDonald's worldwide organization.

Second, the attention that the McWrap idea attracted from the headquarters was driven by a strategic interest in search of fresher and healthier items to outcompete rivals in the Fresh Wars. Specifically, it was the search for local responsiveness—in this case, primarily in McDonald's home country—that identified the wrap to be a potential good fit. Americans are eating more chicken and prefer more fresh food, and the wrap might enable McDonald's to respond to such changing tastes.

Third, significant experimentation, learning, and innovation went into the process. While the idea seemed appealing, McDonald's did not operate on gut feelings. Led by Dan Courfreaut, executive chef and vice president of culinary innovation (whose nick name is Chef Dan), McDonald's menu innovation team undertook intense research and numerous experiments that ultimately took two years (2011–2013) to finish. To introduce new items to a restaurant chain as large as McDonald's was mind-boggling. The food had to be tasty, the cost low, and the time to serve short—without compromising quality. "My job," according to Chef Dan, "is pushing ourselves without breaking the system." To enhance freshness, two slices of English cucumber were added for the first time to McDonald's offerings. Although adding a tiny bit of cucumber did not sound like a big deal, it actually was quite a challenge to McDonald's supply chain structure. About a decade ago, McDonald's introduced sliced apples to its menu, and it quickly became one of the largest buyers of apples in the United States. Initially, a half-breast of chicken was used for the wrap. But focus groups thought the wrap was a salad—with too much vegetable. Despite rising health awareness, customers actually wanted more meat—as long as it was chicken. So the final version of the wrap had a full breast of chicken. The wrap's name also went through intense testing. In the first trial in Chicago, it was called the Grande Wrap. But customers could not figure out what "grande" was. Then the name Fresh Garden Wrap was tested in Orlando, and it flopped too. Eventually, McWrap was chosen.

In a leaked, internal memo obtained by the media, McDonald's admitted that it was not even in the top ten of the Millennial Generation's list of favorite restaurant chains. Calling the McWrap a "Subway buster," the memo suggested that "McWrap offers us the perfect food offering to address the needs of this very important customer to McDonald's." When asked to elaborate, a McDonald's spokesperson noted: "We don't think we have a problem with Millennials, but we want to remain relevant to all of our customers." Whether McWrap will prove to be relevant to customers remains to be seen—or tasted.

Sources: Author's interviews; "McFresh," *Bloomberg Businessweek*, 8 July 2013: 44–49; "Have we reached peak burger?" *Bloomberg Businessweek*, 8 September 2014: 21–22; "8 reasons McDonald's is praying the McWrap is a smash hit," *Wall Street Cheat Sheet*, 10 July 2013: wallstcheatsheet.com; www.mcdonalds.com; www.subway.com.

How can multinational enterprises (MNEs) such as McDonald's strategically manage growth around the world so that they can be successful both locally and internationally? How can they learn country tastes and global trends? How can they improve the odds for better innovation? These are some of the key questions we address in this chapter, which focuses on relatively large MNEs. We start by discussing the crucial relationship between four strategies and four structures. Next, we consider how the institution-based and resource-based views shed light on these issues. Then, we discuss worldwide learning, innovation, and knowledge management and look at a debate over whether control should be centralized or decentralized. Managerial implications follow.

EXHIBIT 12.1 MULTINATIONAL STRATEGIES AND STRUCTURES: THE INTEGRATION-RESPONSIVENESS FRAMEWORK

Note: In some textbooks, "home replication" may be referred to as "international" or "export" strategy, "localization" as "multidomestic" strategy, and "global standardization" as "global" strategy. Some of these labels are confusing because one can argue that all four strategies here are "international" or "global," thus resulting in some confusion if we label one of these strategies as "international" and another as "global." The present set of labels is more descriptive and less confusing.

12-1 MULTINATIONAL STRATEGIES AND STRUCTURES

This section first introduces an integration-responsiveness framework centered on the pressures for cost reduction and local responsiveness. We then outline the four strategic choices and the four corresponding organizational structures that MNEs typically adopt.

12-1a Pressures for Cost Reduction and Local Responsiveness

MNEs confront primarily two sets of pressures: cost reduction and local responsiveness. These two sets of pressures are dealt with in the **integration-responsiveness framework**, which allows managers to deal with the pressures for both global integration and local responsiveness. Cost pressures often call for global integration while local responsiveness pushes MNEs to adapt locally. In both domestic and international competition, pressures to reduce costs are almost universal. What is unique in international competition is the pressures for **local responsiveness**, which means reacting to different consumer preferences and host-country demands. Consumer preferences vary tremendously around the world. For example, McDonald's beef-based hamburgers would obviously find few customers in India, a land where cows are held sacred by the Hindu majority. Thus, changing McDonald's menu is a must in India. Host-country demands and expectations add to the pressures for local responsiveness. Throughout Europe, Bombardier manufactures an Austrian version of rail-cars in Austria, a Belgian version in Belgium, and so on. Bombardier believes that such local responsiveness, although not required, is essential for making sales to railway operators in Europe, which tend to be state owned.

Taken together, being locally responsive certainly makes local customers and governments happy, but unfortunately increases costs. Given the universal interest in lowering cost, a natural tendency is to downplay or ignore the different needs and wants of various local markets and instead market a global version of products and services. The movement to globalize offerings can be traced to a 1983 article by Theodore Levitt: "The Globalization of Markets."[1] Levitt argued that worldwide consumer tastes are converging. As evidence, Levitt pointed to the worldwide success of Coke Classic, Levi Strauss jeans, and Sony color TV. Levitt predicted that such convergence would characterize most product markets in the future.

Levitt's idea has often been the intellectual force propelling many MNEs to globally integrate their products

integration-responsiveness framework An MNE management framework for simultaneously dealing with the pressures for both global integration and local responsiveness.

local responsiveness The need to be responsive to different customer preferences around the world.

while minimizing local adaptation. Ford experimented with "world car" designs. MTV pushed ahead with the belief that viewers would flock to global (essentially American) programming. Unfortunately, most of these experiments are not successful. Ford found that consumer tastes ranged widely around the globe. MTV eventually realized that there is no "global song." In a nutshell, one size does not fit all. This leads us to look at how MNEs can pay attention to *both* dimensions: cost reduction and local responsiveness.

12-1b Four Strategic Choices

Based on the integration-responsiveness framework, Exhibit 12.1 plots the four strategic choices: (1) home replication, (2) localization, (3) global standardization, and (4) transnational. Each strategy has a set of pros and cons outlined in Exhibit 12.2. (Their corresponding structures in Exhibit 12.1 are discussed in the next section.)

Home replication strategy, often known as international (or export) strategy, duplicates home-country-based competencies in foreign countries. Such competencies include production scales, distribution efficiencies, and brand power. In manufacturing, this is usually manifested in an export strategy. In services, this is often done through licensing and franchising. This strategy is relatively easy to implement and usually the first one adopted when firms venture abroad.

On the disadvantage side, home replication strategy often lacks local responsiveness because it focuses on the home country. This strategy makes sense when the majority of a firm's customers are domestic. However, when a firm aspires to broaden its international scope, failing to be mindful of foreign customers' needs and wants may alienate those potential customers. When Walmart entered Brazil, the stores had exactly the same inventory as its US stores, including a large number of *American* footballs. Considering that Brazil is the land of soccer that has won soccer's World Cup five times, more wins than any other country, nobody (except a few homesick American expatriates in their spare time) plays *American* football there.

Localization strategy is an extension of the home replication strategy. **Localization (multidomestic) strategy** focuses on a number of foreign countries/regions, each of which is regarded as a stand-alone local (domestic) market worthy of significant attention and adaptation. While sacrificing global efficiencies, this strategy is effective when differences among national and regional markets are clear and pressures for cost reductions are low. For example, Disney has attempted to localize some of its offerings in its five theme parks in Anaheim, California; Orlando, Florida; Hong Kong; Paris; and Tokyo. Its newest theme park in Shanghai has dropped a standard feature common in Disney parks, Main Street USA, and replaced it with Mickey Avenue—a unique first-time creation for all Disney parks. In fact, 80% of the Shanghai rides are unique.[2]

In terms of disadvantages, the localization strategy has high costs due to duplication of efforts in multiple countries. The costs of producing a variety of programming for MTV are obviously greater than the costs of producing one set of programming. As a result, this strategy is only appropriate in industries where the pressures for cost reductions are not significant. Another potential drawback is too

Photo credit: MATTHIAS G. ZIEGLER/SHUTTERSTOCK.COM

EXHIBIT 12.2 FOUR STRATEGIC CHOICES FOR MULTINATIONAL ENTERPRISES

	Advantages	Disadvantages
Home replication	▸ Leverages home country-based advantages ▸ Relatively easy to implement	▸ Lack of local responsiveness ▸ May alienate foreign customers
Localization	▸ Maximizes local responsiveness	▸ High costs due to duplication of efforts in multiple countries ▸ Too much local autonomy
Global standardization	▸ Leverages low-cost advantages	▸ Lack of local responsiveness ▸ Too much centralized control
Transnational	▸ Cost-efficient while being locally responsive ▸ Engages in global learning and diffusion of innovations	▸ Organizationally complex ▸ Difficult to implement

home replication strategy A strategy that emphasizes duplicating home-country-based competencies in foreign countries.

localization (multidomestic) strategy A strategy that focuses on a number of foreign countries/regions, each of which is regarded as a stand-alone local (domestic) market worthy of significant attention and adaptation.

A potential drawback of localization is too much local autonomy. For example, it took Unilever four years to persuade its 17 European subsidiaries to introduce a single new detergent across the continent.

much local autonomy, which happens when each subsidiary regards its country as so unique that it is difficult to introduce corporate-wide changes. For example, in the 1980s Unilever had 17 country subsidiaries in Europe and it took four years to persuade all 17 subsidiaries to introduce a single new detergent across Europe.

As the opposite of the localization strategy, **global standardization strategy** is sometimes referred to simply as global strategy. Its hallmark is the development and distribution of standardized products worldwide in order to reap the maximum benefits from low cost advantages. While both the home replication and global standardization strategies minimize local responsiveness, a crucial difference is that an MNE pursuing a global standardization strategy is not limited to its major operations at home. In a number of countries, the MNE may designate **centers of excellence**, defined as subsidiaries explicitly recognized as a source of important capabilities, with the intention that these capabilities be leveraged by and/or disseminated to other subsidiaries. Centers of excellence are often given

a **worldwide (or global) mandate**—namely, a charter to be responsible for one MNE function throughout the world. For example, Huawei's Sweden subsidiary has a worldwide mandate in network consulting.

In terms of disadvantages, a global standardization strategy obviously sacrifices local responsiveness. This strategy makes great sense in industries where pressures for cost reductions are paramount and pressures for local responsiveness are relatively minor (particularly commodity industries such as semiconductors and tires). However, as noted earlier, in industries ranging from automobiles to consumer products, a one-size-fits-all strategy may be inappropriate. Consequently, arguments such as "all industries are becoming global" and "all firms need to pursue a global (standardization) strategy" are potentially misleading.

Transnational strategy aims to capture the best of both worlds by endeavoring to be both cost efficient and locally responsive.[3] In addition to cost efficiency and local responsiveness, a third hallmark of this strategy is global learning and diffusion of innovations. Traditionally, the diffusion of innovations in MNEs is a one-way flow from the home country to various host countries— the label "home replication" says it all (!). Underpinning the traditional one-way flow is the assumption that the home country is the best location for generating innovations. However, given that innovations are inherently risky and uncertain, there is no guarantee that the home country will generate the highest-quality innovations (see Opening Case).

MNEs that engage in a transnational strategy promote global learning and diffusion of innovations in multiple ways. Innovations not only flow from the home country to host countries (which is the traditional flow), but also flow from host countries to the home country and flow among subsidiaries in multiple host countries (see Opening Case). Kia Motors, for example, not only operates a design center in Seoul, but also has two other design centers in Los Angeles and Frankfurt, tapping into innovations generated in North America and Europe.

On the disadvantage side, a transnational strategy is organizationally complex and difficult to implement. The large amount of knowledge sharing and coordination may slow down decision making. Trying to achieve cost efficiencies, local responsiveness, and global learning simultaneously places contradictory demands on MNEs (to be discussed in the next section).

Overall, it is important to note that given the various pros and cons, there is no optimal strategy. The new trend in favor of a transnational strategy needs to be qualified with an understanding of its significant organizational challenges. This point leads to our next topic.

global standardization strategy A strategy that relies on the development and distribution of standardized products worldwide to reap the maximum benefits from low-cost advantages.

center of excellence An MNE subsidiary explicitly recognized as a source of important capabilities that can be leveraged by and/or disseminated to other subsidiaries.

worldwide (global) mandate A charter to be responsible for one MNE function throughout the world.

transnational strategy A strategy that endeavors to be simultaneously cost efficient, locally responsive, and learning driven around the world.

EXHIBIT 12.3 INTERNATIONAL DIVISION STRUCTURE AT STARBUCKS

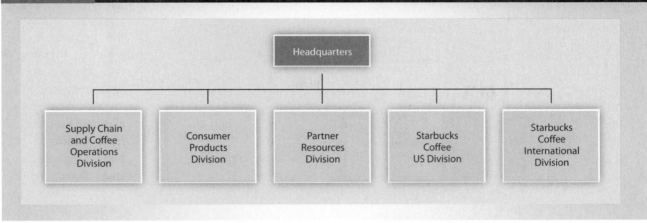

Sources: Adapted from www.cogmap.com; www.starbucks.com. Headquartered in Seattle, Starbucks is a leading international coffee and coffeehouse company.

EXHIBIT 12.4 GEOGRAPHIC AREA STRUCTURE AT AVON PRODUCTS

Source: Adapted from www.avoncompany.com. Headquartered in New York, Avon is a leading global beauty products company.

12-1c Four Organizational Structures

Exhibit 12.1 also shows four organizational structures that are appropriate for each of the strategic choices: (1) international division, (2) geographic area, (3) global product division, and (4) global matrix.

International division is typically used when firms initially expand abroad, often engaging in a home replication strategy. Exhibit 12.3 shows that Starbucks has an international division, in addition to the four divisions that primarily focus on the United States. Although this structure is intuitively appealing, it often leads to two problems. First, foreign subsidiary managers, whose input is channeled through the international division, are not given sufficient voice relative to the heads of domestic divisions. Second, by design, the international division serves as a silo whose activities are not coordinated with the rest of the firm, which is focusing on domestic activities. Consequently, many firms phase out this structure after their initial stage of overseas expansion.

Geographic area structure organizes the MNE according to different geographic areas (countries and regions). It is the most appropriate structure for a localization strategy. Exhibit 12.4 illustrates such a structure for Avon Products. A geographic area can be a country or a region, led by a **country (regional) manager**. Each area is largely stand-alone. In contrast to the limited voice of subsidiary managers in the international division structure, country (and regional) managers carry a great deal of weight in a geographic area structure. Interestingly and paradoxically, *both* the strengths and weaknesses of this structure lie in its local responsiveness. While being locally responsive can be a

international division An organizational structure that is typically set up when a firm initially expands abroad, often engaging in a home replication strategy.

geographic area structure An organizational structure that organizes the MNE according to different countries and regions.

country (regional) manager The business leader of a specific country (or a geographic region).

EXHIBIT 12.5　GLOBAL PRODUCT DIVISION STRUCTURE AT AIRBUS GROUP

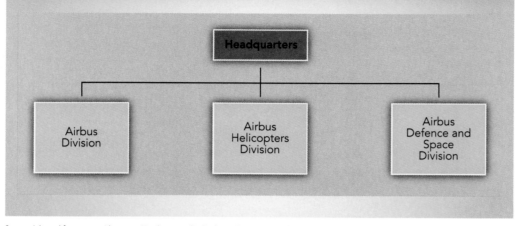

Source: Adapted from www.airbus.com. Headquartered in Toulouse, France, Airbus Group is the largest commercial aircraft maker and the largest defense contractor in Europe. Between 2000 and 2014, it was known as European Aeronautic Defense and Space Company (EADS).

virtue, it also encourages the fragmentation of the MNE into fiefdoms.

Global product division structure, which is the opposite of the geographic area structure, supports the global standardization strategy by assigning global responsibilities to each product division. Exhibit 12.5 shows such an example from Airbus Group. This structure treats each product division as a stand-alone entity with full worldwide responsibilities. This structure is highly responsive to pressures for cost efficiencies, because it allows for consolidation on a worldwide (or at least regional) basis and reduces inefficient duplication in multiple countries. For example, Unilever reduced the number of soap-producing factories in Europe from ten to two after adopting this structure. Recently, because of the popularity of the global standardization strategy (noted earlier), the global product division structure is on the rise. The structure's main drawback is that local

responsiveness suffers, as Ford discovered when it phased out the geographic area structure in favor of the global product division structure.

A **global matrix** alleviates the disadvantages associated with both geographic area and global product division structures, especially for MNEs adopting a transnational strategy. Shown in Exhibit 12.6, its hallmark is the coordination of responsibilities between product divisions and geographic areas in order to be both cost efficient and locally responsive. In this hypothetical example, the country manager in charge of Japan—in short, the Japan manager—reports to Product Division 1 and Asia Division, both of which have equal power.

In theory this structure supports the goals of the transnational strategy, but in practice it is often difficult to deliver. The reason is simple: While managers (such as the Japan manager in Exhibit 12.6) usually find dealing with one boss headache enough, they do not appreciate having two bosses who are often in conflict. For example, Product Division 1 may decide that Japan is too tough a nut to crack and that there are more promising markets

global product division structure An organizational structure that assigns global responsibilities to each product division.

global matrix An organizational structure often used to alleviate the disadvantages associated with both geographic area and global product division structures, particularly when adopting a transnational strategy.

EXHIBIT 12.6　A HYPOTHETICAL GLOBAL MATRIX STRUCTURE

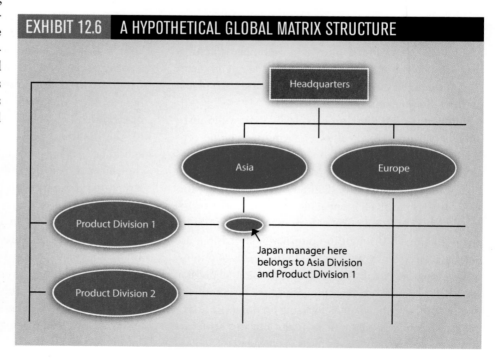

elsewhere, thus ordering the Japan manager to *curtail* his investment and channel resources elsewhere. This makes sense because Product Division 1 cares about its global market position and is not wedded to any particular country. However, Asia Division, which is evaluated by how well it does in Asia, may beg to differ. Asia Division argues that it cannot afford to be a laggard in Japan if it expects to be a leading player in Asia. Therefore, Asia Division demands that the Japan manager *increase* his investment in the country. Facing these conflicting demands, the Japan manager, who prefers to be politically correct, does not want to make any move before consulting corporate headquarters. Eventually, headquarters may provide a resolution. But crucial time may be lost in the process, and important windows of opportunity for competitive actions may be missed.

Despite its merits on paper, the matrix structure may add layers of management, slow down decision speed, and increase costs while not showing significant performance improvement. There is no conclusive evidence for the superiority of the matrix structure. The following quote from the CEO of Dow Chemical, an early adopter of the matrix structure, is sobering:

> *We were an organization that was matrixed and depended on teamwork, but there was no one in charge. When things went well, we didn't know whom to reward; and when things went poorly, we didn't know whom to blame. So we created a global product division structure, and cut out layers of management. There used to be 11 layers of management between me and the lowest level employees, now there are five.*[4]

Overall, the positioning of the four structures in Exhibit 12.1 is not random. They develop from the relatively simple international division through either geographic area or global product division structures and may eventually reach the more complex global matrix stage. It is important to note that not every MNE experiences all of these structural stages, and that the movement is not necessarily in one direction. For example, the matrix structure's poster child, the Swedish-Swiss conglomerate ABB, recently withdrew from this structure.

12-1d The Reciprocal Relationship between Multinational Strategy and Structure

In one word, the relationship between strategy and structure is *reciprocal*. Three key ideas stand out.

▶ Strategy usually drives structure. The fit between strategy and structure, as exemplified by the *pairs* in each of the four cells in Exhibit 12.1, is crucial. A misfit, such as combining a global standardization strategy with a geographic area structure, may have grave performance consequences.

▶ The relationship is not one way. As much as strategy drives structure, structure also drives strategy. The withdrawal from the unworkable matrix structure at MNEs such as ABB has called into question the wisdom of the transnational strategy.

▶ Neither strategy nor structure is static. It is often necessary to change strategy, structure, or both. In an effort to move toward a global standardization strategy, many MNEs have adopted a global product division structure while de-emphasizing the role of country headquarters. However, unique challenges in certain countries, especially China, have now pushed some MNEs to revive the country headquarters to more effectively coordinate numerous activities within a large, complex, and important host country.[5] Panasonic, for example, set up Panasonic Corporation of China to manage its over 40 operations in China.[6] A further experimentation is to have an emerging economies division, which is not dedicated to any single country but dedicated to pursuing opportunities in a series of emerging economies ranging from Brazil to Saudi Arabia. Cisco pioneered this structure, which has been followed by rivals such as IBM.

RELATIONSHIPS ARE TWO-WAY STREETS

MASTER3D/SHUTTERSTOCK.COM

12-2 HOW INSTITUTIONS AND RESOURCES AFFECT MULTINATIONAL STRATEGY, STRUCTURE, AND LEARNING

Having outlined the basic strategy/structure configurations, let us now introduce how the institution-based and resource-based views shed light on these issues. This is mapped out in Exhibit 12.7.

12-2a Institution-Based Considerations

MNEs face two sets of rules of the game: formal and informal institutions governing (1) *external* relationships and (2) *internal* relationships. Each is discussed in turn.

Externally, MNEs are subject to the formal institutional frameworks erected by various home-country and host-country governments (see Closing Case). For example, in order to protect domestic employment, the British government taxes the foreign earnings of British MNEs at a higher rate than their domestic earnings.

Host-country governments, on the other hand, often attract, encourage, or coerce MNEs into undertaking activities that they otherwise would not. For example, basic manufacturing generates low-paying jobs, does not provide sufficient technology spillovers, and carries little prestige. Advanced manufacturing, R&D, and regional headquarters, on the other hand, generate better and higher-paying jobs, provide more technology spillovers, and lead to better prestige. Therefore, host-country governments (such as those in China, Hungary, and Singapore) often use a combination of carrots (such as tax incentives and free infrastructure upgrades) and sticks (such as threats to block market access) to attract MNE investments in higher value-added areas.

In addition to formal institutions, MNEs also confront a series of informal institutions governing their relationships with *home* countries. In the United States, few laws ban MNEs from aggressively setting up overseas subsidiaries, although the issue is a hot button in public debate and is always subject to changes in political policy. Therefore, managers contemplating such moves must consider the informal but vocal backlash against such activities due to the associated losses in domestic jobs.

Dealing with *host* countries also involves numerous informal institutions. For example, Airbus spends 40% of its procurement budget with US suppliers in 40 states. While there is no formal requirement for Airbus to farm out supply contracts, its sourcing is guided by the informal norm of reciprocity: If one country's suppliers are involved with Airbus, airlines based in that country are more likely to buy Airbus aircraft.

Institutional factors affecting MNEs are not only external. How MNEs are governed *internally* is also determined by various formal and informal rules of the game. Formally, organizational charts, such as those in Exhibits 12.3 to 12.6, specify the scope of responsibilities for various parties. Most MNEs have systems of evaluation, reward, and punishment in place based on these formal rules.

What the formal organizational charts do not reveal are the informal rules of the game, such as organizational norms, values, and networks. The nationality of the head of foreign subsidiaries is an example. Given the lack of formal regulations, MNEs essentially have three choices:

▸ A home-country national as the head of a subsidiary (such as an American for a subsidiary of a US-headquartered MNE in India).

▸ A host-country national (such as an Indian for the same subsidiary).

▸ A third-country national (such as an Australian for the same subsidiary above).

MNEs from different countries have different norms when making these appointments. Most Japanese MNEs follow an informal rule: Heads of foreign subsidiaries, at least initially, need to be Japanese nationals. In comparison, European MNEs are more likely to appoint host-country and third-country nationals to lead subsidiaries. As a group, US MNEs are somewhere between Japanese and European practices. These staffing approaches may reflect strategic differences. Home-country nationals, especially long-time employees of the same MNE

ISTOCK.COM/TERRY HANKINS

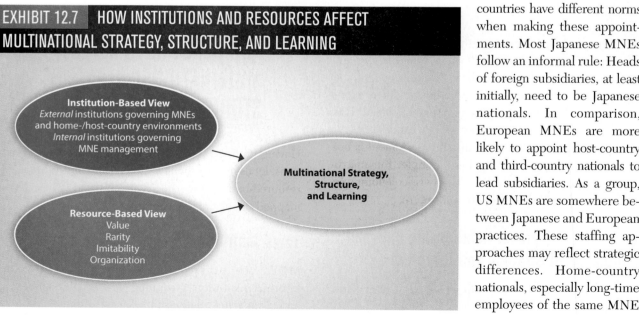

EXHIBIT 12.7 **HOW INSTITUTIONS AND RESOURCES AFFECT MULTINATIONAL STRATEGY, STRUCTURE, AND LEARNING**

Institution-Based View
External institutions governing MNEs and home-/host-country environments
Internal institutions governing MNE management

Resource-Based View
Value
Rarity
Imitability
Organization

Multinational Strategy, Structure, and Learning

at home, are more likely to have developed a better understanding of the informal workings of the firm and to be better socialized into its dominant norms and values. Consequently, the Japanese propensity to appoint home-country nationals is conducive to their preferred global standardization strategy, which values globally coordinated and controlled actions. Conversely, the European comfort in appointing host-country and third-country nationals is indicative of European MNEs' (traditional) preference for a localization strategy.

Beyond the nationality of subsidiary heads, the nationality of top executives at the highest level (such as chairman, CEO, and board members) seems to follow another informal rule: They are almost always home-country nationals. To the extent that top executives are ambassadors of the firm and that the MNE's country of origin is a source of differentiation (for example, a German MNE is often perceived to be different from an Italian MNE), home-country nationals would seem to be the most natural candidates for top positions.

In the eyes of stakeholders such as employees and governments around the world, however, a top echelon consisting of largely one nationality does not bode well for an MNE aspiring to globalize everything it does. Some critics even argue that this "glass ceiling" reflects "corporate imperialism."[7] Consequently, such leading MNEs as BP, Citigroup, Coca-Cola, Electrolux, GSK, HP, Lenovo, Microsoft, Nissan, Nokia, PepsiCo, P&G, and Sony have appointed foreign-born executives to top posts. Nestlé boasts executive board members from eight countries other than Switzerland. Such foreign-born executives bring substantial diversity to the organization, which may be a plus. However, such diversity puts an enormous burden on these nonnative top executives to clearly articulate the values and exhibit behaviors expected of senior managers of an MNE associated with a particular country. For example, in 2010 HP appointed Léo Apotheker, a native of Germany, to be its CEO. Unfortunately, HP lost $30 billion in market capitalization during his short tenure (over ten months), thanks to his numerous change initiatives. He was quickly fired in 2011. Since then, the old rule is back: HP is again led by an American executive.

12-2b Resource-Based Considerations

Shown in Exhibit 12.7, the resource-based view—exemplified by the value, rarity, imitability, and organization (VRIO) framework—adds a number of insights.[8] First, when looking at structural changes, it is critical to consider whether a new structure (such as a matrix) adds concrete value. The value of innovation must also be considered.[9] A vast majority of innovations simply fail to reach market, and most new products that do reach market end up being financial failures. The difference between an innovator and a *profitable* innovator is that the latter not only has plenty of good ideas, but also lots of complementary assets (such as appropriate organizational structures and marketing muscles) to add value to innovation (see Chapter 4). Philips, for example, is a great innovator. The company invented rotary shavers, video cassettes, and CDs. Still, its ability to profit from these innovations lags behind that of Sony and Matsushita, which have much stronger complementary assets.

A second question is rarity. Certain strategies or structures may be in vogue at a given point in time. For example, when a company's rivals all move toward a global standardization strategy, this strategy cannot be a source of differentiation. To improve global coordination, many MNEs spend millions of dollars to equip themselves with enterprise resource planning (ERP)

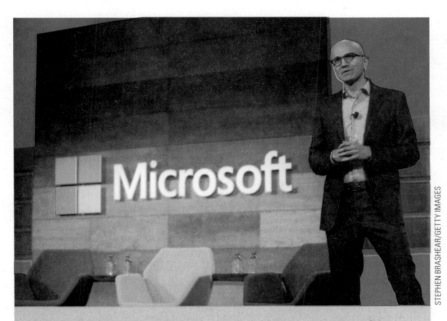

Indian-born Satya Nadella was named CEO of Microsoft in 2014. Here, Nadella addresses shareholders during Microsoft's 2016 Shareholders Meeting in Bellevue, Washington. Microsoft has boomed under Nadella, posting a $22.3 billion profit for the 2016 fiscal year.

STEPHEN BRASHEAR/GETTY IMAGES

Debate: Corporate Controls versus Subsidiary Initiatives

Ethical Dilemma

One of the leading debates on how to manage large firms is whether control should be centralized or decentralized. In an MNE setting, the debate boils down to corporate controls versus subsidiary initiatives.

SUBSIDIARY CONTROL

Subsidiaries are not necessarily receptive to headquarters' commands. When headquarters requires that certain practices (such as ethics training) be adopted, some subsidiaries may be in full compliance, others may pay lip service, and still others may simply refuse to adopt the practice, citing local differences. In addition to reacting to headquarters' demands differently, some subsidiaries may actively pursue their own, subsidiary-level strategies and agendas. These activities are known as **subsidiary initiatives**, defined as the proactive and deliberate pursuit of new opportunities by a subsidiary to expand its scope of responsibility. For example, LEGO's North American subsidiary proposed the idea of licensing *Star Wars* characters for LEGO toys. Advocates argue that such initiatives may inject a much-needed spirit of entrepreneurship throughout the larger, more bureaucratic corporation.

CORPORATE CONTROL

From corporate headquarters' perspective, however, it is hard to distinguish between good-faith subsidiary initiative and opportunistic empire building on the part of subsidiary managers. Much is at stake when determining whether subsidiaries should be named

LEVENT KONUK/SHUTTERSTOCK.COM

"centers of excellence" with worldwide mandates. Subsidiaries that fail to attain this status may see their roles marginalized or, worse, their facilities closed. Subsidiary managers are often host-country nationals who would naturally prefer to strengthen their subsidiary, if only to protect local (and their own!) employment and not necessarily to be patriotic. However natural and legitimate these tendencies, they are not necessarily consistent with the MNE's corporate-wide goals. These tendencies, if not checked and controlled, can surely lead to chaos for the MNE as a whole.

The best way, according to the title of an influential article authored by the former chairman and CEO of Intel, Andy Grove, seems to be: "Let chaos reign, then reign in chaos—repeatedly."

Sources: T. Ambos, U. Andersson, and J. Birkinshaw, "What are the consequences of initiative-taking in multinational subsidiaries?" *Journal of International Business Studies* 41 (2010): 1099–1118; R. Burgelman and A. Grove, "Let chaos reign, then reign in chaos—repeatedly," *Strategic Management Journal* 28 (2007): 965–979; F. Ciabuschi, M. Forsgren, and O. Martin, "Rationality versus ignorance," *Journal of International Business Studies* 42 (2011): 958–970; "It's complicated," *Economist*, 23 November 2013: 68; S. Wang, Y. Luo, X. Lu, J. Sun, and V. Maksimov, "Autonomy delegation to foreign subsidiaries," *Journal of International Business Studies* 45 (2014): 111–130.

packages provided by SAP and Oracle. However, such packages are designed to be implemented widely and appeal to a broad range of firms, thus providing no firm-specific advantage for the particular adopting firm.

Even when capabilities are valuable and rare, they have to pass a third hurdle—imitability. Formal structures are easier to observe and imitate than informal structures. This is one of the reasons why the informal, flexible matrix is in vogue now.

The informal, flexible matrix "is less a structural classification than a broad organizational concept or philosophy, manifested in organizational capability and management mentality."[10] Obviously imitating an intangible mentality is much harder than imitating a tangible structure.

The last hurdle is organization—namely, how MNEs are organized, both formally and informally, around the world (see Debate). One elusive but important concept is organizational culture. Recall from Chapter 3 that culture is defined by Hofstede as "the collective programming of the mind which distinguishes the members of one group or category of people from another." We can extend this concept to define **organizational culture** as the collective programming of the mind that distinguishes

subsidiary initiative The proactive and deliberate pursuit of new opportunities by a subsidiary to expand its scope of responsibility.

organizational culture The collective programming of the mind that distinguishes members of one organization from another.

EXHIBIT 12.8 KNOWLEDGE MANAGEMENT IN FOUR TYPES OF MULTINATIONAL ENTERPRISES

Strategy	Home replication	Localization	Global standardization	Transnational
Examples	Apple, Baidu, Carrefour, Google, Harley Davison, Kraft, P&G, Starbucks, Walmart	Heinz, Johnson & Johnson, KFC, Nestlé, Pfizer, Unilever	Canon, Caterpillar, Haier, HP, Huawei, LVMH, Otis, Texas Instruments, Toyota	GE, Häagen-Dazs, IBM, Kikkoman, Panasonic, Tata, Zara
Interdependence	Moderate	Low	Moderate	High
Role of foreign subsidiaries	Adapting and leveraging parent-company competencies	Sensing and exploiting local opportunities	Implementing parent-company initiatives	Differentiated contributions by subsidiaries to integrate worldwide operations
Development and diffusion of knowledge	Knowledge developed at the center and transferred to subsidiaries	Knowledge developed and retained within each subsidiary	Knowledge mostly developed and retained at the center and key locations	Knowledge developed jointly and shared worldwide
Flow of knowledge	Extensive flow of knowledge and people from headquarters to subsidiaries	Limited flow of knowledge and people to and from the center	Extensive flow of knowledge and people from the center and key locations to other subsidiaries	Extensive flow of knowledge and people in multiple directions

Sources: Adapted from C. Bartlett and S. Ghoshal, *Managing Across Borders: The Transnational Solution* (Boston: Harvard Business School Press, 1989) 65; T. Kostova and K. Roth, "Social capital in multinational corporations and a micro-macro model of its formation," *Academy of Management Review* 28 (2003): 299. Examples are added by M. W. Peng.

members of one organization from another. Huawei, for example, is known to have a distinctive "wolf" culture, which centers on "continuous hunting" and "relentless pursuit" with highly motivated employees who routinely work overtime and sleep in their offices. Although rivals can imitate everything Huawei does technologically, their biggest hurdle lies in their lack of ability to wrap their arms around Huawei's "wolf" culture.

12-3 WORLDWIDE LEARNING, INNOVATION, AND KNOWLEDGE MANAGEMENT

12-3a Knowledge Management

Underpinning the recent emphasis on worldwide learning and innovation is the emerging interest in knowledge management. **Knowledge management** can be defined as the structures, processes, and systems that actively develop, leverage, and transfer knowledge.

Many managers regard knowledge management as simply information management. Taken to an extreme, "such a perspective can result in a profoundly mistaken belief that the installation of sophisticated information technology (IT) infrastructure is the be-all and end-all of knowledge management."[11] Knowledge management depends not only on IT, but also on informal social relationships within the MNE.[12] This is because there are two categories of knowledge: (1) explicit knowledge and (2) tacit knowledge. **Explicit knowledge** is codifiable— it can be written down and transferred with little loss of richness. Virtually all of the knowledge captured, stored, and transmitted by IT is explicit. **Tacit knowledge** is noncodifiable, and its acquisition and transfer require hands-on practice. For example, reading a driver's manual (which contains a ton of explicit knowledge) without any road practice does not make you a good driver. Tacit knowledge is evidently more important and harder to transfer and learn; it can only be acquired through learning by doing (driving in this case). Consequently, from a resource-based view, explicit knowledge captured by IT may be strategically less important. What counts is the hard-to-codify and hard-to-transfer tacit knowledge.

12-3b Knowledge Management in Four Types of Multinational Enterprises

Differences in knowledge management among four types of MNEs in Exhibit 12.1 fundamentally stem from the interdependence (1) between the headquarters and foreign subsidiaries and (2) among various subsidiaries, as illustrated in Exhibit 12.8.[13] In MNEs pursuing a home

knowledge management The structures, processes, and systems that actively develop, leverage, and transfer knowledge.

explicit knowledge Knowledge that is codifiable (that is, can be written down and transferred with little loss of richness).

tacit knowledge Knowledge that is noncodifiable, whose acquisition and transfer require hands-on practice.

EXHIBIT 12.9   MARY KAY AROUND 2005

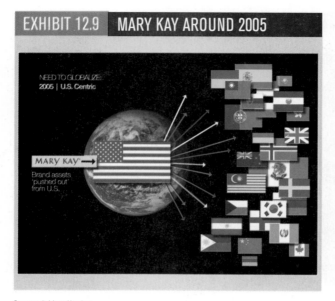

Source: © Mary Kay Inc.

EXHIBIT 12.10   MARY KAY NOW

Source: © Mary Kay Inc.

replication strategy, such interdependence is moderate and the role of subsidiaries is largely to adapt and leverage parent-company competencies (see Exhibit 12.9 on Mary Kay around 2005). Thus, knowledge on new products and technologies is mostly developed at the center and flown to subsidiaries, representing the traditional one-way flow. Starbucks, for example, insists on replicating its US coffee shop concept around the world, down to the elusive "atmosphere."

When MNEs adopt a localization strategy, the interdependence is low. Knowledge management centers on developing insights that can best serve local markets. Ford of Europe used to develop cars for Europe, with a limited flow of knowledge to and from headquarters. In MNEs pursuing a global standardization strategy, on the other hand, the interdependence is increased. Knowledge is developed and retained at the headquarters and a few centers of excellence. Consequently, knowledge and people typically flow from headquarters and these centers to other subsidiaries. For example, Yokogawa Hewlett-Packard, HP's subsidiary in Japan, won a coveted Japanese Deming Award for quality. The subsidiary was then charged with transferring such knowledge to the rest of HP, which resulted in a tenfold improvement in *corporate*-wide quality in ten years.

A hallmark of transnational MNEs is a high degree of interdependence and extensive and bi-directional flows of knowledge. For example, Kikkoman first developed teriyaki sauce specifically for the US market as a barbecue glaze. It was then marketed to Japan and the rest of the world. Similarly, Häagen-Dazs developed a popular ice cream in Argentina that was based on a locally popular caramelized milk dessert. The company then sold the flavor as Dulce De Leche throughout the United States and Europe. Within one year, it became the second most popular Häagen-Dazs ice cream, next only to vanilla. Particularly fundamental to transnational MNEs are knowledge flows among dispersed subsidiaries. Instead of a top-down hierarchy, the MNE thus can be conceptualized as an integrated network of subsidiaries. Each subsidiary not only develops locally relevant knowledge, but also aspires to contribute knowledge to benefit the MNE as a whole (see Exhibit 12.10 on Mary Kay today).

IN FOCUS: Emerging Markets

Panasonic in China and Beyond

Although Panasonic started manufacturing in China in 1987, most product development and engineering had been done in Japan, and local adaptation had been minimal. In a radical departure from its traditional practice, in 2005 it set up the Shanghai-based China Lifestyle Research Center, which was its first serious effort to gain a deep understanding of consumer lifestyles anywhere outside of Japan. Led by a high-caliber executive, center staff undertook a series of meticulous research. For example, visits to Chinese households uncovered that the kitchen space for a refrigerator was small, typically only 55 centimeters wide. Panasonic's standard refrigerator was 65 centimeters wide. In response, Panasonic's engineers in Kusatsu, Japan, and Hangzhou, China, worked together to downsize refrigerators—especially low-end ones—for China. The market reaction was swift. In one year, its most popular model of refrigerators increased its sales ten times compared with the sales in the previous year.

In another example, the Shanghai-based center found that in more than 90% of Chinese households with washing machines, consumers still washed their underwear by hand. Consumer interviews revealed a fear that bacteria picked up by other clothing would spread to underwear during the wash, resulting in infections. Although the fear was never proven, the solution clearly was to sterilize the clothing in the wash. Close collaboration between China-based and Japan-based teams led to the 2007 launch of Panasonic's sterilizing washing machines in China. In less than a year, its market share for front-loading machines rose from 3% to 15% in China. In a departure from the conventional flow of innovation from Japan to emerging economies, Panasonic brought the sterilization concept from China back to Japan.

While these two examples are high-profile successes, they were enabled by numerous efforts to foster formal and informal relationships among (1) the Shanghai-based market researchers, (2) engineers and managers throughout the over 40 operations in China, and (3) engineers and managers throughout Panasonic units in Japan and beyond. Overall, knowledge flowed in both directions:

GUOZHONGHUA/SHUTTERSTOCK.COM

from the rest of Panasonic to China and from China to the rest of Panasonic. To better manage the extensive flows of knowledge, Panasonic set up a China headquarters: Beijing-based Panasonic Corporation of China. China operations were gradually given more autonomy—rare among multinationals in general and among Japanese firms in particular. Since 2008, the China subsidiary has had almost complete autonomy in new product decisions for China.

Going beyond China, Panasonic has leveraged its learning from the China experience by transforming its organization on a global basis. Encouraged by the fruits from paying close attention to local consumer needs in China, Panasonic also developed air conditioners in India and refrigerators in Vietnam. In 2009, Panasonic established a lifestyle research center for Europe (in Wiesbaden, Germany). In 2010, it set up a similar center for India (in Delhi). In 2012, Panasonic created the Global Consumer Marketing organization to facilitate the diffusion of learning from the most insightful research and best practices outside Japan, especially in emerging economies.

Sources: S. Ichii, S. Hattori, and D. Michael, "How to win in emerging markets," *Harvard Business Review* (May 2012): 126–130; T. Wakayama, J. Shintaku, and T. Amano, "What Panasonic learned in China," *Harvard Business Review* (December 2012): 109–113; www.panasonic.co.jp; www.panasonic.com.cn; www.panasonic.net.

12-3c Globalizing Research and Development

R&D represents an especially crucial arena for knowledge management. Relative to production and marketing, only more recently has R&D emerged as an important function to be internationalized—often known as innovation-seeking investment (see In Focus). For example, Airbus has a significant R&D presence in Wichita, Kansas. Huawei has R&D units in China, India, Sweden, and the United States. Intense competition for

innovation drives the globalization of R&D. Such R&D provides access to foreign countries' local talents.

From a resource-based standpoint, a fundamental basis for competitive advantage is innovation-based firm heterogeneity (that is, being different). Decentralized R&D work performed by different locations and teams around the world virtually guarantees that there will be persistent heterogeneity in the solutions generated. GSK, for example, began aggressively spinning off R&D units as it became clear that simply adding more researchers in centralized R&D units did not necessarily enhance global learning and innovation.[14] GE's China units have developed low-cost, portable ultrasound machines at a fraction of the cost of existing machines developed in the United States. GE has not only been selling the developed-in-China machines throughout emerging economies, but has also brought them back to the United States and other developed economies.

12-4 MANAGEMENT SAVVY

MNEs are the ultimate large, complex, and geographically dispersed business organizations. What determines the success or failure of multinational strategies, structures, and learning? The answer boils down to the institution-based and resource-based dimensions. The institution-based view calls for thorough understanding and skillful manipulation of the rules of the game, both at home and abroad. The resource-based view focuses on the development and deployment of firm-specific capabilities to enhance the odds for success.

Consequently, three clear implications emerge for savvy managers (see Exhibit 12.11). First, understanding and mastering the external rules of the game governing MNEs and home/host country environments become a must.[15] For example, some MNEs abandon their original countries of origin and move their headquarters to be governed by more market-friendly laws and regulations in their new countries of domicile (see Closing Case). Despite the Swedish flags in front of its stores, IKEA is now a *Dutch* company, having registered in the Netherlands and enjoyed lower taxes there.

Second, managers need to understand and be prepared to change the internal rules of the game governing MNE management. Different strategies and structures

EXHIBIT 12.11 IMPLICATIONS FOR ACTION

▶ Understand and master the external rules of the game governing MNEs and home-country/host-country environments.

▶ Understand and be prepared to change the internal rules of the game governing MNE management.

▶ Develop learning and innovation capabilities to leverage multinational presence as an asset—"think global, act local."

call for different internal rules. Some facilitate and others constrain MNE actions. A firm using a home replication strategy should not appoint a foreigner as its CEO. Yet, as operations become more global, an MNE's managerial outlook needs to be broadened as well.

Finally, managers need to actively develop learning and innovation capabilities to leverage multinational presence. A winning formula is: *Think global, act local*.[16] Failing to do so may be costly. From 1999 until 2000, Ford Explorer SUVs were involved in numerous fatal rollover accidents in the United States. Most of these accidents were blamed on faulty tires made by Japan's Bridgestone and its US subsidiary Firestone. However, before the increase in US accidents, an alarming number of similar accidents had already taken place in warmer-weather countries such as Brazil and Saudi Arabia—tires wear out faster in warmer weather. Local Firestone managers dutifully reported the accidents to headquarters in Japan and the United States. Unfortunately, these reports were dismissed by the higher-ups as due to driver error or road conditions. Bridgestone/Firestone thus failed to leverage its multinational presence as an asset. It should have learned from these reports and proactively probed into the potential for similar accidents in cooler-weather countries. In the end, lives were lost unnecessarily, and informed car buyers abandoned the Bridgestone/Firestone brand.

EMERGING MARKETS/ETHICAL DILEMMA
Closing Case: Moving Headquarters Overseas

A number of MNEs have moved headquarters (HQ) overseas (see Exhibit 12.12). In general, there are two levels of HQ: *business unit* HQ and *corporate* HQ. The question is: Why?

If you have moved from one house to another in the same city, you can easily appreciate the logistical challenges (and nightmares!) associated with relocating HQ overseas. One simple answer is that the benefits must significantly outweigh the drawbacks. At the business unit level, the answer is straightforward: the "center of gravity" of the activities of a business unit may pull its HQ toward a host country. See the following letter to suppliers from IBM's chief procurement officer informing them of the move to China:

EXHIBIT 12.12 EXAMPLES OF MOVING HEADQUARTERS OVERSEAS

Corporate Headquarters	From	To
HSBC	Hong Kong	London, UK
IKEA	Stockholm, Sweden	Leiden, Netherlands
Lenovo	Beijing, China*	Raleigh (suburb), North Carolina, USA
News Corporation	Melbourne, Australia	New York, USA
Old Mutual	Cape Town, South Africa	London, UK
Tetra Pak	Lund, Sweden	Lausanne (suburb), Switzerland
Business Unit Headquarters		
Chevron Asia Pacific Division	San Francisco (suburb), California, USA	Singapore
IBM Global Procurement Division	Armonk, New York, USA	Shenzhen, China
P&G Global Cosmetics and Personal Care	Cincinnati, Ohio, USA	Singapore
Nokia Finance Division	Helsinki, Finland	New York, USA
Nomura Investment Banking Division	Tokyo, Japan	London, UK

* Lenovo maintains dual headquarters in both Beijing and North Carolina.

IBM Global Procurement is taking a major step toward developing a more geographically distributed executive structure . . . By anchoring the organization in this location, we will be better positioned to continue developing the skills and talents of our internal organization in the region . . . Clearly, this places us closer to the core of the technology supply chain which is important, not only for IBM's own internal needs, but increasingly for the needs of external clients whose supply chains we are managing via our Procurement Services offerings. As IBM's business offerings continue to grow, we must develop a deeper supply chain in the region to provide services and human resource skills to clients both within Asia and around the world.

At the corporate level, there are at least five strategic rationales. First, a leading symbolic value is an unambiguous statement to various stakeholders that the firm is a global player. News Corporation's new corporate HQ in New York is indicative of its global status, as opposed to being a relatively parochial firm from "down under." Lenovo's coming of age is undoubtedly underpinned by the establishment of its second HQ in the United States.

Second, there may be significant efficiency gains. If the new corporate HQ is in a major financial center, such as New York or London, the MNE can have more efficient and more frequent communication with institutional shareholders, financial analysts, and investment banks. The MNE also increases its visibility in a financial market, resulting in a broader shareholder base and greater market capitalization. Three leading (former) South African firms—Anglo American, Old Mutual, and SABMiller—have now joined the FTSE 100, the top 100 UK firms by capitalization.

Third, firms may benefit from their visible commitment to the laws of the new host country. They can also benefit from the higher quality legal and regulatory regime under which

they now operate. These benefits are especially crucial for firms from emerging economies where local rules are not world class. A lack of confidence about South Africa's political stability drove Anglo American, Old Mutual, and SABMiller to London. By moving to London in 1992, HSBC likewise deviated from its Hong Kong roots at a time when the political future of Hong Kong was uncertain.

Fourth, moving corporate HQ to a new country clearly indicates a commitment to that country. In addition to political motivation, HSBC's move to London signaled its determination to become a more global player, instead of being a regional player centered on Asia. HSBC indeed carried out this more global strategy since the 1990s. However, in an interesting twist of events, HSBC's CEO relocated back to Hong Kong in 2010. Technically, HSBC's corporate HQ is still in London, and its chairman remains in London. But the symbolism of the CEO's return to Hong Kong is clear. As China becomes more economically powerful, HSBC is interested in demonstrating its commitment to that important part of the world, which was where HSBC started. (HSBC was set up in Hong Kong in 1865 as Hongkong and Shanghai Banking Corporation.)

Finally, by moving (or threatening to move) HQ, firms enhance their bargaining power vis-à-vis that of their (original) home-country governments. Tetra Pak's move of its HQ to Switzerland was driven primarily by the owners' tax disputes with the Swedish government. Likewise, as three of Britain's large banks—Barclays, HSBC, and Standard Chartered, the three best-run ones that did not need bailouts during the Great Recession of 2008–2009—now face higher taxes and more government intervention, they too have threatened to move their HQ out of London. The message is clear: if the home-country government treats us harshly, we will pack our bags.

The last point, of course, is where the ethical and social responsibility controversies erupt. In 2014, Fiat announced its plan to merge itself and Chrysler into a new Netherlands-based holding company Fiat Chrysler Automobiles NV. So Fiat will in the end leave Italy—on paper at least. Although the absolute number of jobs lost is not great, these are high-quality (and high-paying) jobs that every government would prefer to see. For MNEs' home countries, if a sufficient number of HQ move overseas, there is a serious ramification that other high-quality service providers, such as lawyers, bankers, and accountants, will follow them. In response, proposals are floating to offer tax incentives for these "footloose" MNEs to keep HQ at home. However, critics question why these wealthy MNEs (and executives) need to be subsidized (or bribed), while many other sectors and individuals are struggling.

Case Discussion Questions

1. What are the drawbacks and benefits associated with moving business unit HQ and corporate HQ to another country?

2. **ON ETHICS:** If you were a CEO or a business unit head, under what conditions would you consider moving HQ?

3. If you were a government official in the MNE's home country, what can you do to discourage such moves of multinational HQ out of the country?

Sources: M. Baaij and A. Slangen, "The role of headquarters-subsidiary geographic distance in strategic decisions by spatially disaggregated headquarters," *Journal of International Business Studies* 44 (2013): 941–952; G. Benito, R. Lunnan, and S. Tomassen, "Distant encounters of the third kind: Multinational companies locating divisional headquarters abroad," *Journal of Management Studies* 48 (2011): 373–394; "HSBC: Gulliver's travels," *Economist*, 16 April 2011: 75–77; "Here, there and everywhere," *Economist*, 22 February 2014: 56–57; IBM, "IBM Procurement headquarters moves to Shenzhen, China," 22 May 2006: www-03.ibm.com; T. Laamanen, T. Simula, and S. Torstila, "Cross-border relocations of headquarters in Europe," *Journal of International Business Studies* 43 (2012): 187–210; P. Nell and B. Ambos, "Parenting advantage in the MNC," *Strategic Management Journal* 34 (2013): 1086–1103; M. W. Peng and W. Su, "Cross-listing and the scope of the firm," *Journal of World Business* 49 (2014): 42–50; "HSBC re-emphasizes its 'H,'" *Wall Street Journal*, 26 September 2009: www.wsj.com; "Chevron is placing big bets on Australia," *Wall Street Journal*, 8 July 2013: www.wsj.com.

STUDY TOOLS 12

LOCATED AT THE BACK OF YOUR BOOK:

☐ Rip out and study the Chapter Review Card at the end of the book

LOG IN TO WWW.CENGAGEBRAIN.COM TO:

☐ Review key term flashcards

☐ Complete a practice quiz to test your knowledge of key concepts

☐ View animated PengAtlas Maps

☐ Complete interactive content, watch chapter videos, and take a graded quiz

☐ Track your knowledge of key concepts in Global Business

☐ Read and discuss additional case study content

13 Managing Human Resources Globally

LEARNING OBJECTIVES

After studying this chapter, you will be able to . . .

 13-1 Explain staffing decisions, with a focus on expatriates.

 13-2 Identify training and development needs for expatriates and host-country nationals.

 13-3 Discuss compensation and performance appraisal issues.

 13-4 List factors that affect labor relations in both home and host countries.

13-5 Understand how the institution-based and resource-based views shed additional light on human resource management.

13-6 Identify the five Cs of human resource management.

After you finish this chapter, go to **PAGE 218** for STUDY TOOLS

Opening Case: IKEA Manages Human Resources in the United States

Active in 48 countries with approximately 400 stores, IKEA is the world's largest furniture retailer. In 1985, IKEA came to the United States. It struggled quite a bit in the beginning, not opening a single store between 1993 and 1999. It eventually figured out the right recipe for this market. Currently operating 44 stores with 14,000 employees, US operations contribute $5 billion of IKEA's global sales ($36 billion), ahead of its home country sales in Sweden (but behind those in Germany).

While keeping prices low has always been a hallmark of IKEA's strategy, directly supporting it is its efforts in human resource management (HRM). Its HRM centers on radically reducing staff turnover and creating a stable and nurturing working environment in an industry notorious for high turnover. Toward that end, IKEA US offers generous wages and benefits compared with its rivals. Hourly employees receive an average of $15.45 an hour, and entry-level employees $11.87 an hour—nearly five bucks higher than the federal minimum wage of $7.25. In comparison, Walmart hourly employees receive an average of $13.38 an hour, and entry-level employees merely a dollar above the federal minimum wage. Influenced by the home-country norms, IKEA's benefits are extraordinary by US standards. Even part-time employees enjoy health benefits for just 20 hours of work per week. Full-time employees annually receive 24 paid vacation days and five sick days—essentially "unheard of" in the United States, according to *Fortune*. Employees working for more than ten years can get 34 days of paid time off plus five sick days.

The IKEA culture also discourages workaholics. Instead, work-life balance is a big deal. "If you can't do your job in a reasonable amount of time," head of human resources for IKEA US, an American executive, told a reporter, "you're doing something wrong." Few stick around after work hours, and everybody takes weekends off—of course, except those on-duty running the stores during weekends. Most employees take a "European-style" long vacation of several weeks.

At IKEA, egalitarianism runs deep. Similar to the parent company, IKEA US is not very hierarchical. All in-store employees are called "shopkeepers." Few executives have business cards. Everyone sits side-by-side at no-frills IKEA desks in an open floor plan at the firm's US "service office" (IKEA-speak for "headquarters") in Conshohocken, Pennsylvania (a suburb of Philadelphia). IKEA US's number-one executive, the country manager, on one of his store visits in Miami directly worked with a "shopkeeper" on how to most effectively move trash from the warehouse to the dumpster.

Inclusion and diversity are also part of IKEA's DNA. Not only are half of its US employees women, more than half of its senior managers and executives are women too. Some IKEA commercials feature gay couples. Since 1995, IKEA has offered domestic partner benefits. Starting in 2016, IKEA has covered gender reassignment surgery. Sometimes, its policies are viewed as "going too far" in more conservative markets. For example, in Italy, a politician called for a boycott after IKEA organized an event in support of gay marriage.

Country manager Lars Petersson, an expatriate from Sweden, is proud to put a Swedish spin on notions such as egalitarianism, work-life balance, and inclusion in an American workplace. "We don't make different considerations in different countries," he shared. "It's not that we aren't appreciative and interested in local culture. We are very much. But there are some fundamental things that we are not negotiating."

In 2016, IKEA US is one of the only four proud non-US-owned firms that join the ranks of *Fortune* 100 Best Companies to Work for. The other three are Allianz from Germany, Four Seasons from Canada, and Novo Nordisk from Denmark. (According to that *Fortune* survey, the best company to work for is Google.)

Sources: "This is how we successfully invaded the US market," *Business Insider*, 6 June 2012: www.businessinsider.com; "At IKEA: No ranks, no rancor," *Fortune*, 15 March 2016: 202–203; "The 100 best companies to work for," *Fortune*, 15 March 2016: 141–165; "The magic in the warehouse," *Fortune*, 15 December 2016: 183–189.

How can firms such as IKEA select, retain, reward, and motivate the best employees that they can attract? How can they link the management of people from diverse cultural and professional backgrounds with firm performance? These are some of the crucial questions we will address in this chapter. This chapter is devoted to **human resource management (HRM)**—activities that attract, select, and manage employees. As a function, HRM used to be called "personnel" and before that "records management." Few of you are HRM experts, but everyone can appreciate HRM's rising importance

> **human resource management (HRM)** Activities that attract, select, and manage employees.

just by looking at the evolution of the terminology. The term "HRM" clearly indicates that people are key resources of the firm to be actively managed and developed. From a lowly administrative support function, HRM has now increasingly been recognized as a strategic function that, together with other crucial functions such as finance and marketing, helps accomplish organizational goals and financial performance.[1]

This chapter first reviews the four main areas of HRM: (1) staffing, (2) training and development, (3) compensation and performance appraisal, and (4) labor relations. Then, we use the institution-based and resource-based views to shed light on these issues. To conclude, we outline the five Cs of HRM.

13-1 STAFFING

Staffing refers to HRM activities associated with hiring employees and filling positions. In multinational enterprises (MNEs), there are two types of employees: **host-country nationals (HCNs,** often known as "locals") and expatriates (expats for short). First introduced in Chapter 1, expatriates are nonnative employees working in a foreign country. Among expatriates, there are two types: (1) **Parent-country nationals (PCNs)** come from the parent country of the MNE and work at its local subsidiary. (2) **Third-country nationals (TCNs)** come from neither the parent country nor the host country.

The majority of an MNE's employees would be HCNs. For example, of Siemens's 400,000 employees worldwide, only a small cadre of 300 executives are expatriates and another 2,000 executives are short-term assignees abroad. Of these 2,300 executives, about 60% are PCNs (Germans) and 40% are TCNs (from countries other than Germany and the host country). A leading concern is how to staff the *top* positions abroad, such as the subsidiary CEO, country manager, and key functional heads such as CFO and CIO. The three choices for top positions, PCNs, TCNs, and

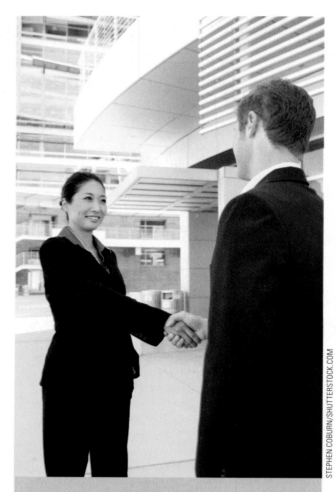

In multinational enterprises, there are two types of employees: host-country nationals and expatriates.

STEPHEN COBURN/SHUTTERSTOCK.COM

HCNs, all have their pros and cons (see Exhibit 13.1). The staffing choices are not random and are often a reflection of the strategic posture of the MNE—as discussed next.

13-1a Ethnocentric, Polycentric, and Geocentric Approaches in Staffing

There are three primary approaches for making staffing decisions for top positions at subsidiaries. An **ethnocentric approach** emphasizes the norms and practices of the parent company (and the parent country of the MNE) by relying on PCNs. Not only can PCNs ensure and facilitate control and coordination by headquarters, they may also be the best qualified people for the job because of special skills and experience. A perceived lack of talent and skills among HCNs often necessitates an ethnocentric approach. In addition, a cadre of

staffing HRM activities associated with hiring employees and filling positions.

host-country national (HCN) An individual from the host country who works for an MNE.

parent-country national (PCN) An employee who comes from the parent (home) country of the MNE and works at its local subsidiary.

third-country national (TCN) An employee who comes from neither the parent country nor the host country of the MNE.

ethnocentric approach A staffing approach that emphasizes the norms and practices of the parent company (and the parent country of the MNE) by relying on PCNs.

EXHIBIT 13.1 PARENT-COUNTRY, THIRD-COUNTRY, AND HOST-COUNTRY NATIONALS

	Advantages	Disadvantages
Parent-country nationals (PCNs)	▶ Control by headquarters is facilitated ▶ PCNs may be the most qualified people ▶ PCNs gain international experience	▶ Opportunities for HCNs are limited ▶ PCNs' adaptation may take a long time ▶ PCNs are usually very expensive
Third-country nationals (TCNs)	▶ TCNs may bridge the gap between headquarters and the subsidiary (and between PCNs and HCNs) ▶ TCNs may be less expensive than PCNs	▶ Host government and employees may resent TCNs ▶ Similar to disadvantages for PCNs
Host-country nationals (HCNs)	▶ Language and cultural barriers are eliminated ▶ Better continuity of management ▶ Usually cheaper	▶ Control and coordination by headquarters may be impeded ▶ HCNs may have limited career opportunity ▶ International experience for PCNs is limited

Source: Adapted from P. Dowling and D. Welch, *International Human Resource Management*, 4th ed. (Cincinnati: Cengage, 2005) 63.

EXHIBIT 13.2 MULTINATIONAL STRATEGIES AND STAFFING APPROACHES

MNE strategies	Typical staffing approaches	Typical top managers at local subsidiaries
Home replication	Ethnocentric	Parent-country nationals
Localization	Polycentric	Host-country nationals
Global standardization	Geocentric	A mix of parent-country, host-country, and third-country nationals
Transnational	Geocentric	A mix of parent-country, host-country, and third-country nationals

internationally mobile and experienced managers, who are often PCNs, can emerge to spearhead further expansion around the world.

As the opposite of an ethnocentric approach, a **polycentric approach** focuses on the norms and practices of the host country. In short, "when in Rome, do as the Romans do." Who would make the best managers in Rome? Naturally, Roman (or Italian) managers—technically, HCNs. HCNs have no language or cultural barriers. Unlike PCNs who often pack their bags and move after several years, HCNs stay in their positions longer, thus providing more continuity of management. Further, placing HCNs in top subsidiary positions sends a morale-boosting signal to other HCNs who may feel they can reach the top as well (at least in that subsidiary).

Disregarding nationality, a **geocentric approach** focuses on finding the most suitable managers, who can be PCNs, HCNs, or TCNs. In other words, a geocentric approach is *color-blind*—the color of a manager's passport does not matter. For a geographically dispersed MNE, a geocentric approach can help create a corporate-wide culture and identity. This can reduce the typical us-versus-them feeling in firms that use either ethnocentric or polycentric

approaches. On the other hand, molding managers from a variety of nationalities is a lot more complex than integrating individuals from two (parent and host) countries.

Overall, there is a systematic link between MNEs' strategic postures (see Chapter 12) and staffing approaches (see Exhibit 13.2). MNEs pursuing a home replication strategy usually use an ethnocentric approach, staffing subsidiaries with PCNs. MNEs interested in a localization strategy are typically polycentric in nature, hiring HCNs to head subsidiaries. Global standardization or transnational strategies often require a geocentric approach, resulting in a mix of HCNs, PCNs, and TCNs. As more firms such as Samsung become more global in their operations, they increasingly have to look beyond the pool of their PCNs to attract and nurture talented HCNs and TCNs. In Focus features some foreign-born bosses at MNEs aspiring to globalize their operations.

polycentric approach A staffing approach that emphasizes the norms and practices of the host country.

geocentric approach A staffing approach that focuses on finding the most suitable managers, who can be PCNs, HCNs, or TCNs.

Foreign-Born Bosses at the Top of Multinationals

BP. Citigroup. Coca-Cola. Electrolux. Google. GSK. Lenovo. Microsoft. Mitsubishi. Nissan. Nokia. PepsiCo. Siemens. Sony. The list of foreign-born bosses running the show at some of the world's most visible MNEs keeps growing. Since 1999, Nissan's chief executive officer (CEO) has been Carlos Ghosn, who more recently (since 2005) has also become CEO of Renault. Born in Brazil to Lebanese immigrants, Ghosn was educated in France and rose through the ranks in French MNEs Michelin and Renault. Soon after Ghosn took over Nissan, he was receiving hate mail from Japanese employees slated to lose their jobs. Now he is revered in Japan and considered a national hero for his success in turning Nissan around. At present he is chairman and CEO of Renault, chairman and CEO of Nissan, and chairman of Mitsubishi Motors.

Because of Renault's acquisition of a chunk of Nissan's equity, Ghosn was initially appointed to Nissan. However, at many other MNEs, foreign-born CEOs were promoted from within. In 1993, Scottish-born Alex Trotman took over as Ford's chairman and CEO, who then in 1999 promoted Lebanese-born Australian Jacques Nasser as his successor. In 2005, Sony appointed Welsh-born American Howard Stringer as its CEO. In 2006, Pepsi promoted Indian-born Indra Nooyi to be its CEO. In 2014, Satya Nadella, also Indian-born, was appointed to be CEO of Microsoft.

Do foreign-born bosses deliver? The record is mixed. In addition to Ghosn's successful turnaround of Nissan, inspiring stories include Turkish-born Mehta Kent, who was appointed chairman and CEO of Coca-Cola in 2008. Coca-Cola's performance improved under his leadership. PepsiCo under Nooyi has also enjoyed strong growth. On the other hand, uninspiring stories are also plenty. Sony under Stringer failed to impress—while rivals such as Samsung and Apple rocketed ahead. Sony's products simply became uninspiring, unpopular, and expensive. In 2012, Stringer was replaced by a Japanese CEO. In 2010, Hewlett-Packard (HP) hired a new CEO, German-born Léo Apotheker. He bought a software maker, Autonomy, with a lavish price of $10 billion—ten times its annual revenue. Apotheker first announced all HP devices would be equipped with Palm software, and then after a few months announced that Palm would be abandoned. During his 11-month tenure as CEO, HP lost $30 billion in market capitalization. The board fired him in 2011.

Despite the hits and misses, appointing foreign-born executives has become a trend for some (although not all) companies aspiring to globalize. After Lenovo acquired IBM's PC Division (PCD) in 2004, Lenovo first appointed PCD's former head, an American, to be its CEO. Then Lenovo replaced him with another American CEO recruited from Dell. In 2007, LG embarked on a drive to globalize its top echelon. Its chairman and CEO were still Korean, but five of its key units—namely, marketing, procurement, supply chain, HRM, and retailer relations—were headed by Western executives recruited from HP, Novartis, Pfizer, and Unilever.

However, not all is rosy. In addition to firm performance challenges confronting all executives, two sources of stress have emerged for foreign-born executives. First, relative to native-born bosses, foreign-born bosses are under heavier scrutiny, confront bigger leadership challenges, and thus suffer from higher levels of stress. A CEO is supposed to be the ambassador representing the firm. Most stakeholders, for example, expect a German firm and its CEO to behave differently from an Italian firm and its CEO, because countries of origin matter. As a result, foreign-born bosses often experience an identity crisis, which does not enhance managerial effectiveness. Second, internal political winds within some of these multinationals change. When the global recession hit Lenovo in 2008, the American CEO left the firm and was replaced by a Chinese one. LG's bold experiments with foreign-born talents abruptly ended after three years. In 2010, its more globally minded Korean CEO was fired due to lackluster firm performance and replaced by the founder's grandson. Within 48 hours, 25 of the 27 non-Korean directors were fired, causing tremendous bitterness.

Sources: "Coke's last round," *Bloomberg Businessweek*, 1 November 2010: 54–61; "Sony needs a hit," *Bloomberg Businessweek*, 21 November 2011: 72–77; "Free fall: Inside Meg Whitman's plan to keep HP from going . . . splat," *Bloomberg Businessweek*, 14 January 2013: 44–50; "The foreigners at the top of LG," *BusinessWeek*, 22 December 2009: 56–57; "Stringer theory," *Economist*, 28 May 2011: 70; "Loosening their ties," *Economist*, 28 November 2015: 61; "Satya Nadella," *Fortune*, 1 December 2016: 77–83.

13-1b The Role of Expatriates

Expatriation is leaving one's home country to work in another country. Shown in Exhibit 13.3, expatriates play four important roles.

▶ Expatriates are *strategists* representing the interests of the MNE's headquarters.[2] Expatriates, especially PCNs who have a long tenure with a particular MNE, may have internalized the parent firm's values and norms (see Opening Case). They may not only enable headquarters to control subsidiaries, but also facilitate the socialization process to bring subsidiaries into an MNE's global orbit.

▶ Expatriates are *daily managers* who run operations and build local capabilities where local management talent is lacking.

▶ Expatriates are *ambassadors*.[3] Representing headquarters' interests, they build relationships with host-country stakeholders such as local managers, employees, suppliers, customers, and government officials. Importantly, expatriates also serve as ambassadors representing the interests of the *subsidiaries* when interacting with headquarters.

▶ Expatriates are *trainers* for their replacements. Over time, some localization in staffing is inevitable, calling for expatriates to train local employees.[4]

13-1c Expatriate Failure and Selection

Few expatriates can play the challenging multidimensional roles effectively. It is not surprising that expatriate failure rates are high. Expatriate failure can be measured in three ways: (1) premature (earlier-than-expected) return, (2) unmet business objectives, and (3) unfulfilled career development objectives. Using the easiest-to-observe measure of premature return, studies in the 1980s reported that 76% of US MNEs had expatriate failure rates of more than 10%, and that 41% and 24% of

Expatriate failure can be measured in three ways: (1) premature (earlier-than-expected) return, (2) unmet business objectives, and (3) unfulfilled career development objectives.

European and Japanese MNEs, respectively, had comparable failure rates.[5] More recent studies find that the failure rates may have declined slightly. However, given the much larger number of expatriates now (1.3 million from the United States alone), expatriate failure rates are still high enough to justify attention. Since expatriates typically are the most expensive group of managers, the cost of each failure is tremendous—between a quarter of a million and one million dollars.

Expatriation can fail for a variety of reasons. Surveys of US and European MNEs find that the leading cause is the spouse and family's inability to adjust to life in a foreign country. In the case of Japanese MNEs, the leading cause is the inability to cope with the larger scope of responsibilities overseas. It usually is a *combination* of work-related and family-related problems that leads to expatriate failures.

Given the importance of expatriates and their reported high failure rates, how can firms enhance the odds for expatriate success? Exhibit 13.4 outlines a model for expatriate selection, with six underlying factors grouped along situation and individual dimensions. In terms of situation dimensions, the preferences of both headquarters and the subsidiary are important. The subsidiary may also have specific

EXHIBIT 13.3   THE ROLES OF EXPATRIATES

MNE headquarters in parent country ⟷ **Expatriate Roles**: • Strategist • Daily manager • Ambassador • Trainer ⟷ Subsidiary in host country

expatriation Leaving one's home country to work in another country.

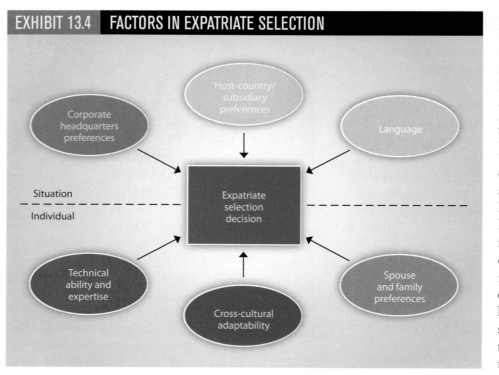

EXHIBIT 13.4 FACTORS IN EXPATRIATE SELECTION

Corporate headquarters preferences

Host-country/ subsidiary preferences

Language

Situation

Individual

Expatriate selection decision

Technical ability and expertise

Cross-cultural adaptability

Spouse and family preferences

Source: Adapted from P. Dowling and D. Welch, *International Human Resource Management*, 4th ed. (Cincinnati: Cengage, 2005) 98.

requests, such as "Send a Spanish speaker." It is preferable for expatriates to have some command of the local language.

In terms of individual dimensions, both technical ability and cross-cultural adaptability are a must. Desirable attributes include a positive attitude, emotional stability, and previous international experience. Last (but certainly not least), spouse and family preferences must be considered. The accompanying spouse often leaves behind a career and a social network. The spouse has to find meaningful endeavors abroad, but many countries protect local jobs by not permitting the spouse to work. Thus, many families find expatriation frustrating.

Expatriates are expensive and failure rates are high in general, but middle-aged expatriates (forty-somethings) are the most expensive. This age group typically has children still in school, so the employer often has to provide a heavy allowance for the children's education. High-quality schools can be expensive. In places such as Manila, Mexico City, and Moscow, international or American schools cost $15,000 to $35,000 per year. Unfortunately, these expatriates also have the highest percentage of failure rates in part because

training Specific preparation to do a particular job.

development Longer-term, broader preparation to improve managerial skills for a better career.

of their family responsibilities. In response, many MNEs either select expatriates in their fifties, who are less likely to have school-age children, and/or promote younger expatriates in their late twenties and early thirties who may not yet have children. Younger expatriates typically do not need a large home or education allowance. Further, given the importance of international experience, many younger managers are eager to go overseas. This development has strong implications for students studying this book now: overseas opportunities may come sooner than you expect. Are *you* ready?

13-2 TRAINING AND DEVELOPMENT

Training is specific preparation to do a particular job. **Development** refers to longer-term, broader preparation to improve managerial skills for a better career. Training and development programs focus on two groups: expatriates and HCNs. Each is discussed in turn.

13-2a Training for Expatriates

The importance and cost of expatriates and their reported high failure rates make training necessary. Yet, many MNEs do not provide any pre-departure training for expatriates—other than wishing them "good luck." Even for firms that provide training, many offer short, one-day-type programs that are inadequate. Not surprisingly, many MNEs and expatriates get burned by such underinvestment in preparation for what are arguably some of the most challenging managerial assignments.

Ideally, training length and rigor should correspond to the expatriate's expected length of stay. For a short stay, training can be short and less rigorous. Sometimes survival-level language training—such as how to say "Where is the lady's room?" and "I'd like a beer"—would suffice. However, for a long stay of several years, it is imperative that more in-depth and rigorous training be provided, especially for first-time expatriates. Preparation should involve more extensive language as well as sensitivity training, preferably with an immersion approach (training conducted in a foreign language/culture environment). Enlightened firms concerned about failure rates now often involve the spouse in expatriate training as well.

13-2b Development for Returning Expatriates (Repatriates)

Many expatriate assignments are not one-shot deals. Instead, they are viewed as part of a manager's accumulated experience and expertise and enhance a long-term career in the firm (see Closing Case). Thus, at some point, expatriates may become repatriates, individuals who return to their home countries to stay after working abroad for a length of time. While the idea to develop a repatriate's long-term career sounds good in theory, in practice, many MNEs do a lousy job managing **repatriation**, which is the process of returning to the expatriate's home country after an extended period overseas.

Chief among the problems experienced by repatriates is career anxiety. A leading concern is "What kind of position will I have when I return?" Prior to departure, many expatriates are encouraged by their boss: "You should take (or volunteer for) this overseas assignment. It's a smart move for your career." Theoretically, this is known as a **psychological contract**, an informal understanding of expected delivery of benefits in the future for current services (see Closing Case). A psychological contract is easy to violate. Bosses may change their minds. Or they may be replaced by new bosses. Violated psychological contracts naturally lead to disappointments.

Many returning expatriates find readjusting to the domestic workplace to be a painful experience. Ethnocentrism continues to characterize many MNEs. Many employees at headquarters have a bias when it comes to knowledge transfer, which typically moves from headquarters to subsidiaries via expatriates. Consequently, they are not interested in learning from returning expatriates, which would mean knowledge moving from subsidiaries to headquarters. This attitude typically leads repatriates to feel that their international experience is not appreciated. After being

Carlos Ghosn

"big fish in a small pond" at the subsidiary, repatriates often feel like "small fish in a big pond" at headquarters. Instead of being promoted, many end up taking comparable (or lower-level) positions.

Repatriates may also experience a loss of status. Overseas, they are big shots, rubbing shoulders with local politicians and visiting dignitaries. They often command lavish expatriate premiums, with chauffeured cars and maids. But most of these perks disappear once they return.

Lastly, the spouse and the children may also find it difficult to adjust back home. The feeling of being a part of a relatively high-class, close-knit expatriate community is gone. Instead, life at home may now seem lonely, dull, unexciting, and in some cases, dreadful. Children, being out of touch with current slang, sports, and fashion, may struggle to regain acceptance into peer groups back home. Having been brought up overseas, (re)adjusting back to the home-country educational system may be especially problematic. Some returning Japanese teenagers have committed suicide after failing to make the grade back home.

Overall, if not managed well, repatriation can be traumatic not only for expatriates and their families, but also for the firm. Unhappy returning expatriates do not stay around long. Approximately one in four or one in three repatriates leave the firm within one year. Since a US MNE spends on average approximately $1 million on each expatriate over the duration of a foreign assignment, losing that individual can wipe out any return on investment. Worse yet, the returnee may end up working for a rival firm.

The best way to reduce expatriate turnover is a career development plan. A good plan also comes with a mentor (also known as champion, sponsor, or godfather).[6] The mentor helps alleviate the out-of-sight, out-of-mind feeling by ensuring that the expatriate is not forgotten at headquarters and by helping secure a challenging position for the expatriate upon return. Another way to reduce expatriate turnover is to send more expatriates on short-term or commuter-type assignments, and rely more on local staff.

Overall, despite the numerous horror stories, many expatriates do succeed. Carlos Ghosn, after successfully

FREDERIC LEGRAND - COMEO/SHUTTERSTOCK.COM

repatriation Returning to an expatriate's home country after an extended period overseas.

psychological contract An informal understanding of expected delivery of benefits in the future for current services.

turning around Nissan as a PCN, went on to become CEO of the parent company, Renault. To reach the top at most MNEs today, international experience is a must. Therefore, despite the drawbacks, aspiring managers should not be deterred from taking overseas assignments. Who said being a manager was easy?

13-2c Training and Development for Host-Country Nationals

While most international HRM practice and research focus on expatriates, it is important to note that the training and development needs of HCNs deserve significant attention as well. In the ongoing "war for talent" in China, a key factor in retaining or losing top talent is which employer can provide better training and development opportunities.[7] To slow turnover, many MNEs in China now have formal career development plans and processes for HCNs. GE, for example, has endeavored to make promising managers in China stimulated, energized, and recognized. This has resulted in a managerial turnover rate of "only" 7% per year, substantially lower than the nationwide average of 30% to 40% for HCNs at the managerial rank working at multinationals in China.

13-3 COMPENSATION AND PERFORMANCE APPRAISAL

compensation Salary and benefits.

performance appraisal The evaluation of employee performance for the purposes of promotion, retention, or ending employment.

going rate approach A compensation approach that pays expatriates the prevailing (going) rate for comparable positions in a host country.

balance sheet approach A compensation approach that balances the cost-of-living differences based on parent-country levels and adds a financial inducement to make the package attractive.

As part of HRM, **compensation** refers to salary and benefits. **Performance appraisal** is the evaluation of employee performance for the purpose of promotion, retention, or ending employment. Three related issues are: (1) compensation for expatriates, (2) compensation for HCNs, and (3) performance appraisal.

	Advantages	Disadvantages
Going rate	▶ Equality among parent-country, third-country, and host-country nationals in the same location ▶ Simplicity ▶ Identification with host country	▶ Variation between assignments in different locations for the same employee ▶ Reentry problem if the going rate in the parent country is less than that in the host country
Balance sheet	▶ Equity between assignments for the same employee ▶ Facilitates expatriate reentry	▶ Costly and complex to administer ▶ Great disparities between expatriates and host-country nationals

13-3a Compensation for Expatriates

A leading issue in international HRM is how to properly compensate, motivate, and retain expatriates. Exhibit 13.5 shows two primary approaches: going rate and balance sheet. The **going rate approach** pays expatriates the prevailing (going) rate for comparable positions in a host country. When Lenovo acquired IBM's PC division, it sent Chinese expatriates to New York and paid them the going rate for comparable positions for HCNs and other expatriates in New York. The going rate approach fosters equality among PCNs, TCNs, and HCNs within the same subsidiary. It also makes locations where pay is higher than the home country a more attractive place to work for PCNs and TCNs. Overall, this approach excels in its simplicity and fosters strong identification with the host country.

However, the going rate for the same position differs around the world, with the United States leading in managerial compensation. The typical US CEO commands a total compensation package of over $2 million, whereas a British CEO fetches less than $1 million, a Japanese CEO $500,000, and a Chinese CEO $200,000. According to the going rate approach, returning Lenovo expatriates, accustomed to New York-level salaries, will have a hard time accepting relatively lower Beijing-level salaries, thus triggering repatriation problems.

A second approach is the **balance sheet approach**, which balances the cost of living differences relative to parent-country levels and adds a financial inducement to make the package attractive. This method is the most widely used in expatriate compensation. Historically, this approach has been justified on the grounds that a majority of expatriates would come from higher-pay, developed economies and go to lower-pay locations. Under these conditions, the going rate approach would not work because an expatriate from New York probably would not accept the lower going rate in Beijing. The balance sheet approach essentially pays Beijing-bound expatriates "New York Plus." The "Plus" is nontrivial: additional financial inducement (premium), cost of living allowance (for housing and children's education), and a hardship allowance (fewer companies now pay a hardship allowance for Beijing, but many MNEs used to). Exhibit 13.6 shows one hypothetical example. Adding housing and taxation that the MNE pays (not shown in the exhibit), the total cost may reach $350,000 to $400,000 a year.

EXHIBIT 13.6	A HYPOTHETICAL ANNUAL EXPATRIATE COMPENSATION PACKAGE USING THE BALANCE SHEET APPROACH	
Items for a hypothetical US expatriate		**Amount (US$)**
Base salary		$200,000
Cost-of-living allowance (25%)		$50,000
Overseas premium (20%)		$40,000
Hardship allowance (20%)		$40,000
Housing deduction (−7%)		−$14,000
TOTAL (pretax)		$316,000

Note: The host country has a cost-of-living index of 150 relative to the United States. Not shown here are (1) the full cost of housing and (2) the cost to pay the difference between a higher income tax in a host country and a lower income tax in the parent country. Adding housing and taxation, the net cost of the MNE can reach $350,000 to $400,000 in this case.

The balance sheet approach has two advantages (see Exhibit 13.5). First, there is equity between assignments for the same employee, whose compensation is always anchored to the going rate in the parent country. Second, it also facilitates repatriation, because there is relatively little fluctuation between overseas and parent-country pay despite the cost-of-living differences around the world.

However, there are three disadvantages. The first is cost. Using the example in Exhibit 13.6, the cost can add up to $1 million for a three-year tour of duty. The second disadvantage is the great disparities between expatriates (especially PCNs) and HCNs. Such unequal pay naturally causes resentment by HCNs.

Lastly, the balance sheet approach is organizationally complex to administer. For a US firm operating in South Africa, both the American PCNs and Australian TCNs are typically compensated more than the South African HCNs. The situation becomes more complicated when the US firm recruits South African MBAs before they finish business school training in the United States. Should they be paid as locally hired HCNs in South Africa or as expatriates from the United States? What about TCNs from Kenya and Nigeria who also finish US MBA training and are interested in going to work for the US MNE in South Africa? Ideally, firms pay for a position regardless of passport color. However, the market for expatriate compensation is not quite there yet.

13-3b Compensation for Host-Country Nationals

At the bottom end of the compensation scale, low-level HCNs, especially those in developing countries, have relatively little bargaining power. The very reason that they have jobs at MNE subsidiaries is often because of their low labor cost—that is, they are willing to accept wage levels substantially lower than those in developed countries. The HCNs compare their pay to the farmhands sweating in the fields and making much less, or to the army of unemployed who make nothing but still have a family to feed (see PengAtlas Maps 15 and 16). Despite accusations of exploitation by some activists, MNEs in developing countries typically pay *higher* wages compared to similar positions in the local market.

On the other hand, HCNs in management and professional positions increasingly have bargaining power. MNEs are rushing into Brazil, Russia, India, and China (BRIC), where local supply of top talent is limited. Some executives in China reportedly receive calls from headhunters every *day*. It is not surprising that high-caliber HCNs, because of their scarcity, will fetch more pay. The question is: How much more? Most MNEs plan to eventually replace even top-level expatriates with HCNs, in part to save on costs. However, if HCNs occupying the same top-level positions are paid the same as expatriates, then there will be no cost savings. But MNEs unwilling to pay top dollar for local talent may end up losing high-caliber HCNs to competitors who are willing to do so. The war for talent is essentially a bidding war for top HCNs. MNEs may eventually have to pay international rates regardless of nationality.

13-3c Performance Appraisal

While initial compensation is determined upon entering a firm, follow-up compensation usually depends on performance appraisal. Performance appraisal helps managers make decisions about pay and promotion, development, documentation, and subordinate expression. In our case, performance appraisal is based on how expatriates evaluate HCNs and how expatriates themselves are evaluated.

When expatriates evaluate HCNs, cultural differences may create problems. Typically from low power distance countries, Western MNEs often see performance appraisals as an opportunity for subordinates to express themselves. In high power distance countries such as those in Asia and Latin America, however,

> **labor relations** A firm's relation with organized labor (unions) in both home and host countries.

such an expression could potentially undermine the power and status of supervisors. Employees themselves do not place a lot of importance on self-expression. Therefore, Western expatriates who push HCNs in these cultures to express themselves in performance appraisal meetings would be viewed as indecisive and lacking integrity.

Expatriates need to be evaluated by their own supervisors. In some cases, however, expatriates are the top manager in a subsidiary (such as country manager), and their supervisors are more senior executives based at headquarters. Some of these off-site managers have no experience as expatriates themselves. A study of 1,000 largest US and EU MNEs reports that 76% of CEOs in US firms and 60% of CEOs in EU firms never had a foreign posting.[8] Such internationally inexperienced managers often evaluate expatriates based on hard numbers (such as productivity and market growth), but sometimes these numbers are beyond expatriates' control (such as a currency crisis). This is one of the reasons why many expatriates think they are not evaluated fairly. The solution lies in fostering more visits and communication between on-site expatriates and off-site supervisors.

Always sensitive, compensation and performance evaluation are even more important during tough economic times. Facing grave financial situations, should the firm impose across-the-board pay cut or engage in reduction in force, which is massive layoffs? If someone has to go, according to what criteria based on performance evaluation should the firm decide who will receive the pink slip first? These are crucial questions that HR managers need to be prepared.

13-4 LABOR RELATIONS

The term **labor relations** refers to a firm's relations with organized labor (unions) in both home and host countries. Each is discussed in turn.

13-4a Managing Labor Relations at Home

In developed economies, a firm's key concern is to cut costs and enhance competitiveness to fight off low-cost rivals from emerging economies. Labor unions, on the other hand, are organized with the purpose of helping workers earn higher wages and obtain more benefits through collective bargaining. In the United States, unionized employees earn 30% more than nonunionized employees. As a result, disagreements and conflicts between managers and unions are natural.

The bargaining chip of labor unions is their credible threat to strike, slow down, refuse to work overtime, or some other form of disruption. The bargaining chip of managers is the threat to shut down operations and move jobs overseas. It is clear which side is winning. In the United States, union membership dropped from 20% of the workforce in 1983 to 11% now (just 7% in the private sector and 36% in the public sector). Membership of United Auto Workers (UAW), for example, fell from 1.5 million to less than 400,000 at present.[9] The trend is similar in other developed countries exposed to globalization, such as Britain, France, Germany, and Japan.[10]

Unlike MNEs, which can move operations around the world, unions are organized on a country-by-country basis. Efforts to establish multinational labor organizations have not been effective. In the 1990s, US MNEs moved aggressively to Mexico to take advantage of NAFTA. The leading US union, the AFL-CIO, contacted the Mexican government and requested permission to recruit members in Mexico. It was flatly rejected.

13-4b Managing Labor Relations Abroad

If given a choice, MNEs prefer to deal with nonunionized workforces. When Japanese and German automakers came to the United States, they avoided the Midwest, a union stronghold. Instead, these MNEs went to the rural South and set up nonunion plants in small towns in Alabama (Mercedes and Hyundai), Kentucky (Toyota), and South Carolina (BMW). When MNEs have to deal with unions abroad, they often rely on experienced HCNs instead of locally inexperienced PCNs or TCNs.

Throughout many developing countries, governments typically welcome MNEs and simultaneously silence unions. However, things are changing. In 2010, a series of high-profile strikes took place at plants run by Taiwan's Foxconn and Japan's Honda in China. Instead of cracking down, the Chinese government chose to look the other way. Emboldened

workers ended up forcing these MNEs to accept 30% to 40% pay increases. The media widely reported that "the days of cheap labor (in China) are gone."[11]

13-5 INSTITUTIONS, RESOURCES, AND HUMAN RESOURCE MANAGEMENT

Having outlined the four basic areas of HRM, let us now turn to the institution-based and resource-based views to see how they shed additional light (see Exhibit 13.7).

13-5a Institutions and Human Resource Management

Formal and informal rules of the game shape HRM significantly, both at home and abroad. Every country has *formal* rules, laws, and regulations governing the do's and don'ts of HRM. Foreign firms ignoring such rules do so at their own peril. For example, in Japan, firms routinely discriminate against women and minorities. However, when Japanese MNEs engage in such usual practices in the United States, they face legal challenges.

On the other hand, foreign firms well versed in local regulations may take advantage of them. For example, the legal hurdles for firing full-time workers in France are legendary. When HP announced a plan to lay off 1,200 employees in France, then-president Jacques Chirac called HP directly and complained. However,

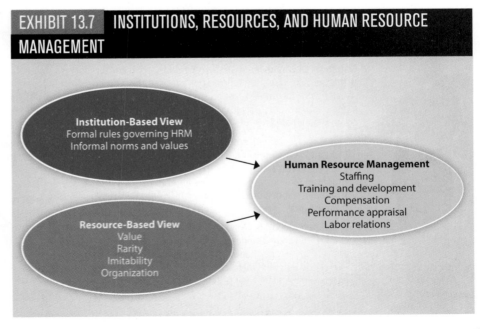

EXHIBIT 13.7 INSTITUTIONS, RESOURCES, AND HUMAN RESOURCE MANAGEMENT

Institution-Based View
Formal rules governing HRM
Informal norms and values

Resource-Based View
Value
Rarity
Imitability
Organization

Human Resource Management
Staffing
Training and development
Compensation
Performance appraisal
Labor relations

it is this very difficulty in firing full-time workers that has made France a highly lucrative market for the US-based Manpower. French firms reluctant or unwilling to hire full-time employees value Manpower's expertise in providing part-time workers. France is now Manpower's *largest* market ahead of the United States.

Informal rules of the game, embodied in cultures, norms, and values, also assert powerful influence (see Exhibit 13.8). MNEs from different countries have different norms in staffing. Most Japanese MNEs follow an informal rule: Heads of foreign subsidiaries, at least initially, need to be PCNs. In comparison, European MNEs are more likely to appoint HCNs and TCNs to lead subsidiaries. There is a historical reason for such differences: Most European MNEs expanded globally before low-cost telephones, faxes, email, and Skype were available. Thus, a localization strategy relying on HCNs and TCNs was necessary.

Most Japanese MNEs went abroad in the 1980s, when modern communication technology enabled more centralized control from headquarters. In addition, the Japanese cultural preference for low uncertainty also translated into higher interest in headquarters control. Thus, Japanese MNEs often implemented a home replication strategy that relied on PCNs who constantly communicated with headquarters.

Interestingly, the emerging Chinese MNEs are more likely to appoint HCNs as managers. This may be due to the lack of international talents among their ranks or due to the more open-minded nature of some Chinese MNEs. Regardless of the reason, the upshot is the same: more managerial jobs for locals.[12]

While informal cultures, norms, and values are important, HR managers need to avoid stereotyping and instead consider changes. In the area of compensation, one study hypothesized that presumably collectivistic Chinese managers would prefer a more egalitarian compensation compared to what their individualistic US counterparts would prefer. The results turn out to be surprising: Chinese managers actually prefer *more* merit-based pay, whereas US managers behave exactly the opposite.[13] In other words, the Chinese seem more "American" than Americans (!). Further digging has revealed that these are not average Chinese—they are HCNs working for some of the most competitive Western MNEs in China. The upshot? Naïve adaptation to presumed local norms and values based on outdated stereotypes may backfire. HR managers must do more homework to better understand their HCNs.

One norm that is changing is the necessity to pay extra compensation to attract higher caliber and more senior expatriates. Since overseas experience, especially in major emerging economies such as China, is now viewed as a necessary step to advance one's career, demand is outstripping supply of such opportunities. Therefore, many firms do not feel compelled to offer financial inducements, because, according to Siemen's HRM chief, "we don't want people to take the job merely for the money." Many Western managers are willing to accept a "local plus" package instead of the traditional expatriate package full of perks. Further, more expatriates are now younger. They may be sent abroad to gain experience—often with more down-to-earth titles such as "assignees" or "secondees." In addition, more expatriates

---

EXHIBIT 13.8   SOME BLUNDERS IN INTERNATIONAL HRM

► A Spanish company sent a team of expatriates to Saudi Arabia. The group included a number of young, intelligent women dressed in current Spanish style. Upon arrival, the Saudi immigration official took a look at the women's short skirts and immediately put the entire team on the next flight back to Spain. The expatriate team and the company belatedly learned that despite the heat, women in Saudi Arabia never show their bare legs.

► In Malaysia, an American expatriate was introduced to an important potential client he thought was named "Roger." He proceeded to call this person "Rog." Unfortunately, this person was a "Rajah," which is an important title of nobility. In this case, the American tendency to liberally use another person's first name—and to proactively shorten it—appeared disrespectful and insensitive. The Rajah walked away from the deal.

► A Japanese CEO of a subsidiary in New York held a meeting of his staff, all of whom were Americans, to inform them that the firm had grave financial losses and that headquarters in Japan had requested that everybody redouble their efforts. After the meeting, the staff immediately redoubled their efforts—by sending their résumés out to other employers.

KAZOKA/SHUTTERSTOCK.COM

ISTOCKPHOTO.COM/GEOTRAC

Source: Based on D. Ricks, *Blunders in International Business*, 3rd ed. (Oxford, UK: Blackwell, 1999) 95–105.

are now sent on short-term, commuter-type assignments for which they do not need to uproot their family—a major source of stress for the family and a cost item for the firm. Overall, the norms and images associated with the stereotypical expatriate, a more senior executive leading a life of luxury to compensate for hardship overseas, are changing rapidly.

13-5b Resources and Human Resource Management

As HRM becomes more strategic, the VRIO dimensions are increasingly at center stage. To start, managers have to ask: Does a particular HR activity add *value*? Consider two examples. First, labor-intensive chores such as administering payroll, benefits, and basic training may not add value. They can often be outsourced. Second, training is expensive—$160 billion in the United States and $350 billion globally in 2015.[14] Does it really add value? Results pooled from 397 studies find that, on average, training adds value by improving individual performance by approximately 20%.[15] Thus, training is often justified.

Next, are particular HR activities *rare*? The relentless drive to learn, share, and adopt best practices may reduce their rarity and thus usefulness. If every MNE in Brazil provides training to high-caliber HCNs, such training, which is valuable, will be taken for granted, but no longer viewed as rare.

Further, how *imitable* are certain HR activities? It is relatively easy to imitate a single practice, but it is much more difficult to imitate a complex HR *system* (or *architecture*) consisting of multiple, mutually reinforcing practices that work together. Consider the five-star Portman Ritz-Carlton Hotel in Shanghai. Its expatriate general manager personally interviews *every* new hire. It selects HCNs genuinely interested in helping guests. It cares deeply about employee satisfaction, which has led to superb guest satisfaction. Each single practice here may be imitable, and the Portman Ritz-Carlton, which has been voted the "Best Employer in Asia," has been studied meticulously by rivals (and numerous nonrivals) in China and around the world. Yet, none has been able to successfully imitate its system. On the surface, every firm says, "We care about our people." But the reality at many firms is increasing underinvestment by both employers and employees with declining loyalty and commitment. A mutual investment approach is likely to result in excellent performance, as exemplified by IKEA (see Opening Case). However, it is very difficult to imitate a mutual investment approach that comes together as a system (or architecture).

Finally, do HR practices support *organizational capabilities* to help accomplish performance goals? Consider teamwork and diversity, especially multinational teams that have members from different subsidiaries.[16] While most firms promote some sort of teamwork and diversity, it is challenging to organizationally leverage such teamwork and diversity to enhance performance. Too little or too much diversity may hurt performance. In teamwork, certain disagreements may help promote learning. But obviously too many disagreements may lead to conflict and destroy team effectiveness. However, few managers (and few firms) know where to draw the line to keep team disagreements from getting out of control.[17]

13-6 MANAGEMENT SAVVY

How much does effective HRM impact firm performance? Results from 3,200 firms show that change of one standard deviation in the HR system affects 10% to 20% of a firm's market value.[18] Findings from 92 studies suggest that an increase of one standard deviation in the use of an effective HR system is associated with a 4.6% increase in return on assets (ROA).[19] These recent findings validate a long-held belief among HRM practitioners and scholars: HRM is indeed *strategic*. In other words, HRM has become a direct answer to the fundamental question of our field: What determines the success and failure of firms around the world?

Consequently, we identify implications for actions, listed in Exhibit 13.9, that center on the four Cs developed by Susan Meisinger, president of the Society for Human Resource Management.[20] These insights have important implications for HR managers.

EXHIBIT 13.9 IMPLICATIONS FOR ACTION

For HR managers: The four Cs

▶ Be *curious*. Know formal and informal rules of the game governing HRM in all regions of operations.

▶ Be *competent*. Develop organizational capabilities that drive business success.

▶ Be *courageous* and *caring*. As guardians of talent, HR managers need to nurture and develop people.

For non-HR managers: The fifth C

▶ Be proactive in managing your (international) *career*.

Debate: A Radical Proposal

Ethical Dilemma

Ram Charan is one of the most influential consultants in the world. He finds most HR executives to have expertise in compensation, benefits, and labor relations. They tend to focus on internal matters, such as engagement, empowerment, and cultural sensitivity. But they do not seem to do well as advisors to CEOs on the talent implications of firms' strategy. In response, in 2014 Charan proposed a radical solution in *Harvard Business Review*. In his own words:

> It is radical, but it is grounded in practicality. My proposal is to eliminate the position of chief human resource officer (CHRO) and split HR into two strands. One—we might call it HR-A (for administration)—would primarily manage compensation and benefits. It would report to the CFO, who would have to see compensation as a talent magnet, not just a major cost. The other, HR-LO (for leadership and organization), would focus on improving the people capabilities of the business and would report to the CEO.

According to Charan, the ideal candidates to serve as HR-LO would not be traditional HR managers. Instead, HR-LO positions ideally would be better served by high-potential line managers

VECTORGURU/SHUTTERSTOCK.COM

from operations or finance. They can develop people skills and link the HR system with operational or financial performance. After a few years, these executives may move to horizontal or higher-level line management positions. Although Charan expects "plenty of opposition" to his proposal, he is convinced that it is time to split HR. What do you think?

Sources: Extracted from R. Charan, 2014, "It's time to split HR," *Harvard Business Review* (July 2014): 34. For more recent thinking, see R. Charan, D. Barton, and D. Carey, "People before strategy: A new role for the CHRO," *Harvard Business Review* (July 2015): 62–71.

First, savvy HR managers need to be *curious*. They need to be well versed in the numerous formal and informal rules of the game governing HRM worldwide. They must be curious about emerging trends in the world and be prepared to respond to these trends. For example, HR managers need to consider how artificial intelligence and robotics are going to affect the future of work.[21] Second, HR managers must be *competent*. Far from its lowly roots as a lackluster administrative support function, HRM is now acknowledged as a strategic function. Many HR managers may have been trained more narrowly and with a more micro (nonstrategic) focus. Now, HR managers must be able not only to contribute to the strategy conversation, but also to take things off the CEO's desk as full-fledged business partners (see Debate).

Finally, HR managers must be *courageous* and *caring*. As guardians of talent, HR managers need to nurture and develop employees (see Opening Case).[22] This often means that as employee advocates, HR managers sometimes need to be courageous enough to disagree with the CEO and other line managers. GE's recently retired head of HR, William Conaty, is such an example. "If you just get closer to the CEO, you're dead," Conaty shared with a reporter, "I need to be independent. I need to be credible." GE's CEO Jeff Immelt called Conaty "the first friend, the guy that could walk in my office and kick my butt when it needed to be"—exactly how a full-fledged business partner should behave.[23]

In addition, there is a fifth C for non-HR managers: proactively manage your *career* in order to develop a global mindset (see Closing Case). Since international experience is a prerequisite for reaching the top at many firms, managers need to prepare by investing in their own technical expertise, cross-cultural adaptability, and language training. Some of these investments (such as language) are long term in nature. This point thus has strategic implications for students who are studying this book *now*: Have you learned a foreign language? Have you spent one semester or year abroad? Have you made any friends from abroad, perhaps fellow students who are taking *this* class with you now? Have you put this course on your resume? Arm yourself with the knowledge now, make proper investments, and advance your career. Remember: your career is in your hands.

EMERGING MARKETS/ETHICAL DILEMMA
Closing Case: Chicago versus Shanghai

Richard Wang is president (country manager) for Dream Hotel China, whose corporate headquarters is in Chicago. Wang has an engineering degree from Shanghai Jiao Tong University and an MBA from the University of Texas at Dallas. After obtaining his MBA in 1995, Wang worked at Dream Hotel Chicago and picked up a green card (US permanent residency) while maintaining his Chinese passport. In 2005, when Dream Hotel opened its first location in China—in Wang's hometown Shanghai—he was tapped to be one of the first managers sent from the United States. China of the 21st century was certainly different from China of the 1990s that Wang had left behind. Reforms were in the air, multinationals coming left and right, and his two phones ringing off the hook from headhunters shouting to him about "career opportunities."

As a manager, Wang has shined in Shanghai. He has been promoted to replace an expat to be the number one executive in charge of all Dream Hotel locations in China. His wife and two children (born in 2001 and 2003 in Chicago) are also happy. After all, Chinese food in Shanghai is a lot more authentic than that in Chicago. Grandparents, relatives, and friends are all happy to see the family back. In Chicago, Wang's wife, Lily, a Chinese language teacher by training, taught on a part-time basis, but could not secure a full-time teaching position because so few schools offered Chinese. Now she is principal of a great school in Shanghai. The two children are enrolled in the elite Shanghai International School, the cost of which is paid for by the

Chicago, Illinois

RUDY BALASKO/SHUTTERSTOCK.COM

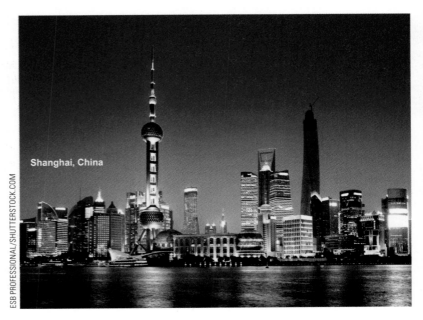

Shanghai, China

ESB PROFESSIONAL/SHUTTERSTOCK.COM

company. Shanghai is not perfect, but the Wangs feel good about coming back.

At the end of 2017, president of Dream Hotel Asia Pacific, an American expat who is co-located with Wang in the same building in Shanghai, has a conversation with him:

Richard, I have great news for you! Headquarters wants you to move back to Chicago. You'll be in charge of strategy development for global expansion, working directly under the group vice president. Isn't that exciting?! They want someone with proven success. You are my best candidate. I don't know what design they have for you after this assignment, but I suspect it'll be highly promising. Don't quote me, but I'd say you may have a shot to eventually replace me or the next Asia Pacific president here. While I personally enjoy the work here, my family is really fed up with the air pollution, especially on a winter day like this. Or folks in Chicago may eventually want you to go somewhere else like Russia or Brazil or Turkey or Cuba. As you know, some of our earlier experience in sensitive countries tells us that a fantastic third-country national may be an awesome Dream Hotel manager. And you can be that awesome third-country national! Frankly, I don't know but I'm just trying to help

you speculate. I know it's a big decision. Talk to Lily and the kids. But they lived in Chicago before, so they should be fine going back. Of course, I'll put you in touch with the folks in Chicago directly so that you can ask them all kinds of questions. Let me know what you think in a week.

Instead of calling his wife immediately, Wang has decided to wait till he gets home in the evening so that he can have a few hours to think about this. Going from Chicago to Shanghai, Wang, with his Chinese passport, is a host-country national (HCN). However, with his green card, he is also considered a US national and thus an expatriate. He wonders whether he should accept the new assignment. He thinks this will be an exciting career move for him, but he is not sure if his family will like it.

Case Discussion Questions

1. What questions should Wang ask the people at headquarters in Chicago? Please help him prepare a list.

2. Will Lily and the children be happy about this move? Why?

3. Should Wang accept or decline this opportunity? Why?

Sources: Author's interviews. All individual and corporate names are fictitious.

STUDY TOOLS 13

LOCATED AT THE BACK OF YOUR BOOK:

☐ Rip out and study the Chapter Review Card at the end of the book

LOG IN TO WWW.CENGAGEBRAIN.COM TO:

☐ Review key term flashcards

☐ Complete a practice quiz to test your knowledge of key concepts

☐ View animated PengAtlas Maps

☐ Complete interactive content, watch chapter videos, and take a graded quiz

☐ Track your knowledge of key concepts in Global Business

☐ Read and discuss additional case study content

GLOBAL ONLINE

ACCESS TEXTBOOK CONTENT ONLINE— INCLUDING ON SMARTPHONES!

Includes Videos & Other Interactive Resources!

MANAGE MY COURSE ∨   STUDENT

GLOBAL4

CHAPTER
1

Globalizing Business

CHAPTER
2

Understanding Politics, Laws, & Economics

4LTR
PRESS

Access GLOBAL4 ONLINE at www.cengagebrain.com

14 Competing in Marketing & Supply Chain Management

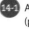

LEARNING OBJECTIVES

After studying this chapter, you will be able to . . .

14-1 Articulate three of the four Ps in marketing (product, price, and promotion) in a global context.

14-2 Explain how the fourth P in marketing (place) has evolved to be labeled supply chain management.

14-3 Outline the triple As in supply chain management (agility, adaptability, and alignment).

14-4 Discuss how institutions and resources affect marketing and supply chain management.

14-5 Draw three implications for action.

After you finish this chapter, go to

PAGE 233 for

STUDY TOOLS

Opening Case: Marketing Aflac in the United States and Japan

Founded in 1955 and based in Columbus, Georgia, Aflac is the largest provider of supplemental insurance in the United States. It also operates in one other country—Japan. In fact, it sells more insurance in Japan than at home. It insures one of four Japanese households and is the largest life insurer in Japan in terms of individual insurance policies in force. Approximately four-fifths of its $20 billion revenues come from Japan.

Although Aflac's business has been successful, its name has been problematic from the beginning. It first started as American Family Life Insurance Company. But a Wisconsin insurance company had an identical name (!). As a result of a gentlemen's coin toss between the two owners, "Assurance" was used instead of "Insurance." But the company still had difficulty differentiating itself from numerous other insurance and noninsurance companies whose names start with "American." In the 1990s, the company decided to go with the acronym only: Aflac. But Aflac still struggled with its unnatural (and "weird") name.

In 1999, in an effort to market itself better, Aflac engaged Kaplan Thaler Group, an advertising agency based in New York. But the agency had a hard time coming up with an idea that would make the relatively obscure insurance company's name memorable. During one lunch break, one of the agency's frustrated directors took a walk around Central Park and still scratched his head, uttering "Aflac, Aflac." As he walked around the duck pond, in a moment of inspiration he realized how much "Aflac" sounded like a duck's quack. In the absence of other more effective ideas, Kaplan Thaler Group pitched the duck to Aflac, hoping Aflac would not be offended by the commercial's making fun of its name. Although this idea convinced CEO Daniel Amos, he had a hard time selling the idea to his colleagues and board members. In his own words:

When I tried explaining to people what we were thinking about, no one got it. "Well, there's this duck," I'd say. "And he quacks Aflac." The response was always the same: a silent stare. So I stopped telling people. I didn't even tell our board; I just said we're trying to do something very bold and creative for our advertising campaign.

DANNY SMYTHE/SHUTTERSTOCK.COM

The Aflac Duck debut was aired on CNN on New Year's Day, 2000, with the Duck quacking "Aflac" to prospective policyholders. It ran four times an hour. The world watched CNN to see if the Y2K bug would wreak havoc, thus giving the Duck the maximum exposure. The response was overwhelming. After the first day on the air, Aflac had more visits to its website than in the entire year 1999. In the first year, Aflac sales in the United States went up by 29%, and in three years they doubled. Thanks to the Duck, Aflac's name recognition was up to 67% after two years of running the commercial and is now higher than 90%. The Aflac Duck went on to be enshrined on Madison Avenue's Walk of Fame as one of America's Favorite Advertising Icons.

The famous American duck, however, had a hard time making itself heard in Japan. In Japan, a duck does not yell "quack-quack;" it says "ga-ga." In Japan since 1973, Aflac did not suffer from being in the middle of a crowd of firms named "American." Instead, in Japan it was known for its full name: American Family Life Assurance Company. While the Japan subsidiary was not wholehearted in its support for the new ad, the Aflac Duck debuted in Japan in 2003. After some mild adaptation (such as toning down the yelling voice to a softer, more courteous tone), the Duck became a rock star in Japan, and sales increased by 12% in 2003. Encouraged by the Duck's success, the Japanese marketing team introduced a new incarnation: a mix of the Duck and the traditional Asian good-luck white cat Maneki Neko—simply known as the Maneki Neko Duck or the cat duck. The cat duck became so popular that it was voted number-one commercial in Japan. The jingle from the commercial became the number-one downloaded mobile-phone ringtone in Japan, and the Maneki Neko Duck attracted thousands of followers on Facebook, Twitter, and YouTube. Aflac rocketed ahead to become the number-one insurance company in Japan, an honor held by Nippon Life for more than 100 years. Now when people come to visit Aflac's headquarters in Georgia, they want to see the Aflac Duck. So the company has added a duck pond to its headquarters—probably the first and only duck pond among all American (and Japanese) company headquarters.

Sources: D. Amos, "Aflac's CEO explains how he fell for the duck," *Harvard Business Review* (January 2010): 13–134; "Aflac Duck in Japan," *BuzzFeed* (October 2014): www.buzzfeed.com; www.aflac.com; www.japanprobe.com.

How can firms such as Aflac market themselves to attract customers around the world? How can they tailor and adapt their messages to capture the hearts, minds, and wallets of different customers who have different tastes and preferences? Having attracted customers, how can firms ensure a steady supply of products and services? This chapter deals with these and other important questions associated with marketing and supply chain management. **Marketing** refers to efforts to create, develop, and defend markets that satisfy individual and business customers. **Supply chain** is the flow of products, services, finances, and information that passes through a set of entities from a source to the customer. **Supply chain management** refers to activities to plan, organize, lead, and control the supply chain. Although marketing and supply chain used to operate separately, today their boundaries are blurred. In the newest frontier, the competition for online and mobile shoppers, retailers such as H&M, Tesco, and Walmart have had to transform themselves to become logistics and supply chain management companies (see Closing Case). In this chapter, instead of viewing marketing and supply chain as two stand-alone, separate functions, we view them as one crucial, integrated function.

We first outline major marketing and supply chain activities in global business. Then we discuss how the institution-based and resource-based views enhance our understanding of the drivers behind marketing and supply chain management success. Finally, managerial implications follow.

EXHIBIT 14.1   MARKETING AND FIRM PERFORMANCE

"What's your marketing plan?"

BILL ABBOTT CARTOONS

14-1 THREE OF THE FOUR Ps IN MARKETING

EXHIBIT 14.2   THE FOUR Ps OF MARKETING MIX

Product

Price

Promotion

Place

Shown in Exhibit 14.1, marketing is crucial for firm performance. Exhibit 14.2 shows the four Ps that collectively consist of the **marketing mix**: (1) product, (2) price, (3) promotion, and (4) place. We start with the first three Ps. The last P—place (where the product is sourced, produced, and distributed)—will be discussed in the next section.

14-1a Product

Product refers to offerings that customers purchase. Even for a single category (such as women's dress or sports car),

marketing Efforts to create, develop, and defend markets that satisfy the needs and wants of individual and business customers.

supply chain Flow of products, services, finances, and information that passes through a set of entities from a source to the customer.

supply chain management Activities to plan, organize, lead, and control the supply chain.

marketing mix The four underlying components of marketing: (1) product, (2) price, (3) promotion, and (4) place.

product Offerings that customers purchase.

product attributes vary tremendously. For multinational enterprises (MNEs) doing business around the world, a leading concern is standardization versus localization. Localization is natural. McDonald's, for example, sells wine in France, beer in Germany, mutton pot pies in Australia, and Maharaja Mac and McCurry Pan in India. In China, Kentucky Fried Chicken (KFC) features menu items that would not be recognizable to its customers in the United States. Alongside the Colonel's "secret recipe" fried chicken, KFC in China also markets congee, a chicken wrap in a Peking duck–type sauce, and spicy tofu chicken rice. In Japan, Wendy's sells a $16 *Foie Gras Rossini* (goose-liver pâté) hamburger.[1]

Chinese Kentucky Fried Chicken locations such as this one in Nanchang, Jiangxi, feature menu items that may not be recognizable to customers in the United States.

What is interesting is the rise of standardization, which is often attributed to Theodore Levitt's 1983 article, "The Globalization of Markets."[2] First discussed in Chapter 12, this article advocated globally standardized products and services, as evidenced by Hollywood movies and Coke Classic. However, numerous subsequent experiments such as Ford's "world" car and MTV's "global" (essentially American) programming backfired. Marketers thus face a dilemma: While one size does not fit all, most firms cannot afford to create products and services for just one group of customers when trying to serve many groups around the world.

As first noted in Chapter 12, localization is appealing (in the eyes of local consumers and governments) but expensive. One sensible solution is to have a product that *appears* to be locally adapted while deriving as much synergy (commonality) as possible in ways that customers cannot easily recognize. Consider the two global business weekly magazines, the US-based *Bloomberg Businessweek* and the UK-based *Economist*. In addition to its US edition, *Bloomberg Businessweek* publishes two English (language) editions for Asia and Europe and a Chinese edition for China. While these four editions share certain content, there is a lot of local edition–only material that is expensive to produce. In comparison, each issue of the *Economist* has the following regional sections (in alphabetical order): (1) the Americas (excluding the United States), (2) Asia (excluding China), (3) Britain, (4) China, (5) Europe (excluding Britain), (6) the Middle East and Africa, and (7) the United States.

While the content for each issue is identical, the order of appearance of the regional sections is different. For US subscribers, their *Economist* would start with the US section. For Chinese subscribers, their magazine would start with the China section. By doing that, the *Economist* appears to be responsive to readers with different regional interests without incurring the costs of running multiple editions for different regions, as *Bloomberg Businessweek* does. Therefore, how many editions does one issue of the *Economist* have? We can say one—or seven if we count the seven different ways of stapling regional sections together.

One of the major concerns for MNEs is to decide whether to market global brands or local brands in their portfolio.[3] The key is **market segmentation**—identifying segments of consumers who differ from others in purchasing behavior.[4] There are limitless ways of segmenting the market (males versus females, urban dwellers versus rural residents, Africans versus Latin Americans).

For international marketers, the million-dollar question is: How does one generalize from a wide variety of market segmentation in different countries to generate products that can cater to a few of these segments *around the world*? One globally useful way of segmentation is to divide consumers into four categories:[5]

- Global citizens (who are in favor of buying global brands that signal prestige and cachet).

- Global dreamers (who may not be able to afford, but nevertheless admire, global brands).

- Antiglobals (who are skeptical about whether global brands deliver higher-quality goods).

- Global agnostics (who are most likely to lead antiglobalization demonstrations smashing McDonald's windows).

The implications are clear. For the first two categories of global citizens and global dreamers, firms are advised to leverage the global brands and their relatively more standardized products and services. "Global brands make us feel like citizens of the world," an Argentine consumer observed. However, MNEs do not necessarily have to write off the antiglobals and

market segmentation
Identifying segments of consumers who differ from others in purchasing behavior.

global agnostics as lost customers, because they can market localized products and services under local brands. Nestlé, for example, owns thousands of brands around the world, most of which are local, country-specific (or region-specific) brands not marketed elsewhere.

Overall, Levitt may be *both* right and wrong. A large percentage of consumers around the world indeed have converging interests and preferences centered on global brands. However, a substantial percentage of them also resist globally standardized brands, products, and services. Armed with this knowledge, both MNEs and local firms can better craft their products and services.

14-1b Price

Price refers to the expenditures that customers are willing to pay for a product. Most consumers are "price sensitive." The jargon is **price elasticity**—how demand changes when price changes. Basic economic theory of supply and demand suggests that when price drops, consumers will buy more and generate stronger demand. Such strong demand, in turn, motivates firms to expand production to meet this demand. This theory, of course, underpins numerous firms' relentless drive around the world to cut costs and then prices. The question is *how* price sensitive consumers are. Holding the product (such as shampoo) constant, in general the lower income the consumers are, the more price sensitive they are. While American, European, and Japanese consumers buy shampoo by the bottle, in India shampoo is often sold in single-use sachets, each costing about one to ten cents. Many consumers there find the cost for a bottle of shampoo to be prohibitive. Some African telecom operators charge customers by the *second*—a big deal for those making pennies a day.[6]

ASWADIE/SHUTTERSTOCK.COM

price Expenditures that customers are willing to pay for a product.

price elasticity How demand changes when price changes.

promotion Communications that marketers insert into the marketplace.

14-1c Promotion

Promotion refers to all the communications that marketers insert into the marketplace. Promotion includes TV, radio, print, and online advertising, as well as coupons, direct mail, billboards, direct marketing (personal selling), and public relations. Marketers face a strategic choice of whether to standardize or localize promotional efforts. Standardized promotion not only projects a globally consistent message (crucial for global brands), but can also save a lot of money.

However, there is a limit to the effectiveness of standardized promotion. In the 1990s, Coca-Cola ran a worldwide campaign featuring a cute polar bear cartoon character. Research later found that viewers in warmer-weather countries had a hard time relating to this ice-bound animal with which they had no direct experience. In response, Coca-Cola switched to more costly, but more effective, country-specific advertisements. For instance, the Indian subsidiary launched a campaign that equated Coke with "thanda," the Hindi word for "cold." The German subsidiary developed commercials that showed a "hidden" kind of eroticism (!). While this is merely one example, it does suggest that even some of the most global brands (such as Coca-Cola) can benefit from localized promotion.

Many firms promote products and services overseas without doing their "homework" and end up with blunders (huge mistakes). GM marketed its Chevrolet Nova in Latin America without realizing that "no va" means "no go" in Spanish. Coors Beer translated its successful slogan "Turn it loose" from English to Spanish as "Drink Coors, get diarrhea." Exhibit 14.3 outlines some blunders that are hilarious to readers but *painful* to marketers, some of whom were fired because of these blunders.

In international marketing, country-of-origin effect refers to the positive or negative perception of firms and products from a certain country (first discussed in Chapter 10). Marketers have to decide whether to enhance or downplay such an effect. This can be very tricky. Disneyland Tokyo became popular in Japan because it played up its American image. But Disneyland Paris received relentless negative press coverage in France, because it insisted on its "wholesome American look." Singapore Airlines projects a "Singapore girl" image around the world. In contrast, Li Ning downplays its Chinese origin by using American NBA players in its commercials. What is the nationality of Häagen-Dazs ice cream?

EXHIBIT 14.3 | SOME BLUNDERS IN INTERNATIONAL MARKETING

EXHIBIT 14.3 | SOME BLUNDERS IN INTERNATIONAL MARKETING

▶ One US toymaker received numerous complaints from American mothers, because a talking doll told their children, "Kill mommy!" Made in Hong Kong, the dolls were shipped around the world. They carried messages in the language of the country of destination. A packing error sent some Spanish-speaking dolls to the United States. The message in Spanish "Quiero mommy!" means "I love mommy!" (This is also a supply chain blunder.)

▶ AT&T submitted a proposal to sell phone equipment in Thailand. Despite its excellent technology, the proposal was rejected out of hand by telecom authorities, because Thailand required a ten-year warranty but AT&T only offered a five-year warranty—thanks to standardization on warranty imposed by US headquarters.

▶ Japan's Olympia tried to market a photocopier to Latin America under the name "Roto." Sales were minimal. Why? "Roto" means "broken" in Spanish.

▶ Chinese exporters have marketed the following products overseas: White Elephant brand batteries, Sea Cucumber brand shirts, and Maxipuke brand poker cards (the two Chinese characters, *pu ke*, means poker, and the product should have been translated as Maxi brand poker cards—but its package said "Maxipuke").

Sources: Based on text in (1) T. Dalgic and R. Heijblom, "International marketing blunders revisited—some lessons for managers," *Journal of International Marketing* 4 (1996): 81–91; (2) D. Ricks, *Blunders in International Business*, 3rd ed. (Oxford, UK: Blackwell, 1999).

EXHIBIT 14.4 | SUPPLY CHAIN MANAGEMENT

If you thought Häagen-Dazs was a German, Austrian, or Belgium brand and had been happily paying a premium price for "European" ice cream, you were fooled. Häagen-Dazs is a US brand. Sometimes, multiple countries of origin are disclosed. For example, Apple stamped on the back of every iPhone: "Designed in California. Assembled in China." Some Toyota cars' dealer stickers disclose: "Made in USA. Engine made in Japan."

Overall, marketers need to experiment with a variety of configurations of the three Ps (product, price, and promotion) around the world in order to optimize the marketing mix (see In Focus). Next, we discuss the fourth P, place.

14-2 FROM DISTRIBUTION CHANNEL TO SUPPLY CHAIN MANAGEMENT

As the fourth P in the marketing mix, **place** refers to the location where products and services are provided (which now, of course, includes the online marketplace). Technically, place is also often referred to as the **distribution channel**—the set of firms that facilitates the movement of goods from producers to consumers. Until the 1980s, many producers made most goods in-house and one of the key concerns was distribution. Since then, production outsourcing has grown significantly. Many firms (such as Apple) do not physically produce their branded products at all. They rely on contract manufacturers (such as Foxconn) to get the job done. Other firms that still produce in-house (such as Dell and Boeing) rely on their suppliers to provide an increasingly higher percentage of the value added. Therefore, the new challenge is how to manage the longer distribution channel—more specifically, the distribution from suppliers (and contract manufacturers) all the way to consumers (see Exhibit 14.4).

Consequently, a new term, "supply chain," has been coined, and it has now almost replaced the old-fashioned "distribution channel." To be sure, the focal firm has always dealt with suppliers. Strategy guru Michael Porter labels this function as "inbound logistics" (and the traditional distribution channel as "outbound logistics").[7] In a broad sense, the new term "supply chain" is almost synonymous with "value chain,"

place The location where products and services are provided.

distribution channel The set of firms that facilitates the movement of goods from producers to consumers.

encompassing both inbound and outbound logistics (see Chapter 4). In the military, logistics is widely acknowledged as a contributor to wartime success. But no army recruitment material would brag about a glamorous career in logistics in the military to attract new soldiers. Similarly, business logistics tends to be tactical and lacks prestige. However, if supply chain is value chain, then supply chain management essentially handles the *entire* process of value creation, which is the core mission of the firm. Consequently, supply chain management has now taken on new strategic importance and gained tremendous prestige.

One indication that supply chain management has gained traction is that instead of being obscure players, leading supply chain management firms, such as Alibaba, Amazon, DHL, FedEx, and UPS, have now become household names. On any given day, 2% of the world's GDP can be found in UPS trucks and planes. "FedEx" has become a verb, and even live *whales* have reportedly been "FedExed." Modern supply chains aim to "get the right product to the right place at the right time—all the time."[8] Next, we discuss the triple As underpinning supply chains: (1) agility, (2) adaptability, and (3) alignment.

DARYL LANG/SHUTTERSTOCK.COM

14-3 | TRIPLE As IN SUPPLY CHAIN MANAGEMENT[9]

14-3a Agility

Agility refers to the ability to quickly react to unexpected shifts in supply and demand. To reduce inventory, many firms now use the trucks, ships, and planes of their suppliers and carriers as their warehouse. In their quest for supply chain speed, cost, and efficiency, many firms fail to realize the cost they have to pay for disregarding agility. Zara thrives in large part because of the agility of its supply chain (see In Focus). Zara's agility permeates throughout its entire operations, starting with design processes. As soon as designers spot certain trends, they create

agility The ability to react quickly to unexpected shifts in supply and demand.

adaptability The ability to change supply chain configurations in response to long-term changes in the environment and technology.

sketches and go ahead to order fabrics without finalizing designs. This speeds things up because fabric suppliers require a long lead time. Designs are finalized when stores receive reliable data. Production commences as soon as designs are complete. In addition, Zara's factories only run one shift, easily allowing for overtime production if demand calls for it. Its distribution centers are also highly efficient, allowing it to handle demand fluctuation without creating bottlenecks.

Agility may become more important in the 21st century, because shocks to supply chains are now more frequent. Recently, notable disruptions have included terrorist attacks (such as 9/11), civil wars (such as those in Syria and Ukraine), political unrest (such as Arab Spring, Hong Kong, and Libya), and natural disasters (such as Ebola, H1N1 swine flu, Icelandic volcano eruption, and Japanese earthquake).

Under shocks, an agile supply chain can rise to the challenge, while a static one can pull a firm down.[10] In 2000, Nokia and Ericsson fought in the mobile handset market. Consider how Nokia and Ericsson reacted differently to a fire caused by thunderstorm at a New Mexico factory of their handset chip supplier, Philips. The damage was minor, and Philips expected to resume production within a week. However, Nokia took no chances, and it quickly carried out design changes so that two other suppliers, one in Japan and another in the United States, could manufacture similar chips for Nokia. (These were the only two suppliers in the world other than Philips that were capable of delivering similar chips.) Nokia then quickly placed orders from these two suppliers. In contrast, Ericsson's supply chain had no such agility. Set up to function exclusively with the damaged Philips plant in New Mexico, it had no plan B. Unfortunately, Philips later found out that the damage was larger than first reported, and production would be delayed for months. By that time Ericsson scrambled to contact the other two suppliers, only to find out that Nokia had locked up all of their output for the next few months. The upshot? By 2001, Ericsson was driven out of the handset market as an independent player.

14-3b Adaptability

While agility focuses on flexibility that can overcome short-term fluctuation in the supply chain, **adaptability** refers to the ability to change supply chain configurations in response to long-term changes in the environment

IN FOCUS

Zara Excels in Marketing and Supply Chain Management

Zara is one of the hottest fashion chains. Founded in 1975, Zara's parent, Inditex, has become the world's largest apparel retailer. Since its initial public offering (IPO) in 2001, Inditex quadrupled its sales (to $19.1 billion or €13.8 billion) and profits. It doubled the number of its stores of eight brands, of which Zara contributes two-thirds of total sales. In this intensely competitive industry, Zara excels in both marketing and supply chain management. Zara succeeds by first breaking and then rewriting industry rules—also known as industry norms.

Rule number one: The origin of a fashion house usually carries some cachet. However, Zara does not hail from Italy or France—it is from Spain. Even within Spain, Zara is not based in a cosmopolitan city such as Barcelona or Madrid. It is headquartered in Arteixo, a town of only 25,000 people in a remote corner of northwestern Spain that a majority of this book's readers would have never heard of. Yet, Zara is active not only throughout Europe, but also in Asia and North America. Currently, the total number of stores is over 2,100 in 88 countries. Zara stores occupy some of the priciest top locations: Champs-Elysées in Paris, Fifth Avenue in New York, Galleria in Dallas, Ginza in Tokyo, Queen's Road Central in Hong Kong, and Huaihai Road in Shanghai.

Rule number two: Avoid stock-outs (a store running out of items in demand). Zara's answer? Occasional shortages contribute to an urge to buy now. With new items arriving at stores twice a week, experienced Zara shoppers know that "If you see something and don't buy it, you can forget about coming back for it because it will be gone." The small batch of merchandise during a short window of opportunity for purchasing motivates shoppers to visit Zara stores more frequently. In London, shoppers visit the average store four times a year, but frequent Zara 17 times. There is a good reason to do so: Zara makes about 20,000 items per year, about triple what Gap does. "At Gap, everything is the same," according to a Zara fan, "and buying from Zara, you'll never end up looking like someone else."

Rule number three: Bombarding shoppers with ads is a must. Gap and H&M spend on average 3% to 4% of their sales on ads. Zara begs to differ: it devotes just 0.3% of its sales to ads. The high traffic in the stores alleviates some needs for advertising in the media, most of which only serves as a reminder to visit the stores.

Rule number four: Outsource. Gap and H&M do not own any production facilities. However, outsourcing production (mostly to Asia) requires a long lead time, usually several months. Again, Zara has decisively deviated from the norm. By concentrating (more than half of) its production in-house (in Spain, Portugal, and Morocco), Zara has developed a super-responsive supply chain. It designs, produces, and delivers a new garment to its

VYTAUTAS KIELAITIS/SHUTTERSTOCK.COM

stores worldwide in a mere 15 days, a pace that is unheard of in the industry. The best speed the rivals can achieve is two months. Outsourcing may not necessarily be "low cost," because errors in prediction can easily lead to unsold inventory, forcing retailers to offer steep discounts. The industry average is to offer 40% discounts across all merchandise. In contrast, Zara sells more at full price, and when it discounts, it averages only 15%.

Rule number five: Strive for efficiency through large batches. In contrast, Zara intentionally deals with small batches. Because of its flexibility, Zara does not worry about "missing the boat" for a season. When new trends emerge, Zara can react quickly. It runs its supply chain like clockwork with a fast but predictable rhythm. Every store places orders on Tuesday/Wednesday and Friday/Saturday. Trucks and cargo flights run on established schedules—like a bus service. From Spain, shipments reach most European stores in 24 hours, North American stores in 48 hours, and Asian stores in 72 hours. Not only do store staff know exactly when shipments will arrive, but regular customers know that too, thus motivating them to check out the new merchandise more frequently on those days, which are known as "Z days" in some cities.

Zara has no shortage of competitors. Why has no one successfully copied its business model of "fast fashion"? "I would love to organize our business like Inditex [Zara's parent]," noted an executive from Gap, "but I would have to knock my company down and rebuild it from scratch." This does not mean Gap and other rivals are not trying to copy Zara. The question is how long it takes for rivals to out-Zara Zara.

Sources: "Zara's fast-fashion edge," *Bloomberg*, 14 November 2013: www.bloomberg.com; "Fashion conquistador," *BusinessWeek*, 4 September 2006: 38–39; "Fashion forward," *Economist*, 24 March 2012: 63–64; Inditex, "Presencia internacional," 2016, www.inditex.com; K. Ferdows, M. Lewis, and J. Machuca, "Rapid-fire fulfillment," *Harvard Business Review* (November 2004): 104–110; www.zara.com.

and technology. Enhancing adaptability often entails making a series of **make-or-buy decisions**.[11] This requires firms to *continuously* monitor major geopolitical, social, and technological trends, make sense of them, and reconfigure the supply chain accordingly. The damage for failing to do so may not be visible immediately, but across a number of years firms failing to do so may be selected out of market.

Consider Lucent, an American telecommunications equipment giant. In the 1990s, in response to competitive pressures from its rivals Alcatel and Siemens that benefited from low-cost, Asia-based production, Lucent successfully adapted its supply chain by phasing out more production in high-cost developed economies and setting up plants in China and Taiwan. However, Lucent then failed to adapt continuously. It concentrated its production in its own Asia-based plants, whereas rivals outsourced such manufacturing to Asian suppliers that became more capable of taking on more complex work. In other words, Lucent used foreign direct investment (FDI) to "make," whereas rivals adopted outsourcing to "buy." Ultimately, Lucent was stuck with its own relatively higher cost (although Asia-based) plants and was overwhelmed by rivals. By 2006, Lucent lost its independence and was acquired by its archrival Alcatel.

14-3c Alignment

Alignment refers to the alignment of interests of various players in the supply chain. In a broad sense, every supply chain is a strategic alliance involving a variety of players, each of which is a profit-maximizing, standalone firm.[12] As a result, conflicts are natural. However, players associated with one supply chain must effectively coordinate to achieve desirable outcomes. Therefore, this is a crucial dilemma. Supply chains that can better solve this dilemma may outperform other supply chains. For example, for Boeing's 787 Dreamliner, some 70% of the $8 billion development cost is outsourced to suppliers: Mitsubishi makes the wings, Messier-Dowty provides the landing gear, and so forth. Many suppliers are responsible for end-to-end design of whole subsections. Headed by a vice

MIROUNGA/SHUTTERSTOCK.COM

president for global partnerships, Boeing treats its suppliers as partners, has "partner councils" with regular meetings, and fosters long-term collaboration.

Conceptually, there are two key elements to achieve alignment: (1) power and (2) trust.[13] Not all players in a supply chain are equal, and more powerful players such as Boeing naturally exercise greater bargaining power.[14] Having a recognized leader exercising power, such as De Beers in diamonds, facilitates legitimacy and efficiency of the whole supply chain. Otherwise, supply chain members of more or less equal standing may end up engaging in excessive bargaining.

Trust stems from perceived fairness and justice from all supply chain members. While supply chains have become ever more complex, modern practices—such as low (or zero) inventory, frequent just-in-time (JIT) deliveries, and more geographic dispersion of production—have made all parties more vulnerable if the *weakest* link breaks down. This happened during the Japanese earthquake in 2011 and 2016. Therefore, it is in the best interest of all parties to invest in trust-building mechanisms in order to foster more collaboration.

For instance, Seven-Eleven Japan exercises a great deal of power by dictating that vendors resupply its 9,000 stores at three *specific* times a day. If a truck is late by more than 30 minutes, the vendor has to pay a penalty equal to the gross margin of the products carried to the store. This may seem harsh, but it is necessary. This is because Seven-Eleven Japan staff reconfigure store shelves three times a day to cater to different consumers at different *hours*, such as commuters in the morning and school kids in the afternoon—time, literally, means money. However, Seven-Eleven Japan softens the blow by trusting its vendors. It does not verify the contents of deliveries. This allows vendors to save time and money, because after deliveries, truck drivers do not have to wait for verification and can immediately move on to make other trips. The alignment of interest of such a supply chain is legendary. Hours after the earthquake in March 2011, when relief trucks moved at two miles per hour (if they moved at all) on the damaged roads, Seven-Eleven Japan's vendors went the extra mile by deploying helicopters and motorcycles to deliver much-needed food and supplies to the devastated region.

Sometimes, introducing a neutral intermediary (middleman)—more specifically, **third-party logistics (3PL) providers**—may more effectively align the interests in the supply chain. In the case of outsourcing in Asia, buyers (importers) tend to be large Western MNEs such as Gap, Nike, and Marks & Spencer, and suppliers

make-or-buy decision The decision on whether to produce in-house ("make") or to outsource ("buy").

alignment Alignment of interests of various players.

third-party logistics (3PL) provider A neutral, third-party intermediary in the supply chain that provides logistics and other support services.

(exporters) are often smaller Asian manufacturers. Despite best intentions, both sides may still distrust each other.[15] MNE buyers are not sure of the quality and timeliness of delivery. Further, MNE buyers are unable to control labor practices in supplier factories, some of which may be dubious (such as running "sweatshops"). In the 1990s, Nike's reputation took a severe hit due to alleged questionable labor practices at its supplier factories. However, suppliers may also be suspicious. Since most contracts for shoes, clothing, toys, and electronics are written several months ahead, suppliers are not confident about MNE buyers' ability to forecast demand correctly. Suppliers thus worry that in case of lower-than-anticipated demand, buyers may reject shipments to reduce excess inventory, by opportunistically citing excuses such as labor practices or quality issues. One solution lies in the involvement of 3PL intermediaries, such as Hong Kong-based Li & Fung. Overall, 3PL firms may add value by aligning the interests of all parties.

14-4 HOW INSTITUTIONS AND RESOURCES AFFECT MARKETING AND SUPPLY CHAIN MANAGEMENT

Having outlined the basic features of marketing and supply chain management, let us now use the institution-based and resource-based views to shed additional light on these topics (Exhibit 14.5).

14-4a Institutions, Marketing, and Supply Chain Management

As an important form of institutions, formal rules of the game obviously have a significant impact. Most countries impose restrictions, ranging from taboos in advertising to constraints on the equity level held by foreign retailers and 3PL providers. Germany bans advertising that portrays another product as inferior. Goodyear Tire exported to Germany a successful commercial used in the United States, by showing that its tire

cord could break a steel chain. Because the commercial was viewed as insulting the German steel chain manufacturers, the German government banned it. China forbids foreign retailers from operating wholly owned stores and only approves joint-venture (JV) stores. In China, France's Carrefour is the most aggressive foreign retailer, with sales ahead of Walmart. In some cities, Carrefour struck sweetheart deals with officials and operated wholly owned stores, which eventually provoked Beijing's wrath. The upshot? Carrefour was forced to sell a portion of its equity to Chinese partners and convert its wholly owned stores to JV stores to be in compliance with regulations.

Informal rules also place significant constraints on marketing and supply chain management (see Debate). In marketing, most of the blunders documented in Exhibit 14.3 happen due to firms' failure to appreciate the deep underlying differences in cultures, languages, and norms—all part of the informal institutions. In supply chains, leading firms headquartered in developed economies may be able to diffuse leading-edge practices. In the 1990s, as a new norm, many European firms adopted the ISO 9000 series of quality management systems. They then imposed the standard on their suppliers and partners throughout the world. Over time, these suppliers and partners spread ISO 9000 to other domestic firms. At present, over 560,000 sites in over 150 countries have been ISO 9000 certified. In other words, due to the normative influence, suppliers and partners that export goods and services to a particular country in a supply chain may

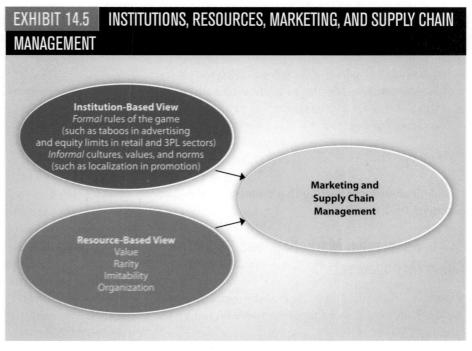

EXHIBIT 14.5 INSTITUTIONS, RESOURCES, MARKETING, AND SUPPLY CHAIN MANAGEMENT

Institution-Based View
Formal rules of the game
(such as taboos in advertising
and equity limits in retail and 3PL sectors)
Informal cultures, values, and norms
(such as localization in promotion)

Resource-Based View
Value
Rarity
Imitability
Organization

Marketing and Supply Chain Management

Debate: IKEA's Marketing Challenge in Saudi Arabia

Emerging Markets/Ethical Dilemma

In October 2012, Swedish furniture company IKEA was criticized on the BBC World Service radio for airbrushing women out of IKEA's catalogs distributed in Saudi Arabia. Some women's rights activists throughout Europe and around the world were outraged. They threatened to boycott IKEA stores in Europe, especially in Sweden. IKEA felt pressured to issue an apology, stating that the marketing catalog was inconsistent with its culture and did not reflect its approach to equality of women in society. In its own words:

We should have reacted and realized that excluding women from the Saudi Arabian version of the catalogue is in conflict with the IKEA Group values.

What went wrong? From the perspective of a marketing manager of the IKEA store in Saudi Arabia, the decision seemed to be straightforward: to distribute a catalog, it needed to comply with the law of the land. Any picture of women who were not totally covered would be illegal, per Saudi Arabia censorship rules. IKEA had operated in Saudi Arabia for 30 years. It possessed significant knowledge about the do's and don'ts in the local institutional framework.

A particularly "offensive" picture that circulated throughout the world media had a man helping two children in the bathroom. Nothing wrong you may think. Except in the original version provided by IKEA headquarters, there was a woman standing in the middle, helping one of the kids. When the two versions were viewed side by side, it appeared that the woman had been erased (or Photoshopped out). This act was fingered as condoning what many Europeans consider the suppression of women in Saudi society.

One of the basic points in international marketing is the need to adapt products and marketing strategies to local contexts. Given that Saudi Arabia censorship rules dictated that using the original Swedish pictures would not be an option, editing the pictures became inevitable. Most pictures in advertising are heavily Photoshopped anyway. One side of the debate argues: What's wrong?

Another side of the debate claims that what the Saudi marketing manager overlooked—and what IKEA as a multinational organization overlooked—was an ethical challenge of an interconnected world. Local practices must also be acceptable to stakeholders back home—even though they may not understand the local context and why local institutions (in this case, formal censorship regulations) would not accept the original pictures. How would *you* participate in this debate?

Sources: BBC WorldService, Radio broadcast, 2 October 2012; "No women please, we're Saudi Arabian IKEA," *The Guardian*, 2 October 2012; M. W. Peng and K. E. Meyer, *International Business*, 2nd ed. (London: Cengage EMEA, 2016): 283–284.

---

be simultaneously *importing* that country's norms and practices.

14-4b Resources, Marketing, and Supply Chain Management

Shown in Exhibit 14.5, we can evaluate marketing and supply chain management activities based on the VRIO criteria.

VALUE Do these activities add *value*?[16] Marketers now increasingly scratch their heads, as traditional media are losing viewers, readers, and thus effectiveness. But marketers do not have a good handle on how advertising in the new online media adds value.[17] As the first cohort to grow up Internet savvy, today's teens and twenty-somethings in many countries flock to social networks such as Facebook, Twitter, and their equivalents around the world. What is challenging is how marketers can reach such youth.[18] A basic threat to such social networks is the whim of their users, whose interest in certain topics and networks themselves may change or even evaporate overnight.

RARITY Managers need to assess the *rarity* of marketing and supply chain activities. If all rival firms use FedEx to manage logistics (which does add value), these activities, in themselves, are not rare. In supply chain management, first movers in radio frequency identification (RFID) tags may derive benefits, because they are rare. However, as RFID becomes more available, its rarity (novelty value) will drop. Capabilities to operate e-commerce platforms are valuable, but not rare. Capabilities to fill every order in a metropolitan city such as Shanghai in less than three hours would be rare—a goal Yihaodian is endeavoring to attain (see Closing Case).

INIMITABILITY Having identified valuable and rare capabilities, managers need to assess how likely it is for rivals and partners to *imitate*. While there is no need to waste more ink on the necessity to watch out for rivals, firms also need to be careful about partners in the supply chain. As more Western MNEs outsource production to suppliers (or, using new jargon, contract manufacturers), it is always possible that some of the aggressive contract manufacturers may bite the hand that feeds them by directly imitating and competing with Western MNEs. This is not necessarily "opportunism." It is natural for ambitious contract manufacturers such as Foxconn and Flextronics to flex their muscle. While it is possible to imitate and acquire world-class manufacturing capabilities, marketing prowess and brand power are more intangible and thus harder to imitate. Thus, Western MNEs often cope by (1) being careful about what they outsource and (2) strengthening customer loyalty to their brands (such as Apple) to fend off contract manufacturers.

ORGANIZATION Managers need to ask: Is our firm *organizationally* ready to accomplish our objectives? Oddly, in many firms, Marketing and Sales functions do not get along well—to avoid confusion, here we use the two terms with capital letters, "Marketing" and "Sales," to refer to these functions. When revenues are disappointing, the blame game begins: Marketing blames Sales for failing to execute a brilliant plan, and Sales blames Marketing for setting the price too high and burning too much cash in high-flying but useless commercials. Marketing staff tend to be better educated, more analytical, and more disappointed when certain initiatives fail. Sales people are often "street smart," persuasive, and used to rejections all the time. It is not surprising that Marketing and Sales have a hard time working together.[19] Yet, work together they must. Some leading firms have disbanded Marketing and Sales as separate functions and have created an integrated function—called Channel Enablement at IBM.

14-5 MANAGEMENT SAVVY

What determines the success and failure in marketing and supply chain management? The institution-based view points out the impact of formal and informal rules of the game. In a nonmarket economy (think of North Korea), marketing would be irrelevant. In a world with high trade and investment barriers, globe-trotting DHL, FedEx, and UPS jets would be unimaginable. The resource-based view argues that holding institutions constant, firms such as Aflac (see Opening Case), IKEA (see Debate), Yihaodian (see Closing Case), and Zara (see In Focus) that develop the best capabilities in marketing and supply chain management will emerge as winners.[20]

Consequently, three implications for action emerge (Exhibit 14.6). First, marketers and supply chain managers need to know the rules of the game inside and out in order to craft savvy responses. For instance, given the limitations of formal regulatory frameworks in prosecuting cross-border credit card crimes, many US e-commerce firms refuse to ship to overseas addresses. Legitimate overseas purchasers are, in turn, denied business. As online shopping became a more widespread informal norm, FedEx acquired Kinkos (which was turned into FedEx Office stores), and UPS took over Mail Boxes (which was turned into UPS Stores). E-commerce firms can now ship to the US addresses of FedEx Offices and UPS Stores, and FedEx and UPS can then forward products to the overseas purchasers from these stores. This is but one example of superb problem solving in the face of cumbersome formal rules and changing informal norms.

Second, in marketing, focus on the four Ps. This obviously is a cliché. However, in international marketing, managers need to do all it takes to avoid costly and embarrassing blunders (see Exhibit 14.3). Remember:

EXHIBIT 14.6 IMPLICATIONS FOR ACTION

▸ Know the formal and informal rules of the game on marketing and supply chain management inside and out.

▸ In marketing, focus on product, price, promotion, and place (the four Ps) and do all it takes to avoid blunders.

▸ In supply chain management, focus on agility, adaptability, and alignment (the triple As).

despite their magnitude, blunders are *avoidable* mistakes. At the very least, international marketers should try very hard to avoid being written up as blunders in a new edition of this textbook.

Finally, in supply chain management, focus on the triple As. This is not a cliché, as the idea was just published a few years ago. Not aware of the importance of the triple As, many firms would only deliver container loads to minimize the number of deliveries and freight costs. When demand for a particular product suddenly rises, these firms often fail to react quickly—they have to wait until the container (or sometimes even the whole container *ship*) is full. Such a "best" practice typically delays shipment by a week or more, forcing stock-outs in stores that disappoint consumers. When firms eventually ship container loads, they often result in excess inventory because most buyers do not need a full container load. To get rid of such inventory, as much as a third of the merchandise carried by department stores ends up in sales. Such discounts not only destroy profits for every firm in the supply chain, but also undermine brand equity by upsetting consumers who recently bought the discounted items at full price. In contrast, the triple As urge savvy supply chain managers to focus on agility, adaptability, and alignment of interests of the entire chain.

EMERGING MARKETS
Closing Case: Online Shop Number One

Online shopping has become the new normal in urban China. Rather than heading for a local supermarket, many consumers in Shanghai turn to the Web, click, and pay—a few hours later, a deliveryman on motorcycle comes to drop a box of food, household goods, or the latest fashion at the doorstep. Why carry home a crate of beer from the supermarket, and then up to the 20th floor? Let the deliveryman do it for you! A revolution in retailing is under way.

One of the latest entrants into the market is Yihaodian, which is literally translated "Number-One Shop." Founded in 2008, it became the third largest online retailer in China—after Alibaba and JD.com. It was founded by Gang Yu, a Chinese-American returnee who had been a professor of logistics at the University of Texas at Austin and who had managed Asia Pacific supply chains for Dell and Amazon.

In 2008, Yihaodian started with food, beverages, and household goods. In 2009, it expanded into cosmetics and consumer electronics. Clothing was its latest offering. The growth has been spectacular. In 2009, Yihaodian celebrated receiving 1,000 orders an hour. By 2014, that number increased to 300,000–400,000.

Between 2010 and 2015, the number of product items carried grew from 50,000 to eight million, and the number of registered customers from four million to 100 million. At present, it operates over 200 distribution centers in 40 cities throughout China, and employs 10,000 people, mainly in the "last mile" delivery.

Yihaodian's strategy is supported by the latest marketing and supply chain management practices. The company does all its technological development in-house, and controls its information systems, including supplier relationships, warehouse management, and delivery stations. One-tenth of its employees are IT engineers. In the central control room,

16 screens allow managers to track online traffic in real time, by region and by category. For example, one screen displays a word cloud with the keywords most frequently entered in the search engine on Yihaodian's website in the last minute. Such tools enable the "instant" capturing of new consumer trends and the targeting of consumers far more precisely than in traditional retail outlets. This includes consumers on the move. With the spread of smartphones and tablets in China, the mobile sector has become an important part of e-commerce, accounting for 10% of all e-commerce in 2013 and predicted to reach 30% in 2018.

In 2011, Walmart acquired 51% of the equity of Yihaodian, but the two companies operated largely independently—apart from cooperating in sourcing and supply management. Both believed they could learn from each other. Walmart had long been famous for its capabilities in supply chain management, yet it had not been successful in translating that expertise to e-commerce. Yihaodian thus became a source of new ideas and inspirations. At one meeting, Walmart executives shared their ambition to fill every order in two *days* in the next two years. Yihaodian executives laughed at this idea. Their ambition was to fill every order in Shanghai in three *hours*. Yihaodian has not attained this goal yet, but it is close. In part, this capability stems from high urban population density and relatively cheap "last mile" delivery using an army of deliverymen on electric motorcycles. Yet, it is enabled by groundbreaking new technologies that analyze mountains of data and coordinate numerous players in a vast supply chain. So impressed was Walmart that in 2015, it went ahead to acquire all the remaining 49% of the shares of Yihaodian at $760 million. "Yihaodian will continue operating under its existing name and will maintain its focus on having strong local leadership with a clear understanding of the needs of online consumers in China," according to a Walmart press release announcing the acquisition. Walmart's faith in Yihaodian was short-lived, however. The US retailer sold its entire stake in Yihaodian to JD.com in June 2016. The deal was valued at $1.5 billion.

Case Discussion Questions

1. What does it take to run a successful e-commerce business in China, in the face of strong competitors such as Alibaba and JD.com?

2. What are the most impressive resources and capabilities in marketing and supply chain management that Yihaodian possesses to attract Walmart?

3. In the competition for the "last mile" delivery in urban China, why was Yihaodian so outstanding, and Walmart was lackluster?

Sources: Author's interviews; M. W. Peng and K. E. Meyer, *International Business*, 2nd ed. (London: Cengage EMEA, 2016): 488–489; Walmart, "Walmart acquires remaining shares to take full ownership of Yihaodian e-commerce business in China," 23 July 2015: corporate.walmart.com; www.yhd.com.

STUDY TOOLS 14

LOCATED AT THE BACK OF YOUR BOOK:

☐ Rip out and study the Chapter Review Card at the end of the book

LOG IN TO WWW.CENGAGEBRAIN.COM TO:

☐ Review key term flashcards

☐ Complete a practice quiz to test your knowledge of key concepts

☐ View animated PengAtlas Maps

☐ Complete interactive content, watch chapter videos, and take a graded quiz

☐ Track your knowledge of key concepts in Global Business

☐ Read and discuss additional case study content

15 Managing Corporate Social Responsibility Globally

 VLADIMIR BOROZENETS/SHUTTERSTOCK.COM

LEARNING OBJECTIVES

After studying this chapter, you will be able to . . .

15-1 Articulate a stakeholder view of the firm.

15-2 Apply the institution-based and resource-based views to analyze corporate social responsibility.

15-3 Identify three ways you can manage corporate social responsibility.

After you finish
this chapter, go to

PAGE 247 for

STUDY TOOLS

Opening Case: Foxconn

Until 2010, the vast majority of end users of Apple iPhones and iPads, Hewlett-Packard laptops, Amazon Kindles, and Microsoft Xboxes around the world had no clue about the firm that manufactured their beloved gadgets. The firm is Foxconn, which is headquartered in Taipei, Taiwan. Foxconn's shares (under the name of Hon Hai) are not only listed in Taipei on the Taiwan World Stock Exchange (TWSE: 2317), but also in Hong Kong (SEHK: 2038), London (LSE: HHPD), and NASDAQ (HNHPF). With US$132 billion in annual revenue, Foxconn is the global leader in contract manufacturing services. In other words, everybody has heard that leading firms such as Cisco, Dell, Ericsson, Intel, Motorola, Nintendo, Nokia, and Sony—in addition to those named in the first four lines of this box above—have outsourced a large chunk of their manufacturing to "low-cost producers." But to *whom*? Prior to 2010, only a small number of people knew the answer: Foxconn has been scooping up a tremendous number of outsourcing orders.

Starting in 1975 in Taipei with a meager $7,500, Foxconn was founded by Taiwanese entrepreneur Terry Gou, who still serves as its chairman. As Foxconn became a giant, industry insiders knew and respected it. But outside the industry, Foxconn lived in relative obscurity. It is likely to be the largest firm many people around the world never heard of. Just how big is Foxconn? Worldwide, it has 1.3 million employees. In China alone, it employs over 900,000 workers (300,000 on one factory campus in Shenzhen). To put these mind-boggling numbers in perspective, its worldwide headcount is as large as the entire US military, and its headcount in China is three times the size of the Taiwanese military. In addition to China, Foxconn has factories in 11 countries: Brazil, the Czech Republic, Hungary, India, Japan, Malaysia, Mexico, Pakistan, Slovakia, South Korea, and the United States. Foxconn is the largest private employer and the largest exporter in China and the second largest exporter in the Czech Republic.

In 2010, Foxconn stumbled into media spotlight, not because of its accomplishments, but because of a dozen suicides committed by employees in Shenzhen, China, in a span of several months. Most of them died by jumping from high-rise Foxconn dormitories. This was one of the biggest paradoxes associated with Foxconn. What were Foxconn's secrets for being so successful? Just as when 100 years ago Henry Ford created the mass assembly line by standardizing each worker's job, Foxconn pioneered a business model that it called e-enabled Components, Modules, Moves, and Services (eCMMS) that helped its clients save a ton of money. But why were there so many worker suicides that shocked the world? The business model was certainly a culprit. Working at Foxconn demands a great deal of concentration and repetition, which breeds enormous stress. *Bloomberg Businessweek* described Gou as "a ruthless taskmaster."

Although the media and corporate social responsibility (CSR) gurus criticized Foxconn for treating workers like machines and exploiting cheap labor, there was no evidence—according to audits run by Apple and other clients as well as the Chinese government—that Foxconn mistreated or abused employees. Instead, in China, labor watchdogs gave Foxconn credit for exceeding the norms, by paying workers (relatively) higher salaries, on time, and for overtime. In both 2005 and 2006, it was among the Best Employers in China, according to a ChinaHR.com poll. In response to the suicides, Foxconn in 2010 installed nets outside dormitories to prevent suicides, and increased Shenzhen factory workers' pay by 30% to an average of $176 a month. Such raises cut earnings per share by about 5% in 2010 and by 12% in 2011. As a result, Gou recently scaled back his annual growth target from 30% to 15%.

Given Apple's "green" image, it reportedly entertained the notion of dropping Foxconn as a supplier, which had spilled some "blood" on pristine iPhones and iPads. But Apple quickly and quietly dropped this idea, which would be suicidal—thanks to Foxconn's unrivaled bargaining power. Foxconn, for its part, promised to beef up CSR. Virtually all workers in Shenzhen were away from their families and friends. Just across the border from Hong Kong, Shenzhen itself was a "new" city that became a boomtown since the 1980s. Although Shenzhen now has more than ten million people, it had a trivial population before the economic reforms took off. Practically no twenty-somethings or thirty-somethings were raised in Shenzhen. They all came to Shenzhen in search of jobs. A majority of such migrant workers (who were known as "low-cost" laborers in the West) came from poor inland provinces. Thanks to the loneliness and boredom, some of the most depressed employees ended up killing themselves. Wouldn't it be better if Foxconn could set up factories in inland provinces so that workers would stay close to their families and friends instead of migrating over a long distance to work in Shenzhen? Hopefully, not many of them would commit suicide, which would be very embarrassing to Foxconn and Apple. Because cost of living in Shenzhen rose sharply, it recently became a high-cost city in China. So moving some production inland would also help Foxconn reduce labor costs.

As a result, Foxconn recently constructed a huge new factory in Zhengzhou, Henan province, which is one of the poorest provinces south of Beijing and a major source of migrant workers. This major undertaking also earned CSR kudos from the Chinese government, which encouraged more multinationals to invest in inland, underdeveloped regions such as Henan. Now with 120,000 employees, Foxconn's Zhengzhou factory made your iPhone 6. While no worker suicide or other incidents were reported in Zhengzhou, Foxconn for the first time also installed a large number of robots—known as Foxbots—to handle repetitive work. Robots can break down, but they will never commit suicide.

In May 2016, Foxconn fired 60,000 employees in China, citing progress in automation. In its press release, Foxconn noted, "We will continue to harness automation and manpower in our manufacturing operations, and we expect to maintain our significant workforce in China."

Sources: "Foxconn replaces 60,000 factory workers with robots," BBC News, 25 May 2016: www.bbc.com; "Chairman Gou," *Bloomberg Businessweek*, 13 September 2010: 58–69; "How to beat the high cost of happy workers," *Bloomberg Businessweek*, 9 May 2011: 39–40; W. Su, 2014, "Foxconn," in M. W. Peng, *Global Business*, 3rd ed. (Boston: Cengage, 2014) 595–597; W. Su, M. W. Peng, W. Tan, and Y. Cheung, "The signaling effect of corporate social responsibility in emerging economies," *Journal of Business Ethics* 134 (2015): 479–491; www.foxconn.com.

Why were Foxconn and Apple so embarrassed by worker suicides? Why was having designed and produced highly popular products such as iPhones and iPads not enough? What else were Foxconn and Apple expected to do? This chapter helps you answer these and other questions. **Corporate social responsibility (CSR)** refers to "consideration of, and response to, issues beyond the narrow economic, technical, and legal requirements of the firm to accomplish social benefits along with the traditional economic gains which the firm seeks."[1] Historically, CSR issues have been on the back burner for many managers, but these issues are now increasingly being brought to the forefront of corporate agendas.[2] While this chapter is the last in this book, by no means do we suggest that CSR is the least important topic. Instead, we believe that this chapter is one of the best ways to *integrate* all previous chapters concerning international trade, investment, strategy, and human resources. The comprehensive nature of CSR is evident in our Opening Case.

At the heart of CSR is the concept of **stakeholder**, which is any group or individual who can affect or is affected by a firm's actions. Shown in Exhibit 15.1, shareholders are important but are not the only group of stakeholders. Other groups include managers, non-managerial employees (hereafter "employees"), suppliers, customers, communities, governments, and social and environmental groups. This chapter focuses on *non-shareholder stakeholders*, which we call "stakeholders" here for simplicity. A leading debate on CSR is whether managers' efforts to promote the interests of these other stakeholders are at odds with their fiduciary duty to safeguard shareholder interests. To the extent that firms are *not* social agencies and that their primary function is to serve as economic enterprises, it is certainly true that firms should not (and are not able to) take on all of the social problems of the world. However, failing to heed certain CSR imperatives may be self-defeating in the long run (see Closing Case).

The remainder of this chapter first introduces a stakeholder view of the firm. Next, we discuss how the institution-based and resource-based views inform the CSR discussion. Finally, we consider how savvy managers can best manage CSR.

15-1 A STAKEHOLDER VIEW OF THE FIRM

15-1a A Big Picture Perspective

A stakeholder view of the firm represents a big picture. A key goal for CSR is **global sustainability**, which is defined as the ability to meet the needs of the present without compromising the ability of future generations to meet their needs. It not only refers to a sustainable social and natural environment, but also sustainable capitalism. Globally, the urgency of sustainability in the 21st century is driven by at least three concerns. First, increasing population, poverty, and inequity require new solutions. The repeated protests, chaos, and terrorist attacks around the world are but the tip of the iceberg of antiglobalization sentiments. Second, the relative power of national governments has eroded in the wake of globalization, but the influence of nongovernmental organizations (NGOs) and other civil society stakeholders has increased. Finally, industrialization has created some irreversible effects on the environment. Global warming, air and water pollution, soil erosion, deforestation, and overfishing have become problems that demand creative solutions (see In Focus). Because firms contribute to many of these problems, many citizens believe that firms should also take on at least some responsibility for solving them.

corporate social responsibility (CSR) Consideration of, and response to, issues beyond the narrow economic, technical, and legal requirements of the firm to accomplish social benefits along with the traditional economic gains that the firm seeks.

stakeholder Any group or individual who can affect or is affected by a firm's actions.

global sustainability The ability to meet the needs of the present without compromising the ability of future generations to meet their needs around the world.

EXHIBIT 15.1 A STAKEHOLDER VIEW OF THE FIRM

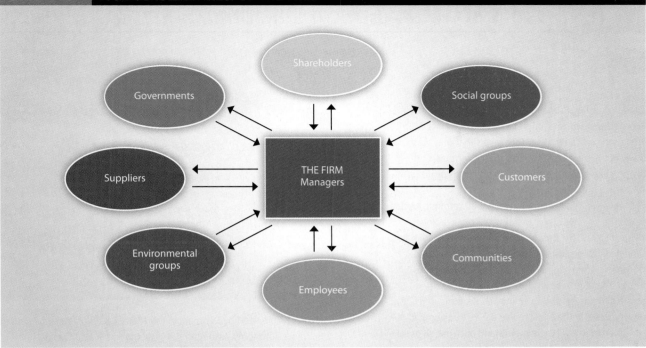

Source: T. Donaldson and L. Preston, "The stakeholder theory of the corporation: Concepts, evidence, and implications," *Academy of Management Review* 20 (1995): 69.

Drivers underpinning global sustainability are complex and multidimensional. This bewilderingly complex big picture forces managers to *prioritize*. To be able to do that, primary and secondary stakeholders must be identified (see Opening Case).

15-1b Primary and Secondary Stakeholder Groups

Primary stakeholder groups are constituents on which the firm relies for its continuous survival and prosperity. Primary stakeholders typically refer to shareholders, managers, employees, suppliers, customers, and governments and communities whose laws and regulations must be obeyed and to whom taxes and other obligations may be due.

Secondary stakeholder groups are groups or individuals who can indirectly affect or are indirectly affected by a firm's actions. Examples include environmental groups (such as Greenpeace) and labor practice groups (such as Fair Labor Association). While firms do not depend on secondary stakeholder groups for survival, such groups may have the potential to cause significant embarrassment and damage. Think of Nike in the 1990s.

A key proposition of the stakeholder view is that firms should not simply pursue the economic bottom line (such as profits and shareholder returns). Instead, firms should pursue a more balanced **triple bottom line**,

consisting of *economic, social,* and *environmental* performances that simultaneously satisfy the demands of all stakeholder groups. To the extent that some competing demands obviously exist, it seems evident that the CSR proposition represents a dilemma (see Opening Case and Closing Case). In fact, it has provoked a fundamental debate, which is introduced next.

15-1c The Fundamental Debate on CSR

The CSR debate centers on the nature of the firm in society. Why does the firm exist? Most people would intuitively answer: "to make money." Milton Friedman was a former University of Chicago economist and a Nobel laureate who passed away in 2006. In an influential article published in 1970, he eloquently suggested: "The business of business is business."[3] The idea that the firm is an economic enterprise seems to be uncontroversial. At issue is whether the firm is *only* an economic enterprise.

primary stakeholder group Constituent on which a firm relies for its continuous survival and prosperity.

secondary stakeholder group Group or individual who can indirectly affect or are indirectly affected by a firm's actions.

triple bottom line Economic, social, and environmental performance that simultaneously satisfies the demands of all stakeholder groups.

IN FOCUS: Ethical Dilemma/Emerging Markets

Global Warming and Arctic Boom

Global warming is one of the most dreadful terms in recent times. Hotter summers. Longer droughts. More frequent hurricanes. Rising sea levels that may wash away many island nations and coastal regions. Can anyone like global warming? Can any firms profit from it? It turns out: plenty.

As a stunning illustration of global warming, Arctic sea ice has lost half of its area since record keeping began in 1979. The Intergovernmental Panel on Climate Change (IPCC) predicted that Arctic summers would become ice-free beginning in 2070. Other estimates moved the date to around 2035. Instead of being terrified by such warming, many people, firms, and governments in the Arctic region are excited about it.

BIGROLOIMAGES/SHUTTERSTOCK.COM

Two sources of excitement stand out. First, ships sailing between the Pacific Ocean and the Atlantic Ocean can go through the Arctic Ocean. The distance between Shanghai and Rotterdam can be shortened by 15% if ships use the Northwest Passage going through the Canadian Arctic Archipelago and by 22% if ships sail through the Northeast Passage, which the Russians call the Northern Sea Route (NSR), by hugging the northern Siberian coast. An expert noted that "the Arctic stands to become a central passageway for global maritime transportation, just as it already is for aviation." It is likely to become "an emerging epicenter of industry and trade akin to the Mediterranean Sea." While Canada and Russia look forward to profiting from maritime services such as refueling and pilotage, "such cities as Anchorage and Reykjavik could someday become major shipping centers and financial capitals—the high-latitude equivalents of Singapore and Dubai."

Second, the melting north can unearth tremendous oil and mineral wealth in the Arctic region. Canada, Norway, Russia, and the United States have all recently opened more of their Arctic offshore to oil exploration. Although Greenland only has 60,000 people, it is the world's largest island and its area is larger than all of Western Europe. Global warming not only means mining riches, but also Greenland's ultimate freedom: independence.

Colonized by Denmark in the 1700s, Greenland in 2009 gained more autonomy, assuming self-government in all affairs except foreign affairs and defense. Denmark provided Greenland an annual grant of 3.6 billion Danish kroner ($660 million), which is roughly a quarter of Greenland's GDP and close to half of the government budget. Both sides agreed to split revenue from oil, gas, and minerals until Greenland could earn enough so that it would not need the subsidy, which meant $12,000 for every Greenlander. Then Greenland can gain its full independence. The Greenlandic government thus has been eager to grant permissions for energy and mining companies to explore the underground and offshore riches. For example, an Australian company called Greenland Minerals and Energy has been developing Greenland's first open pit uranium and rare earth mine. However, some environmentalists and traditionalists are not happy with such development.

Overall, how to strike the right balance between exploitation and environmentalism is not only a challenge for Greenland, but also for all the communities, firms, and governments that aspire to take advantage of the coming Arctic boom.

Sources: "Drill sergeant," *Bloomberg Businessweek*, 5 May 2014: 62–67; S. Borgerson, "The coming Arctic boom," *Foreign Affairs*, July 2013: 76–89; "The melting north," *Economist*, 16 June 2012 (special report): 3–5; "Short and sharp," *Economist*, 16 June 2012 (special report): 14–15; "The Arctic: Not so cool," *Economist*, 3 January 2015: 51–52.

One side of the debate argues that "the social responsibility of business is to increase its profits." In fact, that is the title of Friedman's 1970 article. The free market school of thought goes back to Adam Smith's idea that pursuit of economic self-interest (within legal and ethical bounds) leads to efficient markets. Free market advocates such as Friedman believe that the firm's first and foremost stakeholder group is the shareholders, and managers have a fiduciary duty (required by law) to look after shareholder interests. To the extent that the hallmark of our economic system remains capitalism, the providers of capital—namely, capitalists or shareholders—deserve a commanding height in managerial attention. In fact, since the 1980s, the idea of *shareholder capitalism* has explicitly placed shareholders as the single most important stakeholder group and has become increasingly influential around the world.

Free market advocates argue that if firms attempt to attain social goals such as providing employment and social welfare, managers will lose their focus on profit maximization (and its derivative, shareholder value maximization). Consequently, firms may lose their character as capitalistic enterprises and become *socialist* organizations. The idea of a socialist organization is not a pure argumentative point. It is derived from accurate characterization of numerous state-owned enterprises (SOEs) throughout the pre-reform Soviet Union, Central and Eastern Europe, and China as well as other developing countries in Africa, Asia, and Latin America. Privatization, in essence, removes the social function of SOEs and restores their economic focus through private ownership. Overall, the free market school has provided much of the intellectual underpinning for globalization spearheaded by multinational enterprises (MNEs).

It is against such a formidable and influential school of thought that the CSR movement has emerged. A free market system is, in theory, constrained by rules, contracts, and property rights. But CSR advocates argue that in practice, a free market system that takes the pursuit of self-interest and profit as its guiding light may fail to constrain itself, thus often breeding greed, excesses, and abuses (see Debate). Firms and managers, if left to their own devices, may choose self-interest over public interest. The financial meltdown in 2008–2009 is often fingered as a case in point. While not denying that shareholders are important stakeholders, CSR advocates argue that all stakeholders have an *equal* right to bargain for a fair deal. Given stakeholders' often conflicting demands, a very thorny issue in the debate is whether all stakeholders indeed have an equal right and how to manage their (sometimes inevitable) conflicts (see Opening Case and Closing Case).

Starting in the 1970s as a peripheral voice in an ocean of free market believers, the CSR school of thought has slowly but surely become a more central part of management discussions. There are two driving forces. First, even as free markets spread around the world, the gap between the haves and have-nots has *widened*. While 2% of the world's children who live in America enjoy 50% of the world's toys, one-quarter of the children in Bangladesh and Nigeria are in the workforces of these two countries. Even within developed economies such as the United States, the income gap between the upper and lower echelons of society has widened. In 1980, the average American CEO was paid 40 times more than the average worker. The ratio is now above 400. Although American society accepts greater income inequality than many others do, aggregate data of such widening inequality, which both inform and numb, often serve as a stimulus for reforming a leaner and meaner capitalism. Such sentiments have become especially strong since the Great Recession of 2008–2009. However, the response from free market advocates is that to the extent there is competition, there will always be *both* winners and losers. What CSR critics describe as "greed" is often translated as "incentive" in the vocabulary of free market advocates.

Second, disasters and scandals also drive the CSR movement. In 2001–2002, scandals at Enron, World-Com, Royal Ahold, and Parmalat rocked the world. In 2008–2009, excessive amounts of Wall Street bonuses distributed by financial services firms receiving government bailout funds were criticized of being socially

Nobel Prize-winning economist Milton Friedman eloquently suggested that "The business of business is business."

BROOKS KRAFT/GETTY IMAGES

Debate: Race to the Bottom ("Pollution Haven") versus Race to the Top

Emerging Markets/Ethical Dilemma

One side of this debate argues that because of heavier environmental regulation in developed economies, multinational enterprises (MNEs) may shift pollution-intensive production to developing countries with lower environmental standards. To attract investment, developing countries may enter a "race to the bottom" by lowering (or at least not tightening) environmental standards, and some may become "pollution havens."

The other side argues that globalization does not necessarily have negative effects on the environment in developing countries to the extent suggested by the "pollution haven" hypothesis. This is largely due to many MNEs' *voluntary* adherence to environmental standards higher than those required by host countries. Most MNEs reportedly outperform local firms in environmental management. The underlying motivations behind MNEs' voluntary "green practices" can be attributed to (1) worldwide CSR pressures in general, (2) CSR demands made by customers in developed economies, and (3) requirements of MNE headquarters for worldwide compliance of higher CSR standards (such as ISO 14001). Although it is difficult to suggest that the "race to the bottom" does not exist, MNEs as a group do not necessarily add to the environmental

burden in developing countries. Some MNEs, such as Dow, GM, Toyota, and Siemens, have facilitated the diffusion of better environmental technologies to developing countries where they and their suppliers operate.

Sources: P. Christmann and G. Taylor, "Firm self-regulation through international certifiable standards," *Journal of International Business Studies* 37 (2006): 863–878; P. Madsen, "Does corporate investment drive a 'race to the bottom' in environmental protection?" *Academy of Management Journal* 52 (2009): 1297–1318; www.dow.com.

GRYNOLD/SHUTTERSTOCK.COM

---

insensitive and irresponsible. In 2010, BP made a huge mess in the Gulf of Mexico. Not surprisingly, new disasters and scandals often propel CSR to the forefront of public policy and management discussions.

Overall, managers as a stakeholder group are unique in that they are the only group that is positioned at the center of all these relationships. It is important to understand how they make decisions concerning CSR, as illustrated next.

15-2 INSTITUTIONS, RESOURCES, AND CORPORATE SOCIAL RESPONSIBILITY

While some people do not consider CSR an integral part of global business, Exhibit 15.2 shows that the institution-based and resource-based views can inform the

CSR discussion with relatively little adaptation. This section articulates why this is the case.

15-2a Institutions and Corporate Social Responsibility

The institution-based view sheds considerable light on the gradual diffusion of the CSR movement and the strategic responses of firms. At the most fundamental level, regulatory pressures underpin *formal* institutions, whereas normative and cognitive pressures support *informal* institutions. The strategic response framework consists of (1) reactive, (2) defensive, (3) accommodative, and (4) proactive strategies, as first introduced in Chapter 3 (see Exhibit 3.6). This framework can be extended to explore how firms make CSR decisions, as illustrated in Exhibit 15.3.

EXHIBIT 15.2   INSTITUTIONS, RESOURCES, AND CORPORATE SOCIAL RESPONSIBILITY

and cognitive beliefs, formal regulatory pressures are the only feasible way to push firms ahead. A key insight of the institution-based view—in fact, the very first proposition discussed in Chapter 2—is that individuals and organizations make *rational* choices given the right kind of incentives. For example, one efficient way to control pollution is to make polluters pay some "green" taxes—ranging from gasoline retail taxes to landfill charges. But how demanding these regulatory pressures should be remains controversial. One side of the debate argues that tough environmental regulation may lead to higher costs and reduced competitiveness, especially when competing with foreign rivals not subject to such demanding regulations (see Debate). Others argue, however, that "green" taxes simply force firms to pay real costs that they otherwise place on others. If a firm pollutes, it is imposing a cost on the surrounding community that must either live with the pollution or pay to clean it up. By imposing a pollution tax that roughly equals the cost to the community, the firm has to account for pollution as a real cost. Economists refer to this as "internalizing an externality."

A **reactive strategy** is indicated by relatively little or no support by top management for CSR causes. Firms do not feel compelled to act in the absence of disasters and outcries. Even when problems arise, denial is usually the first line of defense. Put another way, the need to accept some CSR is neither internalized through cognitive beliefs, nor does it result in any norms in practice. That leaves only formal regulatory pressures to compel firms to comply. For example, in the United States, food and drug safety standards that we take for granted today were fought by food and drug companies in the first half of the 20th century. The basic idea that food and drugs should be tested before being sold to customers and patients was bitterly contested even as unsafe foods and drugs killed thousands of people. As a result, the Food and Drug Administration (FDA) was progressively granted more powers. This era is not necessarily over. Today, many dietary supplement makers, whose products are beyond the FDA's regulatory reach, continue to sell untested supplements and deny responsibility.

A **defensive strategy** focuses on regulatory compliance. Top management involvement is piecemeal at best, and the general attitude is that CSR is an added cost or nuisance. Firms admit responsibility but often fight it. After the establishment of the Environmental Protection Agency (EPA) in 1970, the US chemical industry resisted the EPA's intrusion (see Exhibit 15.3). The regulatory requirements were at significant odds with the norms and cognitive beliefs held by the industry at that time.

How do various institutional pressures change firm behavior? In the absence of informal normative

CSR advocates further argue that stringent environmental regulation may force firms to innovate, however reluctantly, thus benefiting the competitiveness of both the industry and country.[4] For example, a Japanese law set standards to make products easier to disassemble. Although Hitachi initially resisted the law, it responded by redesigning products to simplify disassembly. The company reduced the parts in its washing machines by 16% and in vacuum cleaners by 30%. The products became not only easier to disassemble, but also easier and cheaper to *assemble* in the first place, thus providing Hitachi with a significant cost advantage.

reactive strategy A strategy that would only respond to CSR causes when required by disasters and outcries.

defensive strategy A strategy that focuses on regulatory compliance but with little actual commitment to CSR by top management.

An **accommodative strategy** is characterized by some support from top managers, who may increasingly view CSR as a worthwhile endeavor. Since formal regulations may be in place and informal social and environmental pressures may be increasing, a number of firms themselves may be concerned about CSR, leading to the emergence of some new industry norms. Further, new managers who are passionate about or sympathetic toward CSR causes may join the organization, or some traditional managers may change their outlook, leading to increasingly strong cognitive beliefs that CSR is the right thing to do. In other words, from both normative and cognitive standpoints, it becomes legitimate or a matter of social obligation to accept responsibility and do all that is required. For example, in the US chemical industry, such a transformation probably took place in the early 1980s (see Exhibit 15.3). More recently, Burger King, Kraft, Nestlé, and Unilever were pressured by Greenpeace to be concerned about the deforestation practices undertaken by their major palm oil supplier, Sinar Mas in Indonesia. Eventually, the food giants accommodated Greenpeace's demands and dumped Sinar Mas as a supplier, leading to a new industry norm that is more earth-friendly.[5]

Demonstrators demand justice in the wake of the 2010 BP oil spill in the Gulf of Mexico.

ALBERT H. TEICH/SHUTTERSTOCK.COM

accommodative strategy A strategy characterized by some support from top managers, who may increasingly view CSR as a worthwhile endeavor.

Adopting a code of conduct is a tangible indication of a firm's willingness to accept CSR. A code of conduct (sometimes called a code of ethics) is a set of written policies and standards outlining the proper practices for a firm. The global diffusion of codes of conduct is subject to intense debate. First, some argue that firms adopting these codes may not necessarily be sincere. This *negative* view suggests that an apparent interest in CSR may simply be window dressing. Some firms feel compelled to appear sensitive to CSR, following what others are doing, but have not truly and genuinely internalized CSR concerns. For example, in 2009, BP implemented a new safety-oriented operating management system. But after the 2010 oil spill in the Gulf of Mexico, it became apparent that this system had not been seriously implemented, and the result was a huge catastrophe. Second, an *instrumental* view suggests that CSR activities simply represent a useful instrument to make good profits.[6] Firms are not necessarily becoming more ethical. For example, after the 2010 oil spill, BP reshuffled management and created a new worldwide safety division. The instrumental view would argue that these actions did not really mean that BP became more ethical. Finally, a *positive* view believes that (at least some) firms and managers may be self-motivated to do it right regardless of social pressures.[7] Codes of conduct tangibly express values that organizational members view as central and enduring.

The institution-based view suggests that all three perspectives are probably valid. This is to be expected given how institutional pressures work to instill value. Regardless of actual motive, the fact that firms are practicing CSR is indicative of the rising *legitimacy* of CSR on the management agenda. Even firms that adopt a code of conduct simply as window dressing open doors for more scrutiny by stakeholders. Such pressures are likely to transform the firms internally into more self-motivated, better corporate citizens. It probably is fair to suggest that Nike is a more responsible corporate citizen in 2020 than it was in 1990.

From a CSR perspective, the best firms embrace a **proactive strategy**, constantly anticipating responsibility and endeavoring to do more than is required. Top management at a proactive firm not only supports and champions CSR activities, but also views CSR as a source of differentiation that permeates throughout the corporate DNA. Starbucks since 2001 has voluntarily published an annual report on CSR, which embodies its founder, chairman, and CEO Howard Schultz's vision that "we must balance our responsibility to create value for shareholders with a social conscience."[8] Whole Foods' co-founder and co-CEO John Mackey commented:

When people are really happy in their jobs, they provide much higher degrees of service to the customers. Happy team members result in happy customers. Happy customers do more business with you. They become advocates for your enterprise, which results in happy investors. That is a win, win, win, win strategy. You can expand it to include your suppliers and the communities where you do business, which are tied in to this prosperity circle.[9]

Proactive firms often engage in three areas of activity. First, some firms such as Swiss Re and Duke Energy actively participate in regional, national, and international policy and standards discussions. To the extent that policy and standards discussions today may become regulations in the future, it seems better to get involved early and (hopefully) steer the course toward a

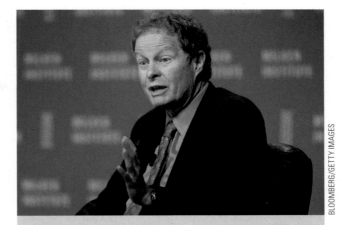

BLOOMBERG/GETTY IMAGES

Whole Foods co-founder and co-CEO John Mackey speaks during the 2016 Milken Institute Global Conference.

favorable direction. Otherwise—as the saying goes—if you're not at the table, you're on the menu. For example, Duke Energy operates 20 coal-fired power plants in five states. It is the third largest US emitter of CO_2 and the 12th largest in the world. But its CEO Jim Rogers has proactively worked with green technology producers, activists, and politicians to engage in policy and legislative discussions. These are not merely defensive moves to protect his firm and the power utility industry. Unlike his industry peers, Rogers has been "bitten by the climate bug" and is genuinely interested in reducing greenhouse gas emissions.

Second, proactive firms often build alliances with stakeholder groups. For example, many firms collaborate with NGOs. Because of the historical tension and distrust, these "sleeping-with-the-enemy" alliances are not easy to handle. The key lies in identifying relatively short-term, manageable projects of mutual interests. For instance, Starbucks collaborated with Conservation International to help reduce deforestation practices.

Third, proactive firms often engage in *voluntary* activities that go beyond what is required by regulations. While examples of industry-specific self-regulation abound, an area of intense global interest is the pursuit of the International Standards Organization (ISO) 14001 certification of the environment management system (EMS). Headquartered in Geneva, Switzerland, the ISO is an influential NGO consisting of national standards bodies in more than 100 countries. Launched in 1996, the ISO 14001 EMS has become the gold standard for CSR-conscious firms. Although not required by law, many MNEs, such as

proactive strategy A strategy that anticipates CSR and endeavors to do more than is required.

Ford and IBM, have adopted ISO 14001 standards in all their facilities worldwide. Firms such as Toyota, Siemens, and General Motors have demanded that all of their top-tier suppliers be ISO 14001 certified.

From an institutional perspective, these proactive activities are indicative of the normative and cognitive beliefs held by many managers on the importance of doing the right thing. While there is probably a certain element of window dressing and a quest for better profits, it is obvious that these efforts provide some tangible social and environmental benefits.

15-2b Resources and Corporate Social Responsibility

CSR-related resources can include *tangible* technologies and processes as well as *intangible* skills and attitudes. The VRIO framework can shed considerable light on CSR.

VALUE Do CSR-related resources and capabilities add *value*? This is the litmus test for CSR work. Many large firms, especially MNEs, can apply their tremendous financial, technological, and human resources toward a variety of CSR causes. For example, firms can choose to refuse to do business with countries that engage in human rights abuses. Such activities can be categorized as **social issue participation**, which refers to a firm's participation in social causes not directly related to the management of its primary stakeholders. Research suggests that these activities may actually *reduce* shareholder value.[10] Overall, although social issue participation may create some remote social and environmental value, it does not satisfy the economic leg of the triple bottom line, so these abilities do not qualify as value-adding firm resources.

RARITY CSR-related resources are not always *rare*. Remember that even a valuable resource is not likely to provide a significant advantage if competitors also possess it. For example, both Home Depot and Lowe's have NGOs such as the Forest Stewardship Council certify that suppliers in Brazil,

BEVAN GOLDSWAIN/SHUTTERSTOCK.COM

Indonesia, and Malaysia use only material from renewable forests. These complex processes require strong management capabilities such as negotiating with local suppliers, undertaking internal verification, coordinating with NGOs for external verification, and disseminating such information to stakeholders. Such capabilities are valuable. But since both competitors possess capabilities to manage these processes, they are common (not rare) resources.

IMITABILITY Although valuable and rare resources may provide some advantage, the advantage will only be temporary if competitors can *imitate* it. Resources must be not only valuable and rare, but also hard to imitate in order to give firms a sustainable (not merely temporary) competitive advantage. At some firms, CSR-related capabilities are deeply embedded in idiosyncratic managerial and employee skills and attitudes. The socially complex way of channeling their energy and conviction toward CSR at Whole Foods, led by John Mackey, a guru on conscious capitalism, cannot be easily imitated.

ORGANIZATION Does the firm have *organizational* capabilities to do a good job to exploit the full potential of CSR? Numerous components within a firm, such as formal management control systems and informal relationships between managers and employees, may be relevant. These components are often called complementary assets (see Chapter 4), because, by themselves, they typically do not generate advantage. However, complementary assets, when combined with valuable, rare, and hard-to-imitate capabilities, may enable a firm to fully utilize its CSR potential.

THE CSR-ECONOMIC PERFORMANCE PUZZLE The resource-based view helps solve a major puzzle in the CSR debate: the CSR-economic performance puzzle. The puzzle—a source of frustration to CSR advocates—is why there is no conclusive evidence on a direct, positive link between CSR and *economic* performance such as profits and shareholder returns. Some studies do indeed report a *positive* relationship.[11] Others find a *negative* relationship[12] or *no* relationship.[13] Viewed together, "CSR does not hurt [economic] performance, but there is no concrete support to believe that it leads to supranormal [economic] returns."[14]

A resource-based explanation suggests that because of the capability constraints discussed above, many firms are not cut out for a CSR-intensive (differentiation) strategy. Since all studies have some sampling bias (no study is perfect), studies that over-sample firms not yet ready for a high level of CSR activities are likely to report a negative relationship between CSR and economic

social issue participation Firms' participation in social causes not directly related to the management of primary stakeholders.

performance. Likewise, studies that over-sample firms ready for CSR may find a positive relationship. Also, studies with more balanced (more random) samples may fail to find any statistically significant relationship. In summary, since each firm is different (a basic assumption of the resource-based view), not every firm's economic performance is likely to benefit from CSR.

15-3 MANAGEMENT SAVVY

Concerning CSR, the institution-based and resource-based views suggest three clear implications for action (see Exhibit 15.4). First, savvy managers need to understand the formal and informal rules of the game, anticipate changes, and seek to shape such changes. The US government refused to ratify the 1997 Kyoto Protocol and only signed the nonbinding 2009 Copenhagen Accord. In 2015, the US government signed the binding Paris Agreement of the UN Framework Convention on Climate Change. However, in 2017, President Trump withdrew from the Paris Agreement. Despite such institutional uncertainties, many US firms such as Chevron, Dow Chemical, DuPont, ExxonMobil, Google, and Microsoft voluntarily participate in CSR activities not (yet) mandated by law (such as being prepared to pay "green" taxes for carbon emissions—known as carbon pricing), in anticipation of more stringent environmental requirements down the road.[15]

Second, savvy managers need to pick CSR battles carefully. The resource-based view suggests an important lesson, which is captured by Sun Tzu's timeless teaching: "Know yourself, know your opponents." While your opponents may engage in high-profile CSR activities that allow them to earn bragging rights and contribute to their triple bottom line, blindly imitating these practices without knowing enough about yourself as a manager and the firm/unit you lead may result in some disappointment. Instead of always chasing the newest

EXHIBIT 15.4 IMPLICATIONS FOR ACTION

▶ Understand the rules of the game, anticipate changes, and seek to shape and influence changes.

▶ Pick your CSR battles carefully. Don't blindly imitate other firms' CSR activities.

▶ Integrate CSR as part of the core activities and processes of the firm. Faking it doesn't last very long.

best practices, firms are advised to select CSR practices that fit with their *existing* resources, capabilities, and especially complementary assets.[16]

Third, given the increasingly inescapable responsibility to be good corporate citizens, managers may want to integrate CSR as part of the core activities of the firm instead of faking it and making only cosmetic changes. For example, instead of treating NGOs as threats, Home Depot, Lowe's, and Unilever have their sourcing policies certified by NGOs. Dow Chemical has established community advisory panels in most of its locations worldwide. Many managers traditionally treated CSR as a nuisance, involving regulation, added costs, and liability. Such an attitude may underestimate potential business opportunities associated with CSR.

What determines the success and failure of firms around the world? No doubt, CSR will increasingly become an important part of the answer. The best-performing firms are likely to be those that can integrate CSR activities into their core economic functions while addressing social and environmental concerns (see Opening and Closing Cases). In the post–Great Recession and post–Occupy Wall Street world, managers, as a unique group of stakeholders, have an important and challenging responsibility. From a CSR standpoint, this means building more humane, more inclusive, and fairer firms that not only generate wealth and develop economies, but also respond to changing societal expectations concerning firms' social and environmental roles around the world.

EMERGING MARKETS/ETHICAL DILEMMA
Closing Case: The Ebola Challenge

First reported in 1976 in Sudan and Zaire (now called the Democratic Republic of the Congo [DRC]), Ebola has been a known virus for four decades. Yet, there is still no effective vaccine or medicine.

Between 1976 and 2013, there were 24 outbreaks in Sub-Saharan Africa, with 1,716 cases. What really put Ebola on the center stage of global media—and on the pages of this book—was the 2014 outbreak, which was the most devastating outbreak, with 22,000 reported cases and 9,000 deaths. Starting in Guinea,

Liberia, and Sierra Leone, the disease quickly diffused to other West African countries such as the DRC, Nigeria, and Senegal. By September 2014, a Liberian man who traveled to Dallas, Texas, was diagnosed to have Ebola. He died there in early October. Two American nurses who treated the patient became the first confirmed cases to be infected by Ebola in the United States, triggering panic and chaos not only in Texas, but also in other parts of the country. State governments in Connecticut, Illinois, New Jersey, and New York demanded that anyone who traveled from affected West African countries be subject to 21 days of quarantine—the longest period the Ebola virus was thought to need to incubate. In October 2014, President Obama appointed a national Ebola response coordinator. All passengers arriving from affected African countries now had to go through screening, and all patients showing up at a US health care establishment had to answer a questionnaire regarding whether they traveled from these countries.

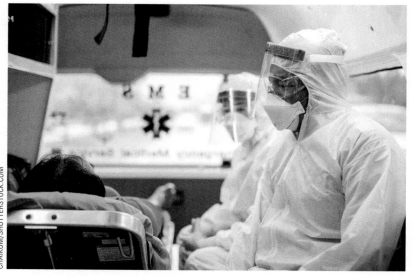

CHAIKOM/SHUTTERSTOCK.COM

In the absence of effective vaccine or medicine, treatment was indirect. It centered on early supportive care with rehydration and symptomatic treatment. The measures would include management of pain, nausea, fever, and anxiety, as well as rehydration via the oral or intravenous (IV) route. Blood products such as packed red blood cells or fresh frozen plasma might also be used. Intensive care was often used in the developed world. This might include maintaining blood volume and electrolytes (salts) balance as well as treating any bacterial infections. Thankfully, the two American nurses recovered after several weeks of treatment. So did the other six American health care workers who went to Africa and came home with Ebola. By December 2014, there had been ten Ebola cases in the United States, and only two resulted in death—the second case of death was an African doctor who was contaminated by his patients in an Ebola-infested country.

Throughout the crisis, the initial silence of the pharmaceutical industry was conspicuous. Dr. Margaret Chan, Director-General of the World Health Organization (WHO), criticized the industry for failing to develop a vaccine for Ebola over the four decades during which the virus threatened poor African countries. She complained that "a profit-driven industry does not invest in products for markets that cannot pay." Initially reluctant, some pharmaceutical firms jumped in. In October 2014, British drugmaker GlaxoSmithKline (GSK) announced that it expedited its R&D in search of a vaccine.

In 2010, the Canadian government developed an experimental vaccine VSV-EBOV and licensed it to a small, virtually unknown biotech firm NewLink Genetics in Ames, Iowa, for clinical trials. However, progress was slow and funding tight. In November 2014, US giant Merck paid NewLink $50 million to buy the rights to the vaccine and to expedite R&D. Also in November 2014, a French Big Pharma player Sanofi announced its intention to work with industry partners to combat Ebola. Another experimental drug ZMapp, developed by a small San Diego, California–based biopharmaceutical firm Mapp, showed encouraging results on primates and had been used on at least seven (human) patients in Africa in 2014. But ZMapp had not received FDA approval. In the absence of the financial, technological, and production capabilities of Big Pharma, ZMapp's stocks quickly ran out. The US government had to provide it with $25 million to scale up production.

The reason that until recently, pharmaceutical firms—especially Big Pharma firms—had been reluctant to apply their significant resources to find a cure for Ebola was simple. Even if successful, these efforts, which would mostly benefit African countries, would not be profitable. In other words, there was "no compelling business case." Now that the disease came to the United States (and a few Western European countries), firms felt compelled to move. Debates continued to rage. One side argued that pharmaceutical firms only focused on markets and products from which they could profit—with "Botox, baldness, and bonus" as their guiding light. Tropical diseases such as malaria and Ebola naturally would receive little (or no) attention. Another side argued that given limited resources, pharmaceutical firms rightly and strategically ignored (relatively) smaller scale diseases such as Ebola, because there were other diseases such as HIV/AIDS that impact a lot more people than does Ebola. A number of pharmaceutical firms jumped onto the "Ebola bandwagon" simply to earn kudos for corporate social responsibility, knowing that they would be unlikely to make any profits for their efforts. Or they were simply driven to do so due to public pressure—the series of eager announcements made in October and November 2014 were defensive in nature. Given the long lead time to develop any effective vaccine and the urgency to have a vaccine at hand when confronting an outbreak of Ebola (and other contagious diseases), how pharmaceutical firms proceed remains one of the leading strategic challenges they face.

Case Discussion Questions

1. ***ON ETHICS***: Dr. Margaret Chan, Director-General of the WHO, criticized the pharmaceutical industry for being "profit driven" and for failing to invest in the development of a vaccine or cure for Ebola. As CEO of a leading pharmaceutical firm, how do you respond to these criticisms?

2. ***ON ETHICS***: You are a shareholder of a pharmaceutical firm that announced its new investment to develop an Ebola vaccine and that, as a result, your dividend would be reduced. Would you support or not support the firm's decision to spend your money to combat Ebola?

3. ***ON ETHICS***: As a US government official, what would be your recommendations to incentivize pharmaceutical firms to develop an Ebola vaccine?

Sources: C. Campos, C. Cole, and J. Steele, "Ebola and corporate social responsibility," EMBA strategy class term project, Jindal School of Management, University of Texas at Dallas, 2014; "Canada should cancel NewLink Ebola vaccine contract," CBC, 19 November 2014: www.cbc.ca; "Ebola: Predictions with a purpose," *Economist*, 7 February 2015: 58; "Ebola outbreak: Why has 'Big Pharma' failed deadly virus' victims?" *Independent*, 7 September 2014: www.independent.co.uk; "Merck partners with NewLink to speed up work on Ebola vaccine," National Public Radio, 24 November 2014: www.npr.org; "WHO pillories drug industry for failure to develop Ebola vaccine," *Time*, 4 November 2014: www.time.com; World Health Organization, "Ebola virus disease fact sheet," November 2014: www.who.int.

STUDY TOOLS 15

LOCATED AT THE BACK OF YOUR BOOK:

☐ Rip out and study the Chapter Review Card at the end of the book

LOG IN TO WWW.CENGAGEBRAIN.COM TO:

☐ Review key term flashcards

☐ Complete a practice quiz to test your knowledge of key concepts

☐ View animated PengAtlas Maps

☐ Complete interactive content, watch chapter videos, and take a graded quiz

☐ Track your knowledge of key concepts in Global Business

☐ Read and discuss additional case study content

ENDNOTES

1

1. J. Dunning, *Multinational Enterprises and the Global Economy* (Reading, MA: Addison-Wesley, 1993) 30.

2. J.-F. Hennart, "Down with MNE-centric models!" *Journal of International Business Studies* 40 (2009): 1432–1454.

3. United Nations, *World Investment Report 2014* (New York and Geneva: UN, 2014) ix.

4. "When giants slow down," *Economist*, 27 July 2013: 20.

5. "Emerge, splurge, purge," *Economist*, 8 March 2014: 65–68.

6. T. London, "Making better investments at the base of the pyramid," *Harvard Business Review* (May 2009): 106–113.

7. K. Meyer and M. W. Peng, "Theoretical foundations of emerging economy business research," *Journal of International Business Studies* 47 (2016): 3–22.

8. M. W. Peng, "Identifying the big question in international business research," *Journal of International Business Studies* 35 (2004): 99–108.

9. J. Dunning and S. Lundan, "Institutions and the OLI paradigm of the multinational enterprise," *Asia Pacific Journal of Management* 25 (2008): 573–593; M. W. Peng, D. Wang, and Y. Jiang, "An institution-based view of international business strategy," *Journal of International Business Studies* 39 (2008): 920–936.

10. M. W. Peng, "The resource-based view and international business," *Journal of Management* 27 (2001): 803–829.

11. J. Johanson and J. Vahlne, "The Uppsala internationalization process model revisited: From liability of foreignness to liability of outsidership," *Journal of International Business Studies* 40 (2009): 1411–1431.

12. K. Meyer, S. Estrin, S. Bhaumik, and M. W. Peng, "Institutions, resources, and entry strategies in emerging economies," *Strategic Management Journal* 30 (2009): 61–80; D. Zoogah, M. W. Peng, and H. Woldu, "Institutions, resources, and organizational effectiveness in Africa," *Academy of Management Perspectives* 29 (2015): 7–31.

13. J. Stiglitz, *Globalization and Its Discontents* (New York: Norton, 2002) 9.

14. "America the relatively beautiful," *Bloomberg Businessweek*, 2 February 2015: 8–10.

15. "The new Davos man," *Economist*, 21 January 2017: 33–34.

16. K. Li, "Economic openness serves everyone better," *Bloomberg Businessweek*, 30 January 2017: 8.

17. P. Ghemawat, "Semiglobalization and international business strategy," *Journal of International Business Studies* 34 (2003): 138–152.

18. International Monetary Fund, *World Economic Outlook* (Washington: IMF, 2015) 168.

19. "Supersized national champs," *Bloomberg Businessweek*, 8 April 2013: 14.

20. United Nations, *World Investment Report 2010* (New York and Geneva: UN, 2010) 10.

21. "The hard truth about globalization," *Fortune*, 1 August 2016: 6.

22. M. W. Peng, "The global strategy of emerging multinationals from China," *Global Strategy Journal* 2 (2012): 97–107.

2

1. M. W. Peng, "Institutional transitions and strategic choices," *Academy of Management Review* 28 (2003): 275.

2. M. W. Peng, D. Wang, and Y. Jiang, "An institution-based view of international business strategy," *Journal of International Business Studies* 39 (2008): 920–936.

3. D. North, *Institutions, Institutional Change, and Economic Performance* (New York: Norton, 1990) 3.

4. W. R. Scott, *Institutions and Organizations*, 3rd ed. (Thousand Oaks, CA: Sage, 2008).

5. "Looking for someone to blame," *Economist*, 13 August 2011: 25–26.

6. O. Williamson, *The Economic Institutions of Capitalism* (New York: Free Press, 1985) 1–2.

7. P. Collier and J. Gunning, "Explaining African economic performance," *Journal of Economic Literature* 37 (1999): 64–111.

8. "The price is wrong," *Economist*, 28 September 2013 (special report): 5.

9. Y. Li, M. W. Peng, and C. Macaulay, "Market-political ambidexterity during institutional transitions," *Strategic Organization* 11 (2013): 205–213.

10. "Trump's K Street office," *Bloomberg Businessweek*, 23 January 2017: 22–24.

11. C. Stevens, E. Xie, and M. W. Peng, "Toward a legitimacy-based view of political risk," *Strategic Management Journal* 37 (2016): 945–963.

12. R. La Porta, F. Lopez-de-Silanes, A. Shleifer, and R. Vishny, "Law and finance," *Journal of Political Economy* 106 (1998): 1118.

13. H. de Soto, *The Mystery of Capital* (New York: Basic Books, 2000).

14. M. W. Peng, D. Ahlstrom, S. Carraher, and W. Shi, "An institution-based view of global IPR history," *Journal of International Business Studies* (2017, in press).

15. P. Hall and D. Soskice, *Varieties of Capitalism* (Oxford, UK: Oxford University Press, 2001).

16. D. North, *Understanding the Process of Economic Change* (Princeton, NJ: Princeton University Press, 2005) 48.

17. D. Acemoglu and J. Robinson, *Why Nations Fail* (New York: Crown, 2012).

18. "Doing business in Africa," *Economist*, 2 July 2005: 61.

19. D. North, *Structure and Change in Economic History* (New York: Norton, 1981) 164.

3

1. G. Hofstede, *Cultures and Organizations* (New York: McGraw-Hill, 1997) xii.

2. Hofstede, *Cultures and Organizations*, 5.

3. K. Leung, R. Bhagat, N. Buchan, M. Erez, and C. Gibson, "Beyond national culture and culture-centrism," *Journal of International Business Studies* 42 (2011): 177–181.

4. R. McCrum, *Globish: How the English Language Became the World's Language* (New York: Norton, 2010).

5. E. Hall and M. Hall, *Hidden Differences* (Garden City, NY: Doubleday, 1987).

6. S. Ronen and O. Shenkar, "Clustering countries on attitudinal dimension," *Academy of Management Review* 10 (1985): 435–454.

7. R. House, P. Hanges, M. Javidan, P. Dorfman, and V. Gupta (eds.), *Culture, Leadership, and Organizations: The GLOBE Study of 62 Societies* (Thousand Oaks, CA: Sage, 2004).

8. S. Huntington, *The Clash of Civilizations and the Remaking of World Order* (New York: Simon & Schuster, 1996) 43.

9. Hofstede, *Cultures and Organizations*, 94.

10. R. Deshpande and A. Raina, "The ordinary heroes of the Taj," *Harvard Business Review* (December 2011): 119–123.

11. This section draws heavily from T. Donaldson, "Values in tension," *Harvard Business Review* (September 1996): 4–11.

12. "How to grease a palm," *Economist*, 23 December 2006: 116.

13. S. Lee and D. Weng, "Does bribery in the home country promote or dampen firm exports?" *Strategic Management Journal* 34 (2013): 1472–1487.

14. S. Wei, "How taxing is corruption on international investors?" *Review of Economics and Statistics* 82 (2000): 1–11.

15. C. Kwok and S. Tadesse, "The MNC as an agent of change for host-country institutions," *Journal of International Business Studies* 37 (2006): 767–785.

4

1. M. W. Peng, "The resource-based view and international business," *Journal of Management* 27 (2001): 803–829.

2. J. Barney, "Is the resource-based view a useful perspective for strategic management research? Yes," *Academy of Management Review* 26 (2001): 54.

3. D. Teece, "Explicating dynamic capabilities," *Strategic Management Journal* 28 (2007): 1319–1350.

4. J. Barney, *Gaining and Sustaining Competitive Advantage*, 2nd ed. (Upper Saddle River, NJ: Prentice Hall, 2002) 157.

5. S. Kotha and K. Srikanth, "Managing a global partnership model," *Global Strategy Journal* 3 (2013): 41–66.

6. D. Levy, "Offshoring in the new global political economy," *Journal of Management Studies* 42 (2005): 685–693.

7. J. Schmidt and T. Keil, "What makes a resource valuable?" *Academy of Management Review* 38 (2013): 206–228.

8. "Can this IBMer keep Big Blue's edge?" *Bloomberg Businessweek*, 31 October 2011: 31–32.

9. "Apple: iThrone," *Economist*, 31 January 2015: 53.

10. Y. Luo, S. Wang, Q. Zheng, and V. Jayaraman, "Task attributes and process integration in business

process offshoring," *Journal of International Business Studies* 43 (2012): 498–524.

11. T. Chi and A. Seth, "A dynamic model of the choice of mode for exploiting complementary capabilities," *Journal of International Business Studies* 40 (2009): 365–387; A. Hess and F. Rothaermel, "When are assets complementary?" *Strategic Management Journal* 32 (2011): 895–909.

12. J. Barney, *Gaining and Sustaining Competitive Advantage* (Reading, MA: Addison-Wesley, 1997) 155.

13. Y. Li, M. W. Peng, and C. Macaulay, "Market-political ambidexterity during institutional transitions," *Strategic Organization* 11 (2013): 205–213; M. W. Peng, S. Sun, and L. Markoczy, "Human capital and CEO compensation during institutional transitions," *Journal of Management Studies* 52 (2015): 117–147.

14. A. Chatterji and A. Patro, "Dynamic capabilities and managing human capital," *Academy of Management Perspectives* 28 (2014): 395–408.

15. D. Burrus, *Flash Foresight* (New York: HarperCollins, 2011) 11.

16. "It's not us, it's you: Why customers are breaking up with IBM," *Bloomberg Businessweek*, 26 May 2014: 58–63.

17. The author's paraphrase based on T. Friedman, *The World Is Flat* (New York: Farrar, Straus, & Giroux, 2005) 237.

5

1. C. Arkolakis, S. Demidova, P. Kelnow, and A. Rodriguez-Clare, "Endogenous variety and the gains from trade," *American Economic Review* 98 (2008): 444–450; A. Smith, "Follow me to the innovation frontier?" *Journal of International Business Studies* 45 (2014): 248–274.

2. M. W. Peng and K. Meyer, *Winning the Future Markets for UK Manufacturing Output* (London: UK Government Office for Science, 2013).

3. I. Colantone and L. Sleuwaegen, "International trade, exit, and entry," *Journal of International Business Studies* 41 (2010): 1240–1257.

4. M. W. Peng, "The resource-based view and international business," *Journal of Management* 27 (2001): 803–829.

5. B. Cassiman and E. Golovko, "Innovation and internationalization through exports," *Journal of International Business Studies* 42 (2011): 56–75; R. Salomon and B. Jin, "Do leading or lagging firms learn more from exporting?" *Strategic Management Journal* 31 (2010): 1088–1113.

6. "Obama: Venture capitalist-in-chief," *Bloomberg Businessweek*, 9 August 2010: 28–31.

7. M. Porter, *Competitive Advantage of Nations* (New York: Free Press, 1990).

8. D. Bernhofen and J. Brown, "An empirical assessment of the comparative advantage gains from trade," *American Economic Review* 95 (2005): 208–225.

9. "Don't go to Rio for a deal on an iPad," *Bloomberg Businessweek*, 13 December 2010: 13–14.

10. Tire Industry Association, "Tire Industry Association expresses disappointment with President's decision concerning Chinese tire tariff," Bowie, MD: TIA (14 September 2009: www.tireindustry.org).

11. "Japan's micro farms face extinction," *Bloomberg Businessweek*, 6 January 2014: 14–15.

12. "A row over cows," *Economist*, 17 February 2011: www.economist.com.

13. "DHL will pay $9.4M fine to settle shipping dispute," *USA Today*, 7 August 2009: 2A.

14. US-China Business Council, *Understanding the US-China Trade Relationship* (Washington: USCBC, January 2017).

6

1. United Nations, *World Investment Report 2016* (New York and Geneva: UN, 2016).

2. T. Khoury and M. W. Peng, "Does institutional reform of intellectual property rights lead to more inbound FDI?" *Journal of World Business* 46 (2011): 337–345; S. Sun, M. W. Peng, R. Lee, and W. Tan, "Institutional open access at home and outward internationalization," *Journal of World Business* 50 (2015): 234–246.

3. R. Aggarwal, J. Berrill, E. Hutson, and C. Kearney, "What is a multinational corporation?" *International Business Review* 20 (2011): 557–577.

4. United Nations, *World Investment Report 2009* (New York and Geneva: UN, 2009) xxi.

5. J. Dunning, *Multinational Enterprises and the Global Economy* (Reading, MA: Addison-Wesley, 1993).

6. R. Tasker, "Pepperoni power," *Far Eastern Economic Review*, 14 November 2002: 59–60.

7. B. Nielson, C. Asmussen, & C. Weatherall, "The location choice of foreign direct investments," *Journal of World Business* 52 (2017): 62–82.

8. B. Pinkham and M. W. Peng, "Overcoming institutional voids via arbitration," *Journal of International Business Studies* 48 (2017): 344–359.

9. S. Chen, "A general TCE model of international business institutions," *Journal of International Business Studies* 41 (2010): 935–959.

10. K. Meyer and E. Sinani, "When and where does FDI generate positive spillovers," *Journal of International Business Studies* 40 (2009): 1075–1094.

11. United Nations, *World Investment Report 2010* (New York and Geneva: UN, 2010) 17.

12. F. Barry and C. Kearney, "MNEs and industrial structure in host countries," *Journal of International Business Studies* 37 (2006): 392–406.

13. M. Zhao, S. Park, and N. Zhou, 2014, "MNC strategy and social adaptation in emerging markets," *Journal of International Business Studies* 45 (2014): 842–861.

7

1. "The all-meaty dollar," *Economist*, 14 January 2017: 66–67.

2. "McCurrencies," *Economist*, 27 May 2006: 74.

3. "Taking a pounding," *Economist*, 15 October 2016: 14.

4. R. Lyons, *The Microstructure Approach to Exchange Rates* (Cambridge, MA: MIT Press, 2001) 1.

5. "Bretton Woods II," *Guardian*, 14 November 2008: www.guardian.co.uk.

6. "Life amid the ruins," *Bloomberg Businessweek*, 28 June 2010: 52–60.

7. R. Carbaugh, *International Economics*, 11th ed. (Cincinnati: Cengage 2007) 360.

8. "Global foreign-exchange turnover," *Economist*, 14 September 2013: 97.

9. S. Lee and M. Makhija, "The effect of domestic uncertainty on the real options value of international investments," *Journal of International Business Studies* 40 (2009): 405–420.

10. D. Boehe, "Strategic hedging," *Journal of World Business* 49 (2014): 290–300; S. Song, "Exchange

rate challenges, flexible intra-firm adjustments, and subsidiary longevity," *Journal of World Business* 50 (2015): 36–45.

8

1. World Trade Organization, *10 Benefits of the WTO Trading System* (Geneva: WTO, 2005) 3.

2. "The future of globalization," *Economist*, 29 July 2006: 11.

3. "WTO: No more grand bargains," *Economist*, 9 August 2014: 10.

4. "In the twilight of Doha," *Economist*, 29 July 2006: 63.

5. P. Bustos, "Trade liberalization, exports, and technology upgrading," *American Economic Review* 101 (2011): 304–340.

6. Delegation of the European Commission to the USA, *The European Union: A Guide for Americans* (Washington: Delegation of the European Commission to the USA, 2005) 2.

7. M. Feldstein, "The failure of the euro," *Foreign Affairs*, January 2012: 105–116.

8. N. Berggruen and N. Gardels, "The next Europe," *Foreign Affairs*, July 2013: 134–142.

9. "Europe's reluctant hegemon," *Economist*, 15 June 2013: special report.

10. "Mexico: Was NAFTA worth it?" *BusinessWeek*, 22 December 2003: www.businessweek.com.

11. "The stranger next door," *Bloomberg Businessweek*, 6 May 2013: 8–9; M. W. Peng, "What happens if NAFTA goes away," *Texas CEO Magazine*, January 2017: 26-27; M. W. Peng, "What happens to Texas if the US withdraws from NAFTA?" *Dallas Morning News*, 9 May 2017: 13A.

12. "Deeper, better NAFTA," *Economist*, 4 January 2014: 8.

13. "Latin America's great divide," *Bloomberg Businessweek*, 9 June 2014: 18–20.

14. US Trade Representative, *The Case for CAFTA*, February 2005: www.ustr.gov.

15. A. Rugman, *The Regional Multinationals* (Cambridge, UK: Cambridge University Press, 2005) 215.

16. G. Qian, T. Khoury, M. W. Peng, and Z. Qian, "The performance implications of intra- and inter-regional geographic diversification," *Strategic Management Journal* 31 (2010): 1018–1030.

9

1. M. Hitt, R. D. Ireland, S. M. Camp, and D. Sexton, "Strategic entrepreneurship," *Strategic Management Journal* 22 (2001): 480.

2. S. Shane and S. Venkataraman, "The promise of entrepreneurship as a field of research," *Academy of Management Review* 25 (2000): 218.

3. M. W. Peng, S. Lee, and S. Hong, "Entrepreneurs as intermediaries," *Journal of World Business* 49 (2014): 21–31.

4. P. McDougall and B. Oviatt, "International entrepreneurship," *Academy of Management Journal* 43 (2000): 903.

5. S. Lee, M. W. Peng, and S. Song, "Governments, entrepreneurs, and positive externalities," *European Management Journal* 31 (2013): 333–347.

6. D. Kelley, N. Bosma, and J. Amoros, *Global Entrepreneurship Monitor 2010 Global Report* (Wellesley, MA: Babson College/GEM, 2011).

7. M. W. Peng, Y. Yamakawa, and S. Lee, "Bankruptcy laws and entrepreneur-friendliness," *Entrepreneur Theory and Practice* 34 (2010): 517–530; Y. Zhu,

X. Wittman, and M. W. Peng, "Institution-based barriers to innovation in SMEs in China," *Asia Pacific Journal of Management* 29 (2012): 1131–1142.

8. "Son also rises," *Economist*, 27 November 2010: 71–72.

9. "In Russia, Facebook is more than a social network," *Bloomberg Businessweek*, 3 January 2011: 32–33.

10. S. Lee, Y. Yamakawa, M. W. Peng, and J. Barney, "How do bankruptcy laws affect entrepreneurship development around the world?" *Journal of Business Venturing* 26 (2011): 505–520.

11. Y. Lu, L. Zhou, G. Bruton, and W. Li, "Capabilities as a mediator linking resources and the international performance of entrepreneurial firms in an emerging economy," *Journal of International Business Studies* 41 (2010): 419–436; Y. Yamakawa, M. W. Peng, and D. Deeds, "Rising from the ashes: Cognitive determinants of venture growth after entrepreneurial failure," *Entrepreneurship Theory and Practice* 39 (2015): 209–236.

12. "The Megabus effect," *Bloomberg Businessweek*, 11 April 2011: 62–67.

13. "The dirtiest job on the Internet," *Bloomberg Businessweek*, 5 December 2011: 95–97.

14. Y. Yamakawa, M. W. Peng, and D. Deeds, "What drives new ventures to internationalize from emerging to developed economies?" *Entrepreneurship Theory and Practice* 32 (2008): 59–82.

15. D. Ahlstrom, G. Bruton, and K. Yeh, "Venture capital in China," *Asia Pacific Journal of Management* 24 (2007): 247–268.

16. Y. Yamakawa, S. Khavul, M. W. Peng, and D. Deeds, "Venturing from emerging economies," *Strategic Entrepreneurship Journal* 7 (2013): 181–196.

17. M. W. Peng and A. York, "Behind intermediary performance in export trade," *Journal of International Business Studies* 32 (2001): 327–346.

10

1. K. Meyer, S. Estrin, S. Bhaumik, and M. W. Peng, "Institutions, resources, and entry strategies in emerging economies," *Strategic Management Journal* 30 (2009): 61–80.

2. M. Guillen and E. Garcia-Canal, "How to conquer new markets with old skills," *Harvard Business Review*, November (2010): 118–122; M. W. Peng, "The resource-based view and international business," *Journal of Management* 27 (2001): 803–829.

3. S. Newman, C. Rickert, and R. Schaap, "Investing in the post-recession world," *Harvard Business Review* (January 2011): 150–155.

4. "Rulers of the new silk world," *Economist*, 5 June 2010: 75–77.

5. "Short takes: Autos," *China Business Review* (January 2011): 8.

6. M. W. Peng and D. Wang, "Innovation capability and foreign direct investment," *Management International Review* 40 (2000): 80.

7. D. Xu and O. Shenkar, "Institutional distance and the multinational enterprise," *Academy of Management Review* 27 (2002): 608.

8. M. W. Peng, "The global strategy of emerging multinationals from China," *Global Strategy Journal* 2 (2012): 97–107.

9. J. G. Frynas, K. Mellahi, and G. Pigman, "First mover advantages in international business and firm-specific political resources," *Strategic Management Journal* 27 (2006): 321–345.

10. M. W. Peng, S. Lee, and J. Tan, "The *keiretsu* in Asia," *Journal of International Management* 7 (2001): 253–276.

11. "Land of war and opportunity," *Bloomberg Businessweek*, 10 January 2011: 46–54.

12. "Cisco's brave new world," *BusinessWeek*, 24 November 2008: 56–68.

13. G. Gao and Y. Pan, "The pace of MNEs' sequential entries," *Journal of International Business Studies* 41 (2010): 1572–1580; Y. Luo and M. W. Peng, "Learning to compete in a transition economy," *Journal of International Business Studies* 30 (1999): 269–296.

14. M. W. Peng, Y. Zhou, and A. York, "Behind make or buy decisions in export strategy," *Journal of World Business* 41 (2006): 289–300.

15. A. Chintakananda, A. York, H. O'Neill, and M. W. Peng, "Structuring dyadic relationships between export producers and intermediaries," *European Journal of International Management* 3 (2009): 302–327.

16. United Nations, *World Investment Report 2014* (New York and Geneva: UN, 2014) 81.

11

1. J. Reuer, T. Tong, B. Tyler, and A. Arino, "Executive preferences for governance modes and exchange partners," *Strategic Management Journal* 34 (2013): 1104–1122; H. Yang, Z. Lin, and M. W. Peng, "Behind acquisitions of alliance partners," *Academy of Management Journal* 54 (2011): 1069–1080.

2. Z. Lin, M. W. Peng, H. Yang, and S. Sun, "How do networking and learning drive M&As?" *Strategic Management Journal* 30 (2009): 1113–1132.

3. W. Shi, S. Sun, and M. W. Peng, "Sub-national institutional contingencies, network positions, and IJV partner selection," *Journal of Management Studies* 49 (2012): 1221–1245.

4. S. Lebedev, M. W. Peng, E. Xie, and C. Stevens, "Mergers and acquisitions in and out of emerging economies," *Journal of World Business* 50 (2015): 651–662; M. W. Peng, "Making M&As fly in China," *Harvard Business Review* (March 2006): 26–27.

5. "The surprising strength of Spain's Santander," *Bloomberg Businessweek*, 5 July 2010: 41–42.

6. "Open skies and flights of fancy," *Economist*, 4 October 2003: 67.

7. T. Tong, J. Reuer, and M. W. Peng, "International joint ventures and the value of growth options," *Academy of Management Journal* 51 (2008): 1014–1029.

8. D. Zoogah and M. W. Peng, "What determines the performance of strategic alliance managers?" *Asia Pacific Journal of Management* 28 (2011): 483–508.

9. W. Shi, S. Sun, B. Pinkham, and M. W. Peng, "Domestic alliance network to attract foreign partners," *Journal of International Business Studies* 45 (2014): 338–362.

10. A. Phene, S. Tallman, and P. Almeida, "When do acquisitions facilitate technological exploration and exploitation?" *Journal of Management* 38 (2012): 753–783.

11. "Mergers and acquisitions: The new rules of attraction," *Economist*, 15 November 2014: 67.

12. C. Moschieri and J. Campa, "The European M&A industry," *Academy of Management Perspectives* 23 (2009): 71–87.

13. G. Andrade, M. Mitchell, and E. Stafford, "New evidence and perspectives on mergers," *Journal of Economic Perspectives* 15 (2001): 103–120.

14. "Jackpot! How Lenovo found treasure in the PC industry's trash," *Bloomberg Businessweek*, 12 May 2014: 46–51.

15. M. W. Peng and O. Shenkar, "Joint venture dissolution as corporate divorce," *Academy of Management Executive* 16 (2002): 92–105.

16. D. Siegel and K. Simons, "Assessing the effects of M&As on firm performance," *Strategic Management Journal* 31 (2010): 903–916.

17. "Bank of America-Merrill Lynch: A $50 billion deal from hell," *Wall Street Journal*, 29 January 2009: blogs.wsj.com.

18. "Hi-yah! Alcatel-Lucent chops away at years of failure," *Bloomberg Businessweek*, 2 May 2011: 29.

19. "Coming unstuck," *Economist*, 9 August 2014: 53–54.

12

1. T. Levitt, "The globalization of markets," *Harvard Business Review* (May–June 1983): 92–102.

2. "How China won the keys to Disney's Magic Kingdom," *New York Times*, 14 June 2016: www.nytimes.com.

3. C. Bartlett and S. Ghoshal, *Managing Across Borders* (Boston: Harvard Business School Press, 1989).

4. R. Hodgetts, "Dow Chemical CEO William Stavropoulos on structure," *Academy of Management Executive* 13 (1999): 30.

5. X. Ma and A. Delios, "Home-country headquarters and an MNE's subsequent within-country diversification," *Journal of International Business Studies* 41 (2010): 517–525.

6. T. Wakayama, J. Shintaku, and T. Amano, "What Panasonic learned in China," *Harvard Business Review* (December 2012): 109–113.

7. C. K. Prahalad and K. Lieberthal, "The end of corporate imperialism," *Harvard Business Review* (August 1998): 68–79.

8. S. Morris, R. Hammond, and S. Snell, "A micro-foundations approach to transnational capabilities," *Journal of International Business Studies* 45 (2014): 405–427.

9. "The great innovation debate," *Economist*, 12 January 2013: 11.

10. Bartlett and Ghoshal, *Managing Across Borders*, 209.

11. A. Gupta and V. Govindarajan, *Global Strategy and Organization* (New York: Wiley, 2004) 104.

12. P. Gooderham, D. Minbaeva, and T. Pedersen, "Governance mechanisms for the promotion of social capital for knowledge transfer in multinational corporations," *Journal of Management Studies* 48 (2011): 123–150.

13. M. Kotabe, D. Dunlap-Hinkler, R. Parente, and H. Mishra, "Determinants of cross-national knowledge transfer and its effect on firm innovation," *Journal of International Business Studies* 38 (2007): 259–282.

14. A. Witty, "Research and develop," *The World in 2011* (London: The Economist, 2011) 140. Witty is CEO of GSK.

15. K. Meyer, R. Mudambi, and R. Narula, "Multinational enterprises and local contexts," *Journal of Management Studies* 48 (2011): 235–252.

16. P. Ghemawat, "The cosmopolitan corporation," *Harvard Business Review* (May 2011): 92–99.

13

1. P. Cappelli, "HR for neophytes," *Harvard Business Review* (October 2013): 25–27; C. Fey, S. Morgulis-Yukushev, H. Park, and I. Bjorkman,

"Opening the black box of the relationship between HRM practices and firm performance," *Journal of International Business Studies* 40 (2009): 690–712.

2. G. Peng and P. Beamish, "MNC subsidiary size and expatriate control," *Journal of World Business* 49 (2014): 51–62.

3. D. Vora and T. Kostova, "A model of dual organizational identification in the context of the multinational enterprise," *Journal of Organizational Behavior* 28 (2007): 327–350.

4. Y. Chang, Y. Gong, and M. W. Peng, "Expatriate knowledge transfer, subsidiary absorptive capacity, and subsidiary performance," *Academy of Management Journal* 55 (2012): 927–948.

5. R. L. Tung, "Selection and training procedures for US, European, and Japanese multinationals," *California Management Review* 25 (1982): 57–71.

6. S. Carraher, S. Sullivan, and M. Crocitto, "Mentoring across global boundaries," *Journal of International Business Studies* 39 (2009): 1310–1326.

7. F. Cooke, D. Saini, and J. Wang, "Talent management in China and India," *Journal of World Business* 49 (2014): 225–235.

8. "Not-so-happy returns," *Economist*, 7 November 2015: 62.

9. "Chattanooga shoo-shoo," *Economist*, 22 February 2014: 57.

10. "Unions, Inc.," *Economist*, 6 April 2013: 68.

11. "A new labor movement is born in China," *Bloomberg Businessweek*, 14 June 2010: 8.

12. M. W. Peng, "The global strategy of emerging multinationals from China," *Global Strategy Journal* 2 (2012): 97–107.

13. C. Chen, "New trends in allocation preferences," *Academy of Management Journal* 38 (1995): 408–428.

14. M. Beer, M. Finnstrom, and D. Shrader, "Why leadership training fails," *Harvard Business Review* (October 2016): 51.

15. W. Arthur, W. Bennett, P. Edens, and S. Bell, "Effectiveness of training in organizations," *Journal of Applied Psychology* 88 (2003): 234–245.

16. D. Zoogah, D. Vora, O. Richard, and M. W. Peng, "Strategic alliance team diversity, coordination, and effectiveness," *International Journal of Human Resource Management* 22 (2011): 510–529.

17. F. Dobbin and A. Kalev, "Why diversity programs fail," *Harvard Business Review* (July 2016): 52–60.

18. B. Becker and M. Huselid, "Strategic human resource management," *Journal of Management* 32 (2006): 907.

19. J. Combs, D. Ketchen, A. Hall, and Y. Liu, "Do high performance work practices matter?" *Personnel Psychology* 59 (2006): 501–528; K. Jiang, D. Lepak, J. Hu, and J. Baer, "How does human resource management influence organizational outcomes?" *Academy of Management Journal* 55 (2012): 1264–1294.

20. S. Meisinger, "The four Cs of the HR profession," *Human Resource Management* 44 (2005): 189–194.

21. "Globalization, robots, and the future of work," *Harvard Business Review* (October 2016): 74–79.

22. A. Ariss, W. Cascio, and J. Paauwe, "Talent management," *Journal of World Business* 49 (2014): 173–179

23. "Secrets of an HR superstar," *BusinessWeek*, 19 April 2007: 66.

14

1. "Wendy's goes beyond the dollar menu in Japan," *Bloomberg Businessweek*, 9 January 2012: 25–26.

2. T. Levitt, "The globalization of markets," *Harvard Business Review* (May–June 1983): 92–102.

3. D. Alden, J. Kelley, P. Riefler, J. Lee, and G. Soutar, "The effect of global company animosity on global brand attitudes in emerging and developed markets," *Journal of International Marketing* 21 (2013): 17–38.

4. D. Griffith, "Understanding multi-institutional convergence effects on international market segments and global marketing strategy," *Journal of World Business* 45 (2010): 59–67.

5. D. Holt, J. Quelch, and E. Taylor, "How global brands compete," *Harvard Business Review* (September 2004): 68–75.

6. "Africa calling," *Economist*, 7 June 2008: 78.

7. M. Porter, *Competitive Advantage* (New York: Free Press, 1985).

8. R. Slone, "Leading a supply chain turnaround," *Harvard Business Review* (October 2004): 116.

9. The following discussion draws heavily from H. Lee, "The triple-A supply chain," *Harvard Business Review* (October 2004): 102–112.

10. C. Bode, S. Wagner, K. Petersen, and L. Ellram, "Understanding responses to supply chain disruptions," *Academy of Management Journal* 54 (2011): 833–856.

11. M. W. Peng, Y. Zhou, and A. York, "Behind make or buy decisions in export strategy," *Journal of World Business* 41 (2006): 289–300.

12. L. Mesquita and T. Brush, "Untangling safeguard and production coordination effects in long-term buyer-supplier relationships," *Academy of Management Journal* 51 (2008): 785–807.

13. Y. Li, E. Xie, H. Teo, and M. W. Peng, "Formal control and social control in domestic and international buyer-supplier relationships," *Journal of Operations Management* 28 (2010): 333–344.

14. E. Katok and V. Pavlov, "Fairness in supply chain contracts," *Journal of Operations Management* 31 (2013): 129–137.

15. L. Leonidou, B. Aykol, T. Fotiadis, P. Christodoulides, and A. Zeriti, "Betrayal in international buyer-seller relationship," *Journal of World Business* 52 (2017): 28–44.

16. P. Skilton, "Value creation, value capture, and supply chain structure," *Journal of Supply Chain Management* 50 (2014): 74–93.

17. C. Schulze and B. Skiera, "Not all fun and games," *Journal of Marketing* 78 (2014): 1–19.

18. J. Schumann, F. von Wangenheim, and N. Groene, "Targeted online advertising," *Journal of Marketing* 78 (2014): 59–75.

19. P. Kotler, N. Rackham, and S. Krishnaswamy, "Ending the war between sales and marketing," *Harvard Business Review* (July 2006): 68–78.

20. R. Leuschner, D. Rogers, and F. Charvet, "A meta-analysis of supply chain integration and firm performance," *Journal of Supply Chain Management* 49 (2013): 34–57.

15

1. K. Davis, "The case for and against business assumption of social responsibilities," *Academy of Management Journal* 16 (1973): 312.

2. T. Devinney, A. McGahan, and M. Zollo, "A research agenda for global stakeholder strategy," *Global Strategy Journal* 3 (2013): 325–337 .

3. M. Friedman, "The social responsibility of business is to increase its profits," *New York Times Magazine*, 13 September 1970: 32–33.

4. A. Gore, *An Inconvenient Truth* (Emmaus, PA: Rodale Press, 2006).

5. "The other oil spill," *Economist*, 26 June 2010: 71–73.

6. D. Siegel, "Green management matters only if it yields more green," *Academy of Management Perspectives* 23 (2009): 5–16.

7. A. Marcus and A. Fremeth, "Green management matters regardless," *Academy of Management Perspectives* 23 (2009): 17–26.

8. "Message from Howard Schultz," *Starbucks Global Responsibility Report 2010* (Seattle: Starbucks, 2011, www.starbucks.com).

9. J. Mackey, "What is it that only I can do?" *Harvard Business Review* (January 2011): 119–123.

10. A. Hillman and G. Keim, "Shareholder value, stakeholder management, and social issues," *Strategic Management Journal* 22 (2001): 125–139.

11. B. Lev, C. Petrovits, and S. Radhakrishnan, "Is doing good good for you?" *Strategic Management Journal* 31 (2010): 182–200.

12. T. Wang and P. Bansal, "Social responsibility in new ventures," *Strategic Management Journal* 33 (2012): 1135–1153.

13. J. Surroca, J. Tribo, and S. Waddock, "Corporate responsibility and financial performance," *Strategic Management Journal* 31 (2010): 463–490.

14. T. Devinney, "Is the socially responsible corporation a myth?" *Academy of Management Perspectives* 23 (2009): 53.

15. "If it's good enough for Big Oil …" *Bloomberg Businessweek*, 17 November 2014: 10–11.

16. W. Su, M. W. Peng, W. Tan, and Y. Cheung, "The signaling effect of corporate social responsibility in emerging economies," *Journal of Business Ethics* 134 (2016): 479–491.

INDEX

Pages followed by an *e* indicate exhibits and an *f* indicates figures.

A

ABB, 191
Abe, Shinzo, 134
absolute advantage theory
  comparative advantage theory and, 71–72
  defined, 70
  examples of, 71*e*
  factor endowments and, 72
  free trade and, 70–71
  productivity and, 72
absolute productivity, 72
Abu Dhabi Investment Authority, 98
accommodative strategy, 48–49, 242, 242*e*
ACFTA. *See* ASEAN-China Free Trade Agreement (ACFTA)
acquisition premium, 174
acquisitions, 169–183
  cross-border, 171*e*, 174*e*
  defined, 170
  failures in, 180*e*
  hard-to-imitate capabilities, 175
  implications for action, 182*e*
  institutions and, 170–171, 171*e*, 172
  integration difficulties in, 180–181
  management of, 182
  motives for, 178–179, 179*e*
  organizational fit, 176
  performance of, 179–181
  real options, 173
  resources and, 170, 171*e*, 172, 174
  strategic fit, 176
  value and, 174–175
  wholly owned subsidiaries and, 165, 172
adaptability, 226, 228
administrative policies, 82
advertising agencies, 221
aerospace industry. *See* airline and aerospace industry
Aflac, 221, 231
AFL-CIO, 213
Africa
  Coca-Cola in, 153
  Ebola virus in, 245–246
  foreign direct investment in, 115
  trade with China, 115
agglomeration, 92–93, 156
agility, 226
agricultural subsidies, 125–126, 134
AH Industries, 157
Airbus, 60, 67, 74–75, 82, 154, 190, 190*e*, 192, 197
Airbus Group, 154
airline and aerospace industry
  Airbus, 60, 67, 74–75, 82, 134, 154, 190*e*, 192, 197
  alliances in, 164, 169, 171–173
  American Airlines, 171
  Boeing, 14, 57, 60, 67, 74–75, 82, 104, 154, 225, 228
  British Airways, 171
  competition in, 67
  competitive advantage and, 60
  distribution channels, 225
  Emirates Airlines, 169, 172–173
  Etihad Airways, 169, 172–173
  European Union (EU), 172
  foreign market entry and, 67–68, 154

fuel consumption and, 67
  joint ventures (JV), 173
  One World, 164, 169, 171–172
  rarity in, 60
  reciprocity and, 192
  research and development (R&D) in, 197
  resource-based view and, 10
  Sky Team, 164, 169, 172
  Star Alliance, 164, 169, 172
  supply chain management, 228
Alaska Permanent Fund, 98
Alberta Heritage Fund, 98
Alcatel, 228
Alcatel-Lucent, 156, 180–181
Alibaba, 14, 62–64, 104, 143, 150, 226, 232
Alifinance, 64
alignment, 228–229
Alipay system, 64
alliances, 169–183
  advantages and disadvantages, 172, 172*e*, 173–174
  airline industry, 164, 169, 171–173
  contractual (nonequity-based), 170
  cross-shareholding, 170
  dissolution of, 177–178, 178*e*
  equity-based, 170
  formation of, 176–177, 177*e*
  implications for action, 182*e*
  institutions and, 170–171, 171*e*, 172
  joint ventures (JV), 170–172
  management of, 182
  performance of, 178
  resources and, 170, 171*e*, 172–174
  strategic, 169–170, 170*e*, 172*e*, 172*f*
  strategic investment, 170
Allianz, 203
Amazon, 63–64, 149, 226, 232, 235
ambidexterity, 61
AMC Theaters, 174
American Airlines, 171
American exceptionalism, 38
Amos, Daniel, 221
Andean Community, 132
Anglo American, 199
antidumping duties, 82
anti-failure bias, 150
anti-globalization, 12, 236
ANZCERTA. *See* Australia-New Zealand Closer Economic Relations Trade Agreement (ANZCERTA or CER)
AOL Time Warner, 181
APEC. *See* Asia-Pacific Economic Cooperation (APEC)
Apotheker, Léo, 193, 206
Apple, 14, 15*e*, 57, 61, 159, 175, 206, 225, 235–236
Applebee's, 139
appreciation, 104
Arab Spring, 27
Arctic region, 238
Argentina
  domestic industries in, 12
  political risk and, 26
  small business in, 142
ASEAN. *See* Association of Southeast Asian Nations (ASEAN)
ASEAN-China Free Trade Agreement (ACFTA), 133
ASEAN Free Trade Area (AFTA), 133
Asian Infrastructure Investment Bank, 112–113
Asia-Pacific Economic Cooperation (APEC), 133–135
asset of foreignness, 154–155

Association of Southeast Asian Nations (ASEAN), 133
AT&T, 156, 171, 225*e*
Australia, 81, 133–134
Australia-New Zealand Closer Economic Relations Trade Agreement (ANZCERTA or CER), 133
automobile industry. *See also specific companies*
  acquisitions in, 178–179, 181–183, 200
  agglomeration in, 93
  bankruptcy and, 182
  Brazilian, 93
  Chinese, 172
  corporate headquarters, 200
  FDI and, 89–90
  first-mover advantages, 160
  flexible-fuel cars, 93
  foreign-born bosses, 206, 210
  foreign direct investment in, 93
  global product division structure, 190
  late-mover advantages, 160
  local responsiveness, 187
  "mergers of equals" in, 181
  Mexican, 92–93
  oligopolistic nature of, 94
  output of, 183
  rarity in, 60
Autonomy, 206
Avenue Strategies, 24
Avon Products, 55, 189, 189*e*
awareness, 49
Azevedo, Roberto, 124*f*

B

backward compatibility, 53
BAE Systems, 172
Baidu, 64
balance of payments (BOP), 107, 107*e*, 108
balance of trade, 69, 107
balance sheet approach, 210, 210*e*, 211
bandwagon effect, 109
Bangalore, 158
Bangladesh, 5
banking industry
  acquisitions in, 24, 176, 176*f*, 180–181
  corporate headquarters, 199
  dollar and, 103–104
  EU and, 121–122
  financing in, 144–145
  foreign exchange market and, 113–114, 117–118
  global, 103
  gold standard and, 110
  IMF and, 111–113
  letter of credit (L/C), 146
  post-Bretton Woods system, 110
Bank of America, 24, 146, 180
Bank of China, 146
bankruptcy, 149–151
Barclays Bank, 199
base of the pyramid (BoP), 6
beauty products, 55
Belgium, 128, 144
Bellini, Danilo, 117–119
Bellini do Brasil, 117–119
benchmarking, 56, 62
Benelux countries, 128
Best Price, 101
Bharti, 101
bid rates, 114

Big Data, 64
Big Mac index, 105–106, 106*e*
Big Pharma, 246
Bloomberg Businessweek, 223, 235
BMW, 49, 89–90, 160, 181
Boeing, 14, 57, 60, 67, 74–75, 82, 104, 154, 176, 225, 228
Bolivia, 97
Bombardier, 186
Bon Appétit, 139
born global firms (international new ventures), 145
Bosch, 171
BP, 15, 15*e*, 94–95, 240, 242*f*, 243
Brazil
    auto industry in, 93
    beauty products in, 55
    currency, 117–118
    domestic and export sales, 118*e*
    domestic industries in, 12
    economic growth in, 6
    emerging economies divisions, 5
    entrepreneurship in, 149
    ethanol fuel, 93
    exchange rates, 118*e*
    foreign exchange, 117–119
    GDP of, 34
    global economy and, 16
    gray market in, 23
    informal investment, 144
    institutional transitions in, 23
    small business in, 142
    taxation in, 23
Bretton Woods II, 111
Bretton Woods system, 110
Brexit (British exit), 13, 27, 121–122, 127, 131
bribery, 48
BRIC countries (Brazil, Russia, India, China)
    defined, 5
    de-globalization and, 17–18
    globalization and, 12, 16
BRICET countries (BRIC + Eastern Europe and Turkey), 5
BRICM countries (BRIC + Mexico), 5
BRICS countries (Brazil, Russia, India, China, South Africa)
    defined, 5
    exports to, 121
BRICS Development Bank, 113
Bridgestone, 198
Brin, Sergey, 149
British Airways, 171
build-operate-transfer (BOT) agreements, 163
Bulgaria, 130
Bumble Bee Foods, 166
Burger King, 242
Burundi, 141
business process outsourcing (BPO), 58
business-to-business (B2B) portals, 63
business-to-consumer (B2C) portals, 63

C

Cameron, David, 121
Canada
    EU bilateral trade and, 78
    exports to the US by, 78
    global warming and, 238
    NAFTA and, 132
    regional economic integration, 132–133
    trade diversification in, 78
    US imports, 132, 136
Canadian Arctic Archipelago, 238
capabilities, 54. *See also* resources and capabilities
capital flight, 109
capitalism
    income inequality, 239
    shareholder, 238–239
    sustainable, 236
captive sourcing, 57, 57*e*
Carlsberg, 33–34

Carrefour, 229
Carrier, 14, 21, 99, 132
Castro, Fidel, 25*f*
Castro, Raúl, 25*f*
causal ambiguity, 60–61
centers of excellence, 188
Central Europe
    EU and, 130
    globalization and, 12
    totalitarianism in, 25
    transition economy of, 21
CER. *See* Australia-New Zealand Closer Economic Relations Trade Agreement (ANZCERTA or CER)
Chan, Jackie, 40
Chan, Margaret, 246
Chansiri, Thiraphong, 166
Charan, Ram, 216
Chavez, Hugo, 97
ChemChina, 174
chemical industry, 242*e*
Chevrolet Nova, 224
Chevron, 14, 245
Chicken of the Sea, 166
chief human resource officer (CHRO), 216
Chile, 132–133, 142
China
    acquisitions case, 174–175
    Disney and, 3
    e-commerce and, 63–64
    economic growth in, 6, 27–28
    economic relationship with the US, 84*e*
    emerging economies divisions, 5
    entrepreneurship in, 149
    exports and, 67, 83–84, 132–133
    FDI and, 107, 174
    free trade agreements (FTAs), 134–135
    GDP of, 34
    global economy and, 16
    globalization and, 12–13
    gray market in, 24
    informal investment, 144
    joint ventures (JV), 229
    labor market, 158
    labor relations, 213
    manufacturing, 80–81
    MNEs and, 191, 214
    online shopping, 232–233
    Panasonic in, 197
    per capita income in, 5
    regional economic integration, 134–135
    relations with Japan, 26
    self-sufficiency in, 12
    sovereign wealth funds (SWF), 98
    state-owned enterprises (SOEs), 175
    stock market, 103
    taxation in, 23
    totalitarianism in, 25
    trade surplus, 69
    trade with Africa, 115
    training and development, 210
    transition economy of, 21, 23
    US autos in, 157
    US trade deficit with, 85*e*
    venture capital (VC) investment, 144
    wholly owned subsidiary (WOS), 229
China Investment Corporation (CIC), 98
China Lifestyle Research Center, 197
China National Petroleum Corp., 15*e*
Chirac, Jacques, 213
Christian-Muslim tensions, 130
Christiansen, Ole Kirk, 53
Chrysler, 39, 60, 160, 181–183
Cisco, 14, 160, 191
Citibank, 181
Citibank Islamic Bank, 161
Citigroup, 14, 98, 159
civilization, 42
civil law, 28
clean (free) float exchange rate policy, 108
Clemens, Randy, 139

climate change, 238, 243, 245
Clinton, Hillary, 134
cluster approach to culture, 41–42
coal industry, 128, 243
Coca-Cola, 7, 9–10, 97, 153–154, 163, 206, 224
codes of conduct, 46–47, 242–243
cognitive pillar, 22, 48
Colgate, 159
collectivism, 43
Colombia, 132
co-marketing, 164, 170
command economy, 31
commoditization, 56
Common Agricultural Policy (CAP), 81
common denominator, 110
common law, 28
common market, 127
comparative advantage theory, 72*e*–73*e*
    absolute advantage and, 71–72
    defined, 72
    evaluating, 83
    factor endowments and, 72
    opportunity cost and, 72
    productivity and, 72
compensation
    balance sheet approach, 210–211, 211*e*
    expatriates, 210–211, 211*e*
    going rate approach, 210
    going rate vs. balance sheet approach, 210*e*
    host-country nationals (HCNs), 211–212
complementary assets, 61
Components, Modules, Moves, and Services (eCMMS), 235
Comprehensive Economic and Trade Agreement (CETA), 78
Conaty, William, 216
Conservation International, 243
consumer convergence, 186–187
consumer-to-consumer (C2C) portals, 63
contagion (imitation) effect, 96
context
    cultural difference and, 40–41
    defined, 40
    importance of, 41
continued globalization, 16–17
contractual (nonequity-based) alliances, 162*e*, 163–164, 170
Cook, Tim, 61
Cooks Illustrated, 139
Coors Beer, 224
Copenhagen Accord, 245
copyrights, 30
corporate control, 194
corporate headquarters, 198–199, 199*e*, 200
corporate social responsibility (CSR), 234–247
    accommodative strategies, 242–243
    codes of conduct, 242–243
    defensive strategies, 241
    defined, 236
    disasters and scandals, 239–240
    economic performance and, 244–245
    environmentalism and, 236, 238, 240, 243
    Foxconn case, 235–236
    free market and, 237–239
    fundamental debate on, 237–238
    global sustainability and, 236–238
    implications for action, 245*e*
    importance of, 239
    institutions and, 240–241, 241*e*, 242–245
    legitimacy of, 243
    Maasai Tribal name case, 50
    managers and, 240, 245
    MNEs and, 14
    offshoring and, 58
    proactive strategies, 243–244
    profits and, 237–239
    reactive strategies, 241
    resources and, 241*e*, 244–245
    shareholders and, 238–239
    stakeholders and, 236–239, 243
    VRIO framework, 244

taxation in, 23
US imports, 132, 136
MHI Vestas Offshore Wind, 157
Michelin, 206
microfinance, 144–145
Microsoft, 14, 160, 179, 193*f*, 206, 235, 245
Midea, 174–175
migrant crisis, 131
Milken Institute Global Conference, 243*f*
Minor Group, 148
Mitsubishi Heavy Industries (MHI), 157
Mitsubishi Motors, 45, 206
mixed economy, 31
mobile phones
  online shopping, 233
  pioneer, 73*f*, 74
modes of entry
  advantages and disadvantages, 162*e*
  build-operate-transfer (BOT) agreements, 163
  co-marketing, 164
  comprehensive model of, 161*e*
  contractual agreements and, 163–164
  equity, 161–164
  formal institutions and, 171–172
  joint ventures (JV), 164–165
  nonequity, 161–162
  research and development (R&D) contracts, 164
  selection of, 163–165
  turnkey projects, 163
  wholly owned subsidiary (WOS), 164–165
monetary policy, 129
monetary union, 128
Morgan Stanley, 98
Motorola Mobility, 175
movie industry, 180
MTV, 187
Multifiber Arrangement (MFA), 124
multilateral trading systems, 123
multinational corporation (MNC), 89
multinational enterprise (MNE)
  acquisitions and, 174–175
  career development, 210
  centers of excellence, 188
  Chinese, 174–175, 182
  corporate controls in, 194
  corporate headquarters, 198–200
  criticism of, 12
  debates on, 14
  defined, 4, 89
  diffusion of innovation in, 188
  effects on home and host countries, 96–97
  efficiency-seeking, 157
  equity modes, 160, 162
  ethnocentrism in, 209
  expatriation and, 204, 207–210
  FDI and, 89–92, 95–102
  foreign-born bosses, 206
  foreign market entry, 165
  free market and, 239
  globalization and, 15–16
  global strategy, 188
  growth in, 89, 186
  host-country nationals (HCNs), 204
  Indian, 174–175, 182
  ISO standards and, 243–244
  joint ventures and, 164–165
  labor relations, 212–213
  localization and, 15, 196, 222–224
  management of, 198
  market failure and, 94–95
  market segmentation, 223–224
  Nordic countries, 87
  OLI advantages, 90, 93, 95
  outsourcing, 228–229, 231
  pollution-intensive production and, 240
  repatriation and, 209
  staffing, 204–205, 205*e*, 206–214
  standardization and, 222–224
  subsidiary control in, 194
  technology spillovers, 96
  transnational strategy, 190, 196

voluntary "green practices," 240
multinational structure and strategy, 184–200
  cost reduction and local responsiveness, 186–191
  entrepreneurship and, 146–148
  geographic area, 189*e*
  global standardization strategy, 188
  home replication strategy, 187
  implications for action, 198
  institution-based considerations, 191–192, 192*e*, 193
  integration-responsiveness framework, 186, 186*e*, 187
  international divisions in, 189*e*
  knowledge management, 195, 195*e*, 196–197
  learning and, 195–196
  LEGO case, 194
  localization (multidomestic) strategy, 187–188, 196
  organizational, 189–193
  reciprocal relationship between, 191
  research and development (R&D) in, 197–198
  resource-based considerations, 192*e*, 193–195
  strategic choices for, 187, 187*e*, 188
  transnational strategy, 188, 190
MW Brands, 166

N

Nadella, Satya, 193*f*, 206
NAFTA. *See* North American Free Trade Agreement (NAFTA)
Nasser, Jacques, 206
Natale, 117–118
national boundaries, 44
national culture, 38
Natura, 55, 62
NEC, 159, 165
Nestlé, 224, 242
Netherlands, 128
Netscape, 160
New Development Bank, 112–113
NewLink Genetics, 246
News Corporation, 199
New Zealand, 133
"Nexit" (Netherlands exit), 131
Next Eleven countries (N-11: Bangladesh, Egypt, Indonesia, Iran, Korea, Mexico, Nigeria, Pakistan, the Philippines, Turkey, and Vietnam), 5
Nicaragua, 132
Nigeria, 5
Nigerian National Petroleum Corp. (NNPC), 94–95
Nike, 48, 57, 101, 228–229, 237, 243
Nissan, 121, 160, 170, 206, 210
Nixon, Richard, 110
Nobel Peace Prize, 129, 145
Nokia, 226
Nomura Securities, 176, 176*f*, 180
nondiscrimination, 123
nonequity modes, 161–163
nonfinancial companies
  currency risks, 115
  foreign exchange strategies, 115–116
  strategic hedging, 115–116
nongovernmental organizations (NGOs), 236, 243, 245
non-multinational enterprises, 160, 162
non-shareholder stakeholders, 236
nontariff barriers (NTB), 78, 81–82, 124
Nooyi, Indra, 206
Nordic multinationals, 87
normative pillar, 22, 48
norms
  culturally sensitive, 50
  defined, 48
  ethical challenges and, 48–49
North, Douglass, 22
North American Free Trade Agreement (NAFTA), 13, 21, 24, 68, 78

Canada and, 132
  consequences of withdrawing from, 136–137
  controversies in, 136
  defined, 131
  economic integration and, 131–132
  jobs and, 132, 136–137
  maquiladora plants, 132
  Mexico and, 131
Northern Sea Route (NSR), 238
North Korea, 25
Northrop Grumman, 14, 154, 175–176
Norway, 87
Novo Nordisk, 203

O

Obama administration
  Ebola and, 246
  TPP and, 134
O Boticário, 55
OECD Convention on Combating Bribery of Foreign Public Officials, 48
offer rates, 114
offshoring, 57–58, 58*e*, 59, 63
Ohlin, Bertil, 72
oil and gas industries, 97, 142, 172, 238
Old Mutual, 199
O'Leary, Michael, 169
OLI advantages, 90, 90*e*, 92–93, 95
oligopolistic industries, 94
Olympia, 225*e*
O'Neil, Jim, 16
O'Neill, Paul, 84
One World, 164, 169, 171–172
online shopping, 231–233
onshoring, 57, 59
opportunism, 23
opportunistic behavior, 95
opportunity cost, 72
organization
  alliances and acquisitions and, 173–174, 176
  ambidexterity in, 61
  competitive advantage and, 61
  complementary assets and, 61
  marketing and, 231
  MNEs and, 194
  resource-based view and, 61–62
  social complexity in, 62
  in VRIO framework, 61–62
organizational culture, 194–195
organizational fit, 176, 180
Organization for Economic Cooperation and Development (OECD), 16
outbound logistics, 225–226
outsourcing
  alignment in, 228–229
  business process outsourcing (BPO), 58
  captive sourcing, 57, 57*e*, 59
  commoditization and, 56
  controversies in, 57–59
  defined, 56–57
  ethics of, 58
  geographic dimension of, 57, 57*e*, 58–59
  in-house vs., 57*e*
  manufacturing, 228, 235
  offshoring, 57–59, 63
  onshoring, 57, 59
  reshoring, 59
  of service activities, 57
  Zara case, 227
ownership advantages
  benefits of, 91–92
  defined, 90

P

Pakistan, 5
Panama, 132

CHAPTER 1 LEARNING OBJECTIVES / KEY TERMS

1-1 Explain the concepts of international business and global business.
- International business (IB) is typically defined as (1) a business (firm) that engages in international (cross-border) economic activities, or (2) the action of doing business abroad.
- Multinational enterprises (MNEs) are firms that engage in foreign direct investment (FDI).
- Global business is defined in this book as business around the globe.
- Emerging economies contribute about 50% of global gross domestic product (measured by purchasing power parity, PPP).
- Viewed as a pyramid, the global economy has one billion people at the top and another billion in the second tier. The majority of humanity, approximately five billion people, makes up the base of the pyramid.

international business (IB) (1) A business (firm) that engages in international (cross-border) economic activities or (2) the action of doing business abroad. (p. 4)

multinational enterprise (MNE) A firm that engages in foreign direct investment and operates in multiple countries. (p. 4)

foreign direct investment (FDI) Investment in, controlling, and managing value-added activities in other countries. (p. 4)

global business Business around the globe. (p. 4)

emerging economy (emerging market) A developing country. (p. 5)

gross domestic product (GDP) The sum of value added by resident firms, households, and governments operating in an economy. (p. 5)

purchasing power parity (PPP) A conversion that determines the equivalent amount of goods and services different currencies can purchase. This conversion is usually used to capture the differences in cost of living in different countries. (p. 5)

BRIC An acronym for the emerging economies of Brazil, Russia, India, and China. (p. 5)

BRICS An acronym for the emerging economies of Brazil, Russia, India, China, and South Africa. (p. 5)

Triad Three regions of developed economies (North America, Western Europe, and Japan). (p. 6)

base of the pyramid (BoP) The vast majority of humanity, about five billion people, who make less than $2,000 a year. (p. 6)

1-2 Give three reasons why it is important to study global business.
- To better advance your employability and career in the global economy.
- To better prepare for possible expatriate assignments abroad.
- Expatriate managers generally command an international premium for taking overseas positions.
- To enhance your competence in interacting with foreign suppliers, partners, and competitors; and in working for foreign-owned employers in your country.

expatriate manager (expat) A manager who works outside his or her native country. (p. 6)

international premium A significant pay raise commanded by expatriates when working overseas. (p. 7)

1-3 Articulate the fundamental question that the study of global business seeks to answer and the two perspectives from which to answer it.
- Our most fundamental question is: What determines the success and failure of firms around the globe?
- The two core perspectives are (1) the institution-based view and (2) the resource-based view.
- The institution-based view suggests that the success and failure of firms are enabled and constrained by different rules of the game.
- The resource-based view says that successful firms have certain valuable and unique firm-specific resources and capabilities that are not shared by competitors in the same environments.
- We develop a unified framework by organizing materials in every chapter according to the two perspectives guided by the fundamental question.

institution-based view A leading perspective in global business that suggests that firm performance is, at least in part, determined by the institutional frameworks governing firm behavior around the world. (p. 9)

institution Formal and informal rules of the game. (p. 9)

institutional framework Formal and informal institutions that govern individual and firm behavior. (p. 9)

resource-based view A leading perspective in global business that suggests that firm performance is, at least in part, determined by its internal resources and capabilities. (p. 10)

liability of foreignness The inherent disadvantage that foreign firms experience in host countries because of their nonnative status. (p. 10)

1-4 Identify three ways of understanding what globalization is.

- The three views of globalization are (1) that it is a recent phenomenon, (2) that it is a one-directional evolution since the dawn of human history, and (3) that it is a process similar to the swing of a pendulum.
- Advocates of globalization say that it increases economic growth, standards of living, technology sharing, and cultural integration.

- Critics argue that globalization undermines wages in rich countries, exploits workers in poor countries, gives MNEs too much power, destroys the environment, and promotes inequality.
- Semiglobalization is more complex than extremes of total isolation and total globalization and provides a more accurate picture of the current global economy.

globalization The close integration of countries and peoples of the world. (p. 10)

risk management Identification and assessment of risks and preparation to minimize the impact of high-risk, unfortunate events. (p. 13)

scenario planning A technique to prepare and plan for multiple scenarios (either high or low risk). (p. 13)

semiglobalization A perspective that suggests that barriers to market integration at borders are high, but not high enough to completely insulate countries from each other. (p. 13)

1-5 Appreciate the size of the global economy and the strengths of multinationals.

- MNEs, especially large ones from developed economies, are sizeable economic entities.
- Emerging economies have numerous MNEs in the *Fortune* Global 500 as well.

- Current and would-be business leaders need to be aware of their own hidden pro-globalization bias.
- The rapid globalization of the 1990s saw significant backlash around the turn of the century marked by protests and terrorist attacks, largely attributed to a sense of powerlessness in the face of rapid global change.

1-6 Understand the organization of this book.

- This book has three parts.
- Part 1 is *foundations*. Chapters 1, 2, 3, and 4 deal with the two leading perspectives: institution-based and resource-based views.
- Part 2 covers tools, focusing on trade (Chapter 5), foreign investment (Chapter 6), foreign exchange (Chapter 7), and global and regional integration (Chapter 8).

- Part 3 focuses on *managing* around the world. We start with the internationalization of small, entrepreneurial firms (Chapter 9), followed by ways to enter foreign markets (Chapter 10), to make alliances and acquisitions work (Chapter 11), to strategize, structure, and learn (Chapter 12), to manage human resources (Chapter 13), to deal with marketing and supply chain management (Chapter 14), and finally to manage corporate social responsibility (Chapter 15).

CHAPTER 2 LEARNING OBJECTIVES / KEY TERMS

2-1 Identify two types of institutions.
- Institutions are commonly defined as "the rules of the game."
- There are two types of institutions: formal and informal. Each has different supportive pillars.

institutional transition Fundamental and comprehensive changes introduced to the formal and informal rules of the game that affect organizations as players. (p. 22)

regulatory pillar The coercive power of governments exercised through laws, regulations, and rules. (p. 22)

normative pillar The mechanisms through which norms influence individual and firm behavior. (p. 22)

cognitive pillar The internalized, taken-for-granted values and beliefs that guide individual and firm behavior. (p. 22)

2-2 Explain how institutions reduce uncertainty.
- Institutions' key function is to reduce uncertainty, curtail transaction costs, and combat opportunism. Institutions accomplish these things by reducing the range of acceptable actions.

transaction cost Cost associated with economic transactions or, more broadly, the cost of doing business. (p. 23)

opportunism The act of seeking self-interest with guile. (p. 23)

2-3 Identify the two core propositions underpinning an institution-based view of global business.
- Proposition 1: Managers and firms *rationally* pursue their interests and make choices within formal and informal institutional constraints in a given institutional framework.
- Proposition 2: When formal constraints are unclear or fail, informal constraints will play a *larger* role.

2-4 List the differences between democracy and totalitarianism.
- Democracy is a political system in which citizens elect representatives to govern the country.
- Freedom of expression is a fundamental aspect of democracy.
- Totalitarianism is a political system in which one person or party exercises absolute political control.
- Totalitarian systems can be communist, right-wing, theocratic, or tribal.
- Totalitarian systems generally carry a greater degree of political risk than democracies do.

political system The rules of the game on how a country is governed politically. (p. 24)

democracy A political system in which citizens elect representatives to govern the country on their behalf. (p. 25)

totalitarianism (dictatorship) A political system in which one person or party exercises absolute political control over the population. (p. 25)

political risk Risk associated with political changes that may negatively impact domestic and foreign firms. (p. 26)

2-5 List the differences among civil law, common law, and theocratic law.
- Civil law uses comprehensive statutes and codes as a primary means to form legal judgments and as such is less confrontational.
- Common law is shaped by precedents and traditions from previous judicial decisions and is more confrontational as plaintiffs and defendants argue the relevance of precedent to specific cases.
- Theocratic law is a legal system based on religious teachings, such as Islamic law.

legal system The rules of the game on how a country's laws are enacted and enforced. (p. 28)

civil law A legal tradition that uses comprehensive statutes and codes as a primary means to form legal judgments. (p. 28)

common law A legal tradition that is shaped by precedents from previous judicial decisions. (p. 28)

theocratic law A legal system based on religious teachings. (p. 29)

CHAPTER REVIEW

CHAPTER 2 LEARNING OBJECTIVES / KEY TERMS

2-6 Articulate the importance of property rights and intellectual property rights.

- Protection of property rights by a functioning legal system is fundamental to economic development.
- Patents, copyrights, and trademarks are the three primary ways that intellectual property is recognized and protected.
- The intangible nature of intellectual property rights makes enforcement difficult, and weak enforcement makes counterfeiting a rational choice for certain firms.

property right Legal right to use an economic property (resource) and to derive income and benefits from it. (p. 29)

intellectual property (IP) Intangible property that results from intellectual activity (such as the content of books, videos, and websites). (p. 29)

intellectual property right (IPR) Legal right associated with the ownership of intellectual property. (p. 30)

patent Exclusive legal right of inventors to derive income from their inventions through activities such as manufacturing, licensing, or selling. (p. 30)

copyright Exclusive legal right of authors and publishers to publish and disseminate their work. (p. 30)

trademark Exclusive legal right of firms to use specific names, brands, and designs to differentiate their products from others. (p. 30)

piracy The unauthorized use of intellectual property rights. (p. 30)

2-7 List the differences among market economy, command economy, and mixed economy.

- A pure market economy is characterized by *laissez faire* and total control by market forces.
- A pure command economy is defined by government ownership and control of all means of production, distribution, and pricing.
- Most countries operate mixed economies, with a different emphasis on market versus command forces.

economic system The rules of the game on how a country is governed economically. (p. 30)

market economy An economy that is characterized by the "invisible hand" of market forces. (p. 30)

command economy An economy in which theoretically all factors of production are state owned and state controlled, and all supply, demand, and pricing are planned by the government. (p. 31)

mixed economy An economy that has elements of both a market economy and a command economy. (p. 31)

2-8 Explain why it is important to understand the different institutions when doing business abroad.

- Have a thorough understanding of the formal institutions before entering a country.
- Recognize when informal relationships must be developed before business can be conducted due to generally weak formal institutions.

3-1 Explain where informal institutions come from.

- Informal institutions are a pervasive feature of every economy.
- Societies tend to perceive their own culture, ethics, and norms as "natural, rational, and morally right"—a self-centered mentality is known as ethnocentrism.

ethnocentrism A self-centered mentality held by a group of people who perceive their own culture, ethics, and norms as natural, rational, and morally right. (p. 38)

3-2 Define culture and articulate its two main manifestations.

- Culture is the collective programming of the mind that distinguishes one group from another.
- Managers and firms ignorant of foreign languages and religious traditions may end up with embarrassments and, worse, disasters when doing business around the globe.
- English is the *lingua franca* because of the need in a global market for a common language.
- The four leading religions in the world are Christianity, Islam, Hinduism, and Buddhism.

culture The collective programming of the mind that distinguishes the members of one group or category of people from another. (p. 38)

lingua franca A global business language. (p. 39)

3-3 Articulate three ways to understand cultural differences.

- The context approach differentiates cultures based on the high- versus low-context dimension.
- The cluster approach groups similar cultures together as clusters and civilizations.
- Hofstede and colleagues have identified five cultural dimensions: (1) power distance, (2) individualism/collectivism, (3) masculinity/femininity, (4) uncertainty avoidance, and (5) long-term orientation.

context The background against which interaction takes place. (p. 40)

low-context culture A culture in which communication is usually taken at face value without much reliance on unspoken conditions or assumptions. (p. 41)

high-context culture A culture in which communication relies heavily on the underlying unspoken conditions or assumptions, which are as important as the words used. (p. 41)

cluster A group of countries that have similar cultures. (p. 41)

civilization The highest cultural grouping of people and the broadest level of cultural identity people have. (p. 42)

power distance The extent to which less powerful members within a culture expect and accept that power is distributed unequally. (p. 42)

individualism The idea that the identity of an individual is fundamentally his or her own. (p. 42)

collectivism The idea that an individual's identity is fundamentally tied to the identity of his or her collective group. (p. 42)

masculinity A relatively strong form of societal-level sex-role differentiation whereby men tend to have occupations that reward assertiveness and women tend to work in caring professions. (p. 43)

femininity A relatively weak form of societal-level sex-role differentiation whereby more women occupy positions that reward assertiveness and more men work in caring professions. (p. 43)

uncertainty avoidance The extent to which members of a culture accept or avoid ambiguous situations and uncertainty. (p. 44)

long-term orientation A perspective that emphasizes perseverance and savings for future betterment. (p. 45)

3-4 Explain why understanding cultural differences is crucial for global business.

- A great deal of global business activity is consistent with the context, cluster, and dimension approaches to cultural differences.

3-5 **Explain why ethics is important.**
- Ethics refers to the principles, standards, and norms of conduct governing individual and firm behavior.

- When managing ethics overseas, two schools of thought are ethical relativism and ethical imperialism.

ethics The principles, standards, and norms of conduct that govern individual and firm behavior. (p. 46)

code of conduct A set of guidelines for making ethical decisions. (p. 46)

ethical relativism A perspective that suggests that all ethical standards are relative. (p. 46)

ethical imperialism The absolute belief that "there is only one set of

Ethics (with a capital E), and we have it." (p. 46)

3-6 **Identify ways to combat corruption.**
- The fight against corruption around the world is a long-term, global battle.
- Corruption distorts the basis for competition.

- High levels of corruption and low levels of economic development are strongly correlated.
- Legislation criminalizing corruption must not only be institutionalized, but also must be enforced to be effective.

corruption The abuse of public power for private benefits, usually in the form of bribery. (p. 47)

3-7 **Identify norms associated with strategic responses when firms deal with ethical challenges.**
- When confronting ethical challenges, individual firms have four strategic choices: (1) reactive, (2) defensive, (3) accommodative, and (4) proactive strategies.
- Using a reactive strategy, a firm is passive and does not feel compelled to act even when problems arise.

- Using a defensive strategy, a firm fights informal pressure and is only concerned with required regulatory compliance.
- Using an accommodative strategy, a firm accepts responsibility and will act beyond what is simply required.
- Using a proactive strategy, a firm anticipates institutional changes and does more than required by current regulations.

norm The prevailing practices of relevant players that affect the focal individuals and firms. (p. 48)

reactive strategy A response to an ethical challenge that often involves denial and belated action to correct problems. (p. 48)

defensive strategy A response to an ethical challenge that focuses on regulatory compliance. (p. 48)

accommodative strategy A response to an ethical challenge that involves accepting responsibility. (p. 48)

proactive strategy A strategy that anticipates ethical challenges and addresses them before they happen. (p. 49)

3-8 **Explain how you can acquire cross-cultural literacy.**
- It is important to enhance cultural intelligence, leading to cross-cultural literacy.
- Acquisition of cultural intelligence passes through three phases: (1) awareness, (2) knowledge, and (3) skills.

- The most effective way to acquire cultural intelligence is through total immersion in a foreign culture.
- It is crucial to understand and adapt to the changing norms globally.

cultural intelligence An individual's ability to understand and adjust to new cultures. (p. 49)

CHAPTER 4 LEARNING OBJECTIVES / KEY TERMS

4-1 **Define resources and capabilities.**
- Resources and capabilities are tangible and intangible assets a firm uses to choose and implement its strategies.
- Although some scholars define resources and capabilities differently, in practice the distinctions become blurred.
- Tangible resources and capabilities can be financial, physical, technological, and organizational.
- Intangible resources and capabilities can be human, innovation, and reputational.

SWOT analysis An analytical tool for determining a firm's strengths (S), weaknesses (W), opportunities (O), and threats (T). (p. 54)

resource (capability) The tangible and intangible assets a firm uses to choose and implement its strategies. (p. 54)

tangible resource and capability Assets that are observable and easily quantified. (p. 54)

intangible resource and capability Assets that are hard to observe and difficult to quantify. (p. 54)

4-2 **Explain how value is created from a firm's resources and capabilities.**
- A value chain consists of a stream of activities from upstream to downstream that add value.
- A SWOT analysis engages managers to ascertain a firm's strengths and weaknesses on an activity-by-activity basis relative to rivals, a process known as benchmarking.
- If a firm's particular activity is unsatisfactory, the manager uses a two-stage decision model to remedy the situation.

value chain A series of activities used in the production of goods and services that make a product or service more valuable. (p. 55)

benchmarking Examining whether a firm has the resources and capabilities to perform a particular activity in a manner superior to competitors. (p. 56)

4-3 **Articulate the difference between keeping an activity in-house and outsourcing it.**
- Outsourcing is defined as turning over all or part of an organizational activity to an outside supplier.
- An activity with a high degree of industry commonality and a high degree of commoditization can be outsourced.
- An industry-specific and firm-specific (proprietary) activity is better performed in-house.
- On any given activity, the four choices for managers in terms of modes and locations are (1) offshoring, (2) onshoring, (3) captive sourcing/FDI, and (4) domestic in-house activity.

commoditization A process of market competition through which unique products that command high prices and high margins gradually lose their ability to do so, thus becoming commodities. (p. 56)

outsourcing Turning over an activity to an outside supplier that will perform it on behalf of the focal firm. (p. 57)

offshoring Outsourcing to an international or foreign firm. (p. 57)

onshoring Outsourcing to a domestic firm. (p. 57)

captive sourcing Setting up subsidiaries abroad so that the work done is in-house but the location is foreign. Also known as foreign direct investment (FDI). (p. 57)

business process outsourcing (BPO) The outsourcing of business processes such as loan origination, credit card processing, and call center operations. (p. 58)

reshoring Moving formerly offshored activities back to the home country of the focal firm. (p. 59)

4-4 **Explain how to use a VRIO framework to understand a firm's resources and capabilities.**
- A VRIO framework suggests that only resources and capabilities that are valuable, rare, inimitable, and organizationally embedded will generate sustainable competitive advantage.
- Non-value-adding resources and capabilities may become weaknesses instead of strengths.
- Valuable but common resources and capabilities will lead to competitive parity but no advantage.
- Valuable and rare resources and capabilities can be a source of competitive advantage only if they are difficult for competitors to imitate.
- Causal ambiguity refers to the difficulty of identifying the actual cause of a firm's successful performance.
- Only valuable, rare, and hard-to-imitate resources and capabilities that are organizationally embedded and exploited can possibly lead to persistently above average performance.

VRIO framework The resource-based framework that focuses on the value (V), rarity (R), imitability (I), and organizational (O) aspects of resources and capabilities. (p. 59)

causal ambiguity The difficulty of identifying the actual cause of a firm's successful performance. (p. 60)

complementary asset The combination of numerous resources and assets that enable a firm to gain a competitive advantage. (p. 61)

ambidexterity Ability to use one's both hands equally well. In management jargon, this term has been used to describe capabilities to simultaneously deal with paradoxes (such as exploration versus exploitation). (p. 61)

social complexity The socially intricate and interdependent ways that firms are typically organized. (p. 62)

4-5 **Identify four things you need to do as part of a successful career and business strategy.**
- Managers need to distinguish resources and capabilities that are valuable, rare, hard-to-imitate, and organizationally embedded from those that do not share these attributes.
- Relentless imitation or benchmarking, while important, is not likely to be a successful strategy.
- A sustainable competitive advantage does not imply that it will last forever.
- Managers need to build up resources and capabilities for future competition.
- Students are advised to make themselves into "untouchables" whose jobs cannot be outsourced, by nurturing valuable, rare, and hard-to-imitate capabilities indispensable to an organization.

CHAPTER 5 LEARNING OBJECTIVES / KEY TERMS

5-1 Use the resource-based and institution-based views to explain why nations trade.
- The resource-based view suggests that nations trade because firms in one nation generate valuable, unique, and hard-to-imitate exports that firms in other nations find it beneficial to import.
- The institution-based view argues that as "rules of the game," different laws and regulations governing international trade determine how the gains from trade are shared or not shared.

export To sell abroad. (p. 68)

import To buy from abroad. (p. 68)

merchandise (goods) trade Tangible products being bought and sold. (p. 68)

service trade Intangible services being bought and sold. (p. 68)

trade deficit An economic condition in which a nation imports more than it exports. (p. 68)

trade surplus An economic condition in which a nation exports more than it imports. (p. 69)

balance of trade The country-level trade surplus or deficit. (p. 69)

5-2 Identify and define the classical and modern theories of international trade.
- Classical theories include (1) mercantilism, (2) absolute advantage, and (3) comparative advantage.
- Mercantilism was widely practiced during the 17th and 18th centuries. It viewed international trade as a zero-sum game, and is the forerunner of modern protectionism.
- The theory of absolute advantage was proposed by Adam Smith in 1776 and advocates specialization and trade as a win-win game for all.
- David Ricardo developed the theory of comparative advantage in 1817 as an explanation for how countries can benefit from trade even when one of them does not have an absolute advantage.
- Modern theories include (1) product life cycles, (2) strategic trade, and (3) national competitive advantage of industries or "diamond."
- The product life cycle theory was developed in 1966 by Raymond Verson to explain the changes in trade patterns over time.
- The strategic trade theory was developed in the 1970s to address the question of whether government intervention can actually add value.
- Developed by Michael Porter in 1990, the theory of national competitive advantage of industries is presented in a diamond-shaped diagram to show why nations are competitive internationally in some industries but not in others.

mercantilism A theory that holds that the wealth of the world (measured in gold and silver) is fixed and that a nation that exports more than it imports will enjoy the net inflows of gold and silver and become richer. (p. 70)

protectionism The idea that governments should actively protect domestic industries from imports and vigorously promote exports. (p. 70)

free trade The idea that free market forces should determine the buying and selling of goods and services with little or no government intervention. (p. 70)

theory of absolute advantage A theory that suggests that under free trade, each nation gains by specializing in economic activities in which it is the most efficient producer. (p. 70)

absolute advantage The economic advantage one nation enjoys because it can produce a good or service more efficiently than anyone else. (p. 70)

theory of comparative advantage A theory that suggests that a nation gains by specializing in production of one good in which it has comparative advantage. (p. 72)

comparative advantage The relative (not absolute) advantage in one economic activity that one nation enjoys in comparison with other nations. (p. 72)

opportunity cost The cost of pursuing one activity at the expense of another activity. (p. 72)

factor endowment The extent to which different countries possess various factors of production such as labor, land, and technology. (p. 72)

factor endowment theory (Heckscher–Ohlin theory) A theory that suggests that nations will develop comparative advantages based on their locally abundant factors. (p. 72)

product life cycle theory A theory that suggests that patterns of trade change over time as production shifts and as the product moves from new to maturing to standardized stages. (p. 73)

strategic trade theory A theory that suggests that strategic intervention by governments in certain industries can enhance their odds for international success. (p. 74)

first-mover advantage Advantage that first entrants enjoy and do not share with late entrants. (p. 74)

strategic trade policy Economic policy that provides companies a strategic advantage through government subsidies. (p. 75)

theory of national competitive advantage of industries (or diamond theory) A theory that suggests that the competitive advantage of certain industries in different nations depends on four aspects that form a "diamond" shape when diagrammed. (p. 75)

resource mobility The assumption that a resource used in producing a product in one industry can be shifted and put to use in another industry. (p. 77)

5-3 | **Explain the importance of political realities governing international trade.**

- The net impact of various tariffs and nontariff barriers is that the nation as a whole is worse off while certain special interest groups (such as specific industries, firms, and regions) benefit.

- Economic arguments against free trade center on (1) protectionism and (2) infant industries.
- Political arguments against free trade focus on (1) national security, (2) consumer protection, (3) foreign policy, and (4) environmental and social responsibility.

tariff barrier A means of discouraging imports by placing a tariff (tax) on imported goods. (p. 79)

import tariff A tax imposed on imports. (p. 79)

deadweight cost Net losses that occur in an economy as the result of tariffs. (p. 79)

nontariff barrier (NTB) A means of discouraging imports using means other than taxes on imported goods. (p. 81)

subsidy A government payment to domestic firms. (p. 81)

import quota A restriction on the quantity of goods brought into a country. (p. 81)

voluntary export restraint (VER) An international agreement that shows that an exporting country voluntarily agrees to restrict its exports. (p. 81)

local content requirement A rule that stipulates that a certain proportion of the value of a good must originate from the domestic market. (p. 82)

administrative policy A bureaucratic rule that makes it harder to import foreign goods. (p. 82)

antidumping duty A cost levied on imports that have been "dumped," or sold below cost, to unfairly drive domestic firms out of business. (p. 82)

trade embargo Politically motivated trade sanctions against foreign countries to signal displeasure. (p. 83)

5-4 | **Identify factors that should be considered when your firm participates in international trade.**

- Be aware of the comparative advantage of certain locations, and leverage their potential.

- Monitor and nurture the comparative advantage of current locations, and take advantage of new locations.
- Be politically active to demonstrate, safeguard, and advance the gains from international trade.

CHAPTER 6 LEARNING OBJECTIVES / KEY TERMS

6-1 Identify and define the key terms associated with foreign direct investment (FDI).
- The resource-based view suggests that *direct* is the key word in FDI, which reflects firms' interest in directly managing, developing, and leveraging their firm-specific resources and capabilities abroad.
- The institution-based view argues that recent expansion of FDI is indicative of generally more friendly formal policies and informal norms and values associated with FDI (despite some setbacks).

foreign portfolio investment (FPI) Holding securities, such as stocks and bonds, of firms in other countries but without a controlling interest. (p. 88)

management control right The right to appoint key managers and establish control mechanisms. (p. 88)

horizontal FDI A type of FDI in which a firm produces the same products or offers the same services in a host country as at home. (p. 88)

vertical FDI A type of FDI in which a firm moves upstream or downstream in different value chain stages in a host country. (p. 88)

upstream vertical FDI A type of vertical FDI in which a firm engages in an upstream stage of the value chain. (p. 88)

downstream vertical FDI A type of vertical FDI in which a firm engages in a downstream stage of the value chain. (p. 88)

FDI flow The amount of FDI moving in a given period (usually a year) in a certain direction. (p. 88)

FDI inflow FDI moving into a country in a year. (p. 88)

FDI outflow FDI moving out of a country in a year. (p. 88)

FDI stock The total accumulation of inbound FDI in a country or outbound FDI from a country across a given period of time (usually several years). (p. 88)

6-2 Use the resource-based and institution-based views to answer why FDI takes place.
- FDI takes place due to the quest for ownership, location, and internalization (OLI) advantages.

OLI advantages The advantages of ownership (O), location (L), and internalization (I) that come from engaging in FDI. (p. 90)

ownership Possessing and leveraging of certain valuable, rare, hard-to-imitate, and organizationally embedded (VRIO) assets overseas in the context of FDI. (p. 90)

location Advantages enjoyed by a firm that derive from the places in which it operates. (p. 90)

internalization The replacement of cross-border markets (such as exporting and importing) with one firm (the MNE) located in two or more countries. (p. 90)

licensing Buying and selling technology and intellectual property rights. (p. 90)

market imperfection (market failure) The imperfect rules governing international market transactions. (p. 90)

6-3 Explain how FDI results in ownership advantages.
- MNEs generally prefer ownership over licensing because ownership reduces dissemination risks, provides greater control over foreign operations, and makes firm-specific know-how easier to implement.

dissemination risk The possibility of unauthorized diffusion of firm-specific know-how. (p. 91)

6-4 Identify the ways you can acquire and neutralize location advantages.
- Location advantages refer to certain advantages that can help MNEs attain strategic goals, whether it is access to labor, natural resources, or markets.

agglomeration Clustering of economic activities in certain locations. (p. 92)

6-5 List the benefits of internalization.
- Internalization refers to the replacement of a cross-border market relationship with a single firm (the MNE) with locations in two or more countries.
- Internalization helps combat market imperfections and failures.

intrafirm trade International trade between two subsidiaries in two countries controlled by the same MNE. (p. 95)

6-6 **Identify different political views on FDI and understand its benefits and costs to host and home countries.**

- The radical view, with its roots in Marxism, is hostile to FDI, and the free market view calls for minimum intervention in FDI.
- Since the 1980s, many countries, including Brazil, China, Hungary, India, Ireland, and Russia, have moved from radical to more FDI-friendly policies.
- Most countries practice pragmatic nationalism, weighing the costs and benefits of FDI.

- FDI brings a different (and often opposing) set of benefits and costs to host and home countries.
- Host-country benefits include capital inflow, technology spillover, advanced management know-how, and job creation. Costs include loss of sovereignty, adverse competition, and capital outflow.
- Home-country benefits include repatriated earnings, increased exports of components and services, and knowledge gains from operations abroad. Costs include capital outflow and job losses.

radical view on FDI A political view that sees FDI as an instrument of imperialism and a vehicle for foreign exploitation. (p. 95)

free market view on FDI A political view that holds that FDI, unrestricted by government intervention, will enable countries to tap into their absolute or comparative advantages by specializing in the production of certain goods and services. (p. 96)

pragmatic nationalism view on FDI A political view that approves FDI only when its benefits outweigh its costs. (p. 96)

technology spillover The domestic diffusion of foreign technical knowledge and processes. (p. 96)

demonstration effect (contagion or imitation effect) The effect that occurs when local rivals

recognize the feasibility of foreign technology and imitate it. (p. 96)

sovereign wealth fund (SWF) A state-owned investment fund composed of financial assets such as stocks, bonds, real estate, or other financial instruments funded by foreign exchange assets. (p. 98)

6-7 **List three things you need to do as your firm considers FDI.**

- Carefully assess whether FDI is justified, in light of other options such as outsourcing and licensing.

- Pay careful attention to the location advantages in combination with the firm's strategic goals.
- Be aware of the institutional constraints governing FDI, and enhance legitimacy in host countries.

7-1 List the factors that determine foreign exchange rates.

- Currency is a commodity, and its price is fundamentally determined by supply and demand.
- A foreign exchange rate is the price of one currency expressed in terms of another.
- Basic determinants of foreign exchange rates include (1) relative price differences and purchasing power parity (PPP), (2) interest rates, (3) productivity and balance of payments, (4) exchange rate policies, and (5) investor psychology.
- The theory of PPP, the "law of one price," suggests that in the absence of trade barriers (such as tariffs), the price for identical products sold in different countries must be the same.
- Variations in interest rates have a powerful effect in the short run, with a high domestic interest rate increasing

the demand for a country's currency and a low interest rate decreasing demand.
- A country's rate of inflation, relative to that in other countries, affects its ability to attract foreign funds and thereby its exchange rate. Thus, exchange rates are highly sensitive to changes in monetary policy.
- A rise in a country's productivity, relative to other countries, will improve its competitive position. In turn, more foreign direct investment will be attracted to the country, fueling demand for its home currency and affecting its balance of payments.
- Most countries practice a dirty (or managed) float, with selective government interventions.
- Short-run movements in the exchange rate are largely determined by investor psychology and are thus difficult to predict.

foreign exchange rate The price of one currency in terms of another. (p. 104)

appreciation An increase in the value of the currency. (p. 104)

depreciation A loss in the value of the currency. (p. 104)

balance of payments (BOP) A country's international transaction statement, which includes merchandise trade, service trade, and capital movement. (p. 107)

floating (flexible) exchange rate policy A government policy to let demand and supply conditions determine exchange rates. (p. 108)

clean (free) float A pure market solution to determine exchange rates. (p. 108)

dirty (managed) float Using selective government intervention to determine exchange rates. (p. 108)

target exchange rate (crawling band) Specified upper or lower bounds within which an exchange rate is allowed to fluctuate. (p. 108)

fixed exchange rate policy A government policy to set the exchange rate of a currency relative to other currencies. (p. 109)

bandwagon effect The effect of investors moving in the same direction at the same time, like a herd. (p. 109)

capital flight A phenomenon in which a large number of individuals and companies exchange a domestic currency for foreign currencies. (p. 109)

7-2 Articulate and explain the steps in the evolution of the international monetary system.

- The gold standard (1870–1914) pegged the value of each country's currency to gold, providing a predictable and stable system but forcing countries to maintain gold reserves.
- The Bretton Woods system (1944–1973) emerged after World War II and pegged all currencies to the US dollar,

which in turn was convertible to gold at a fixed $35 per ounce.
- The current post–Bretton Woods system (1973–present) has various floating and fixed rates, making it a flexible and diverse exchange system. However, the current system is also turbulent and uncertain.
- The International Monetary Fund (IMF) serves as a lender of last resort to help member countries correct balance-of-payments problems.

gold standard A system in which the value of most major currencies was maintained by fixing their prices in terms of gold. (p. 109)

common denominator A currency or commodity to which the value of all currencies are pegged. (p. 110)

Bretton Woods system A system in which all currencies were pegged at a fixed rate to the US dollar. (p. 110)

post–Bretton Woods system A system of flexible exchange rate regimes with no official common denominator. (p. 110)

International Monetary Fund (IMF) An international organization that was established to promote international monetary cooperation, exchange stability, and orderly exchange arrangements. (p. 111)

quota The weight a member country carries within the IMF, which determines the amount of its financial contribution (technically known as its "subscription"), its capacity to borrow from the IMF, and its voting power. (p. 111)

foreign exchange market The market where individuals, firms, governments, and banks buy and sell currencies of other countries. (p. 113)

7-3 **Identify strategic responses firms can take to deal with foreign exchange movements.**

- The three foreign exchange transactions are (1) spot transactions, (2) forward transactions, and (3) swaps.

- Firms' strategic responses to the risk of losses from fluctuations in the foreign exchange market include (1) invoicing in their own currencies, (2) currency hedging, or (3) strategic hedging.

spot transaction The classic single-shot exchange of one currency for another. (p. 113)

forward transaction A foreign exchange transaction in which participants buy and sell currencies now for future delivery. (p. 113)

currency hedging A transaction that protects traders and investors from exposure to the fluctuations of the spot rate. (p. 114)

forward discount A condition under which the forward rate of one currency relative to another currency is higher than the spot rate. (p. 114)

forward premium A condition under which the forward rate of one currency relative to another currency is lower than the spot rate. (p. 114)

currency swap A foreign exchange transaction between two firms in which one currency is converted into another at Time 1, with an agreement to revert it back to the original currency at a specified Time 2 in the future. (p. 114)

offer rate The price at which a bank is willing to sell a currency. (p. 114)

bid rate The price at which a bank is willing to buy a currency. (p. 114)

spread The difference between the offer price and the bid price. (p. 114)

currency risk The potential for loss associated with fluctuations in the foreign exchange market. (p. 115)

strategic hedging Spreading out activities in a number of countries in different currency zones to offset any currency losses in one region through gains in other regions. (p. 115)

7-4 **Identify three things you need to know about currency when doing business internationally.**

- Fostering foreign exchange literacy is a must.
- Risk analysis of any country must include an analysis of its currency risks.

- A currency risk management strategy is necessary, be it via currency hedging, strategic hedging, or invoicing in one's own currency.

CHAPTER 8 LEARNING OBJECTIVES / KEY TERMS

8-1 **Make the case for global economic integration.**
- There are both political and economic benefits for global economic integration.
- The biggest expected political benefit is peace.
- The three economic benefits of global integration are constructive dispute settlement, streamlined trade policies, and increased worldwide income through job creation and economic growth.

European Union (EU) The official title of European economic integration since 1993. (p. 122)

World Trade Organization (WTO) The official title of the multilateral trading system and the organization underpinning this system since 1995. (p. 122)

regional economic integration Efforts to reduce trade and investment barriers within one region. (p. 122)

global economic integration Efforts to reduce trade and investment barriers around the globe. (p. 122)

General Agreement on Tariffs and Trade (GATT) A multilateral agreement governing the international trade of goods (merchandise). (p. 122)

multilateral trading system The global system that governs international trade among countries—otherwise known as the GATT/WTO system. (p. 123)

nondiscrimination A principle that a country cannot discriminate among its trading partners. (p. 123)

8-2 **Explain the evolution of the GATT and the WTO, including current challenges.**
- The GATT (1948–1994) significantly reduced tariff rates on merchandise trade.
- The WTO (1995–present) was set up not only to incorporate the GATT, but also to cover trade in services and intellectual property, settle trade disputes, and provide a peer review of trade policy.
- The Doha Round was intended to promote more trade and development but has so far failed to accomplish its goals.

General Agreement on Trade in Services (GATS) A WTO agreement governing the international trade of services. (p. 124)

Trade-Related Aspects of Intellectual Property Rights

(TRIPS) A WTO agreement governing intellectual property rights. (p. 124)

Doha Round A round of WTO negotiations to reduce agricultural subsidies, slash tariffs, and strengthen intellectual property protection that started in Doha, Qatar, in 2001. Officially known as the "Doha Development Agenda," it was suspended in 2006 due to disagreements. (p. 125)

8-3 **Make the case for regional economic integration.**
- Political and economic benefits for regional integration are similar to those for global integration.
- Regional integration may undermine global integration and lead to some loss of countries' sovereignty.
- The five levels of regional economic integration are (1) free trade area, (2) customs union, (3) common market, (4) economic union, and (5) political union.

free trade area (FTA) A group of countries that remove trade barriers among themselves. (p. 127)

customs union One step beyond a free trade area, a customs union imposes common external policies on nonparticipating countries. (p. 127)

common market Combining everything a customs union has, a common market additionally permits the free movement of goods and people. (p. 127)

economic union Having all the features of a common market, members also coordinate and harmonize economic policies (in areas such as monetary, fiscal, and taxation) to blend their economies into a single economic entity. (p. 127)

monetary union A group of countries that use a common currency. (p. 128)

political union The integration of political and economic affairs of a region. (p. 128)

8-4 **List the accomplishments, benefits, and costs of the European Union.**
- The EU has delivered more than 60 years of peace and prosperity, launched a single currency, and constructed a single market.
- The EU's challenges include (1) enlargement concerns, (2) internal divisions, and (3) existential crisis.

Schengen A passport-free travel zone within the EU. (p. 129)

euro The currency currently used in 19 EU countries. (p. 129)

euro zone The 19 EU countries that currently use the euro as the official currency. (p. 129)

8-5 **Identify the five organizations that promote regional trade in the Americas and describe their benefits and costs.**
- Despite initial misgivings, NAFTA has significantly boosted trade and investment among members.

- The two South American customs unions, the Andean Community and Mercosur, have not been effective, because only a relatively small part of any member's trade is within the union and the region's largest trading partner, the United States, is outside the union.

Andean Community A customs union in South America that was launched in 1969. (p. 132)

Mercosur A customs union in South America that was launched in 1991. (p. 132)

Union of South American Nations (USAN/UNASUR) A regional integration mechanism integrating two existing customs unions (Andean Community and Mercosur) in South America. (p. 132)

United States–Dominican Republic–Central America Free Trade Agreement (CAFTA) A free trade agreement between the United States and five Central American countries and the Dominican Republic. (p. 132)

8-6 **Identify the four organizations that promote regional trade in the Asia Pacific and describe their benefits and costs.**
- Regional integration in the Asia Pacific centers on CER, ASEAN, APEC, and TPP.

- APEC is the largest regional integration by both geographic area and GDP.
- TPP is a multilateral free trade agreement that has been signed but that is not likely to be ratified.

Australia–New Zealand Closer Economic Relations Trade Agreement (ANZCERTA or CER) A free trade agreement between Australia and New Zealand. (p. 133)

Association of Southeast Asian Nations (ASEAN) The organization underpinning regional economic integration in Southeast Asia. (p. 133)

Asia-Pacific Economic Cooperation (APEC) The official title for regional economic integration involving 21 member economies around the Pacific. (p. 133)

Trans-Pacific Partnership (TPP) A multilateral free trade agreement being signed (but not yet ratified) by 12 Asia Pacific countries. (p. 135)

8-7 **Articulate how global and regional integration may influence your thinking about global business.**
- Think regional, downplay global.

- Understand the rules of the game and their transitions at both global and regional levels.

9-1 Define entrepreneurship, entrepreneurs, and entrepreneurial firms.

- Entrepreneurship is the identification and exploitation of previously unexplored opportunities.
- Entrepreneurs may be founders and owners of new businesses or managers of existing firms.
- Entrepreneurial firms in this chapter are defined as small- and medium-sized (SMEs) that employ less than 500 people.

small and medium-sized enterprise (SME) A firm with fewer than 500 employees in the United States or with fewer than 250 employees in the European Union. (p. 139)

entrepreneurship The identification and exploitation of previously unexplored opportunities. (p. 140)

entrepreneur Founders and owners of new businesses or managers of existing firms who identify and exploit new opportunities. (p. 140)

international entrepreneurship A combination of innovative, proactive, and risk-seeking behavior that crosses national borders and is intended to create wealth in organizations. (p. 140)

9-2 Identify the institutions and resources that affect entrepreneurship.

- Institutions—both formal and informal—enable and constrain entrepreneurship around the world.
- The more entrepreneur-friendly the formal institutional requirements are, the more flourishing entrepreneurship is and the more developed the economies become.
- Resources and capabilities largely determine entrepreneurial success and failure.

9-3 Highlight three characteristics of a growing entrepreneurial firm.

- Growth of an entrepreneurial firm is an attempt to more fully utilize currently under-utilized resources and capabilities, particularly entrepreneurial vision, drive, and leadership.
- Innovation is at the heart of entrepreneurship and allows for a more sustainable basis for competitive advantage.
- The primary sources of entrepreneurial financing are founders, family, friends, and strategic investors.
- The extent to which entrepreneurs draw on resources from outside investors versus family and friends varies from country to country.
- Microfinance has emerged in response to the lack of financing for entrepreneurial opportunities in many developing countries.

microfinance Lending small sums ($50–$300) used to start small businesses with the intention of ultimately lifting the entrepreneurs out of poverty. (p. 145)

9-4 Describe how international strategies for entering foreign markets are different from those for staying in domestic markets.

- Compared with domestic transaction costs (the costs of doing business), international transaction costs are qualitatively higher, so entrepreneurial opportunities exist where innovation can lower transaction costs and bring distant groups of people, firms, and countries together.
- Entrepreneurial firms can internationalize by entering foreign markets through entry modes such as (1) direct exports, (2) licensing and franchising, and (3) foreign direct investment.
- Direct exports are attractive because entrepreneurial firms are able to reach foreign customers directly, but SMEs may not have enough resources to turn overseas opportunities into profits.
- With licensing and franchising, the SME can expand abroad while risking relatively little of its own capital, but may suffer a loss of control over how its technology and brand names are used.
- Foreign direct investment gives a firm better control over how its proprietary technology and brand name are used, but requires both a nontrivial sum of capital and a significant managerial commitment.
- Entrepreneurial firms can also internationalize without venturing abroad by (1) exporting indirectly, (2) supplying foreign firms, (3) becoming licensees/franchisees of foreign firms, (4) joining foreign entrants as alliance partners, and (5) harvesting and exiting through sell-offs to foreign entrants.

CHAPTER REVIEW

CHAPTER 9 LEARNING OBJECTIVES / KEY TERMS

born global firm (International new venture) A start-up company that attempts to do business abroad from inception. (p. 145)

direct export The sale of products made by firms in their home country to customers in other countries. (p. 146)

sporadic (passive) exporting The sale of products prompted by unsolicited inquiries from abroad. (p. 146)

letter of credit (L/C) A financial contract that states that the importer's bank will pay a specific sum of money to the exporter upon delivery of the merchandise. (p. 146)

licensing Firm A's agreement to give Firm B the rights to use A's proprietary technology (such as a patent) or trademark (such as a corporate logo) for a royalty fee paid to A by B. This is typically done in manufacturing industries. (p. 146)

franchising Firm A's agreement to give Firm B the rights to use A's proprietary assets for a royalty fee paid to A by B. This is typically done in service industries. (p. 147)

stage model Model of internationalization that involves a slow step-by-step (stage-by-stage) process a firm must go through to internationalize its business. (p. 147)

indirect export A way for SMEs to reach overseas customers by exporting through domestically based export intermediaries. (p. 148)

export intermediary A firm that acts as a middleman by linking domestic sellers and foreign buyers that otherwise would not have been connected. (p. 148)

9-5 **Articulate what you should do to strengthen your entrepreneurial ability.**

- Push for both formal and informal institutions that facilitate entrepreneurship development.
- When internationalizing, be bold but not too bold.

CHAPTER 10 LEARNING OBJECTIVES / KEY TERMS

10-1 **Identify ways in which institutions and resources affect the liability of foreignness.**
- When entering foreign markets, firms confront a liability of foreignness.
- The institution-based view suggests that firms need to undertake actions deemed legitimate and appropriate by the various formal and informal institutions governing market entries.
- The resource-based view advises foreign firms to deploy *overwhelming* resources and capabilities to offset the liability of foreignness in order to achieve competitive advantage.

country-of-origin effect The positive or negative perception of firms and products from a certain country. (p. 155)

10-2 **Match the quest for location-specific advantages with strategic goals.**
- Where to enter depends on the location-specific advantages of certain foreign countries and the strategic goals of firms involved.
- Firms seeking natural resources have to go to particular foreign locations where those resources are found.
- Market-seeking firms go to countries that have a strong demand for their products and services.
- Efficiency-seeking firms often single out the most efficient locations featuring a combination of scale economies and low cost factors.
- Innovation-seeking firms target countries and regions renowned for generating world-class innovations.
- Firms must also consider cultural and institutional distance when considering foreign locations.

location-specific advantage The benefit a firm reaps from the features specific to a place. (p. 156)

cultural distance The difference between two cultures along identifiable dimensions such as individualism. (p. 158)

institutional distance The extent of similarity or dissimilarity between the regulatory, normative, and cognitive institutions of two countries. (p. 158)

10-3 **Compare and contrast first-mover and late-mover advantages.**
- First movers may gain advantages through proprietary technology, preemptive investments, erecting barriers to entry, and building relationships with key stakeholders.
- First movers may be disadvantaged when late movers free ride on their investments as well as by technological and market uncertainties and being locked into fixed assets or existing product lines.
- Late-mover advantages may include free riding on the investments of first movers, resolution of technological and market uncertainties, and leapfrogging the first mover's fixed assets or existing products.
- Late movers may be disadvantaged by lack of access to proprietary technology, barriers to entry, and difficulty in building relationships with key stakeholders who are already loyal to the first mover.
- Each has pros and cons, and there is no conclusive evidence pointing to one direction.

first-mover advantage Benefit that accrues to firms that enter the market first and that later entrants do not enjoy. (p. 159)

late-mover advantage Benefit that accrues to firms that enter the market later and that early entrants do not enjoy. (p. 159)

10-4 **List the steps in the comprehensive model of foreign market entries.**
- How to enter depends on the scale of entry, whether large scale or small scale.

- A comprehensive model of foreign market entries first focuses on the equity (ownership) issue.
- The second step focuses on making the actual selection within that mode, be it exports, contractual agreements, joint ventures, or wholly owned subsidiaries.

scale of entry The amount of resources committed to entering a foreign market. (p. 160)

mode of entry Method used to enter a foreign market. (p. 161)

nonequity mode A mode of entering foreign markets through exports and/or contractual agreements that tends to reflect relatively smaller commitments to overseas markets. (p. 161)

equity mode A mode of entering foreign markets through joint ventures and/or wholly owned subsidiaries that indicates a relatively larger, harder-to-reverse commitment. (p. 161)

dumping Exporting products at prices that are below what it costs to manufacture them, with the intent to raise prices after eliminating local rivals. (p. 163)

turnkey project A project in which clients pay contractors to design and construct new facilities and train personnel. (p. 163)

build-operate-transfer (BOT) agreement A nonequity mode of entry used to build a longer-term presence by building and then operating a facility for a period of time before transferring operations to a domestic agency or firm. (p. 163)

research and development (R&D) contract Outsourcing agreement in R&D between firms. (p. 164)

co-marketing Efforts among a number of firms to jointly market their products and services. (p. 164)

joint venture (JV) A new corporate entity jointly created and owned by two or more parent companies. (p. 164)

wholly owned subsidiary (WOS) A subsidiary located in a foreign country that is entirely owned by the parent multinational. (p. 164)

greenfield operation Building factories and offices from scratch (on a proverbial piece of "green field" formerly used for agricultural purposes). (p. 164)

10-5 **Explain what you should do to make your firm's entry into a foreign market successful.**
- Understand the rules of game—both formal and informal—governing competition in foreign markets.

- Develop overwhelming resources and capabilities to offset the liability of foreignness.
- Match efforts in market entry with strategic goals.

CHAPTER 11 LEARNING OBJECTIVES / KEY TERMS

11-1 Define alliances and acquisitions.
- Strategic alliance is a voluntary agreement of cooperation between firms.
- Acquisition is a transfer of the control of operations and management from one firm (target) to another (acquirer).

strategic alliance Voluntary agreement of cooperation between firms. (p. 169)

contractual (nonequity-based) alliance An association between firms that is based on a contract and does not involve the sharing of ownership. (p. 170)

equity-based alliance An association between firms that is based on shared ownership or financial interest. (p. 170)

strategic investment A business strategy in which one firm invests in another. (p. 170)

cross-shareholding A business strategy in which each partner in an alliance holds stock in the other firm. (p. 170)

acquisition The transfer of the control of operations and management from one firm (target) to another (acquirer), the former becoming a unit of the latter. (p. 170)

merger The combination of operations and management of two firms to establish a new legal entity. (p. 170)

11-2 Articulate how institutions and resources influence alliances and acquisitions.
- Formal institutions influence alliances and acquisitions through antitrust and entry mode concerns.
- Informal institutions affect alliances and acquisitions through normative and cognitive pillars.
- The impact of resources on alliances and acquisitions is illustrated by the VRIO framework.
- Alliances and acquisitions must create value.
- The abilities to successfully manage interfirm relationships may be rare.
- Imitability can occur at the firm level or at the alliance level.
- The organization of a successful alliance relationship or an acquisition may be difficult to replicate.

real option An investment in real operations as opposed to financial capital. (p. 173)

relational (collaborative) capability The ability to successfully manage interfirm relationships. (p. 173)

acquisition premium The difference between the acquisition price and the market value of target firms. (p. 175)

strategic fit The effective matching of complementary strategic capabilities. (p. 176)

organizational fit The similarity in cultures, systems, and structures between two or more firms. (p. 176)

11-3 Describe how alliances are formed.
- Managers typically go through a three-stage decision process when considering alliances.
- Stage one is the decision to cooperate with another firm or to grow purely by market transactions (not cooperate).
- Stage two is the decision whether to use a contract or equity mode.
- Stage three is specifying which specific type of relationship to pursue.

11-4 Outline how alliances are dissolved.
- The phases of dissolution are initiation, going public, uncoupling, and aftermath.
- Managers need to combat opportunism and, if necessary, manage the dissolution process.

11-5 Discuss how alliances perform.
- Alliance performance may be affected by (1) equity, (2) learning and experience, (3) nationality, and (4) relational capabilities.

11-6 Explain why firms make acquisitions.
- Acquisitions are often driven by synergistic, hubristic, and/or managerial motives.

hubris Exaggerated pride or overconfidence. (p. 179)

managerial motive Managers' desire for power, prestige, and money, which may lead to decisions that do not benefit the firm overall in the long run. (p. 179)

11-7 Describe what performance problems firms tend to encounter with acquisitions.
- Many acquisitions fail because managers fail to address pre- and post-acquisition problems.
- Pre-acquisition problems include managers over-estimating their ability to create value; inadequate pre-acquisition screening; poor strategic fit; a lack of familiarity with foreign cultures, institutions, and business systems; or nationalistic concerns.
- Post-acquisition problems include poor organizational fit, failure to address multiple stakeholder groups' concerns, clashes of organizational cultures and/or national cultures, and nationalistic concerns.

11-8 Articulate what you can do to make global alliances and acquisitions successful.
- Understand and master the rules of the game governing alliances and acquisitions around the world.
- When managing alliances, pay attention to the soft relationship aspects.
- When managing acquisitions, do not overpay. Focus on both strategic and organizational fit.

CHAPTER 12 LEARNING OBJECTIVES / KEY TERMS

12-1 Describe the relationship between multinational strategy and structure.

- An integration-responsiveness framework governs multinational strategy and structure.
- Strategy and structure work in four pairs.
- Home replication strategy duplicates home country strengths in foreign countries and adds an international division to the existing company structure.
- Localization strategy focuses on a number of foreign countries, each of which is regarded as a stand-alone local market supported by a geographic area structure.

- Global standardization strategy relies on the development and distribution of standardized products worldwide in order to reap the maximum benefits from low cost advantages by organizing each product division as a stand-alone entity with full worldwide responsibilities.
- Transnational strategy, which is often supported by a global matrix structure, seeks to be simultaneously cost efficient, locally responsive, and learning driven around the world.

integration-responsiveness framework An MNE management framework for simultaneously dealing with the pressures for both global integration and local responsiveness. (p. 186)

local responsiveness The need to be responsive to different customer preferences around the world. (p. 186)

home replication strategy A strategy that emphasizes duplicating home-country-based competencies in foreign countries. (p. 187)

localization (multidomestic) strategy A strategy that focuses on a number of foreign countries/regions, each of which is regarded as a stand-alone local (domestic) market worthy of significant attention and adaptation. (p. 187)

global standardization strategy A strategy that relies on the development and distribution of standardized products worldwide to reap the maximum benefits from low-cost advantages. (p. 188)

center of excellence An MNE subsidiary explicitly recognized as a source of important capabilities that can be leveraged by and/or disseminated to other subsidiaries. (p. 188)

worldwide (global) mandate A charter to be responsible for one MNE function throughout the world. (p. 188)

transnational strategy A strategy that endeavors to be simultaneously cost efficient, locally responsive, and learning driven around the world. (p. 188)

international division An organizational structure that is typically set up

when a firm initially expands abroad, often engaging in a home replication strategy. (p. 189)

geographic area structure An organizational structure that organizes the MNE according to different countries and regions. (p. 189)

country (regional) manager The business leader of a specific country (or a geographic region). (p. 189)

global product division structure An organizational structure that assigns global responsibilities to each product division. (p. 190)

global matrix An organizational structure often used to alleviate the disadvantages associated with both geographic area and global product division structures, particularly when adopting a transnational strategy. (p. 190)

12-2 Explain how institutions and resources affect multinational strategy, structure, and learning.

- "Rules of the game" for multinational enterprises (MNEs) are set by both formal and informal institutions governing (1) external relationships and (2) internal relationships.

- According to the resource-based view, management of MNE structure, learning, and innovation must be handled within the VRIO framework.

subsidiary initiative The proactive and deliberate pursuit of new opportunities by a subsidiary to expand its scope of responsibility. (p. 194)

organizational culture The collective programming of the mind that distinguishes members of one organization from another. (p. 194)

12-3 **Outline the challenges associated with learning, innovation, and knowledge management.**

- Knowledge management should primarily focus on tacit knowledge, which is more important than explicit knowledge but also harder to transfer and learn.
- Differences in knowledge management among four types of MNEs fundamentally stem from the interdependence (1) between the headquarters and foreign subsidiaries and (2) among various subsidiaries.
- Globalization of research and development (R&D) calls for capabilities to combat a number of problems associated with knowledge creation, retention, outflow, transmission, and inflow.

knowledge management The structures, processes, and systems that actively develop, leverage, and transfer knowledge. (p. 195)

explicit knowledge Knowledge that is codifiable (that is, can be written down and transferred with little loss of richness). (p. 195)

tacit knowledge Knowledge that is noncodifiable, whose acquisition and transfer require hands-on practice. (p. 195)

12-4 **List three things you can do to make a multinational firm successful.**

- Understand and master the external rules of the game from host/home country environments.
- Understand and be prepared to change the internal rules of the game governing MNE management.
- Develop learning and innovation capabilities around the world: "Think global, act local."

CHAPTER 13 LEARNING OBJECTIVES / KEY TERMS

13-1 **Explain staffing decisions, with a focus on expatriates.**

- International staffing primarily uses one of three approaches: ethnocentric, polycentric, or geocentric.
- Expatriates (primarily parent-county nationals [PCNs] and to a lesser extent third-country nationals [TCNs]) play multiple challenging roles and often have high failure rates, defined by (1) premature return, (2) unmet business objectives, and (3) unfulfilled career development objectives.
- Expatriates need to be carefully selected, taking into account a variety of factors in terms of both the individual and the situation.

human resource management (HRM) Activities that attract, select, and manage employees. (p. 203)

staffing HRM activities associated with hiring employees and filling positions. (p. 204)

host-country national (HCN) An individual from the host country who works for an MNE. (p. 204)

parent-country national (PCN) An employee who comes from the parent (home) country of the MNE and works at its local subsidiary. (p. 204)

third-country national (TCN) An employee who comes from neither the parent country nor the host country of the MNE. (p. 204)

ethnocentric approach A staffing approach that emphasizes the norms and practices of the parent company (and the parent country of the MNE) by relying on PCNs. (p. 204)

polycentric approach A staffing approach that emphasizes the norms and practices of the host country. (p. 205)

geocentric approach A staffing approach that focuses on finding the most suitable managers, who can be PCNs, HCNs, or TCNs. (p. 205)

expatriation Leaving one's home country to work in another country. (p. 207)

13-2 **Identify training and development needs for expatriates and host-country nationals.**

- Training length and rigor should correspond to the expatriates' expected length of stay.
- Expatriates need to be properly trained and cared for during repatriation.
- Training and development of host-country nationals (HCNs) is now an area of differentiation among many multinational enterprises (MNEs).

training Specific preparation to do a particular job. (p. 208)

development Longer-term, broader preparation to improve managerial skills for a better career. (p. 208)

repatriation Returning to an expatriate's home country after an extended period overseas. (p. 209)

psychological contract An informal understanding of expected delivery of benefits in the future for current services. (p. 209)

13-3 **Identify and discuss compensation and performance appraisal issues.**

- Expatriates are compensated using the going rate and balance sheet approaches.
- The going rate approach fosters equality among PCNs, TCNs, and HCNs within the same subsidiary, but the going rate for the same position differs around the world, making it potentially problematic to attract or possibly repatriate talent.
- The balance sheet approach balances the cost-of-living differences relative to parent-country levels and adds a financial inducement to make the package attractive. But this approach can be expensive, can create disparities between expatriates and HCNs, and can be organizationally complex to administer.
- Top talent HCNs now increasingly command higher compensation.
- Performance appraisal needs to be carefully provided to achieve its intended purposes.

compensation Salary and benefits. (p. 210)

performance appraisal The evaluation of employee performance for the purposes of promotion, retention, or ending employment. (p. 210)

going rate approach A compensation approach that pays expatriates the prevailing (going) rate for comparable positions in a host country. (p. 210)

balance sheet approach A compensation approach that balances the cost-of-living differences based on parent-country levels and adds a financial inducement to make the package attractive. (p. 210)

13-4 List factors that affect labor relations in both home and host countries.
- Despite revival efforts, unions have been declining in developed countries.

- MNEs prefer to deal with nonunionized workforces, but the power of unions in developing countries deserves some attention.

labor relations A firm's relation with organized labor (unions) in both home and host countries. (p. 212)

13-5 Discuss how the institution-based and resource-based views shed additional light on human resource management.
- Formal and informal rules of the game shape HRM significantly, both at home and abroad.

- While informal cultures, norms, and values are important, HR managers need to avoid stereotyping and instead consider changes.
- As HRM becomes more strategic, VRIO dimensions are now more important.

13-6 Identify the five Cs of human resource management.
- HR managers need to be *curious*, *competent*, *courageous*, and *caring* about people.

- Non-HR managers need to proactively develop their *careers*.

CHAPTER 14 LEARNING OBJECTIVES / KEY TERMS

14-1 Articulate three of the four Ps in marketing (product, price, and promotion) in a global context.

- Product refers to offerings that customers purchase.
- There are limitless ways of segmenting the market—males vs. females; urban dwellers vs. rural residents; Africans vs. Latin Americans.
- Price refers to the expenditures that customers are willing to pay for a product.
- Promotion refers to all the communications that marketers insert into the marketplace.

marketing Efforts to create, develop, and defend markets that satisfy the needs and wants of individual and business customers. (p. 222)

supply chain Flow of products, services, finances, and information that passes through a set of entities from a source to the customer. (p. 222)

supply chain management Activities to plan, organize, lead, and control the supply chain. (p. 222)

marketing mix The four underlying components of marketing: (1) product, (2) price, (3) promotion, and (4) place. (p. 222)

product Offerings that customers purchase. (p. 222)

market segmentation Identifying segments of consumers who differ from others in purchasing behavior. (p. 223)

price Expenditures that customers are willing to pay for a product. (p. 224)

price elasticity How demand changes when price changes. (p. 224)

promotion Communications that marketers insert into the marketplace. (p. 224)

14-2 Explain how the fourth P in marketing (place) has evolved to be labeled supply chain management.

- The fourth P in the marketing mix refers to "place." Place is often referred to as distribution channel.
- The new challenge facing companies is how to manage the longer distribution channel—the distribution from suppliers all the way to consumers.

place The location where products and services are provided. (p. 225)

distribution channel The set of firms that facilitates the movement of goods from producers to consumers. (p. 225)

14-3 Outline the triple As in supply chain management (agility, adaptability, and alignment).

- Agility refers to the ability to quickly react to unexpected shifts in supply and demand.
- To reduce inventory, many firms now use trucks, ships, and planes of their suppliers and carriers as their warehouse.
- Adaptability refers to the ability to change supply chain configurations in response to longer-term changes in the environment and technology.
- Alignment refers to the alignment of interests of various players in the supply chain.
- Trust along the supply chain stems from perceived fairness and justice from all members of the chain.

agility The ability to react quickly to unexpected shifts in supply and demand. (p. 226)

adaptability The ability to change supply chain configurations in response to long-term changes in the environment and technology. (p. 226)

make-or-buy decision The decision on whether to produce in-house ("make") or to outsource ("buy"). (p. 228)

alignment Alignment of interests of various players. (p. 228)

third-party logistics (3PL) provider A neutral, third-party intermediary in the supply chain that provides logistics and other support services. (p. 228)

14-4 **Discuss how institutions and resources affect marketing and supply chain management.**
- Most countries impose restrictions, ranging from taboos in advertising to constraints on the equity level held by foreign retailers and 3PL providers.

14-5 **Draw three implications for action.**
- Marketers and supply chain managers need to know the rules of the game inside and out in order to craft savvy responses to process changes.

- Informal rules also place significant constraints on marketing and supply chain management.
- Marketing and supply chain activities can be evaluated using VRIO—value, rarity, inimitability, and organization.

- They must focus on the four Ps in marketing—product, price, promotion, and place.
- They also must focus on the triple As in supply chain management—agility, adaptability, and alignment.

CHAPTER 15 LEARNING OBJECTIVES / KEY TERMS

15-1 **Articulate a stakeholder view of the firm.**
- A stakeholder view of the firm urges managers to pursue a balanced triple bottom line consisting of economic, social, and environmental performance.
- Despite the fierce defense of the free market school, especially the shareholder capitalism variant, the corporate social responsibility (CSR) movement has now become a more central part of management discussions.
- The CSR debate centers on the nature of the firm in society.

- Free market advocates argue that the social responsibility of business is to increase its profits, and, if firms attempt to attain social goals, such as providing employment and social welfare, managers will lose their focus on profit maximization.
- CSR advocates argue that a free market system that takes the pursuit of self-interest and profit as its guiding light—although in theory constrained by rules, contracts, and property rights—may in practice fail to constrain itself, thus often breeding greed, excesses, and abuses.

corporate social responsibility (CSR) Consideration of, and response to, issues beyond the narrow economic, technical, and legal requirements of the firm to accomplish social benefits along with the traditional economic gains that the firm seeks. (p. 236)

stakeholder Any group or individual who can affect or is affected by a firm's actions. (p. 236)

global sustainability The ability to meet the needs of the present without compromising the ability of future generations to meet their needs around the world. (p. 236)

primary stakeholder group Constituent on which a firm relies for its continuous survival and prosperity. (p. 237)

secondary stakeholder group Group or individual who can indirectly affect or are indirectly affected by a firm's actions. (p. 237)

triple bottom line Economic, social, and environmental performance that simultaneously satisfies the demands of all stakeholder groups. (p. 237)

15-2 **Apply the institution-based and resource-based views to analyze corporate social responsibility.**
- The institution-based view suggests that when confronting CSR pressures, firms may employ (1) reactive, (2) defensive, (3) accommodative, or (4) proactive strategies.
- A code of conduct (sometimes called a code of ethics) is a tangible indication of a firm's willingness to accept CSR.

- CSR-related resources can include *tangible* technologies and processes as well as *intangible* skills and attitudes.
- The resource-based view argues that not all CSRs satisfy the VRIO requirements.
- The resource-based view suggests that because of capability constraints, many firms are not cut out for a CSR-intensive (differentiation) strategy.

reactive strategy A strategy that would only respond to CSR causes when required by disasters and outcries. (p. 241)

defensive strategy A strategy that focuses on regulatory compliance but with little actual commitment to CSR by top management. (p. 241)

accommodative strategy A strategy characterized by some support from top managers, who may increasingly view CSR as a worthwhile endeavor. (p. 242)

proactive strategy A strategy that anticipates CSR and endeavors to do more than is required. (p. 243)

social issue participation Firms' participation in social causes not directly related to the management of primary stakeholders. (p. 244)

15-3 **Identify three ways you can manage corporate social responsibility.**
- Understand the rules of the game, anticipate changes, and seek to influence such changes.

- Pick your CSR battles carefully. Don't blindly imitate other firms' CSR activities.
- Integrate CSR as part of the core activities and processes of the firm.

GLOBAL
ONLINE

STUDY YOUR WAY
WITH STUDYBITS!

WEAK

FAIR

STRONG

UNASSIGNED

Rate and Organize StudyBits

Collect What's Important

Create Flashcards From Your StudyBits

Track/Monitor Your Progress

85%

CORRECT

INCORRECT

INCORRECT

INCORRECT

Personalize Your Quizzes

4LTR PRESS

MAP 1

MAP 1   Developed Economies and Emerging Economies

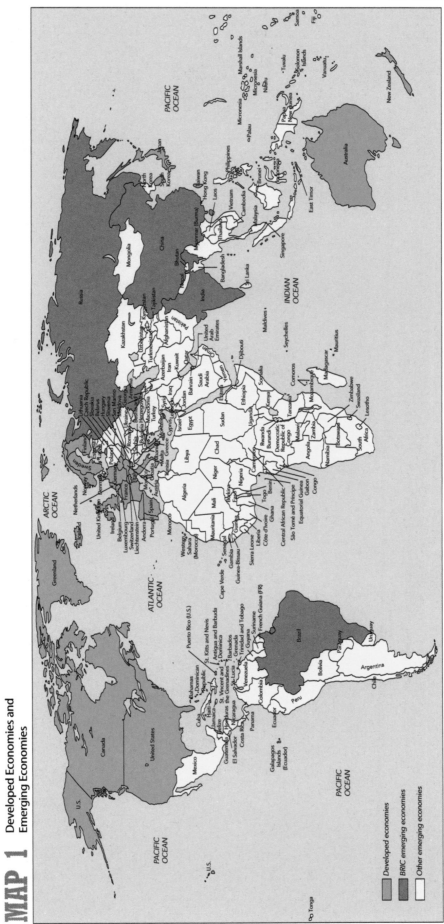

Developed economies

BRIC emerging economies

Other emerging economies

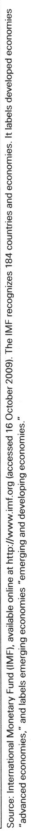

Source: International Monetary Fund (IMF), available online at http://www.imf.org (accessed 16 October 2009). The IMF recognizes 184 countries and economies. It labels developed economies "advanced economies," and labels emerging economies "emerging and developing economies."

MAP 2

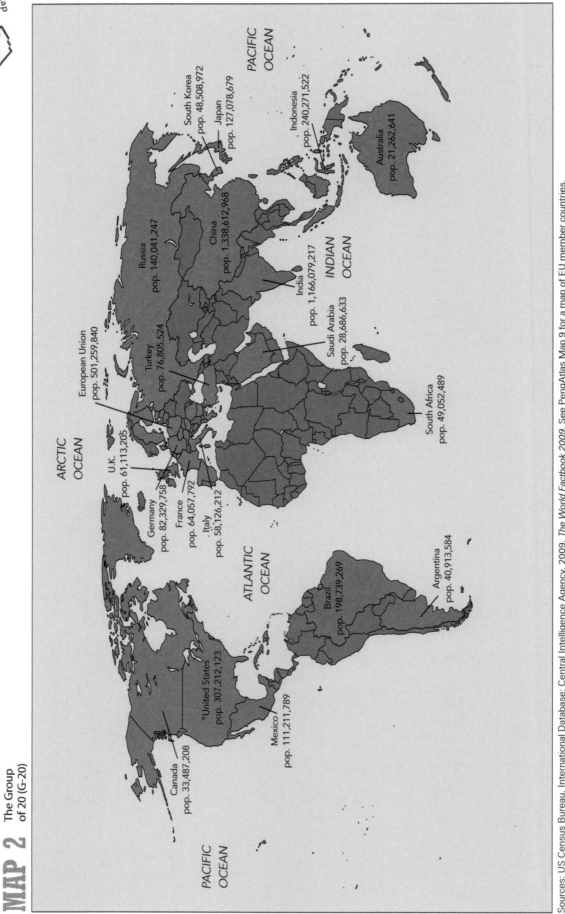

MAP 2 The Group of 20 (G-20)

Canada pop. 33,487,208

United States pop. 307,212,123

Mexico pop. 111,211,789

PACIFIC OCEAN

ATLANTIC OCEAN

Brazil 198,739,269

Argentina pop. 40,913,584

ARCTIC OCEAN

U.K. pop. 61,113,205

European Union pop. 501,259,840

Germany pop. 82,329,758

France pop. 64,057,792

Italy pop. 58,126,212

Turkey pop. 76,805,524

Russia pop. 140,041,247

China pop. 1,338,612,968

South Korea pop. 48,508,972

Japan pop. 127,078,679

PACIFIC OCEAN

Indonesia pop. 240,271,522

India pop. 1,166,079,217

Saudi Arabia pop. 28,686,633

INDIAN OCEAN

Australia pop. 21,262,641

South Africa pop. 49,052,489

Sources: US Census Bureau, International Database; Central Intelligence Agency, 2009, *The World Factbook 2009*. See PengAtlas Map 9 for a map of EU member countries.

MAP 3

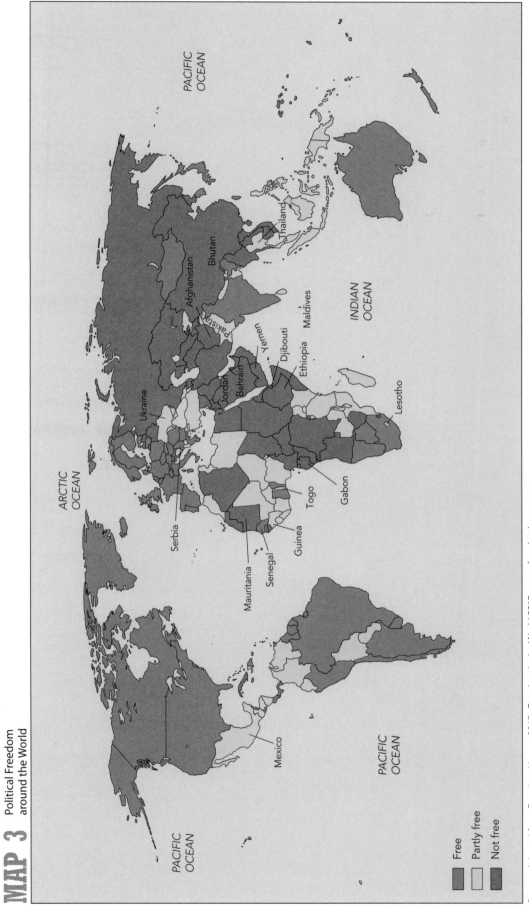

MAP 3 — Political Freedom around the World

PACIFIC OCEAN

ARCTIC OCEAN

PACIFIC OCEAN

INDIAN OCEAN

PACIFIC OCEAN

Bhutan

Afghanistan

Pakistan

Ukraine

Thailand

Maldives

Yemen

Djibouti

Ethiopia

Jordan

Bahrain

Lesotho

Gabon

Togo

Serbia

Guinea

Senegal

Mauritania

Mexico

Free

Partly free

Not free

Source: Adapted from Freedom House, 2015, *Freedom in the World 2015*, www.freedomhouse.org.

MAP 4

MAP 4 Top Ten and Bottom Ten Countries
by Per Capita Income

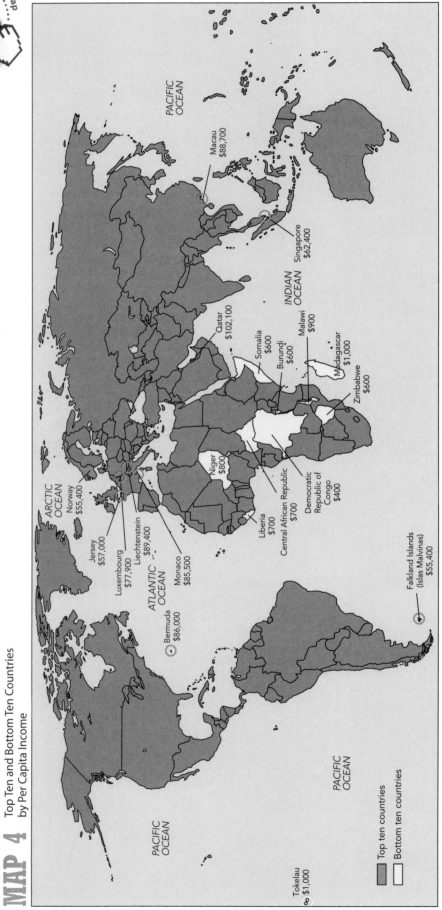

PACIFIC
OCEAN

Macau
$88,700

Singapore
$62,400

INDIAN
OCEAN

Qatar
$102,100

Somalia
$600

Burundi
$600

Malawi
$900

Madagascar
$1,000

Zimbabwe
$600

Niger
$800

Democratic
Republic of
Congo
$400

Liberia
$700

Central African Republic
$700

ARCTIC
OCEAN

Norway
$55,400

Jersey
$57,000

Luxembourg
$77,900

Liechtenstein
$89,400

Monaco
$85,500

ATLANTIC
OCEAN

Bermuda
$86,000

Falkland Islands
(Islas Malvinas)
$55,400

PACIFIC
OCEAN

PACIFIC
OCEAN

PACIFIC
OCEAN

Tokelau
$1,000

Top ten countries

Bottom ten countries

Source: Adapted from Central Intelligence Agency, 2013, *The World Factbook 2013*. Amounts in US dollars.

MAP 5

Religious Heritage
around the World

Source: *World Factbook*, 2000. Note that Confucianism, strictly speaking, is not a religion, but a set of moral codes guiding interpersonal relationships.

Religious beliefs among 70% or more of the population

Atheist
Buddhism
Confucian
Christian, other
Christian, Roman Catholic
Hindu
Indigenous
Judaism
Muslim
Orthodox, no major sects

MAP 6

MAP 6 Top Merchandise Exporters and Importers

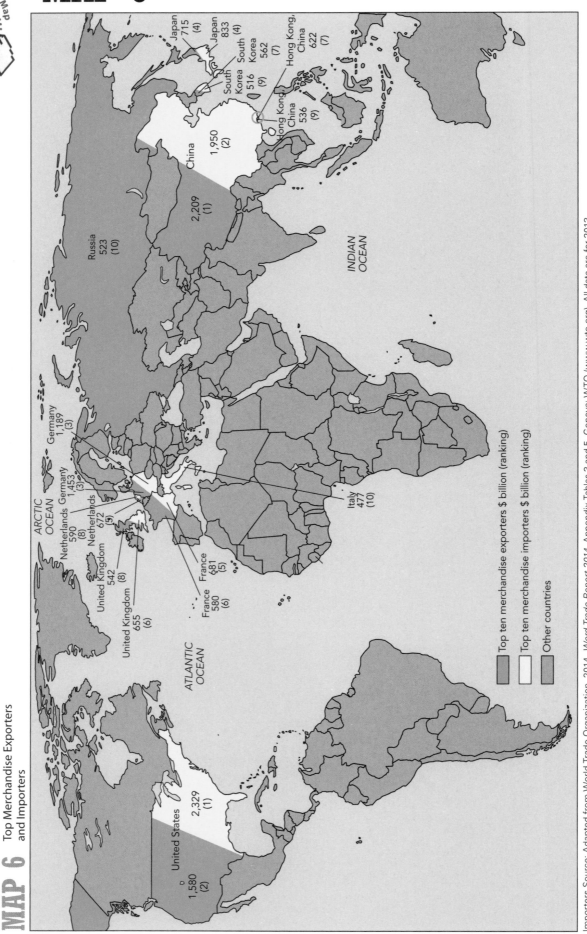

Japan 715 (4)

Japan 833 (4)

South Korea 562 (7)

Hong Kong, China 622 (7)

South Korea 516 (9)

Hong Kong, China 536 (9)

China 1,950 (2)

China 2,209 (1)

Russia 523 (10)

INDIAN OCEAN

ARCTIC OCEAN

Germany 1,189 (3)

Germany 1,453 (3)

Netherlands 590 (8)

Netherlands 672 (5)

United Kingdom 542 (8)

United Kingdom 655 (6)

France 681 (5)

France 580 (6)

Italy 477 (10)

ATLANTIC OCEAN

United States 2,329 (1)

1,580 (2)

Top ten merchandise exporters $ billion (ranking)

Top ten merchandise importers $ billion (ranking)

Other countries

Importers Source: Adapted from World Trade Organization, 2014, *World Trade Report 2014*, Appendix Tables 3 and 5, Geneva: WTO (www.wto.org). All data are for 2013.

MAP 7

MAP 7 Top Service Exporters and Importers

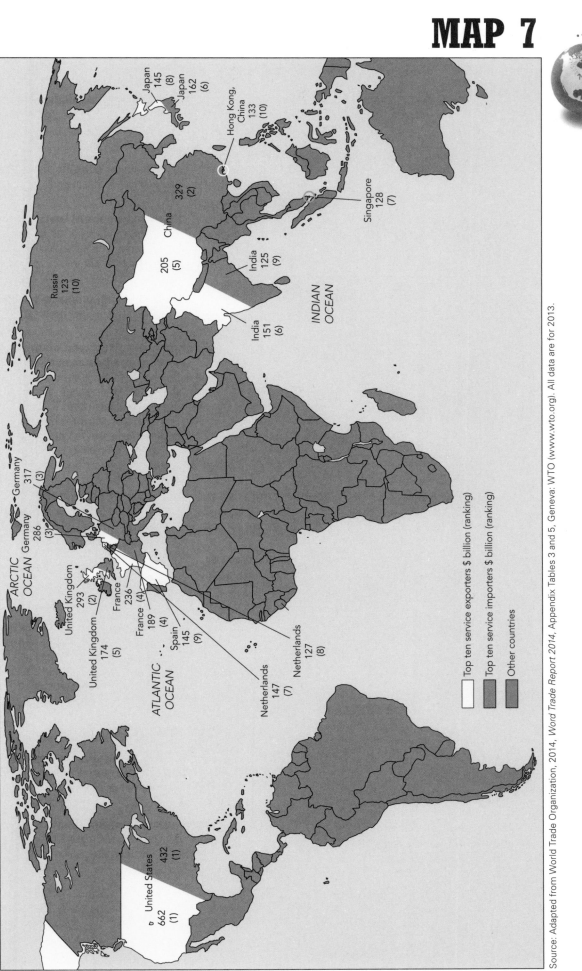

United States 662 (1)

United States 432 (1)

Russia 123 (10)

China 329 (2)

China 205 (5)

India 151 (6)

India 125 (9)

Japan 145 (8)

Japan 162 (6)

Hong Kong, China 133 (10)

Singapore 128 (7)

Germany 317 (3)

Germany 286 (3)

United Kingdom 293 (2)

United Kingdom 174 (5)

France 236 (4)

France 189 (4)

Spain 145 (9)

Netherlands 147 (7)

Netherlands 127 (8)

ARCTIC OCEAN

ATLANTIC OCEAN

INDIAN OCEAN

Top ten service exporters $ billion (ranking)

Top ten service importers $ billion (ranking)

Other countries

Source: Adapted from World Trade Organization, 2014, *Word Trade Report 2014*, Appendix Tables 3 and 5, Geneva: WTO (www.wto.org). All data are for 2013.

MAP 8   FDI Inflows and Outflows

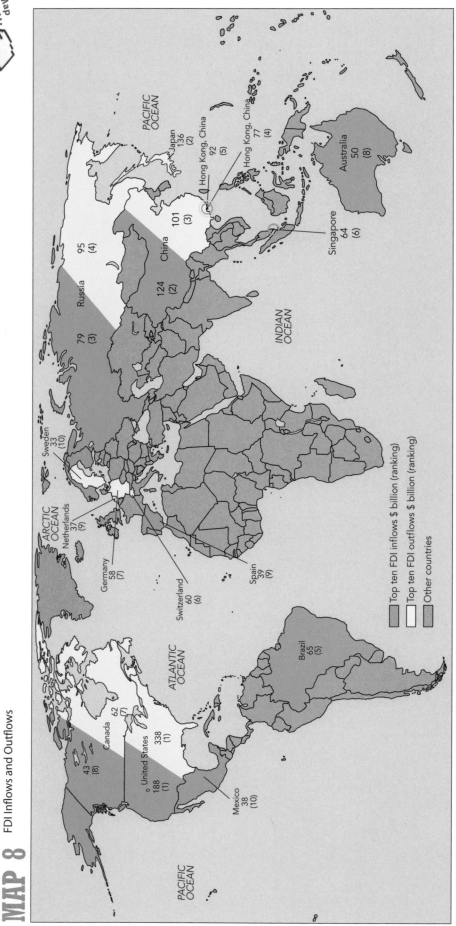

Source: Adapted from United Nations, 2014, *World Investment Report 2014* (p. xvi), New York and Geneva: UN. Data refer to 2013.

MAP 9

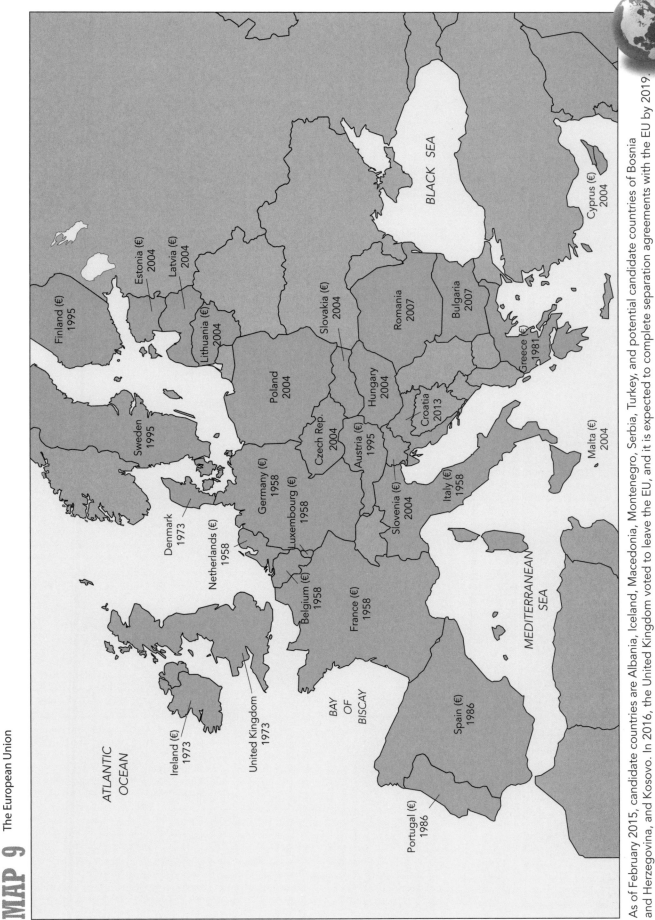

MAP 9   The European Union

ATLANTIC
OCEAN

Ireland (€)
1973

United Kingdom
1973

Portugal (€)
1986

Spain (€)
1986

BAY
OF
BISCAY

France (€)
1958

Belgium (€)
1958

Netherlands (€)
1958

Denmark
1973

Luxembourg (€)
1958

Germany (€)
1958

Sweden
1995

Finland (€)
1995

Estonia (€)
2004

Latvia (€)
2004

Lithuania (€)
2004

Poland
2004

Czech Rep.
2004

Austria (€)
1995

Slovenia (€)
2004

Italy (€)
1958

Hungary
2004

Slovakia (€)
2004

Croatia
2013

Romania
2007

Bulgaria
2007

Greece
1981

Malta (€)
2004

MEDITERRANEAN
SEA

BLACK   SEA

Cyprus (€)
2004

As of February 2015, candidate countries are Albania, Iceland, Macedonia, Montenegro, Serbia, Turkey, and potential candidate countries of Bosnia and Herzegovina, and Kosovo. In 2016, the United Kingdom voted to leave the EU, and it is expected to complete separation agreements with the EU by 2019.

Source: Adapted from http://europa.eueuropa.eu.

PengAtlas Map

MAP 10

PengAtlas Map

MAP 10 Regional Integration in
South America

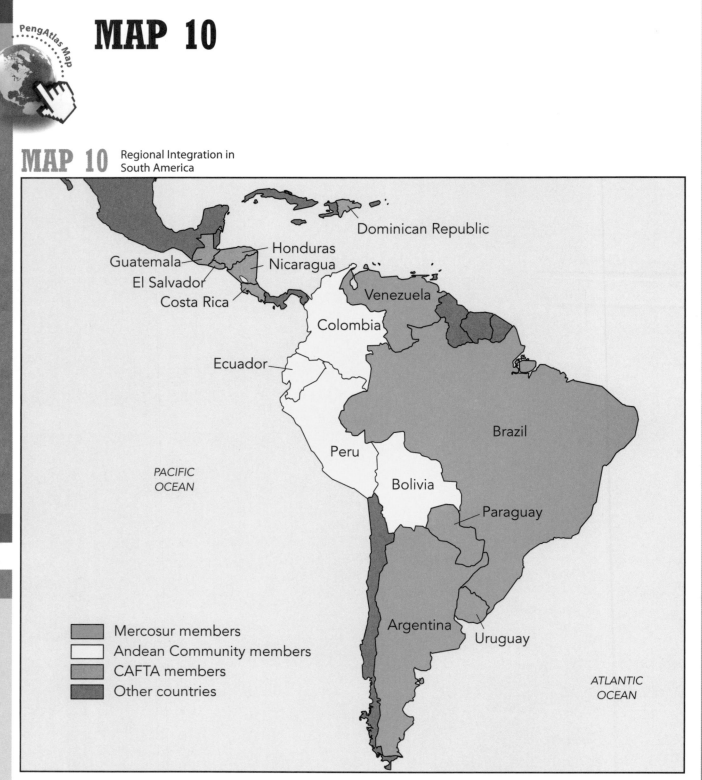

In May 2008, Andean Community and Mercosur agreed to merge to form the Union of South American Nations (USAN, more commonly known by its Spanish acronym, UNASUR, which refers to Unión de Naciones Suramericanas).

MAP 11

MAP 11 Regional Integration in the Asia Pacific

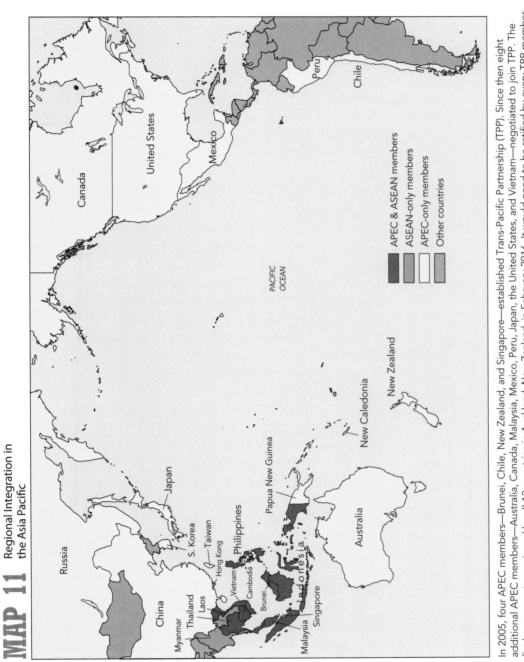

China
Russia
Myanmar
Thailand
Laos
Japan
S. Korea
Taiwan
Hong Kong
Vietnam
Cambodia
Philippines
Brunei
Papua New Guinea
Indonesia
Singapore
Malaysia
Australia
New Caledonia
New Zealand

Canada
United States
Mexico
Peru
Chile

PACIFIC
OCEAN

APEC & ASEAN members
ASEAN-only members
APEC-only members
Other countries

In 2005, four APEC members—Brunei, Chile, New Zealand, and Singapore—established Trans-Pacific Partnership (TPP). Since then eight additional APEC members—Australia, Canada, Malaysia, Mexico, Peru, Japan, the United States, and Vietnam—negotiated to join TPP. The final agreement was signed by all 12 countries in Auckland, New Zealand, in February 2016. It would need to be ratified by every TPP member in two years of signing. As of this writing (June 2017), only Japan has ratified it. In January 2017, President Donald Trump withdrew the US signature from TPP.

MAP 12   Ease of Doing Business

Legend:
- Top ten countries
- Bottom ten countries
- All other countries

Map labels:
- New Zealand 2
- Australia 10
- South Korea 5
- Hong Kong, China 3
- Singapore 1
- Afghanistan 183
- Eritrea 189
- South Sudan 186
- Democratic Republic of the Congo 184
- Angola 181
- Central African Republic 187
- Chad 185
- Libya 188
- Finland 9
- Norway 6
- Denmark 4
- United Kingdom 8
- United States 7
- Haiti 180
- Venezuela 182

Source: Data extracted from www.doingbusiness.org/rankings. *Doing Business 2014.*

MAP 13

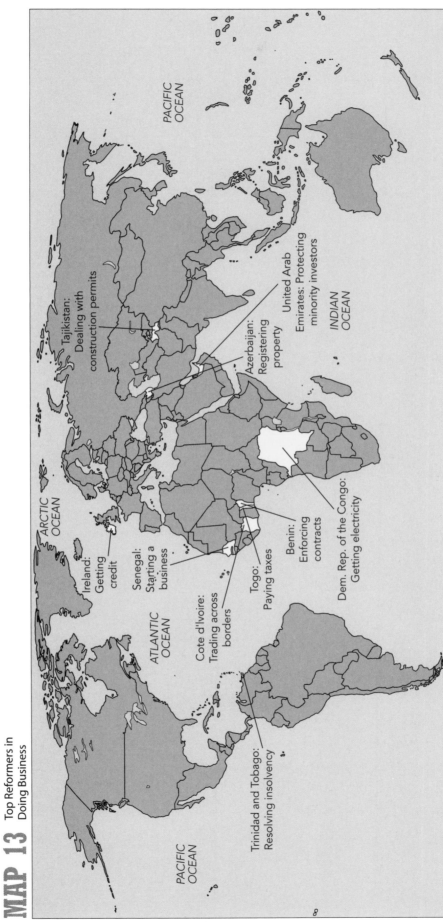

MAP 13 Top Reformers in Doing Business

PACIFIC OCEAN

Tajikistan: Dealing with construction permits

United Arab Emirates: Protecting minority investors

Azerbaijan: Registering property

INDIAN OCEAN

ARCTIC OCEAN

Ireland: Getting credit

Senegal: Starting a business

Dem. Rep. of the Congo: Getting electricity

Benin: Enforcing contracts

Togo: Paying taxes

ATLANTIC OCEAN

Cote d'Ivoire: Trading across borders

Trinidad and Tobago: Resolving insolvency

PACIFIC OCEAN

Source: Data extracted from http://www.doingbusiness.org/reforms/top-reformers-2015.

MAP 14

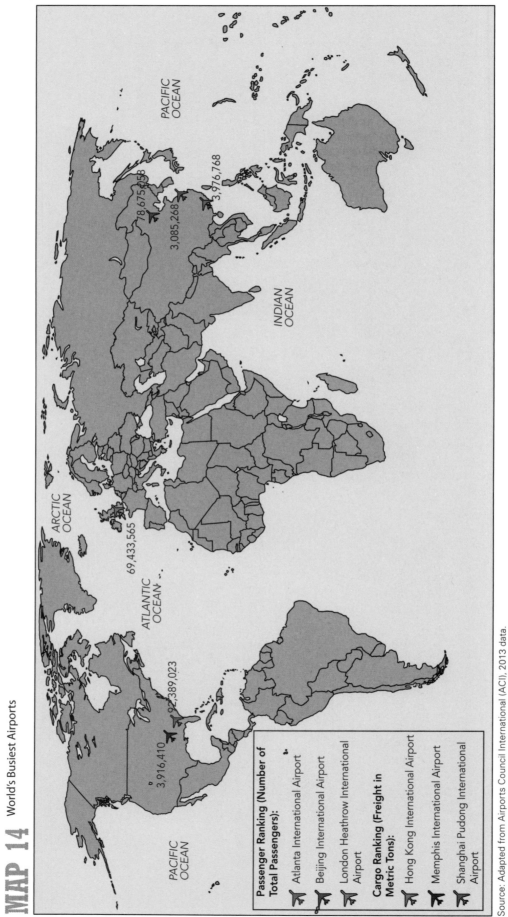

MAP 14 World's Busiest Airports

PACIFIC OCEAN

PACIFIC OCEAN

ARCTIC OCEAN

ATLANTIC OCEAN

INDIAN OCEAN

78,675,058

3,085,268

3,976,768

69,433,565

92,389,023

3,916,410

Passenger Ranking (Number of Total Passengers):

Atlanta International Airport

Beijing International Airport

London Heathrow International Airport

Cargo Ranking (Freight in Metric Tons):

Hong Kong International Airport

Memphis International Airport

Shanghai Pudong International Airport

Source: Adapted from Airports Council International (ACI), 2013 data.

MAP 15

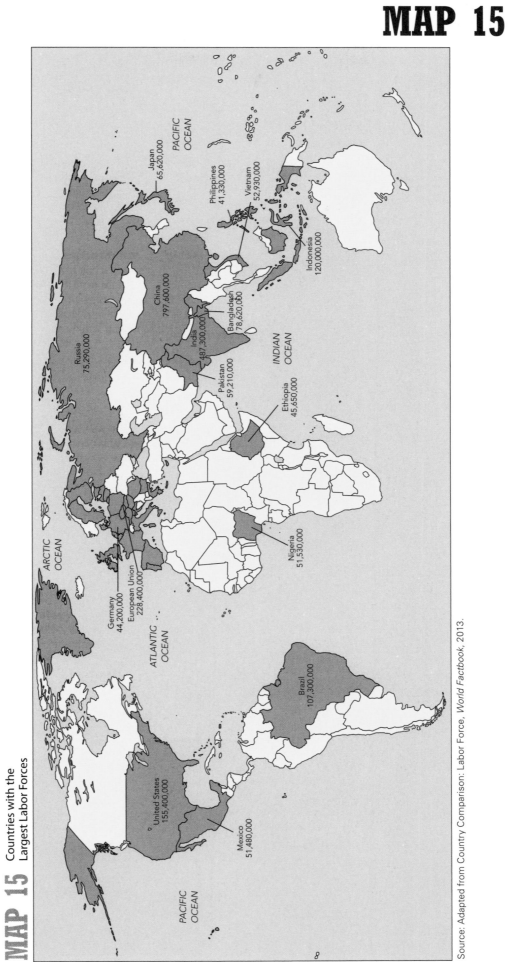

MAP 15   Countries with the Largest Labor Forces

Source: Adapted from Country Comparison: Labor Force, *World Factbook*, 2013.

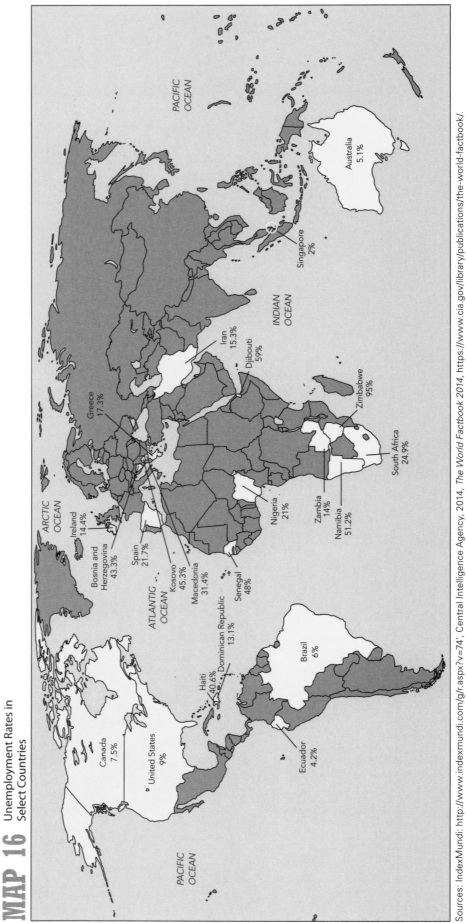

MAP 16 Unemployment Rates in Select Countries

Canada
7.5%

United States
9%

Haiti
40.6%

Dominican Republic
13.1%

Ecuador
4.2%

Brazil
6%

ARCTIC
OCEAN

Ireland
14.4%

Bosnia and
Herzegovina
43.3%

Spain
21.7%

Kosovo
45.3%

Macedonia
31.4%

Senegal
48%

ATLANTIC
OCEAN

Greece
17.3%

Iran
15.3%

Djibouti
59%

Zimbabwe
95%

South Africa
24.9%

Nigeria
21%

Zambia
14%

Namibia
51.2%

INDIAN
OCEAN

Singapore
2%

Australia
5.1%

PACIFIC
OCEAN

PACIFIC
OCEAN

Sources: IndexMundi: http://www.indexmundi.com/g/r.aspx?v=74', Central Intelligence Agency, 2014, *The World Factbook 2014*, https://www.cia.gov/library/publications/the-world-factbook/.